KU-775-796

Introduction to
Financial
Accounting

**seventh
edition**

McGraw-Hill
Higher Education

London Boston Burr Ridge, IL Dubuque, IA Madison, WI New York San Francisco
St. Louis Bangkok Bogotá Caracas Kuala Lumpur Lisbon Madrid Mexico City
Milan Montreal New Delhi Santiago Seoul Singapore Sydney Taipei Toronto

Introduction to Financial Accounting, seventh edition
Andrew Thomas & Anne Marie Ward
ISBN-13 9780077132682
ISBN-10 0077132688

**McGraw-Hill
Higher Education**

Published by McGraw-Hill Education
Shoppenhangers Road
Maidenhead
Berkshire
SL6 2QL
Telephone: 44 (0) 1628 502 500
Fax: 44 (0) 1628 770 224
Website: www.mcgraw-hill.co.uk

British Library Cataloguing in Publication Data
A catalogue record for this book is available from the British Library

Library of Congress Cataloguing in Publication Data
The Library of Congress data for this book has been applied for from the Library of Congress

Acquisitions Editor: Leiah Batchelor
Development Editor: Stephanie Frosch
Production Editor: James Bishop
Marketing Manager: Alexis Thomas

Text Design by Hardlines
Cover design by Adam Renvoize
Printed and bound in Singapore by Markono Print Media Pte Ltd

Published by McGraw-Hill Education (UK) Limited an imprint of The McGraw-Hill Companies, Inc., 1221 Avenue of the Americas, New York, NY 10020. Copyright © 2012 by McGraw-Hill Education (UK) Limited. All rights reserved. No part of this publication may be reproduced or distributed in any form or by any means, or stored in a database or retrieval system, without the prior written consent of The McGraw-Hill Companies, Inc., including, but not limited to, in any network or other electronic storage or transmission, or broadcast for distance learning.

Fictitious names of companies, products, people, characters and/or data that may be used herein (in case studies or in examples) are not intended to represent any real individual, company, product or event.

ISBN-13 9780077132682
ISBN-10 0077132688
© 2012. Exclusive rights by The McGraw-Hill Companies, Inc. for manufacture and export. This book cannot be re-exported from the country to which it is sold by McGraw-Hill.

The McGraw·Hill Companies

For Martin

Anne Marie Ward

Brief Table of Contents

Continued

The following chapters are available online at www.mcgrawhill.co.uk/textbooks/thomas:

Detailed Table of Contents

Introduction to
Financial Accounting

seventh edition

700316541 £46.99

Andrew Thomas &
Anne Marie Ward

BLACKPOOL AND THE FYLDE COLLEGE

3 8049 00141 6992

Detailed Table of Contents

Continued

Detailed Table of Contents

Continued

Detailed Table of Contents

Continued

The following chapters are available online at www.mcgraw-hill.co.uk/textbooks/thomas:

Preface to seventh edition

What's new

1 New material and structural changes

- The sequencing of topics covered in Part 1 has changed.

  a) Chapter 5 from the 6th Edition 'The conceptual framework of accounting' has been split into two chapters with the 'History and purpose of the conceptual framework' being introduced earlier as a new chapter and the 'The qualitative characteristics of financial information' forming a chapter on its own (Chapter 6). The authors felt that the student should read the history and purpose of the conceptual framework before starting to study its main components ('The nature and objectives of financial reporting' – Chapter 4, 'Accounting principles concepts and policies' – Chapter 5 and the 'Qualitative characteristics of financial information' – Chapter 6).

  b) Chapter 4 – 'The nature and objectives of financial reporting' has been extended to include more extensive coverage of corporate social responsibility (CSR) and accountability.

  c) A new section on environmental accounting has been included in Chapter 4.

  d) Chapter 2 'International financial reporting: institutional framework and standards' has been rewritten in light of the recent restructuring (which took effect in 2010) of the international bodies which regulate international accounting.

- The textbook has been updated in light of recent changes to relevant international financial reporting standards (IFRS).

- In response to feedback from lecturers, a new example which integrates the opening and closing statements of financial position and the statement of profit and losses has been introduced to Chapter 32 'Statement of cash flows'.

- In response to feedback from lecturers a section (and worked example) on the accounting treatment of debt has been introduced to Chapter 31. A practice question has also been included in the exercises at the end of the chapter.

2 New pedagogical features

- In response to feedback from lecturers and students, over 50 new real world examples have been added to the textbook. These examples highlight the link between the topic being covered academically and the real business world.

- Diagrams have been introduced to several of the chapters, particularly chapters that are quite narrative in nature. This pictorial presentation of information should help student learning by breaking up the text and providing another vehicle to highlight key points and connections between them.

- Additional examples have been included in Chapters 31 and 32.

- End-of-chapter exercises are categorized and ordered progressively by order of difficulty: Basic, Intermediate and Advanced in order to help students and academics identify and assign questions according to ability and to help develop progressive student learning.

- All references, key terms and learning objectives have also been updated as appropriate.

3 New and improved presentation

- In response to feedback from lecturers and students, the new edition now has a new and improved look and feel, with a new four-colour text design. Aimed to present the concept clearly, with greater use of colour than the previous edition in order to engage students and provide improved presentation of materials.

Aim of text

This book is primarily intended to be an introductory text for students taking a degree in accounting or business studies with a substantial element of accounting. It is IFRS compliant, though it also refers to UK terminology in the introductory chapter so that students are aware of the different accounting terms that are currently used in practice in the UK and Ireland.

The textbook also covers the financial accounting syllabus for Part One of the Association of Chartered Certified Accountants, the Foundation stage of the Chartered Institute of Management Accountants and the Introductory, Intermediate and Advanced Levels of the Certified Accounting Technicians. The authors have tried to provide a textbook that deals with all the fundamental basic accounting techniques and practices while at the same time going further to explain the reasons for accounting for transactions in a particular manner. The authors link the accounting techniques to the relevant International Accounting Standard, the *Framework* and real world examples, where possible. In addition, in several of the chapters, the authors highlight how accounting can be used unethically – for example, to smooth earnings. It is hoped that this deeper discussion will stimulate students to think strategically about the important influence that accounting can have on economic decision-making and hence society at large.

The book has been structured into eight parts for ease of reference. The first section covers the framework of accounting, as the authors feel that students should be exposed to the most important issues underlying accounting at the start. It is not expected that students who are only starting to learn accounting, or who have a low level of accounting knowledge, will understand every aspect of these chapters. However, reading the chapters will make students aware of the language of accounting, how accounting information is communicated by companies and the regulation of world accounting. Students are unlikely to comprehend in full the framework of accounting at the start of any accounting course, but understanding of the framework should start to become clearer as the student progresses through their accounting studies.

Knowledge of Part 2 (Double-entry bookkeeping and the books of account) is required before Part 3 (Preparing final financial statements of sole traders) can be fully appreciated and this section needs to be studied before Part 4 'Internal control and check' is taught. However, the sections from then on, Manufacturing entities (Part 5), Clubs (Part 6) Partnerships (Part 7) and Companies (Part 8) are stand alone and can be approached in any order, so long as the first four parts have been studied.

The structure within each chapter also follows a deliberate pattern. These usually start by examining the purpose, theoretical foundation and practical relevance of the topic. This is followed by a description of the accounting methods and then a comprehensive example. A further unique feature of the book is that after most examples there is a series of notes. These are intended to explain the unfamiliar and more difficult aspects of the example in order that the reader is able to follow the example. The notes also provide guidance on further aspects of the topic that may be encountered in examination questions, such as alternative forms of wording.

Each chapter also contains a set of written review questions and numerical exercises designed by the authors to test whether the student has fulfilled the learning objectives set out in the chapter, as well as past questions from various examining bodies. The review questions and exercises are presented in a coherent progressive sequence designed to test understanding of terminology, legal requirements, theoretical foundations, etc. The exercises are categorized into three levels (Basic, Intermediate and Advanced) according to their level of difficulty. This is rather subjective for a book that focuses on the introductory level, but it is hoped that the following classification may be useful to students and lecturers:

Basic exercises are of a standard lower than those commonly found in the first year of an undergraduate degree in accounting or the professional accountancy bodies examinations and can usually be completed in a relatively short time (i.e. less than about 35 minutes).

Intermediate exercises are of a standard commonly found in the first year of an undergraduate degree in accounting or the professional accountancy bodies' examinations and can usually be completed in about 35 minutes.

Advanced exercises are of a standard slightly higher than those commonly found in the first year of an undergraduate degree in accounting or the professional accountancy bodies examinations or will take longer to complete. They should be completed in between 45 to 60 minutes.

All users, especially lecturers, should also be aware that some exercises are extensions of other exercises in previous chapters. This is intended to provide a more comprehensive understanding of the relationship between different topics in accounting, such as day books and cash books, and provisions for depreciation and bad debts. Suggested solutions to some of the numerical exercises are included on the Online Learning Centre for student self-study. The answers to the rest of the numerical exercises are contained in a *Teachers' Solutions Manual* that is on the website for this book.

Each chapter also includes learning objectives, learning activities, a summary, a list of key terms and concepts, a real world example showing how a company is applying the topic or detailing a real-life scenario. The learning objectives at the start of each chapter set out the abilities and skills that the student should be able to demonstrate after reading the chapter. Students should also refer back to these after reading each chapter. Similarly, students should satisfy themselves that they can explain the meaning of the key terms and concepts listed at the end of each chapter. The summaries provide a comprehensive but concise review of the contents of each chapter that students should find useful for revision purposes. The learning activities are mostly real-life activities of a project/case study type which require students to apply their knowledge to practical situations. They frequently necessitate students collecting publicly available data from actual companies, or their own financial affairs.

The authors are **Andrew Thomas**, who has been a senior lecturer in accounting at the University of Birmingham, and **Anne Marie Ward**, a professor of accounting at the University of Ulster at Jordanstown and a Chartered Accountant, who has taught the professional examinations of Chartered Accountants Ireland for their student services department for the past 12 years and also lectures for the Institute of Accounting Techniques Ireland.

Summary of international accounting standards covered by the seventh edition

(Note: the versions referred to include all the changes made by the IASB up to 2010.)

International Accounting Standards Committee, (1989), adopted by the International Accounting Standards Board 2001, *Framework for the Preparation and Presentation of Financial Statements*, (IASC).

International Accounting Standards Board, (2010), *International Accounting Standard 1 – Presentation of Financial Statements*, (IASB).

International Accounting Standards Board, (2010), *International Accounting Standard 2 – Inventories*, (IASB).

International Accounting Standards Board, (2010), *International Accounting Standard 7 – Statement of Cash Flows*, (IASB).

International Accounting Standards Board, (2010), *International Accounting Standard 8 – Accounting Policies, Changes in Accounting Estimates and Errors*, (IASB).

International Accounting Standards Board, (2010), *International Accounting Standard 10 – Events after the Reporting Period*, (IASB).

International Accounting Standards Board, (2010), *International Accounting Standard 16 – Property, Plant and Equipment*, (IASB).

International Accounting Standards Board, (2010), *International Accounting Standard 18 – Revenue*, (IASB).

International Accounting Standards Board, (2010), *International Accounting Standard 37 – Provisions, Contingent Liabilities and Contingent Assets*, (IASB).

International Accounting Standards Board, (2010), *International Accounting Standard 38 – Intangible Assets*, (IASB).

International Accounting Standards Board, (2010), *International Financial Reporting Standard 3 – Business Combinations*, (IASB).

International Accounting Standards Board, (2010), *International Financial Reporting Standard 5 – Non-current Assets Held for Sale and Discontinuing Operations*, (IASB).

Anne Marie Ward and Andrew Thomas

Guided Tour

Learning Objectives

After reading this chapter you should be able to do th

1. Explain the meaning of the key terms and conce

2. Describe the contents of a typical statement of pr

3. Describe the contents of a typical statement of profit a

4. Outline the differences in the presentation of financial
and partnership financial statements.

5. Describe the contents of a typical statement of compre

6. Outline the differences in the presentation of financial
and both a sole trader and a partnership.

7. List the typical contents of an annual report.

8. Describe the contents of a typical statement of financi

Learning Objectives

Each chapter opens with a set of learning objectives, summarizing what you should learn from each chapter.

Key terms and concepts

annual report	4	listed comp
appropriation account	8	long-term l
asset	4	minority in
available-for-sale assets	5	non-contro
balance sheet	4	non-curren
comparatives	18	non-curren
corporation tax	13	notes to the
cost of services	8	other incon
current assets	5	other comp
current liabilities	5	partnership
equity	5	private limi
equity shareholder	5	profit and l
expenses	4	profit or los
ial statements	5	property, pl
sets	17	public limit
statement	6	revenue
le assets	5	sole traders
ry	5	statement o
ents in associates	5	statement o
s	5	statement

Key Terms and Concepts

These are highlighted throughout the chapter, with page number references at the end of each chapter so they can be found quickly and easily. A full glossary of definitions can be downloaded from the online learning centre.

	Note: Statement of changes in owners' equity			
	Capital		Current	
	X	Y	X	
	£	£	£	
Opening capital	3,000	2,000	200	
Capital introduced	–	500	–	
Profit for the year	–	–	13,558	
Drawings	–	–	(13,258)	
Closing capital	3,000	2,500	500	

Figure 1.5 An example of the layout of the statement of cha[nges in owners'] equity (capital and current accounts) for a partnership

It is also normal to provide some detail in partnership financial statemen[ts]... owners' equity (see Figure 1.5). A reconciliation based on the guidance given... Standard (IAS) 1 – *Presentation of Financial Statements* (IASB, 2010) discu[sses]... to portray this information.

Figures and Tables

Figures and tables help you to visualize the various accounting documents, and to illustrate and summarize important concepts.

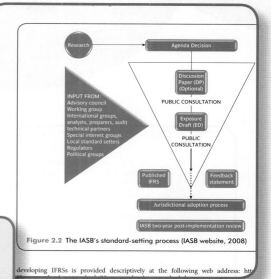

Figure 2.2 The IASB's standard-setting process (IASB website, 2008)

developing IFRSs is provided descriptively at the following web address: htt[p]...

Learning Activities

These quick activities give opportunities to test your learning and practise accountancy methods throughout the book.

As can be seen, this comprehensive accounting policy covers how... chased assets and internally generated assets, the method of accoun... ments are determined and when the company no longer recognizes...

LEARNING ACTIVITY 16.1

Using the financial statements of any plc for gui... with tangible assets), draft a pro forma note on... show the typical movements in a cost account ar... with the resultant opening and closing written-d...

Note how the property, plant and equipment note in the comp... the figure that is disclosed on the face of the company's stateme...

REAL WORLD EXAMPLE 12.1

Bookkeeping in practice – M...

'CONTROL of money sets apart the survivors in... grams that can help, even at the cheap end of the...

Software giant Microsoft has released its own, called Money 200... after personal finances and the accounting needs of small busin...

The program can clash with some anti-virus software, so prote... you can install it. It then grills the user for personal information... asks you to select from a range of popular financial ideals. Then... current bank accounts, credit cards, unit trusts.

On personal income the program is intolerant of random pay... regular payslips, even if from different sources. The business part... sys...

S...

Real World Examples

The chapters contain many and varied examples, including real-life accounting situations and mini case studies which bring accounting to life.

Guided Tour

amount he or she is to invest/pay into the firm.

EXAMPLE 28.5

Using the data in Example 28.4 this can be illustrated as follows. C is to b[e] partner with a one-half interest in both capital and profits in exchange for £42[,] in the capital/assets is computed as follows:

Capital/assets/equity of old partnership (£15,000 + £20,000)	
Investment by C	
Capital/assets/equity of new partnership	
C's share of equity of new partnership	
$(\frac{1}{2} \times £77,000)$	

The premium which C is being charged is therefore £42,000 – £38,500 = £3,500. The[n] similar to those in Method 3. However, these can be shortened to the following:

Journal			
		Debit	Cre[dit]
		£	£
Debit:	Bank	42,000	
Credit:	Capital – C		38,500
Credit:	Capital – A		2,100
Credit:	Capital – B		1,400
		42,000	42,000

Extracts and worked problems

Extracts from financial statements and worked problems will help you apply theory to practice.

disclosed in financial statements regardless of entity type.

Summary

Financial accounting today emerged from demand for quality financial information [on] financial performance and financial position by stakeholders who are external to the [entity.] information on performance, a statement of comprehensive income has evolved sho[wing] from normal activities, other types of gains and the total comprehensive income (the [bottom] figures) for the period. To provide information on the state of a company's affairs, the s[tatement of] [financ]ial position has evolved. It shows the total assets of the entity split into non-current a[nd current] [asse]ts. The bottom half of the statement of financial position shows how the entity is fina[nced] [from] the owner's equity invested and the liabilities (split into non-current and current) [The] [su]m of the equity and liabilities should equal the total assets (it should balance).

[Fi]ve types of business entity are covered in this book: sole traders, manufacturing entities, [partnerships] [an]d companies. In this chapter, standard information is provided for sole traders, part[nerships, governing bodies] [go]verned bodies and companies, and differences between the standard pro forma state[ments are highlighted.] [F]or example, sole traders and partnerships have more detail on their expenses and asset[s in their financial] [st]atements than companies do, as this information is required for an individual owner's [tax] [r]eturns. These entities also provide more detail in the statement of financial position of [the] owner's equity, whereas the detail of this is provided in the notes to company financial [statements.]

Chapter Summaries

These briefly review and reinforce the main topics covered in each chapter to ensure you have acquired a solid understanding of the key topics.

Continued

*An asterisk after the question number indicates that there is a s...
Centre (www.mcgraw-hill.co.uk/textbooks/thomas).*

Review questions

3.1*   Provide two definitions for the 'conceptual framework of a...

3.2   Describe the purposes of a conceptual framework of acco...

3.3   Describe the nature and contents of a conceptual framewo...

3.4   'It is unrealistic to expect a conceptual framework of acco...
or even generally accepted accounting standards in the...
conflicts and inconsistencies between, for example, the q...
information as well as the differing information needs and...

3.5   Outline the main differences between the ASB (UK) and t...

Review Questions

These questions encourage you to review and apply the knowledge you have acquired from each chapter.

Exercises

This end-of-chapter feature is the perfect way to practise the techniques you have been taught and apply methodology to real-world situations. They are pitched at different levels to ensure all readers have questions appropriate to their stage of learning.

b   What is the justification for adjusting the say, the total prime/direct cost?

connect Exercises

| BASIC | 25.5 |

Inventories, 1 January 20X3
Raw materials
Finished goods
Work-in-progress
Wages and salaries
Factory direct
Factory indirect
Purchases – raw materials
Power and fuel
Sales revenue
Insurance

APPENDIX

Case studies

Case Studies Appendix

The Appendix contains case studies designed to test how well you can apply the main techniques learned. Each case study has its own set of questions, and answers can be found on the Online Learning Centre.

Case study 1

The following case study shows how to track entries from the book of original the preparation of final financial statements for a sole trader. Details and instru to complete the relevant sections for Part 2, 'Double-entry Bookkeeping' and fo Financial Statements for Sole Traders'.

Trading details and supporting documentation

Mr O'Donnell, a sole trader, has owned and operated an antique furniture sto

connect™
ACCOUNTING

STUDENTS...

Want to get **better grades**? *(Who doesn't?)*

Prefer to do your **homework online**? *(After all, you are online anyway.)*

Need **a better way** to **study** before the big test?

(A little peace of mind is a good thing...)

With **McGraw-Hill's** *Connect*™ *Plus Accounting,*

STUDENTS GET:

- **Easy online access** to homework, tests, and quizzes assigned by your instructor.

- **Immediate feedback** on how you're doing. (No more wishing you could call your instructor at 1 a.m.)

- **Quick access** to lectures, practice materials, eBook, and more. (All the material you need to be successful is right at your fingertips.)

- A Self-Quiz and Study tool that **assesses your knowledge** and **recommends** specific readings, supplemental study materials, and additional practice work.*

- **LearnSmart** – intelligent flash cards that adapt to your specific needs and provide you with **24 x 7 personalized** study.*

*Available with select McGraw-Hill titles.

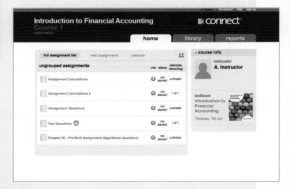

Less managing. More teaching. Greater learning.

 ## INSTRUCTORS...

Would you like your **students** to show up for class **more prepared**?
(Let's face it, class is much more fun if everyone is engaged and prepared...)

Want an **easy way to assign** homework online and track student **progress**?
(Less time grading means more time teaching...)

Want an **instant view** of student or class performance relative to learning objectives? *(No more wondering if students understand...)*

Need to **collect data and generate reports** required for administration or accreditation? *(Say goodbye to manually tracking student learning outcomes...)*

Want to **record and post your lectures** for students to view online?

 ## With **McGraw-Hill's *Connect*™ *Plus Accounting*,**

INSTRUCTORS GET:

- Simple **assignment management**, allowing you to spend more time teaching.
- **Auto-graded** assignments, quizzes, and tests.
- **Detailed Visual Reporting** where student and section results can be viewed and analyzed.
- Sophisticated **online testing** capability.
- A **filtering and reporting** function that allows you to easily assign and report on materials that are correlated to accreditation standards, learning outcomes, and Bloom's taxonomy.
- An easy-to-use **lecture capture** tool.
- The option to **upload course documents** for student access.

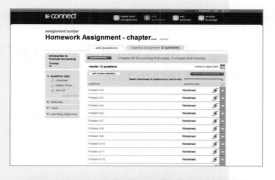

Want an online, **searchable version** of your textbook?

Wish your textbook could be **available online** while you're doing your assignments?

 ## Connect™ Plus Accounting eBook

If you choose to use *Connect™ Plus Accounting*, you have an affordable and searchable online version of your book integrated with your other online tools.

Connect™ Plus Accounting eBook offers features like:

- Topic search
- Direct links from assignments
- Adjustable text size
- Jump to page number
- Print by section

 Want to get more **value** from your textbook purchase?

Think learning accounting should be a bit more **interesting**?

 ## Check out the STUDENT RESOURCES section under the *Connect™* Library tab.

Here you'll find a wealth of resources designed to help you achieve your goals in the course. You'll find things like **quizzes, PowerPoints, and Internet activities** to help you study. Every student has different needs, so explore the STUDENT RESOURCES to find the materials best suited to you.

Technology to enhance learning and teaching

Visit www.mcgraw-hill.co.uk/textbooks/thomas today!

Online Learning Centre

Lecturer support- Helping you to help your students

In addition to the assignments, questions, problems and activities McGraw-Hill provides within Connect, we also offer a host of resources to support your teaching.

- **Faster course preparation** – time-saving support for your module.

- **High-calibre content to support your students** – resources written by your academic peers, who understand your need for rigorous and reliable content.

- **Flexibility** – edit, adapt or repurpose; test in Connect or test through EZ Test Online. The choice is yours.

The materials created specifically for lecturers adopting this textbook include:

- *Solutions Manual*

- *PowerPoint Slides*

- *Additional Tutorial Exercises*

- *Test Bank*

The following resources are available for students:

- *Mock Exams*

- *Additional Chapters*

- *A Glossary*

- *Answers to Selected End-of-Chapter Questions*

To request your password to access these resources, contact your McGraw-Hill representative or visit:

www.mcgraw-hill.co.uk/textbooks/thomas

Technology to enhance learning and teaching

EZTest

Test Bank available in McGraw-Hill EZ Test Online

A test bank of hundreds of questions is available to lecturers adopting this book for their module. For flexibility, this is available for adopters of this book to use through Connect or through the EZ Test online website. For each chapter you will find:

- A range of multiple choice questions

- Questions identified by type and difficulty to help you to select questions that best suit your needs

McGraw-Hill EZ Test Online is:

- **Accessible** anywhere with an internet connection – your unique login provides you access to all your tests and material in any location

- **Simple** to set up and easy to use

- **Flexible,** offering a choice from question banks associated with your adopted textbook or allowing you to create your own questions

- **Comprehensive,** with access to hundreds of banks and thousands of questions created for other McGraw-Hill titles

- **Compatible** with Blackboard and other course management systems

- **Time-saving** students' tests can be immediately marked and results and feedback delivered directly to your students to help them to monitor their progress.

To register for this FREE resource, visit www.eztestonline.com

Custom Publishing Solutions:

Let us help make our content your solution

At McGraw-Hill Education our aim is to help lecturers to find the most suitable content for their needs delivered to their students in the most appropriate way. Our custom publishing solutions offer the ideal combination of content delivered in the way which best suits lecturer and students.

Our custom publishing programme offers lecturers the opportunity to select just the chapters or sections of material they wish to deliver to their students from a database called CREATE™ at www.mcgrawhillcreate.co.uk

CREATE™ contains over two million pages of content from:

- Textbooks
- Professional books
- Case books – Harvard Articles, Insead, Ivey, Darden, Thunderbird and BusinessWeek
- Taking Sides – debate materials

Across the following imprints:

- McGraw-Hill Education
- Open University Press
- Harvard Business Publishing
- US and European material

There is also the option to include additional material authored by lecturers in the custom product – this does not necessarily have to be in English.

We will take care of everything from start to finish in the process of developing and delivering a custom product to ensure that lecturers and students receive exactly the material needed in the most suitable way.

With a Custom Publishing Solution, students enjoy the best selection of material deemed to be the most suitable for learning everything they need for their courses – something of real value to support their learning. Teachers are able to use exactly the material they want, in the way they want, to support their teaching on the course.

Please contact your local McGraw-Hill representative with any questions or alternatively contact Warren Eels, email: warren_eels@mcgraw-hill.com.

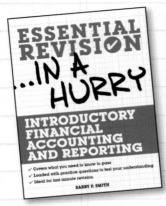

Improve your grades!

20% off any Study Skills book!

ESSENTIAL REVISION ...IN A HURRY
INTRODUCTORY FINANCIAL ACCOUNTING AND REPORTING
✓ Covers what you need to know to pass
✓ Loaded with practice questions to test your understanding
✓ Ideal for last minute revision
BARRY P. SMITH

Student-Friendly Guides
Excellent dissertations!
Peter Levin

Open UP Study Skills
The Complete Guide to Referencing and Avoiding Plagiarism
Second Edition
Colin Neville

Our Study Skills books are packed with practical advice and tips that are easy to put into practice and will really improve the way you study. Our books will help you:

- ✓ Improve your grades
- ✓ Avoid plagiarism
- ✓ Save time
- ✓ Develop new skills
- ✓ Write confidently
- ✓ Undertake research projects
- ✓ Sail through exams
- ✓ Find the perfect job

Special offer!

As a valued customer, buy online and receive 20% off any of our Study Skills books by entering the promo code **BRILLIANT**

www.openup.co.uk/studyskills

Acknowledgements

Publisher's Acknowledgements

Our thanks go to the following reviewers for their comments at various stages in the text's development:

Mary Bishop, University of West of England

Juliet Cottingham, Kingston

Ian Crawford, University of Bath

Robert Devlin, University of Ulster

Ellie Franklin, Middlesex University

Alan Graham, University of Portsmouth

Matthew W. Guah, Erasmus University Rotterdam

Helena Isidro, Cass Business School

Robert Jupe, Kent University

Jim O'Hare, University of Leicester

Nick Rowbottom, University of Birmingham

Thomas Spencer, Nottingham Trent University

Thanks to Bridger McNally, NUI Maynooth, and Thomas Spencer, Nottingham Trent University, for their work on the online resources.

Author's Acknowledgements

My family – for being supportive.

The lecturers who adopted the last edition of the text and anyone who has purchased the textbook.

The reviewers as listed above for their comments.

Sandra Brosnan and Robert Jupe for contributing case studies.

Leiah Batchelor, Tom Hill, James Bishop, Stephanie Frosch and the production team at McGraw-Hill.

Michael Monaghan, the Copy Editor.

The Association of Chartered Certified Accountants (ACCA), The Association of Accounting Technicians (AAT), The Associated Examining Board (AEB) and The Joint Matriculation Board (JMB) for allowing us to reproduce copies of their questions in the text.

Anne Marie Ward

Every effort has been made to trace and acknowledge ownership of copyright and to clear permission for material reproduced in this book. The publishers will be pleased to make suitable arrangements to clear permission with any copyright holders whom it has not been possible to contact.

The framework of accounting

Part contents

Entities and financial reporting statements

Learning Objectives

After reading this chapter you should be able to do the following:

1. Explain the meaning of the key terms and concepts listed at the end of the chapter.

2. Describe the contents of a typical statement of profit and loss for a sole trader.

3. Describe the contents of a typical statement of profit and loss for a partnership.

4. Outline the differences in the presentation of financial information between sole trader and partnership financial statements.

5. Describe the contents of a typical statement of comprehensive income for a company.

6. Outline the differences in the presentation of financial information between a company and both a sole trader and a partnership.

7. List the typical contents of an annual report.

8. Describe the contents of a typical statement of financial position.

1.1 Introduction

Accounting is a necessity in every entity, regardless of type or size. It is so important that a full-time international body, the International Accounting Standards Board (IASB), representing accounting experts from several countries exists to provide guidance on how to account for items and transactions and how to communicate (present) this information. This book is prepared using the most recent accounting guidance as produced by the IASB.

In its earliest form accounting involved keeping a count of items. The first form of accounting was known as **stewardship accounting** as stewards were employed by wealthy individuals to keep 'a count' of items they owned (assets) and items they owed (liabilities). The difference between these two 'elements' represents the individuals' financial position (their net worth). Evidence from archaeological digs would suggest that this form of accounting might be 7000 years old (stone tablets inscribed with hieroglyphic records of counts of assets were uncovered in Egypt). In Europe, archaeological evidence (wooden tally sticks which are argued to represent counts of assets and liabilities) from about 2000 BC were found and considered to be evidence of stewardship accounting. The information collected under this ancient form of accounting is still in existence today and is captured in one of the most important statements provided in an entity's **annual report** – the **statement of financial position** (assets, liabilities and owners' capital). This statement is referred to as the '**balance sheet**' under UK accounting. The whole purpose of this statement is to identify the net worth of the entity. It provides information on what the entity owns (assets) and what the entity owes (liabilities). The difference represents 'capital' being the amount that the company owes the owners, or to consider it another way, it is the amount the owners have invested in the company either directly or indirectly.

The industrial revolution advanced the role and nature of accounting. For the first time the general public were able to purchase shares in companies. Before this time, most company managers were the company's owners. Accounting was more for internal control purposes. After the separation of ownership and control, accounting had to progress to provide information to people who were external to the company and who had little knowledge of what went on in the company. To help the external owners assess the performance of a company and the performance of management, legislation at this time required that companies provided their owners with statements of financial position and also required that they provide a statement detailing the performance of the company in the period. This statement is now called the **statement of profit and loss** or the **statement of comprehensive income**. In the UK this statement is also called the **profit and loss account**. This statement outlines the income for the period and the expenses incurred in the period. The difference between income and expenses is profit or loss. The requirement to produce the two statements is generally regarded as the start of financial accounting as we now know it. When the two statements are published together with other related information, the combined document is called the **annual report**.

1.2 Accounting language

Before progressing to discuss accounting and financial statements, this section details the main terminology used in financial statements (in brief). More detail and other phrases are introduced throughout this textbook.

Statement of profit and loss terminology

Profit or loss is the total income made by the entity in the period less the total expenses incurred by the entity in the period. **Revenue** is income earned in the period from normal trading activities. When an entity has income from activities that are not its core business, such as receiving interest, then this is disclosed separately as '**other income**'. This is so the reader of the financial information can gauge management's performance in generating income from the business and income from investing activities. **Expenses** are yearly running costs. They are used up in the period being reported on. Examples include staff wages, electricity used to generate heat and light for the business and rent of the business premises for the period. The user is interested to see these costs as again they can assess management's performance in their efficient use of resources. Information on expenses can enable the reader of the statement of profit and loss to determine how risky an entity's profits are.

Statement of financial position terminology

Assets

In simple terms, an **asset** is an item of value held by an entity that is going to generate income in the future. This income might, for example, come from the sale of an asset, or from its use. Assets are categorized into four types and have descriptions that signify how long the entity is likely to keep the asset. The four types of asset are tangible assets, intangible assets, investments in associate companies (other companies over which the company has some influence) and available-for-sale investments.

1 **Tangible assets**, referred to in the statement of financial position as **property, plant and equipment**, can be seen and touched (they are tangible in nature); for example, a car, a house or a desk.

2 **Intangible assets** cannot be seen or touched but have value. An example is your education. You will be able to earn more income in the future because of your education. You are building up intellectual capital (your human value) as you progress through your studies. Companies/firms, and so on, will pay a premium to get access to your knowledge in the future.

3 **Available-for-sale assets** are investments that are denominated in money, or in paper (e.g. shares and bonds), which the entity holds for financial gain and which will be sold by the entity in the future.

4 **Investments in associates** are also investments in paper shares; however, the intention is to retain this investment as part of the entity's normal activities.

As mentioned, assets are presented in the financial statements according to the length of time an entity expects to hold on to the asset. Assets that the entity expects to turn to cash within one year (and cash itself) are called **current assets**, and assets that the entity expects to use for periods that extend beyond one year are called **non-current assets**.

Inventory (stock) is the name for goods that have been purchased for resale but are not yet sold. They are current assets. A **trade receivable** (debtor) is the term given to the money that is owed from a customer, to whom the entity has sold goods on credit (the goods were given in advance of the entity receiving money for the goods).

Liabilities

In simple terms, **liabilities** represent obligations that the entity has to meet in the future. For example, a loan from a bank is a liability because at some point in the future the entity has to pay this back. Getting goods on credit (in advance of having to pay for them) from a supplier is a liability because the supplier has to be paid in the future. A **trade payable** (creditor) is the term given to the money that is owed from a supplier who provided goods on credit. Like assets, liabilities are presented in the financial statements according to the length of time an entity expects the liability to be outstanding. Liabilities that the entity expects to pay within one year are called **current liabilities** and liabilities that the entity expects to pay in periods that extend beyond one year are called **non-current liabilities**.

Equity or **equity shareholder** is another name for owner. It is usually used in reference to limited companies to refer to the shareholders who own ordinary shares.

1.3 Financial statements

As mentioned in the introduction, all entities have to produce a document periodically (usually yearly), which details what has been made in the period (profit or loss) and the entity's financial position. This information is provided in a number of short statements. The first statement provides details on the profits/losses made by the entity in the period. There is choice in the way that this information can be presented. The information can either be presented in one statement called the **statement of comprehensive income** which shows the profits and losses for the period from realized activities in the first section followed by a section providing information on other comprehensive income (typically unrealized gains/losses). The second alternative splits the information into two consecutive statements the first of which is called the **statement of profit and loss** and the second the **statement of other comprehensive income**. This format is effective from 1 January 2012 (IASplus, 2011).

The second statement provides information on the financial position of the entity and is called the **statement of financial position**. The two statements together are called **financial statements** (otherwise known as '**accounts**'). Larger companies also have to provide a third statement, showing the source and use of cash in the period. This third statement is called the **statement of cash flows**. As all the financial information about an entity is summarized in the three statements, which usually do not extend beyond one page each, more detail is provided in the **notes to the financial statements**. The financial statements and notes are included in an entity's '**annual report**' along with reports from management telling the owners what they are doing and what they plan to do: the operating and financial review, the directors' report, the chief executive's report, the chairman's statement and the corporate social responsibility report. They also provide information on how they govern themselves in a corporate governance report and remuneration report. The narrative part of the report also highlights in narrative form key information about the company and outlines the principle risks that the company faces. A plc's annual report can extend to over 100 pages.

LEARNING ACTIVITY 1.1

Visit the Ryanair plc website and view a copy of their most recent annual report. Familiarize yourself with the reports provided by the directors at the front of the annual report. Note that this part of the annual report extends to over 100 pages. The latter part of the annual report contains the **income statement** (also called the statement of comprehensive income), the balance sheet (now called the statement of financial position), the statement of cash flows and the notes to the financial statements for the Group and separately for the company.

Having financial information that is useful for financial statement users is so important that international standards of accounting, which cover how we account and how we present the information we have accounted for, have been established over the past four decades. The institutional framework underlying the establishment of international accounting standards is covered in the next chapter in detail. The standards are prepared with companies in mind; however, other types of entity exist.

1.4 Types of entity

Changes in accounting practices and disclosures usually arise from the need to provide quality financial information that is regarded as useful for the external stakeholders of a company. The stakeholders are discussed in detail in Chapter 4, 'The Nature and Objectives of Financial Reporting'. They include the owners of the company, investors, creditors, employees, customers, the government and the public. There are several types of entity, for example owner-managed entities (wherein the owners are the managers and there are no external owners) and publicly-owned companies that are owned predominately by the public and are managed by paid employees. Owner-managed entities include sole traders, partnerships and some limited companies and public-owned companies include companies that are listed on stock exchanges.

The type of information required in financial statements depends on the type of entity and the information needs of its stakeholders (users). The main difference in the accounting requirements for each type of entity is in respect of presentation. Though most entities follow guidance provided by the accountancy bodies, which are geared towards companies with external owners, differences in presentation arise because the accounting information being prepared by different entities may be for different purposes. For example, owner-managed entities may have full knowledge of the performance of their business. They do not have to formalize this knowledge into a set of written financial statements. However, the tax authorities (HM Revenue and Customs) will require financial statements to determine the tax bill, or the bank which has given the entity a loan may require information to determine if the entity will be able to repay the loan. There are other differences in the information that an entity itself will wish to highlight for the benefit of its stakeholders. For example, a charity will wish to provide more information on the sources of its income, and what it is doing with that income, than a conventional business which will not wish such detail to be provided as this may give too much information to competitors. Therefore, different entities tend to present their financial information in slightly different ways. This chapter highlights some of the main types of entity and provides proforma layouts of both the statement of profit and loss (the statement of comprehensive income) and the statement of financial position for each type of entity covered in this book.

1.5 Sole traders

Sole traders are individuals who have started a business on their own. In a sole-trader business there is only one owner, the sole trader. Sole-trader businesses are **unincorporated businesses** – they are not separate legal entities, not companies. As such, the sole trader is responsible for the debts of the business. This means that creditors have a claim over the sole trader's personal wealth for unpaid debts when the business runs out of funds. There is no legal distinction between the assets of the business and the assets of the sole trader.

Profits made in sole trader businesses are regarded as their owner's by the tax authorities and are subject to income tax. Sole traders usually have to get financial statements prepared for the purposes of completing their self-assessment tax return that has to be filed annually. This return requires quite a bit of expense detail, therefore sole-trader statements of profit and loss are more detailed (have less aggregation of expenses) than occurs in company financial statements. The statement of financial position disclosures are similar to those required for companies; however, more detail is provided in this statement on non-current assets and changes in the owner's capital.

Simple examples of a statement of profit and loss and a statement of financial position for a sole trader who operates a child-minding business are shown in Figures 1.1 and 1.2. Note the extensive detail

T. Sole: Trading as T. Child Minding Services		
Statement of profit and loss for the year ended 31 March 20X3		
	£	£
Revenue		6,470
Less: cost of services		
Purchases		1,527
Gross profit		4,943
Other income		100
Less: expenses		
Travel and mileage	530	
Sundry expenses	33	
General running expenses	975	
Stationery	41	
Depreciation – toys	143	
Depreciation – equipment	67	
Depreciation – house fixtures	64	1,853
Profit for the year		3,190

Figure 1.1 A simple example of the layout of a statement of profit and loss for a sole trader

Note: depreciation is an allocation of the cost, or value of tangible non-current asset, to the statement of profit and loss over the period the business expects to use and generate revenue from the asset. This is covered in detail in Chapter 16.

T. Sole: Trading as T. Child Minding Services Statement of financial position as at 31 March 20X3		
ASSETS	Note	£
Non-current assets		
Property, plant and equipment	2	824
Current assets		
Trade receivables		350
Bank		100
		450
Total assets		1,274
EQUITY AND LIABILITIES		
Owners' capital		
Opening capital		243
Capital introduced		0
Profit for the year		3,190
		3,433
Drawings		(2,609)
Closing capital		824
Current liabilities		
Trade and other payables		450
Total equity and liabilities		1,274
I approve these financial statements and confirm that all relevant information and explanations have been provided		
T. Sole	28th August 20X3	

Figure 1.2 A simple example of the layout of a statement of financial position for a sole trader

provided on expenses. As mentioned, this is primarily to suit the tax authorities who require similar detail in an individual's self-assessment return. Many of the terms used have been explained earlier in this chapter and are not repeated here. The **cost of services** section includes those expenses that are directly related to the child-minding service that is being sold by the business. Typical costs might include food for the children, nappies and toiletries. In a business that sells goods, this description usually changes to cost of goods sold.

The format of sole trader financial statements is explained in more detail in Part 3.

1.6 Partnerships

Partnerships occur when two or more individuals get together to form a business. A partnership can be incorporated as a limited liability partnership or as an unincorporated business. If it is unincorporated then the same principles as outlined above for sole traders apply, except that the partners will be jointly liable for the partnership's debts. In many instances the partnership will have a partnership

X & Y: Trading as X & Y Hair Salon		
Statement of profit and loss for the year ended 31 March 20X3		
	£	£
Revenue		101,433
Less: cost of goods sold		
Opening inventory	200	
Purchases	15,836	
	16,036	
Less: closing inventory	500	15,536
Gross profit		85,897
Less: expenses		
Salaries	29,569	
Rent and rates	16,504	
Heat and light	2,386	
Telephone	200	
Advertising and stationery	817	
Laundry and cleaning	547	
Professional fees and insurance	1,600	
Bank interest and fees	2,144	
Accountancy fees	260	
Refreshments, papers, etc.	342	
Repairs	3,199	
Sundry expenses	544	
Travel	636	
Depreciation	33	58,781
Profit for the year		27,116
Apportioned between:		
X current account		13,558
Y current account		13,558
		27,116

Figure 1.3 An example of the layout of a statement of profit and loss for a partnership

agreement that may alter the profit-sharing ratios between the partners. The partners usually have to get financial statements prepared for the partnership for the purposes of completing a partnership return for the tax authorities, and for completing their personal self-assessment tax return, which has to be filed annually. The partners have to pay income tax on the profits of the partnership. The partnership return requires quite a bit of expense detail; therefore, partnership statements of profit and loss are more detailed (have less aggregation of expenses) than company statements of profit and loss. If the partnership is limited, then the same principles as detailed under companies (discussed in Part 8) are relevant. A typical layout of a partnership statement of profit and loss can be seen in Figure 1.3.

X & Y: Trading as X & Y Hair Salon			
Statement of financial position as at 31st March 20X3			
ASSETS			£
Non-current assets			
Tangible assets			
Equipment			100
Current assets			
Inventories			500
Trade and other receivables			7,743
Bank			7,095
Cash			200
			15,538
Total assets			15,638
OWNERS' EQUITY AND LIABILITIES			
Owners' equity:	Capital	Current	Total
	£	£	£
Partner X	3,000	500	3,500
Partner Y	2,500	791	3,291
	5,500	1,291	6,791
Non-current liabilities			
Loan			5,000
Current liabilities			
Trade and other payables			3,847
Total equity and liabilities			15,638

I approve these financial statements and confirm that all relevant information and explanations have been provided

X (Signature) _____   Y (Signature) _____

31st May 20X3   31st May 20X3

Figure 1.4 An example of the layout of a statement of financial position for a partnership

The profit or loss for the period is apportioned between the partners using an **appropriation account** that is typically included at the base of the statement of profit and loss. This disclosure is unique to partnerships.

The statement of financial position is similar to that prepared for sole traders and companies, except the capital attributable to each owner is disclosed separately. Like sole traders more detail on tangible non-current assets is also typically provided in the statement of financial position than is disclosed on the face of company financial statements, wherein the detail is provided in the notes (see Chapter 31). An example of a statement of financial position for a partnership can be seen in Figure 1.4.

Note: Statement of changes in owners' equity					
	Capital		Current		
	X	Y	X	Y	Total
	£	£	£	£	£
Opening capital	3,000	2,000	200	300	5,500
Capital introduced	–	500	–	–	500
Profit for the year	–	–	13,558	13,558	27,116
Drawings	–	–	(13,258)	(13,067)	(26,325)
Closing capital	3,000	2,500	500	791	6,791

Figure 1.5 An example of the layout of the statement of changes in owners' equity (capital and current accounts) for a partnership

It is also normal to provide some detail in partnership financial statements on the movements within owners' equity (see Figure 1.5). A reconciliation based on the guidance given in International Accounting Standard (IAS) 1 – *Presentation of Financial Statements* (IASB, 2010) discussed below has been adapted to portray this information.

The preparation of partnership financial statements is covered in detail in Part 7.

1.7 Member-governed bodies

Some entities are run by its members for the benefit of the members. Many are unincorporated (not established under law as a company). Some of these entities are large, formal and subject to their own legislation (not company legislation). However, their disclosure requirements usually follow those recommended by the accounting bodies. Examples of this type of organization include mutual building societies, sports clubs and life assurance companies. In many instances, to protect members' private wealth, these entities become incorporated; however, unlike normal companies, they are not limited by share opting to become limited by guarantee instead. Therefore, they do not have a share capital or shareholders. The guarantor members agree to pay a fixed sum of money towards the debts of the entity in the event of the entity being unable to do so. The sums guaranteed by each member are small, typically £1. This text does not consider the presentation requirements of all these different types of organization; however, it does cover unincorporated clubs (see Part 6). An example of a typical format is now provided. Reading University Students' Union has been prepared in accordance with UK Generally Accepted Accounting Practice, hence the terminology and formats are not IAS compliant.

Reading University Students' Union Financial Statements

Reading University Students' Union Income and Expenditure Account For the year ended 31st July 2010	Notes	2010 £	2009 £
INCOME			
Block Grant		886,611	886,611
Net Trading Income	2	211,285	262,971
Interest Receivable		804	4,117
Profit on Disposal of Fixed Assets		648	–
		1,099,348	1,153,699
EXPENDITURE			
Support Services Activities	3	319,255	351,019
Membership Services	4	263,691	353,022
Affiliations	5	52,492	51,305
Democracy and Elected Committees	6	195,330	157,417
Clubs and Societies	7	209,641	181,342
		1,040,409	1,094,105
SURPLUS FOR THE YEAR TO ACCUMULATED FUND		£58,939	£59,594

Reading University Students' Union Balance Sheet As at 31st July 2010	Note	2010 £	2010 £	2009 £	2009 £
FIXED ASSETS					
Tangible Assets	8		782,745		754,065
Investments	9		1,862		1,862
			784,607		755,927
CURRENT ASSETS					
Stocks	10	91,956		86,912	
Debtors	11	243,426		180,843	
Cash at Bank and In Hand		67,403		90,255	
		402,785		357,980	

CREDITORS: Amounts falling due within one year	12	(428,184)		(551,797)
NET CURRENT LIABILITIES			(25,399)	(193,817)
TOTAL ASSETS LESS CURRENT LIABILITIES			759,208	562,110
CREDITORS: Amounts falling due more than one year	13	(400,375)		(262,216)
			£358,833	£299,894
RESERVES				
Accumulated Fund	19		£358,833	£299,894

Source: http://www.rusu.co.uk/asset/event/6013/RUSUFinancialStatements31stJuly2010.pdf (accessed August 2011)

LEARNING ACTIVITY 1.2

Re-prepare Reading University Students' Union Financial Statements using IFRS terminology and formats.

1.8 Companies

Companies are incorporated by law as separate legal entities. Companies can own assets and can take action in their own right. Companies are regulated by legislation (the Companies Act 2006), the accounting profession and the stock exchanges (if listed). Companies are subject to more stringent regulation than other forms of business entity. Companies have to pay **corporation tax** (company income tax). The two most common forms of company are **public limited companies** (plc) and **private limited companies** (Ltd). Under law incorporated companies have to include the abbreviated 'plc' or 'Ltd' in their name so that stakeholders (interested parties) are aware of their status. Plcs offer shares to the public on recognized share exchanges, such as the London Stock Exchange (LSE), the Irish Stock Exchange (ISE) or the New York Share Exchange (NYSE). When a company is formed its ownership is split into shares. These shares are then sold on stock exchanges to members of the public. For example, if a company is set up with an authorized share capital of 1,000 shares and you purchase 100 shares, you will own 10 per cent of the company. Plcs are commonly referred to as **listed companies** (because they are listed as members of a stock exchange). Limited companies are privately owned, usually by a family or a small group of investors. The owners in private companies also hold shares in the company. These shares may be sold privately but are not publicly sold on exchanges. In both public and private limited companies, owners' private wealth is protected from creditors by legislation. They have what is referred to as **limited liability** – owners will only lose their investment (represented by monies paid for shares held) in the company if it fails. Creditors cannot sue them for their private assets. Therefore, their liability is limited to the amount invested in the company. The most up-to-date guidance on how to present company financial statements is provided in IAS 1. According to this standard, a company should prepare

Milky Chocolate Ltd	
Statement of comprehensive income for the year ended 31 March 20X3	
	£
Revenue	101,433
Cost of sales	(15,537)
Gross profit	85,896
Other income	3,000
Distribution costs	(28,000)
Administration expenses	(41,285)
Other expenses	(895)
Finance costs	(2,514)
Profit before tax	16,202
Income tax expense	(3,850)
Profit for the year from continuing activities	12,352
Loss for the year from discontinuing activities	(1,895)
Profit for the year	10,457
Other comprehensive income	
Gains on property revaluation	2,500
Exchange differences on translating foreign operations	(365)
Income tax on other comprehensive income	(256)
Other comprehensive income net of tax	1,879
Total comprehensive income for the year	12,336
Profit attributable to:	
Owners	9,850
Non-controlling interests	607
	10,457
Total comprehensive income attributable to:	
Owners	11,490
Non-controlling interests	846
	12,336

Figure 1.6 A detailed example of the layout of a statement of comprehensive income for a company

a statement of comprehensive income showing the **profit or loss for the period** (revenue less expenses) in the first part of the statement and **other comprehensive income** in the second part of the statement, with the final line showing the **total comprehensive income** for the period. IAS 1 contains an example in its appendices, which is similar to the one as seen in Figure 1.6. In an exposure draft, issued May 2010, the IASB suggested changes to the format of this statement and the title, which they suggest should change to 'statement of comprehensive income'.

Milky Chocolate Ltd	
Statement of comprehensive income for the year ended 31 March 20X3	
	£'000
Revenue	101,433
Cost of sales	(25,537)
Gross profit	75,896
Other income	3,000
Distribution costs	(28,000)
Administration expenses	(41,285)
Other expenses	(895)
Finance costs	(2,514)
Profit before tax	6,202
Income tax expense	(2,850)
Profit for the year from continuing activities	3,352
Other comprehensive income	
Gains on property revaluation	1,500
Other comprehensive income net of tax	1,500
Total comprehensive income for the year	4,852

Figure 1.7 A simple example of the layout of a statement of comprehensive income for a company

At this stage you will not be expected to prepare anything as comprehensive at this. You will not have to show income from continuing and discontinuing activities separately. It is assumed that all the businesses you will be preparing the financial statements for will be continuing into the foreseeable future. In addition, the revaluation of non-current assets is the only 'other comprehensive income' entry referred to in this book – it will not be addressed until Parts 7 and 8. You will also not have to deal with non-controlling interests in the book, though this is covered in the chapter on group financial statements in the website. **Non-controlling interests** are otherwise known as **minority interests**. They arise when one company controls another company by virtue of having the majority of the shares/voting rights in that company. As such, this dominant shareholder is regarded as the owner (the parent), and the people/entities who own the remainder of the shares are called non-controlling interests.

These more obscure entries have been omitted from the statement of comprehensive income provided in Figure 1.7. It is more likely than not that any statement of comprehensive income you have to prepare for a company will look like the one shown in Figure 1.7.

A standard format for reporting a company's financial position (assets, liabilities and owners' capital) is also provided in the appendix to IAS 1. Figure 1.8 has been prepared in light of the example provided in IAS 1.

Total assets equals total equity and liabilities (both amount to £27,160,000). This balancing concept is explored fully in Chapter 8, 'The Accounting Equation and its Components' and forms the underlying principles behind double entry that is covered in Chapter 10, 'Double Entry and the General Ledger' and subsequent chapters. It is hoped that you will now be familiar with the consistencies and differences in the reporting between different types of entity. As presentation is so important in accounting, the IAS dealing with this is now briefly explained.

Milky Chocolate Ltd	
Statement of financial position as at 31 March 20X3	
ASSETS	**£'000**
Non-current assets	
Property, plant and equipment	21,520
Goodwill	800
Other intangible assets	400
Available-for-sale investments	1,200
	23,920
Current assets	
Inventories	1,560
Trade receivables	1,480
Other current assets	120
Cash and cash equivalents	80
	3,240
Total assets	27,160
EQUITY AND LIABILITIES	
Capital and reserves	
Share capital	8,000
Retained earnings	6,528
Other components of equity	2,500
Total equity	17,028
Non-current liabilities	
Long-term borrowing	3,000
Long-term provisions	2,580
Total non-current liabilities	5,580
Current liabilities	
Trade and other payables	1,540
Short-term borrowing	520
Current portion of long-term borrowing	932
Current tax payable	980
Short-term provision	580
Total current liabilities	4,552
Total liabilities	10,132
Total equity and liabilities	27,160

Figure 1.8 A simple example of the layout of a statement of financial position for a company

1.9 IAS 1 – Presentation of Financial Statements[1]

The components of financial statements required by IAS 1 (IASB, 2010) are as follows:

1 To report on profit or loss in the period, two options are available. The first involves producing a single statement called a 'statement of comprehensive income' (as portrayed in Figure 1.7). The first half of this statement contains conventional profit and loss items (income and expenses) and is subtotalled to provide one figure to represent the profit or loss from the entity's normal trading activities. Other comprehensive income (equity gains/losses not arising from normal trading activities) is then set out and subtotalled. Finally, a total comprehensive income amount (the profit or loss for the period plus the other comprehensive income) is provided at the bottom of the statement.

The second option is to produce an **income statement** that details the profit or loss for the period (the statement of profit and loss) and a separate statement dealing with all non-owner changes in equity (the statement of other comprehensive income). At the time of writing the IASB had just finished a consultation period on the presentation of the profits and losses of an entity. The result is that the two options for presentation remain (IASplus, 2011). In this text book the statement of profit and loss is used for sole traders and partnerships as they rarely have other comprehensive income, whereas the statement of comprehensive income is used for companies as this is more common in practice (for plcs).

2 To report the net worth of the business, a statement of financial position has to be prepared at the reporting date. This lists the entity's assets, liabilities and capital on that date.

3 A **statement of changes in equity** is required to show all owner changes in equity, such as dividends paid to owners, or new share issues (see Chapter 31, 'The Final Financial Statements of Limited Companies').

4 Finally, a statement of cash flows is also required (see Chapter 32, 'Statements of Cash Flows').

The minimum contents of the statement of financial position specified in IAS 1 are also similar to that required by the UK Generally Accepted Accounting Practice (GAAP), but the format and terminology are slightly different. In particular, under UK GAAP, the statement of financial position is called the **balance sheet** and the statement of profits and losses is referred to as the **profit and loss account**. The ordering of presentation is also quite different (this is highlighted in an online chapter 'UK Accounting: Institutional Framework and Standards'; available at: www.mcgrawhill.co.uk/textbooks/thomas). In terms of terminology, non-current assets are referred to as **fixed assets** in UK legislation, non-current liabilities are referred to as **long-term liabilities**, trade receivables are referred to as **trade debtors**, and the trade and other payables are referred to as **trade creditors**. **Property, plant and equipment** is equivalent to the **tangible fixed assets** shown in the UK format and is made up of land and buildings, plant and machinery, and fixtures, fittings, tools and equipment. The retained earnings are equivalent to the balance on the profit and loss account as shown in the UK balance sheet format. The remaining items should be self-explanatory.

LEARNING ACTIVITY 1.3

Access the financial statements of Morrison Supermarkets PLC for 2010. Note this company is adopting a UK GAAP format for its 'Balance Sheet'. Note the terminology and different presentation style.

---

[1] The UK equivalent is FRS 3 – Reporting Financial Performance.

In practice prior year figures (called **comparatives**) are provided for nearly all financial information disclosed in financial statements regardless of entity type.

Summary

Financial accounting today emerged from demand for quality financial information about an entity's financial performance and financial position by stakeholders who are external to the entity. To provide information on performance, a statement of comprehensive income has evolved showing profit or loss from normal activities, other types of gains and the total comprehensive income (the sum of both these figures) for the period. To provide information on the state of a company's affairs, the statement of financial position has evolved. It shows the total assets of the entity split into non-current and current categories. The bottom half of the statement of financial position shows how the entity is financed. The amount of the owner's equity invested and the liabilities (split into non-current and current) are disclosed. The sum of the equity and liabilities should equal the total assets (it should balance).

Five types of business entity are covered in this book: sole traders, manufacturing entities, clubs, partnerships and companies. In this chapter, standard information is provided for sole traders, partnerships, member-governed bodies and companies, and differences between the standard pro forma statements are outlined. For example, sole traders and partnerships have more detail on their expenses and assets in their reporting statements than companies do, as this information is required for an individual owner's self-assessment tax returns. These entities also provide more detail in the statement of financial position of movements in the owner's equity, whereas the detail of this is provided in the notes to company financial statements.

Key terms and concepts

An asterisk after the question number indicates that there is a suggested answer on the Online Learning Centre (www.mcgraw-hill.co.uk/textbooks/thomas).

Review questions

connect

1.1 List the typical contents of an annual report for a public limited company.

1.2 Outline the differences between the information provided in the financial statements of sole traders and partnerships.

1.3 Outline the differences in the information provided in the financial statements of sole traders and companies.

Exercises

connect

1.4*

BASIC

In which statement will the following appear, and under which heading will it be included:

a Furniture and fixtures;

b Rent;

c Wages;

d Amounts owing to a supplier;

e Amounts due from a customer.

1.5

BASIC

Why are financial statements prepared by companies?

1.6

BASIC

What do you think is the objective of financial statements?

1.7

BASIC

Who do you think the stakeholders (users) of financial statement might be?

References

IASplus (2011) 'Information on the changes to IAS 1 on the presentation of financial statements', website http://www.iasplus.com/standard/ias01.htm (accessed March 2011).

International Accounting Standards Board (2010) *International Accounting Standard 1 – Presentation of Financial Statements* (IASB).

Reading University Students' Union (2010) 'Financial Statements for 2010', website http://www.rusu.co.uk/asset/event/6013/RUSUFinancialStatements31stJuly2010.pdf (accessed March 2011).

Tesco annual report (2010) Website http://www.tesco.com (accessed March 2011).

When you have read this chapter, log on to the Online Learning Centre for *Introduction to Financial Accounting* at www.mcgraw-hill.co.uk/textbooks/thomas, where you will find multiple choice quizzes, case studies, a glossary and mock exams.

International financial reporting: institutional framework and standards

Learning Objectives

After reading this chapter you should be able to do the following:

1. Explain the meaning of the key terms and concepts listed at the end of the chapter.

2. Describe the regulatory framework of international accounting.

3. Describe the objectives and role of the International Accounting Standards Board.

4. Explain the process adopted by the International Accounting Standards Board when preparing a new standard/revising an existing standard.

5. Discuss the current activities of the International Accounting Standards Board.

6. Describe in brief the main elements of each of the International Accounting Standards that will be referred to in this book.

2.1 Introduction

Accounting is not meant to be creative. It is meant to portray the economic substance of a transaction. This is not always as easy as it may seem. For example, in some instances it may be difficult to determine whether a transaction actually results in an asset. In other instances it is difficult to determine whether a liability should be created, or not. Not all transactions are straightforward and there are incentives to account in a manner which best serves management (who are in charge of accounting). Guidance on how to account is required to protect stakeholders (users of accounting information) and to provide information that is useful for their economic decision-making.

Most countries have a country-specific accounting body which provides guidance to entities within that country on how to account. The UK has one such body, the **Accounting Standards Board (ASB)**. The ASB issues accounting standards which outline recommended practice on how to account for certain transactions/elements (such as inventories, taxation, income, leases, etc.). At the time of writing the ASB have introduced 30 **Financial Reporting Standards (FRS)** and they have adopted and retained 8 Statements of Standard Accounting Practice (SSAP). These were originally introduced by the ASB's predecessor the Accounting Standard's Committee. They also promulgate 12 **Statements of Recommended Practice**

(SORP) and 30 of the 47 **Urgent Issue Task Force (UITF)** Abstracts that were issued. The ASB strongly believe that consistent accounting standards should be adopted across the globe, and a major aim of the ASB is to achieve convergence between UK accounting standards and the standards that are introduced by the **International Accounting Standards Board (IASB)**. The IASB is a worldwide umbrella accounting standards board which aims to issue one set of accounting standards which are agreed upon and adopted in every country in the world. Convergence has been achieved in many instances and both bodies are working hard to achieve full convergence. For this reason, the textbook has been prepared in line with IFRS not UK FRS, though a full chapter on the UK institutional framework and standards is available on the textbook's website (www.mcgraw-hill.co.uk/textbooks/thomas).

This chapter examines the role of the IASB and describes in brief the 11 main **International Accounting Standards (IASs)** that are referred to in this book. IASs is the name given to the standards that were issued by the International Accounting Standards Committee (IASC), the predecessor of the IASB. The IASB have adopted a number of the IASC's standards and the name (IAS) has not been changed, though new standards are called **International Financial Reporting Standards (IFRSs)**.

 2.2 The institutional framework for setting IFRSs

The institutional framework for setting IFRSs is shown in Figure 2.1.

According to the IFRS website the IASB is 'an independent standard-setting board, appointed and overseen by a geographically and professionally diverse group of trustees (the IFRS Foundation Trustees) that are publicly accountable to a Monitoring Board of public capital market authorities'. The new constitution as detailed in Figure 2.1 was introduced after a two-year consultation (2008 and 2009) and was effective from 1 March 2010. The IASB are supported by an external 'IFRS Advisory Council' and an 'IFRS Interpretations Committee' that offers guidance where divergence in practice occurs (IASB and the IFRS Foundation, 2010). Some brief detail is now provided on each of the main bodies involved.

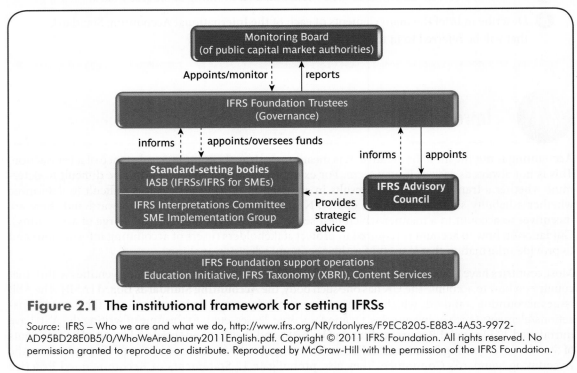

Figure 2.1 The institutional framework for setting IFRSs

Source: IFRS – Who we are and what we do, http://www.ifrs.org/NR/rdonlyres/F9EC8205-E883-4A53-9972-AD95BD28E0B5/0/WhoWeAreJanuary2011English.pdf. Copyright © 2011 IFRS Foundation. All rights reserved. No permission granted to reproduce or distribute. Reproduced by McGraw-Hill with the permission of the IFRS Foundation.

2.3 The International Accounting Standards Board (IASB)

The predecessor to the IASB, the **International Accounting Standards Committee (IASC)** was formed in 1973. Up until 2000 the IASC was governed by representatives from some of its member countries. In 2001 the IASC was renamed the IASB when it became governed by an independent board whose members are appointed by trustees. The members are drawn from the world's financial community, who represent the public interest. The IASB has 15 full-time members, though this is to increase to 16 by 2012 under the rules of the new constitution (effective from 2010). These members have a variety of functional backgrounds – from academics, to former chief executives of financial institutions, to former partners in professional accounting firms. Each member has one vote. As mentioned previously, standards that are issued by the IASB are known as **International Financial Reporting Standards (IFRSs)**. The IASC issued 41 IASs and a conceptual framework called *The Framework for the Preparation and Presentation of Financial Statements* (IASC, 1989).

Currently, 29 IASs are still in existence and are promulgated by the IASB. Nine IFRSs have been produced by the IASB.

The main objective of the IASB is 'to develop a single set of high quality, understandable, enforceable and globally accepted financial reporting standards based upon clearly articulated principles.' (IASB and the IFRS Foundation, 2010).

To achieve this, the IASB has reorganized its internal structure (see Figure 2.1 and discussion thereof) and aims to establish:

1 'A thorough, open, participatory and transparent due process;

2 Engagement with investors, regulators, business leaders and the global accountancy profession at every stage of the process;

3 Collaborative efforts with the worldwide standard-setting community.'

(IASB and the IFRS Foundation, 2010)

2.4 SME Implementation Group

The **SME Implementation Group (SMEIG)** was established on 1 January 2010. Its aim is to support the international adoption of the IFRS for Small and Medium-sized Entities (IFRS for SMEs) and to monitor its implementation. The **IFRS for SMEs** is a separate IFRS that was issued by the IASB in July 2009 to cater for the needs of smaller entities that deemed full IFRSs to be too onerous and inappropriate for their needs. It is based on the same principles as full IFRS, however, contains certain omissions, simplifications, reduced disclosures and has been written for clarity.

2.5 The IFRS Foundation Trustees

From 1 March 2010 the **International Accounting Standards Committee Foundation (IASCF)** was renamed the **IFRS Foundation Trustees**. The aim of the trustees is to promote the work of the IASB and the rigorous application of IFRSs. However, they are not involved in any technical matters relating to the standards. The Trustees are accountable to an external body, the **Monitoring Board of Public and Capital Market Authorities** (hereafter called the Monitoring Board). The Monitoring Board appoints the trustees. The objectives of the trustees are:

1 'to develop, in the public interest, a single set of high-quality, understandable, enforceable and globally accepted financial reporting standards based upon clearly articulated principles. These standards should require high quality, transparent and comparable information in financial statements and other financial reporting to help investors, other participants in the world's capital markets and other users of financial information make economic decisions;

2 to promote the use and rigorous application of those standards;

3 in fulfilling the objectives associated with (1) and (2), to take account of, as appropriate, the needs of a range of sizes and types of entities in diverse economic settings;

4 to promote and facilitate adoption of IFRSs, through the convergence of national accounting standards IFRS.'

(IFRS website, 2010)

Ultimately the trustees are responsible for the governance of all the bodies that are directly involved in the development of international accounting standards. The IFRS website states that the responsibilities of the trustees' include:

1 'appointing trustees, members of the IASB, the IFRS Interpretations Committee and the IFRS Advisory Council;

2 establishing and amending the operating procedures, consultative arrangements and due process for the IASB, the Interpretations Committee and the Advisory Council;

3 reviewing annually the strategy of the IASB and assessing its effectiveness;

4 ensuring the financing of the IFRS Foundation and approving annually its budget'.

(IFRS website, 2010)

2.6   The Monitoring Board of Public and Capital Market Authorities

In 2009 the trustees of the **IFRS Foundation** established the Monitoring Board to enhance the public accountability of the IFRS Foundation whilst not impairing the independence of the standard-setting process. The Monitoring Board serves as a formal link and a forum for interaction between representatives of the main capital market authorities worldwide (nominated and appointed to the Board) and the IFRS Foundation. The aim of the Monitoring Board is to appoint members of the IFRS Foundation and to hold them accountable in their role.

2.7   The IFRS Interpretations Committee

The **IFRS Interpretations Committee** replaced the **International Financial Reporting Interpretations Committee (IFRIC)** on 1 March 2010. It is the interpretive body of the IASB. The IFRS Interpretations Committee's mandate is to 'review on a timely basis widespread accounting issues that have arisen within the context of current IFRSs and to provide authoritative guidance on those issues' (IFRS website, 2010). The authoritative guidance is called 'IFRIC Interpretations' (these are published and have the same authority as IFRSs). They cover:

1 'newly identified financial reporting issues not specifically dealt with in IFRSs;

2 issues where unsatisfactory or conflicting interpretations have developed, or seem likely to develop in the absence of authoritative guidance'.

(IFRS website, 2010)

IFRIC Interpretations have to be approved by the IASB before publication.

2.8 The IFRS Advisory Council

The **IFRS Advisory Council** replaced the **Standards Advisory Council (SAC)** as part of the IFRS Foundation Trustees constitutional change on 1 March 2010. The IFRS Advisory Council is 'made up of a wide range of representatives from user groups, preparers, financial analysts, academics, auditors, regulators, professional accounting bodies and investor groups that are affected by and interested in the IASB's work' (IFRS, 2010). The primary objective of the Advisory Council is to give the IASB advice on issues including:

1 'input on the IASB's agenda;

2 input on the IASB's project timetable including project priorities, and consultation on any changes in agenda and priorities;

3 advice on projects, with particular emphasis on practical application and implementation issues, including matters relating to existing standards that may warrant consideration by the IFRS Interpretations Committee'.

The IFRS Advisory Council also supports the IASB in the promotion and adoption of IFRSs throughout the world.

2.9 IFRS Foundation Support Operations

To promote and support the worldwide use of IFRS, the IFRS Foundation also has a number of supporting initiatives going on, including:

1 the creation of a XBRL taxonomy for IFRSs and the IFRS for SMEs. The XBRL taxonomy is standardized formats and labels (called tags) which should enable the electronic use, exchange and comparability of financial data across countries;

2 The production of high-quality, understandable and up-to-date material (including training material) for the IFRS for SMEs and the organization of workshops and conferences on IFRSs;

3 Promotion of the IFRS brand and the support of global convergence.

2.10 The standard-setting process

The standard-setting process formally starts with the publication of a **Discussion Paper (DP)** which is prepared by the IASB and distributed for public consultation to various interested parties. This discussion paper is prepared after the IASB has undertaken thorough research of the area and after it has been included in their agenda. The feedback received from the public consultation on the DP is incorporated into an **Exposure Draft (ED)** which is reissued to interested parties and the general public for comment. The IASB then reviews the comments/feedback received and may decide to revise and publish the ED again. Finally, a new IFRS is issued and is adopted by the various accounting bodies around the world who have signed up to IFRS. After two years the IASB review the IFRS and any communications/feedback that they have received in the intervening period. At this stage they may revise the IFRS or leave it as it is.

The standard-setting process was displayed in diagram form in the IASB's website in 2008 and is reproduced in Figure 2.2. This diagram is no longer available on the website but more detail on the process of

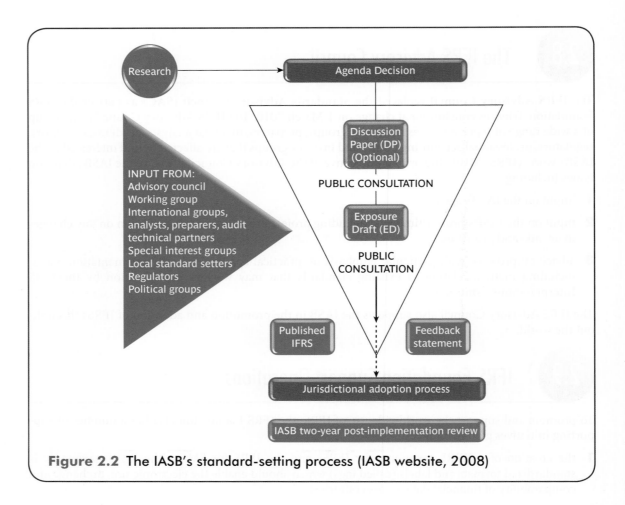

Figure 2.2 The IASB's standard-setting process (IASB website, 2008)

developing IFRSs is provided descriptively at the following web address: http://www.ifrs.org/How+we+develop+standards/How+we+develop+standards.htm.

LEARNING ACTIVITY 2.1

Go to the IASBs website and read up on current issues that the IASB are working on.

2.11 Harmonization

Many accountancy and standard setting bodies throughout the world are involved in the work of the IASB, as are various government agencies and stock market regulators. For example, all the countries of the EU, the USA, Australia, China and many of the African countries use IFRSs. Indeed, almost 120 countries have required or permitted the use of IFRSs and according to the IASB 'all remaining major economies have established time lines to converge with or adopt IFRSs in the near future' (IASB and the IFRS Foundation, 2010). The UK and the USA have a long tradition of standard setting and as a result these two countries have probably had the greatest influence on the development of IFRSs, especially given that the working language of the IASB is English. Moreover, many IFRSs are very similar to either UK standards and/or their US equivalent. **Statements of Financial Accounting Standards (SFASs)** as produced by the **Financial Accounting Standards Board (FASB)**. This is because some of the UK and US standards were formulated jointly, while others have been either wholly or partly adopted by each of the bodies from each other's standards. However, there are still some differences between IFRSs and UK and US standards that are subject to much heated debate.

From 2005 all EU listed companies have had to prepare their financial statements in accordance with IFRSs. Since that date the IASB (International), FASB (USA) and ASB (UK) have also been engaged in what is known as a 'convergence project' to harmonize international, US and UK accounting standards.

REAL WORLD EXAMPLE 2.1 Update on the convergence to IFRS by US accounting standard setter

The independence and funding of the International Accounting Standards Board (IASB) will be among the key issues to be examined by the US before it finally makes a decision on whether to buy into international standards.

The SEC will look at whether the current governance structure will maintain the standard setter's independence. As part of this it will look at the work of the IASB's supreme oversight body, the Monitoring Board, in reviewing current governance structures.

The SEC will also look at the IASB's mission of developing standards for investors. The work plan report said SEC staff would 'analyse stakeholder perspectives in this area'.

Jim Kroeker, the SEC's chief accountant, said: 'The staff has invested significant time and effort in executing the Work Plan, and we've made great progress to date. This progress report emphasizes the importance of transparency in the staff's activities, and can help the public's understanding of the magnitude of this project and the staff's progress.'

The SEC's decision will be guided by an examination of six key areas: sufficient development and application of IFRS for the US; the independence of standard setting for the benefit of investors.; investors' education and understanding; the regulatory systems that would be affected by adoption; the impact on public companies both large and small; human resource readiness.

Source: Hinks, G. (2010) 'US tests standard setter's independence', *Accountancy Age*, 29 October 2010, www.accountancyage.com

The EU has given up much of its work on formulating accounting practices in favour of extending IFRSs to all companies in the EU. In the light of these developments many people have predicted that national accounting standards will disappear within the next decade. However, before this happens there are some major differences of opinion between the IASB, the EU, USA and UK standard setters that need to be resolved. One major issue was the fact that IFRS were deemed to be inappropriate for **small and medium-sized entities (SMEs)**. However, with the formation of the SMEIG and the creation of the IFRS for SMEs, this problem should be removed over time as countries adopt the new standard.

The IASB clearly has enormous status and authority stemming from the impact of IFRSs worldwide and the focus of the global harmonization of national accounting standards. However, it is easy to overlook that unlike, for example, the Financial Reporting Council in the UK, the IASB really has no power to enforce IFRSs. Compliance depends on their adoption and enforcement by nation states and their respective stock market regulatory bodies such as the SEC and the London Stock Exchange (LSE).

International Financial Reporting Standards (IFRSs)

The following is a list of the main IFRSs/IASs that are referred to in this book.

Framework for the Preparation and Presentation of Financial Statements

IAS 1 – Presentation of Financial Statements

IAS 2 – Inventories

IAS 7 – Statement of Cash Flows

IAS 8 – Accounting Policies, Changes in Accounting Estimates and Errors

IAS 10 – Events after the Reporting Period

IAS 16 – Property, Plant and Equipment

IAS 18 – Revenue

IAS 37 – Provisions, Contingent Liabilities and Contingent Assets

IAS 38 – Intangible Assets

IFRS 3 – Business Combinations

IFRS 5 – Non-current Assets Held for Sale and Discontinuing Operations

The remainder of this chapter outlines a brief summary of the international framework for accounting and each of the above IASs (the equivalent UK standard is identified as a footnote). At this stage these brief summaries are only intended to provide you with a sense of the type of information that is provided in IFRSs. You will have to return to study these summaries when you complete the book. They will be more understandable to you then.

Framework for the Preparation and Presentation of Financial Statements[1]

The *Framework* (IASC, 1989) sets out the concepts that underlie the preparation and presentation of financial statements. It provides guidance on the fundamentals of accounting. The key issues considered by the framework document include:

1 What is the objective of financial statements?

2 What are the qualitative characteristics that determine the usefulness of information in financial statements?

3 What is an asset, a liability, equity, income and expenses? How are these elements recognized and measured?

4 What is the concept of capital and capital maintenance?

These questions are examined in depth in Chapters 3, 4, 5, 6 and 8.

---

[1] The UK equivalent is the Statement of Principles for Financial Reporting.

2.13 IAS 1 — Presentation of Financial Statements[2]

IAS 1 (IASB, 2010a) was discussed in Chapter 1, 'Entities and Financial Reporting Statements'. It provides guidance on how to present financial information in the financial statements. It tries to promote standardization of accounting formats and terminology.

2.14 IAS 2 — Inventories[3]

IAS 2 (IASB, 2010b) requires that inventories should be measured at the lower of cost and net realizable value. Cost includes all costs to bring inventories to their present condition and location. Where specific cost is not appropriate, the benchmark treatment is to use either the first-in-first-out (FIFO) or the weighted average cost (AVCO) methods for determining inventory value. Inventory valuation is covered in depth in Chapter 24.

2.15 IAS 7 — Statement of Cash Flows[4]

In IAS 7 (IASB, 2010c) cash flows are classified under the headings: operating activities, investing activities and financing activities. Within the operating activities section of the statement of cash flows, a reconciliation of operation profit before tax from the statement of profit and loss to net cash inflows from operating activities is provided. IAS 7 permits the use of either the direct or indirect method of reporting cash flows from operating activities. Separate disclosure is required of the movement in cash equivalents and details should be provided for any significant non-cash transactions. The appendix to IAS 7 contains illustrations of a typical statement of cash flows using both of these methods.

2.16 IAS 8 — Accounting Policies, Changes in Accounting Estimates and Errors[5]

IAS 8 (IASB, 2010d) covers changes in accounting policies and the correction of errors. Changes in accounting policies and the correction of errors should be treated as prior year adjustments. This involves restating the **comparative figures** (previous year's figures) to take account of the adjustment. For financial statements being prepared for periods starting on or after 1 January 2010, IAS 1 requires that entities that have a change in accounting policy provide two years of comparatives in respect of the statement of financial position (assets, liabilities and owners' capital) and one year of comparatives for most other disclosures. Changes in accounting policy are only allowed in restricted circumstances. The spirit seems to be that a change is allowable if it produces better quality financial information. This usually occurs when a new standard is introduced, or updated with new measurement or recognition guidance.

---

[2] The UK equivalent is FRS 3 – Reporting Financial Performance.
[3] The UK equivalent is SSAP 9 – Stocks and Long-term Contracts.
[4] The UK equivalent is FRS 1 – Cash Flow Statements.
[5] The UK equivalent is SSAP 2 – Disclosure of Accounting Policies. Some of the issues are also covered in FRS 3 – Reporting Financial Performance and FRS 28 – Corresponding Amounts.

In contrast, changes in accounting estimates should only be included in the financial statements of the current and future accounting periods, and their classification will be unchanged (e.g. depreciation arising from a change in the estimated useful life of a non-current asset).

 ## IAS 10 – Events after the Reporting Period[6]

IAS 10 (IASB, 2010e) states that events occurring after the reporting date that provide additional information on conditions existing at the reporting date should lead to adjustment of the financial statements. In addition, disclosure should be made for other non-adjusting events, if necessary, for a proper evaluation.

 ## IAS 16 – Property, Plant and Equipment[7]

Under IAS 16 (IASB, 2010f) all tangible non-current assets are recognized at historic cost and depreciated over the asset's useful economic life. The value to appear in the statement of financial position should equal the tangible assets' cost less accumulated (built-up) depreciation. An alternative treatment is allowed, wherein the tangible non-current assets can be revalued to fair value and depreciated. Under IAS 16, **fair value** is the amount that an entity would expect to receive for the asset in an arm's-length transaction between two unconnected parties. This usually equates to market price, replacement cost or economic value. When an asset is revalued, the whole class of assets has to be revalued and the valuations have to be kept up to date.

 ## IAS 18 – Revenue[8]

IAS 18 (IASB, 2010g) is concerned with revenue recognition. In particular, it sets out the following rules for determining the accounting year in which sales revenue should be included in the statement of profit and loss in the sale of goods:

> 'In a transaction involving the sale of goods, performance should be regarded as being achieved when the following conditions have been fulfilled:
>
> a the seller of the goods has transferred to the buyer the significant risks and rewards of ownership, in that all significant acts have been completed and the seller retains no continuing managerial involvement in, or effective control of, the goods transferred to a degree usually associated with ownership; and
>
> b no significant uncertainty exists regarding:
>   i the consideration that will be derived from the sale of the goods;
>   ii the associated costs incurred or to be incurred in producing or purchasing the goods;
>   iii the extent to which the goods may be returned
>
> (IASB, 2010g)

Revenue from the rendering of services should be recognized by reference to the state of completion of the transaction at the reporting date (i.e. the percentage of completion).

---

[6] The UK Equivalent is FRS 21 – Events after the Balance Sheet Date.
[7] The UK standards dealing with this topic are FRS 15 – Tangible Fixed Assets and FRS 11 – Impairment of Fixed Assets and Goodwill.
[8] The UK equivalent is FRS 5 – Reporting the Substance of Transactions.

2.20 IAS 37 – Provisions, Contingent Liabilities and Contingent Assets[9]

Under IAS 37 (IASB, 2010i) a provision has to be recognized when the enterprise has a present obligation to transfer economic benefits as a result of past events and it is probable (more likely than not) that such a transfer will be required and a reliable estimate of the obligation can be made. A present obligation exists when an entity has little or no discretion to avoid incurring the economic outflow. This means that the item comes into the statement of financial position as a liability and as an expense in the statement of profit and loss.

Contingent liabilities are liabilities whose outcome will be confirmed on the occurrence or non-occurrence of uncertain future events that are outside the entity's control. They are recognized in the financial statements (as a liability and an expense) if it is more likely than not (probable) that a transfer of economic benefits will result from past events and a reliable estimate of the amount can be made. When this condition cannot be fulfilled, disclosures of the nature and amount (if possible) should be provided in the notes to the financial statements.

Contingent assets should not be recognized unless they are reasonably certain, then they are treated as assets. If they are not reasonably certain they should be disclosed in the notes to the financial statements.

2.21 IAS 38 – Intangible Assets[10]

Under IAS 38 (IASB, 2010j) intangible assets can only be recognized if they meet the definition of an asset (i.e. if it is probable that future economic benefits attributable to the asset will flow to the enterprise and that cost of the asset can be measured reliably). Like IAS 16 an intangible asset can be carried at cost or at fair value. Fair value can only be determined in this instance with reference to an active market for the asset. Internally generated assets cannot be recognized unless they meet the recognition criteria for capitalizing development expenditure. The criteria are that the expenditure should be on a clearly defined product or process, capable of reliable measurement, technically feasible, there should be evidence of an intention to sell the product being developed for a profit (i.e. there should be evidence of the existence of a market in which to sell the product, or the product being developed should be demonstrated to be useful internally) and the entity should have the technical expertise and resources to complete the project. Intangible assets have to be amortized over their useful economic lives.

2.22 IFRS 3 – Business Combinations[11]

Under IFRS 3 (IASB, 2010k) any goodwill arising on a business combination (i.e. the excess amount given for a business over and above the value of its separately identifiable assets, liabilities and contingent liabilities) should be capitalized as an intangible non-current asset and impaired. This is covered in the section on partnerships and companies.

---

[9] The UK equivalent is FRS 12 – Provisions, Contingent Liabilities and Contingent Assets.
[10] The UK standards dealing with this topic are FRS 10 – Goodwill and Intangible Assets and FRS 11 – Impairment of Fixed Assets and Goodwill.
[11] The UK standards dealing with this topic are FRS 2 – Accounting for Subsidiary Undertakings; FRS 6 – Acquisitions and Mergers; FRS 9 – Associates and Joint Ventures; FRS 7 – Fair Values in Acquisition Accounting.

2.23 IFRS 5 – Non-current Assets Held for Sale and Discontinuing Operations[12]

Under IFRS 5 (IASB, 2010h) discontinuing operations includes operations that actually discontinued in the reporting period and operations that are likely to be discontinued in the next reporting period. The assets, liabilities, revenue and expenses from those operations/assets should be presented separately from the assets, liabilities, revenues and expenses from continuing activities. All required disclosures in respect of these items should also be provided separately. In the statement of financial position, the assets and liabilities are disclosed separately for each main category (e.g. non-current assets). In the statement of profit and loss the approach is different, the revenue and expenses from the discontinuing activity are shown in a note to the financial statements, with the profit or loss for the period being added to the profit for the period from continuing operations. This is covered in Part 8, 'Companies'.

> **LEARNING ACTIVITY 2.2**
>
> Go to the UK Accounting Standards Board's (ASBs) website and read the summaries on each of the footnoted UK accounting standards. Note the similarities between these and the summaries provided in this chapter for the international equivalent.

2.24 Current issues

In response to criticism received after the financial crises, the IASB have been and are actively discussing current standards, or introducing new standards to deal with:

1 *Off-balance-sheet finance*: The IASB has revised IFRS 3 Business Combinations and is currently working on a standard to provide guidance on how to account for lease transactions.

2 *Fair value in illiquid markets*: The IASB is currently working on a general standard on fair value, which will support all other standards, rather than having all standards separately identifying how they measure fair value. In addition, in 2009 a new standard, IFRS 9 *Financial Instruments*, was introduced. This new standard is scheduled to eventually replace IAS 39 *Financial Instruments: Recognition and Measurement* by June 2011, though mandatory adoption is not required until 1 January 2013. IFRS 9 deals with the classification and measurement of financial instruments and reduces the variety of accounting treatments that were available for financial instruments under IAS 39. Hedge accounting is currently under consultation and the final agreed approach will be incorporated into IFRS 9.

3 *Disclosure*: The IASB implemented changes to the standard on disclosures on financial instruments (IFRS 7) and discussion on this area is still ongoing. This process been ongoing before the credit crisis came to the fore, when it was felt that the accounting and disclosure requirements for derivative products needed simplifying, standardizing and strengthening.

4 The IASB is also currently revisiting the conceptual framework and the presentation of financial statements.

---

[12] The UK equivalent is FRS 3 – Reporting Financial Performance.

Summary

In 2010 the international framework for the preparation and promulgation of IFRS was restructured to make it more accountable. A Monitoring Board was established and charged with making the IFRS Foundation Trustees accountable in their role. The IASB continues to have independent control over issuing IFRS and revising IAS. They are supported by the IFRS Interpretation Committee (publish authoritative guidance on new issues, issues that are unclear or are omitted from an IFRS) and the SMEIG (monitors the implementation of the IFRS for SMEs, publishes questions and answers on issues raised by users, makes suggestions for changes to the IFRS for SMEs to the IASB in light of the issues raised and in light of changes to the full IFRS). The IFRS Advisory Council represents the major stakeholders of accounting information and provides strategic advice to the IASB. Finally the IFRS Foundation Support Operations provide policy on education, champions the development and implementation of an IFRS Taxonomy (XBRL) and deals with the general running of all the bodies that make up the institutional international regulatory framework.

The objectives of the IASB are 'to develop a single set of high quality, understandable, enforceable and globally accepted financial reporting standards based on clearly articulated principles'. At the time of writing almost 120 countries have either adopted IFRSs in their entirety, have converged national accounting standards with IFRSs, or allow IFRS to be used. The IASB, the FASB and the ASB are currently engaged in a convergence project aimed at harmonizing international, US and UK accounting standards. This has been greatly assisted by the publication of the IFRS for SMEs in July 2009.

Key terms and concepts

Websites

For more information on topics covered in this chapter visit:

http://www.frc.org.uk/asb/ Provides details on the UK framework and standards.

www.ifrs.org/ Provides guidance on the institutional framework underlying the production of IFRSs and new issues.

www.iasplus.com/ Provides a summary of IFRSs, the institutional framework and the objectives of all the bodies that are party to the framework.

An asterisk after the question number indicates that there is a suggested answer on the Online Learning Centre (www.mcgraw-hill.co.uk/textbooks/thomas).

connect Review questions

2.1* Describe the objectives of the International Accounting Standards Board (IASB).

2.2 Discuss the current activities of the International Accounting Standards Board (IASB) in the convergence/harmonization of accounting standards.

2.3 Explain the role of the IFRS Interpretations Committee.

2.4 Explain the role and objectives of the IFRS Advisory Council.

2.5 Describe the standard setting process for International Financial Reporting Standards (IFRSs).

2.6 Describe the accounting treatment for measuring the value of inventories under *IAS 2 – Inventories.*

2.7 Describe the rules relating to the recognition of product revenue set out in *IAS 18 – Revenue.*

2.8 State the two measurement methods recommended by *IAS 16 – Property, Plant and Equipment* for recording the value of tangible non-current assets.

References

Hinks, G. (2010) 'US tests standard setter's independence', *Accountancy Age*, 29, October 2010, www.accountancyage.com.

International Accounting Standards Board (2010a) *International Accounting Standard 1 – Presentation of Financial Statements* (IASB).

International Accounting Standards Board (2010b) *International Accounting Standard 2 – Inventories* (IASB).

International Accounting Standards Board (2010c) *International Accounting Standard 7 – Statement of Cash Flows* (IASB).

International Accounting Standards Board (2010d) *International Accounting Standard 8 – Accounting Policies, Changes in Accounting Estimates and Errors* (IASB).

International Accounting Standards Board (2010e) *International Accounting Standard 10 – Events after the Reporting Period* (IASB).

International Accounting Standards Board (2010f) *International Accounting Standard 16 – Property, Plant and Equipment* (IASB).

International Accounting Standards Board (2010g) *International Accounting Standard 18 – Revenue* (IASB).

International Accounting Standards Board (2010h) *International Financial Reporting Standard 5 – Non-current Assets Held for Sale and Discontinuing Operations* (IASB).

International Accounting Standards Board (2010i) *International Accounting Standard 37 – Provisions, Contingent Liabilities and Contingent Assets* (IASB).

International Accounting Standards Board (2010j) *International Accounting Standard 38 – Intangible Assets* (IASB).

International Accounting Standards Board (2010k) *International Financial Reporting Standard 3 – Business Combinations* (IASB).

International Accounting Standards Committee (1989) Adopted by the International Accounting Standards Board 2001, *Framework for the Preparation and Presentation of Financial Statements* (IASC).

International Accounting Standards Board and the IFRS Foundation (March 2010) *Who We Are and What We Do* (IFRS Foundation, 2010).

When you have read this chapter, log on to the Online Learning Centre for *Introduction to Financial Accounting* at www.mcgraw-hill.co.uk/textbooks/thomas, where you will find multiple choice quizzes, case studies, a glossary and mock exams.

History and purpose of the conceptual framework

Learning Objectives

After reading this chapter you should be able to do the following:

1 Explain the meaning of the key terms and concepts listed at the end of the chapter.

2 Explain the nature, purpose and scope of the conceptual framework of accounting, including the main contents of the International Accounting Standards Committee's *Framework for the Preparation and Presentation of Financial Statements* (IASC, 1989).

3 Describe the conceptual framework and standardization debates and discuss related issues.

4 Describe the main types of accounting theory and their implications for a conceptual framework of accounting.

3.1 The conceptual framework of accounting

The nature of a conceptual framework – an analogy

At some point in their studies students may feel rather confused and frustrated by accounting theory. It is a hurdle that has to be overcome. On the one hand, students frequently have a perception of accounting as being definitive, because much of it is based on the law, and they have been taught a simplified set of rules about double-entry bookkeeping that is very systematic. On the other hand, they frequently think that accountants tend to bend the rules (or 'cook the books'), also known as **creative accounting**. Many of the later chapters of this book may reinforce this view because some transactions can be treated in different ways, thus giving possible alternative figures of profit.

It is important to appreciate the difference between 'cooking the books' and the professional judgement involved in decisions between alternative methods (bases) of accounting. An analogy may prove useful. Imagine you went to a private consultant because you had backache. In order to maximize his or her fee, the consultant might decide to operate on you. If this was the sole consideration, it would be unethical of the surgeon. Similarly, an accountant who chose a particular form of accounting treatment with the sole intention of reducing net profit would be acting unethically. However, an ethical physician or accountant is still faced with a number of possible forms of treatment. The physician might prescribe a number of different drugs, but needs to ascertain which is likely to be most appropriate for you. Similarly, the accountant has to choose which accounting treatment for, say, development costs is the most appropriate in the circumstances.

This analogy can be extended further to illustrate another very important relevant idea. The physician's judgement about your treatment for backache is guided by a body of expert knowledge and research, loosely known as 'medical science'. This includes such disciplines as anatomy and chemistry, which are based on generally accepted theories and concepts similar, in principle, to those discussed in this chapter relating to accounting. Similarly, the accountant's judgement about the most appropriate treatment of certain types of transaction is guided by a body of expert knowledge and research, which is loosely referred to as the theoretical or **conceptual framework of accounting**.

However, unlike medical science, the conceptual framework of accounting is not well developed and thus may contain apparent inconsistencies. It is also unlikely that a conceptual framework of accounting could be as definitive as, say, medical science in the foreseeable future since accounting theory, like other social sciences, is fundamentally different from natural sciences, such as medical science.

This tension between the need for a set of concepts/principles to guide the practice of accounting, and the awareness that these are unlikely to be conclusive/definitive, has given rise to an extensive debate over the past three decades about the development of a conceptual framework of accounting or what are sometimes called **generally accepted accounting principles (GAAP)**.

(*Note*: The abbreviation GAAP is commonly taken as referring to generally accepted accounting practice; that is, accounting standards.)

The conceptual framework of accounting – a brief history

In order to appreciate fully the sources of authoritative pronouncements about the nature, purpose and scope of a conceptual framework of accounting, it is necessary to start with a brief history of the accountancy profession's attempts to develop a conceptual framework. The earliest comprehensive conceptual framework project was started in the mid-1970s in the USA by the Financial Accounting Standards Board (FASB), which is the US equivalent of the IASB. This work has been a major influence on subsequent conceptual framework projects by the IASC and the Accounting Standards Board (ASB) (the UK standard setting body).

In 1989 the IASC published what might be described as an abbreviated conceptual framework entitled *Framework for the Preparation and Presentation of Financial Statements* (IASC, 1989) (the *Framework*). This was adopted by the IASB in 2001. This was supplemented by a standard on disclosure and presentation: *IAS 1 – Presentation of Financial Statements* (IASB, 2010a) and a standard on selecting and applying accounting policies: *IAS 8 – Accounting Policies, Changes in Accounting Estimates and Errors* (IASB, 2010b). The *Framework* provides the conceptual framework for the process of accounting and the two IASs provide a framework for the application and disclosure of accounting items.

In 1999 the ASB published a *Statement of Principles for Financial Reporting* (ASB, 1999), which is generally interpreted as being the conceptual framework of accounting in the UK for entities who do not apply IASs. This document closely follows the structure of the IASC framework. Indeed, the ASB stated explicitly that 'it proposes to use wherever possible the IASC text'. It includes additional principles on presentation and disclosure. The contents of these frameworks and the US framework are outlined later in this chapter.

The conceptual framework of accounting – definition and purpose

The conceptual framework of accounting is defined, by UK accounting standard setters, in the report *Setting Accounting Standards: A Consultative Document* (ASC, 1978) as 'a set of broad, internally consistent fundamentals and definitions of key terms'.

Another slightly more informative definition is provided by the FASB (1976) (US standard setters) in its *Scope and Implications of the Conceptual Framework Project* – a conceptual framework of accounting is 'a constitution, a coherent system of interrelated objectives and fundamentals that can lead to consistent standards and that prescribe the nature, function and limits of financial accounting and financial statements'.

 LEARNING ACTIVITY 3.1

Visit the IASB and the ASB websites and obtain a copy of their definition of a conceptual framework of Accounting.

The definitions highlight one of the main purposes of a conceptual framework; that is, to provide standard setting bodies with a set of internally consistent definitions of accounting principles that can be used as a basis for setting accounting standards that are not contradictory or in conflict with each other. The other main purpose of a conceptual framework, explained earlier using the analogy with medicine, is to provide guidance to accountants in their day-to-day work of choosing appropriate forms of accounting treatments for various transactions and items. Though the conceptual framework that is currently in existence is well intentioned, the recent financial crises has fuelled the debate on whether the international accounting standards that have been prepared under the framework are appropriate (as highlighted in an article in the *Daily Telegraph* on accounting in UK banks).

REAL WORLD EXAMPLE 3.1

UK bank accounting

'UK bank accounting rules "fatally flawed", warns influential watchdog

The Government has been warned of a "regulatory fiasco" in which British banks have apparently adhered to flawed reporting standards for more than five years.

An influential watchdog has written to the Department of Business listing a catalogue of staggering regulatory errors that allegedly contributed to the collapse of several banks in 2008 – and still threatens the system today.

While reviewing the proposed expansion of the International Financial Reporting Standards for accounting, Tim Bush, a member of the "Urgent Issues Task Force" that scrutinises the work of the Accounting Standards Board (ASB), claims to have uncovered "fatal" and "dangerous" flaws in the system.

The City veteran has argued that applied to banks, the standards "produced false profits and overstated capital" which have "misled creditors, misled shareholders, the Bank of England, FSA and others".

In a devastating assessment, Mr Bush alleges the regulations, and specifically the way they have been implemented in the UK and Ireland, have led to "mistakes [being made] of such severity that it is difficult to overstate".'

Source: Armitstead (2010) (see References).

3.2 The international framework

The international framework: purpose

As detailed in the introduction to the *Framework*, the purpose of a conceptual framework is to:

1 'assist the board of the IASB in the development of future International Financial Reporting Standards (IFRSs);

2 assist the board of the IASB in promoting harmonization of regulations, accounting standards and procedures relating to the presentation of financial statements by providing a basis for reducing the number of alternative accounting treatments permitted by IFRSs;

3 assist national standard setting bodies in developing national standards;

4 assist preparers of financial statements in applying IFRSs and in dealing with topics that have yet to form the subject of an IFRS;

5 assist auditors in forming an opinion as to whether financial statements conform with IFRSs;

6 assist users of financial statements in interpreting the information contained in financial statements prepared in conformity with IFRSs;

7 provide those who are interested in the work of the IASB with information about its approach to the formulation of IFRSs.'

The international framework: nature and scope

One approach to determining the nature and scope of a conceptual framework of accounting is to answer questions in respect of information required from accounting (financial statements). Questions put forward in this respect include: 'For whom are financial statements to be prepared? For what purposes do they want to use them? What kind of accounting reports do they want? How far are present financial statements suitable for these purposes, and how could we improve accounting practice to make them more suitable?' (ASC, 1978).

The scope of the international conceptual framework, as detailed in the *Framework* is summarized as key aims that the IASC, now the IASB, are trying to define and provide guidance on. The key areas are divided into four main chapters in the *Framework* as follows:

Chapter 1   The objective of financial statements

Chapter 2   The qualitative characteristics that determine the usefulness of information in financial statements

Chapter 3   The definition, recognition and measurement of the elements from which financial statements are constructed

Chapter 4   Concepts of capital and capital maintenance

The international framework: scope restrictions

The guidance provided in Chapters 1 to 4 of the framework is restricted to accounting in general purpose financial statements only. In addition, accounting is considered to provide information for a predefined group of users. Seven types of user are mentioned in the *Framework*. These are discussed in depth in this book in Chapter 4, 'The Nature and Objectives of Financial Accounting'. To recap: the users are investors, employees, lenders, suppliers and other trade creditors, customers, governments and their agencies and the public.

3.3   The UK framework (in brief)

The UK equivalent, the ASB framework, is set out in the *Statement of Principles for Financial Reporting* (ASB, 1999). The contents are similar to those of the IASC. The chapters covered in the *Statement of Principles for Financial Reporting* are as follows:

Chapter 1   The objective of financial statements

Chapter 2   The reporting entity

Chapter 3   The qualitative characteristics of financial information

Chapter 4   The elements of financial statements

Chapter 5   Recognition in financial statements

Chapter 6   Measurement in financial statements

Chapter 7   Presentation of financial information

There are two notable differences. The UK framework has a chapter on defining the reporting entity and on presentation of financial information. The guidance provided in the additional chapter on the reporting entity is deemed to be covered by *IFRS 3 – Business Combinations* (IASB, 2010c), *IAS 28 – Investments in Associates* (IASB, 2010d), *IAS 31 – Interests in Joint Ventures* (IASB, 2010e) and by the entity concept. The guidance provided in Chapter 7 of the *Statement of Principles*, 'Presentation of financial information', is deemed to be covered in IAS 1.

3.4   Framework to compare the international, UK and US conceptual frameworks

The content of both the UK and the international frameworks can be compared with the FASB's conceptual framework and is shown in diagrammatic form in Figure 3.1. Notice in particular its hierarchical nature and the similar concepts referred to.

Typical framework

Having identified the scope or structure of the conceptual frameworks produced to date (the IASC, the ASB and the FASB's have been considered) it is clear that common themes emerge. It would seem that a conceptual framework for accounting comprises the following:

1   Setting out *the objective of financial reporting*, including identifying users of financial statements and their information needs.

2   Determining *the attributes or qualitative characteristics* of accounting information that enable financial statements to fulfil their objective. Determining what useful information is and providing criteria for choosing among alternative accounting methods.

3   Providing definitions of the *elements* of financial statements, such as the nature of income, expenses, assets, liabilities and ownership interest.

4   Providing a set of criteria for deciding when the elements are to be *recognized* in financial statements. According to the *Framework*, recognition is the process of including an item in either the statement of financial position or the statement of comprehensive income (statement of profit and loss). In general, to be included the item must meet the definition for income, an expense, an asset, a liability

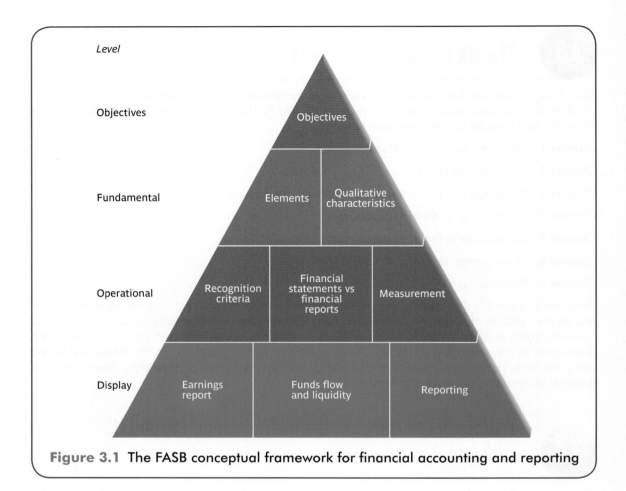

Figure 3.1 The FASB conceptual framework for financial accounting and reporting

or owner's equity. In addition, the transaction can only be recognized if it is 'probable that any future economic benefit associated with the item will flow to, or from the entity and the item has a cost or value that can be measured with reliability'.

5 Providing a set of *measurement* rules for determining the monetary amounts at which the elements of financial statements are to be recognized and carried in the accounts. For example, these might comprise historical cost, fair value, market value, current cost, realizable (settlement) value or present value.

6 Providing guidelines for the *presentation and disclosure* of the elements in financial statements. These currently take the form of statements of financial performance (i.e. a statement of comprehensive income, a statement of financial position and a statement of cash flows, as detailed in IAS 1).

Some aspects of the conceptual framework for accounting are discussed in subsequent chapters of this book. The objective of financial reporting, users and the information needs of users are covered in Chapter 4, 'The Nature and Objectives of Financial Reporting'. Definitions for the elements, recognition criteria and measurement bases are provided in Chapter 5, 'Accounting Principles, Concepts and Policies' and the qualitative characteristic are presented in Chapter 6, 'The Qualitative Characteristics of Financial Information'. The presentation and disclosure of the elements in financial statements were covered in Chapter 1, 'Entities and Financial Reporting Statements'. It is beyond the introductory nature of this book to deal with capital maintenance, measurement and recognition in detail; however, a simple explanation is provided in Chapter 8, 'The Accounting Equation and its Components'.

3.5 The conceptual framework debate, standardization and choice

Much controversy has surrounded the idea of developing a conceptual framework of accounting, particularly in the UK where the self-regulatory standard setting institutions have limited resources. There are two main related issues. The first is whether the cost of preparing a conceptual framework is justified in terms of its benefits, including the questions of whether it is possible to develop a set of consistent fundamentals and whether these will lead to improvements in accounting standard setting. The second issue concerns whether accounting standards just make published financial statements more consistent rather than comparable, or alternatively whether more meaningful comparisons would result from allowing companies to choose those accounting policies that are appropriate to their individual circumstances. This has always been an issue in standard setting, but the development of a conceptual framework accentuates the debate because it will presumably lead to greater standardization.

There is a wide variety of schools of thought on the conceptual framework debate, but for the sake of structuring and simplifying the discussion, these can be grouped into two extremes comprising the normative/deductive approach and the positive/empiricist approach.

The normative/deductive approach regards a conceptual framework as absolutely essential. **Normative theories** view accounting as a technical process that is capable of measuring the 'true income' of a business given a set of theories that specify how this should be done (e.g. Hicks, 1946). They often use the analogy that financial statements are like maps, which have the potential to provide a **faithful representation** of reality given a set of underlying consistent rules (i.e. a conceptual framework). Similarly, **deductive theories** view accounting as a technical process but advocates a user needs' approach based on identifying the objectives of financial statements similar to that taken in all the conceptual framework projects to date.

In contrast, the positive/empiricist approach regards a conceptual framework as at best unnecessary, and at worst positively dysfunctional. **Empirical theories** view accounting as an economic process, and the objective of financial statements as being to facilitate predictions (of profits, insolvency, etc.). Thus, accounting methods should be selected on the basis of which give the best predictions – that is, not according to some conceptual framework. Many **positive theories** view accounting, and particularly standard setting, as a political process that may be used to provide information for some stakeholders (equity shareholders) to the detriment of other stakeholders (employees, creditors). They maintain that standard setting should be as a result of consensus and not dictatorial pronouncements based on a conceptual framework which, itself, is the product of a particular set of class interests (e.g. equity shareholders' interests).

At present the international accounting standard setters seem to have taken a deductive view – emphasizing the need for accounting information to satisfy user information needs, though standards are created after an extensive consultation period wherein all stakeholders are encouraged to contribute their view.

It is difficult to determine if the monetary costs of preparing a conceptual framework is justified in terms of the benefits (in the form of improvements in standard setting). In recent years some of the standards have been considered to have been poor (for example the standard on accounting for derivative transactions – see Deutsche Bank real world example). Furthermore, the development of a conceptual framework is unlikely to quieten those who argue that accounting standards may promote more consistency of accounting policies between companies but this does not necessarily result in greater comparability. There are said to be 'circumstantial variables' or 'differences in circumstances' between companies that necessitate the exercise of managerial discretion in the choice of accounting methods. It is argued that standardization forces companies to use the same accounting policies, but it does not necessarily mean that they are the most appropriate accounting policies for each company and thus comparisons may be misleading. The existence of a conceptual framework is likely to lead to greater standardization and, it is said, more rigidity, a lack of flexibility, and thus less innovation. It is easy to be cynical about innovation when it takes the form of creative accounting, but it must be recognized that standardization taken to the extreme (as uniformity) would probably reduce innovation, which is said to be the case in some countries with uniform national accounting systems specified solely by law.

Problems with standards (accounting for derivatives)

Accounting for derivatives: IFRS vs GAAP

Deutsche Bank is among the few banks that report their balance sheets under both GAAP and IFRS. Under IFRS, its balance sheet shows assets of around €2 trillion for 2008. In order to show how much its leverage has fallen, Deutsche Bank has published its own evaluation of how large its balance would be under GAAP, arriving at only €1 trillion – but roughly the same level of equity. This implies that its leverage would be halved if judged under the US accounting system (see Figure 1).

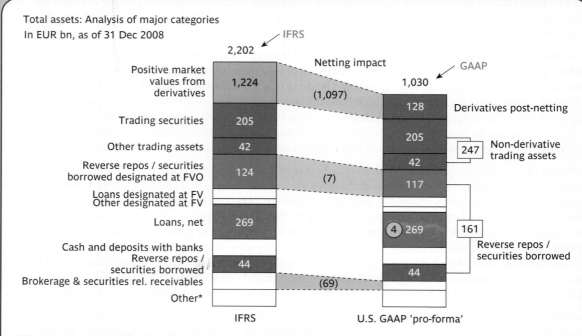

Figure 1 Deutsche Bank results: IFRS vs GAAP

Source: Ackermann (2009), www.deutsche-bank.de/ir/de/download/Roadshow_Canada_Ackermann_19–20_Feb.pdf, (accessed March 2010).

The key difference between IFRS and GAAP is the treatment of the item called (under IFRS) 'positive market values from derivatives', which equals €1.224 billion on Deutsche Bank's IFRS balance sheet. Under GAAP, however, this item would shrink to about one-tenth of that figure, with only €128 billion appearing under 'derivatives post netting'. A similar observation applies to the liability side of the balance sheet. With IFRS, Deutsche Bank also shows over €1.2 billion in liabilities under 'market values of derivatives', which presumably would also be reduced by a factor of about 10 under GAAP. For other categories (loans, repos, etc.) the difference in the results between IFRS and GAAP are minor.

Source: Gros (2010), www.voxeu.org/index.php?q=node/4524 (accessed March 2011).

Summary

All professions need a body of theological, empirical and/or theoretical knowledge to guide the actions of their practitioners. In accounting this is not as well developed as in some other professions, such as medicine, nor is it likely to be in the foreseeable future. The tension between this need for a set of rules to guide practice, and the awareness that these are unlikely to be definitive, has given rise to extensive debate about the current development of a conceptual framework of accounting, also known as generally accepted accounting principles (GAAP).

The FASB, IASC/IASB and ASC/ASB have all published conceptual frameworks of accounting. The main purposes of a conceptual framework of accounting are to provide a basis for the development and review of accounting standards, and to assist preparers, users and auditors of financial statements. This takes the form of an internally consistent set of interrelated objectives and fundamentals that prescribe the nature, function and limits of financial statements.

The IASC conceptual framework is contained in its *Framework for the Preparation and Presentation of Financial Statements* (IASC, 1989). This sets out the objectives of financial statements, the qualitative characteristics of financial information, the elements of financial statements, recognition criteria, measurement rules and concepts of capital and capital maintenance.

Key terms and concepts

conceptual framework of accounting	38	faithful representation	43
creative accounting	37	generally accepted accounting principles (GAAP)	38
deductive theories	43	normative theories	43
empirical theories	43	positive theories	43

An asterisk after the question number indicates that there is a suggested answer on the Online Learning Centre (www.mcgraw-hill.co.uk/textbooks/thomas).

Review questions

connect

3.1* Provide two definitions for the 'conceptual framework of accounting'.

3.2 Describe the purposes of a conceptual framework of accounting.

3.3 Describe the nature and contents of a conceptual framework of accounting.

3.4 'It is unrealistic to expect a conceptual framework of accounting to provide a basis for definitive or even generally accepted accounting standards in the foreseeable future because of inherent conflicts and inconsistencies between, for example, the qualitative characteristics of accounting information as well as the differing information needs and abilities of users'. Discuss.

3.5 Outline the main differences between the ASB (UK) and the IASC conceptual frameworks.

3.6   'A conceptual framework of accounting is likely to lead to greater standardization, less choice, less innovation and thus reduced comparability because of the existence of fundamental differences between companies in the way they conduct their activities'. Discuss.

References

Accounting Standards Board (1999) *Statement of Principles for Financial Reporting* (ASB).

Accounting Standard Committee (1978) *Setting Accounting Standards: A Consultative Document* (ASC).

Ackermann, J. (2009) 'Financial Transparency', presentation, Montreal and Toronto, 19–20 February 2010. Website http://www.deutsche-bank.de/ir/de/download/Roadshow_Canada_Ackermann_19_-_20_Feb.pdf (accessed March 2010)

Armitstead, L. (2010) 'UK Bank Accounting Rules Fatally Flawed warns Influential Watchdog', *Daily Telegraph*, 26 Aug. 2010, website (accessed March 2011), http://www.telegraph.co.uk/finance/newsbysector/banksandfinance/7964816/UK-bank-accounting-rules-fatally-flawed-warns-influential-watchdog.html.

Financial Accounting Standards Board (1976) *Scope and Implications of the Conceptual Framework Project* (FASB).

Gros, D. (2010) 'Too interconnected to Fail = Too big to fail: What is in a Leverage Ratio?', Vox website (Research-based policy analysis and commentary from leading economists), Source: http://www.voxeu.org/index.php?q=node/4524 (accessed March 2011).

Hicks, J.R. (1946) *Value and Capital* (2nd edn) Oxford: Clarendon Press.

International Accounting Standards Board (2010a) *International Accounting Standard 1 – Presentation of Financial Statements* (IASB).

International Accounting Standards Board (2010b) *International Accounting Standard 8 – Accounting Policies, Changes in Accounting Estimates and Errors* (IASB).

International Accounting Standards Board (2010c) *International Financial Reporting Standard 3 – Business Combinations* (IASB).

International Accounting Standards Board (2010d) *International Accounting Standard 28 – Investments in Associates* (IASB).

International Accounting Standards Board (2010e) *International Accounting Standard 31 – Interests in Joint Ventures* (IASB).

International Accounting Standards Committee (1989) *Framework for the Preparation and Presentation of Financial Statements* (IASC).

When you have read this chapter, log on to the Online Learning Centre for *Introduction to Financial Accounting* at www.mcgraw-hill.co.uk/textbooks/thomas, where you will find multiple choice quizzes, case studies, a glossary and mock exams.

The nature and objectives of financial reporting
(including corporate social responsibility, environmental accounting and accountability)

Learning Objectives

After reading this chapter you should be able to do the following:

1. Explain the meaning of the key terms and concepts listed at the end of the chapter.

2. Describe the nature and functions of double-entry bookkeeping and financial accounting.

3. Discuss the objectives of company financial statements.

4. Explain corporate social responsibility and discuss the type of information included in a corporate social responsibility report.

5. Discuss the type of information a company includes under environmental reporting.

6. Define accountability and explain how management use financial reports to discharge their accountability requirements.

7. Identify the users of annual reports and describe their information needs.

8. Describe the three regulatory influences on financial reporting.

9. Outline the limitations of financial statements.

4.1   The nature and functions of financial accounting

Financial accounting may be defined as the process of designing and operating an information system for collecting, measuring and recording an enterprise's transactions, and summarizing and communicating the results of these transactions to users to facilitate making financial/economic decisions.

The first part of this definition, relating to collecting and recording transactions, refers to the accounting system within an organization. This is typically a **double-entry bookkeeping** system, which consists of maintaining a record of the nature and money value of the transactions of an enterprise. In many businesses these records are maintained on computer systems (see Chapter 38 'The Role of Computers in Accounting' for more detail. This chapter is available on the website www.mcgraw-hill.co.uk/textbooks/thomas). The second part of the definition, relating to communicating the results, refers to preparing

final financial statements from the books of account (or any other system of recording) showing the profit earned during a given period and the financial position at the end of that period.

These two functions of financial accounting may be broken down further as described below.

4.2 The objectives of an appropriate accounting system

The recording and control of business transactions

This includes keeping a record of:

1 The amount of cash and cheques received, for what and from whom;

2 The amount of cash and cheques paid, for what and to whom. Records of money received and paid are kept so that the business knows how much money it has at any time;

3 Liabilities, expenses and goods purchased on credit. This is so that the business knows to whom it owes money and how much. These are referred to as **payables**. Payables are further categorized as either sundry (expenses) or trade (goods);

4 Assets and goods sold on credit. This is so that the business knows its resources and who owes it money and how much. These are referred to as **receivables**. Receivables are further categorized as either sundry (other income, for example interest receivable) or trade (goods).

The owners of a business wish to safeguard their assets and to ensure that they are being utilized efficiently to produce wealth. They employ accountants to put in place controls to protect business assets and to advise them on how the company is performing. To safeguard assets accountants normally introduce a variety of controls over transactions and processes. The control aspect of the accounting function includes ensuring that the correct amounts are paid to those entitled to them at the appropriate time, to ensure that the business's debts are paid when due, and to ensure that assets (e.g. goods or cash) are safeguarded against fraud and misappropriation. For example, accountants usually require that a list of all non-current assets is kept, including their location and state of condition. These will be inspected periodically to verify that they have not been misappropriated. The latter function is often referred to as **internal control**. Control is considered further in Chapter 7 'Auditing, Corporate Governance and Ethics'.

To maintain accuracy in recording

Double-entry bookkeeping is generally regarded as the most accurate method of bookkeeping, primarily because each transaction is entered in the books twice. This duplication, considered to be a form of **internal check**, highlights any errors.

To meet the requirements of the law

The law, in the form of the Companies Act 2006, states that companies must keep a proper record of their transactions. There is no legislation that specifically requires sole traders or partnerships to keep records of their transactions. However, HM Revenue and Customs expects financial statements to be prepared and proper accounting records to be kept for the purpose of determining the proprietor's income tax liability. In addition, any trader who does not keep proper records and goes bankrupt will find it more difficult to obtain discharge from bankruptcy.

To present final financial statements to the owners of the business

Final financial statements comprise a statement of profit and loss showing the amount of profit or loss for the period and a statement of the financial position showing the **financial position** at

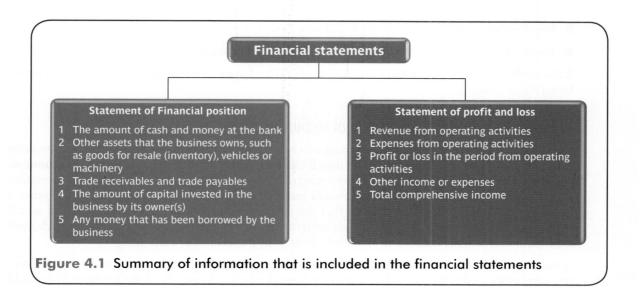

Figure 4.1 Summary of information that is included in the financial statements

the end of that period. **Financial statements** were introduced in Chapter 1, 'Entities and Financial Reporting Statements'. In summary, the financial statements will include the items detailed in Figure 4.1 above.

In the case of a sole trader, these final financial statements are primarily used to determine the owner's tax liability, though they also show the owner his or her 'earnings' for the period and can be used by others (such as the bank) to evaluate the profitability of the business. Final financial statements perform similar functions in the case of companies, though the primary aim of the final financial statements is to give information to third parties to enable them to evaluate the profitability and financial stability of the company. The third parties include current and prospective equity shareholders, trade unions and employees, customers, creditors and those who have lent the company money, government departments, social pressure groups and the public. Stakeholders and their information needs are discussed later in this chapter.

This function of financial accounting is often referred to as **stewardship**, which may be defined as the accountability of an enterprise's management for the resources entrusted to them. **Accountability** refers to management's responsibility to provide an account/report on the way in which the resources entrusted to them have been used.

To present other financial reports and analyses

Financial statements are contained within an annual report which includes other reports which provide a vehicle for the management team (directors) to communicate directly with the stakeholders. For example, the operating and financial review, the directors' report, the chairman's statement, the remuneration report and the **corporate social responsibility** report (discussed later). Summary analysis of the performance and financial standing of the business are usually provided in these other reports. They typically include the use of ratio analysis to evaluate the following matters:

1 the profitability of the business;

2 the level of activity and productivity;

3 the solvency and liquidity position (i.e. whether the business will be able to pay its debts);

4 the efficiency of credit control procedures;

5 the efficiency of inventory control procedures;

6 the effect of any loans on the business's profitability and financial stability.

Ratio analysis is examined in detail in Chapter 33, 'The Appraisal of Company Financial Statements Using Ratio Analysis'.

To facilitate the efficient allocation of resources

Viewing the function of financial accounting at a more general abstract level, its ultimate *raison d'être* is usually described as being to facilitate the efficient and effective allocation of resources (**economic decision-making**). This is generally given a macroeconomic interpretation as providing information to investors so that capital is directed towards more efficient firms. By viewing financial statements investors can determine the companies that are efficient in the utilization of resources and which entities are not. Investors will channel their investment monies into the more efficient firms, who will expand; hence, provide benefits for the economy and the population as a whole.

A less common but similar interpretation would be to extend this to providing information to prospective employees so that labour is directed towards more efficient firms. The same interpretation could also be extended to other potential users of final financial statements and providers of resources in a broad sense that embraces quality of life and environmental considerations, and so on. This would include others such as bank lenders, payables/suppliers, the government and the public in general. Therefore, everyone will be more interested in more efficient entities.

This function of financial accounting can also be viewed at a microeconomic or individual firm level. One of the main purposes of financial accounting may be said to be to enable an organization's management to operate the enterprise efficiently and effectively. This embraces at least three of the functions referred to above, namely, the recording and control of business transactions, accuracy in recording and the preparation of final financial statements (for management use). For example, by viewing financial information about internal departments, or products, management can direct resources to those that are more profitable and may even close down those that are not providing appropriate returns. This will improve the entity overall. This 'internal' function of accounting is more commonly attributed to management accounting, particularly in larger organizations.

Management accounting can be defined as the provision of information to an organization's management for the purposes of planning, control and decision-making. The latter includes production, marketing, investment and financing decisions.

LEARNING ACTIVITY 4.1

Imagine that you are in business in a small general store or as a plumber. Prepare a list of the financial information about the business that you would expect to be able to obtain from your records. Compare this with the above and consider any differences.

4.3 The objectives of company financial statements

As explained above, one of the main functions of financial accounting is **financial reporting**, which involves the preparation of final financial statements, also referred to as **financial accounts**. These consist of a statement of comprehensive income and a statement of financial position. In the case of companies, the final financial statements are often referred to as **published financial statements**. These are sent to equity shareholders in the form of a pamphlet known as the **annual or corporate report**.

It is therefore usual to discuss the objectives of company final financial statements in terms of the functions of annual reports.

Function of annual reports

The function of annual reports is related to beliefs about the role of business organizations in society and their objectives. Up until about the mid-1970s the accountancy profession took the view that the primary objective of a business enterprise was to maximize its profit and the wealth of its equity shareholders. This was reinforced by disciplines such as economics that gave prominence to the classical theory of the firm. The function of annual reports was thus regarded as being to provide information about the profitability and financial position of a company to those with whom it has a capital contractual relationship, namely, equity shareholders and loan creditors.

However, during the 1970s there was a swing in society's beliefs towards the idea that business enterprises exist for the benefit of the community as a whole. Similarly, developments in disciplines such as economics and modern organization theory cast doubt on whether profit maximization was a meaningful description of business objectives. For example, Herbert Simon argues that business enterprises are 'satisficers', that is, they seek to earn a satisfactory level of profit. Also, a survey of large UK companies undertaken by the accountancy profession found that 'the majority view of those replying to the survey seems to be that their primary objective is to make a profit for the benefit of a number of groups. It is not the majority view that the maximization of equity shareholder's profit is the primary objective'. Other respondents to this survey described their primary objective as being survival, or in terms of the service that they provide.

REAL WORLD EXAMPLE 4.1

Companies have objectives that cater for different stakeholders

Paddy Power's main mission is customer focused:

'Our mission is "to make risk-based entertainment" more accessible and fun. To offer customers an unparalleled betting experience that is great value; great fun and has the best service.'

Source: www.paddypower.com/bet/about-us (accessed May 2011).

British Telecom has several objectives. Two are included here. The first focuses on maximizing customer satisfaction, the second on ensuring there are equal opportunities for everyone employed by the company.

'Our vision is to be dedicated to helping customers thrive in a changing world. The world we live in and the way we communicate are changing, and we believe in progress, growth and possibility. We want to help all our customers make their lives and businesses better with products and services that are tailored to their needs and easy to use.'

Source: www.btplc.com/Thegroup/Ourcompany/Companyprofile/Ourvalues/index.htm (accessed May 2011).

We continue to support an inclusive working environment in which our people can develop their careers regardless of their race, sex, religion/beliefs, disability, marital or civil partnership status, age, sexual orientation, gender identity, gender expression or caring responsibilities and we are proud of our performance benchmarks. Our policy is for people to be paid fairly, regardless of gender, ethnic origin or disability.

Source: BT Annual Report and Form 20-F (2010) http://www.btplc.com/Sharesandperformance/Annualreportandreview/pdf/BTGroupAnnualReportSmart2010.pdf (accessed May 2011).

CHAPTER 4 The nature and objectives of financial reporting

It follows from this that enterprises are accountable to a number of different groups (employees, the public, etc.), and that the function of annual reports is to provide each of them with information. This is the view taken by *The Corporate Report* (ASSC, 1975) which is the UK accountancy bodies' most detailed statement on the function/objective of annual reports, their users and the information that they need. It is not mandatory but represents one of the most comprehensive pieces of published work in this area and has probably led to a number of new developments in accounting practices and more recent UK statements on these matters.

 ## 4.4 Corporate social responsibility (CSR)

During the 1980s there was a swing in society's beliefs back to an emphasis on the profit objective and equity shareholders as a result of the political philosophy known as 'enterprise culture'. In the past two decades, EU Directives on company law and other matters (e.g. employee participation) require greater disclosure of information that is primarily for the benefit of other users in the annual report. Furthermore, the privatization of government-owned enterprises and greater environmental awareness has resulted in more demand from members of the public, such as small investors and environmental activist groups, for annual reports. To cater for these wider interests directors in public listed companies include a *corporate social responsibility report* in the company's annual report.

Corporate social responsibility (CSR) describes how entities adopt policies by their own free will which benefit:

- local communities within which they operate (purchasing produce from the locality, volunteering in local schools, providing money donations to local charities, sponsoring prizes for educational programmes, etc.);
- their employees (health and safety, fair wages, pensions, etc.);
- customers (warranties, customer support, guarantees, etc.);
- the environment (pollution, recycling, energy saving); and
- in general conducting business in an ethical manner.

 ## CSR: objectives, areas of focus and actual projects

REAL WORLD EXAMPLE 4.2

British Gas objective:

British Gas has made 'environmental responsibility a top priority by investing in green energy and developing clear plans to reduce our own impact on the planet'.

Boots UK – the areas of their CSR focus:

'To support good governance of our behaviour and approach to corporate social responsibility, the Group has produced a number of key policy statements. These cover environment, health and safety, charity, product testing, customer safety and diversity'.

Source: Allianceboots (2010), Corporate Social Responsibility Report, 2009–10 http://www.allianceboots.com/CorporateSocialResponsibilityReport2009–10/strategic-approach/ourapproach.html (accessed 2011).

Marks and Spencer (an example of a community project):

'Marks and Spencer are committed to a fair trade relationship, with a number of regions in Africa, to pay fair prices to local farmers for their flower and fruit produce'.

Shell Foundation (an example of a community project):

'The Shell Foundation set up an early-learning centre in the Flower Valley in South Africa to help educate the community's children'.

Source: http://www.shellfoundation.org/pages/core_lines.php?p=corelines_inside_content&page=trading&newsID=100; http://www.ecofast-africa.com/community-projects/ (both accessed August 2011).

The function of the CSR report is to communicate social and environmental effects of a company's actions to interested parties within society and to society at large (Gray et al., 1987). CSR activities are mooted to bring benefits to an organization. Bhattacharya et al. (2008) argue that CSR can help with the recruitment and retention of employees, as they have a better perception of the company if they have policies such as payroll giving, active fundraising or releasing staff to do community volunteering (on full pay). It is also argued that CSR is good risk management. Promoting a culture of doing good means that, when deviant behavior does occur, the markets and public will react less negatively as the behaviour will be seen as being out of character. CSR activities also lead to brand enhancement and a stronger brand reputation; this can lead to investor loyalty and customer loyalty, which is beneficial for the organization.

On the downside, some environmentalists argue that UK companies 'greenwash' their annual reports highlighting what they do for the environment and the community; however, they do not identify the environmental risks that their entity creates for the community/environment, nor the steps taken to hedge against these risks. BP is one example of a company that champions CSR, even changing its brand name to 'BP – beyond petroleum' to emphasise its environmental objectives. However, the environmental catastrophe that occurred in 2010 in the Gulf of Mexico (the deepwater oil leek) was caused by reckless practice that had not been identified as a potential environmental risk (Thornton, 2010).

4.5 Environmental accounting (social accounting)

Sometimes referred to as 'green accounting' or 'social accounting', environmental accounting has many aims. At government level it tries to highlight the contribution that the natural environment makes to the economy both in terms of the economic contribution earned from the environments resources and the impact that a clean economy has on social well-being. In addition, it tries to determine the expenditure that is incurred in ensuring that the environment is protected (for example, expenditure on controlling pollution or controlling resource depletion such as the destruction of the Amazon forest).

At company level environmental reporting is be used to raise public/stakeholder awareness about the steps that an entity is taking to protect the environment. It typically identifies the costs incurred in, for example, reducing pollution, protecting wildlife and wildlife habitats. The impact that a company's actions has on society and the environment is difficult to ascertain as many of the benefits and costs are intangible, are difficult to identify, and when identified are difficult to quantify as the values may be very subjective. Nonetheless, many companies make reference to environment management in their annual report and prepare a separate report providing details of all their activities that impact on society and the environment. An example of the type of information that is provided and the problems with separately identifying the relevant costs can be seen from the following excerpt from BP's Annual Report for 2010.

BP's Business Review for 2010 – The Mexico Oil Spill

REAL WORLD EXAMPLE 4.3

Environmental expenditure			$ million
	2010	2009	2008
Environmental expenditure relating to the Gulf of Mexico oil spill			
Spill response	**13,628**	–	–
Additions to environmental remediation provision	**929**	–	–
Other environmental expenditure			
Operating expenditure	**716**	701	755
Capital expenditure	**911**	955	1,104
Clean-ups	**55**	70	64
Additions to environmental remediation provision	**361**	588	270
Additions to decommissioning provision	**1,800**	169	327

BP incurred significant costs in 2010 in response to the Gulf of Mexico oil spill. The spill response cost of $13,628 million includes amounts provided during 2010 of $10,883 million, of which $9,840 million has been expended during 2010, and $1,043 million remains as a provision at 31 December 2010. The majority of this remaining amount is expected to be expended during 2011. In addition, a further $2,745 million of clean-up costs were incurred in the year that were not provided for.

Operating and capital expenditure on the prevention, control, abatement or elimination of air, water and solid waste pollution is often not incurred as a separately identifiable transaction. Instead, it forms part of a larger transaction that includes, for example, normal maintenance expenditure. The figures for environmental operating and capital expenditure in the table are therefore estimates, based on the definitions and guidelines of the American Petroleum Institute.

The extent and cost of future environmental restoration, remediation and abatement programmes are inherently difficult to estimate. They often depend on the extent of contamination, and the associated impact and timing of the corrective actions required, technological feasibility and BP's share of liability. Though the costs of future programmes could be significant and may be material to the results of operations in the period in which they are recognized, it is not expected that such costs will be material to the group's overall results of operations or financial position.'

Source: Extract from page 73 of the Annual Report and Form 20-F 2010 for BP, 2010. http://www.bp.com/liveassets/bp_internet/globalbp/STAGING/global_assetsdownloads/I/BP_Annual_Report_and_Form_20F.pdf.

4.6 Public accountability

The basic philosophy of *The Corporate Report* (ASSC, 1975) is reflected in the need for what is called **public accountability**:

> there is an implicit responsibility to report publicly . . . incumbent on every entity whose size or format renders it significant; . . . we consider the responsibility to report publicly (referred to . . . as public accountability) is separate from and broader than the legal obligation to report and arises from the custodial role played in the community by economic entities; . . . they are involved in the maintenance of standards of life and the creation of wealth for and on behalf of the community.

The 'custodial role' of business enterprises refers to their responsibility to use the assets with which they have been entrusted to create wealth and maintain the standard of living, and other considerations such as the quality of the environment. It follows from this notion of public accountability that the objective or function of annual reports is: 'to communicate economic measurements of and information about the resources and performance of the reporting entity useful to those having reasonable rights to such information'. 'Reasonable rights' is defined as follows: 'A reasonable right to information exists where the activities of an organisation impinge or may impinge on the interest of a user group'.

A similar study of the function of annual reports was undertaken in 1973 by the American Institute of Certified Public Accountants (AICPA); this is known as *The Objectives of Financial Statements* (AICPA, 1973). This document emphasizes the use to which the information is put: 'The basic objective of financial statements is to provide information useful for making economic decisions.' It also regards annual reports as principally intended for those groups who only have access to limited information about the enterprise: 'An objective of financial statements is to serve primarily those users who have limited authority, ability, or resources to obtain information and who rely on financial statements as their principal source of information about an enterprise's economic activities.'

The most recent pronouncement by the UK accountancy profession on the objective of financial statements is in the *Statement of Principles for Financial Reporting* prepared by the Accounting Standards Board (ASB) in 1999 (ASB, 1999). The fundamental objective of financial statements is also defined by the International Accounting Standards Board (IASB) in its *Framework for the Preparation and Presentation of Financial Statements* (IASC, 1989), hereafter called the *Framework*. The *Framework* (IASC, 1989) states that: 'The objective of financial statements is to provide information about the financial position, performance and changes in financial position of an entity that is useful to a wide range of users for making economic decisions.'

The objective can usually be met by focusing exclusively on the information needs of present and potential investors, the defining class of user. Present and potential investors need information about the reporting entity's financial performance and financial position that is useful to them in evaluating the entity's ability to generate cash (including the timing and certainty of its generation) and in assessing the entity's financial adaptability. The financial statements should also show information to enable users to assess the stewardship of management, or the accountability of management for the resources entrusted to them.

The **financial performance** of an entity comprises the return it obtains on the resources it controls, the components of that return and the characteristics of those components. Profitability in particular is important as this allows users to assess potential changes in the entity's future resources.

An entity's **financial position** encompasses the economic resources it controls, its financial structure, its liquidity and solvency, its risk profile and risk management approach, and its capacity to adapt to changes in the environment in which it operates. This is useful to users in determining the entity's ability to generate cash (cash equivalents) in the future, in determining its future finance requirements, in determining its ability to attract finance and in determining how future profits and cash is likely to be distributed.

Information about the ways in which an entity generates and uses cash in its operations, its investment activities and its financing activities provides an additional perspective on its financial performance – one that is largely free from allocation and valuation issues.

An entity's **financial adaptability** is its ability to take effective action to alter the amount and timing of its cash flows so that it can respond to unexpected needs or opportunities.

4.7   The users of annual reports and their information needs

The users of annual reports identified in the *Framework* are described below.

Investors

Investors are defined in the *Framework* as providers of risk capital. They are concerned with evaluating the 'risk in, and return provided by their investment'. A basic premise in the *Framework* is that 'investors require information to help them determine whether they should buy, hold or sell. Shareholders are also interested in information which enables them to assess the ability of the entity to pay dividends'. Though the *Framework* does not explicitly refer to investors being interested in the stewardship of management, this is implicit in the decision on whether to retain, buy or sell shares. More explicit information needs are set out in the *The Corporate Report* (ASSC, 1975, p. 20) – investors require information for five purposes:

1 To evaluate the performance of the entity and its management, and assess the effectiveness of the entity in achieving its objectives.

2 To assess the economic stability and vulnerability of the reporting entity including its liquidity (i.e. whether it will have enough money to pay its debts), its present or future requirements for additional capital, and its ability to raise long- and short-term finance.

3 To estimate the value of users' own or other users' present or prospective interests in, or claims on, the entity.

4 To ascertain the ownership and control of the entity.

5 To estimate the future prospects of the entity, including its capacity to pay dividends and to predict future levels of investment.

Accountants have traditionally regarded published financial statements as fulfilling two main functions: (1) stewardship, and (2) facilitating share trading and lending decisions. The concept of stewardship roughly corresponds with everyday usage of the word and refers to the directors' responsibility to account for the uses to which they have put the equity shareholders' investment. This is the one function of published financial statements on which most accountants agree. *The Corporate Report* does not discuss this as such but rather emphasizes the share trading and decision-making function of annual reports. However, it is debatable whether past data is likely to be useful in predicting future profits, dividends or share prices. The literature on efficient market theory suggests that the content of annual reports has little, if any, predictive value. Published financial statements may therefore only perform a stewardship and feedback function.

Employees

The *Framework* states that 'employees and their representative groups are interested in information about the stability and profitability of their employers. They are also interested in information which enables them to assess the ability of the entity to provide remuneration, retirement benefits and employment opportunities.' It is considered that entities have a responsibility for the future livelihood and prospects of its employees' (*Corporate Report*, p. 21). Employee representatives (trade unions) will be interested in information for the purpose of wage bargaining. According to *The Corporate Report* such information may relate to 'the ability of the employer to meet wage demands, management's intentions regarding employment levels, locations and working conditions, the pay, conditions and terms of employment of various groups of employees and the contributions made by employees in different divisions. In addition, employees are likely to be interested in indications of the position, progress and prospects of the employing enterprise as a whole and about individual establishments and bargaining units.' Some companies produce employee reports that usually contain a summary of the year's trading results in a simplified form. Ryanair emphasize the training provided by the company to employees in their annual report:

REAL WORLD EXAMPLE 4.4

Ryanair

'Ryanair's pilots, flight attendants, maintenance and ground operations personnel undergo training, both initial and recurrent. A substantial portion of the initial training for Ryanair's flight attendants is devoted to safety procedures, and cabin crews are required to undergo annual evacuation and fire drill training during their tenure with the airline. Ryanair also provides salary increases to its engineers who complete advanced training in certain fields of aircraft maintenance. Ryanair utilizes its own Boeing 737-800 aircraft simulators for pilot training.'

Source: Ryanair plc (2010), Annual Report 2010, http://www.ryanair.com/en/investor/download/2010 (accessed May 2011).

Lenders

According to the *Framework*, lenders are interested in information that enables them to determine whether their loans, and the interest attached to them, will be paid when due. Lenders encapsulate entities like the bank and investors in debt capital (bonds). Holders of debt capital that is traded on a recognized stock exchange will have similar information requirements to equity investors as they will also have to decide whether to hold, buy or sell their bonds. Certain information will be of particular relevance, such as that relating to:

1 The present and likely future cash position; since this will determine whether the company will be able to pay the annual interest on loans and repay the money borrowed as and when it becomes due (liquidity and solvency).

2 The economic stability and vulnerability of the company in so far as this reflects the risk of possible default in repayment of money borrowed by the company (risk).

3 Prior claims on the company's assets in the event of its going into liquidation (security).

Suppliers and other creditors

Suppliers and other creditors will have similar interests to lenders. When a supplier provides goods in advance of receiving payment, this is like giving a loan. Therefore, they will be interested to determine at the outset whether to trade with the entity or not, and will want to make judgements on the length of credit period to give and the amount of credit to allow. According to the *Framework*, 'suppliers and other creditors are interested in information that enables them to determine whether amounts owing to them will be paid when due. Credit suppliers are likely to be interested in an entity over a shorter period than lenders unless they are dependent upon the continuation of the entity as a major customer.' Therefore, they are most interested in liquidity and changes in liquidity. A supplier may be interested in determining whether the company is growing as they may have to decide whether to increase its production capacity in order to meet the reporting entity's future demands.

Customers

According to the *Framework*, 'customers have an interest in information about the continuance of an entity, especially when they have a long-term involvement with, or are dependent on, the entity'. For example, if the reporting entity is engaged in construction work, customers will wish to assess the likelihood of its being able to complete long-term contracts. In the case of manufactured goods, such as computers and vehicles, customers will be concerned about the reporting entity's continued existence because of its warranty obligations and the need for spare parts. Annual reports may thus be useful to customers in assessing the likelihood of a reporting entity's continued existence. Going concern will be of particular interest.

Governments and their agencies

According to the *Framework*, 'Governments and their agencies are interested in the allocation of resources and, therefore, the activities of entities. They also require information in order to regulate the activities of entities, determine taxation policies and as the basis for national income and similar statistics.' For example, HM Revenue and Customs have a statutory right to information about the reporting entity for the purpose of assessing its liability to taxation. The Department of Trade and Industry require industry sector statistics to determine how sectors are performing. The government can utilize this information to provide assistance to particular sectors (e.g. grants and subsidies are awarded to the farming sector) and to penalize other sectors (e.g. a windfall tax was charged on utility companies in 1997). The government also needs to estimate economic trends, including balance of payments figures (imports versus exports), employment figures and inflation levels. In the UK most of this information is collected through special government returns. However, in some other countries corporate reports perform this function.

The public

According to the *Framework*, entities:

> affect members of the public in a variety of ways. For example, entities may make a substantial contribution to a local economy in many ways including the number of people they employ and their patronage of local suppliers. Financial statements may assist the public by providing information about the trends and recent developments in the prosperity of the entity and its range of activities.

The public has a right to information about a local entity as most entities use community-owned assets such as roads and car parks. Their employment requirements may bring an influx of people to the area. More people means more places required in schools, longer waits for the doctor, and so on.

Some members of the public may be concerned about the employment policies of the reporting entity and therefore want information relating to local employment levels or discrimination in employment, for example. Other members of the public may be interested in any plans that the reporting entity has that affect the environment, including issues relating to conservation and pollution, and congestion. Other matters of a political or moral nature may also be of particular concern to some sections of the community, such as contributions to political organizations, pressure groups or charities, and whether the reporting entity is trading with countries having repressive political regimes. Some of this information must be disclosed under the Companies Act 2006 (i.e. donations to political parties and charities). Most companies provide information that is relevant for the public and the local community in their CSR report, others provide it in the directors' report.

Other users

These user groupings and their information needs are more or less identical to those listed in the UK accountancy profession's *Statement of Principles for Financial Reporting* (ASB, 1999) as prepared by the ASB in 1999. The earlier guidance on users, *The Corporate Report*, mentioned two further categories explicitly: the analyst–adviser group and competitor and takeover bidders. These are described next.

REAL WORLD EXAMPLE 4.5

Tesco plc providing information for the local community

'. . . Last year we recruited over 3,000 long-term unemployed people and other disadvantaged job seekers, up on nearly 500 the previous year.' . . . . .

'. . . Our staff broke all records for our Charity of the Year, raising over £6 million for Marie Curie Cancer Care to fund an additional 300,000 hours of nursing care for over 5,000 terminally ill patients and their families.'. . . .

'. . . Our new Tesco for Schools and Clubs scheme is now running in our UK stores . . . We have had successful schools programmes in Ireland for 11 years now, in Poland for eight, and this year is the first year of 'Shop for Schools' in the US . . .'

'In recent months, we have also moved some £11 million worth of business back to UK suppliers, supporting domestic orderbooks and production, and safeguarding employment.'. . .

Source: Tesco plc (2010) Annual Report 2010, www.ar2010.tescoplc.com (accessed May 2011).

The analyst–adviser group

This group's information needs are satisfied under each of the user groups identified in the *Framework*. This grouping is explicitly referred to in *The Corporate Report*, which states that 'the information needs of the analyst–adviser group are likely to be similar to the needs of the users who are being advised. For example, the information needs of stockbrokers are likely to be similar to the needs of investors and those of trade unions are likely to be similar to the needs of employees.' *The Corporate Report* makes the point that this group, because of their expertise, will tend to demand more elaborate information than other groups.

Competitors and takeover bidders

This grouping comes under 'the business contact group' in *The Corporate Report*. The rationale for competitors having a right to information is a little vague but seems to rest on the premise that inter-firm comparisons of performance and costs can facilitate improvements in efficiency. Similarly, given that mergers and takeovers of less efficient firms are in the public interest, a case can be made for the disclosure of information to potential bidders.

Management

One of the duties required of management is to prepare financial statements that give a true and fair view of the state of the company's affairs for the period and its financial position at the end of the period. This involves ensuring that they comply with the *Framework*, the accounting standards and legislation. The *Framework* recognizes that management are users of financial statements. However, it takes the view that financial statements should not be prepared with management's information needs in mind. Management have access to information which can be, and is, tailored to their information needs. As their needs are varied and bespoke given the decision being made, it is considered that the *Framework* and the information included in financial statements should ignore their needs. Regardless, management usually do find the information useful, as they use it to assess their performance in the past and to determine if their projections of what will happen in the future are realistic or not.

The limitations of financial statements

This section provides a summary of the debate relating to whether financial statements achieve the objective of financial statements given in the *Framework*. The debate involves a broad range of issues, and thus is confined to those addressed in the *Framework*. There are four main themes:

- The first is often referred to as the adequacy of financial statements in meeting users' information needs, and includes a debate about general-purpose versus specific-purpose financial reports.

- The second relates to problems of classification, aggregation and allocation.

- The third involves the lack of non-financial information in financial statements.

- The fourth theme in the debate concerns the use of largely historical information. This includes the use of historical cost accounting, which refers to recording transactions at cost price on the date the item is recognized in the financial statements – where the price reflects the price that has been agreed in an arm's-length transaction.

The limitations of historical cost accounting are discussed in depth in Chapter 5, 'Accounting Principles, Concepts and Policies'. Problems with classification, aggregation and allocation embrace a wide range of issues discussed throughout the book. For example, a classification problem might be the treatment of overdrafts. In most financial statements these are classified as current liabilities because they are repayable on demand. In practice the entity may be using an overdraft as a long-term source of funds and in practice the bank is not likely to ask for the overdraft to be repaid. In these circumstances the company might look as though it is having liquidity problems (problems paying its short-term commitments), when it does not. An example of how aggregation limits the quality of information is the disclosure on the face of the statement of financial position in company financial statements of trade receivables. One figure is provided, yet it represents two accounts; one showing the money owing to the company from trade customers (a positive account) and the other showing the amount of these trade customers who are not likely to pay (a negative account). Only the net amount is disclosed, yet information on bad debts is vital for highlighting the efficiency of the credit control policies of the entity. Finally, an example of the limitations associated with allocation can be found in the treatment of non-current tangible assets. The cost of these assets is allocated to the statement of profit and loss in the years that the assets help to generate revenue. This is a process called 'depreciation'. The concept is simple, yet in practice there are a variety of methods used to allocate this cost, all ending up with different profit or loss figures.

Some companies voluntarily publish specific-purpose financial reports, each of which is aimed at a particular class or classes of users of financial statements. These include a statement of value added, an employment report, an employee report, an environmental report and simplified financial statements. Some of these are included in the annual report with the financial statements, and others are published as separate documents. However, there is a fundamental presumption underlying most of the authoritative pronouncements on financial reporting that financial statements should be general purpose documents. This is based on the premise that the main information needs of users other than investors are the same as those of investors. That is, they all need information about the financial performance and financial position of the reporting entity in order to assess its ability to provide rewards (dividends, wages, etc.) and the likelihood of its continued existence, respectively. This is explained in the *Framework* as follows:

 While all of the information needs of these users cannot be met by financial statements, there are needs which are common to all users. As investors are providers of risk capital to the entity, the provision of financial statements that meet their needs will also meet most of the needs of other users that financial statements can satisfy.

The other three main themes in the debate about the limitations of financial statements, introduced above, are described in the UK's *Statement of Principles for Financial Reporting* (ASB, 1999) as follows:

financial statements have various inherent limitations that make them an imperfect vehicle for reflecting the full effects of transactions and other events on a reporting entity's financial performance and financial position. For example:

a they are a conventionalised representation of transactions and other events that involves a substantial degree of classification and aggregation and the allocation of the effects of continuous operations to discrete reporting periods.

b they focus on the financial effects of transactions and other events and do not focus to any significant extent on their non-financial effects or on non-financial information in general.

c they provide information that is largely historical and therefore does not reflect future events or transactions that may enhance or impair the entity's operations, nor do they anticipate the impact of potential changes in the economic environment.

These inherent limitations mean that some information on the financial performance and financial position of the reporting entity can be provided only by general purpose financial reports other than financial statements – or in some cases is better provided by such reports.

LEARNING ACTIVITY 4.2

Download Ryanair plc's annual report and financial statements.

Read through the financial statements (statement of profit and loss, statement of financial position, statement of cash flows and the related notes) and make a list of whatever information you find that is likely to be useful to a potential investor. Then draw up a different list of any other information that is missing and that you think would be useful to a potential investor. Then read the narrative reports at the start of the annual report.

Do these reports provide the information you listed as being useful for investors, but not present in the financial statements?

4.9 The regulatory framework of accounting

The **regulatory framework of accounting** is a general term used to describe the legislation and other rules that govern the content and format of company final financial statements. There is no legislation or other regulation covering the final financial statements of sole traders and partnerships. However, it is generally accepted that their financial statements should closely follow the rules and regulations relating to companies since these are regarded as 'best practice'. There are three main sources of rules and regulations governing the content and format of company final financial statements in the UK:

1 The Companies Act 2006, with which all companies are required to comply.

2 The Rules of the London Stock Exchange, with which all companies whose shares are listed on the London Stock Exchange are expected to comply.

3 The accounting standards, of which there are two possibilities: International Financial Reporting Standards (IFRSs) or UK Financial Reporting Standards (FRSs). The regulatory framework for setting IFRS is described in Chapter 2, 'International Financial Reporting: Institutional Framework and Standards'. IFRSs are compulsory for all publicly listed companies though can be adopted by all other types of entity also. The regulatory framework for setting UK FRSs is described in the chapter on the website, 'UK Accounting: Institutional Framework and Standards, available at www.mcgraw-hill.co.uk/textbooks/thomas. UK FRSs cannot be applied by publicly listed companies though can be used for all other entities. Over the last decade the international accounting standard setters and the UK accounting standard setters have focused on achieving convergence between the standards and several of the standards are now similar. However, there are still many differences, particularly in respect of the presentation of financial information. In practice, the financial statements of unincorporated entities (e.g. sole traders and partnerships) are prepared using FRSs. The wheels of change are in motion and it is expected that full convergence will happen in the future; therefore, a decision has been taken by most academic institutions to be proactive and to teach students how to prepare financial statements using IFRSs. That is the position adopted in this book.

Summary

Financial accounting is the process of designing and operating an information system for collecting, measuring and recording business transactions, and summarizing and communicating the results of these transactions to users to facilitate the making of financial/economic decisions. The first part of this definition, relating to collecting and recording business transactions, is called double-entry bookkeeping. The purposes of financial accounting systems are to record and control business transactions, maintain accuracy in recording, meet the requirements of the law, present final financial statements and other financial reports to the owners of the enterprise, and facilitate the efficient allocation of resources.

The final financial statements of companies are often referred to as published financial statements, and include a statement of comprehensive income and a statement of financial position. These are contained in a document called the 'annual report and **financial statements**' (or 'annual report and accounts'). The functions of annual reports are related to society's beliefs about the objective(s) of business enterprises. It is recognized that businesses have objectives that go beyond creating value for shareholders only, that they also have a duty to promote the local community and to be environmentally friendly. Most plc companies provide information on their activities towards the local community and the environment within a CSR report.

The basic philosophy of the accountancy bodies is that of public accountability. This underlies their view of the objective of financial statements as being to provide information about the reporting entity's financial performance and financial position that is useful to a wide range of users for assessing the stewardship of management and for making economic decisions. These users include investors, employees, lenders, suppliers and other trade creditors, customers, governments and their agencies, and the public. Each of these will have particular information needs.

The contents of company financial statements are governed by the regulatory framework. In the UK this comprises the Companies Act 2006, London Stock Exchange regulations, and accounting standards. The latter includes IASs and IFRSs as issued by the IASC/IASB and SSAPs and FRSs as issued by the ASC/ASB.

Key terms and concepts

accountability	49	financial reporting	50
annual or corporate report	50	financial statements	49
corporate social responsibility	49	internal check	48
double-entry bookkeeping	47	internal control	48
economic decision-making	50	management accounting	50
final financial statements	48	payables	48
financial accounting	47	public accountability	54
financial accounts	50	published financial statements	50
financial adaptability	55	receivables	48
financial performance	55	regulatory framework of accounting	61
financial position	48	stewardship	49

An asterisk after the question number indicates that there is a suggested answer on the Online Learning Centre (www.mcgraw-hill.co.uk/textbooks/thomas).

Review questions

4.1 Explain the nature and functions of financial accounting.

4.2* Explain briefly each of the following: internal control; internal check; stewardship; and accountability.

4.3   a Describe the recording and control function of financial accounting.

     b Explain the role of financial accounting with regard to the presentation of final financial statements.

4.4   a Outline the objective of financial statements as set out in the IASC's *Framework for the Preparation and Presentation of Financial Statements* (1989).

     b Identify the users of financial statements and briefly describe their information needs as set out in the IASC's *Framework for the Preparation and Presentation of Financial Statements* (1989).

4.5   The objective of financial statements is to provide information about the reporting entity's financial performance and financial position that is useful to a wide range of users for assessing the stewardship of the entity's management and for making economic decisions (*Statement of Principles for Financial Reporting*).

Required

a State five potential users of company published financial statements, briefly explaining for each one their likely information needs from those statements.

b Briefly discuss whether you think that UK company published financial statements achieve the objective stated above, giving your reasons. Include in your answer two ways in which you think the quality of the information disclosed in financial statements could be improved.

(ACCA)

Websites

Alliance Boots CSR report (2010) can be accessed on: http://www.allianceboots.com

BP's Annual Report (2010) can be accessed on: http://www.bp.com/liveassets/bp_internet/globalbp/ STAGING/global_assets/downloads/I/BP_Annual_Report_and_Form_20F.pdf.

Ryanair plc Annual Report (2010) including its CSR report can be found on: http://ryanair.com/en/ investor/download/2010.

Tesco plc's CSR report can be found on: http://tesco.com

References

Accounting Standards Board (1999) *Statement of Principles for Financial Reporting* (ASB).

Accounting Standards Steering Committee (ASSC) (1975) *The Corporate Report* (ICAEW).

American Institute of Certified Public Accountants (1973) *The Objectives of Financial Statements* (AICPA).

Bhattacharya, C.B., Sen, S. and Korschun, D. (2008) 'Using Corporate Social Responsibility to Win the War for Talent', *Sloan Management Review*, 49, 2. 37–44.

Gray, R.H., Owen, D.L. and Maunders, K.T. (1987) *Corporate Social Responsibility: Accounting and Accountability*, Prentice Hall, Hemel Hempstead.

International Accounting Standards Committee (IASC) (1989) Adopted by the International Accounting Standards Board in 2001, *Framework for the Preparation and Presentation of Financial Statements* (IASB).

Thornton, J. (2010) 'Companies put on Notice to Report Environmental Impact of their Work', *Guardian*, Thursday, 4 November 2010, www.guardian.co.uk.

When you have read this chapter, log on to the Online Learning Centre for *Introduction to Financial Accounting* at www.mcgraw-hill.co.uk/textbooks/thomas, where you will find multiple choice quizzes, case studies, a glossary and mock exams.

Accounting principles, concepts and policies

Learning Objectives

After reading this chapter you should be able to do the following:

1. Explain the meaning of the key terms and concepts listed at the end of this chapter.

2. Explain the nature of accounting principles, accounting concepts, measurement bases, accounting policies and estimation techniques.

3. Explain the nature of the going concern concept, the accruals concept, the matching concept, the entity concept, the materiality concept, the time period concept, the cost concept, the money measurement concept, the prudence concept, the duality concept, the substance over form concept, the consistency concept and the separate determination concept, including their implications for the preparation of financial statements.

4. Outline the recognition criteria required before transactions can be included in financial statements.

5. Describe the objectives against which an entity should judge the appropriateness of accounting policies, that is, relevance and reliability.

6. Describe the constraints that an entity should take into account in judging the appropriateness of accounting policies.

7. Describe the requirements of *IAS 8 – Accounting Policies, Changes in Accounting Estimates and Errors* (IASB, 2010a) with regard to the selection, review, change in and disclosure of accounting policies, estimation techniques and errors.

5.1 Introduction

An appreciation of the conceptual and theoretical foundations of financial accounting is fundamental to the preparation, understanding and interpretation of financial statements. The conceptual and theoretical foundations can be described as a set of rules, principles, postulates, conventions and methods. The first part of this chapter explains the nature of the underlying concepts of accounting. Some of the concepts are referred to specifically in the International Accounting Standard Committee's (IASC's) *Framework for the Preparation and Presentation of Financial Statements* (the *Framework*) (IASC, 1989). This framework is the main source of guidance underpinning the accounting for any transaction in financial statements that are prepared using International Accounting Standards (IASs). The *Framework* is supported by *IAS 1 – Presentation of Financial Statements* (IASB, 2010d) and by IAS 8. IAS 8 focuses on the selection, change in and disclosure of accounting policies, accounting estimates and errors. The latter part of this chapter provides a summary of the relevant parts of IAS 8.

 ## The nature of accounting principles

The *Framework* provides conceptual guidance on international generally accepted **accounting principles**. Each chapter within the *Framework* deals with a different principle. The chapters of the *Framework* include the following topics:

1 The objective of financial statements, as explained in Chapter 4, 'The Nature and Objectives of Financial Accounting: Including Corporate Social Responsibility, Environmental Accounting and Accountability'.

2 Underlying assumptions of accounting. These are explained in this chapter.

3 The qualitative characteristics of financial statements, comprising understandability, relevance, reliability and comparability. These are explained in Chapter 6, 'The Qualitative Characteristics of Financial Information.

4 The elements of financial statements such as assets, liabilities, **ownership interest** (equity), performance, income, expenditure and capital maintenance. These are explained briefly in this chapter.

5 Recognition of the elements financial statements. This is explained briefly in this chapter.

6 Measurement of the elements in financial statements. This is explained briefly in this chapter.

7 Concepts of capital maintenance. This is explained briefly in Chapter 8, 'The Accounting Equation and its Components'.

 ## Key accounting concepts

Accounting concepts were defined in the UK standard *SSAP 2 – Disclosure of Accounting Policies* (ASSC, 1971) as 'broad basic assumptions that underlie the periodic financial statements of business enterprises'. There are several, though two are specifically singled out for explicit mention in the *Framework* as they are regarded as being fundamental for ensuring that financial statements meet their objective (i.e. providing useful information). These comprise the going concern concept and the accruals concept.

Going concern

The **going concern** concept is the assumption that an entity will continue in operational existence for the foreseeable future. Any user when looking at an entity's financial statements has the right to assume that the company is not going to liquidate or curtail materially the scale of its operations. Users should be able to look at the financial implications of prior activity as captured in the financial statements and use this as an indication of future activity.

The implication of the going concern assumption is that assets are valued at their historical cost (or fair value), not their scrap value. It is assumed that the entity will continue to operate for the remaining useful life of the non-current assets; hence, the asset's cost will be allocated to the statement of profit and loss over the useful life of the asset to match against the revenues that the asset helps to generate. If, however, the entity were going to close, the asset cost would have to be written down to the net revenue that it is expected to generate on sale; that is, the sales price less any costs associated with the sale. This may be significantly lower than the book value recorded in the statement of financial position, particularly where the asset is unique, bespoke or specialized, as there will be a limited second-hand market for the sale of the asset.

If there is reason to believe that the entity will not be able to continue in business, then the going concern principle no longer holds and the assets should be valued on a cessation basis; that is, at their net **realizable value**. For example a £10,000 machine, which can easily generate output for the next 10 years, would be recognized in the statement of financial position at cost price less depreciation, if the company is a going concern. However, if the company decides to go into voluntary liquidation, then this machine is not going to produce revenue for the next 10 years, hence should be written down to the value expected to be received on its sale (its net realizable value). This may be zero.

In terms of disclosures, IAS 1 states that 'when an entity does not prepare financial statements on a going concern basis, it shall disclose that fact, together with the basis on which it prepared the financial statements and the reasons why the entity is not regarded as a going concern'. There are real economic consequences of this disclosure as highlighted in the following real world example.

REAL WORLD EXAMPLE 5.1 Standard & Poor's reaction to Clearwire Corp.'s disclosure

Standard & Poor's Ratings downgraded Clearwire Corp. to highly speculative territory, citing the company's recent disclosure questioning its ability to continue as a going concern. Its shares declined 1.7 per cent to $6.42 in recent premarket trading. The stock was down 3.4 per cent this year as of Monday's close.

Clearwire may run out of cash and investments to cover its liquidity by mid-2011, it indicated last week. The company also disclosed uncertainty about its ability to obtain additional capital and continue as a going concern.

Source: Jarzemsky, M. (2010) Dow Jones Newswires, http://www.totaltele.com/view.aspx?ID=460127

Accruals concept

According to the *Framework* and IAS 1, to meet their objectives, financial statements should be prepared on the accruals basis of accounting.

The **accruals concept** is concerned with allocating expenses and income to the periods to which they relate (when the **expenses** were used by the entity, or when the income was earned, as distinctly different to when cash is paid out for expenses and when cash is received from a sale). The *Framework* states that the transactions should be 'recorded in the accounting records and reported in the financial statements in the periods to which they relate'. In most instances this refers to the accounting period in which the goods or services physically pass from the seller to the buyer. Accrual accounting provides useful information to users of financial statements as it identifies past payments involving the receipt (deferred income) or payment of cash (prepayments) and also highlights future commitments to pay cash in the future (for example, trade payables) and resources that represent cash to be received in the future (for example, trade receivables).

In the case of sales revenue, this notion has traditionally been referred to as **revenue recognition**. It relates to the assumption that a sale is deemed to have taken place at the time at which the goods are delivered or services provided (i.e. when the revenue is earned), and not when the proceeds of sale are received. In practice this is normally also the date of the invoice. However, where the invoice is rendered some time after the date of delivery, the sale is deemed to have taken place on the date of delivery and not the date of the invoice. Though coming under the remit of the accruals concept, revenue recognition is such an important principle that a whole standard has been dedicated to provide guidance on the accounting for certain types of revenue: *IAS 18 – Revenue* (IASB, 2010b). This standard applies to the accounting for revenue arising from the sale of goods, the rendering of services and the use by others of entity assets yielding interest, royalties and dividends.

Legislation has also impacted on the interpretation of the accruals concept. Companies legislation requires that only profits realized at the period end should be included in the statement of profit and loss. 'It is generally accepted that profits shall be treated as realized, for these purposes, only when realized in the form either of cash or of other assets, the ultimate cash realization of which can be assessed with reasonable certainty.' This is known as the **realization concept**. Unrealized profits are shown in the statement of comprehensive income for the year net of tax.

The accruals concept also assumes that costs should be recognized when they occur, and not when money is paid: that is, goods and services are deemed to have been purchased on the date they are received and services consumed, for which no invoice has been received at the end of an accounting year (e.g. electricity, gas, telephone), are treated as a cost for that year. The amount due is treated as a liability. These are referred to as **accrued expenses**. In contrast, services paid for in advance (e.g. rent, insurance, road tax, local government taxes) that have not been received at the end of an accounting year are treated as a cost of the following accounting year, and thus carried forward as an asset at the end of the current year. These are referred to as **prepaid expenses** or **prepayments**. Accrued and prepaid expenses are dealt with in more depth in Chapter 18 'Accruals and Prepayments'.

Matching concept

The **matching concept/principle** refers to the assumption that in the measurement of profit, costs should be set against the revenue that they generate at the time when this arises. A classic example of the application of the matching principle is inventory. Where goods are bought in one accounting year but sold in the next, their cost is carried forward as inventory at the end of the year and set against the proceeds of sale in the accounting year in which it occurs. This is expounded in *IAS 2 – Inventories* (IASB, 2010c) as follows: 'When inventories are sold, the carrying amount of those inventories shall be recognised as an expense in the period in which the related revenue is recognised.'

In terms of the calculation of the gross profit in the statement of profit and loss, this process of carrying forward costs takes the form of the computation of the cost of sales. The cost is carried forward by being deducted from purchases in the form of the inventory at the end of the year. It is brought forward to the following year in the form of the opening inventory, which is matched against the proceeds of sale by virtue of its being included in the cost of sales.

A more theoretical view of the matching principle is that it refers to ascertaining profit on the basis of a cause and effect relationship. Costs cause or give rise to certain effects that take the form of revenue. Matching is thus the determination of profit by attributing specific causes to particular effects at the time at which the effects occur.

The accruals concept and matching principle can be illustrated vividly by a simplified example (see Example 5.1).

> **EXAMPLE 5.1**
>
> Suppose a business only had the following transactions:
>
> **15 Jan**   Purchased goods costing £100 on credit
>
> **15 Feb**   Paid for the goods purchased on 15 January
>
> **15 Mar**   Sold on credit for £150 the goods purchased on 15 January
>
> **15 Apr**   Received payment for the goods sold on 15 March
>
> The accruals (and matching) concept dictates that:
>
> **1** The cost of the goods was *incurred* in January.
>
> **2** The sales revenue was *earned* in March.
>
> **3** There was no profit or loss in January, February or April. The profit of £50 arose in March, the cost of the goods being carried forward as inventory at the end of January and February.

Unfortunately, the application of the accruals concept in general, and the revenue recognition concept and matching principle in particular, is not always as simple as implied above. Although the contents of this section thus far would usually be sufficient to answer most examination questions at this level, students might be expected to demonstrate an awareness of its relevance to current issues. There have recently been several high-profile cases of large companies throughout the world where abuses of the revenue recognition and the matching principle have resulted in the overstatement of profits, and in some cases, corporate bankruptcy. Moreover, standard setting bodies have been reviewing revenue recognition rules for some years.

Many of the issues concerning revenue recognition arise where the revenue received in one accounting year relates to goods or services that the business will provide in the next, or future, accounting year(s).

As noted in the next real world example, the revenue from the creation of IT systems was recognized before it should have been causing profits to be overstated.

REAL WORLD EXAMPLE 5.2 — iSOFT Group Plc

iSOFT Group Plc, a software firm charged with developing a £6 billion computer upgrade for the National Health Service (NHS) was investigated by the Financial Services Authority (FSA) because of accounting irregularities. In particular, it emerged that iSOFT were stating revenues earlier than they should have been. The auditors, 'Deloitte', were unable to state whether the financial statements in 2004 and 2005 provided a true and fair view of the company's performance and their financial position at the reporting period end in each year.

According to a communication document posted on the FSA website: 'On 6 January 2010 the FSA announced that it had just commenced criminal proceedings against four former directors of iSOFT Group Plc for the offence of conspiracy to make misleading statements, contrary to section 397 (1)(a) and (2) of the Financial Services and Markets Act 2000 and section 1 of the Criminal Law Act 1977.'

Source: FSA 2010, 'FSA starts criminal proceedings against former iSOFT directors', FSA website, www.FSA.gov.uk/pages/Library/Communication/PR/2010/002.shtml (accessed May 2011).

Other examples include revenue from the installation of security and IT systems, different forms of prepayments associated with various mobile phone and other telecommunication services including television, extended warranties and maintenance agreements, and so on. The latter provides a good illustration of the general issues and underlying principles.

When consumers purchase electrical goods they are often encouraged to buy an extended warranty. The consumer pays a one-off premium at the time of purchase, and the seller undertakes to maintain and/or repair the item for some fixed future period of often three to five years. The customer is invoiced at the time of sale. Thus, applying the revenue recognition concept, as described above, might suggest that the premium would be treated as earned/realized in the statement of profit and loss in the year of sale, which is a practice that some companies have sought to adopt in their financial statements.

However, this does not accord with the matching principle. The costs of the repairs that the seller is obliged to make under the extended warranty will be incurred over several future accounting years, and thus the matching principle dictates that the premium received should be spread over this period. This is referred to as **deferred income**.

This is not the end of the problem. The issue now arises as to how much of the premium should be recognized as revenue in each of the future accounting years. The repairs to the item in question are likely to be more common and more costly as the item becomes older. A proper matching would thus require a higher proportion of the premium to be recognized in each of the later years. The precise proportion to be recognized in each year will thus be highly subjective/arbitrary, which is where the further possibility of abuse arises (allocation limitation).

Furthermore, the extended warranty illustration does not highlight another very subjective decision. Extended warranties cover a fixed number of years, whereas other goods and services of a similar nature often do not relate to a given period. In applying the matching principle it will thus be necessary to determine over how many years the income should be recognized. This again gives scope for revenue manipulation.

Similar issues arise in deciding whether expenditure should be treated as capital (i.e. on non-current assets) or revenue (i.e. expenses), and in the case of capital expenditure, over what period to write off the asset and how much should be charged to each year (classification and allocation limitations). This is discussed further in Chapter 16, 'Depreciation and Non-current Assets'.

 ## 5.4 Other concepts

The fundamental concepts (going concern and accruals) and the related concepts (revenue recognition, realization and matching) are discussed above. There are a number of other concepts that are implicit in the preparation of financial statements and are so engrained in the process of accounting that they are not explicitly mentioned in the *Framework*. Some have already been mentioned in earlier chapters and some will be focused on in later chapters. To be comprehensive, a short explanation of each is given in this chapter.

Entity concept

The first is the **entity concept**, otherwise known as the **accounting entity** or the **business entity** concept. This concept is discussed in detail in Chapter 1, 'Entities and Financial Reporting Statements'. In simple terms this concept allows the user to look at a reporting entity's financial statements and to know that these represent the performance and financial position of the business unit and do not include any **assets**, **liabilities**, **income** or expenditure that are not related to the business. Therefore, when a sole trader uses the business cheque book to buy a car for personal use, this car will not form part of the business's assets; it will be treated as the owner withdrawing equity capital. This is called a 'drawing'.

Materiality concept

The **materiality concept** affects every transaction and every set of financial statements. This concept affects two main areas: presentation and application of accounting standards. In respect of the first, this concept assumes that only material items should be disclosed in financial statements. This is important for achieving the objective of financial statements as attention being afforded to immaterial items can mislead the user. The user should be able to look at a set of financial statements and focus on the important figures, not see a mass of information, much of which is of no use for economic decision-making. For example, it is irrelevant to disclose a yearly spend on stationery of £100 and a yearly spend on coffee of £75, if the company has a turnover of £10 million and total expenditure of £8 million. The immaterial items need to be grouped together, or grouped into categories that are material. For example, the stationery and coffee could be combined into administration expenses that might have a total of £2.5 million. Knowing about the £100 spend on stationery, or the £75 spend on coffee, will not influence users' economic decision-making. Indeed, if such detail was provided, the user might not easily see that total expenses are £8 million.

The second area of relevance is when deciding whether to comply with guidance given in accounting standards. As a general rule of thumb, accounting standards only apply to material items. Therefore, a company that spends £2,000 per year on heating oil (with other expenditure of £8 million) does not have to apply the cost flow inventory valuation techniques as detailed in *IAS 2 – Inventories* (see Chapter 24, 'Inventory Valuation') when valuing its oil inventories. This saves the company time, hence money. Whether the final value for the year ended up as £2,000 or £2,100 would not affect users' economic decision-making.

The only time that immaterial-sized items become 'material' is when the nature of the item makes them so. For example, when an entity experiences theft by staff, or the directors have borrowed money from the entity, then even though the amounts may be small relative to the entity's overall performance and financial position, they indicate weaknesses that users should be aware of. Theft by staff indicates weak internal controls and directors borrowing money may highlight fiduciary problems.

Time period concept

Another concept, the **time period concept**, otherwise known as the **time interval** concept, refers to the practice of dividing the life of an entity into discrete periods for the purpose of preparing financial statements. The norm, as required by company law, is one year. Therefore, a user has the right to assume that the figures shown in a set of financial statements refer to a one-year period. When the period is different to one year, the financial statements need to make it clear that this is the case. Indeed, company law limits the ability of companies to change their accounting year-end date. Entities can of course elect to report for different time periods; however, to comply with law and the tax authorities they will also need to prepare financial statements every 12 months.

Historical cost concept/fair value

The **historical cost concept** allows a user to assume that all the transactions in an entity's financial statements reflect the actual cost price billed, or revenue charged, for items. In addition, it allows the reader to see the history of the management team's investment decision-making from the statement of financial position. This concept is becoming less relevant now as it is widely believed that historical cost information does not support financial statements in their aim of producing information that is useful for economic decision-making. In particular the impact of inflation means that many of the items recorded at historic cost, do not reflect current value. The ASC tried to introduce a standard (*SSAP 16 current cost accounting*) to enable entities to incorporate inflation into their financial statements; however, this standard had to be withdrawn due to lack of support from the business community. Measuring items at fair value is deemed to provide more relevant information. **Fair value** is defined by the International Accounting Standards Board (IASB) as 'the amount for which an asset could be exchanged, or a liability settled, between knowledgeable, willing parties in an arm's length transaction'.

Money measurement concept

The **money measurement concept** allows the user to assume that the performance and financial position of a reporting entity will be expressed in monetary amounts (usually in the currency of the country where the business is registered). In this book it is assumed that the relevant currency is the sterling pound (£).

Duality concept

The **duality concept**, otherwise known as the **dual aspect** concept or **double entry**, assumes that every transaction has two aspects. Every transaction affects two accounts in a set of financial statements in such a manner as to keep the accounting equation in balance (i.e. assets will always equal liabilities plus owners' capital). This is discussed in detail in Chapter 8, 'The Accounting Equation and its Components'.

Prudence concept

The **prudence concept**, as the name implies, assumes that the financial statements have been prepared on a prudent basis. This allows the user to have confidence that no profits are included that are not earned and, if not yet received, are reasonably certain to be received. The user can also be confident that expenses are complete and are not understated, that assets are not overstated and liabilities are complete and are not understated. At one time this concept was deemed to be fundamental to the objective of financial statements (i.e. to provide relevant information to a wide range of users for economic decision-making). However, it was abused by some companies. When companies did well they tended to overstate expenses (by creating provisions for expenditure) and understate revenue. Then, in years when performance was not strong, the companies reversed the adjustments – reducing the provisions and the expenses in the year and increasing revenue. The result was that users could not quite work out how the company really performed. For this reason prudence was downgraded and provisions and manipulations that were based on the prudence concept are no longer allowed.

These transactions did not follow the spirit of this concept. They manipulated it for earnings management purposes. **Earnings management** is where the preparers of financial statements use accounting adjustments to alter the reported performance of the reporting entity. They usually try to smooth profits, that is, to show steady profits. The concept still is applicable; however, it cannot be used as a defence for earnings management or earnings manipulation.

Substance over form concept

The **substance over form concept** was formally introduced in the UK with the implementation of *FRS 5 – Substance Over Form* (ASB, 1994). This concept assumes that when accounting for transactions the preparer should look at the economic substance of a transaction, not its legal form. This was a reactive concept/standard that was introduced to try to stop the accounting practices that had emerged of creating complicated legal transactions which, because of their legal form, allowed transactions to be omitted from the financial statements. In particular, debts/liabilities were arranged in such a manner as to enable them to be left off the statement of financial position. This would make the company look stronger, healthier and in general masked the real debt commitment that the entity had, from the users. This is no longer allowed. Regardless of the legal contract underlying a transaction, the preparer of the financial statements has to determine whether the transaction creates an asset or a liability as defined by the *Framework* (IASC, 1989). If the transaction does, then the preparer has to account for it as such.

Consistency concept

The **consistency concept** allows the user to look at a set of financial statements over a number of years for an entity and to assume that the same methods, policies and **estimation techniques** have been used from year to year. This allows the user to compare the performance of the entity over time. Financial information should allow users to determine trends in the performance of an entity over time. If accounting policies, techniques and methods used were allowed to vary from year to year, this would make comparisons meaningless. Similarly, users should be able to look at the financial statements of several entities within the same industry and make informed comparisons in the performance and financial standing of each entity, relative to each other. If consistent accounting policies and practices are not adopted, this process would be very difficult. Consistency is one of the qualities that financial information should have, as detailed in the *Framework*. As such, it is discussed later in this chapter.

Separate determination concept

The **separate determination concept** also protects the user. IAS 1 states that 'an entity shall not offset assets and liabilities or income and expenses, unless required or permitted by an IFRS'. Company law does not allow netting, except in some limited instances. For example, netting is allowed in the disclosure of hedged derivative products, which is beyond the scope of this book. Under this concept, netting transactions is only allowed when offsetting reflects the substance of the transactions, or other event. For example, trade discounts and volume rebates can be offset against sales revenue under *IAS 18 – Revenue* as this net amount reflects the fair value of the consideration to be received.

This concept allows the user to look at the assets, liabilities, income and expenditure and to know that the reported figure is the total value for each of these elements. The entity should have a separate record of every asset held. The asset category in the financial statement should not be just a big bath that includes a whole host of untraceable past transactions. This concept also does not allow a company to net one element against another. This is important as netting can mislead users. For example, if a company were able to net its debt against some assets so that less debt is shown in the statement of financial position, then the user would be unable to make a proper assessment of the entity's ability to pay back the debt as the user would assume the repayments required to clear it were less than they actually were.

5.5 Recognition

Recognition is the process of including an item in either the statement of financial position or in the statement of comprehensive income. To be included two conditions must be met: the item must meet the definition of one of the elements as set out in the *Framework* and must also meet the criteria for recognition as detailed by the *Framework* (IASC, 1989) – summarized in Figure 5.1.

In addition to meeting the definition of an element, the transaction can only be recognized if it is 'probable that any future economic benefit associated with the item will flow to, or from the entity; and the item has a cost or value that can be measured with reliability'.

5.6 Measurement

Measurement is defined in the *Framework* as: 'the process of determining the monetary amounts at which the elements of the financial statements are to be recognised and carried in the statement of financial position and the statement of comprehensive income'.

Measurement bases are the methods used to determine the monetary value. The main bases are outlined in Figure 5.2.

Many entities use a combination of these measurement bases for measuring the value of different items, deeming that some of the bases are better for some items than others. For example, inventory is commonly recorded at the lower of historic cost or net realizable value. Many oil companies use **current**

Assets

- 'resources controlled by an entity as a result of past events and from which future economic benefits are expected to flow to the entity'

Liabilities

- 'present obligations of an entity arising from past events, the settlement of which is expected to result in an outflow from the entity of resources embodying economic benefits'

Ownership interest

- 'the residual interest in the assets of the entity after deducting all its liabilities'

Income

- 'increases in economic benefits during the accounting period in the form of inflows or enhancements of assets or decreases of liabilities that result in increases in equity, other than those relating to contributions from equity participants' (owners)

Expenses

- 'decreases in economic benefits during the accounting period in the form of outflows or depletions of assets or incurrences of liabilities that result in decreases in equity, other than those relating to distributions to equity participants' (owners)

Figure 5.1 The elements as defined in the *Framework* (IASC, 1989)

Measurement bases

1 ***Historical cost**: Assets are recorded at the amount of cash or cash equivalents paid, or the fair value of the consideration given to acquire them, at the time of their acquisition. Liabilities are recorded at the amount of proceeds received in exchange for the obligation, or in some circumstances (for example, income taxes) at the amounts of cash or cash equivalents expected to be paid.*

2 ***Current cost**: Assets are carried at the amount of cash or cash equivalents that would have to be paid if the same or an equivalent asset was acquired currently. Liabilities are carried at the undiscounted amount of cash or cash equivalents that would be required to settle the obligation currently.*

3 ***Realizable (settlement) value**: Assets are carried at the amount of cash or cash equivalents that could currently be obtained by selling the asset in an orderly disposal. Liabilities are carried at their settlement values; that is, the undiscounted amounts of cash or cash equivalents expected to be paid to satisfy the liabilities.*

4 ***Present value**: Assets are carried at the present discounted value of the future net cash inflows that the item is expected to generate in the normal course of business. Liabilities are carried at the present discounted value of the future net cash outflows that are expected to be required to settle the liabilities.*

Figure 5.2 The four main measurement bases as provided in the *Framework* (IASC, 1989).

cost techniques to value their cost of goods sold. Lease liabilities, or pension liabilities are usually measured at the **present value** of the future expected economic outflows.

The historical cost concept is revisited again in more depth in Chapter 8, 'The Accounting Equation and its Components'.

5.7 Accounting policies

Accounting policies are defined in IAS 8 as: 'the specific principles, bases, conventions, rules and practices applied by an entity in preparing and presenting financial statements. An accounting policy will deal with three issues, recognising, selecting measurement bases for, and presenting assets, liabilities, income, expenses and changes to owners funds' (IASB, 2010a).

Some simple examples of accounting policies are the choice between treating expenditure on items such as tools and equipment or development expenditure, as expenses in the statement of profit or loss or as non-current assets in the statement of financial position. A real world example of three accounting policies currently being followed by Tesco plc is as follows:

Tesco Plc

Inventories

Inventories comprise goods held for resale and properties held for, or in the course of, development and are valued at the lower of cost and fair value less costs to sell using the weighted average cost basis.

Revenue (Retailing)

Revenue consists of sales through retail outlets. Revenue is recorded net of returns, relevant vouchers/offers and value added taxes, when the significant risks and rewards of ownership have been transferred to the buyer. Relevant vouchers/offers include: money-off coupons, conditional spend vouchers and offers such as buy one get one free (BOGOF) and 3 for 2. Commission income is recorded based on the terms of the contracts and is recognized when the service is provided.

Trade payables

Trade payables are non interest-bearing and are stated at amortised cost.

Source: Annual Report and Financial Statements, 2009, Accounting policies extract, www.tescoplc.com.

As is notable from Tesco plc's accounting policies, the measurement bases and recognition criteria are detailed where relevant. For example, lower of cost and fair value are two measurement bases. This is an example of the prudence concept in practice. The revenue accounting policy focuses on detailing the recognition criteria (i.e. Revenue is recorded . . . when the significant risks and rewards of ownership have been transferred to the buyer) which corresponds exactly with the criteria laid down in the *Framework*. The policy also details the measurement bases (Revenue is recorded net of returns, relevant vouchers/offers and value added taxes). Again this policy can be used as an example to show the use of the accruals concept in practice – commission income is recorded based on the terms of the contracts and is recognized when the service is provided.

Accounting policies are dealt with in more detail later. The most important part of this topic at this stage comprises the objectives and constraints in selecting accounting policies discussed below.

Estimation techniques

Estimation techniques are the methods that are used to apply accounting policies. They are not measurement bases. For example, methods of depreciation, such as straight line, reducing balance and sum of digits are different estimation techniques that can be used to allocate the cost of a non-current asset that has been recorded using the measurement basis – historical cost, to the statement of profit and loss in each accounting period. In the real world example on Tesco plc's accounting policies, inventory is valued using the weighted average cost method of valuation. This is the estimation technique used.

 ## 5.8 Selecting accounting policies

According to IAS 8,

> management should develop and apply an accounting policy that results in information that is:
>
> a relevant to the economic decision-making needs of users; and
>
> b reliable, in that the financial statements:
>   i   represent faithfully the financial position, financial performance and cash flows of the entity;
>   ii   reflect the economic substance of transactions, other events and conditions, and not merely their legal form;
>   iii are neutral, i.e. free from bias;
>   iv   are prudent; and
>   v   are complete in all material respects.
>
> (IASB, 2010a)

These attributes are the qualities that financial information included in financial statements should have. They are discussed in depth in the next chapter. In addition IAS 8 explicitly refers to the consistency concept, recommending that entities 'select and apply its accounting policies consistently for similar transactions, other events and conditions, unless a standard or an interpretation specifically requires or permits categorisation of items for which different policies may be appropriate'. In these circumstances 'an appropriate accounting policy needs to be selected and applied consistently to each category'. IAS 8 also reminds management not to forget that the recognition criteria as detailed in the *Framework* and guidance given in IASs is also influential. Selecting the most appropriate policy is important, IAS 1 highlights this by stating that 'inappropriate accounting policies are not rectified either by disclosure of the accounting policies used or by notes or explanatory material'.

5.9 Changing accounting policies

As mentioned in the previous paragraph consistency in the application of accounting policies is very important. Changes in accounting policy can impact on profit or loss and on the values presented in the statement of financial position. The result of this is that users are unable to assess trends in the performance of an entity over time as they are not comparing like with like. Therefore, IAS 8 sets out limits on what is deemed to be acceptable reasons for changing an accounting policy:

> An entity shall change an accounting policy only if the change:
>
> a is required by a Standard or an Interpretation; or
>
> b results in the financial statements providing reliable and more relevant information about the effects of transactions, other events or conditions on the entity's financial position, financial performance or cash flows.
>
> (IASB, 2010a)

When a change in accounting policy is permitted, the financial statements of the previous period (the comparatives), which are included in a set of financial statements, and the opening balances, are amended to take account of the cumulative change and a specific disclosure on the reason for the change and the impact of the change on profit or loss is disclosed. IAS 1 requires that two years' comparative figures for the statement of financial position be provided, amended to reflect application of the new accounting policy. This helps the user to compare the results of the current year with previous years. More detail on disclosures when there is a change in accounting policy is provided in the next section.

IAS 8 outlines two occasions that involve adopting a new approach, which are *not* considered to be changes in accounting policy:

a   the application of an accounting policy for transactions, other events or conditions that differ in substance from those previously occurring: and

b   the application of a new accounting policy for transactions, other events or conditions that did not occur previously or were immaterial.

(IASB, 2010a)

5.10 The disclosure of accounting policies and estimation techniques

To achieve fair presentation of accounting information, IAS 1 states that an entity has to 'select and apply accounting policies in accordance with IAS 8 and to present information, including accounting policies, in a manner that provides relevant, reliable, comparable and understandable information'. IAS 1 recommends that an entity has a section in its financial statements called the '**summary of significant accounting policies**', which should highlight 'the measurement basis (or bases) used in preparing the financial statements and the other accounting policies used that are relevant to an understanding of the financial statements'. The disclosure should also include any judgements (not judgements in respect of estimations as these are included in the note, not the accounting policy) made by management when applying accounting policies within the accounting policy note. Not all accounting policies need to be disclosed, only those that management consider to be material. An accounting policy is deemed to be material when it is considered that disclosing details of the policy will 'assist users in understanding how transactions, other events and conditions are reflected in the reported financial performance and financial position' (IAS 8).

When the disclosures in relation to any change made in accounting policies as a result of the implementation of a new standard have material consequences on the reported performance and/or reported financial position of an entity, then IAS 8 requires that additional information is provided in the year of the change to explain the nature of the change, the transitional arrangements (if any), the impact of these transitional arrangements on future performance, the change made to the figures reported in the financial statements (on a line-by-line basis), the cumulative impact on previous years' results and financial position and limits on the ability to determine the cumulative impact of the change where it has been impractical to determine the cumulative impact.

In terms of accounting estimates used as part of an accounting policy, such as the level of bad debts or inventory obsolescence, IAS 8 recommends that an entity should 'disclose the nature and amount of a change in an accounting estimate that has an effect in the current period or is expected to have an effect in future periods, except for the disclosure of the effect on future periods when it is impracticable to estimate that effect'. Changes in accounting estimate are not changes in accounting policy; therefore, changes should be included in the current period only.

Summary

The IASB's conceptual/theoretical *Framework* of accounting may be described as essentially being a set of accounting principles. These are said to comprise the objective of financial statements, the underlying assumptions of accounting (the concepts), the qualitative characteristics of financial information, the elements of financial statements, recognition in financial statements, measurement in financial statements and concepts of capital maintenance.

Recognition and measurement in financial statements include two accounting concepts that have been described as 'part of the bedrock of accounting': namely, the accruals concept and the going concern assumption, respectively. Accounting concepts can be defined as broad basic assumptions that underlie the accounting for transactions or events in the periodic financial statements of business enterprises.

The going concern assumption is described as follows: the information provided by financial statements is usually most relevant if prepared on the hypothesis that the entity is to continue in operational existence for the foreseeable future. The implication of this is that assets will normally be valued, and shown in the statement of financial position at their historical cost or, if more appropriate, fair value.

The accruals concept is described as follows: the non-cash effects of transactions and other events should be reflected, as far as is possible, in the financial statements for the accounting period in which they occur and not, for example, in the period in which any cash involved is received or paid. It is also considered to refer to the notion that revenue and costs are accrued (that is, recognized as they are earned or incurred not when money is received or paid). In most instances this refers to the accounting period in which the goods or services physically pass from the seller to the buyer. The accruals concept has traditionally been taken to include the matching principle. This refers to the assumption that in the measurement of profit, costs should be set against the revenue that they generate at the time when this arises. A classic example of the application of the matching principle is inventory. Other concepts are also regarded as underlying assumptions of accounting, though are not explicitly referred to in the *Framework*; these include the entity concept, materiality concept, time period concept, historical cost concept, fair value concept, money measurement concept, duality concept, prudence concept, substance over form concept, consistency concept and the separate determination concept.

The preparation of financial statements also involves selecting measurement bases, accounting policies and estimation techniques. Measurement bases are defined as the monetary attributes of the elements of financial statements – assets, liabilities, income, expenses and changes to owners' funds – that are reflected in financial statements. Accounting policies are defined as those principles, bases, conventions, rules and practices applied by an entity that specify how the effects of transactions and other events are to be reflected in its financial statements through recognizing, selecting measurement bases for, and presenting assets, liabilities, income, expenditure and changes to owners' funds. Estimation techniques are defined as the methods adopted by an entity to arrive at estimated monetary amounts, corresponding to the measurement bases selected, for assets, liabilities, income, expenses and changes to owners' funds.

The objectives against which an entity should judge the appropriateness of accounting policies to its particular circumstances are relevance, reliability, comparability and understandability. These are discussed in the next chapter. IAS 8 provides detailed guidance relating to the selection, review, change in and disclosure of accounting policies and estimation techniques.

There are two constraints that an entity should take into account in judging the appropriateness of accounting policies to its particular circumstances, which are the need to balance the different objectives set out above, and the need to balance the cost of providing information with the likely benefit of such information to users of the entity's financial statements.

Key terms and concepts

An asterisk after the question number indicates that there is a suggested answer on the Online Learning Centre (www.mcgraw-hill.co.uk/textbooks/thomas).

Review questions

5.1* Describe the accounting concept that would be relevant when deciding on how to account for a transaction, which involves an owner of a business taking inventory for his own use.

5.2 Describe the nature of accounting principles.

5.3* Define each of the following:

a assets

b liabilities

c ownership interest

d income

e expenses.

5.4 Explain the nature of the going concern assumption and its implications for the preparation of financial statements.

5.5 Explain the nature of the accruals concept and the matching concept. Give an example of the application of each.

5.6 Describe the nature of each of the following:

    a measurement bases

    b accounting policies

    c estimation techniques.

    Give one example of each.

5.7 According to *IAS 8 – Accounting Policies, Changes in Accounting Estimates and Errors* (IASB, 2010a) management should develop and apply an accounting policy that provides quality information that will be of benefit to users. Outline the main attributes that information resulting from the application of an accounting policy should have.

5.8 Explain the relevance of prudence to the appropriateness of accounting policies.

5.9 Outline the circumstances that must be prevalent before a change in accounting policy is permitted under *IAS 8 – Accounting Policies, Changes in Accounting Estimates and Errors* (IASB, 2010a).

5.10 Describe the information that should be disclosed in financial statements relating to an entity's accounting policies and estimation techniques.

5.11 Describe the nature of any adjustments required and the information that should be disclosed when an entity changes an accounting policy.

5.12 Describe the nature of any adjustments required and the information that should be disclosed when an entity changes an accounting estimate.

connect Exercises

BASIC

5.13

An acquaintance of yours, H. Gee, has recently set up in business for the first time as a general dealer. The majority of his sales will be on credit to trade buyers but he will sell some goods to the public for cash. He is not sure at which point of the business cycle he can regard his cash and credit sales to have taken place.

After seeking guidance on this matter from his friends, he is thoroughly confused by the conflicting advice he has received. Samples of the advice he has been given include:

The sale takes place when:

1 you have bought goods which you know you should be able to sell easily;

2 the customer places the order;

3 you deliver the goods to the customer;

4 you invoice the goods to the customer;

5 the customer pays for the goods;

6 the customer's cheque has been cleared by the bank.

He now asks you to clarify the position for him.

Required

a Write notes for Gee setting out, in as easily understood a manner as possible, the accounting conventions and principles that should generally be followed when recognizing sales revenue.

b Examine each of the statements 1–6 above and advise Gee (stating your reasons) whether the method advocated is appropriate to the particular circumstances of his business.

(ACCA)

5.14

On 20 December 20X2 your client paid £10,000 for an advertising campaign. The advertisements will be heard on local radio stations between 1 January and 31 January 20X3. Your client believes that as a result sales will increase by 60 per cent in 20X3 (over 20X2 levels) and by 40 per cent in 20X4 (over 20X2 levels). There will be no further benefits.

Required

Write a memorandum to your client explaining your views on how this item should be treated in the financial statements for the three years, 20X2 to 20X4. Your answer should include explicit reference to at least *three* relevant traditional accounting conventions, and to the requirements of *two* classes of user of published financial statements.

(ACCA)

5.15*

'If a business invests in shares, and the market value of the shares increases above cost then, until and unless the business sells them, no profit is made. If the business invests in inventory for resale, and the market value of the inventory falls below cost then the loss is recognized even though no sale has taken place'.

'If a business undertakes an intensive advertising campaign which will probably result in increased sales (and profit) in succeeding years it will nevertheless usually write off the cost of the campaign in the year in which it is incurred'.

Required

Explain the reasoning behind the application of accounting principles in situations such as these and discuss the effect on the usefulness of accounting information in relation to users' needs.

(ACCA)

5.16

Classify each of the following as either a measurement basis, an accounting policy or an estimation technique, and explain your reasons:

a Advertising expenditure that has been treated as a non-current asset rather than an expense.

b The use of the straight-line method of depreciation.

c The valuation of an asset at the lower of cost or net realizable value.

d Provision for bad debts of 5 per cent of the amount of trade receivables at the end of the accounting period.

e Land and buildings have been shown on the statement of financial position at their current replacement cost.

f Listed investments have been shown on the statement of financial position as a current asset.

g The historical cost of inventory has been ascertained by taking a weighted average of the prices paid during the accounting period.

5.17

One of your clients is a beef farmer. She informs you that the price of beef has fallen dramatically over the past few months and that she expects it to fall even further over the next three months. She therefore argues that the prudence principle should be applied to the valuation of her beef herd, stating that it should be valued at the lower of cost or net realizable value; in this case at the latter value. She further asserts that this treatment is reasonable on the grounds that it will reduce her profit for tax purposes by the loss in value of her herd.

One of your colleagues has advised you that this may be a misinterpretation of the prudence principle and could contravene the neutrality principle. Discuss.

INTERMEDIATE 5.18

Nesales plc, a large food manufacturer, has purchased the brand name of a chocolate bar from one of its competitors for £5 million. It proposes to include this on its statement of financial position as a non-current asset.

Cadberry plc, another large food and soft drinks manufacturer, has spent £5 million this year on promoting a new brand of chocolate bar. It proposes to include this on its statement of financial position as a non-current asset.

You are required to discuss whether the proposed accounting treatment of these two items is likely to achieve quality financial information, as outlined in the IASC's *Framework for the Preparation and Presentation of Financial Statement* (IASC, 1989).

INTERMEDIATE 5.19

Minisoft plc, a manufacturer of computer software, has spent £10 million in the current accounting year on staff recruitment, training and development. It proposes to include this on its statement of financial position as a non-current asset. Discuss.

References

Accounting Standards Board (1994) *Financial Reporting Standard 5 – Substance Over Form* (ASB).

Accounting Standards Steering Committee (1971) *Statement of Standard Accounting Practice 2 – Disclosure of Accounting Policies* (ASSC).

International Accounting Standards Board (2010a), *International Accounting Standard 8 – Accounting Policies, Changes in Accounting Estimates and Errors* (IASB).

International Accounting Standards Board (2010b) *International Accounting Standard 18 – Revenue* (IASB).

International Accounting Standards Board (2010c) *International Accounting Standard 2 – Inventories* (IASB).

International Accounting Standards Board (2010d) *International Accounting Standard 1 – Presentation of Financial Statements* (IASB).

International Accounting Standards Committee (1989) *Framework for the Preparation and Presentation of Financial Statement* (IASC).

Jarzemsky, M., (2010), 'S&P cuts Clearwire on liquidity, "going concern" worries', *Dow Jones Newswires*, Total Telecom, Tuesday 9 November 2010. http://www.totaltele.com/view.aspx?ID=460127

When you have read this chapter, log on to the Online Learning Centre for *Introduction to Financial Accounting* at www.mcgraw-hill.co.uk/textbooks/thomas, where you will find multiple choice quizzes, case studies, a glossary and mock exams.

The qualitative characteristics of financial information

Learning Objectives

After reading this chapter you should be able to do the following:

1. Explain the meaning of the key terms and concepts listed at the end of the chapter.

2. Describe the qualitative characteristics of financial information contained in the IASC's *Framework for the Preparation and Presentation of Financial Statements* (IASC, 1989).

3. Discuss the conflict that can arise between the qualitative characteristics of financial information.

6.1 The qualitative characteristics of financial information

According to the *Framework* 'qualitative characteristics are attributes that make the information provided in financial statements useful to users'. The *Framework* identifies four principle **qualitative characteristics**. These are summarized in Figure 6.1:

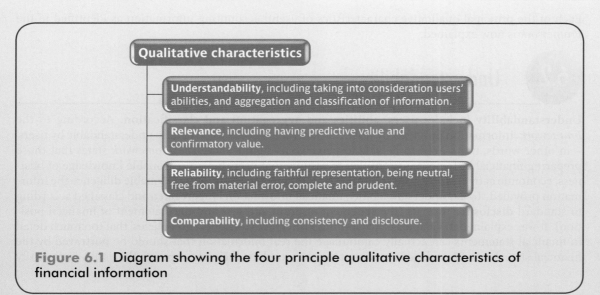

Qualitative characteristics

Understandability, including taking into consideration users' abilities, and aggregation and classification of information.

Relevance, including having predictive value and confirmatory value.

Reliability, including faithful representation, being neutral, free from material error, complete and prudent.

Comparability, including consistency and disclosure.

Figure 6.1 Diagram showing the four principle qualitative characteristics of financial information

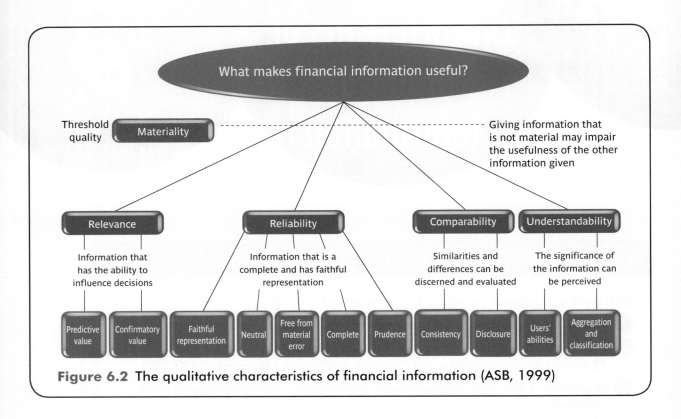

Figure 6.2 The qualitative characteristics of financial information (ASB, 1999)

The ASB developed a diagram showing the qualitative characteristics of financial information and how these characteristics are related to each other. This is shown in Figure 6.2. Though this book focuses on the international framework for accounting, this diagram is reproduced as it is an excellent *aide-memoire*. There is one difference between the ASB's interpretation of the qualitative characteristics of useful information and the IASB's interpretation. According to the ASB's (1999) *Statement of Principles for Financial Reporting*, as shown by the diagram (Figure 6.1), there is a **threshold quality** (of materiality); whereas the *Framework* includes materiality as being an attribute of **relevance**, that is, only material information is relevant.

Each of the principal qualitative characteristics of useful accounting information as identified in the *Framework* is now explained.

 ## 6.2 Understandability

Understandability includes **users' abilities** and **aggregation and classification**. According to the *Framework* 'information provided by financial statements needs to be readily understandable by users' – in other words, users need to be able to perceive its significance. The *Framework* states that those preparing financial statements are entitled to assume that users have a reasonable knowledge of business, economic activities and accounting and a willingness to study with reasonable diligence the information provided. To aid understandability, financial information is aggregated and classified according to standard **disclosure** formats (the statement of profit and loss and the statement of financial position). It was explained in Chapter 5 'Accounting Principles, Concepts and Policies' that too much detail in financial statements can actually camouflage the real information that should be portrayed by the financial statements. The adage 'one cannot see the wood for the trees' captures this issue. Each entity has numerous different ledger accounts; indeed, large companies will have thousands of these. To provide a list of all the balances would be meaningless to users. For example, the benefit of providing a list of all the credit customer balances at the year end is limited, whereas a total figure for all the trade receivables does provide information that can be of use to users. They can compare the trade receivables this year to those last year. This will give some indication as to how credit management has changed over time.

> **LEARNING ACTIVITY 6.1**
>
> Obtain the financial statements for Tesco plc, Ryanair plc, Diageo plc and Morrison Supermarkets plc. Go to the pages showing the statement of comprehensive income and statement of financial position. Note the standardized presentation adopted by all of the companies. They are following the presentation rules set out in IAS 1. This consistent format aids understandability.

6.3 Relevance

According to the *Framework* information is relevant if it has 'the ability to influence the economic decisions of users by helping them to evaluate past, present or future events or confirming, or correcting, their past evaluations'. Therefore, according to the *Framework* relevant information should have predictive value or confirmatory value. Information has **predictive value** if it helps users to evaluate or assess past, present or future events. To have predictive value, information need not be in the form of an explicit forecast. However, the ability to make predictions from financial statements is enhanced by the manner in which the information on the past is presented. For this reason, comparatives are provided and exceptional, one-off and abnormal items are identified separately in the financial statements from normal activities. In addition, transactions involving newly acquired businesses, or businesses that are being disposed of, are reanalysed and separately disclosed from transactions from continuing operations. Therefore, a diligent user can determine changes in the performance and financial position of the entity that resulted from normal activities that are expected to continue into the future.

Information has **confirmatory value** if it helps users to confirm or correct their past evaluations and assessments. Information may have both predictive and confirmatory value. Though not mentioned in the *Framework*, it is commonly considered that relevant information is more relevant when it is provided in a timely manner as it is more likely to influence decision-making (**timeliness concept**).

Materiality

As mentioned in the previous chapter, materiality is an underlying accounting concept. According to the *Framework* the relevance of information is affected by its nature and materiality.

Materiality provides guidance as to how a transaction or item of information should be classified in financial statements and/or whether it should be disclosed separately rather than being aggregated with other similar items. This depends on whether the item is of a significant amount, relative to the size of the enterprise. Whether or not a transaction or item is material or significant is generally taken to be a matter of professional judgement. In practice, this is usually regarded as dependent on how large the amount is in relation to an entity's total sales revenue, its profitability, the value of its assets or other items of the same type. However, sometimes an item is taken as not being material simply because the absolute amount is small.

A common application of materiality concerns whether an item of expenditure is to be regarded as a non-current asset or an expense. Where the amount is not material, the item would be treated as an expense even though it is expected to have a useful life of more than one accounting period and thus normally regarded as a non-current asset (e.g. relatively inexpensive tools (a spanner), sundry items of office equipment/stationery (hole punch, stapler) and sundry fixtures and fittings (picture hooks)).

Another common application of materiality relates to the separate disclosure of certain items in financial statements. There are numerous references to materiality in the Companies Act 2006, IFRSs that require separate disclosure of items such as plant hire charges and rents receivable, where the amounts are material. In most instances separate disclosure of an income or an expense is required if it is considered that the separate disclosure will be useful to users when making economic decisions in respect of the entity.

A related, but slightly different, way of explaining materiality is in terms of the degree of aggregation of data in financial statements. Users are unable to assimilate large amounts of detailed information. This necessitates considerable aggregation of data. Materiality provides guidance on what transactions are to be aggregated by virtue of its specifying which items should be disclosed separately.

Finally, another interpretation of materiality concerns whether the separate disclosure of certain items is likely to influence decisions made by the users of financial statements. One criterion that can be used to decide whether an item is material is whether or not it may be expected to influence the judgements, decisions or actions of users of financial statements. If this is expected to occur, then the item is said to be material and should be disclosed separately from other similar items. This interpretation of materiality is contained in the *Framework* that states that 'information is material if its omission or misstatement could influence the economic decisions of users taken on the basis of financial statements. Materiality depends on the size of the item or error judged in the particular circumstances of its omission or misstatement. Thus, materiality provides a **threshold** or cut-off point rather than being a primary qualitative characteristic which information must have if it is to be useful.'

Methods of determining materiality levels

The principal factors to be taken into account when determining if information is material are set out below. It will usually be a combination of these factors, rather than any one in particular, that will determine materiality.

a An item's size is judged in the context both of the financial statements as a whole and of the other information available to users that would affect their evaluation of the financial statements. If the item is likely to influence users' perceptions of the trends in the performance and financial position of the entity, then it is material. For example, if the item were to cause a profit to turn to a loss, then it is more likely to be material. If there are two or more similar items, the materiality of the items in aggregate as well as the materiality of the items individually needs to be considered.

b Consideration should also be given to the item's nature. In particular, in relation to:

   i   what gave rise to the item;

   ii   how legal, sensitive and normal the transaction is;

   iii   the potential consequences of the event or transaction underlying the item;

   iv   the identity of the parties involved;

   v   the particular headings and disclosures that are affected.

An example provided in the *Framework* is that of the reporting of a new segment. The *Framework* suggests that this may affect the assessment of the risks and opportunities facing the entity irrespective of the materiality of the results achieved by the new segment in the reporting period. This would be particularly important if the new segment were located in a risky country such as Afghanistan or Iraq (given the current unstable economic climates in both countries).

6.4 Reliability

According to the *Framework*, 'to be useful, information must also be reliable'. Information has the quality of **reliability** when:

1 it is free from material error;

2 it is free from deliberate or systematic bias (i.e. it is neutral);

3 it can be depended upon by users to represent faithfully that which it either purports to represent or could reasonably be expected to represent.

To be reliable, information should faithfully represent the underlying transaction or event, reflect the substance of the underlying transaction or event, be neutral (free from bias and material error), be prudent and **complete**. These attributes are now discussed in more detail.

Free from material error

Though not mentioned in the *Framework*, the UK equivalent, the ASB's *Statement of Principles for Financial Reporting,* states that to be reliable and to faithfully represent what it purports to, information should also be **free from material error**. Information that contains a material error can cause the financial statements to be false or misleading and thus unreliable and deficient in terms of their relevance.

Neutrality

According to the *Framework*, to be reliable, information provided in financial statements needs to be neutral – in other words, free from bias. Financial statements are not neutral if, by the selection or presentation of information, they influence the making of a decision or judgement in order to achieve a predetermined result or outcome.

Faithful representation/substance over form

According to the *Framework*, reliable information is 'information that represents faithfully the transactions and other events it either purports to represent or could reasonably be expected to represent'. It involves identifying all the rights and obligations arising from a transaction or event, and accounting for the transaction or event in a way that reflects its economic **substance**. Information must be accounted for and presented with regard for the economic **substance of a transaction** and not merely its **legal form** (although the effects of the legal characteristics of a transaction or other event are themselves a part of its substance and commercial effect). The legal form of a transaction or event is not always consistent with the economic reality of the transaction. For example, an entity may pass legal ownership of an item of property to another party, yet, when the circumstances are looked into in full, it may be that the entity continues to have access to all the future economic benefits of the item of property. In such circumstances, the reporting of a sale of the property would not represent faithfully the transaction entered into. In this instance it might be more appropriate to account for this as obtaining a loan using the property as security.

The classic example of the relevance of substance relates to certain types of lease, such as where a company has contracted to lease a motor vehicle at a given monthly rental for a period of, say, three years, at the end of which it has the option to purchase the vehicle for a nominal/small amount. The legal form of this transaction is a rental agreement. If the legal form were to dictate the accounting entries, the rental payments would appear as an expense in the statement of comprehensive income and the vehicle would not be included in the non-current assets on the statement of financial position. This is why such transactions are referred to as a form of **off-balance-sheet finance**. However, the economic substance of this transaction is the purchase of a vehicle payable by instalments, very similar to a hire purchase transaction. Thus, the substance characteristic dictates that the rental payments are not treated as an expense; instead, they are capitalized. This means that the vehicle is recorded as the purchase of a non-current asset and the total rental payments for the three years are shown as a finance lease liability.

To sum up, a statement of financial position should represent faithfully the transactions and other events that give rise to assets, liabilities and owners' equity and the statement of profit and losses should represent faithfully the transactions that give rise to income and expenditure in the period. Therefore, a transaction or other event is faithfully represented in the financial statements if the way in which it is recognized, measured and presented in those statements corresponds closely to the economic effect of that transaction or event.

Prudence

Prudence is historically one of the fundamental accounting concepts as discussed in the previous chapter. The crux of this concept is that preparers of accounting information should exercise prudent views when making judgements about uncertain items such as provisions for doubtful debts, asset lives or the number of warranty claims that might occur. It is also highlighted as one of the qualitative characteristics of accounting information. According to the *Framework* information included in financial statements should be prudent. The *Framework* defines prudence as 'the inclusion of a degree of caution in the exercise of the judgements needed in making the estimates required under conditions of uncertainty, such that assets and income are not overstated and liabilities and expenses are not understated'. In the past more emphasis was placed on ensuring that assets and incomes were not overstated. However, this is no longer the case, as prudence had been used in the past as a reason to overstate liabilities (provisions) and expenses, particularly in years when the entity performed well. The *Framework* makes particular reference to this by stating 'the exercise of prudence does not allow, for example, the creation of hidden reserves or excessive provisions, the deliberate understatement of assets or income, or the deliberate overstatement of liabilities or expenses, because the financial statements would not be neutral and, therefore, not have the quality of reliability'. An example of where prudence was used inappropriately to the extent that it undermined the reliability of the financial statements is now provided.

 REAL WORLD EXAMPLE 6.1

Nortel – accounting irregularities involving the manipulation of reserves to obtain bonuses

'In November 2002, three senior managers of Nortel – Dunn, Beatty and Gollogly – learned that Nortel was carrying over $300 million in excess reserves. Dunn, Beatty and Gollogly did not release these excess reserves into income as required under US GAAP. Instead, they concealed their existence and maintained them for later use. Further, in early January 2003, Beatty, Dunn and Gollogly directed the establishment of yet another $151 million in unnecessary reserves during the 2002 year-end closing process to avoid posting a profit and paying bonuses earlier than Dunn had predicted publicly. These reserve manipulations erased Nortel's *pro forma* profit for the fourth quarter of 2002 and caused it to report a loss instead.

In the first and second quarters of 2003 Dunn, Beatty and Gollogly directed the release of at least $490 million of excess reserves specifically to boost earnings, fabricate profits and pay bonuses. These efforts turned Nortel's first quarter 2003 loss into a reported profit under US GAAP, which allowed Dunn to claim that he had brought Nortel to profitability a quarter ahead of schedule. In the second quarter of 2003, their efforts largely erased Nortel's quarterly loss and generated a *pro forma* profit. In both quarters, Nortel posted sufficient earnings to pay tens of millions of dollars in so-called "return to profitability" bonuses, largely to a select group of senior managers.'

Source: USSEC Press Release (http://www.sec.gov/news/press/2007/2007-39.htm, November 2010).

Prudence is deeply embedded in accounting and possibly even in the personality of many accountants. It is one of the main reasons why accountants are often described as conservative, prudent, cautious, pessimistic, and so on. Correctly applied, prudence refers to not overstating the profit in the statement of profit and loss and the financial position in the statement of financial position. This is achieved by making cautious estimates of items such as the amount of potential bad debts and the depreciation of non-current assets; that is, where the estimate is a range of amounts, prudence dictates that the amount entered in the financial statements will be the highest figure of a probable loss or liability, and the lowest figure of a gain or asset.

Completeness

According to the *Framework*, to be reliable the information in financial statements must be complete within the bounds of materiality and cost. An omission can cause the financial statements to be false or misleading and thus unreliable and deficient in terms of its relevance.

6.5 Comparability

According to the *Framework*, users must be able to compare the financial statements of an entity: (**1**) over time; and (**2**) relative to other entities, in order to properly assess the entity's relative financial position, performance and changes in financial position. Therefore, financial statements should include the current year statements, the statement of comprehensive income and statement of financial position, presented beside the prior year statements (called **comparatives**). In the following example, Tesco plc provide their previous years income and expense figures alongside the current years items to aid comparison.

REAL WORLD EXAMPLE 6.2

Tesco plc

Group income statement

Year ended 27 February 2010	Points	52 weeks 2010 £m	53 weeks 2009 Restated* £m
Continuing operations			
Revenue (sales excluding VAT)	2	56,910	53,898
Cost of sales		(52,303)	(49,713)
Gross profit		4,607	4,185
Administrative expenses		(1,527)	(1,252)
Profit arising on property-related items	3	377	236
Operating profit		3,457	3,169
Share of post-tax profits of joint ventures and associates	13	33	110
Finance income	5	265	116
Finance costs	5	(579)	(478)
Profit before tax	3	3,176	2,917
Taxation	6	(840)	(779)
Profit for the year		2,336	2,138

Source: Tesco plc (2010) p. 70, Annual Report 2010, http://at2010.tescoplc.com (accessed May 2011).

To be able to view similarly prepared financial statements over time allows users to make judgements about trends in performance and in changes in financial position and to use this information to predict into the future. This is required for economic decision-making, such as deciding whether to buy, sell or retain a holding of equity shares in the entity.

As well as providing a copy of the previous period's statement of profit and loss and statement of financial position, the user needs to be able to ascertain if the figures have been prepared using the same methods of recognition and measurement; therefore, the material accounting policies should be disclosed and consistently applied.

Consistency

According to the *Framework*, consistency in the application of accounting policies is vital for producing comparable information. Any changes to the accounting policies and the impact of these changes should be disclosed (discussed in detail in Chapter 5, 'Accounting Principles, Concepts and Policies').

LEARNING ACTIVITY 6.2

Go to the website of the following companies – Tesco plc, Ryanair plc, Diageo plc and Morrison Supermarkets plc. You already have copies of their most recent financial statements. For each company access the financial statements for the preceding two years. Go to the pages showing the accounting policies. Select two items (for example, turnover or inventory) and read the accounting policy being adopted. Note the consistency in application of accounting treatments.

Disclosure

According to the *Framework*, 'compliance with IASs, including disclosure of the accounting policies adopted by the entity, helps to achieve **comparability**'. To assist in the making of comparisons despite inconsistencies, users need to be able to identify any differences between:

1 the accounting policies adopted by an entity to account for some transactions relative to others;

2 the accounting policies adopted from period to period by an entity;

3 the accounting policies adopted by different entities.

Users also need to be able to assess the impact of changes in the accounting policies of the entity. Therefore, disclosures are required detailing the reason for the change, the impact and cumulative impact on two years' statements of financial position and the opening balances.

Some academics regard disclosure as a fundamental qualitative characteristic of financial statements. In crude terms, it is argued that if companies use different accounting policies and/or these change over time (i.e. there is a lack of consistency) and/or if companies do not comply with accounting standards, this is not critical; provided there is full disclosure of how the figures are derived, users can make the necessary adjustments in order to achieve comparability. This view is in conflict with the understandability principle as users would need to have a sophisticated knowledge of accounting to perform some of the adjustments that would be required to make the financial statements comparable.

6.6 Constraints on the qualitative characteristics

The *Framework* explicitly refers to three underlying constraints on relevant and reliable information (timeliness, balance between benefit and cost, and balance between qualitative characteristics).

Timeliness

Conflict between relevance and reliability can arise over the timeliness of information. If there is undue delay in the reporting of information making it out of date, then this will affect its relevance. On the other hand, reporting on transactions and other events before all the uncertainties involved are resolved may affect the information's reliability. This information cannot be omitted as omitting information from the financial statements because of reliability concerns may affect the completeness, and therefore reliability of the information provided. If reporting is delayed until the underlying information is reliable, it may be of little use to users who have economic decisions to make in the interim. In achieving a balance between timeliness and relevance and reliability, the entity should take all steps possible to produce reliable information in a timely manner. The overriding consideration affecting the timing of reporting should be 'how best to satisfy the information needs of users for economic decision-making'.

Balance between benefit and cost

The general rule laid down in the *Framework* is that 'the benefits derived from information should exceed the cost of providing that information'. The evaluation of the benefits and costs is regarded as judgemental and the costs may not fall on the users who benefit from that particular piece of information. It is difficult to undertake a practical cost–benefit study on the provision of a particular type of information; nevertheless, the *Framework* states that the preparers and indeed standard setters should be aware of this general constraint.

Balance between qualitative characteristics

In some instances, a conflict may arise between the characteristics of relevance, reliability, comparability and understandability. In such circumstances, a trade-off needs to be found that still enables the objective of financial statements to be met. The relative importance of some of the characteristics in different instances is a matter for professional judgement. Some examples include the following:

1 *Relevance and reliability.* Sometimes information that is the most relevant is not the most reliable and vice versa. Choosing the amount at which to measure an asset or liability will sometimes involve such a conflict. In such circumstances, it will usually be appropriate to use the information that is the most relevant of whichever information is reliable. For example, when a realistic estimate of the impact of a transaction or an event (such as the potential damages to be paid on a legal claim) cannot be made, that fact and details of the transaction or event should be disclosed.

2 *Neutrality and prudence.* There can also be tension between two aspects of reliability – neutrality and prudence – because, while neutrality involves freedom from bias, prudence is a potentially biased concept that seeks to ensure that, under conditions of uncertainty, gains and assets are not overstated and losses and liabilities are not understated. This tension exists only where there is uncertainty, because it is only then that prudence needs to be exercised. When there is uncertainty, the competing demands of **neutrality** and prudence are reconciled by finding a balance that ensures that the deliberate and systematic understatement of income and assets and overstatement of expenses and liabilities do not occur.

3 *Understandability.* It may not always be possible to present a piece of relevant, reliable and comparable information in a way that can be understood by all users. However, information that is relevant and reliable should not be excluded from the financial statements simply because it is too difficult for some users to understand.

4 *Consistency and relevance and reliability.* Consistency should not be confused with mere uniformity. It is not an end in itself and it should not be allowed to become an impediment to the introduction of improved accounting practices and accounting standards. It is not appropriate to keep accounting for an item in the same manner as before, when a new treatment emerges that provides more relevant and reliable information.

True and fair view/fair presentation

The *Framework* does not specifically deal with the concept of **fair presentation**; however, the *Framework* does state that it considers that the application of the principal qualitative characteristics of information and the application of appropriate accounting standards will result in financial statements that portray a **true and fair view** of the entities' financial performance and financial position.

Summary

Qualitative characteristics are the attributes that make the information provided in financial statements useful to users. According to the *Framework* the qualitative characteristics of financial information comprise four principal characteristics that make financial information useful. These comprise understandability, relevance, reliability and comparability. Understandability includes users' abilities, and aggregation and classification. Relevance includes materiality, predictive value and confirmatory value. Reliability includes faithful representation, substance over form, neutrality, prudence, completeness and being free from material error. Comparability includes consistency and disclosure. There are several constraints on the qualitative characteristics that relate to timeliness, cost versus benefit, relevance versus reliability, neutrality versus prudence and understandability versus consistency.

Overall summary (conceptual framework)

The major issues considered in this chapter and in the previous chapters can be briefly summarized as follows:

1 The accounting entity is used to determine the boundaries of the organizational unit to be reported upon. The accounting entity is created as an artificial construct, and as such cannot own itself. The external owners' interests are identified as owners' capital (equity).

2 The life of an accounting entity is divided into accounting periods usually of a year, each seen as a separate entity. Financial statements are produced to show the results relating to a particular period. Division into periods is reflected by the emphasis given to periodic reporting.

3 Profit can be defined in terms of changes in capital represented in the statement of financial position at the start and end of the period.

Another approach is to calculate profit using a transaction-based, or a net production approach. Here, revenues are recognized in the period when they are realized and the matching principle identifies the costs to be traced to the appropriate period. Critical in this process is the classification of expenditure as either capital or revenue. Costs that are capitalized are carried forward from period to period as statement of financial position items. Assets in the statement of financial position are carried forward in anticipation of providing benefits to future periods and this may then lead to matching in those periods.

4 Recognition and measurement in financial statements involves the application of two accounting concepts – the accruals concept and the going concern assumption – as well as the selection of measurement bases, estimation techniques and accounting policies.

5 Any system of accounting for profit has to define either explicitly or implicitly three basic dimensions. These are the unit of measurement, the valuation model and the concept of capital maintenance.

6 Selecting and applying appropriate accounting policies are necessary for the proper application of the conceptual framework of accounting. To be appropriate, accounting policies should be relevant, reliable and comparable from period to period.

Key terms and concepts

aggregation and classification	84	qualitative characteristics	83
comparability	90	relevance	84
comparatives	89	reliability	87
complete	87	substance	87
confirmatory value	85	substance of a transaction	87
disclosure	84	threshold	86
fair presentation	92	threshold quality	84
free from material error	87	timeliness concept	85
legal form	87	true and fair view	92
neutrality	91	understandability	84
off-balance-sheet finance	87	users' abilities	84
predictive value	85		

An asterisk after the question number indicates that there is a suggested answer on the Online Learning Centre (www.mcgraw-hill.co.uk/textbooks/thomas).

Review questions

connect

6.1   a   Briefly explain the nature of a qualitative characteristic of financial information.

　　　b   Prepare a diagram showing the qualitative characteristics of financial information and the relationship between each of them as identified in the ASB *Statement of Principles for Financial Reporting* (1999).

6.2   Define and explain the qualitative characteristic of relevance, including its predictive value and confirmatory value.

6.3   Define and explain the qualitative characteristic of reliability, including the attributes of faithful representation, substance over form, neutrality, free from material error, completeness and prudence.

6.4   Define and explain the qualitative characteristics of comparability and understandability.

6.5   Define and explain materiality.

6.6   Describe the constraints on the qualitative characteristics of financial information.

6.7   According to the *Framework* there is a potential 'conflict between the characteristics of relevance and reliability. There can also be tension between two aspects of reliability – neutrality and prudence'. Explain the nature of these conflicts/tensions and how they can be reconciled.

6.8* Define the following terms: Off-Balance sheet finance; Substance over form; Threshold quality.

References

Accounting Standards Board (1999) *Statement of Principles for Financial Reporting* (ASB).

International Accounting Standards Committee (1989) *Framework for the Preparation and Presentation of Financial Statements* (IASC).

Securities and Exchange Commission, (2007), 'SEC Charges Four Former Senior Executives of Nortel Networks Corporation in Wide-Ranging Financial Fraud Scheme', *U.S. Securities and Exchange Commission Press Release*, 12 March 2007, http://www.sec.gov/news/press/2007/2007-39.htm.

Auditing, corporate governance and ethics

Learning Objectives

After reading this chapter you should be able to the following:

1. Explain the meaning of the key terms and concepts listed at the end of this chapter.

2. Describe briefly the history of auditing and the change in the nature of auditing.

3. Explain the objective and principles of auditing as identified in International Standard on Auditing (UK and Ireland) 200 – *Overall Objectives of the Independent Auditor and the Conduct of an Audit in Accordance with International Standards on Auditing* (APB, 2009a).

4. Describe the auditing assertions.

5. Describe the audit process.

6. Outline the content of a typical 'clean' audit report.

7. Explain the term *audit risk*.

8. Explain the expectations gap.

9. Define corporate governance and outline the reasons for the growth in its importance over the past few decades.

10. Describe some of the ethical conflicts facing management in the UK.

11. Explain auditor ethics and the importance of an auditor being ethical.

7.1   Auditing

History of auditing

The word 'auditing' is derived from the Latin word 'audire', which means to listen. Auditing received its name from the earliest form of auditing that involved an individual publicly reading out an entity's transactions for validation by interested parties. Prior to AD 1500 evidence of accounting and auditing were more likely to be found in the keeping of records of government. Auditing usually involved the setting up of two parallel bookkeeping functions to record transactions. The aim of this was to detect fraud, minimize the risk of error and to ensure the honesty of the custodians of public funds. In the period 1500 to 1980 accounting systems with controls were gradually introduced and this reduced the need to have two separate functions. The main changes to the role of auditing came about because of the Industrial Revolution. The Industrial Revolution was the impetus for the creation of public limited companies. In general, these companies are owned by the public but are run by separate management teams. This separation of ownership from management increased the importance placed on having published financial statements available to the owning public that have been appropriately audited by independent, suitably qualified individuals. At this stage the approach to auditing also changed with auditors testing a sample of transactions, as opposed to testing all the transactions, which was the approach taken in the earliest form of auditing.

In the early 1900s the remit of an audit in the USA changed even more so, to that of providing an *opinion* on the fair presentation of financial statements, from trying to detect fraud and error (though the latter remained the primary purpose of an audit in the UK until the early 1980s).

From the 1980s the practical approach to auditing also changed, from detailed testing of individual transactions and checking of balances (substantive testing) to placing reliance on internal controls and checking the operation of these controls (compliance testing or systems-based testing). At this stage the use of statistical sampling and computer-based audit techniques (CATs) were utilized as audit tools. With constant pressure on cost, in more recent decades many audit firms have adopted a 'risk-based approach', which identifies the most risky areas and focuses audit attention in these areas.

In the past decade the UK Auditing Practice Board (APB) has taken steps to harmonize UK auditing practices with the rest of the world and have actively adopted International Standards on Auditing (ISAs), which focus on the auditor providing an opinion on whether the financial statements give a true and fair view. The approaches to auditing in the UK are now detailed in ISAs (UK and Ireland).

True and fair view

The financial statements of limited companies are required by the Companies Act 2006 to give a true and fair view of the company's financial position at the reporting period date and of its profit or loss for the reporting period. Financial statements provide a true and fair view if they contain sufficient information (in quantity and quality) to satisfy the reasonable expectations of the users of financial statements. Auditors provide an informed professional independent opinion on this, and that is all. This opinion is based on the company's compliance with accounting practices, principles and norms. These are captured in accounting standards. Therefore, any financial statements that comply with accounting standards can be regarded as giving a true and fair view. Likewise, deviations from accounting standards will result in financial statements that do not provide a true and fair view.

Why is a statutory external audit required?

All the companies that are listed on stock exchanges are publicly owned. Indeed, many limited companies have owners who are not involved in the management of the company. Companies produce financial statements that portray the performance and financial position of an entity. However, these are open to manipulation by management, so owners require an independent audit to assess if management are discharging their stewardship function appropriately (i.e. looking after the owner's assets). A statutory audit is required for all listed companies and larger companies – those with a turnover of over £6.5 million and net assets total of £3.26 million (Companies Act 2006 as amended by the Companies Act 2006 (Amendment) (Accounts and Reports) Regulations, 2008).

Objective, scope and principles of auditing

The auditor performs an audit on behalf of the members or equity shareholders of an entity. An **audit** is an independent check on reported financial statements that are produced from an entity's accounting system. Therefore, the audit also has to determine whether the accounting system is appropriate or not. In 1973 the American Accounting Association (AAA), in a statement of basic auditing concepts, defined auditing as 'a systematic process of objectively obtaining and evaluating evidence regarding assertions about economic actions and events, to ascertain the degree of correspondence between those assertions and established criteria and communicating the results to interested users'. **Auditing assertions** are indications that information is complete, accurate, properly prepared, applied in the correct period (cut-off), classified correctly, exists, is correctly valued, treated and disclosed in an understandable manner, in accordance with accounting standards and applicable law. ISA (UK and Ireland) 200 – *Overall Objectives of the Independent Auditor and the Conduct of an Audit in Accordance with International Standards on Auditing* (APB, 2009a) states that: 'The purpose of an audit is to enhance the degree of confidence of intended users in the financial statements. This is achieved by the expression of an opinion by the auditor on whether the financial statements are prepared, in all material respects, in accordance with an applicable financial reporting framework.' As is stated in the IASC's *Framework for the Preparation and Presentation of Financial Statements* (IASC, 1989), it is assumed that financial statements that are properly prepared in accordance with the *Framework* and International Financial Reporting Standards will show a true and fair view of the financial performance for the period being reported on and state of a company's affairs at the period end.

When preparing their opinion on whether the financial statements have been prepared, in all material respects, in accordance with the ISA (UK and Ireland), the auditor should:

1 Conduct the audit in accordance with ISAs (UK and Ireland) (APB, 2009a).

2 Comply with relevant ethical principles (the APB's *Ethical Standard for Auditors* [APB, 2008a] in the UK).

3 Obtain reasonable assurance that the financial statements, as a whole, are free from material misstatement whether due to fraud or error (APB, 2009a).

4 'Exercise professional judgment and maintain professional scepticism throughout the planning and performance of the audit and among other things: identify and assess risks of material misstatement, whether due to fraud or error, based on an understanding of the entity and its environment, including the entity's internal control; and obtain sufficient appropriate audit evidence about whether material misstatements exist, through designing and implementing appropriate responses to the assessed risks' (APB, 2009a).

An audit is not only restricted to providing an opinion on financial statements; some companies have to get grant applications verified, hospitals have to have their systems for processing patients checked, and so on.

Audit risk

Audit risk is the risk that the auditor will express an inappropriate audit opinion: for example, by giving a positive opinion when the financial statements include material misstatements. As auditors do not test every single transaction, there will be a certain amount of audit risk. What the auditor has to evaluate is the acceptable level of audit risk. This is influenced by the auditor's knowledge of the entity, the financial statements, audit assertions, internal controls and materiality level. Audit risk is prevalent at every stage of an audit. The auditor's view of audit risk is not stationary. It may change as the audit progresses through the main audit stages (outlined in the next paragraph). The higher the audit risk, the more testing required and vice versa.

The audit process

There are five main stages to every audit: client acceptance or retention; audit planning stage; control testing stage; substantive testing stage; and opinion formulation stage. A brief description of these processes is now provided.

Client acceptance or retention

At this point the auditor has to decide whether to accept or reject a potential client, or to retain an existing client. The auditor has to be mindful of ethical considerations (discussed later). After an initial analysis the auditor, on deciding to accept the client, will issue a **letter of engagement** that sets out the terms of engagement as under ISA (UK and Ireland) 210 – *Agreeing the terms of audit engagements* (APB, 2009b). The engagement letter includes a summary of responsibilities of the auditor and management towards the audit, defines the objective of the audit, the scope of the work to be carried out and how the audit will be reported on.

Audit planning stage

Recommended practice on audit planning is given in ISA (UK and Ireland) 300 – *Planning an Audit of Financial Statements* (APB, 2009c). The planning stage is regarded as the most important part of the audit process. It determines the audit approach to take. The plan will be influenced by the auditors' knowledge of the business, risk assessment of the entity's controls and records, the risk of fraud and an analytical review of the financial statements and other provided information at the planning stage. Effective audit planning should result in a more focused, prompt, efficient, cost-effective and higher quality audit for the client. It should result in the focus on risky areas; that is, **auditing by exception**. The audit plan is detailed in the **audit planning memorandum**. The auditor will have to complete an **audit plan** for every type of item being audited, such as inventories, trade receivables, income, and so on.

Control testing stage

The planning stage will detail the extent of testing required on information systems controls (**compliance testing**). At this stage the systems will be thoroughly recorded and controls noted. ISA (UK and Ireland) 330 – *The Auditor's Responses to Assessed Risks* (APB, 2009d) requires that the auditor should carry out tests of controls when the risk assessment relies on those controls (both when the operating effectiveness of the controls are relied on and when it is believed that the controls reduce the potential for material misstatement) and when substantive tests alone do not provide sufficient appropriate audit evidence at assertion level.

Substantive testing stage

Substantive testing involves testing in detail individual transactions that have been selected using statistical techniques to ensure that they have been properly authorized, processed and accounted for correctly. They focus on ensuring that audit assertions can be made (see Figure 7.1).

Opinion formulation stage

This involves determining whether, based on the risk assessment, based on the results of tests completed and based on management assertions; the auditor believes that the financial statements show a true and fair view of the entity's financial performance and financial position. Before the opinion is provided, the audit work will be reviewed by an audit manager, then by an audit partner and management will have been asked to formally provide assertions about the completeness, validity and accuracy of the information provided in the financial statements. This is important as an audit is provided on a test basis. In general, an assertion about **completeness** is management stating that all items that should be included are included. An assertion about **validity** is management stating that the financial statements

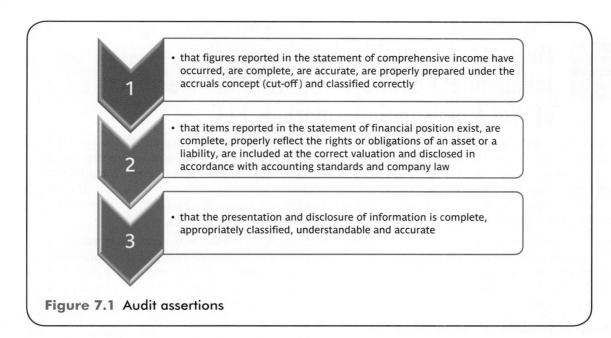

1
• that figures reported in the statement of comprehensive income have occurred, are complete, are accurate, are properly prepared under the accruals concept (cut-off) and classified correctly

2
• that items reported in the statement of financial position exist, are complete, properly reflect the rights or obligations of an asset or a liability, are included at the correct valuation and disclosed in accordance with accounting standards and company law

3
• that the presentation and disclosure of information is complete, appropriately classified, understandable and accurate

Figure 7.1 Audit assertions

do not include any information that should not be included and an assertion about **accuracy** is management confirming that items that are included are included correctly.

The audit report

An audit opinion is provided in an **audit report**. The audit report is included with a company's financial statements in a company's annual return. Indeed, the financial statements cannot be issued without it. The form and content of an audit report is provided in ISA (UK and Ireland) 700 – *The Auditors Report on Financial Statements* (APB, 2009e). The audit report has standard form and content – it is argued that this helps to promote users' understandability and highlights variations/problems when they occur. An audit report with a positive opinion on a company's financial statements is called an **unmodified**, **unqualified** or a **clean audit report**. The main contents of a clean audit report include:

1 title (independent audit report);

2 addressee (to the shareholders of company name);

3 introductory paragraph – provides the date of the financial statements, the period covered and the location of the audited financial statements within the annual report;

4 paragraph dealing with the responsibilities of management (governors) and auditors;

5 the **audit scope** paragraph – describes the nature of an audit, the standards adopted and a description of the work performed (sample basis). This information can be provided in the body of the audit report or the paragraph can be cross-referenced to the FRC's website (see real world example);

6 opinion paragraph – contains reference to the financial reporting framework used to prepare the financial statements (i.e. IFRSs) and the opinion on the financial statements. If a clean audit report is being issued, then this paragraph must state that the auditor believes that that financial statements give a true and fair view;

7 date of the report;

8 auditor's address;

9 auditor's signature.

An example of an unmodified audit report, as included in the annual report of Morrison Supermarkets PLC in 2010, is as follows:

REAL WORLD EXAMPLE 7.1

Morrison's unmodified audit report. Independent auditors' report to the members of Wm Morrison Supermarkets PLC

We have audited the financial statements of Wm Morrison Supermarkets PLC for the 52 weeks ended 31 January 2010 set out. The financial reporting framework that has been applied in the preparation of the Group financial statements is applicable law and International Financial Reporting Standards (IFRS) as adopted by the EU. The financial reporting framework that has been applied in the preparation of the Parent Company financial statements is applicable law and UK Accounting Standards (UK Generally Accepted Accounting Practice).

This report is made solely to the Company's members, as a body, in accordance with chapter 3 of part 16 of the Companies Act 2006. Our audit work has been undertaken so that we might state to the Company's members those matters we are required to state to them in an auditors' report and for no other purpose. To the fullest extent permitted by law, we do not accept or assume responsibility to anyone other than the Company and the Company's members, as a body, for our audit work, for this report, or for the opinions we have formed.

Respective responsibilities of directors and auditors

As explained more fully in the Directors' Responsibilities Statement, the Directors are responsible for the preparation of the financial statements and for being satisfied that they give a true and fair view. Our responsibility is to audit the financial statements in accordance with applicable law and International Standards on Auditing (UK and Ireland). Those standards require us to comply with the Auditing Practices Board's (APB) Ethical Standards for Auditors.

Scope of the audit of the financial statements

A description of the scope of an audit of financial statements is provided on the APB's website at www.frc.org.uk/apb/scope/UKP

Opinion on financial statements

In our opinion:

- The financial statements give a true and fair view of the state of the Group's and of the Parent Company's affairs as at 31 January 2010 and of the Group's profit for the year then ended;

- The Group financial statements have been properly prepared in accordance with IFRS as adopted by the EU;

- The Parent Company financial statements have been properly prepared in accordance with UK Generally Accepted Accounting Practice; and

- The financial statements have been prepared in accordance with the requirements of the Companies Act 2006; and, as regards the Group financial statements, Article 4 of the IAS Regulation.

Opinion on other matters prescribed by the Companies Act 2006

In our opinion:

- The part of the Directors' remuneration report to be audited has been properly prepared in accordance with the Companies Act 2006; and

- The information given in the Directors' report for the financial year for which the financial statements are prepared is consistent with the financial statements.

◀ **Matters on which we are required to report by exception**

We have nothing to report in respect of the following:

Under the Companies Act 2006 we are required to report to you if, in our opinion:

- Adequate accounting records have not been kept by the Parent Company, or returns adequate for our audit have not been received from branches not visited by us; or

- The Parent Company financial statements and the part of the Directors' remuneration report to be audited are not in agreement with the accounting records and returns; or

- Certain disclosures of Directors' remuneration specified by law are not made; or

- We have not received all the information and explanations we require for our audit.

Under the Listing Rules we are required to review:

- The Directors' statement, in relation to going concern; and

- The part of the corporate governance statement relating to the Company's compliance with the nine provisions of the June 2008 Combined Code specified for our review.

Chris Hearld (Senior Statutory Auditor) for and
on behalf of KPMG Audit Plc

Chartered Accountants

1 The Embankment
Neville Street
Leeds
LS1 4DW

Source: Wm Morrison Supermarkets plc (2010), Annual Report 2010, http://www.morrisons.co.uk/Global/Images/Corporate/Annual%20Report/Morrisons_AnRep10.pdf (accessed May 2011).

There are two types of **modified audit report** (also called **adverse opinion**, or **qualified audit report**): those where (1) matters arise that do not affect the auditor's opinion; and (2) matters arise that do affect the auditor's opinion.

There is only one type of modified audit report that can also be regarded as clean (i.e. not affecting the audit opinion) and that is when the auditor wants to emphasize some matter to the reader of the financial statements. In this instance the auditor includes an 'emphasis of matter paragraph' usually after the opinion paragraph so the reader is in no doubt that the financial statements are 'clean'. This paragraph refers to the issue briefly and usually cross-references the audit report to a note in the financial statements where more detail is provided.

Expectations gap

The **expectations gap** is the gap between the auditors' role and opinion and the public's perception of the auditors' role. Many members of the public believe that auditors are looking for fraud when they undertake an audit, that auditors say the financial statements are accurate (many believe the financial statements to be 100 per cent accurate if audited), that auditors certify financial statements, that a 'clean' audit report is stating the financial statements are accurate, that the auditors are responsible for the financial statements and that auditors should give warnings about the future of the entity when they suspect it is going to fail.

However, in practice auditors' argue that managers prepare the financial statements, therefore are responsible for them. Auditors are quick to argue that an audit report is only an opinion that at best provides reasonable assurance that the financial statements are free from **material misstatement**. The important word here is 'material' which has been defined in the *Framework* as follows:

> information is material if its omission or misstatement could influence the economic decisions of users taken on the basis of financial statements. Materiality depends on the size of the item or error judged in the particular circumstances of its omission or misstatement.

The audit report does not say the financial statements are correct. Auditors only check a sample of transactions, not every transaction; therefore, they cannot guarantee that fraud will be detected, though they plan their tests so as to uncover any fraud that may cause material misstatement in the financial statements. An audit does not guarantee that a company will succeed in the future.

As is noted in this section and highlighted in previous paragraphs, management are responsible for the financial statements that they prepare, or that are prepared on their behalf. Management are also fully responsible for the running of the company. The next section 'Corporate governance' outlines in brief the responsibility that management have for the proper conduct of their management of affairs on behalf of a company's equity shareholders.

7.2 Corporate governance

Corporate governance has been defined by O'Donovan (2003) as:

> an internal system encompassing policies, processes and people, which serves the needs of shareholders and other stakeholders, by directing and controlling management activities with good business savvy, objectivity and integrity. Sound corporate governance is reliant on external marketplace commitment and legislation, plus a healthy board culture which safeguards policies and processes. [The] perceived quality of a company's corporate governance can influence its share price as well as the cost of raising capital. Quality is determined by the financial markets, legislation and other external market forces plus the international organizational environment; how policies and processes are implemented and how people are led. External forces are, to a large extent, outside the circle of control of any board. The internal environment is quite a different matter, and offers companies the opportunity to differentiate from competitors through their board culture.

Agency theory (the equity holder and director conflict)

Corporate governance is important because of the conflict that arises between owners and management. Management are employed by a company's owners (its equity shareholders) to manage the company on their behalf; therefore, they are agents for the equity shareholders (who are the principals). However, management have difficulty making decisions which, though in shareholders' best interests, may damage their own interests. For example, equity shareholder value is enhanced by taking decisions that maximize the long-run earnings of a company. However, these decisions may result in the rejection of other investments that provide higher short-term returns. Directors' bonus packages may be tied into short-term profitability. This conflict is discussed in the relevant literature under '**agency theory**'.

A commonly used method to encourage congruence between the aims of directors and equity shareholders is to align the financial rewards available to the board of directors with those of the equity shareholders. The financial rewards might include setting bonuses and rewards for meeting long-term performance targets. The performance targets might include achieving a certain growth in earnings per share over a three-to-five-year period, achieving a minimum return on equity over a three-to-five-year period or achieving a minimum return on assets over a three-to-five-year period.

Another method is to award share options to directors as part of their salary package. **Share options** allow the holder to purchase shares at a set price on a future date – usually in three-to-ten years' time.

If management has performed well and taken decisions that maximize equity holder value, then share price on the exercise date will exceed the target exercise price when the options were first issued. Management can then purchase the shares at the lower exercise price and can either sell them immediately, realizing a financial gain, or retain the shares and benefit from future capital value increases. A problem with share option schemes is that they do not indicate whether an increased share price is due to genuine value creation caused by management decision-making or whether it is due to positive changes in the economy. Equally so, they mask good performance when there has been a general downturn.

Every company incurs a considerable amount of expenditure in trying to reduce/monitor the agency problem. These costs are termed '**agency costs**' and include audit fees, costs associated with the remuneration committee and costs of aligning salaries with equity holder objectives. The costs of policing corporate governance are agency costs. Ensuring that a company has strong corporate governance is the responsibility of company directors, not the equity shareholders – though they suffer the cost of it. Good corporate governance practices help to reduce agency conflicts.

The rise in the importance of corporate governance

A number of high-profile company scandals and collapses in Britain (Robert Maxwell, Mint and Boxed, Levitt, Polly Peck, Barings Bank, Royal Bank of Scotland (RBS)), in Ireland (Powerscreen, Allied Irish Banks (AIB)) and in the US (WorldCom, Enron, Lehman Bros) have increased the attention afforded by regulators to the corporate governance of companies. The scandals reduced public confidence in financial reporting, the audit process and the worth of regulatory watchdogs (e.g. the London Stock Exchange, auditors and the government). To build confidence, the London Stock Exchange set up a committee in 1991, to investigate the responsibilities of executive and non-executive directors, to determine whether an audit committee is required, to clarify the principal responsibilities of auditors and to consider the responsibilities the board of directors has to other stakeholders. This committee issued a report in 1992: the first '*code of best practices*' for the governance of a company. This report is known as the *Cadbury Report* (Cadbury, 1992) after Sir Adrian Cadbury, the lead investigator. The *Cadbury Report* defined corporate governance as 'the system by which companies are directed and controlled'.

The *Cadbury Report* detailed the composition of a typical board of directors in a company with good corporate governance practices and outlined the board's recommended responsibilities. It suggested that the board of directors meet regularly, take steps to ensure that they have control of the company at all times and ensure that the board has sufficient segregation of duties so that no one director has ultimate control – as in the case of Robert Maxwell. The report recommended conditions to ensure the independence of non-executive directors (they should not be awarded share options as remuneration, have no dealings with the company and be able to obtain independent advice at the company's expense). The report recommended that executive directors (and non-executive directors) hold office for only three years, though they could be reappointed by equity holders. The report also recommended the establishment of two committees: a remuneration committee to deal with remuneration packages, and an audit committee to control the internal audit within a company. Companies listed on the London Stock Exchange had to disclose the extent of compliance with the *Cadbury Report*. Non-public limited companies were not required to disclose the extent of their compliance; however, it was recommended by professional accounting bodies that it be included.

The *Greenbury Report* (Greenbury, 1995) strengthened some of the suggestions made in the *Cadbury Report* by recommending that all members of the remuneration committee be non-executive directors, and a remuneration report setting out all the remuneration details for each director (executive and non-executive) should be made available in the annual report of a company. A further report, the *Hampel Report* (Hampel, 1998), recommended that the role of the chairman and chief executive be segregated and that directors receive training on corporate governance. This report recommends that directors narrow their responsibilities to their primary duty – the enhancement of equity holders' value. These reports were integrated to form the *Combined Code* in 1999 (FRC, 1999).

Corporate governance and risk

Risk is inherent in virtually every strategic decision taken by a company. Most boards direct specific attention to identifying the risks that a company faces and creating strategies to manage those risks. This may involve, for example, hedging transactions. The level of risk faced by a company is influenced by the nature of a business, its capital structure, foreign risk and exposures that might arise when there are changes in microeconomic conditions. For example, a manufacturing company that imports most of its supplies from one country, hires a labour force in another country (an emerging economy) and exports its products to yet another country, will face far higher risks when compared to a similar company that purchases and sells its products in one country (that has a stable economy). Were the future expected income from both companies the same, the latter company would be valued at a premium by the market, due to its lower exposure to the various risks.

Corporate governance, risk and strategic management

Risk identification, evaluation and management have become more important over the past two decades. After the establishment of the *Combined Code* of practice for corporate governance (FRC, 1999), a working party was established to provide best practice guidance on how to comply with the *Combined Code*. This group was led by Nigel Turnbull and their recommendations were published in 1999, in a report called *Internal Control – Guidance for Directors on the Combined Code* (referred to as the ***Turnbull Report***) (LSE, 1999). The report suggests that a risk-based approach should be taken when establishing internal controls and when reviewing their effectiveness. The ethos of the report is not that a company should undertake a box-ticking exercise to ensure compliance, but should embrace the principles of risk-based management as a means of increasing company value. This approach is captured by Sir Brian Jenkins, the Chairman of the Corporate Governance Group of the ICEAW, in the preface to the guidance report: *Implementing Turnbull: A Board Room Briefing,* 1999 (LSE, 1999) when he stated:

> for directors the task ahead is to implement control over the wider aspects of business risk in such a way as to add value rather than merely go through a compliance exercise. There is also a need to get the buy-in of people at all levels of the organisation and to focus on risk management and internal controls in such a way as to improve the business.

The *Combined Code* (1999) was updated in 2003 to include the *Turnbull Report* (LSE, 1999) and the ***Smith Report*** (FRC, 2005a) and updated again in 2005 (FRC, 2005b) by a working party led by Douglas Flint. The findings of this recent review were that there is widespread support for the recommendations of Turnbull, with most companies adopting a risk-based approach to their strategic management. Indeed, the US Securities and Exchange Commission (SEC) have identified the Turnbull guidance as a suitable framework for reporting on a company's internal controls for financial reporting. The US legal requirements for disclosures in relation to internal controls are set out in section 404(a) of the Sarbanes–Oxley Act (2002) and the SEC's rules. In contrast to the US's 'rule based' approach, in the UK the approach is 'principle-based', with Flint recommending that this approach remain.

Diageo a large drinks company which owns brand names such as Guinness, Baileys, Smirnoff and Johnny Walker has dedicated pages of information on risk in their 2009 Annual Report. In the business description they identify 15 potential risks which may impact on their future performance and financial position, including an assessment of competition, risks associated with pursuing their strategy, the consequences of systems failure and their exposure to regulatory changes. In the business review, which forms part of the audited part of the financial statements, Diageo provides specific information on the identification and management of currency risk, interest rate risk, liquidity risk, credit risk, commodity price risk and insurance. As recommended by Turnbull, the general risk management policy and procedures are outlined at the start of the business review (see real world example 7.2).

Diageo Annual Report 2009

This section on risk management forms part of the audited financial statements.

The group's funding, liquidity and exposure to interest rate and foreign exchange rate risks are managed by the group's treasury department. The treasury department uses a combination of derivative and conventional financial instruments to manage these underlying risks.

Treasury operations are conducted within a framework of board-approved policies and guidelines, which are recommended and subsequently monitored by the finance committee. This committee is described in the corporate governance report. These policies and guidelines include benchmark exposure and/or hedge cover levels for key areas of treasury risk. The benchmarks, hedge cover and overall appropriateness of Diageo's risk management policies are reviewed by the board following, for example, significant business, strategic or accounting changes. The framework provides for limited defined levels of flexibility in execution to allow for the optimal application of the board-approved strategies. Transactions giving rise to exposures away from the defined benchmark levels arising on the application of this flexibility are separately monitored on a daily basis using value at risk analysis. These derivative financial instruments are carried at fair value and gains or losses are taken to the income statement as they arise. At 30 June 2009 gains and losses on these transactions were not material.

The finance committee receives monthly reports on the activities of the treasury department, including any exposures away from the defined benchmarks.'

Source: Extract from http://209.207.237.32/Lists/Resources/Attachments/214/Diageo_AR09.pdf.

LEARNING ACTIVITY 7.1

Visit the Ryanair plc website and view a copy of their annual report. The qualitative reports at the front of the annual report will contain information on the company's corporate governance. Make a list (in bullet point form) of the corporate governance procedures/structures in place for the company.

Corporate governance – response to the financial crises

In light of the recent failures which occurred because of the financial crises a further review of the corporate governance of companies was undertaken which not only reviewed industry practices but also looked at the Walker Report (2009) *A review of corporate governance in UK banks and other financial industry entities*. The final report, *The UK Corporate Governance Code* (FRC, 2010) replaces the *Combined Code* and was published in May 2010. It is applicable for all listed entities with accounting periods beginning on or after 29 June 2010. The main changes are that – it is now recommended that all directors of FTSE 350 companies be subject to re-election yearly and that directors disclose how they have complied with the code and explain reasons for non-compliance if relevant. In addition the report suggests that: 'More attention be afforded to the spirit of the code as well as its letter. Secondly that the impact of shareholders in monitoring the code could and should be enhanced by better interaction between the boards of listed companies and their shareholders.' To this end the FRC has published the *The UK Stewardship Code* in July 2010 to encourage engagement between investors and investees (Hamill et al., 2010). There is also a requirement that a greater emphasis be placed on risk identification and management.

7.3 Ethics

This text will deal with two streams of ethics: **management ethics** and **auditor ethics**.

Management ethics

As a country the UK has some of the highest ethical business standards in the world. Indeed, in many instances, having regard to ethical practices might restrict the profitability of a company. For example, in a global economy, there is much to be gained by companies that have products that can be made in countries that have no employment laws. For example, profits and company value will increase if a company is able to access cheap labour, or even child labour, for next to nothing (so long as the company does not advertise its policy in this area, as this may cause an adverse reaction in the stock market, as equity holders are likely to react irrationally). In these circumstances, companies justify their actions by arguing that some income to a family is better than none, or by highlighting the fact that, though the salaries paid are low, they are higher than those paid by indigenous companies. Many companies also use some of their profits for social purposes in the communities that they are located in, by for example, building schools, building churches, building hospitals or getting running water. These are deemed to be signs of these companies acting ethically.

The use of bribery or corruption may be seen as part and parcel of normal trade within certain countries, but not in the UK. In a global economy, when there is so much pressure to perform, directors may consider using unethical approaches to secure a contract. However, unethical behaviour cannot be defended on the grounds of it being normal practice in a country, nor can it be defended by the argument 'if I did not do it, someone else would' or 'we would lose the business to a competitor, who does it'.

Acting unethically does not have to be as dramatic as the examples provided in the previous two paragraphs. A company should also act ethically in relation to company stakeholders because doing so is in a company's long-term interest. By treating customers and suppliers correctly, future sales and supplies will be secured. Paying loan creditors the interest and capital repayments they are due on time will ensure that this source of finance can be used again in the future. Avoiding the practice of gearing the company unnecessarily just to make returns to equity holders builds confidence in the management of the company, from creditors' perspectives. Showing concern for employee welfare (and acting on it) will ensure loyalty and increased effort from employees. By taking steps to reduce pollution, the health of employees will not deteriorate, which will reduce staff absenteeism. In addition, the company's image will be improved and future sales may result. Equity shareholders should also be treated fairly; they should be kept well informed about a company's performance, future developments and strategies. Equity shareholders should not be surprised by the dividend that they are paid. If equity holders feel that they are being treated fairly, then the market will value the company higher and the equity holder body is more likely to support director decisions in the future.

Auditor ethics

To be an auditor, an accounting practice must be registered under law with a Recognized Supervisory Body (RSB) and be eligible for appointment as an auditor under the rules of that Body. Under law auditors should be independent, carry out their work with integrity, be technically up to date, be competent and maintain competence and be able to defend their audit work. Most Accounting Institutes are RSBs who apply the ethical standards as set out by the APB's *Ethical Standards for Auditors* (APB, 2008a). These standards are concerned with ensuring the integrity, objectivity and independence of auditors.

An auditor's **integrity** is supported when they are fit and proper persons. This means being sufficiently competent as verified by being appropriately qualified with an up-to-date record of continuing professional development and when they are visibly independent from the audit client.

The *Ethical Standards for Auditors* (APB, 2008a) outlines guidance on circumstances that may be considered to breach an auditor's **independence**. These are now outlined briefly.

● *Financial interests*: an auditor should not have any direct financial interest in an audit client, or any indirect material financial interest that may question their independence. Read *APB Ethical Standard 2 (Revised) – Financial, Business, Employment and Personal Relationships* (2008b) for more detail on indirect financial interests that are not considered to breach independence.

● *Business relationships*: an auditor can only have business relationships with a client if the transactions are in the normal course of business, are at arm's length and are immaterial to both parties.

● *Employment relationships*: an audit member of staff can only work on a part-time basis for a client if the individual will not hold a management role, will not make management decisions and does not direct the audit client into a particular position or accounting treatment. That member of audit staff can never be part of the audit team on that client in the future. If a senior member of the audit team joins employment with the client, then the audit firm should not accept reappointment of the client for two years.

● *Family and other personal relationships*: these should be reported immediately and a decision taken as to whether this reduces independence. It may be necessary to select an audit team that has no links with the client.

● *Length of service*: the audit firm should rotate the engagement partner on audit engagements, as close relationships between the client and individual auditor may foster over time, reducing perceived independence. In plcs, rotation should be at least every five years.

● *Fees, remuneration, litigation, gifts and hospitality*: the fee from a non-listed audit client should not exceed 15 per cent of the audit firm's total fee income and the fee from a listed audit client should not exceed 10 per cent. In these instances the auditors should resign as they are not deemed to be independent. Auditors, or their family, should not accept gifts from audit clients unless insignificant. The provision of non-audit services such as tax advice, and so on is severely restricted by the *Ethical Standards for Auditors*.

REAL WORLD EXAMPLE 7.3

The fall of Arthur Andersen

The fee Enron paid Arthur Andersen was $25 million for audit work the year before it collapsed. In addition to this, Enron paid Arthur Andersen a further $27 million in consultancy fees. The level of fees paid was commonly cited afterwards as an indicator that Arthur Andersen was not independent. The outcome of Arthur Andersen's behaviour in the Enron debacle meant that the public lost confidence in Arthur Andersen as auditors and this huge international audit firm collapsed.

Arthur Andersen's problems started at least a decade earlier, when the audit firm focused on securing lucrative consultancy work with many of their audit firms, which downgraded the less profitable audit work and brought Andersen's independence into question. The seeds of their demise is captured by the following quote from the *Chicago Tribune* (1 September 2002):

> Through the 1990s, Andersen aggressively sold lucrative consulting services to those who relied on them for audits in what turned out to be a profitable strategy. Andersen's top partners tripled their earnings in the '90s, a feat that put them on a par with their Andersen consulting siblings, who had split into their own division in 1989. But the new strategy also planted the seeds of the firm's downfall. Suddenly, partners who faced accounting dilemmas with clients had a lot more at stake when deciding whether to reject questionable practices uncovered in audits. The fallout from those decisions has unfolded in the headlines about shredded documents, restated earnings, shady loans and financial sleight of hand at Enron, WorldCom Inc., and Waste Management Inc., all Andersen clients beset by accounting scandals.

Source: http://www.chicagotribune.com/news/chi-0209010315sep01,0,538751.story?page=1 (accessed November 2010).

Not only has the auditor to be seen to be acting ethically but the auditor also has to prove (using documentation) that they have conducted the audit ethically (independently, objectively and with integrity) and have acted with confidentiality. Part of being ethical is the need to conduct the audit and to treat the financial information obtained about the client with **confidentiality**. This involves not telling anyone outside the audit firm, who the audit firm clients are and taking steps to ensure that client audit records are secure.

Summary

Auditing is defined as an evaluation of an organization, system, process or product. It is performed by a competent, objective and unbiased person or persons who are known as auditors. The purpose of an audit of an entity's financial statements is to verify that the financial statements were completed according to approved and accepted standards, statutes, regulations or practices. An audit also usually evaluates the entity's controls to determine if it is likely that the entity will continue to conform with these standards, and so on. Auditing involves collecting evidence to support auditing assertions. Auditing assertions are indications that information is complete, accurate, properly prepared, applied in the correct period (cut-off), classified correctly, exists, is correctly valued, treated and disclosed in an understandable manner in accordance with accounting standards and applicable law.

According to ISA (UK and Ireland) 200 (APB, 2009a), the objective of an audit of financial statements is 'to enable auditors to give an opinion on whether the financial statements are prepared, in all material respects, in accordance with an applicable financial reporting framework'. An audit typically has five main stages: client acceptance or retention (this involves assessing independence and audit risk and preparing a terms of engagement); audit planning stage (reviewing audit risk, knowledge of the entity, systems, controls, financial statement information, risk of fraud and other material errors and preparing audit planning schedules detailing the work to be performed); control testing stage (this involves undertaking compliance tests of controls to determine if they work properly); substantive testing (sample testing of individual transactions or balances); and opinion formulation stage (taking into account all the evidence obtained during the audit and management assertions). The result of the audit is reported in an independent audit report.

The expectations gap is the difference that exists between the public's perception of what an auditor does and what audited financial statements mean, relative to the auditor's perception of what these mean. The audit report is one step that has been taken by auditors to try to reduce the expectations gap as this report explicitly refers to auditor and management responsibility and details out the restricted nature of audit tests that had been performed. The audit report also provides an opinion only, not a certification.

Corporate governance has become more important over the past two decades when it became clear that a number of large, seemingly successful companies failed unexpectedly (Polly Peck, Worldcom, Enron). Though auditing firms suffered some of the blame, and agency problems were apparent, the corporate world also considered that the systems of ensuring good corporate governance required strengthening. Corporate governance is the system by which companies are directed and controlled. A number of changes to corporate governance have occurred over the past two decades and at present the approach is a risk-based approach based on the *Turnbull Report* of 1999 (LSE, 1999). Underlying all the high-profile corporate collapses was a breakdown in ethics, both in terms of management's governance of the respective entities and in terms of auditors exercising due diligence in their auditing work and adhering to independence principles.

Key terms and concepts

An asterisk after the question number indicates that there is a suggested answer on the Online Learning Centre (www.mcgraw-hill.co.uk/textbooks/thomas).

Review questions

7.1 What is the objective of an audit?

7.2 Explain the term 'audit risk'.

7.3 Describe the five main stages of an audit briefly.

7.4 Explain the audit expectations gap to a new trainee auditor.

7.5 Explain the term 'corporate governance'.

7.6 Why does corporate governance influence company value?

7.7 Outline six characteristics of good corporate governance, detailing how each can influence company value.

7.8 Explain the role of a non-executive director to a company and outline possible benefits of such an appointment to the company.

Exercises

INTERMEDIATE

7.9*

Zonton, a UK public limited company, has been experiencing a downturn in their fortunes. The company's performance in the past seems to have moved in line with the performance of the UK economy. The directors of the company are concerned about the current economic climate in the UK and are looking for suggestions to reduce their risk to the UK economy and to boost profits. Cara Van informed the board at a brain-storming session that a way to alleviate the impact of the expected downturn in the economy would be to open a factory in Tomarat (a fictional emerging economy). She suggests that with a couple of small bribes – to the right people – a suitable factory can be obtained and that the local indigenous population (from the age of 5 upwards) would be delighted to work for a mere fraction of the wages being paid in this country. This would reduce costs and increase profit margins, which would more than outweigh the expected reduction in sales units.

Required

Your father sits on the board of this company and he asks you as an accounting student for advice on the appropriateness of this proposal.

References

Auditing Practice Board (2008a) *Ethical Standards for Auditors* (APB).

Auditing Practice Board (2008b) *Ethical Standards 2 (Revised) – Financial, Business, Employment and Personal Relationships* (APB).

Auditing Practice Board (2009a) International Standard on Auditing (UK and Ireland) 200 – *Overall Objectives of the Independent Auditor and the Conduct of an Audit in Accordance with International Standards on Auditing* (APB).

Auditing Practice Board (2009b) International Standard on Auditing (UK and Ireland) 210 – *Agreeing the Terms of Audit Engagements* (APB).

Auditing Practice Board (2009c) International Standard on Auditing (UK and Ireland) 300 – *Planning an Audit of Financial Statements* (APB).

Auditing Practice Board (2009d) International Standard on Auditing (UK and Ireland) 330 – *The Auditor's Responses to Assessed Risks* (APB).

Auditing Practice Board (2009e) International Standard on Auditing (UK and Ireland) 700 – *The Auditors Report on Financial Statements* (APB).

Cadbury, Sir A. (1992) *Report of the Committee on the Financial Aspects of Corporate Governance (Cadbury Committee Report)*, Gee Publishing.

Department of Trade and Industry (2003) *Review of the Role and Effectiveness of Non-executive Directors*, DETI, The Stationery Office.

Financial Reporting Council (1999) *Committee on Corporate Governance: The Combined Code* (FRC), Gee Publishing.

Financial Reporting Council (2005a) *Guidance on Audit Committees (the Smith Report)*, FRC.

Financial Reporting Council (2005b) *Committee on Corporate Governance: The Combined Code (Revised)* (FRC), Gee Publishing.

Financial Reporting Council (2010) *The UK Stewardship Code* (FRC).

McRoberts, F. (2002) 'The Fall of Andersen', *Chicago Tribune*, 1 September 2002,

http://www.chicagotribune.com/news/chi-0209010315sep01,0,538751.story?page=1 (accessed November 2010).

Greenbury, Sir R. (1995) *Directors' Remuneration: Report of a Study Group Chaired by Sir Richard Greenbury (Greenbury Committee Report)*, Gee Publishing.

Hamill, P., Ward, A.M. and Wylie, J. (2010) 'Corporate Governance Policy: New Dawn in Ireland and the UK', *Accountancy Ireland*, December, 42(6), 56–59.

Hampel, Sir R. (1998) *Committee on Corporate Governance: Final Report (Hampel Committee Report)*, Gee Publishing.

International Accounting Standards Committee (1989) *Framework for the Preparation and Presentation of Financial Statements* (IASC).

London Stock Exchange (1999) *Internal Control: Guidance for Directors on the Combined Code* (Turnbull Report), LSE.

O'Donovan, G. (2003) 'A board culture of corporate governance', *Corporate Governance International Journal*, 6(3).

Note: All International Standards on Auditing were issued by the International Auditing and Assurance Standards Board and adopted by the Auditing Practice Board (UK and Ireland) in 2008.

When you have read this chapter, log on to the Online Learning Centre for *Introduction to Financial Accounting* at www.mcgraw-hill.co.uk/textbooks/thomas, where you will find multiple choice quizzes, case studies, a glossary and mock exams.

Double-entry bookkeeping (recording transactions and the books of account)

Part contents

The accounting equation and its components

Learning Objectives

After reading this chapter you should be able to do the following:

1. Explain the meaning of the key terms and concepts listed at the end of the chapter.

2. Explain the relevance of the accounting entity concept in financial accounting.

3. Describe the accounting equation, including how it is reflected in the statement of financial position.

4. Explain the nature of assets, liabilities and capital.

5. Prepare simple statements of financial position and compute the profit from these.

6. Explain the nature of profit and capital maintenance, including their interrelationship.

7. Explain the relevance of the accounting period concept in financial accounting.

8. Distinguish between revenue expenditure and capital expenditure, including their effects on the statement of financial position.

9. Discuss the relevance and limitations of the historical cost concept in financial accounting.

8.1 The accounting entity

The entity concept was introduced in Chapter 5 'Accounting Principles, Concepts and Policies' briefly and is now revisited in more detail. A **reporting entity** is defined in the *Statement of Principles for Financial Reporting* (ASB, 1999) as 'an entity for which there are users who rely on the financial statements as their major source of financial information about the entity'. Accounting for a reporting entity focuses on setting up a means of recording all accounting information in relation to that entity, as distinct from information that does not relate to the entity. The reporting entity may be, for example, a particular company, club or business partnership. We are used to hearing that a financial report relates to a specific organization, but now the organization is called an 'entity'. The use of the word 'entity' emphasizes the properties of being separate and discrete. Greater precision is demanded by accounting in deciding what is, and is not, part of the entity. Boundaries are created to separate out the **accounting entity**. Realizing that these boundaries are necessary, even though they may be artificial, is the key to the entity concept. It becomes possible to accept that a business may be separate from its sole proprietor.

EXAMPLE 8.1

A trainee accountant is starting to prepare the financial statements for a sole proprietor who has a retail shop as his business. The following items appear in the list of cheques written by the businessman. The trainee accountant has been asked to state whether or not the items of expenditure below should be included in the financial statements of the retail shop.

1 Cheque paying the shop's rates.

2 Cheque paying the sole proprietor's house rates.

3 Cheque paying for a new cash till.

4 Cheque paying for a new washing machine for the proprietor's wife's birthday.

5 Cheque for stationery (90 per cent is for the shop, 10 per cent is for his kids).

6 Cheque purchasing overalls for himself for cleaning the shop.

7 Cheque paying for a new outfit, which he can wear to work.

Required

Complete a table detailing whether the items should enter the accounting system of the reporting entity or not.

	Yes	No
1. Shop rates	√	
2. House rates		√
3. Till	√	
4. Washing machine		√
5. Stationery	√ (90%)	√ (10%)
6. Overalls	√	
7. New outfit		√

By defining the boundaries of the organizational unit, the accounting entity concept determines the transactions that will be recorded in the financial statements. For example, when a local plumber buys tools to carry out his work, that action can be regarded as a purchase by the business, while when the same man buys a cinema ticket this would be seen as a personal purchase. In the same way, the salary paid to a company director is treated not as some internal transfer within a company but as a payment to an officer as a separate individual. In general, accounting sets up 'the business', 'the company' and 'the club' as entities that are artificial constructs, separate from their owners and employees as individuals.

In some instances the boundary between business and private expenditure is difficult to determine, particularly where an expense is incurred for both business and private purposes. It is normal to estimate the portion that is business and to allocate that portion to the business entity. This adjustment provides the potential for manipulating an entities reported performance. Where private expenses are treated as business expenditure, a lower profit results, which can have detrimental consequences for users, particularly the tax man and a divorcee (assuming they are making a claim for a share of the value of business). A key part of forensic accounting centres on examining the appropriateness of certain expenditures that are processed as business expenditure, particularly in small sole trader-type entities. This is evident from the following promotional excerpt from the Dolman Bateman Company website (accessed July 2010).

Dolman Bateman – forensic accounting

REAL WORLD EXAMPLE 8.1

'We are often asked to undertake financial investigations in family law proceedings utilizing our forensic accounting skills and experience in a wide range of areas including: Appropriateness of Expenditure. Often in family law proceeding there are arguments as to whether a level of certain expenditure is appropriate for the business or are essentially private in nature. Travel, marketing and entertaining expenses often fall into this category. We can provide a detailed report as to whether the costs are appropriate for the business and the industry as a whole.'

Source: www.dolmanbateman.com.au/ (July 2010)

As will be seen in later chapters, one accounting entity can be a part of another accounting entity. For example, a branch of a retail chain store (such as Marks & Spencer plc) may be treated as a separate accounting entity for internal reporting purposes. However, the branch will also be a part of the business as a whole, which would be treated as another accounting entity for external reporting purposes. Similarly, one company may be a subsidiary of (i.e. owned by) another (holding) company. In this case the subsidiary will be one accounting entity, and its final financial statements must also be consolidated with those of the holding (owner) company into group final financial statements, representing another accounting entity.

In sum, an accounting entity can be a legal entity, part of a legal entity, a combination of several legal entities, part of another accounting entity, or a combination of accounting entities.

The accounting/reporting entity concept is also sometimes referred to as the 'business entity' or simply the 'entity concept'.

8.2 The statement of financial position as an accounting equation

An accounting entity may also be viewed as a set of assets and liabilities. Perhaps the most familiar form this takes is the **statement of financial position**. As an equation this would appear as follows:

Proprietor's **ownership interest** in the business = Net resources of the business

The ownership interest or claims are called owner's **equity** or owner's **capital**. The net resources are analysed into assets and liabilities.

In relatively simple terms, an **asset** can be defined as a tangible or intangible resource that is owned or controlled by an accounting entity, and which is expected to generate future economic benefits. Examples of assets include land and buildings, motor vehicles, plant and machinery, tools, office furniture, fixtures and fittings, office equipment, goods for resale (known as inventory), amounts owed to the accounting entity by its customers (i.e. trade receivables), money in a bank cheque account, and cash in hand.

The use of the word 'net' to describe the resources possessed by the business recognizes that there are some amounts set against or to be deducted from the assets. There are two major types of such deduction: liabilities and provisions. In relatively simple terms, a **liability** can be defined as a legal obligation to transfer assets or provide services to another entity that arises from some past transaction or event. Liabilities represent claims by outsiders (compared to the owners, whose claims are equity or capital) and may include such items as loans made to the business and amounts owed for goods supplied (i.e. trade payables). As the name suggests, **provisions** are amounts provided to allow for liabilities that are anticipated but not yet quantified precisely, or for reductions in asset values. However, although there are some important matters to consider in relation to provisions, it will be entirely appropriate at this stage to think of provisions as simply a special category of liability, and to postpone detailed attention until later. Chapter 16 'Depreciation and Non-current Assets' and Chapter 17 'Bad Debts and Provisions for Bad Debts' are both particularly concerned with provisions.

Given that liabilities can be regarded as being negative in relation to assets, the **accounting equation** can now be stated in the form:

$$\text{Assets} - \text{Liabilities} = \text{Owners' capital}$$

Or alternatively:

$$\text{Assets} = \text{Owners' capital} + \text{Liabilities}$$

This equation is based on what is sometimes referred to as the 'duality' or 'dual aspect concept'. This concept purports that every transaction has two aspects: one represented by an asset and the other a liability, or two changes in either the assets or the liabilities. For example, the purchase of an asset on credit will increase the assets and the liabilities by the same amount. The purchase of a vehicle for cash will increase the value of the vehicle asset but decrease the amount of the cash asset. These two aspects of each transaction are also reflected in the duality of double-entry bookkeeping, as explained in Chapter 5 'Accounting Principles, Concepts and Policies'.

The accounting equation is a fundamental equation and is a valuable basis from which to begin understanding the whole process of accounting. It sets out the financial position of the owners at any point in time, although in practice a complete and detailed statement of financial position may only be produced periodically, such as monthly or yearly. Most accounting activity is concerned with individual transactions; nevertheless, the statement of financial position equation remains a focus towards which the activity is directed. For now we will examine accounting simply in terms of statements of financial position. Let us trace how this approach reflects the setting-up of a plumbing business (see Example 8.2).

EXAMPLE 8.2

Adam Bridgewater decided to start his business by opening a bank account for business transactions and depositing £2,000 into it on 1 July 20X2. This transaction involves a flow of value from Adam Bridgewater to his business and will affect two parts of the accounting equation: owner's capital and assets. Owner's capital will increase by £2,000 as the business in now indebted to Adam for the £2,000 that he provided to the business and cash at the business bank will have increased by £2,000. There are several ways of presenting this. In practice companies usually adopt a vertical approach, placing capital vertically below net assets in the form:

Bridgewater (Plumber) Statement of financial position as at 1 July 20X2	
	£
Assets	
Cash at bank	2,000
Equity	
Owner's capital	2,000

However, a side-by-side or horizontal presentation may illustrate more clearly the accounting equation format. A question arises: on which side should assets be included? There is considerable variation and it is a matter of convention. The most useful convention at this stage is to put assets on the left-hand side, as shown below. However, there is a long, well-established tradition in accounting of putting assets on the right-hand side, and liabilities and capital on the left-hand side. The lack of consistency may seem unnecessarily confusing, but students need to be prepared to encounter either convention.

Bridgewater (Plumber)			
Statement of financial position as at 1 July 20X2			
Assets	**£**	**Equity**	**£**
Cash at bank	2,000	Owner's capital	2,000

EXAMPLE 8.3

Following on from Example 8.2, if on 2 July 20X2 Adam draws out £800 cash and spends it all on purchasing tools, then cash at bank will be decreased by £800 and a new asset, tools, is introduced on the statement of financial position with a balance of £800.

Bridgewater (Plumber)			
Statement of financial position as at 2 July 20X2			
Assets	**£**	**Equity**	**£**
Tools	800	Owner's capital	2,000
Cash at bank	1,200		
	2,000		2,000

In this case one asset is increased by exactly the same amount as another is decreased (£800), so that the accounting equation, assets equals capital plus liabilities, continues to balance.

EXAMPLE 8.4

Following on from Example 8.3, on 3 July Adam buys a range of plumbing accessories for £300 from the local storekeeper, but arranges to pay in the next few days. The arrangement is described as 'on credit'. The credit transaction with the storekeeper becomes a trade payable since he is now owed a debt of £300. There is no problem in maintaining the balance of the equation when including the effects of this transaction in the business statement of financial position, since the new liability of £300 owed to the store exactly complements the £300 increase in assets represented by the inventory of accessories:

Bridgewater (Plumber)			
Statement of financial position as at 3 July 20X2			
Assets	**£**	**Equity and liabilities**	**£**
Tools	800	Owner's capital	2,000
Inventory	300	**Liability**	
Cash at bank	1,200	Trade payable	300
	2,300		2,300

As mentioned, the horizontal approach adopted to portray the outcome of the last three transactions reflects the accounting equation (assets = liabilities + equity). However, in practice this is rarely utilized; therefore, the vertical approach is used throughout the remainder of this book.

The manner in which the two components of the change in the statement of financial position are complementary so that the equality of the two sides remains intact is worthy of note since it underlies the principles of double-entry bookkeeping developed in Chapter 10 'Double Entry and the General Ledger'. Another event in the life of this business offers further illustration.

EXAMPLE 8.5

Following on from Example 8.4, if on the next day, Bridgewater pays the store the £300 to clear the outstanding debt, this will decrease both the cash (from £1,200 to £900) and the trade payable (from £300 to £0) – an asset and a liability – by the same amount, giving:

Bridgewater (Plumber)	
Statement of financial position as at 4 July 20X2	
	£
Assets	
Tools	800
Inventory	300
Cash at bank	900
	2,000
Equity and liabilities	£
Owner's capital	2,000
	2,000

LEARNING ACTIVITY 8.1

Prepare a statement of financial position listing your assets, liabilities and resultant capital, or those of your family. Use the original purchase price of the assets.

8.3 The accounting equation and profit reporting

Drawing up a statement of financial position after each of the enormous number of transactions carried out every day or week in large corporations would be very time consuming and inefficient, and a business cannot be expected to do so. However, it is normal for even small businesses to produce a statement of financial position once a year. Annual reporting has taken on a significance of its own for many reasons. A year's activity encompasses all the seasons, and many statistics of economic and business performance are produced on this basis. Examples include annual inflation rates, annual interest rates, annual salaries, annual tax allowances and, not surprisingly, annual profits.

EXAMPLE 8.6

Bridgewater may be interested to see how his business has progressed in its first year. For him to be able to draw up a statement of financial position he needs to know the amounts to include for assets and liabilities at that date. Suppose he has the following amounts relating to his financial position at the end of the day's trading on 30 June 20X3:

Assets of business: Building £5,000; tools £1,100; inventory of accessories £500; trade receivables £350; cash at bank £200.

Liabilities: Bank loan £3,500; trade payables £450.

Many changes and transactions are likely to have taken place during the year to reach this position, but these have not been tracked from statement of financial position to statement of financial position. The absence of a figure for capital will not prevent the statement of financial position being drawn up, given that it is the only missing figure in the accounting equation. So the statement of financial position becomes:

Bridgewater (Plumber)	
Statement of financial position as at 30 July 20X3	
	£
Assets	
Building	5,000
Tools	1,100
Inventory	500
Trade receivables	350
Cash	200
	7,150
EQUITY AND LIABILITIES	£
Equity	
Owners' capital (to balance)	3,200
Non-current liabilities	
Bank loan	3,500
Trade payables	450
Total non-current liabilities	3,950
Total equity and liabilities	7,150

Capital is the balancing item, and by this means all statements of financial position would inevitably balance. This inevitability is consistent with recognizing that the business is an entity that is an artificial creation. It cannot have any net ownership of its own. However, the capital figure at the end of the year is different to that at the beginning, and analysis and explanation of that change is needed to provide a more complete picture. In this case we see that the increase in the year by the difference between opening and closing capital is £3,200 − £2,000 = £1,200. How could this have arisen?

One possible explanation is that Bridgewater paid some more money into the business. In this case let us decide that we know that he paid in a further £1,000. Of course, the opposite of paying would be taking money out, so let us say that he also took out £750 for personal use. The net effect will produce an increase of £1,000 − £750 = £250. The rest of the increase in capital (i.e. £1,200 − £250 = £950) would be profit – that is, increased capital generated by the business itself.

A simple example will illustrate how profit is able to generate increases in capital. A trader is able to start a small venture with £30 in cash, equivalent to £30 capital. She uses the money to buy a bath. When she sells the bath for £40 she now has £40 cash and has increased capital by £10 (profit).

To provide a more useful definition of profit as increased capital, accounting has made use of explanations given by the economist Hicks (1946) who defines **profit** as the maximum amount that could be withdrawn in a period from the business while leaving the capital intact. In the case of Bridgewater's business, the capital that is kept intact is the £2,000 figure at the start of the period. Measuring profit in relation to capital that is kept intact is commonly described as a **capital maintenance** approach, which forms one of the major pillars of profit measurement theory. It is implicit in all profit measurement approaches that will be drawn upon in this book.

8.4 The accounting period and profit reporting

The **accounting period concept** (sometimes called **periodicity concept**) is a means of dividing up the life of an accounting entity into discrete periods for the purpose of reporting performance for a period of time (in a statement of profit and loss) and showing its financial position at a point in time (in a statement of financial position). The period of time is usually one year and is often referred to as the **accounting year**, **financial year** or **reporting period**. Each accounting year of an entity's life normally ends on the anniversary of its formation, and therefore does not necessarily coincide with the calendar year. It could thus end on any day of the calendar year, but for convenience the accounting year is nearly always taken to be the end of a calendar month, and sometimes adjusted to the end of the calendar year or to the end of a particular month (e.g. for tax reasons). Some companies report on their financial position half-yearly or even quarterly. Thus, the accounting period can be less than one year.

The accounting period concept is also sometimes referred to as the **time interval** or **time period** concept (discussed briefly in Chapter 5 'Accounting Principles, Concepts and Policies').

The previous section commenced by recognizing the significance of annual reporting in assessing business performance. Profit is defined in terms of potential consumption 'in a period'. Although the use of a period of a year is no more than a convention – albeit a very useful one – the idea of periodic reporting is fundamental to present-day accounting. In relation to maintenance of capital, the second year of the plumbing business's performance will be measured in profit terms in relation to that year's opening capital: that is, the £3,200 closing capital from year one. The approach adopted in accounting is an extension of the use of the entity concept. For accounting purposes, each complete period, usually of a year, is treated as a separate entity. It inherits as its opening statement of financial position the closing statement of financial position of the previous period.

One response that follows from the needs of periodic reporting is to classify items into two types: those that will be included in the closing statement of financial position to be properly carried forward as part of the opening position of the new entity commencing next period, and those that are properly attributable to the period just finished. An aspect of this has already been seen in the simple illustration of buying and selling a bath to make a profit. The transactions involved are all treated as being complete by the time the profit figure for the year is calculated. Details of the buying and selling transactions are not part of the next year's position except to the extent that they form an element contained within the total capital figure (i.e. the profit part of £10).

The approach adopted here will be only briefly described now, as it was discussed more fully in Chapter 5 'Accounting Principles, Concepts and Policies'. It is known as the 'matching process'. Sales associated with a particular period are recognized as the revenue of that period. The expenditures used up in that period in creating those sales are matched against them. The aggregate sales less the aggregate expenditures matched against them gives the profit for the year. Before analysing this in-depth, it is necessary to be able to identify period expenditure (called 'revenue expenditure') and statement of financial position expenditure (capital expenditure).

8.5 Revenue expenditure versus capital expenditure

The word 'capital' is associated with items that appear in the statement of financial position (e.g. owners' capital), whereas the word 'revenue' encapsulates items that appear in the statement of profit and loss (comprehensive income). Expenditure of the type that is to be matched against the period's revenue and is used up in the period is called **revenue expenditure**. Revenue expenditure will have no value at the end of the period to which it relates. Revenue expenditure is distinguished from **capital expenditure** – that which represents amounts which it is appropriate to carry forward as part of the next year's opening statement of financial position. Capital expenditure is carried forward because it will be used over a number of periods and contributes to several periods' revenues.

EXAMPLE 8.7

A trainee accountant who has been given the task of listing items of expenditure as being either capital or revenue expenditure approaches you for advice. She specifically wants to know whether the following expenditures (which relate to a builder's yard) should be classed as capital or revenue items:

1 rates charge for the year;

2 a new delivery van;

3 rent for the building;

4 sand that is not yet sold;

5 stationery;

6 telephone bills for the year;

7 a new telephone;

8 a new fence surrounding the yard (this is expected to reduce theft);

9 wages;

10 electricity bills;

11 timber in the yard that is not yet sold.

Required

Complete a table detailing whether the items are capital or revenue in nature.

Solution

	Capital	Revenue
1. Rates		√
2. Delivery van (motor vehicle)	√	
3. Rent		√
4. Sand (inventory)	√	
5. Stationery		√
6. Telephone bill		√
7. New telephone (office equipment)	√	
8. Fence (fixtures and fittings)	√	
9. Wages		√
10. Electricity		√
11. Timber (inventory)	√	

Note

To improve the presentation of financial information, it is common practice to categorize items into accounts that have generic names. These are provided in brackets where they differ to the exact name of the expense. For example, electricity, oil, gas, etc. are commonly grouped into the account named 'heat and light'.

Capital expenditure typically includes the cost of purchasing a non-current asset (including the costs of getting the non-current asset operational at the outset) and the cost of improvements to a non-current asset that lead to increased revenue, or sustained revenue. Expenditure on tools, which represent the long-term equipment of the business, is capital expenditure and is carried forward from statement of financial position to statement of financial position. Rental expenditure on a building used during the year is revenue expenditure – what it provides is used up in the period. The purchase of the building, however, would be capital expenditure, as it is entirely appropriate to represent ownership being carried forward from period to period.

EXAMPLE
8.8

A trainee accountant who has been given the task of analysing items of expenditure in respect of the motor vehicles of the business in the year approaches you for advice. She specifically wants to know whether the following expenditures should be classed as capital or revenue items:

- repair of a lorry (the lorry is already included in the opening statement of financial position);

- purchase of a new van;

- motor tax on the van and lorry;

- cost of removing seats in the van to create more room for transporting goods for the business;

- new tyres for the lorry;

- advertising painted on the side of both the lorry and the van.

Required

Complete a table detailing whether the items are capital or revenue in nature.

	Capital	Revenue
Repair of a lorry		√
Purchase of new van	√	
Motor tax		√
Cost of removing seats – more storage	√	
New tyres		√
Advertising	√	

Allocating expenditure to the incorrect type of account has a major impact on an entity's reported performance and financial position. Revenue expenditure reduces profitability, whereas capital expenditure ends up in the statement of financial position with a portion of the expenditure being allocated to the statement of profit and loss in line with the use of the asset (the reduction in the useful economic life of the asset). The latter is discussed in depth in Chapter 16 'Depreciation and Non-Current Assets'. To allocate capital expenditure as revenue expenditure will cause profitability to fall, and vice versa. To knowingly allocate expenditure to the incorrect type of account is fraud, as users (particularly investors, lenders and the tax authorities) are misled and can suffer a loss. A high-profile example of accounting fraud which used this technique is now outlined.

WorldCom plc

WorldCom was one of the largest telecommunications companies in the world. In the late 1990s it came under increasing pressure to maintain reported cash flow and earnings before interest and taxation levels. However, orders for new telecommunication equipment were declining. This environment led the management of the company to commit one of the largest accounting frauds in world history. The overall reporting irregularities amounted to about $11 billion. The SEC (2003) found four major areas of fraud, one of which was 'the unauthorized movement of line costs to capital as prepaid. Line costs are paid to local telephone companies for originating and terminating long distance calls and account for the largest single expense for long-distance companies. By moving these costs to capital, the costs could be depreciated over time thereby increasing the current year's earnings before interest and tax.'

Source: Scharff, M.M. (2005) 'Understanding WorldCom's Accounting Fraud: Did Groupthink Play a Role?', *Journal of Leadership and Organizational Studies*, 11(3), 109–118.

8.6 Static and dynamic approaches to profit determination

The previous two sections described two approaches to measuring profit in the financial statements of a business. The first can be identified as a **comparative static approach** (statement of financial position approach). It computes profit through a comparison of the opening and closing capital positions, adjusting these for additions and withdrawals of capital made by the owners during the year. Each statement of financial position is a static representation of the elements of the accounting equation at a particular time.

The alternative is a more **dynamic approach** (statement of profit and loss approach) attempting to record increases and decreases in capital values throughout the period by recognizing the increases as revenue items and deducting from these the decreases or costs incurred in producing those revenues. By tracking the changes within a period, the latter 'transaction based or net production method' indicates the sources of profit.

8.7 Measurement

For accounting statements to represent the various values of assets and liabilities and to be able to aggregate these, it is necessary for a **measurement unit** to be established and a **valuation model** to be adopted. We have already been using a measurement unit, the sterling £. Providing this represents a stable unit for expressing economic values, **money measurement** will be appropriate to accounting statements intended to reflect the performance and financial position of business entities. Money provides a common denominator for measuring, aggregating and reporting the performance of an accounting entity and the attributes of transactions and items. Examples of other less plausible alternatives might include the amount of energy (e.g. electrical) or labour hours consumed in creating an asset.

As regards a valuation model, the price that is agreed in an arm's-length transaction when an asset or liability is originally acquired provides a readily available objective valuation expressed in terms of monetary units of measurement. This is the major source of valuation used by **historical cost accounting**. Sales are recorded at the contracted sales value and purchases at the agreed purchase price.

Over the past decade a change in emphasis has occurred in terms of measurement basis, with the standard setters putting more emphasis on **fair value accounting** (at present this change is mostly targeted at listed companies and larger limited companies). The underlying principle behind fair value measurement basis is the view that items stated in the financial statements should reflect their economic value, whether this is market value, or the present value of the expected future revenues expected from the item. In many instances fair value equates to historical cost values. As the focus of this book is accounting for small entities, the historical cost approach is utilized.

8.8 Strengths and limitations of historical cost in accounting measurement

Historical cost accounting has many strengths. It permits financial statements to be produced by collecting information about business transactions. This is particularly useful not only for preparing financial statements but also commercially for managing an entity's finances, as it can assist in tracking down what amounts have to be paid and collected and in determining the cash balances that remain after making payments and collections. Amounts are determined 'automatically' by the transactions themselves rather than being left to the judgement and possible abuse of individuals. For these and other reasons historical cost continues to be the predominant basis for accounting record keeping and reporting in non-plc entities.

However, the historical cost approach is not without disadvantages. These arise largely because there is change over time in prices (both of individual items and because of inflation). As a result, accounting reports based on historical costs may become unrealistic. Statements of financial position will contain values for assets that are out of date, being based on prices when they were originally purchased, which may be several years ago; capital, which is being maintained in the profit measurement process, represents a value that is also out of date, in terms of both its value to the owners, and the capacity of the facilities that it could provide for the business. The matching process becomes debased to the extent that sales may be made at prices which, although above the original purchase price of the items being sold, are below the current replacement price. This would mean that a business might be reporting a profit on a sale even though this put it in the position where it was no longer able to buy the goods it owned prior to the sale.

These limitations must be borne in mind when the appraisal of financial statements is considered in Chapter 33 'The Appraisal of Company Financial Statements Using Ratio Analysis'.

LEARNING ACTIVITY 8.2

As far as is possible, repeat Learning Activity 8.1 for one year ago. Calculate the change in the value of capital over the year and list the main reasons for the change. What do these tell you about the nature of the profit, capital maintenance and the effect of valuing assets at their historical cost?

Summary

The accounting entity concept defines the boundaries of the organizational unit that is the focus of the accounting process, and thus the transactions that will be recorded. An accounting entity may also be viewed as a set of assets and liabilities, the difference between the money values of these being capital. This is referred to as the accounting equation, and can be presented in the form of a statement of financial position in which the assets and liabilities are valued at their historical cost (or fair value if a listed entity).

The accounting period concept divides up the life of an entity into discrete periods (usually of one year) for the purpose of reporting profit and its financial state of affairs. The profit for an accounting year can be measured either in terms of the change in the value of the capital over this period, or by a process of matching sales revenue with the expenditure incurred in generating that revenue. This involves distinguishing between revenue expenditure and capital expenditure. Knowingly allocating a capital transaction as revenue and vice versa is fraud, as this can lead to tax evasion, or to losses being incurred by other users, such as investors or loan creditors. This is a criminal offence that can result in a fine, jail or both!

Key terms and concepts

accounting entity	116	liability	117
accounting equation	118	measurement unit	125
accounting period concept	122	money measurement	125
accounting year	122	ownership interest	117
asset	117	periodicity concept	122
capital	117	profit	121
capital expenditure	122	provisions	117
capital maintenance	121	reporting entity	115
comparative static approach	125	reporting period	122
dynamic approach	125	revenue expenditure	122
equity	117	statement of financial position	117
fair value accounting	126	time interval	122
financial year	122	time period	122
historical cost accounting	125	valuation model	125

An asterisk after the question number indicates that there is a suggested answer on the Online Learning Centre (www.mcgraw-hill.co.uk/textbooks/thomas).

Review questions   connect

8.1*   Explain the relevance of the entity concept in accounting.

8.2   Define and distinguish between the following:

   a   assets and liabilities;

   b   capital and revenue expenditure.

8.3   a   State the accounting equation and explain its components.

       b   The financial position of a business at any time is represented in the statement of financial position. Why is it that every business entity's position should 'balance'?

8.4   Explain briefly what is meant by the following terms: profit; capital; and capital maintenance.

8.5   Explain the relevance of the accounting period concept in accounting.

8.6   Discuss the relevance and limitations of the historical cost concept in accounting.

8.7*

J. Frank commenced business on 1 January 20X3. His position was:

Assets: land and buildings, £7,500; fixtures, £560; balance at bank, £1,740.

Liabilities: mortgage on land and buildings, £4,000.

He traded for a year, withdrawing £500 for his personal use and paying in no additional capital. His position on 31 December 20X3 was:

Assets: land and buildings, £7,500; fixtures, £560; delivery van, £650; sundry receivables, £470; inventory, £940; balance at bank, £1,050; cash in hand, £80.

Liabilities: mortgage on land and buildings, £5,000; sundry payables, £800.

Required

Calculate Frank's profit or loss for 20X3.

8.8

Prepare J. Magee's statement of financial position (vertical format as utilized in the chapter) as at 31 December 20X3 from the following:

	£
Office machinery	18,000
Trade payables	1,000
Sundry payables	800
Inventory of goods	2,900
Stationery inventory	200
Cash at bank	550
Trade receivables	8,150
Sundry receivables	2,000

Note: You have to determine J. Magee's equity capital balance.

connect Exercises

BASIC   8.9   Using the information from question 8.8, re-prepare J. Magee's statement of financial position, using the horizontal format, as at 31 December 20X3.

BASIC   8.10

State whether the following expenditures for a local school are revenue or capital in nature. In addition, state the name of the classification (current asset, non-current asset, etc.) and the generic account name that the item would appear in within the financial statements.

For example: tins of beans on the shelf of a grocery store are a type of current asset called 'inventory'.

1 A filing cabinet

2 Replacement pitched roof (the old roof was a flat roof)

3 Rates bill for the year

4 Insurance paid for the premises

5 Cleaners' wages

6 A till

7 A chair

8 A blackboard in the school

9 Chalk used on the blackboard in the year

10 Oil

11 Double-glazed windows (replaced single-glazed windows)

12 Repainting the classrooms

13 Painting the extension for the first time

14 Teachers' wages

References

Accounting Standards Board (1999) *Statement of Principles for Financial Reporting* (ASB).

DolemanBateman (2010) *Forensic Accounting*, http://www.dolmanbateman.com.au/.

Hicks, J.R. (1946) *Value and Capital* (2nd edn), Oxford: Clarendon Press.

Scharff, M.M. (2005) 'Understanding WorldCom's Accounting Fraud: Did Groupthink Play a Role?', *Journal of Leadership and Organizational Studies*, 11(3), 109–118.

When you have read this chapter, log on to the Online Learning Centre for *Introduction to Financial Accounting* at www.mcgraw-hill.co.uk/textbooks/thomas, where you will find multiple choice quizzes, case studies, a glossary and mock exams.

Basic documentation and books of account

Learning Objectives

After reading this chapter you should be able to do the following:

1 Explain the meaning of the key terms and concepts listed at the end of the chapter.

2 Distinguish between cash transactions and credit transactions.

3 Describe the nature of trade discount and cash discount.

4 List the documents and describe the procedure relating to credit transactions.

5 Describe the contents of those documents that are entered in the books of account.

6 Explain the purpose of books of prime entry.

7 List the books of prime entry and state what each is used to record.

 9.1 Introduction

No two businesses are exactly the same and the same can be said of the accounting systems used by firms. Most firms have their own particular ways of doing things. Some use manual record-keeping, others use off-the-shelf accounting software packages such as Sage, while others create their own bespoke accounting systems. However, there is a certain degree of homogeneity in keeping accounting records that is prevalent among the great majority of firms. This chapter focuses on providing background information on the typical documentation and books of account that are used by most firms.

9.2 Basic documentation for cash and credit transactions

In accounting, a **cash transaction** is one where goods or services are paid for in cash or by cheque when they are received or delivered. A **credit transaction** is one where payment is made or received some time after delivery (normally in one instalment). This should not be confused with hire purchase or credit card transactions. Credit transactions are extremely common in many industries. The credit terms of most UK businesses are that goods which are delivered at any time during a given calendar month should be paid for by the end of the following calendar month.

Credit transactions often involve **trade discount**. This is a discount given by one trader to another. It is usually expressed as a percentage reduction of the recommended retail price of the goods, and is deducted in arriving at the amount the buyer is charged for the goods.

A large number of businesses also allow their customers **cash discounts**. This is a reduction in the amount that the customer has to pay, provided payment is made within a given period stipulated by the seller at the time of sale (e.g. 5 per cent if paid within 10 days).

A cash transaction is recorded in the books of account from the receipt received if paid in cash, or from the cheque book stub if paid by cheque. A credit transaction, in contrast, involves a number of documents, not all of which are recorded in the books of account. Figure 9.1 shows, in chronological order, the documents

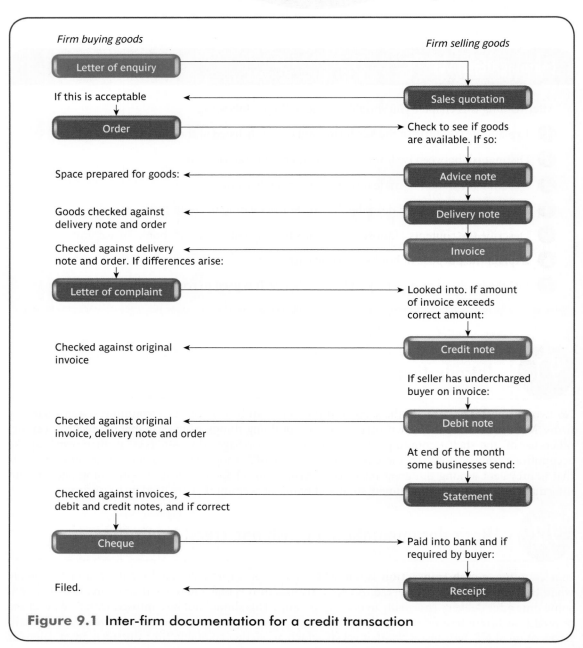

Figure 9.1 Inter-firm documentation for a credit transaction

and procedures relating to a business transaction on credit, including who originates each document. Note that only the invoice, debit note, credit note and cheque are recorded in the books of account.

The main documents involved in a credit transaction are now discussed.

The invoice

The purpose of the **invoice**, which is sent by the seller, is primarily to inform the buyer how much is owed for the goods supplied. It is *not* a demand for payment. A specimen invoice is shown in Figure 9.2.

FROM:	Trendy Gear Ltd			
	High Street			
	London			
TO:	Catalogue Times Ltd	INVOICE NO: 38167		
	Middlesex Street	Date: 30 January 20X3		
	London			
Delivered to: 23 Oxford Road, London				
No. of units	Details		Unit price	Total price
100	Dresses size 14, pattern no. 385		£6.50	£650
50	Leather bags, pattern no. 650		£3.00	£150
				£800
	Less: 25 per cent trade discount			(£200)
				£600
	Add: VAT at 20 per cent			£120
	Total			£720
	Tights unavailable – to follow later			
Date of Delivery:	30 January 20X3			
Mode of Delivery:	Our transport			
Cash Discount Terms:	5 per cent monthly account			
Your Order No:	6382			

Figure 9.2 An example of the layout of a typical invoice

The information shown on an invoice typically consists of the following items:

- the name and address of the seller;
- the name and address of the buyer;
- the invoice and delivery note number of the seller (usually the same);
- the date of the invoice;
- the address to which the goods were delivered;
- the buyer's order number;
- the quantity of goods supplied;
- details of the goods supplied;

- the price per unit of each of the goods;
- the total value of the invoice before value added tax (VAT)*;
- the trade and cash discount;
- VAT payable and the total value of the invoice including VAT;
- when payment should be made;
- the seller's terms of trade.

The buyer checks the invoice against the order and the delivery note (or more usually with a goods received note prepared by the receiving department). If correct, the invoice is then entered in the buyer's books. Similarly, a copy of the invoice would have been entered in the seller's books.

The debit note

A **debit note** is sent by the seller if the buyer has been undercharged on the invoice. It has basically the same layout and information as the invoice except that instead of details of the goods, it shows details of the undercharge. It is recorded in the books of the seller and buyer in the same way as an invoice.

The credit note

A **credit note** may be sent by the seller for a number of reasons. These include:

- The buyer has returned goods because they were not ordered, or they were the wrong type, quantity or quality, or are defective.
- The seller has overcharged the buyer on the invoice. This may be due to an error in the unit price or calculations.

A credit note has basically the same layout and information as an invoice, except that instead of the details of the goods, it will show the reason why it has been issued.

A credit note will be recorded in the books of the seller and buyer in a similar way to the invoice, except that the entries are the reverse. It is perhaps worth mentioning here the reason why this document is called a credit note. This is because it informs the buyer that the account in the books of the seller is being credited. Conversely, a debit note informs the buyer that the account in the seller's books is being debited. This is discussed in more depth in the next chapter. In many instances credit notes are differentiated from invoices by being printed in red ink.

The statement

As explained above, the most common terms of credit in the UK are that a buyer should pay for all the goods invoiced by the seller during a particular calendar month at the end of the following calendar month. The **statement** is a list of the invoices, debit notes and credit notes that the seller has sent to the buyer during a given calendar month, and thus shows how much the buyer owes the seller and when it should be paid. The statement is often a copy of the buyer's account in the seller's books. This is illustrated in Figure 9.3.

The statement may be kept by the buyer for reference purposes or returned to the seller with the buyer's cheque. In either case neither the buyer nor the seller records the statement in the books. Not all businesses use statements.

---

* VAT affects a large number of sales and purchase transactions which, in turn, must be incorporated in the recording of those transactions. Including VAT introduces little in the way of principles but some additional detail. In order to concentrate on the subject matter developed in this book, VAT is recognized here but its treatment is covered in depth in a separate chapter on the OLC – 'Value Added Tax, Columnar Books of Prime Entry and the Payroll' (**www.mcgraw-hill.co.uk/textbooks/thomas**).

Seller's name and address				
Buyer's name and address				Month: January 20X3
Date of invoice	Invoice/Credit note no.	Debits (amount of invoices and debit notes)	Credits (amount of credit notes and payments)	Balance
2 Jan	In426	£23.12		£23.12
9 Jan	In489	£16.24		£39.36
16 Jan	In563	£52.91		£92.27
22 Jan	Cheque		£25.14	£67.13
25 Jan	Cr1326		£6.00	£61.13
Amount due on 28 February: £61.13				
Cash discount terms: 5 per cent monthly				

Figure 9.3 An example of the layout of a typical statement

The cheque

This is the most common form of payment in business because of its convenience and safety. Most cheques are crossed and therefore have to be paid into a bank account. This makes it possible to trace the **cheque** if it is stolen and fraudulently passed on to someone else. A crossed cheque may be paid into anyone's bank account if the payee endorses (i.e. signs) the back of the cheque. However, if the words 'account payee only' are written between the crossings it must be paid into the account of the person named on the cheque.

The information that must be shown on a cheque consists of the following items:

● the date;

● the signature of the drawer (i.e. payer);

● the name of the drawee (i.e. the bank at which the drawer has the account);

● the name of the payee (i.e. who is to receive the money);

● the words 'Pay . . .' or 'Order the sum of . . .';

● the amount of money in figures and in words.

The bank account number of the drawer, and the cheque and bank number are also shown on pre-printed cheques.

Since there is only one copy of a cheque, it is essential to write on the cheque stub or counterfoil to whom the cheque was paid (i.e. the payee), the amount and what the payment was for. Without this information the books of account cannot be written up.

The bank paying-in book

The paying-in book provides a record of the cash and cheques received that have been paid into the business's bank account. The information shown on the **bank paying-in book** stub consists of:

● the date;

● the amounts paid in, from whom they were received, and to what they relate.

Cash and cheques received paid into the business's bank account are recorded in the books of account from the information on the bank paying-in book stub or counterfoil, which must therefore be accurate and complete.

The receipt

The law requires the seller to give the buyer a **receipt** for goods or services that have been paid for in cash. However, there is no legal requirement to do so in the case of payments by cheque.

A receipt must contain the following information:

- the name of the payer;
- the signature of the recipient;
- the amount of money in figures and in words;
- the date.

A receipt is only recorded in the books of account when it relates to cash receipts and payments.

Books of account

The main book of account in which all transactions are recorded is called the **ledger** (otherwise known as the **general ledger**, or the **nominal ledger**). However, before a transaction is recorded in the ledger, it must first be entered in a **book of prime entry**. These books are designed to show more detail relating to each transaction than appears in the ledger. They also facilitate making entries in the ledger, in that transactions of the same type can be posted periodically in total rather than one at a time. Sometimes, there are analysis columns in each book of prime entry in which are collected all those transactions relating to the same type of expenditure or income. For example, the cheque journal may record payments made for credit purchases in one column, for motor expenses in another column and for stationery in a further column. A business may use up to nine books of prime entry, which consist of the following:

1 The **sales day book**, in which is recorded the sale on credit of those goods bought specifically for resale. It is written up from copies of sales invoices and debit notes retained by the seller. The amount entered in the sales day book is after deducting trade discount (but before deducting cash discount).

2 The **purchases day book**, in which is recorded the purchase on credit of goods intended for resale. It is written up from the invoices and debit notes received from suppliers. The amount entered in the purchases day book is after deducting trade discount (but before deducting cash discount).

3 The **sales returns day book**, in which is recorded the goods sold on credit that are returned by customers. It is written up from copies of credit notes retained by the seller.

4 The **purchases returns day book**, in which is recorded the goods purchased on credit that are returned to suppliers. It is written up from the credit notes received from suppliers.

5 The **petty cash book**, in which is recorded cash received and cash paid. This is written up from receipts (or petty cash vouchers where employees are reimbursed expenses).

6 The **cash book**, in which are recorded cheques received (and cash paid into the bank) and payments made by cheque (and cash withdrawn from the bank). This is written up from the bank paying-in book stub and cheque book stubs.

7 The **bills receivable book**, in which are recorded bills of exchange received by the business from customers. A **bill of exchange** can best be described as being similar to a post-dated cheque, except that instead of being written out by the person paying the money, it is prepared by the business to whom the money is owed (the seller) and then signed by the entity/person paying the money (customer) as agreed and returned to the seller. When the period of credit given by the bill of exchange has expired, which is usually 30, 60 or 90 days, the entity in possession of the bill (seller) presents the bill to the customer and receives payment.

8 The **bills payable book**, in which are recorded bills of exchange given to creditors as payment.

9 The **journal**, in which are recorded any transactions that are not included in any of the other books of prime entry. At one time all entries passed through the journal, but now it is primarily used to record the purchase and sale of non-current assets on credit, the correction of errors, opening entries in a new set of books and any remaining transfers. Non-current assets are items not bought

specifically for resale, such as land and buildings, machinery or vehicles. The journal is written up from copies of invoices and adjustments requested by the accountant.

Figure 9.4 provides a summary of the seven main books of prime entry, including the documents from which each is written up. Each of these books of prime entry is discussed in depth in later chapters.

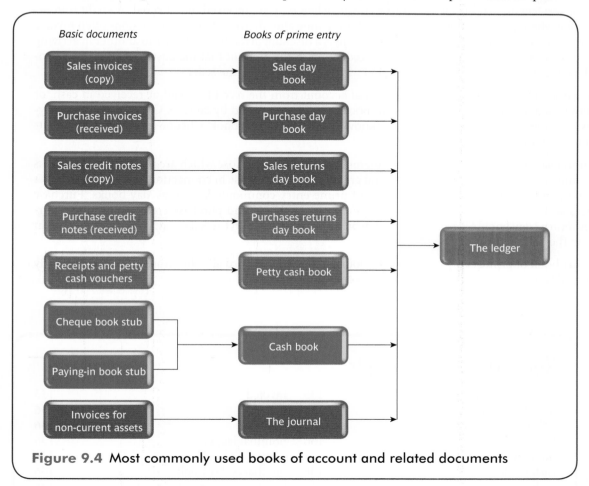

Figure 9.4 Most commonly used books of account and related documents

Finally a real world example referring to two famous worldwide accounting software providers shows that the accounting system described in this chapter is widely accepted.

REAL WORLD EXAMPLE 9.1 Manual and off-the-shelf compared

An example of the homogeneity of various accounting systems can be found when the websites of two major accounting system providers are reviewed. Kalamazoo, a worldwide provider of stationery for manual accounting systems, provides 'business systems' (a system of manual ledgers) to deal with all accounts receivable (and payable) type transactions, all cash reporting systems and ledger systems (general ledger). It also provides a range of other systems for recording payroll information, etc.

Sage, a world famous provider of off-the-shelf accounting software packages provides a variety of accounting systems that have differing levels of sophistication. The most simple of these systems includes the ledgers discussed in this chapter. Sage calls the various ledgers 'modules'.

Source: Author.

Summary

In accounting a distinction is made between cash and credit transactions. A cash transaction is one where goods or services are paid for in cash or by cheque when they are received or delivered. A credit transaction is one where payment is made or received some time after delivery. Credit transactions often involve trade discounts and cash discounts. Trade discount is a discount given by one trader to another in arriving at the price of the goods. Cash discount is a reduction in the amount that the customer has to pay provided payment is made within a given period which is stipulated by the seller.

Cash transactions are recorded in the books of account from the receipt, if paid or received in cash, or from the cheque book and bank paying-in book, if paid or received by cheque. Cash receipts and payments are entered in a book of prime entry known as the 'petty cash book'. Cheque receipts and payments are entered in the 'cash book'.

Credit transactions involve a number of different documents, but those which are recorded in the books of account comprise invoices, debit notes and credit notes. These arise in connection with both purchases and sales, and are entered in a set of books of prime entry commonly known as 'day books'. Purchase invoices and debit notes are entered in the 'purchases day book', and purchase credit notes in the 'purchases returns day book'. Sales invoices and debit notes are entered in the 'sales day book', and sales credit notes in the 'sales returns day book'.

A further book of prime entry known as the 'journal' is used to record all other transactions, particularly the purchase and sale of non-current assets on credit.

Key terms and concepts

bank paying-in book	135	invoice	133
bill of exchange	136	journal	136
bills payable book	136	ledger	136
bills receivable book	136	nominal ledger	136
book of prime entry	136	petty cash book	136
cash book	136	purchases day book	136
cash discount	132	purchases returns day book	136
cash transaction	131	receipt	136
cheque	135	sales day book	136
credit note	134	sales returns day book	136
credit transaction	131	statement	134
debit note	134	trade discount	132
general ledger	136		

An asterisk after the question number indicates that there is a suggested answer on the Online Learning Centre (www.mcgraw-hill.co.uk/textbooks/thomas).

Review questions

9.1 Explain the difference between a cash transaction and a credit transaction.

9.2 Explain the difference between trade discount and cash discount.

9.3 Outline the purpose and content of (a) an invoice; (b) a debit note; and (c) a credit note.

9.4 Explain the difference between an invoice and (a) a statement; (b) a receipt.

9.5 List the books of prime entry with which you are familiar and briefly describe what each is intended to record, including the documents used to write them up.

9.6 Briefly describe the nature of a bill of exchange.

9.7 Explain the purpose of books of prime entry.

Exercises connect

9.8

BASIC

You have received goods from trader X who invoiced you and delivered the invoice with the goods. You have just received a debit note for £100.

a What is a debit note?

b How should the £100 be accounted for?

9.9*

BASIC

List the four books of prime entry that are used to record inventory movements.

9.10*

BASIC

What do you have to do to a cheque to make it safe when sending it to a supplier using the postal system?

 When you have read this chapter, log on to the Online Learning Centre for *Introduction to Financial Accounting* at www.mcgraw-hill.co.uk/textbooks/thomas, where you will find multiple choice quizzes, case studies, a glossary and mock exams.

Double entry and the general ledger

Learning Objectives

After reading this chapter you should be able to do the following:

1. Explain the meaning of the key terms and concepts listed at the end of the chapter.

2. Explain the principles of double-entry bookkeeping, including the purpose of having different ledger accounts.

3. Describe the format and contents of the general ledger and ledger accounts.

4. Distinguish between asset and expense accounts, and between capital, liability and income accounts.

5. Enter cash (including cheque) transactions and credit transactions in the ledger.

10.1 The principles of double-entry bookkeeping

Bookkeeping versus accounting

As mentioned earlier, financial accounting is all about providing useful information in the financial statements to users to enable them to make economic decisions. It is all about communicating information. Recording transactions in the books of an entity is not accounting, it is bookkeeping. Accountants usually come in after the bookkeeper has finished and use the information supplied by the bookkeeper to prepare financial statements. However, to be able to account properly, accountants need to understand bookkeeping. Therefore this section of the book focuses on bookkeeping. **Double-entry bookkeeping** is a systematic method of recording an enterprise's transactions in a book called the **general ledger**, or simply the 'ledger'. Each page of the ledger is split into two halves: the left half is called the **debit side** and the right half is called the **credit side**. The ledger is divided into sections called **accounts**. In practice, each of these accounts is on a separate page. There is usually an 'account' for every class of expenditure, income, asset, and liability. Separate accounts are created to also record transactions into and out of the business by its owner/s. For example, there are typically separate accounts for wages expenses, for stationery, for heat and light, for motor vehicles, loans, drawings, capital introduced by the owner, and so on. There could be 1,000 accounts, depending on the detail required by management. Each of these 'accounts' can be traced to the financial statements. More detail is provided in the ledger than is provided in the statement of profit and loss and in the statement of financial position, as too much detail would reduce the understandability of the information being presented (i.e. the user would not see the wood for the trees). So, the expenses, income, assets and liabilities are usually combined in company financial statements to provide succinct meaningful information.

Indeed, many of the transactions that enter the ledger are summarized in other bookkeeping books beforehand to reduce the entries to the ledger. In this chapter it is assumed that all transactions are posted directly to the ledger (i.e. sales are recorded in the sales day book, of which the daily/weekly total is entered into the general ledger). The role of the other supporting bookkeeping books and how they feed into the ledger is examined in forthcoming chapters.

Double-entry bookkeeping

Double-entry bookkeeping is an application of the dual aspect concept. Under this concept each transaction affects two accounts (hence the name 'double-entry') and records a flow of value between the accounts. In accounting, a language has developed to indicate the direction of the flow, to debit an account means to have value flow into that account, whereas to credit an account means to have value flow out of that account. Convention has it that a debit always means an adjustment to the left-hand side of the ledger account, whereas a credit means an adjustment to the right-hand side of the ledger account. Some people find it easier to think of debits as being a '+' and a credit as being a '−'.

The money value of each transaction is entered once on each side of the general ledger in different accounts. The actual process of placing the bookkeeping entry in each account is called '**posting the transaction**' or simply '**posting**'. For example, if we take one transaction such as the sale of goods for cash of £100 on 6 January, this would be recorded (posted) as follows:

Ledger

	Debit				Credit		
Date	Details	Folio	Amount	Date	Details	Folio	Amount
			Cash account	(page 1)			
6 Jan	Sales	p. 2	100				

	Debit				Credit		
Date	Details	Folio	Amount	Date	Details	Folio	Amount
			Sales account	(page 2)			
				6 Jan	Cash	p. 1	100

The cash account on page 1 is debited with £100 and the sales account on page 2 is credited with £100.

T accounts

Many academics and textbooks create a simplified version of a ledger account called a 'T' account to teach bookkeeping to students. A 'T' account leaves out some of the detail that is given in ledger accounts, such as the reference to the folio page (the pages in a ledger are typically called folios) and contains less lines. A typical 'T' account looks like the following:

DEBIT			*Account name*		CREDIT	
Date	Details	£	Date	Details		£

The date column is the date of the transaction, the details column outlines the other account being posted to (so that the transaction can be traced) and the £ column records the amount that is being posted. Just like the ledger, flows of value to the account will be debited to the left-hand side, and flows of value from the account are recorded on the right-hand side (credited). A separate T account is opened for every type of expense, asset, liability, income and transaction with the owner (capital introduced and separately, drawings).

Three steps are required for every double-entry transaction:

1 Determine the two accounts to be adjusted.

2 Consider the flow of value (which account does it go to? which account does it leave?).

3 Identify the money value that is transferring.

The transaction noted previously was the sale of goods for cash of £100 on 6 January.

1 The two accounts affected are the sales account and the cash account.

2 Cash comes in (debit); therefore, the value must leave the sales account (credit).

3 The value transferring is £100.

In accounting language this translates as:

Debit:	Cash account		£100	
Credit:	Sales account			£100

and is shown in the two T accounts as follows:

Cash account						Sales account					
Date	Details	£	Date	Details	£	Date	Details	£	Date	Details	£
6 Jan	Sales	100							6 Jan	Cash	100

10.2 Cash and bank transactions

When cash is received, it is entered on the debit side of the **cash account** (as the flow of value is to cash) and credited to the account to which the transaction relates. When cash is paid out, it is entered on the credit side of the cash account (an outflow of value from cash) and on the debit side of the account to which the transaction relates. The same occurs with cheques received and paid, except that they are entered in an account called the **bank account** instead of the cash account.

When someone starts a business they usually put money into the business. This is debited to the cash or bank account (depending on whether it is cash or a cheque) and credited to a **capital introduced account**. Money introduced at a later date by the proprietor as additional capital is treated in the same way. Any money withdrawn by the proprietor is credited in the cash or bank account (depending on whether it is cash or a cheque) and debited to a **drawings account**. These accounts are never netted against each other.

Sometimes businesses also borrow money. The amount received is debited to the cash or bank account (depending on whether it is cash or a cheque) and credited to an account in the name of the lender, who is referred to as a **loan creditor**.

EXAMPLE
10.1

Complete the following table showing which accounts are to be debited and which are to be credited in the spaces provided:

	Debit	Credit
a) Bought office machinery in cash		
b) Bought lorry for cash		
c) A loan of £200 is received by cheque from Earls		
d) Paid stationery by cheque		
e) Paid rates by cash		
f) Owner wrote a cheque to himself		
g) Owner put cash into the business		
h) Owner buys a washing machine for his home and pays by cheque		

Solution

	Debit	Credit
a) Bought office machinery in cash	Office machinery a/c	Cash a/c
b) Bought lorry for cash	Motor vehicles a/c	Cash a/c
c) A loan of £200 is received by cheque from Earls	Bank a/c	Earls a/c (loan creditor)
d) Paid stationery by cheque	Stationery a/c	Bank a/c
e) Paid rates by cash	Rates a/c	Cash a/c
f) Owner wrote a cheque to himself	Drawings a/c	Bank a/c
g) Owner put cash into the business	Cash a/c	Capital introduced a/c
h) Owner buys a washing machine for his home and pays by cheque	Drawings a/c	Bank a/c

Double entry is now taken a step further by introducing monetary values and T account entries. The entries for various cash transactions are illustrated in Example 10.2.

EXAMPLE
10.2

S. Baker started business on 1 January 20X3 as a grocer with capital (in cash) of £1,000. She also borrowed £500 in cash from London Bank Ltd. Her transactions during January, which are all in cash, were as follows:

1 Jan Paid one month's rent for the shop: £100

2 Jan Bought fixtures and fittings for the shop: £300

8 Jan Purchased goods for resale: £400

9 Jan Paid £25 carriage inwards

10 Jan Bought stationery for £50

15 Jan Paid £200 in wages for shop assistant

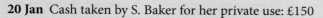

20 Jan Cash taken by S. Baker for her private use: £150

31 Jan Cash takings for the month: £600

You are required to write up the accounts in the general ledger.

Cash account					
20X3	**Details**	**£**	**20X3**	**Details**	**£**
1 Jan	Capital	1,000	1 Jan	Rent	100
1 Jan	Loan – London Bank Ltd	500	2 Jan	Fixtures and fittings	300
31 Jan	Sales revenue	600	8 Jan	Purchases	400
			9 Jan	Carriage inwards	25
			10 Jan	Stationery	50
			15 Jan	Wages	200
			20 Jan	Drawings	150

Capital introduced account					
20X3	**Details**	**£**	**20X3**	**Details**	**£**
			1 Jan	Cash	1,000

Loan–London Bank account					
20X3	**Details**	**£**	**20X3**	**Details**	**£**
			1 Jan	Cash	500

Rent account					
20X3	**Details**	**£**	**20X3**	**Details**	**£**
1 Jan	Cash	100			

Fixtures and fittings account					
20X3	**Details**	**£**	**20X3**	**Details**	**£**
2 Jan	Cash	300			

Purchases account					
20X3	**Details**	**£**	**20X3**	**Details**	**£**
8 Jan	Cash	400			

Carriage inwards account					
20X3	**Details**	**£**	**20X3**	**Details**	**£**
9 Jan	Cash	25			

Stationery account					
20X3	**Details**	**£**	**20X3**	**Details**	**£**
10 Jan	Cash	50			

Wages account					
20X3	**Details**	**£**	**20X3**	**Details**	**£**
15 Jan	Cash	200			

Drawings account					
20X3	**Details**	**£**	**20X3**	**Details**	**£**
20 Jan	Cash	150			

Sales revenue account					
20X3	**Details**	**£**	**20X3**	**Details**	**£**
			31 Jan	Cash	600

Notes

1 The narrative in the details column of an account specifies the name of the account that contains the other entry for each transaction.

2 **Carriage inwards** refers to haulage costs relating to goods that this business has purchased and is responsible for transporting from the sellers' premises.

LEARNING ACTIVITY 10.1

Prepare a cash account for your cash transactions over the forthcoming week or month. Make the necessary double-entry in the other ledger accounts.

10.3 Ledger entries for credit transactions

The entries in the ledger for credit transactions are more complicated than those for cash transactions. This is because a credit transaction involves at least two (and sometimes three) events, each of which is recorded in double-entry form. In this section, credit bookkeeping is explained using the most common types of credit transactions – the purchase and sale of inventory. Movements in inventory are not recorded in an inventory account because the value moving out of the account (sale) is different to the value moving into the account (the purchase). Putting the two transactions in the one account would be an example of netting (off-set), which is not allowed under law and is an accounting concept. Users are interested in knowing sales figures; it is one of the growth indicators. They are also interested in knowing how much the items cost that were sold. Therefore, they want to see purchases. The difference between the sales value and the purchase value of the item(s) sold is the gross profit on the item(s) and this information is disclosed separately in the statement of profit and loss (covered later). In addition to sales and purchases, there are two other types of inventory movement that have to be recorded separately: purchase returns and sales returns. The level of sales returns gives an indication of the quality of the entity's products and the level of purchase returns provides information on the entity's purchasing policy. Therefore, inventory movements are recorded in four separate accounts (see Figure 10.1).

Movements inwards	Posting	Movements outwards	Posting
Purchases	Debit	Sales	Credit
Sales returns (returns inward)	Debit	Purchase returns (returns outward)	Credit

Figure 10.1 The recording of purchase and sales returns inventory

Postings to the purchases and sales returns ledger accounts will always be on the debit side and these accounts will always have a debit balance, and postings to the sales and purchase returns ledger accounts will always be on the credit side and these accounts will always have a credit balance. A walked-through example of the double-entry posting to the appropriate T accounts is now provided. At this stage it is assumed that the sales ledger and the purchase ledger are not kept separate from the general ledger, so each credit customer and credit supplier has their own account in the general ledger. These accounts are typically recorded in separate day books with only the total 'trade receivables' and total 'trade payables' entering the general ledger. This is not covered in this chapter but will be examined in depth in Chapter 12 'Day Books and the Journal'.

Credit sales

The first event consists of the purchase or sale of goods on credit as evidenced by an invoice. The invoice is recorded in the ledger as follows:

1 Feb	Sold goods on credit to AB Ltd for £500

The first step is to identify the two accounts affected: The sales account and AB Ltd account.

The next step is to identify the flow of value: The goods represent the value and the goods physically go to AB Ltd (so the value leaves the sales account (credit) and flows to AB Ltd's account (debit)).

The next step is to identify the monetary value flowing between the accounts: In this case it is £500.

	Sales account				AB Ltd account					
20X3	Details	£	20X3	Details	£	20X3	Details	£	20X3	Details	£
			1 Feb	AB Ltd	500	1 Feb	Sales	500			

The amount outstanding on credit from a credit customer is referred to as a **trade receivable**. In the above example, the balance owing from AB Ltd is a trade receivable of the business whose books are being prepared. In the UK, trade receivables are commonly called 'debtors'. The term '**debtor**' arises from the existence of an account in the seller's books that contains more on the debit side than on the credit side. International Accounting Standards (IASs) do not use the term 'debtor'.

Credit purchases

2 Feb	Purchased goods on credit from CD Ltd for £250.

The first step is to identify the two accounts affected: The purchases account and CD Ltd account.

The next step is to identify the flow of value: The goods represent the value and they physically come from CD Ltd (so the value flows to the purchases account (debit) and from CD Ltd's account (credit)).

The next step is to identify the monetary value flowing between the accounts: In this case it is £250.

CD Ltd account						Purchases account					
20X3	Details	£	20X3	Details	£	20X3	Details	£	20X3	Details	£
			2 Feb	Purchases	250	2 Feb	CD Ltd	250			

The amount owing to a business or person from whom goods are purchased on credit is referred to as a **trade payable**. In the above example, the balance owing to CD Ltd is a trade payable of the business whose books are being prepared. In the UK, trade payables are commonly called 'creditors'. The term '**creditor**' arises from the existence of an account in the purchaser's books which contains more on the credit side than on the debit side. IASs do not use the term 'creditor'.

Sales returns

A second event that may occur when goods are bought and sold on credit is the return of goods. This can arise for example when some of the goods delivered were not ordered, or are defective. When goods are returned the seller sends the buyer a credit note. This is recorded in the ledger as follows:

3 Feb	AB Ltd returned goods invoiced for £100.

The first step is to identify the two accounts affected: The returns inward account and AB Ltd account.

The next step is to identify the flow of value: The goods represent the value and they come from AB Ltd (so the value flows to the returns inward account (debit) and comes from AB Ltd's account (credit)).

The next step is to identify the monetary value flowing between the accounts: In this case it is £100.

Returns inward account						AB Ltd Account					
20X3	Details	£	20X3	Details	£	20X3	Details	£	20X3	Details	£
3 Feb	AB Ltd	100				1 Feb	Sales	500	3 Feb	Returns inward	100

Purchase returns

Similarly, goods received may be defective, or not fit for purpose. These will be returned to the supplier. They are not treated as a reduction in purchases, but are recorded in a separate account, the 'returns outward' account.

Then on 4 Feb	The entity returned goods to CD Ltd invoiced for £50

The first step is to identify the two accounts affected: The returns outward account and CD Ltd account.

The next step is to identify the flow of value: The goods represent the value and they go to CD Ltd (so the value flows to CD Ltd's account (debit) and comes from the returns outward account (credit)).

The next step is to identify the monetary value flowing between the accounts: In this case it is £50.

CD Ltd account						Returns outwards account					
20X3	Details	£	20X3	Details	£	20X3	Details	£	20X3	Details	£
4 Feb	Returns outward	50	2 Feb	Purchases	250				4 Feb	CD Ltd	50

The balance on the customer's (AB Ltd) and supplier's (CD Ltd) accounts thus show the amounts of money owed at any point in time.

Receiving funds from credit customers

The third event that occurs when goods are bought and sold on credit is the transfer of money in settlement of the debt. The entries on settlement of a trade receivable account by a credit customer, is recorded in the ledger as follows:

| 5 Feb | Received from AB Ltd cash of £400 |

The first step is to identify the two accounts affected: The cash account and AB Ltd account.

The next step is to identify the flow of value: Money is the value and it flows to the cash account (debit) and flows from AB Ltd's account (credit).

The next step is to identify the monetary value flowing between the accounts: In this case it is £400.

	Cash account						AB Ltd account				
20X3	**Details**	**£**	**20X3**	**Details**	**£**	**20X3**	**Details**	**£**	**20X3**	**Details**	**£**
5 Feb	AB Ltd	400				1 Feb	Sales	500	3 Feb	Returns inward	100
									5 Feb	Cash	400

Paying credit suppliers

The entries on settlement of a trade payable account by the business, is recorded in the ledger as follows:

| 6 Feb | Paid CD Ltd £200 in cash |

The first step is to identify the two accounts affected: The cash account and CD Ltd account.

The next step is to identify the flow of value: Money is the value and it flows from the cash account (credit) and flows to CD Ltd's account (debit).

The next step is to identify the monetary value flowing between the accounts: In this case it is £200.

	CD Ltd account						Cash account				
20X3	**Details**	**£**	**20X3**	**Details**	**£**	**20X3**	**Details**	**£**	**20X3**	**Details**	**£**
4 Feb	Returns outward	50	2 Feb	Purchases	250	5 Feb	AB Ltd	400	6 Feb	CD Ltd	200
6 Feb	Cash	200									

An illustration of both credit and cheque transactions is shown in Example 10.3. The three steps are not shown in each instance. This is something that is done subconsciously and is not recorded.

A further related complication occurs where a business pays cash sales into its bank account. This can be treated as two transactions. The first transaction is cash sales that are recorded as a debit in the cash account and a credit in the sales account. The second is the payment of this money into the bank that is recorded as in Example 10.3, note 5a. Alternatively, where cash sales are banked on a regular basis, such as daily, the more common method of recording this is simply to debit the bank account and credit the sales account. There are thus no entries in the cash account.

EXAMPLE
10.3

E. Blue commenced business in 1 July 20X2 as a wholesale greengrocer with a capital in the bank of £2,000. His transactions during July were as follows:

1 July Bought a second-hand van by cheque for £800

3 July Paid insurance on the van by cheque for £150

7 July Purchased goods costing £250 on credit from A. Brown

11 July Sold goods on credit to B. Green amounting to £450

14 July Paid carriage outwards by cheque amounting to £20

16 July Returned goods to A. Brown of £50

18 July Repairs to van paid by cheque: £30

20 July B. Green returned goods of £75

23 July Sent A. Brown a cheque for £140

26 July Received a cheque from B. Green for £240

31 July Paid telephone bill by cheque: £65

31 July Paid electric bill by cheque: £45

You are required to write up the accounts in the general ledger.

Bank account					
20X2	**Details**	**£**	**20X2**	**Details**	**£**
1 July	Capital	2,000	1 July	Vehicles	800
26 July	B. Green	240	3 July	Motor expenses	150
			14 July	Carriage outwards	20
			18 July	Motor expenses	30
			23 July	A. Brown	140
			31 July	Telephone and postage	65
			31 July	Light and heat	45

Capital account					
20X2	**Details**	**£**	**20X2**	**Details**	**£**
			1 July	Bank	2,000

Motor vehicles account					
20X2	**Details**	**£**	**20X2**	**Details**	**£**
1 July	Bank	800			

Motor expenses account					
20X2	**Details**	**£**	**20X2**	**Details**	**£**
3 July	Bank	150			
18 July	Bank	30			

Purchases account

20X2	Details	£	20X2	Details	£
7 July	A. Brown	250			

A. Brown account (trade payable)

20X2	Details	£	20X2	Details	£
16 July	Returns	50	7 July	Purchases	250
23 July	Bank	140			

Sales account

20X2	Details	£	20X2	Details	£
			11 July	B. Green	450

B. Green account (trade receivable)

20X2	Details	£	20X2	Details	£
11 July	Sales	450	20 July	Returns	75
			26 July	Bank	240

Purchase returns (outwards) account

20X2	Details	£	20X2	Details	£
			16 July	A. Brown	50

Sales returns (inwards) account

20X2	Details	£	20X2	Details	£
20 July	B. Green	75			

Carriage outwards account

20X2	Details	£	20X2	Details	£
14 July	Bank	20			

Telephone and postage account

20X2	Details	£	20X2	Details	£
31 July	Bank	65			

Light and heat account

20X2	Details	£	20X2	Details	£
31 July	Bank	45			

Notes

1 The narrative in the details column of the expense accounts is 'bank' because the other side of the double entry is in the bank account.

2 Where there is more than one transaction relating to the same type of expenditure these are all entered in the same account (e.g. motor expenses). However, the purchase of a vehicle (capital expenditure) is shown in a different account from the running costs, referred to as an **asset account**.

3 Lighting and heating expenses, such as coal, electricity, gas and heating oil, are usually all entered in an account called 'light and heat'. The same principle is applied in the case of the telephone and postage account, the rent and rates account and the printing and stationery account.

4 **Carriage outwards** refers to haulage costs relating to goods that this business has sold and is responsible for delivering.

5 A business sometimes pays cash into its bank account and at other times withdraws cash from its bank account. The ledger entries for these transactions are as follows:

a Paying cash into the bank:

Debit: Bank account

Credit: Cash account

b Withdrawing cash from a bank account:

Debit: Cash account

Credit: Bank account.

LEARNING ACTIVITY 10.2

Prepare a bank account for your cheque transactions over the forthcoming week or month. Make the necessary double-entry in the ledger accounts.

10.4 Adjustments for drawings and capital introduced

Drawings may take a number of forms in addition to cash. For example, it is common for the owner to take goods out of the business for his or her personal consumption. This requires an adjustment that may be done by either of two entries:

1 debit drawings and credit purchases with the *cost* of the goods to the business; or

2 debit drawings and credit sales where the goods are deemed to be taken at some other value such as the normal selling price.

Another form of drawings occurs where the business pays the owner's personal debts. A common example of this is taxation on the business profits. Sole traders and partnerships are not liable to taxation as such. It is the owner's personal liability and not that of the business; therefore, if taxation is paid by the business, it must be treated as drawings. The ledger entry is to debit drawings and credit the cash book.

A similar form of drawings occurs when the business has paid expenses, some of which relate to the owner's private activities. The most common example is where the business has paid motor expenses, some of which relate to the owner's private vehicle or the use of a business asset for domestic or social purposes. The ledger entry in this case is to debit drawings and credit the relevant expense account. The

EXAMPLE 10.4

6 Feb Owner took £50 worth of vegetables for private use

The first step is to identify the two accounts affected: The drawings account and the purchases account.

The next step is to identify the flow of value: The goods are the value and the flow is from the purchases account (credit) to the drawings account (debit).

The next step is to identify the monetary value flowing between the accounts: In this case it is £50.

Purchases a/c						Drawings account					
20X3	Details	£	20X3	Details	£	20X3	Details	£	20X3	Details	£
			6 Feb	Drawings – vegetables	50	6 Feb	Purchases	50			

principle is exactly the same where the owner takes a non-current asset out of the business for his or her permanent private use.

Some other examples of drawings occasionally found in examination questions include where the owner buys a private asset (e.g. a car, holiday, groceries) for himself or herself, or for a friend or relative (e.g. spouse), and pays for it from the business cash or bank account. The ledger entry is to debit drawings and credit the cash book. A similar but more complicated example is where a credit customer of the business pays their debt to the owner (who pays the money into his or her private bank account), or alternatively the owner accepts some private service (repairs to his or her private assets, a holiday, and so on) in lieu of payment. In this case the ledger entry is to debit drawings and credit the credit customer's trade receivables account.

After all the drawings for the accounting year have been entered in the drawings account, this account must be closed by transferring the balance to the capital account. The entry is to credit the drawings account and debit the capital account.

Capital introduced after the start of a business usually takes the form of either cash/cheques or other assets (e.g. a vehicle). The ledger entry is to credit the capital introduced account and debit the appropriate asset account (e.g. cash book, motor vehicles). A slight variation on this occurs when the owner buys a business asset (e.g. vehicle or goods for resale) or pays a business expense or liability from his or her private cash/bank account. In this case the ledger entry is to credit the capital introduced account and debit the relevant asset (e.g. motor vehicles), liability, expense or purchases account. A more complicated version of the same principle is where the owner privately provides some service to a supplier of the business in lieu of payment. The ledger entry for this will be to credit the capital introduced account and debit the credit suppliers' account.

Some of these examples of drawings and capital introduced are quite common in small businesses, and particularly important in the context of partnerships, as will be seen in Part 7, 'Partnerships'.

10.5 Adjustments for goods on sale or return

Goods that have been sent to potential customers on sale or return or on approval must not be recorded as sales until actually sold. In the ledger, **goods on sale or return** at the end of an accounting year are included in inventories at cost. In many instances it is difficult to determine the exact number of sales that have been made (the cost of finding this out may outweigh the benefits) and an estimate of expected returns is used instead. This approach is evident in the following real world example.

McGraw-Hill Companies' accounting policy

Allowance for sales returns

'A significant estimate in the McGraw-Hill Education segment, and particularly within the HPI Group, is the allowance for sales returns, which is based on the historical rate of return and current market conditions.'

Source: extract from http://investor.mcgraw-hill.com/phoenix.zhtml?c=96562&p=irol-reportsannual

10.6 Ledger account balances

Each account can be totalled to give a balance that represents all the transactions affecting that account in the period. This balance can then be transferred to the statement of profit and loss or the statement of financial position. The main purposes of the ledger accounting system are to provide a means of ascertaining the total amount of each type of income and expenditure, the total value of the assets owned by the business (e.g. cash), and how much is owed to and by the business. For example, the cash account shows how much money the business has at any time. Also, when there are several transactions, the sales account will contain all the sales made during a period and thus it is possible to see at a glance the total sales for that period. Similarly, other accounts, such as wages and postage, will show the total amount spent on each of these types of expense for the period. These are referred to as **nominal accounts** (also called general ledger or simply ledger accounts). The information extracted from the totals of the nominal accounts is used to ascertain the profit or loss for a given period.

When the total amount of money on the debit side of an account is greater than that on the credit side, the account is said to have a **debit balance**. When the reverse is the case, the account is said to have a **credit balance**. An account that contains a debit balance represents either an asset (such as cash) or an expense or loss. An account with a credit balance represents capital, a liability, income (such as sales) or a gain.

Summary of expected balances on particular types of account	
Statement of profit and loss account	
Debit balances	Credit balances
Expenses	Income

Therefore, a profit is a credit balance (as a profit results when income exceeds expenditure) and a loss is a debit balance. The income and expense nominal account balances do not carry forward into the next year (as discussed in Chapter 8 'The Accounting Equation and its Components') but are all transferred to the statement of profit and loss account where they are netted against each other to form either a profit or a loss. This can be regarded as being a statement of financial position account. The statement of financial position accounts are carried into the next year. A summary of the expected balances on nominal accounts in the statement of financial position is as follows:

Statement of financial position	
Debit balances	Credit balances
Assets	Liabilities
Drawings	Capital (opening balance)
Losses	Capital introduced
	Profits

The **capital account** can be regarded as the owner's investment in the entity. From the entity's perspective, the capital account is the liability of the entity to the owner. Hence the capital account usually has a credit balance. Having knowledge of what the owner withdraws and introduces to the business is deemed to be of relevance for users. Hence, the movements in the owner's capital account are recorded in three accounts – drawings, capital introduced and the statement of profit and loss.

As mentioned, the statement of profit and loss is an account that takes the balances of all the revenue type accounts (income and **expense accounts**), summarizes them and presents them in a manner that is deemed to be of use to users and then transfers the balance (profit or loss) to the owner's capital account. In the context of the capital account, it can be assumed that every sale is made on behalf of the owners and increases the liability to them (hence is a credit) and every expense reduces the amount that is due to the owners (hence is a debit).

Therefore, profits and capital introduced will increase the balance on the capital account and drawings and losses will reduce the balance on the capital account.

Owners' capital movement accounts	
Debit balances	Credit balances
Drawings	Capital introduced
Losses	Profits

At the end of each reporting period the balances on each of these accounts are cleared to the capital account, to either increase or decrease the capital balance that has been carried forward from the previous statement of financial position. The closing balance of this account is then carried forward into the statement of financial position in the next period.

Summary

After being recorded in a book of prime entry, all business transactions are entered in another book called the 'ledger'. This is based on the double-entry principle and comprises various accounts. Each account is divided into two halves; the left half is called the debit side and the right half is called the credit side. The money value of every transaction is recorded once on each side of the ledger in different accounts. The main purposes of this system are to provide a means of ascertaining the total amount of each type of income and expenditure for a period, and the value of the assets and liabilities at a point in time. When the total amount on the debit side of an account is greater than that on the credit side, the account is said to have a debit balance. When the reverse is the case, the account is said to have a credit balance. An account that contains a debit balance represents an asset, a drawing, an expense or a loss. An account with a credit balance represents capital, capital introduced, a liability, income or a gain.

The ledger entries for cash transactions are made in a cash account (if in cash) or a bank account (if by cheque). These are then posted to the opposite side of another account representing the nature of the transaction. The ledger entries for credit transactions are more complicated because these are treated in accounting as comprising at least two separate transactions: the purchase (or sale) of goods on credit, and the settlement of the debt. The purchase of goods is debited to the purchases account and credited to the supplier's trade payables account. The sale of goods is credited to the sales account and debited to the customer's trade receivables account. When the supplier is paid this is credited to the cash (or bank) account and debited to the supplier's trade payables account. When money is received from a customer, this is debited to the cash (or bank) account and credited to the customer's trade receivables account.

Key terms and concepts

An asterisk after the question number indicates that there is a suggested answer on the Online Learning Centre (www.mcgraw-hill.co.uk/textbooks/thomas).

connect Exercises

BASIC

10.1 (Statement of profit and loss double-entry)

Complete the following table showing which ledger account is to be debited and which is to be credited:

	Debit	Credit
a) Stationery purchased on credit from Gormley		
b) Rates paid by direct debit		
c) Telephone bill paid by cash		
d) Stationery returned to Gormley		
e) Insurance paid by direct debit		
f) Cash sales		
g) Cheques received for sales		
h) Cash wages		
i) Wages paid by BACS		

10.2 (Inventory movements)

Complete the following table showing which ledger accounts are to be debited and which are to be credited:

	Debit	Credit
a) Goods sold on credit to Gormley		
b) Goods bought on credit from Morgan		
c) Goods bought for cash		
d) Goods bought by cheque		
e) Goods sold for cash		
f) Goods sold on credit to Earls		
g) Goods bought on credit from McAfee		

10.3*

H. George commenced business as a butcher on 1 October 20X2 introducing cash of £5,000 from her personal bank account to the newly opened business bank account. Her transactions during October 20X2, which were all in cash, are as follows:

1 Oct   Rent of shop: £200

2 Oct   Purchases of goods: £970

4 Oct   Bought fixtures and fittings: £1,250

6 Oct   Borrowed £3,500 from S. Ring

9 Oct   Purchased delivery van: £2,650

12 Oct   Sold goods for £1,810

15 Oct   Paid wages of £150

18 Oct   Purchases: £630

19 Oct   Drawings: £350

21 Oct   Petrol for van: £25

22 Oct   Printing costs: £65

24 Oct   Sales: £1,320

25 Oct   Repairs to van: £45

27 Oct   Wages: £250

28 Oct   Purchased stationery costing £35

30 Oct   Rates on shop: £400

31 Oct   Drawings: £175

You are required to record the above transactions in the ledger (use T accounts).

BASIC

10.4*

L. Johnson started business on 1 March 20X3 with capital of £10,000 in a bank current/cheque account. During March 20X3 he made the following transactions:

 1 Mar Paid £5,000 by cheque for a 10-year lease on a shop

 2 Mar Bought office equipment by cheque at a cost of £1,400

 4 Mar Bought goods costing £630 from E. Lamb on credit

 6 Mar Paid postage of £35 by cheque

 9 Mar Purchases by cheque: £420

 11 Mar Sold goods on credit to G. Lion for £880

 13 Mar Drawings by cheque: £250

 16 Mar Returned goods costing £180 to E. Lamb

 18 Mar Sold goods and received a cheque for £540 in payment

 20 Mar Paid telephone bill by cheque: £120

 22 Mar G. Lion returned goods invoiced at £310

 24 Mar Paid gas bill by cheque: £65

 26 Mar Sent E. Lamb a cheque for £230

 28 Mar Received a cheque for £280 from G. Lion

 30 Mar Paid electricity bill of £85 by cheque

 31 Mar Paid bank charges of £45

You are required to enter the above transactions in the ledger (use T accounts).

BASIC

10.5

N. Moss commenced business on 1 May 20X3 with a capital of £5,000 of which £1,000 was in cash and £4,000 was in a bank current/cheque account. Her transactions during May were as follows:

 1 May Borrowed £2,000 from Birmingham Bank Ltd in the form of a cheque

 2 May Paid rent of £750 by cheque

 5 May Paid wages of £120 in cash

 8 May Purchased goods for £1,380 by cheque

 10 May Sold goods for £650 cash

 12 May Withdrew £200 in cash for personal use

 15 May Bought goods on credit for £830 from S. Oak

 18 May Sold goods on credit for £1,250 to K. Heath

 20 May Bought shop fittings of £2,500 by cheque

 23 May Paid water rates of £325 in cash

 25 May Paid gas bill of £230 by cheque

 27 May Returned goods costing £310 to S. Oak

28 May K. Heath returned goods with an invoice value of £480

29 May N. Moss introduced further capital by cheque: £3,000

30 May Bought stationery of £90 in cash

31 May Sent S. Oak a cheque for £300

31 May Received a cheque for £500 from K. Heath.

You are required to show the above transactions in the ledger (use T accounts).

10.6

BASIC

Enter the following transactions in the books of 'Seamus McKee' for November (use T accounts).

 1 Nov Started business with £10,000 in the bank

 2 Nov Paid for advertising by cheque: £130

 3 Nov Paid for stationery by cheque: £50

 5 Nov Bought goods on credit from Red – £900

 5 Nov Sold goods for cash: £300

 6 Nov Paid for insurance in cash: £8

 8 Nov Bought machinery on credit from Black: £700

 9 Nov Paid for machinery expenses in cash: £150

10 Nov Sold goods on credit to Flanagan: £800

11 Nov Returned goods to Red: £200

12 Nov Paid wages in cash: £20

13 Nov Received cheque from Flanagan: £500

15 Nov Paid rent by cheque: £200

20 Nov Bought stationery on credit for £60 from Hutchinson

21 Nov Paid Black £700 by cheque

30 Nov Paid Hutchinson £60 by cheque

30 Nov Sold goods on credit to Flanagan: £500

10.7

BASIC

Enter the following transactions in the books of 'Mary Ward' for December (use T accounts).

 1 Dec Introduced a motor vehicle to the new business worth £8,000

 1 Dec Transferred a computer from home to the business: £500

 1 Dec Withdrew £200 cash from her personal account to cover the cash expenses of the business

 1 Dec Put a cheque in the business bank account to cover business start-up costs: £10,000

 1 Dec Purchased goods for sale by cheque: £4,000

 2 Dec Bought a van using a loan from the bank: £15,000

 2 Dec Bought office equipment using a loan from the bank: £5,000

3 Dec   Received cheques amounting to £5,000 for sales made

4 Dec   Purchased stationery for £450

5 Dec   Purchased envelopes for £25 using cash

6 Dec   Paid wages by cheque: £400

9 Dec   Purchased goods for sale for £2,000 by cheque

10 Dec   Sales lodged: £3,000

10 Dec   Cash sales: £1,000

12 Dec   Cash lodged: £800

14 Dec   Pens purchased in cash: £20

15 Dec   Loan instalment transferred by direct debit (DD): £1,000

18 Dec   Mary wrote a business cheque to her personal account: £2,000

21 Dec   Petrol paid by cheque: £280

22 Dec   Petrol for vehicles paid by cash: £40

23 Dec   Wages paid by cheque: £400

24 Dec   Second loan instalment DD from bank: £1,000

When you have read this chapter, log on to the Online Learning Centre for *Introduction to Financial Accounting* at www.mcgraw-hill.co.uk/textbooks/thomas, where you will find multiple choice quizzes, case studies, a glossary and mock exams.

The balancing of accounts and the trial balance

Learning Objectives

After reading this chapter you should be able to do the following:

1. Explain the meaning of the key terms and concepts listed at the end of the chapter.

2. Balance and close ledger accounts (T accounts).

3. Describe the nature and purposes of a trial balance.

4. Prepare a trial balance from the ledger or a list of ledger account balances (T accounts).

5. Describe the types of error that cause a trial balance to disagree.

6. Make the ledger entries necessary to correct errors that cause a trial balance to disagree.

11.1 The balancing of accounts

At the end of every accounting period it is necessary to balance each account in the ledger. This has to be done at least annually, and more likely monthly.

The procedure for balancing an account is as follows:

1 Leave one blank line under the last entry in the ledger account and draw parallel lines on the top and bottom of the next line in the amounts column on each side. When this happens it marks the end of the period. All the transactions before the totalling lines represent the period that has just ended and the area after the totalling lines represents the new period.

2 Add up each side of the ledger account and calculate the difference using a separate piece of paper (when you become familiar with balancing off accounts you will no longer need to use a separate piece of paper, except perhaps for the bank account).

3 If the amount of the debit side exceeds that on the credit side, enter the difference on the credit side immediately after the last entry on that side (in step one you left a blank line for this purpose). This is the closing balance on the account. Similarly where the amount on the credit side exceeds that on

the debit side, the difference should be entered on the debit side immediately after the last entry on that side. The result is that with the entered closing balance, both sides will total exactly.

4 Enter the total of each side of the ledger account between the parallel lines. These two figures should now be the same.

5 There are three descriptions used to close off accounts. These descriptions identify where the closing balance will end up in the new period.

   a When the ledger account is a statement of financial position account (an asset, capital or liability account, for example the motor vehicles account, bank account, loan account, etc.), the closing balance within the period (before the parallel lines) should be described as the 'balance carried down' (Bal. c/d). Enter the same figure on the opposite side below the parallel lines. This should be described as the 'balance brought down' (Bal. b/d). This is double-entry in practice – the closing balance from one period is being carried forward as the opening balance in the next period. For example, this may involve debiting the current period with the closing balance and crediting the new period with the same amount (the opening balance). Statement of financial position accounts always have opening balances.

   b When the account is a statement of profit and loss account (income or expense accounts for example sales, wages, purchases, heat and light, etc.) the closing balance transfers to the statement of profit and loss account and should be described as such (shortened sometimes to P/L a/c). This is a T account that is set up to determine the profit or loss made in the period. These ledger accounts will typically not have opening balances in the next period as the balance from the previous period has been transferred somewhere else (the statement of profit and loss account), however, whenever there are accruals or adjustments (Chapter 18) these accruals will be carried forward into the ledger T accounts in the next period. The accrual entries are statement of financial position items, however, they typically remain within the statement of profit and loss accounts. The statement of profit and loss account should be the second last account to be closed.

   c Finally, any account that represents a movement in owners' capital (drawings, capital introduced and the statement of profit and loss account) will be balanced off to the owners' capital account. Therefore, the description showing the destination of the closing balance on these accounts will be 'owners' capital'. The owners' capital account is a statement of financial position account. As all movements take place in the latter-mentioned accounts, this account will only have the opening balance. When all the movement accounts are closed and the balances transferred to this account, it will be closed and the balance carried down to the next period. This is the last account to be closed off.

This is illustrated below using the ledger accounts from the answer to Example 10.3 (Chapter 10). It is the period end (31 July) and the ledger accounts are being closed for the purposes of preparing the financial statements. This illustration will take you step by step through the stages of closing off an entity's books. An example of the three different types of account and the different way of closing them off is highlighted by shading.

Closing a statement of financial position account – the bank account

Step one – identify the type of account it is (Bank is a statement of position account. It is the least predictable account as the bank can either be a current asset or a current liability, if in overdraft).

Step two – leave a gap below the longest column of figures (shaded in grey below) and put totals' lines on both the credit and debit sides of the account. Leave room below the totals' lines for the opening balance. In practice, in a ledger there would be enough room after the total rows for several periods' transactions after July.

Bank account						
20X2	**Details**	**£**	**20X2**	**Details**		**£**
1 July	Capital	2,000	1 July	Vehicles		800
26 July	B. Green	240	3 July	Motor expenses		150
			14 July	Carriage outwards		20
			18 July	Motor expenses		30
			23 July	A. Brown		140
			31 July	Telephone and postage		65
			31 July	Light and heat		45

Step three – add up each side of the ledger account and calculate the difference using a separate piece of paper. In this instance the debit side totals £2,240 and the credit side totals £1,250. As the debit side has a larger balance, this will be the expected sign of the opening balance in the next period. This account will be regarded as having a debit balance (debits > credits). The larger of the sides will be the amount that goes in the totals' column (£2,240), as follows.

Bank account						
20X2	**Details**	**£**	**20X2**	**Details**		**£**
1 July	Capital	2,000	1 July	Vehicles		800
26 July	B. Green	240	3 July	Motor expenses		150
			14 July	Carriage outwards		20
			18 July	Motor expenses		30
			23 July	A. Brown		140
			31 July	Telephone and postage		65
			31 July	Light and heat		45
		2,240				2,240

Step four – work out the closing balance and put it in the correct side. In this instance, the closing balance is £990 (£2,240 − £1,250) and the balance will have to go on the credit side of the account, otherwise the numbers on the credit side will not add up to £2,240. This is shown as follows:

Bank account						
20X2	**Details**	**£**	**20X2**	**Details**		**£**
1 July	Capital	2,000	1 July	Vehicles		800
26 July	B. Green	240	3 July	Motor expenses		150
			14 July	Carriage outwards		20
			18 July	Motor expenses		30
			23 July	A. Brown		140
			31 July	Telephone and postage		65
			31 July	Light and heat		45
						990
		2,240				2,240

Step five – complete the double entry (otherwise the books will not balance). If you make an entry into an account, you must carry the value to another account, or in this case to the next period of the same account. At this stage the correct date and description need to be entered beside the closing balance. As a statement of position account, this period will be closed off and the balance carried into the next period (which starts on 1 August).

		Bank account				
20X2	**Details**	**£**	**20X2**	**Details**		**£**
1 July	Capital	2,000	1 July	Vehicles		800
26 July	B. Green	240	3 July	Motor expenses		150
			14 July	Carriage outwards		20
			18 July	Motor expenses		30
			23 July	A. Brown		140
			31 July	Telephone and postage		65
			31 July	Light and heat		45
			31 July	**Balance c/d**		990
		2,240				2,240
1 Aug	**Balance b/d**	990				

Closing a movement in capital account – the capital introduced account

This account is a movement in capital account and the balance on it will be transferred to the capital account at the period end (as this is a new business, this capital account will have to be opened).

		Capital introduced account			
20X2	**Details**	**£**	**20X2**	**Details**	**£**
			1 July	Bank	2,000
31 July	**Capital a/c**	2,000			
		2,000			2,000

The double-entry to close the capital introduced account is provided in journal form to assist student understanding. This is not required to be produced in exams and is not reproduced in the examples from now on. Instead (just in the case of this example), the relevant entries are shaded to highlight the debit–credit relationship.

Debit:	Capital introduced account (to close)	£2,000	
Credit:	Capital account		£2,000

The capital introduced account is now closed and has no opening balance in the new period. This makes sense as users will want to see what the owner has introduced in each period. This information would be difficult to obtain if all the items affecting owners were just pooled into the capital account.

		Capital account			
20X2	**Details**	**£**	**20X2**	**Details**	**£**
			31 July	Capital introduced a/c	2,000

The capital account is not closed yet, it is the last ledger account to close as the statement of profit and loss account is closed off to this account.

The next account to close is the motor vehicles account.

Motor vehicles account					
20X2	**Details**	**£**	**20X2**	**Details**	**£**
1 July	Bank	800			
			31 July	Balance c/d	800
		800			800
1 Aug	**Balance b/d**	800			

As an asset, the motor vehicles account is a statement of financial position account; therefore, the closing balance is carried into the next period.

Closing a revenue type account – the motor expenses account

As a revenue expense, this account will balance into the statement of profit and loss ledger account and will have no opening balance in the next period. The statement of profit and loss ledger account for this period has to be opened to receive this expense.

Motor expenses account					
20X2	**Details**	**£**	**20X2**	**Details**	**£**
3 July	Bank	150			
18 July	Bank	30			
			31 July	**Statement of P&L a/c**	180
		180			180

The motor expenses account is described as having a debit balance as the debit side is greatest and the balance is carried into the debit side of the statement of profit and loss ledger account. The statement of profit and loss ledger account is not closed at this time. It is the second last ledger account to be closed.

Statement of profit and loss account					
20X2	**Details**	**£**	**20X2**	**Details**	**£**
31 July	Motor expenses	180			

The next account to be closed is the purchases account. As a revenue expense, this is a statement of profit and loss account, hence will be closed off in the same manner as the motor vehicles account.

Purchases account					
20X2	**Details**	**£**	**20X2**	**Details**	**£**
7 July	A. Brown	250			
			31 July	**Statement of P&L a/c**	250
		250			250

Statement of profit and loss account					
20X2	**Details**	**£**	**20X2**	**Details**	**£**
31 July	Motor expenses	180			
31 July	Purchases	250			

The next account to be closed is A. Brown's trade payable account. As a liability, this account is a statement of financial position account; hence the balance will be carried into the next period.

A. Brown account (trade payable)					
20X2	Details	£	20X2	Details	£
16 July	Returns	50	7 July	Purchases	250
23 July	Bank	140			
31 July	Balance c/d	60			
		250			250
			1 Aug	Balance b/d	60

The sales revenue account is a revenue account, as such it will be closed off to the statement of profit and loss ledger account.

Sales revenue account					
20X2	Details	£	20X2	Details	£
			11 July	B. Green	450
31 July	Statement of profit and loss a/c	450			
		450			450

Statement of profit and loss account					
20X2	Details	£	20X2	Details	£
31 July	Motor expenses	180	31 July	Sales revenue	450
31 July	Purchases	250			

B. Green's account is a trade receivable. Trade receivables are current assets, which are statements of financial position ledger accounts; therefore, the closing balance will be carried forward into the next period.

B. Green account (trade receivable)					
20X2	Details	£	20X2	Details	£
11 July	Sales revenue	450	20 July	Returns	75
			26 July	Bank	240
			31 July	Balance c/d	135
		450			450
1 Aug	Balance b/d	135			

The purchase returns account is a revenue account; as such the balance is transferred to the statement of profit and loss ledger account.

Purchase returns (outwards) account					
20X2	Details	£	20X2	Details	£
			16 July	A. Brown	50
31 July	Statement of P&L a/c	50			
		50			50

Statement of profit and loss account					
20X2	Details	£	20X2	Details	£
31 July	Motor expenses	180	31 July	Sales revenue	450
31 July	Purchases	250	31 July	Purchase returns	50

Likewise, the sales returns account is a revenue account; as such the balance is transferred to the statement of profit and loss ledger account.

Sales returns (inwards) account					
20X2	Details	£	20X2	Details	£
20 July	B. Green	75			
			31 July	**Statement of P&L a/c**	75
		75			75

Statement of profit and loss account					
20X2	Details	£	20X2	Details	£
31 July	Motor expenses	180	31 July	Sales revenue	450
31 July	Purchases	250	31 July	Purchases returns	50
31 July	Sales returns	75			

Carriage outwards, telephone and postage and heat and light are revenue expenses; therefore, the balances will be transferred to the statement of profit and loss ledger account.

Carriage outwards account					
20X2	Details	£	20X2	Details	£
14 July	Bank	20			
			31 July	**Statement of P&L a/c**	20
		20			20

Telephone and postage account					
20X2	Details	£	20X2	Details	£
31 July	Bank	65			
			31 July	**Statement of P&L a/c**	65
		65			65

Heat and light account					
20X2	Details	£	20X2	Details	£
31 July	Bank	45			
			31 July	**Statement of P&L a/c**	45
		45			45

At this stage all the ledger accounts (except the capital account) have been closed; therefore, the statement of profit and loss ledger account can be closed. The balance represents the period's profit or loss. If the sum of the debit side (expenses) is greater than the sum of the credit entries then the entity has made a loss in the period; if the credit side (income) is greater, then the entity has made a profit in the period. Either way the balance is transferred to the owners' capital account. No balance will appear in the next period. Like the bank, the balance on this account can either be a debit or a credit, so it is good practice to add up each side and determine the largest before proceeding with the closure. In this instance the debit side is larger at £635, whereas the credit side adds to £500. Therefore the balance is a loss.

		Statement of profit and loss account				
20X2	**Details**	**£**	**20X2**	**Details**		**£**
31 July	Motor expenses	180	31 July	Sales revenue		450
31 July	Purchases	250	31 July	Purchase returns		50
31 July	Sales returns	75				
31 July	Carriage outwards	20				
31 July	Telephone and postage	65				
31 July	Heat and light	45				
			31 July	**Capital a/c**		135
		635				635

At this stage the capital ledger account (a statement of financial position account) can be closed with the balance carried forward into the next period to reflect the owner's investment in the business on that date. This becomes the opening capital balance in the new period.

		Capital account			
20X2	**Details**	**£**	**20X2**	**Details**	**£**
31 July	Loss from P/L a/c	135	31 July	Capital introduced a/c	2,000
31 July	**Balance c/d**	1,865			
		2,000			2,000
			31 July	**Balance b/d**	1,865

The ledger accounts are now fully closed for the period.

By now you should have noticed some of the rules outlined in the last chapter happening in practice. Expense accounts always have debit balances. Income accounts have a credit balances. Asset accounts have debit balances. Liability accounts have credit balances. The capital account mostly has a credit balance (though in rare instances an owner may withdraw more than he or she is entitled to, in which cash the capital account balance becomes a debit – because the owner owes the business money).

If the total of each side of an account is the same there will be no balance and thus the total amount is simply entered between the parallel lines.

 ## 11.2 The purposes and preparation of a trial balance

The **trial balance** is neither part of the general ledger nor is it a book of prime entry (although it is often prepared on paper with the same ruling as the journal). It is a list of the balances in the general ledger (nominal ledger, ledger) at the end of an accounting period, divided between those ledger accounts with debit balances and those with credit balances. Since every transaction recorded in the ledger consists of both a debit and a credit entry, the total of the balances on each side should be the same. This is checked by entering on the trial balance the balance of each account in the ledger, and adding up each side.

The purposes of the trial balance may be summarized as follows:

1 To ascertain whether the total of the ledger accounts with debit balances equals the total of the ledger accounts with credit balances. If so, this proves that the same money value of each transaction has been entered on both sides of the general ledger. It also proves the arithmetic accuracy of the ledger accounts. However, a trial balance can agree but there may still be errors in the ledger. For example, an amount may have been entered on the correct side but in the wrong account, or a transaction could have been completely omitted.

2 The trial balance is also used for the preparation of final financial statements that show the profit or loss for the period and the assets and liabilities at the end of that period. In practice this is done in the form of an extended trial balance. This is discussed further in Chapter 19 'The Preparation of Final Financial Statements from the Trial Balance (Advanced)'.

All the ledger accounts end up in two reports in the financial statements: the statement of profit and loss and the statement of financial position. Because the ledger accounts making up the statement of profit and loss are disclosed separately for users' benefits they are separately listed in the trial balance and the statement of profit and loss ledger account is not created until after the trial balance has been prepared. As noted, the trial balance does not form part of the double-entry process; this is shown in detail above. The trial balance is just a memorandum that is used to check that the ledger accounts balance and to assist in preparing the financial statements for disclosure purposes. As mentioned before, it is expected that expenses, returns inward and assets will have debit balances and income, returns outward, capital, and liabilities will have credit balances. An illustration of the preparation of a trial balance is given in Example 11.1. The amounts are taken from the closed ledger accounts noted in the last section of this chapter. *Note*: the capital account and the statement of profit and loss account are not listed as these accounts only include the closing balances of other ledger accounts. To include them in the trial balance would be to account for all their component accounts twice.

EXAMPLE 11.1

	E. Blue	
	Trial balance as at 31 July 20X2	
Name of account	Debit	Credit
	£	£
Bank	990	
Capital introduced		2,000
Motor vehicles	800	
Motor expense	180	
Purchase	250	
A. Brown (trade payable)		60
Sales revenue		450
B. Green (trade receivable)	135	
Purchases returns		50
Sales returns	75	
Carriage outwards	20	
Telephone and postage	65	
Heat and light	45	
	2,560	2,560

If a trial balance does not agree, students often fail to take a systematic approach to ascertaining the reason. It is therefore suggested that the following procedure be adopted, which will minimize effort and time spent looking for the errors.

1 Recast the trial balance.

2 Check that no ledger account has been omitted from the trial balance. This sometimes happens with the cash and bank balances as they are usually in separate books.

3 Check that each amount entered in the trial balance is on the correct side. This is quick to do once you become familiar with the nature of different ledger accounts.

4 Check to see that the amounts entered in the trial balance are the same as those shown in the ledger accounts.

5 If the error has still not been found, it will then be necessary to check all the entries in the general ledger.

6 If the difference between the totals of the trial balance is divisible by nine, then it is likely that a ledger account balance or a transaction has been transposed incorrectly – for example, if the heat and light account had been recorded as £54 instead of £45, or the account B. Green had been recorded at £315 instead of £135. In these instances careful consideration should be given to looking for this type of error.

It is also worth noting that often in examinations no marks are given for correct trial balance totals. The student will therefore only lose marks for the error that caused it to disagree. Thus, do not spend more than a few minutes trying to make a trial balance agree.

A further illustration of the preparation of a trial balance is given in Example 11.2. The data in the question would not be presented in this manner in practice, but the question is a useful way of testing your knowledge of which ledger accounts contain debit balances and which contain credit balances.

EXAMPLE 11.2

The following is a list of the balances appearing in the general ledger of T. Wall at 30 September 20X2:

	£		£
Capital	32,890	Trade payables	4,620
Drawings	5,200	Land and buildings	26,000
Loan from M. Head	10,000	Plant and machinery	13,500
Cash	510	Listed investments	4,800
Bank overdraft	1,720	Interest paid	1,200
Sales revenue	45,600	Interest received	450
Purchases	29,300	Rent received	630
Returns inwards	3,800	Salaries	3,720
Returns outwards	2,700	Repairs to buildings	810
Carriage inwards	960	Plant hire charges	360
Carriage outwards	820	Bank charges	240
Trade receivables	7,390		

You are required to prepare a trial balance.

Solution

Name of account	Debit	Credit
	T. Wall	
	Trial balance as at 30 September 20X2	
Capital		32,890
Drawings	5,200	
Loan from M. Head		10,000
Cash	510	
Bank overdraft		1,720
Sales revenue		45,600
Purchases	29,300	
Returns inwards	3,800	
Returns outwards		2,700
Carriage inwards	960	
Carriage outwards	820	
Trade receivables	7,390	
Trade payables		4,620
Land and buildings	26,000	
Plant and machinery	13,500	
Listed investments	4,800	
Interest paid	1,200	
Interest received		450
Rent received		630
Salaries	3,720	
Repairs to buildings	810	
Plant hire charges	360	
Bank charges	240	
	98,610	98,610

Notes

1 As mentioned before, the cash account can only have a debit balance. However, the bank account may contain either a debit or a credit balance. A credit balance occurs where the business is overdrawn at the bank.

2 The items 'Trade receivables' and 'Trade payables' are common in trial balances. These are the totals of the individual personal accounts of credit customers and suppliers, respectively.

3 The item 'Listed investments' refers to money invested in equity stocks and shares that are listed/quoted on the London Stock Exchange/Irish Stock Exchange.

LEARNING ACTIVITY 11.1

Prepare a trial balance for the ledger entries made for Learning Activities 10.1 and 10.2.

At this point in your studies of accounting you have covered the core systems (accounts, ledgers, posting and the trial balance) that underpin the accounting system in any entity. This information is valuable as highlighted by the following real world recruitment advertisement from late 2009:

REAL WORLD EXAMPLE 11.1

Sigmar Recruitment

A North Dublin-based multi-national company now requires a General Ledger Analyst.

The post is a twelve-month contract and offers a salary of €45,000.

The General Ledger Analyst will be responsible for *(the extract included in this real world example makes reference to the tasks that are relevant to the material covered to date, though the textbook does not extend to general ledgers for multi-national companies. However, the same principles apply)*:

- Closing sub-ledgers for trade and intercompany accounts, clearing interface tables and reconciling sub-ledger to general ledger balances.

- Participate in the intercompany out of balance project, ensuring any unidentified differences between trading countries are investigated and resolved immediately.

Experience required:

- At least 3 years of experience in an accounting, treasury or finance environment

- Strong general ledger accounting background, gained in a multi-national company

Salary will be €45 000

Source: Sigmar Recruitment 2009, www.sigmarrecruitment.com (accessed 2009).

Summary

At the end of each accounting period every account in the ledger must be balanced. The balance is the difference between the monetary amounts on the two sides of an account. There are three ways to close off ledger accounts depending on the nature of the account. If the ledger account is a movement in the owners' capital account, then it is balanced off to the capital account (a statement of financial position account). If the account is revenue ledger account (income or expense), the balance is transferred to the statement of profit and loss ledger account. Finally, if the ledger account is an asset, liability or capital account, then the balance carries forward into the new period. The closing balance is entered in the ledger account as a balance carried down at the end of the period, and as a balance brought down at the start of the following period.

The balances on all the ledger accounts are used to prepare a trial balance on a loose sheet of paper. A trial balance is a list of the balances in a general ledger at a specific time, divided between those with debit balances and those with credit balances. Since every transaction is recorded in the general ledger on both the debit and credit sides, the total of the ledger accounts with debits should equal the total of the ledger accounts with credit balances. The main purpose of the trial balance is to ascertain whether this is the case, and thus to check the accuracy of the ledger. Another function of the trial balance is to facilitate the preparation of final financial statements.

Key term

trial balance   168

An asterisk after the question number indicates that there is a suggested answer on the Online Learning Centre (www.mcgraw-hill.co.uk/textbooks/thomas).

Review question

connect

11.1 Explain the main purposes of a trial balance.

Exercises

connect

11.2*

Close off the ledger accounts in Example 10.2 (Chapter 10) fully transferring the ledger balances into the next period, the capital ledger account or the statement of profit and loss ledger account where appropriate.

BASIC

11.3*

Prepare a trial balance for Example 10.2 (Chapter 10).

BASIC

11.4*

Close off the T accounts and prepare a trial balance from your answer to Question 10.3 in Chapter 10.

BASIC

11.5*

Close off the T accounts and prepare a trial balance from your answer to Question 10.4 in Chapter 10.

BASIC

BASIC

11.6

Close off the T accounts and prepare a trial balance from your answer to Question 10.5 in Chapter 10.

BASIC

11.7

Close off the T accounts and prepare a trial balance from your answer to Question 10.6 in Chapter 10.

BASIC

11.8

Close off the T accounts and prepare a trial balance from your answer to Question 10.7 in Chapter 10.

BASIC

11.9

The following is a list of balances in the ledger of C. Rick at 31 May 20X3:

	£
Cash at bank	2,368
Purchases	12,389
Sales revenue	18,922
Wages and salaries	3,862
Rent and rates	504
Insurance	78
Motor expenses	664
Printing and stationery	216
Light and heat	166
General expenses	314
Premises	10,000
Motor vehicles	3,800
Fixtures and fittings	1,350
Trade receivables	3,896
Trade payables	1,731
Cash in hand	482
Drawings	1,200
Capital	12,636
Bank loan	8,000

Required

Prepare a trial balance.

11.10

The following is a list of balances in the general ledger of R. Keith at 30 June 20X2:

	£
Capital	39,980
Drawings	14,760
Loan – Bromsgrove Bank	20,000
Leasehold premises	52,500
Motor vehicles	13,650
Investment	4,980
Trade receivables	2,630
Trade payables	1,910
Cash	460
Bank overdraft	3,620
Sales revenue	81,640
Purchases	49,870
Returns outwards	960
Returns inwards	840
Carriage	390
Wages and salaries	5,610
Rent and rates	1,420
Light and heat	710
Telephone and postage	540
Printing and stationery	230
Bank interest	140
Interest received	620

Required

Prepare a trial balance.

BASIC **11.11**

The following is a list of balances in the general ledger of J. McKee at 30 June 20X3:

	£'000
Drawings	50
Loan – Mainstreet Bank	500
Freehold premises	1,000
Vans	250
Fixtures and fittings	35
Trade receivables	650
Sundry tools	20
Sundry tools returned	5
Trade payables	500
Cash	2
Bank overdraft	56
Deposit account	100
Sales revenue	3,300
Purchases	1,800
Returns outwards	150
Returns inwards	100
Carriage inwards	80
Carriage outwards	10
Wages and salaries	850
Rent and rates	58
Light and heat	45
Telephone and postage	18
Printing and stationery	25
Bank interest	5
Interest received	6
Rent received	23
Commission received	12

Required

a Prepare a trial balance.

b The trial balance does not balance (on purpose). Which account is missing? How much is the balance on this account (the accounting equation will help you answer this question).

When you have read this chapter, log on to the Online Learning Centre for *Introduction to Financial Accounting* at www.mcgraw-hill.co.uk/textbooks/thomas, where you will find multiple choice quizzes, case studies, a glossary and mock exams.

Day books and the journal

Learning Objectives

After reading this chapter you should be able to do the following:

1 Explain the meaning of the key terms and concepts listed at the end of the chapter.

2 Describe the transactions and documents that are recorded in each of the day books and the journal.

3 Enter credit transactions in the appropriate day books or journal and post these to the relevant ledger accounts.

4 Prepare opening journal entries to record capital introduced other than cash, and the takeover of another sole trader.

12.1 The contents of the day books and the journal

Before a transaction is recorded in the general ledger, it must first be entered in a book of prime entry. These are intended to facilitate the posting of the general ledger, in that transactions of the same type are entered in the same book of prime entry, which is periodically posted to the general ledger in total (rather than one transaction at a time). These initial entries do not form part of double-entry bookkeeping.

There are several books of prime entry. This chapter examines only those that are used to record credit transactions. These consist of: (1) the **sales day book**; (2) the **purchases day book**; (3) the **sales returns day book**; (4) the **purchases returns day book**; and (5) the **journal**. The transactions recorded in these books are as follows.

The sales day book

This is used to record the sale on credit of those goods bought specifically for resale. It is written up from copies of the sales invoices and debit notes retained by the seller. The amount entered in the sales day book is after deducting **trade discount**. At the end of each period, say calendar month, the total of the sales day book is credited to the sales account in the general ledger and the amount of each invoice and debit note is debited to the individual credit customers' trade receivable ledger accounts in the sales ledger. Most entities have several credit customers. Keeping separate ledger accounts for each credit customer in the general ledger and recording these in the trial balance would be cumbersome. Therefore, to reduce clutter in the general ledger and the trial balance and to serve as a control (the latter point is dealt with in Chapter 21 'Control Accounts') individual credit customers are maintained in a separate ledger called the **sales ledger**. The total of the balances on this ledger becomes the trade receivables amount. This total should agree to the balance on the trade receivables account in the general ledger. This balance is included in the statement of financial position.

The purchases day book

This is used to record the purchase on credit of those goods bought specifically for resale. It is written up from the invoices and debit notes received from suppliers. The amount entered in the purchases day book is after deducting any trade discount received. At the end of each period, say calendar month, the total of the purchases day book is debited to the purchases ledger account in the general ledger and the amount of each invoice and debit note received is credited to the individual credit supplier's trade payable ledger account in the purchase ledger. Like credit customers, most entities also have several suppliers who provide goods on credit. Keeping separate ledger accounts for each credit supplier in the general ledger and recording these in the trial balance would be cumbersome. Therefore, to reduce clutter in the general ledger and the trial balance and to serve as a control (the latter point is dealt with in Chapter 21 'Control Accounts') individual credit suppliers ledger accounts are maintained in a separate ledger called the **purchases ledger**. The total of the balances on this ledger becomes the trade payables amount. This total should agree to the balance on the trade payables ledger account in the general ledger. The balance of this account is included in the statement of financial position.

The sales returns day book

This is used to record the credit notes sent to customers relating to goods they have returned or where they have been overcharged on an invoice. Note that the entry is made when a credit note has been issued, and not when the goods are returned or the amount of the invoice is queried. The sales returns day book is written up from copies of the credit notes retained by the seller. The amount shown in the sales returns day book is after deducting trade discount. At the end of each period (for example, calendar month) the total of the sales returns day book is debited to the sales returns ledger account in the general ledger and the amount of each credit note credited to the individual credit customer's trade receivable ledger accounts in the sales ledger.

The purchases returns day book

This is used to record the credit notes received from suppliers relating to goods returned or where there has been an overcharge on the invoice. Note that the entry is made when a credit note is received and not when the goods are returned or the amount of the invoice is queried. The purchases returns day book is written up from the credit notes received from suppliers. The amount entered in the purchases returns day book is after deducting trade discount. At the end of each period (for example, calendar month) the total of the purchases returns day book is credited to the purchases returns ledger account in the general ledger and the amount of each credit note received is debited to the individual credit suppliers' trade payable ledger accounts in the purchases ledger.

The journal

The journal is used to record a variety of things, most of which consist of accounting adjustments, such as the correction of errors, rather than transactions. However, the journal is also used to record transactions that are not appropriate to any other book of prime entry, the most common being the purchase and sale of **non-current assets** on credit. These are items not specifically bought for resale but to be used in the production and distribution of those goods normally sold by the business. Non-current assets are durable goods that usually last for several years and are normally kept by the business for more than one year. Examples include land and buildings, plant and machinery, motor vehicles, furniture, fixtures and fittings, and office equipment.

Unlike the sales, purchases and returns day books, the journal has debit and credit columns. These are not a part of the double entry in the ledger. They are used to indicate what entries are going to be made in the general ledger in respect of a given transaction or adjustment. Each entry in the journal consists of the name of the ledger account that is to be debited (and the amount) and the name of the ledger account that is to be credited (and the amount). The nature of the entry must also be explained in a narrative that commonly starts with the word 'being'. Use of the word 'being' is considered to be old-fashioned and is not as strictly used. However, because it is still commonly used by many firms in practice, we have decided to continue to use it in this text. Having a description is of particular importance because of the variety of entries that are made in the journal. In addition, journals are usually used to record the posting of unusual transactions that may take quite a bit of explaining. Indeed, I recall at one time writing 10 lines of description to explain a complicated adjusting entry made to a client's records when I was a practising accountant.

An illustration of the entries in the above five books of prime entry (sales day book, purchases day book, sales return day book, purchases return day book and the journal) and the three ledgers (general ledger, sales ledger and purchase ledger) is given in Example 12.1.

EXAMPLE 12.1

Bright Spark is an electrical goods wholesaler. The transactions during June 20X3, which are all on credit, were as follows:

1 June Bought on credit from Lights Ltd various bulbs with a retail price of £1,000 and received 20 per cent trade discount

4 June Sold goods on credit to Electrical Retailers Ltd for £500 and allowed them 10 per cent trade discount on this amount

8 June Sent Electrical Retailers Ltd a credit note for goods returned that had a retail value of £300

10 June Sold goods on credit to Smith Retailers Ltd for £600 after deducting 40 per cent trade discount

12 June Purchased goods with a retail value of £1,000 from Switches Ltd who allowed us 30 per cent trade discount

15 June Purchases on credit from Cables Ltd goods costing £550

16 June Sent Smith Retailers Ltd a credit note for goods returned that had a retail value of £100

18 June Switches Ltd sent us a credit note for £300 in respect of goods returned

19 June Received a credit note for goods returned to Lights Ltd that had a retail value of £250

25 June Sold goods to General Retailers Ltd on credit for £250

27 June Sent General Retailers Ltd a credit note for £50 to rectify an overcharge on their invoice

28 June Sold goods on credit to Electrical Retailers Ltd at a price of £560

29 June Purchased on credit a motor van from Brown Ltd that cost £800

30 June Sold on credit to London Trading Co. some fixtures and fittings no longer required in the shop for £350. (Prior to this the business owned fixtures costing £1,000.)

Required

Make the necessary entries in the books of prime entry and general ledger.

Before starting to undertake double entry, the first step is to summarize the transactions in the day books. The first part of this solution deals with the transactions that do not impact on the journal.

The entries are as follows:

Sales day book

Date	Name of credit customer	Our invoice number	Folio	Amount
20X3				£
4 June	Electrical Retailers Ltd	I00446	F34	450
10 June	Smith Retailers Ltd	I00447	F8	600
25 June	General Retailers Ltd	I00448	F45	250
28 June	Electrical Retailers Ltd	I00449	F15	560
				1,860

Sales returns day book

Date	Name of credit customer	Our credit note number	Folio	Amount
20X3				£
8 June	Electrical Retailers Ltd	CRN06	F34	270
16 June	Smith Retailers Ltd	CRN07	F8	60
27 June	General Retailers Ltd	CRN08	F45	50
				380

Purchases day book

Date	Name of credit supplier	Our ref no for Supplier's invoice	Folio	Amount
20X3				£
1 June	Lights Ltd	Inv460	T23	800
12 June	Switches Ltd	I000672	T5	700
15 June	Cables Ltd	S0056932	T10	550
				2,050

Purchases returns day book

Date	Name of credit supplier	Our ref no for Supplier's credit note	Folio	Amount
20X3				£
18 June	Switches Ltd	C00569	T5	300
19 June	Lights Ltd	SC452	T23	200
				500

The next step is to take the day books and to use them to enter the information into the main double-entry bookkeeping system (the general ledger, sales ledger and purchase ledger). These ledger accounts are shown in T account format. In practice they would enter a ledger (which has a similar format).

The first two day books to be closed off and posted are those involving customers (sales day book and the sales return day book). The sales day book is totalled and the total entered into the credit side of the sales account in the general ledger. The corresponding credit entry will be to the four credit customer accounts in the sales ledger (entries highlighted by shading). Similarly, the sales returns day book is totalled and the total entered into the debit side of the sales return general ledger account, with the corresponding credit entry being posted to the three credit customers' accounts in the sales ledger who returned goods (entries highlighted in bold). Note the normal double-entry rules in respect of recording the flow of value are being applied.

General ledger entries					
			Sales account		
20X3	Details	£	20X3	Details	£
			30 June	Total per sales day book	1,860

			Sales returns account		
20X3	Details	£	20X3	Details	£
30 June	Total per sales returns day book	**380**			

Sales ledger entries					
			Electrical Retailers Ltd		
20X3	Details	£	20X3	Details	£
4 June	Sales	450	8 June	Returns	**270**
28 June	Sales	560			

			Smith Retailers Ltd		
20X3	Details	£	20X3	Details	£
10 June	Sales	600	16 June	Returns	**60**

			General Retailers Ltd		
20X3	Details	£	20X3	Details	£
25 June	Sales	250	27 June	Returns	**50**

Next, the two day books involving suppliers (purchases day book and the purchases return day book) are closed and posted. The purchases day book is totalled and the total entered into the debit side of the purchases account in the general ledger. The corresponding credit entry will be to the three credit suppliers' accounts in the purchases ledger (entries highlighted by shading). Similarly, the purchases returns day book is totalled and the total entered into the credit side of the purchases return general ledger account, with the corresponding credit entry being posted to the two credit suppliers accounts in the purchases ledger who we returned goods to (entries highlighted in bold).

General ledger entries

Purchases account

20X3	Details	£	20X3	Details	£
30 June	Total per purchases day book	2,050			

Purchases returns account

20X3	Details	£	20X3	Details	£
			30 June	Total per purchases returns day book	500

Purchase ledger entries

Lights Ltd

20X3	Details	£	20X3	Details	£
19 June	Returns	200	1 June	Purchases	800

Switches Ltd

20X3	Details	£	20X3	Details	£
18 June	Returns	300	12 June	Purchases	700

Cables Ltd

20X3	Details	£	20X3	Details	£
			15 June	Purchases	550

The journal

The entries required to post the motor van on credit and the sale of fixtures and fittings are first recorded in the journal before they enter the general ledger bookkeeping system as follows:

Date	Details (account in which the ledger entry is to be made)	Folio	Debit amount	Credit amount
20X3				
29 June	Motor vehicles	Dr	800	
	To Brown Ltd	Cr		800
	Being purchase on credit of motor van reg no ABC123.			
29 June	London Trading Co	Dr	350	
	To fixtures and fittings	Cr		350
	Being sale on credit of shop fittings.			

Second, the journal is taken and its entries are posted to the individual ledger accounts in the general ledger as follows:

General ledger entries					
Motor vehicles account					
20X3	**Details**	**£**	**20X3**	**Details**	**£**
29 June	Brown Ltd	800			

Brown Ltd account (sundry payable)					
20X3	**Details**	**£**	**20X3**	**Details**	**£**
			29 June	Motor vehicles	800

Fixtures and fittings account					
20X3	**Details**	**£**	**20X3**	**Details**	**£**
1 June	Balance b/d	1,000	30 June	London Trading Co	350
			30 June	Balance c/d	650
		1,000			1,000
1 July	Balance b/d	650			

London Trading Co account (sundry receivable)					
20X3	**Details**	**£**	**20X3**	**Details**	**£**
30 June	Fixtures and fittings	350			

Notes

1 The fixtures and fittings that were sold must obviously have already been owned by the business. Their cost is therefore included in the balance brought down on the debit side of the fixtures and fittings account along with the cost of other fixtures and fittings owned at that date.

2 The London Trading Co. is referred to as a sundry receivable and Brown Ltd as a sundry payable.

 ## 12.2 Opening entries/takeovers and the journal

Another use of the journal is to record and post **opening entries** as part of the double entry bookkeeping system. An opening entry is an entry to record the capital introduced into the business by the owner when it consists of assets in addition to cash and, possibly, liabilities. As the name implies, this entry usually occurs when the business is formed and the books are being opened. However, it is also used to record the takeover of another business. This is illustrated in Example 12.2.

<table>
<tr><td rowspan="2">EXAMPLE
12.2</td><td>A. King went into business on 1 March 20X3 by taking over a firm owned by B. Wright. The purchase consideration was £47,500, which had been computed by valuing the assets and liabilities that were taken over as follows:</td></tr>
</table>

	£
Shop	30,000
Fixtures and fittings	12,500
Inventories	4,600
Trade receivables	3,100
Trade payables	2,700

Required

Show the opening entries in the journal of A. King.

The journal

Date	Details/account		Debit	Credit
20X3				
1 Mar	Land and buildings	Dr	30,000	
	Fixtures and fittings	Dr	12,500	
	Inventories	Dr	4,600	
	Trade receivables	Dr	3,100	
	To: Trade payables	Cr		2,700
	To: Capital	Cr		47,500
			50,200	50,200
	Being assets and liabilities introduced into business by owner from takeover of an existing business			

Notes

1 The ledger entries will consist of debiting and crediting the ledger accounts shown above in the details column. In the case of trade receivables and trade payables the amounts will be entered in the personal accounts of the individuals/firms concerned in the sales ledger and the purchases ledger.

2 The capital of £47,500 is the difference between the total assets and liabilities brought into the business. This will be credited to the capital introduced account.

<table>
<tr><td>LEARNING
ACTIVITY
12.1</td><td>Where possible, approach a local business or a family member who works in the administration function of a business and ask them about the books of account of the business. Ask them to explain the transactions that they record in each type of book. Different names to those used in this chapter may exist, however, they will typically perform the same function.</td></tr>
</table>

The bookkeeping system described in this chapter is manual. In practice most companies use computerised bespoke packages with different modules for each book which are automatically linked into the general nominal ledger. Examples include Sage (caters for all the different books), Dosh Cashbook (focuses on recording cash transactions) or Microsoft (caters for all the different books). The latter two products were discussed in a *Daily Telegraph* article by Murray in 2001.

Bookkeeping in practice – Microsoft

'CONTROL of money sets apart the survivors in business. There are many accounting programs that can help, even at the cheap end of the market.'

Software giant Microsoft has released its own, called Money 2001 Personal & Businesses, designed to look after personal finances and the accounting needs of small businesses and sole traders.

The program can clash with some anti-virus software, so protection may well have to be disabled before you can install it. It then grills the user for personal information. It wants to know about financial goals and asks you to select from a range of popular financial ideals. Then there are figures to be fed in for up to nine current bank accounts, credit cards, unit trusts.

On personal income the program is intolerant of random payments and interested only in details from regular payslips, even if from different sources. The business part has an integrated invoicing and accounting system, and keeps track of suppliers, customers, sales, purchases and nominal ledger.'

Source: Murray, 2001, www.telegraph.co.uk/finance/personalfinance/4477402/Microsoft-helps-you-gain-a-grip-on-money.html.

Summary

Before a transaction is recorded in the ledger, it must first be entered in a book of prime entry. These are intended to facilitate the posting of the general ledger, in that transactions of the same type are entered in the same book of prime entry, the totals of which are periodically posted to the general ledger rather than one transaction at a time.

Credit transactions are recorded in a set of books of prime entry known as day books. The sales day book is used to record the sale of goods on credit of those goods specifically bought for resale, and is written up from copies of the sales invoices. The purchases day book is used to record the purchase on credit of those goods intended for resale, and is written up from the invoices received from suppliers. The sales returns and purchases returns day books are used to record returns, and are written up from the credit notes.

The posting of day books to the general ledger follows a common principle. The total of the day book is entered in the relevant general account (i.e. sales, purchases, sales returns or purchases returns), and the individual invoices or credit notes shown in the day book are posted to the customers' or suppliers' personal trade credit accounts, which are held separately from the general ledger in two ledgers called the 'sales ledger' and the 'purchases ledger'. The total of the balances on these ledgers represents the balance on the trade receivables (sales ledger) and trade payables (purchases ledger) ledger accounts in the trial balance. These balances are used to prepare the subsequent statement of financial position.

Credit transactions not relating to goods for resale (or services), such as the purchase and sale of non-current assets, are recorded in another book of prime entry known as the 'journal'. This is also used to record transactions that are not appropriate to any other book of prime entry, and various accounting adjustments that are not the subject of a transaction such as the correction of errors. The format of the journal includes a details column and two money columns labelled 'debit' and 'credit'. The narrative in the details column and amounts in the money columns indicate the entries that will be made in the ledger in respect of a given transaction or item.

Key terms and concepts

An asterisk after the question number indicates that there is a suggested answer on the Online Learning Centre (www.mcgraw-hill.co.uk/textbooks/thomas).

connect Review questions

12.1 a Outline the purposes of those books of prime entry referred to as day books.

   b Describe the contents, and state which documents are used to write up each of the following:

   i   the sales day book;

   ii the purchases day book;

   iii the sales returns day book;

   iv the purchases returns day book.

12.2 a State two fundamentally different types of transactions/items that are recorded in the journal.

   b Describe how these two transactions are recorded in the journal.

connect Exercises

BASIC

12.3

B. Jones is in business as a builders' merchant. The following credit transactions took place during April 20X3:

1 Apr   Bought goods on credit from Brick Ltd for £725

2 Apr   Sold goods on credit to Oak Ltd for £410

4 Apr   Bought goods costing £315 from Stone Ltd on credit

7 Apr   Sold goods on credit to Pine Ltd for £870

11 Apr Bought goods costing £250 from Slate Ltd on credit

15 Apr Sold goods to Lime Ltd for £630 on credit

17 Apr Bought goods on credit from Brick Ltd for £290

19 Apr Received a credit note for £120 from Brick Ltd

22 Apr Sent Oak Ltd a credit note for £220

24 Apr Stone Ltd sent us a credit note for £75 in respect of goods returned

27 Apr Sent Pine Ltd a credit note for £360

Required

You are required to make the necessary entries in the books of prime entry and the general ledger.

12.4

Veronica Reichester owns a shop. The following transactions happened in November.

 1 Nov   Credit sales, C. Flanagan £456, S. Morgan £300, F. Hutchinson £645, A. Adair £987

 2 Nov   Credit purchases, N. Ward £123, F. Wood £465, S. Duffy £786, N. Hynd £56

 5 Nov   Credit sales, C. Flanagan £560, S. Ruddle £560

 6 Nov   Credit purchases F. Wood £79, N. Hynd £560

 7 Nov   Goods returned to Veronica by F. Hutchinson £45, S. Ruddle £60

10 Nov   Veronica returned goods to N. Ward £19, N. Hynd £60

25 Nov   Veronica sold goods on credit to C. Flanagan £50, S. Morgan £45

28 Nov   Veronica returned goods to N. Ward £4

Required

a   You are required to show the above transactions in the day books of Veronica's shop.

b   Using this information post the transactions to the general ledger, sales ledger and purchase ledger.

c   Close the ledger accounts and extract the trial balance.

12.5*

B. Player buys and sells soft furnishings and office equipment. During August 20X3 she had the following credit transactions:

 1 Aug   Bought goods on credit from Desks Ltd which had a retail price of £1,000 and trade discount of 25 per cent

 3 Aug   Purchased goods with a retail price of £500 from Chairs Ltd who allowed 30 per cent trade discount

 6 Aug   Sold goods on credit to British Cars Ltd for £700 less 10 per cent trade discount

10 Aug   Received a credit note from Desks Ltd in respect of goods returned that had a retail price of £300 and trade discount of 25 per cent

13 Aug   Sold goods to London Beds Ltd on credit. These had a retail value of £800 and trade discount of 15 per cent

16 Aug   Sent British Cars Ltd a credit note in respect of goods returned that were invoiced at a retail price of £300 less 10 per cent trade discount

18 Aug   Purchased goods on credit from Cabinets Ltd that had a retail value of £900 and trade discount of 20 per cent

21 Aug   Received a credit note from Chairs Ltd for goods returned that had a retail price of £200 and 30 per cent trade discount

23 Aug   Sold goods on credit to English Carpets Ltd for £1,300 less 10 per cent trade discount

25 Aug   Sent London Beds Ltd a credit note relating to an overcharge of £100 in the retail value of those goods delivered on 13 August that carried trade discount of 15 per cent

Required

You are required to make the necessary entries in the books of prime entry and the general ledger.

BASIC

12.6*

Show the journal and ledger entries in respect of the following:

a   On 20 April 20X3 purchased on credit a machine (not for resale) from Black Ltd at a cost of £5,300.

b   On 23 April 20X3 sold on credit a motor vehicle for £3,600 to White Ltd. This had previously been used to deliver goods sold.

c   On 26 April 20X3 purchased some shop fittings for £480 on credit from Grey Ltd. These were not for resale.

d   On 28 April 20X3 sold on credit to Yellow Ltd for £270 a typewriter that had previously been used in the sales office.

BASIC

12.7*

W. Green decided to go into business on 1 August 20X2 by purchasing a firm owned by L. House. The purchase consideration was £96,000, which had been computed by valuing the assets and liabilities that were taken over as follows:

	£
Premises	55,000
Plant and machinery	23,000
Goods for resale	14,600
Trade receivables	6,300
Trade payables	2,900

Required

You are required to show the opening entries in the journal and ledger of W. Green.

BASIC

12.8

You are provided with the following details about a company's credit customers for the month of November.

Balances in sales ledger

		£
1 November 20X2	Boycey	200
	Del Boy	100
	Rachel	100
	Rodney	150
		550

Credit sales

		£
8 Nov	Boycey	320
11 Nov	Rodney	250
14 Nov	Del Boy	80
		650

Sales returns

		£
16 Nov	Boycey	70

Required

You are required to update the sales ledger accounts highlighting the balances to be carried down on 1 December and prepare the general ledger accounts to reflect November's transactions.

12.9

BASIC

You are supplied with the following information in respect of B. Score's transactions in September with its suppliers.

The list of opening balances per the purchases ledger is as follows:

J. Smith & Co	£378
A. Brown	£459
C. Jones	£235
M. Mann	£684
Payne & Co	£245
	£2,001
Less Debit – J. Cann & Co	£18
	£1,983

The following are the transactions relating to the suppliers' accounts in September:

		£	£
4 Sept	J. Cann & Co – goods purchased from Brook		48
	A. Gray – Goods		30
11 Sept	C. Jones – goods		39
	A. Brown – goods		75
18 Sept	Goods returned to A. Brown		10
	M. Mann contra for goods purchased by him		90
	Payne & Co – goods		83
25 Sept	A. Read – goods		120
30 Sept	Allowance by Gray for soiled goods		4
	Trade discount allowed by A. Read		24
	(Not previously deducted from the invoice)		

Required

a Prepare the entries to the purchases day book and the purchases returns book.

b Open up ledger accounts for all the other transactions.

c Update the suppliers' accounts in the purchases ledger.

Reference

Murray, R. (2001) 'Microsoft helps you gain a grip on money', *Daily Telegraph*, 8 Jan 2001, http://www.telegraph.co.uk/finance/personalfinance/4477402/Microsoft-helps-you-gain-a-grip-on-money.html

 When you have read this chapter, log on to the Online Learning Centre for *Introduction to Financial Accounting* at www.mcgraw-hill.co.uk/textbooks/thomas, where you will find multiple choice quizzes, case studies, a glossary and mock exams.

The cash book

Learning Objectives

After reading this chapter you should be able to do the following:

1. Explain the meaning of the key terms and concepts listed at the end of the chapter.

2. Describe the format of two- and three-column cash books.

3. Explain the relationship between a cash book and the cash and bank accounts in the ledger, including the implications of its being a book of prime entry as well as a part of the double entry system.

4. Explain the function of the cash discount columns in cash books.

5. Enter transactions in a two- or three-column cash book and post these to the appropriate ledger accounts.

13.1 Introduction

The pages of the **cash book**, like the general ledger, are divided into two halves, the debit side is on the left and the credit side is on the right. A cash book can take one of three forms:

1. A **two-column cash book** in which are recorded cash received and paid in one column on each side, and cheques received and paid in the other column on each side. This essentially combines and replaces the ledger accounts for cash and bank.

2. A two-column cash book in which are recorded cheques received and paid in one column on each side, and cash discount in the other column on each side (discussed further below).

3. A **three-column cash book** in which are recorded: (1) cash received and paid in one column on each side; (2) cheques received and paid in one column on each side; and (3) cash discount in the remaining column on each side (discussed further below).

In practice, cash received and paid is usually recorded in a separate petty cash book. Thus, the cash book normally consists of a two-column cash book of type 2 above.

13.2 The two-column cash book

The two-column cash book is used to record receipts and payments by cheque. It is written up from the bank paying-in book and cheque book stubs. The cash book is used instead of a bank account in the ledger. This is because there are usually a large number of transactions involving the receipt and payment of cheques, and if these were recorded in a bank account in the ledger it would become cumbersome. Moreover, it permits a division of labour in that one person can write up the cash book while another is working on the general ledger. This also reduces the possibility of errors and provides a check on the work of the person who writes up the cash book where it is posted to the general ledger by someone else.

In addition to being a book of prime entry, the cash book is part of the double-entry system. Thus, debits in this book are credited to a ledger account in the general ledger and no further entries are necessary. Similarly, credits in this book are debited to an account in the ledger and no further entries are necessary.

The two-column cash book gets its name from the existence of two money columns on the debit side and two on the credit side. The additional column on the debit side is used to record the cash **discount allowed** to credit customers and the extra column on the credit side is used to record the cash **discount received** from credit suppliers. Both of these additional columns are, like the day books, memorandum columns in that each item entered in these columns requires both a debit and a credit in the general ledger.

Cash discount is a reduction given (in addition to trade discount) by the supplier of goods to a buyer if the latter pays for them within a period stipulated by the seller at the time of sale. Often in practice all goods supplied during a particular calendar month must be paid for by the end of the following calendar month if cash discount is to be obtained. Note that cash discount is not deducted on the invoice but is calculated from the amount shown on the invoice, and deducted at the time of payment.

Apart from the entries in these two additional columns, the cash book is written up in the same way as the bank account. A debit balance on the cash book represents the amount of money the business has in the bank. Unlike the cash account the cash book may have a credit balance, which means that the business has an overdraft at the bank.

An illustration of the entries in the two-column cash book is given in Example 13.1. The question and that part of the answer relating to the entries in the cash book, shown on a separate page, should be read now.

EXAMPLE 13.1

In an extension to Example 12.1, enter the following transactions in a two-column cash book and write up the ledger accounts in the general ledger:

Capital at 1 July 20X3   £5,750

Bank balance at 1 July 20X3   £4,750

Bright Spark has the following cheque receipts and payments during July 20X3:

1 July Cash sales paid into the bank: £625

3 July Received a cheque for £70 for goods sold

4 July Paid rent by cheque: £200

6 July Received a cheque from the London Trading Co. for £350

8 July Paid an electricity bill by cheque: £50

11 July Sent Brown Ltd a cheque for £800

13 July Bought a car that cost £1,000 and paid by cheque

16 July The owner of Bright Spark paid into the business a cheque for £900 as additional capital

20 July Paid wages of £150 by cheque

23 July Purchases paid for by cheque: £670

24 July The proprietor withdrew a cheque for £100

31 July Paid Lights Ltd a cheque for their June account (balance £600) and they allowed us 5 per cent cash discount

31 July Sent Switches Ltd a cheque for their June account of £400 and deducted 2½ per cent cash discount

31 July Paid Cables Ltd a cheque for £300 on account

31 July Received from Smith Retailers Ltd a cheque for £525 after allowing them £15 cash discount

31 July Received a cheque for £720 from Electrical Retailers Ltd in full settlement of their account, which amounted to £740

31 July General Retailers Ltd paid £190 by cheque after deducting cash discount of £10, which was not allowed by us

As explained above, the cheques received and paid shown in the debit and credit amount columns respectively are posted to the relevant ledger accounts in the normal manner. However, the amounts shown in the memorandum columns relating to the discount allowed and received require both a debit and a credit entry in the general ledger. In simple terms, the entry for discount allowed is:

Debit   Discount allowed account

Credit   Customer's personal account (trade receivable)

Similarly, the entry for discount received is:

Debit   Supplier's personal account (trade payable)

Credit   Discount received account

This can be illustrated using just two of the personal accounts in Examples 12.1 and 13.1 as follows (double entry is highlighted by shading):

	Smith Retailers Ltd					
20X3	Details	£	20X3	Details		£
10 June	Sales	600	16 June	Returns		60
			31 July	Bank		525
			31 July	Discount allowed		15
		600				600

	Discount allowed				
20X3	Details	£	20X3	Details	£
31 July	Smith Retailers	15			

20X3	Details		£	20X3	Details		£
			Lights Ltd				
9 June	Returns		200	1 June	Purchases		800
31 July	Bank		570				
31 July	Discount received		30				
			800				800

20X3	Details	£	20X3	Details	£
			Discount received		
			31 July	Lights Ltd	30

However, entering each item of discount in the discount allowed and discount received accounts individually is inefficient, and defeats the main objective of the two-column cash book. The memorandum columns in the two-column cash book are intended to provide a means of ascertaining the total discount allowed and discount received for the period. The total of the memorandum discount allowed column is debited to the discount allowed account and the amount of each item of discount allowed is credited to the individual customers' accounts in the sales ledger. Similarly, the total of the memorandum discount received column is credited to the discount received account and the amount of each item of discount received is debited to the individual suppliers' accounts in the purchase ledger.

It can thus be seen that the memorandum discount columns in the cash book operate on the same principle, and perform the same function, as day books. That is, they facilitate the bulk posting of transactions to the general ledger by aggregating items of the same type. However, since they are not a part of the double-entry system, each item requires both a debit and a credit entry in the general ledger.

The proper ledger entries for discount allowed and discount received can now be illustrated by completing Example 13.1 using the answer to Example 12.1 as follows:

Cash book

Date	Details	Folio	Memo: Discount allowed	Debit amount	Date	Details	Folio	Cheque number	Memo: Discount received	Credit amount
20X3					20X3					
1 July	Balance	b/d		4,750	4 July	Rent and rates		54301		200
1 July	Sales			625	8 July	Light and heat		2		50
3 July	Sales			70	11 July	Brown Ltd		3		800
6 July	London Trading Co.			350	13 July	Motor vehicles		4		1,000
16 July	Capital			900	20 July	Wages		5		150
31 July	Smith Retailers Ltd		15	525	23 July	Purchases		6		670
31 July	Electrical Retailers		20	720	24 July	Drawings		7		100
31 July	General Retailers Ltd			190	31 July	Lights Ltd		8	30	570
					31 July	Switches Ltd		9	10	390
					31 July	Cables Ltd		10		300
					31 July	Balance	c/d		40	3,900
			35	8,130					40	8,130
1 Aug	Balance	b/d		3,900						

The general ledger accounts

Sales returns

20X3	Details	£	20X3	Details	£
30 June	Total per sales returns day book	380			

Sales revenue

20X3	Details	£	20X3	Details	£
			30 June	Total per sales day book	1,860
			1 July	Bank	625
			3 July	Bank	70

London Trading Co. (other payable)

20X3	Details	£	20X3	Details	£
30 June	Fixtures and fittings	350	6 July	Bank	350

Fixtures and fittings

20X3	Details	£	20X3	Details	£
1 June	Balance b/d	1,000	30 June	London Trading Co	350
			31 July	Balance b/d	650
		1,000			1,000
1 Aug	Balance b/d	650			

Capital introduced

20X3	Details	£	20X3	Details	£
31 July	Capital a/c	900	16 July	Bank – capital introduced	900

Drawings

20X3	Details	£	20X3	Details	£
24 July	Bank – drawings	100			
			31 July	Capital a/c	100
		100			100

Capital

20X3	Details	£	20X3	Details	£
31 July	Drawings a/c	100	1 July	Balance b/d	5,750
31 July	Balance c/d	6,550	31 July	Capital introduced a/c	900
		6,650			6,650
			1 Aug	Balance b/d	6,650

Discount allowed

20X3	Details	£	20X3	Details	£
31 July	Total per cash book	35			

Smith Retailers Ltd (trade receivable)

20X3	Details	£	20X3	Details	£
10 June	Sales revenue	600	16 June	Returns	60
			31 July	Bank	525
			31 July	Discount allowed	15
		600			600

Electrical Retailers Ltd (trade receiveds)

20X3	Details	£	20X3	Details	£
4 June	Sales revenue	450	8 June	Returns	270
28 June	Sales revenue	560	31 July	Bank	720
			31 July	Discount allowed	20
		1,010			1,010

General Retailers Ltd (trade receivable)

20X3	Details	£	20X3	Details	£
25 June	Sales revenue	250	27 June	Returns	50
			31 July	Bank	190
			31 July	Balance c/d	10
		250			250
1 Aug	Balance c/d	10			

Rent and rates

20X3	Details	£	20X3	Details	£
4 July	Bank	200			

Light and heat

20X3	Details	£	20X3	Details	£
8 July	Bank	50			

Brown Ltd (other payable)

20X3	Details	£	20X3	Details	£
11 July	Bank	800	29 June	Motor vehicles	800

Motor vehicles

20X3	Details	£	20X3	Details	£
29 June	Brown Ltd	800	31 July	Balance c/d	1,800
13 July	Bank	1,000			
		1,800			1,800
1 Aug	Balance b/d	1,800			

Wages					
20X3	**Details**	**£**	**20X3**	**Details**	**£**
20 July	Bank	150			

Purchase returns					
20X3	**Details**	**£**	**20X3**	**Details**	**£**
			30 June	Total per purchases returns day book	500

Purchases					
20X3	**Details**	**£**	**20X3**	**Details**	**£**
30 June	Total per purchase day book	2,050			
23 July	Bank	670			

Discount received					
20X3	**Details**	**£**	**20X3**	**Details**	**£**
			31 July	Total per cash book	40

Lights Ltd (trade payable)					
20X3	**Details**	**£**	**20X3**	**Details**	**£**
19 June	Returns	200	1 June	Purchases	800
31 July	Bank	570			
31 July	Discount received	30			
		800			800

Switches Ltd (trade payable)					
20X3	**Details**	**£**	**20X3**	**Details**	**£**
18 June	Returns	300	12 June	Purchases	700
31 July	Bank	390			
31 July	Discount received	10			
		700			700

Cables Ltd (trade payable)					
20X3	**Details**	**£**	**20X3**	**Details**	**£**
31 July	Bank	300	15 June	Purchases	550
31 July	Balance c/d	250			
		550			550
			1 Aug	Balance b/d	250

Notes

1 The personal accounts are usually balanced at the end of each month.

13.3   The three-column cash book

The three-column cash book is not common in practice, but is sometimes required in examination questions. It can be seen as an extension of the two-column cash book described above. The additional column on each side is used to record cash received (debit side) and cash payments (credit side). These columns are intended to replace the cash account in the ledger. Thus, the three-column cash book is used instead of the cash account and bank account in the general ledger.

In addition to being a book of prime entry, the three-column cash book is part of the double-entry system. Thus, entries in either the cash or bank columns require only one further entry in another ledger account on the opposite side.

The only additional complication that arises in the case of the three-column cash book concerns cash paid into the bank and cash withdrawn from the bank. At this point the reader may find it useful to refer back to Chapter 10 (Example 10.3, Note 5) which explains the double entry for these items. The form that this takes in the three-column cash book is as follows:

a Paying cash into the bank:

   Debit: Bank account column

   Credit: Cash account column

b Withdrawing cash from the bank:

   Debit: Cash account column

   Credit: Bank account column

The three-column cash book is not common in practice because in most businesses cash received and paid is usually recorded in a separate petty cash book instead of a cash account. This is discussed further in the next chapter.

An illustration of the three-column cash book is given in Example 13.2.

EXAMPLE 13.2

B. Andrews is in business as a motor factor and parts agent. The balances shown in her cash book at 1 December 20X3 were: bank, £1,630 and cash, £820. The following receipts and payments occurred during December 20X3:

2 Dec Received a cheque for £1,000 from J. Sutcliffe as a loan repayable in five years

3 Dec Purchased a personal computer for £1,210 and paid by cheque

4 Dec Purchased in cash goods for resale costing £340

5 Dec Paid wages of £150 in cash

6 Dec Cash sales paid into bank: £480

8 Dec Purchases by cheque: £370

9 Dec Cash sales of £160

11 Dec Cheque sales: £280

12 Dec Paid telephone bill of £320 by cheque

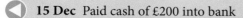

15 Dec Paid cash of £200 into bank

17 Dec Drawings by cheque: £250

18 Dec Bought stationery of £80 in cash

20 Dec Introduced additional capital in the form of a cheque for £500

21 Dec Paid water rates of £430 by cheque

23 Dec Withdrew cash of £100 from the bank

24 Dec Sent K. Vale a cheque for £530 after deducting cash discount of £40

24 Dec Received a cheque for £640 from A. Green who deducted £35 cash discount

27 Dec Paid M. Fenton £720 by cheque after deducting £25 cash discount

28 Dec J. Evans sent us a cheque for £860 after deducting £45 cash discount

29 Dec Received a cheque from B. Court for £920 who deducted £50 cash discount which we did not allow

Required

Enter the above transactions in a three-column cash book.

Cash book

Date	Details	Memo: Discount allowed	Bank	Cash	Date	Details	Memo: Discount received	Bank	Cash
20X3					20X3				
1 Dec	Balance b/d	—	1,630	820	3 Dec	Office Equipment		1,210	
2 Dec	J. Sutcliffe – loan		1,000		4 Dec	Purchases			340
6 Dec	Sales revenue		480		5 Dec	Wages			150
9 Dec	Sales revenue			160	8 Dec	Purchases		370	
11 Dec	Sales revenue		280		12 Dec	Telephone		320	
15 Dec	Cash		200		15 Dec	Bank			200
20 Dec	Capital		500		17 Dec	Drawings		250	
23 Dec	Bank			100	18 Dec	Stationery			80
24 Dec	A. Green	35	640		21 Dec	Rates		430	
28 Dec	J. Evans	45	860		23 Dec	Cash		100	
29 Dec	B. Court		920		24 Dec	K. Vale	40	530	
					27 Dec	M. Fenton	25	720	
					31 Dec	Balance c/d	—	2,580	310
		80	6,510	1080			65	6,510	1,080
1 Aug	Balance b/d	—	2,580	310					

LEARNING ACTIVITY 13.1

Prepare a two-column cash book with cash and bank columns to record your cash and cheque transactions over the forthcoming week or month. Make the necessary double entry in the other general ledger accounts.

Many companies use computerised bespoke packages to record their cash transactions. One such system is the Dosh Cashbook (focuses on recording cash transactions) as described in a *Daily Telegraph* article by Murray (2001).

REAL WORLD EXAMPLE 13.1

Dosh Cashbook

'The producers of the Dosh Cashbook program – designed for the sole trader and small business – claim that it can keep accounts up to date in less than 10 minutes a day without needing bookkeeping experience.

You simply enter receipts and payments and the program can produce:

- cashbook listing receipts and payment details
- summary of receipts and payments analysed by category, with opening and closing balances for any period of months
- opening/closing balances with bank/cash split
- sub-analysis of receipts and payments
- cash flow summary for any period of months
- VAT account (cash accounting) either monthly or quarterly
- VAT input/output sub-lists can link entries with VAT totals
- bank reconciliation.'

Source: Murray, 2001 (see Reference).

Summary

The cash book is both a book of prime entry and part of the double-entry system in the general ledger, and thus has the same format as a general ledger account. It usually takes one of two forms: a two- or a three-column cash book. The two-column cash book has two money columns on each side. One column on each side is used to record cheques received and paid. The other column on each side is used to record cash discount allowed and cash discount received. The two-column cash book replaces the bank account in the general ledger, and is written up from the bank paying-in book and cheque book stubs. The three-column cash book has three money columns on each side. Two of these are the same as the two-column cash book. The third is used to record cash receipts and payments, and is written up from copies of the receipts. The three-column cash book replaces the bank and cash ledger accounts in the general ledger.

Because the cash book is a part of the double-entry system, entries in the cash book in respect of cash and cheque transactions need only to be posted to the opposite side of the relevant general ledger account. However, this is not the case with regard to the entries in the cash discount columns. These columns are memoranda, and essentially intended to serve the same purpose as day books: namely to facilitate the periodic bulk posting of items of the same type. Thus, the total of the memo discount allowed column is debited to the discount allowed account in the ledger, and the individual amounts are credited to the relevant credit customers' personal accounts (sales ledger). Similarly, the total of the memo discount received column of the cash book is credited to the discount received account, and the individual amounts are debited to the relevant credit suppliers' personal accounts (purchase ledger).

Key terms and concepts

cash book	191	discount received	192
cash discount	192	three-column cash book	191
discount allowed	192	two-column cash book	191

An asterisk after the question number indicates that there is a suggested answer on the Online Learning Centre (www.mcgraw-hill.co.uk/textbooks/thomas).

Review questions

connect

13.1 Describe the different forms of two- and three-column cash books with which you are familiar.

13.2 Describe the entries in the cash book and general ledger in respect of discount allowed and discount received.

Exercises

connect

13.3

BASIC

B. Jones is in business as builders' merchants. He had £3,680 in the bank on 1 May 20X3. The following receipts and payments by cheque took place during May 20X3:

3 May Introduced additional capital: £2,000

4 May Sales by cheque: £840

7 May Purchases by cheque: £510

10 May Paid wages by cheque: £200

13 May Paid rent by cheque: £360

15 May Cash sales paid into bank: £490

18 May Purchased shopfittings for £2,450

20 May Paid gas bill of £180

23 May   Bought stationery by cheque: £70

26 May   Drawings by cheque: £250

31 May   Sent Brick Ltd a cheque for £850 after deducting £45 cash discount

31 May   Received a cheque from Oak Ltd for £160 after deducting £30 cash discount

31 May   Paid Stone Ltd £220 after deducting cash discount of £20

31 May   Pine Ltd sent us a cheque for £485 after deducting £25 cash discount

31 May   Sent Slate Ltd a cheque for £480 after deducting cash discount of £40.
         However, Slate Ltd did not allow the discount

31 May   Lime Ltd sent us a cheque for £575

Required

Show the entries in respect of the above in a two-column cash book.

BASIC

13.4

Using your answers to Question 12.3 in Chapter 12 and Question 13.3 above:

a   make the necessary entries in the general ledger given a balance on the capital account at 1 May 20X3 of £3,680;

b   prepare a trial balance at 31 May 20X3.

BASIC

13.5*

B. Player buys and sells soft furnishings and office equipment. On 1 September 20X3 the bank balance per the cash book was £1,950 and the cash balance per the cash book was £860. During September 20X3 the following receipts and payments occurred:

3 Sep   Cash sales paid into bank: £470

4 Sep   Cash purchases: £230

6 Sep   Paid electricity bill of £510 (paid by cheque)

9 Sep   Sales by cheque: £380

10 Sep   Drew a cheque for £250 in respect of wages

12 Sep   Cash sales: £290

15 Sep   Paid £40 in cash for travelling expenses

16 Sep   Paid water rates by cheque: £410

19 Sep   Drawings in cash: £150

20 Sep   Purchases by cheque: £320

21 Sep   Paid postage of £30 in cash

22 Sep   Paid cash of £350 into the bank

24 Sep   Introduced further capital of £500 by cheque

25 Sep   Purchased a delivery vehicle for £2,500 and paid by cheque

26 Sep   Received a cheque for £1,000 from B. Jones as a three-year loan

27 Sep   Returned goods costing £170 and received a cash refund

28 Sep   Paid tax and insurance on delivery vehicle of £280 in cash

29 Sep   Withdrew cash of £180 from bank

30 Sep   Received a cheque from British Cars Ltd for £350 after deducting £10 cash discount

30 Sep   Received a cheque from London Beds Ltd for £580 after deducting £15 cash discount

30 Sep   Paid Desks Ltd a cheque for £500 after deducting £25 cash discount

30 Sep   Paid Chairs Ltd a cheque for £190 after deducting £20 cash discount

30 Sep   Received a cheque from English Carpets Ltd for £1,100 after deducting £70 cash discount. However, this cash discount was not allowed

30 Sep   Paid Cabinets Ltd a cheque for £500 on account

Required

Enter the above in a three-column cash book.

13.6*

Using your answers to Question 12.5 in Chapter 12 and Question 13.5 above:

a   make the necessary entries in the ledger given a balance on the capital account at 1 September 20X3 of £2,810; and

b   prepare a trial balance at 30 September 20X3.

BASIC

13.7

The following information is an extension to Question 12.4 in Chapter 12.

a   Enter the following transactions using a three-column cash book.

The following cash transactions happened in November:

9 Nov   Cash paid to Veronica by A. Adair £900, S. Ruddle £500

12 Nov   Veronica received cheques from F. Hutchinson £600, C. Flanagan £456

26 Nov   Veronica paid by cheque the following: N. Ward £100, F. Wood, £465, N. Hynd £56

b   Make the necessary entries in the ledgers using your answers to Question 12.4 in Chapter 12.

c   Prepare the trial balance at 30 November.

BASIC

13.8

The following information is an extension to Question 12.8 in Chapter 12:

BASIC

Cash book (receipts side)		Discount allowed £	Amount received from customers £
7 Nov	Boycey	20	180
9 Nov	Rodney	15	135
12 Nov	Del Boy	10	90
		45	405

Required

a   Make the necessary entries in the ledgers using your answers to Question 12.8 in Chapter 12.

b   Close the suppliers' accounts at 30 September.

BASIC

13.9

The following information is an extension to Question 12.9 in Chapter 12.

a Enter the following transactions relating to the suppliers' accounts in September using a three-column cash book:

			£	£
4 Sept	Paid	J Smith & Co		150
	Paid	A. Brown	268	
		Discount	7	275
11 Sept	Paid	C. Jones	169	
		Discount	6	175
18 Sept	Paid	M. Mann		300
	Paid	Payne & Co	164	
		Discount	5	169

b Make the necessary entries in the ledgers using your answers to Question 12.9 in Chapter 12.

c Close the suppliers' accounts at 30 September.

BASIC

13.10

Enter the following transactions in ledger accounts of ABC (including a two-column cash book), balance off and extract the trial balance.

1 Jan ABC started business and put £1,000 in the business bank account

2 Jan Bought £200 worth of inventory on credit from Brown

3 Jan Purchased a van by cheque for £300

3 Jan Got a logo painted on the side of the van for £100 paid by cheque

4 Jan Sold goods to Yellow on credit worth £300

8 Jan Purchased pencils by cheque for £50

9 Jan Yellow paid his account in full by cheque

10 Jan Paid Brown his account in full by cheque

12 Jan Purchased more inventory on credit from Brown for £300

14 Jan Sold goods to Yellow on credit for £500

15 Jan Purchased a lorry for £100 paying by cheque

20 Jan ABC put another £100 in the business bank account from his own personal account

Reference

Murray, R. (2001) 'Microsoft helps you gain a grip on money', *Daily Telegraph*, 8 Jan. 2001, www.telegraph.co.uk/finance/personalfinance/4477402/ microsoft-helps-you-gain-a-grip-on-money.html.

When you have read this chapter, log on to the Online Learning Centre for *Introduction to Financial Accounting* at www.mcgraw-hill.co.uk/ textbooks/thomas, where you will find multiple choice quizzes, case studies, a glossary and mock exams.

The petty cash book

Learning Objectives

After reading this chapter you should be able to do the following:

1. Explain the meaning of the key terms and concepts listed at the end of the chapter.

2. Explain the relationship between a petty cash book and the cash account in the general ledger, including the implications of the petty cash book being a book of prime entry as well as being a part of the double-entry system.

3. Describe the format of a columnar petty cash book.

4. Explain the function of the analysis columns in a columnar petty cash book.

5. Describe the petty cash imprest system and its advantages.

6. Enter transactions in a columnar petty cash book using the imprest system, and post these to the appropriate ledger accounts.

 14.1 Introduction

The **petty cash book** is used to record the receipt and payment of small amounts of cash. Any large amounts of cash received and cash takings are usually paid into the bank and thus recorded in the cash book. The petty cash book is written up from receipts and petty cash vouchers (where employees are reimbursed expenses).

The petty cash book is used instead of a cash ledger account in the general ledger. This is because there usually are a large number of transactions in cash, and if these were recorded in a cash ledger account in the general ledger it would become cumbersome. Like the cash book, it also permits a division of labour and facilitates improved control. In addition to being a book of prime entry, the petty cash book is part of the double-entry system. Thus, debits in this book are credited to a ledger account in the general ledger and no further entries are necessary. Similarly, credits in this book are debited to a ledger account in the general ledger and no further entries are necessary.

14.2 The columnar petty cash book

It is usual for a **(columnar) petty cash book** to have analysis columns on the credit side. Each column relates to a particular type of expenditure, such as postage, stationery or travelling expenses. These are intended to facilitate the posting of entries to the general ledger. Every item of expenditure is entered in both the credit column and an appropriate analysis column. At the end of each calendar week or month the total of each analysis column is debited to the relevant ledger account in the general ledger. Thus, instead of posting each transaction to the general ledger separately, expenditure of the same type is collected together in each analysis column and the total for the period posted to the relevant ledger account.

14.3 The imprest system

Many firms also operate their petty cash on an **imprest system**. At the beginning of each period (week or month) the petty cashier has a fixed amount of cash referred to as a **float**. At the end of each period (or the start of the next) the petty cashier is reimbursed the exact amount spent during the period, thus making the float up to its original amount. The reimbursement usually takes the form of a cheque drawn for cash. The amount of the petty cash float is determined by reference to the normal level of petty cash expenditure in each period.

The advantages of the imprest system are as follows:

1 It facilitates control of the total petty cash expenditure in each period as the petty cashier cannot spend more than the amount of the float, except by applying to the management for an increase.

2 It deters theft of cash by the petty cashier since a large cash balance cannot be accumulated by drawing cash from the bank at irregular intervals.

3 The entries in the petty cash book are kept up to date because the cash expenditure is not reimbursed until the petty cash book is written up and the total amount of expenditure for the period is known.

4 It discourages the practice of loans and subs from petty cash since these would have to be accounted for at the end of the period, and in addition may result in insufficient cash to meet the necessary expenditure.

An illustration of a columnar petty cash book and the imprest system is shown in Example 14.1.

EXAMPLE
14.1

A. Stone uses a columnar petty cash book to record his cash payments. He also operates an imprest system with a float of £150. During August 20X2 the cash transactions were as follows:

1 Aug Postage stamps: £5

2 Aug Cleaning materials: £13

4 Aug Recorded delivery: £2

5 Aug Gratuity to delivery man: £4

7 Aug Tea, milk, etc.: £1

9 Aug Rail fare: £11

10 Aug Paper clips and pens: £6

13 Aug Window cleaner: £10

18 Aug Travelling expenses: £7

21 Aug Envelopes: £3

22 Aug Postage stamps: £9

24 Aug Stationery: £14

27 Aug Taxi fare: £12

28 Aug Office cleaning: £8

31 Aug Received reimbursement to make float up to £150

You are required to make the necessary entries in the petty cash book using appropriate analysis columns, and show the relevant general ledger account entries.

The petty cash book

Debit			Credit					
Amount	Date	Details	Amount	Telephone and postage	Cleaning	Printing and stationery	Travelling expenses	Miscellaneous expenses
£			£	£	£	£	£	£
	20X2							
b/d 150	1 Aug	Stamps	5	5				
	2 Aug	Materials	13		13			
	4 Aug	Recorded delivery	2	2				
	5 Aug	Gratuity	4					4
	7 Aug	Tea and milk	1					1
	9 Aug	Rail fare	11				11	
	10 Aug	Clips and pens	6			6		
	13 Aug	Windows	10		10			
	18 Aug	Travelling	7				7	
	21 Aug	Envelopes	3			3		
	22 Aug	Stamps	9	9				
	24 Aug	Stationery	14			14		
	27 Aug	Taxi	12				12	
	28 Aug	Office	8		8			
105	31 Aug	Reimbursement	105	16	31	23	30	5
	31 Aug	Balance c/d	150					
255			255					
b/d 150	1 Sep							

In some firms the cash reimbursement is made at the beginning of the next period, in which case the entries are as follows (highlighted by shading):

Debit				Credit					
Amount	Date	Details	Amount	Telephone and postage	Cleaning	Printing and stationery	Travelling expenses	Miscellaneous expenses	
£			£	£	£	£	£	£	
	31 Aug	Totals	105	16	31	23	30	5	
	31 Aug	Balance c/d	45						
150			150						
b/d 45									
105	1 Sep	Reimbursement							
150									

Ledger entries			
Telephone and postage			
20X2	**Details**	**£**	
31 Aug	Total per PCB	16	

Cleaning			
20X2	**Details**	**£**	
31 Aug	Total per PCB	31	

Printing and stationery			
20X2	**Details**	**£**	
31 Aug	Total per PCB	23	

Travelling expenses			
20X2	**Details**	**£**	
31 Aug	Total per PCB	30	

Miscellaneous expenses			
20X2	**Details**	**£**	
31 Aug	Total per PCB	5	

Cash book (bank account)					
20X2	**Details**	**£**	**20X2**	**Details**	**£**
31 Aug	Balance b/d	xxxx	31 Aug	Total per PCB	105

Notes

1 When designing a columnar petty cash book it is necessary first to decide on the appropriate number of analysis columns. This is done by identifying the number of different types of expenditure for which there is more than one transaction. In Example 14.1 there are four different types, namely postage, cleaning, stationery and travelling expenses. These four, plus a column for miscellaneous expenses, give five columns. The headings for each of these columns should be the same as the name of the general ledger account to which the total of the column will be posted.

2 The details column of the petty cash book is used to describe the nature of each transaction, rather than the name of the general ledger account containing the double entry, since this is given at the head of the analysis column in which the item is entered.

3 The items entered in the miscellaneous expenses column sometimes have to be posted to several different ledger accounts according to the nature of each transaction.

4 When cash is withdrawn from the bank to restore the float to its original amount the ledger entry consists of:

Debit: Petty cash book

Credit: Cash book (bank account)

LEARNING ACTIVITY 14.1

Prepare a columnar petty cash book for your cash transactions over the forthcoming week or month. Make the necessary double entry in the other ledger accounts.

Summary

The petty cash book is both a book of prime entry and a part of the double-entry system in the ledger, and thus has the same format as a ledger account. It is used to record cash receipts and payments, and is written up from copies of the receipts and petty cash vouchers. The petty cash book replaces the cash ledger account in the general ledger, and thus entries in this book need only to be posted to the opposite side of the relevant ledger accounts.

The most common form of petty cash book is a columnar petty cash book. This has several analysis columns on the credit side, each relating to a particular type of expenditure. These columns are memoranda, and essentially intended to serve the same purpose as day books; namely, to facilitate the periodic bulk posting of transactions of the same type.

Many organizations also operate their petty cash on an imprest system. This essentially comprises a fixed cash float that is replenished at the end of each period by an amount equal to that period's cash expenditure. The imprest system has several very important advantages including facilitating control of the total cash expenditure for a period, deterring the theft of cash, discouraging cash loans/subs, and ensuring that the entries in the petty cash book are kept up to date.

Key terms and concepts

An asterisk after the question number indicates that there is a suggested answer on the Online Learning Centre (www.mcgraw-hill.co.uk/textbooks/thomas).

connect Review questions

14.1   a   Describe the purpose and format of a columnar petty cash book.

       b   Explain how you would determine the appropriate number of analysis columns.

14.2   a   Describe how a petty cash imprest system operates.

       b   Explain how such a system facilitates control.

connect Exercises

BASIC

14.3*

C. Harlow has a petty cash book that is used to record his cash receipts and payments. This also incorporates an imprest system that has a float of £400. During February 20X4 the following cash transactions took place:

  1 Feb   Purchases: £31

  3 Feb   Wages: £28

  6 Feb   Petrol for delivery van: £9

  8 Feb   Bus fares: £3

11 Feb   Pens and pencils: £8

12 Feb   Payments for casual labour: £25

14 Feb   Repairs to delivery van: £17

16 Feb   Copying paper: £15

19 Feb   Goods for resale: £22

20 Feb   Train fares: £12

21 Feb   Repairs to premises: £35

22 Feb   Postage stamps: £6

23 Feb   Drawings: £20

24 Feb   Taxi fares: £7

25 Feb   Envelopes: £4

26 Feb   Purchases: £18

27 Feb   Wages: £30

28 Feb   Petrol for delivery van: £14

On 28 February 20X4 the cash float was restored to £400.

Record the above in the petty cash book using appropriate analysis columns and make the necessary entries in the ledger.

14.4

The Oakhill Printing Co. Ltd operates its petty cash account on the imprest system. It is maintained at a figure of £80 on the first day of each month. At 30 April 20X3 the petty cash box held £19.37 in cash. During May 20X3, the following petty cash transactions arose:

		£
1 May	Cash received to restore imprest	to be derived
1 May	Bus fares	0.41
2 May	Stationery	2.35
4 May	Bus fares	0.30
7 May	Postage stamps	1.70
7 May	Trade journal	0.95
8 May	Bus fares	0.64
11 May	Correcting fluid	1.29
12 May	Printer ink cartridge	5.42
14 May	Parcel postage	3.45
15 May	Paper clips	0.42
15 May	Newspapers	2.00
16 May	Photocopier repair	16.80
19 May	Postage stamps	1.50
20 May	Drawing pins	0.38
21 May	Train fare	5.40
22 May	Photocopier paper	5.63
23 May	Display decorations	3.07
23 May	Correcting fluid	1.14
25 May	Wrapping paper	0.78
27 May	String	0.61
27 May	Sellotape	0.75
27 May	Biro pens	0.46
28 May	Replacement laser mouse	13.66
30 May	Bus fares	2.09
1 June	Cash received to restore imprest	to be derived

Required

Open and post the company's petty cash account for the period 1 May to 1 June 20X3 inclusive and balance the account at 30 May 20X3.

In order to facilitate the subsequent double-entry postings, all items of expense appearing in the 'payments' column should then be analysed individually into suitably labelled expense columns.

(ACCA)

BASIC

14.5

Belfast cleaning company operates its petty cash account using an imprest system. It is maintained at a figure of £100 on the first day of each month. At 31 December 20X2 £21.48 was held in the petty cash box. During January 20X3, the following petty cash transactions arose:

		£
1 Jan	Cash received to restore imprest	to be derived
1 Jan	Postage	0.63
2 Jan	Taxi	4.25
4 Jan	Pens	8.56
7 Jan	Bus fare	1.90
8 Jan	Paper clips	3.56
9 Jan	Brown envelopes	5.68
11 Jan	Bus fare	1.90
12 Jan	Taxi fare	5.00
12 Jan	Coffee	8.25
13 Jan	Rulers	6.50
15 Jan	Taxi fare	4.50
17 Jan	Box of envelopes	12.80
19 Jan	Sandwiches for guests	15.60
20 Jan	Toilet roll	4.59
21 Jan	Taxi	5.25
25 Jan	Stamps	1.31
28 Jan	Recorded delivery	2.49
31 Jan	Bus fare	1.45
1 Feb	Cash received to restore imprest	to be derived

Required

Open and post the company's petty cash account for the period 1 January to 1 February 20X3 inclusive and balance the account at 31 January 20X3.

All items of expense appearing in the 'payments' column should be analysed and posted to the respective ledger accounts.

BASIC

14.6

London Printing Co. has an opening balance on its cash account on 1 January of £20.00. A cheque for £100 is cashed on the first of each month to cover that month's potential petty cash requirements. The secretary records the expenses manually for the month in a cash journal which analyses the transactions according to the ledger accounts utilised in the trial balance. The company does not operate an imprest system.

The total petty cash spend for January, February and March is as follows:

January totals					
Stationery	Postage	Travel	Sundries	Cleaning wages	Drawings
£15.68	£25.36	£32.00	£16.58	£36.00	£10.00

February totals					
Stationery	Postage	Travel	Sundries	Cleaning wages	Drawings
£14.50	£3.50	£45.00	£25.00	£36.00	–

March totals					
Stationery	Postage	Travel	Sundries	Cleaning wages	Drawings
£8.56	£5.60	£28.00	£31.50	£36.00	£20.00

Required

Write up the general ledger accounts for the three months January to March.

When you have read this chapter, log on to the Online Learning Centre for *Introduction to Financial Accounting* at www.mcgraw-hill.co.uk/textbooks/thomas, where you will find multiple choice quizzes, case studies, a glossary and mock exams.

Preparing final financial statements for sole traders

The final financial statements of sole traders (introductory)

Learning Objectives

After reading this chapter you should be able to do the following:

1 Explain the meaning of the key terms and concepts listed at the end of the chapter.

2 Explain the purpose and structure of statements of profit and loss.

3 Explain the purpose and structure of statements of financial position.

4 Describe the nature of administrative expenses, selling and distribution expenses, non-current assets, current assets, current liabilities, non-current liabilities and capital.

5 Explain the relevance of inventory and the cost of sales in the determination of gross profit.

6 Prepare a simple statement of profit and loss and statement of financial position from a trial balance using either an account/horizontal format or a vertical format.

7 Make all the necessary general ledger account and journal entries relating to the preparation of a statement of profit and loss account and the resulting statement of profit and loss that is prepared for users.

15.1 Introduction

Final financial statements consist of a **statement of comprehensive income** (or **statement of profit and loss**) and a statement of financial position. These are prepared at the end of a business's accounting year after the trial balance has been completed. Some businesses also produce final financial statements half yearly, quarterly or even monthly. Pro forma financial statements for sole traders, partnerships and companies are provided in Chapter 1, 'Entities and Financial Reporting Statements'. This chapter focuses on the preparation of financial statements for sole traders. The purpose, structure and preparation of the statement of profit and loss and statement of financial position are discussed below. Sole traders rarely have unrealized gains or losses; therefore, a full statement of comprehensive income is not prepared.

15.2 The purpose and structure of statements of profit and loss

The **statement of profit and loss** provides a summary of the results of a business's trading activities during a given accounting year. It shows the profit or loss for the year. The purpose of a statement of profit and loss is to enable users of financial statements, such as the owner, to evaluate the financial performance of a business for a given accounting year. It may be used to determine the amount of taxation on the profit.

Chapter 8, 'The Accounting Equation and its Components', explained that **profit** can be defined as the amount that could be taken out of a business as drawings in the case of a sole trader or partnership, or is available for distribution as dividends to shareholders in the case of a company, after maintaining the value of the **capital** of a business. Profit is not the same as an increase in the amount of money the business possesses. It is the result of applying certain accounting principles to the transactions of the business. These were described in detail in Chapter 5, 'Accounting Principles, Concepts and Policies'.

The basic format of the statement of profit and loss is shown in Figure 15.1.

ABC		
Statement of profit and loss for the year ended . . .		
	£	£
Revenue		X
Less: cost of sales		<u>X</u>
Gross profit		X
Less: other costs and expenses:		
Selling and distribution costs	X	
Administrative expenses	X	
Interest payable on loans	<u>X</u>	
		X
Profit/(Loss) for the period		<u>X</u>

Figure 15.1 An example of the layout of a statement of profit and loss for a sole trader

In the financial statements of sole traders and partnerships, the actual composition of each of the above groupings of costs would be shown in detail. Selling and distribution costs include advertising expenditure, the wages of delivery-van drivers, motor expenses including petrol and repairs, and so on. Administrative expenses usually comprise the salaries of office staff, rent and rates, light and heat, printing and stationery, telephone and postage, and so on. The published final financial statements of companies contain a classification of costs similar to that shown above.

15.3 Gross profit: inventory and the cost of sales

The first stage in the determination of the profit for the year involves calculating gross profit. It is usually carried out in the statement of profit and loss. However, this part of the statement of profit and loss is sometimes presented as a separate account referred to as the 'trading account'.

The **gross profit** for a given period is computed by subtracting the cost of goods sold/cost of sales from sales revenue. It is important to appreciate that the cost of goods sold is not usually the same as the amount of purchases. This is because most businesses will have purchased goods that are unsold at the end of the accounting period. These goods are referred to as **inventory**. The cost of inventory unsold is carried forward into the next accounting period to be matched against the income that it generates (matching concept), by being transferred to the statement of financial position at the end of the year.

A manufacturing business will have a number of different types of inventory. However, for simplicity, the following exposition is confined to non-manufacturing businesses whose inventory consists of goods purchased for resale that have not undergone any further processing by the entity.

The **cost of sales** is determined by taking the cost of goods in inventory at the start of the period, adding to this the cost of goods purchased during the period, and subtracting the cost of goods unsold at the end of the period. The cost of sales is then deducted from the sales revenue to give the gross profit. This is illustrated in Example 15.1.

EXAMPLE 15.1	S. Mann, whose accounting year ends on 30 April, buys and sells one type of product. On 1 May 20X3 there were 50 units in inventory that had cost £100 each. During the subsequent accounting year he purchased a further 500 units at a cost of £100 each and sold 450 units at a price of £150 each. There were 100 units that cost £100 each that had not been sold at 30 April 20X4. You are required to compute the gross profit for the year.	

	S. Mann		
	Trading account for the year ended 30 April 20X4		
Units		**£**	**£**
<u>450</u>	Sales revenue		67,500
	Less: Cost of goods sold:		
50	Inventory of goods at 1 May 20X3	5,000	
<u>500</u>	*Add:* Goods purchased during the year	<u>50,000</u>	
550	Cost of goods available for sale	55,000	
<u>100</u>	*Less:* Inventory of goods at 30 April 20X4	<u>10,000</u>	
<u>450</u>	Cost of sales		45,000
	Gross profit for the year		<u>22,500</u>

Note

1 The number of units is not usually shown in a trading account. They have been included in the above to demonstrate that the cost of sales relates to the number of units that were sold.

The trading account

The **trading account** is an account in the general ledger and is thus a part of the double-entry system. It is used to ascertain the gross profit and is prepared by transferring the balances on the sales revenue, purchases and returns ledger accounts to the trading ledger account. In addition, certain entries are required in respect of inventory. These are as follows:

1 Inventory at the start of the period:

Debit: Trading account

Credit: Inventory account

2 Inventory at the end of the period:

Debit: Inventory account

Credit: Trading account

Note that the inventory at the start of the period will be the inventory at the end of the previous period. This is a statement of financial position account. The ledger entries in respect of inventories are illustrated in Example 15.2 using the data in Example 15.1.

EXAMPLE 15.2

Prior to the preparation of the trading account the ledger will appear as follows:

Sales revenue

20X4	Details	£	20X4	Details	£
			30 Apr	Balance b/d	67,500

Purchases

20X4	Details	£			
30 Apr	Balance b/d	50,000			

Inventory

20X3	Details	£			
30 Apr	Balance b/d	5,000			

The trading income account will then be prepared as follows:

Sales revenue

20X4	Details	£	20X4	Details	£
30 Apr	Trading account	67,500	30 Apr	Balance b/d	67,500

Purchases

20X4	Details	£	20X4	Details	£
30 Apr	Balance b/d	50,000	30 Apr	Trading account	50,000

Inventory

20X3	Details	£	20X4	Details	£
1 May	Balance b/d	5,000	30 Apr	Trading account	5,000
20X4					
30 Apr	Trading account	10,000			

	S. Mann				
	Trading income account for year ending 30 April 20X4				
		£			£
Inventory at 1 May 20X3		5,000	Sales revenue		67,500
Purchases		50,000	Inventory at 30 April 20X4		10,000
Gross profit c/d		22,500			
		77,500			77,500
			Gross profit b/d		22,500

Notes

1 The gross profit is the difference between the two sides of the trading account and must be brought down to the opposite side of the account.

2 No date columns are shown in the trading account since the date appears as part of the heading of the account.

3 When the trading account is prepared in account form the inventory at the end of the year may be shown as either a credit entry or deducted on the debit side as shown below. This has the advantage of showing the cost of sales.

S. Mann				
Trading account for the year ended 30 April 20X4				
	£			£
Opening inventory	5,000	Sales revenue		67,500
Add: Purchases	50,000			
	55,000			
Less: Closing inventory	10,000			
Cost of sales	45,000			
Gross profit c/d	22,500			
	67,500			67,500
		Gross profit b/d		22,500

4 The trading income account is a ledger account in the general ledger and thus part of the double-entry system. However, when it is prepared for submission to the management, the owner(s) of a business or Revenue and Customs, it is often presented vertically as shown at the start of Example 15.1.

5 No entries other than those shown above (and the correction of errors) should be made in an inventory account. It is not a continuous record of the value of inventory.

6 The inventory shown in a trial balance will always be that at the end of the previous year (and thus the opening inventory of the year to which the trial balance relates).

The statement of profit and loss

The statement of profit and loss is taken from a ledger account in the general ledger (called the profit and loss account) and thus is a part of the double-entry system. It is used to ascertain the **profit** (or **loss) for the period** and is prepared in the same way as the trading account. That is, the balances on the income and expense ledger accounts in the general ledger are transferred to the profit and loss account by means of double entry.

An explanation of the statement of profit and loss is provided by Times 100 Advice (Online) as follows:

Times100 advice on the statement of profit and loss

REAL WORLD
EXAMPLE
15.1

The statement of profit and loss (P&L).

This statement can be updated regularly and shows how much profit or loss a business is making. A profit can be made in several ways, for example:

- from trading, in the case of a High Street shop, i.e. buying and selling items such as clothes and furniture
- from manufacturing, for example a company like Kraft produces chocolate bars and other foodstuffs. It buys in raw materials such as cocoa and sugar which it processes to make chocolate.'

Read more: http://www.thetimes100.co.uk/theory/
theory–profit-loss-accounts-balance-sheet–125.php#ixzz1HExBlIi6.

15.4 The purpose and structure of a statement of financial position

The **statement of financial position** is a list of the assets, liabilities and capital of a business at the end of a given accounting period. It therefore provides information about the resources and debts of the reporting entity. The statement of financial position enables users of financial statements to evaluate the entity's financial position, in particular whether the business is likely to be unable to pay its debts. The statement of financial position is like a photograph of the financial state of affairs of a business at a specific time.

Statements of financial position contain five groups of items, as follows.

1 Non-current assets

These are items not specifically bought for resale but to be used in the production or distribution of those goods normally sold by the business. They are utilized to generate economic inflows to the entity. **Non-current assets** are durable goods that usually last for several years, and are normally kept by a business for more than one accounting year. Examples of non-current assets include land and buildings, plant and machinery, motor vehicles, office equipment, furniture, fixtures and fittings. These are tangible assets. The different types are recorded in separate ledger accounts with the balances on each account being disclosed in the statement of financial position.

In company financial statements tangible non-current assets are collectively referred to as 'property, plant and equipment' – only one combined figure would be disclosed in a company's statement of financial position.

2 Current assets

These are items that are normally kept by a business for less than one accounting year. Indeed, the composition of each type of current asset is usually continually changing. Examples include inventories, trade receivables, short-term investments, money in a bank account and cash.

3 Equity capital

This refers to the amount of money invested in the business by the owner(s). This can take the form of cash introduced or profits not withdrawn.

4 Non-current liabilities

These are debts owed by a business that are not due until after one year (often much longer) from the date of the statement of financial position. Examples include loans and mortgages.

5 Current liabilities

These are debts owed by a business that are payable within one year (often considerably less) from the date of the statement of financial position. Examples include trade payables and bank overdrafts.

The structure of a statement of financial position is shown in Figure 15.2. Note that the items shown in bold are subtotals or totals that should be shown on the statement of financial position.

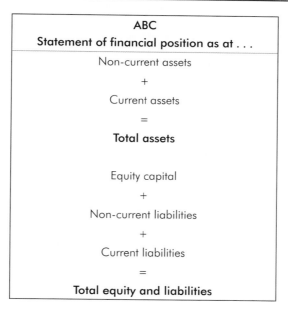

ABC
Statement of financial position as at . . .

Non-current assets

+

Current assets

=

Total assets

Equity capital

+

Non-current liabilities

+

Current liabilities

=

Total equity and liabilities

Figure 15.2 An example of the key areas covered in a statement of financial position for a sole trader

LEARNING ACTIVITY **15.1**

Prepare a statement of financial position listing your assets and liabilities, or those of your family. Use an appropriate method of classifying the assets and liabilities and show the relevant totals and subtotals.

15.5 Preparing financial statements from the trial balance

In practice, and in examinations, it is usual to prepare final financial statements from the information given in the trial balance. However, it is important to appreciate that the general ledger entries described above to close the income and expenditure ledger accounts also have to be done, although students are not normally expected to show them in their answer to examination questions.

An illustration of the preparation of final financial statements, including the required ledger entries, is shown in Example 15.3.

EXAMPLE
15.3

The following is the trial balance of A. Dillon at 31 March 20X3:		
	Debit	Credit
	£	£
Capital		42,140
Drawings	13,600	
Loan from S. Rodd		10,000
Bank	5,800	
Cash	460	
Sales revenue		88,400
Purchases	46,300	
Sales returns	5,700	
Purchases returns		3,100
Inventory at 1 Apr 20X2	8,500	
Carriage inwards	2,400	
Carriage outwards	1,600	
Trade receivables	15,300	
Trade payables		7,200
Motor vehicles	23,100	
Fixtures and fittings	12,400	
Wages and salaries	6,800	
Rent	4,100	
Light and heat	3,200	
Telephone and postage	1,700	
Discount allowed	830	
Discount received		950
	151,790	151,790

The inventory at 31 March 20X3 was valued at £9,800. The loan from S. Rodd is repayable on 1 January 20X5.

Required

Prepare the statement of profit and loss and statement of financial position (horizontal format) for A. Dillon from the trial balance provided.

Sales revenue			
Trading a/c	88,400	Balance b/d	88,400

Sales returns			
Balance b/d	5,700	Trading a/c	5,700

Purchases			
Balance b/d	46,300	Trading a/c	46,300

Purchases returns			
Trading a/c	3,100	Balance b/d	3,100

Inventories			
Balance b/d	8,500	Trading a/c	8,500
Trading a/c	9,800		

Carriage inwards			
Balance b/d	2,400	Trading a/c	2,400

Carriage outwards			
Balance b/d	1,600	Profit and loss a/c	1,600

Wages and salaries			
Balance b/d	6,800	Profit and loss a/c	6,800

Rent			
Balance b/d	4,100	Profit and loss a/c	4,100

Light and heat			
Balance b/d	3,200	Profit and loss a/c	3,200

Telephone and postage			
Balance b/d	1,700	Profit and loss a/c	1,700

Discount allowed			
Balance b/d	830	Profit and loss a/c	830

Discount received			
Profit and loss a/c	950	Balance b/d	950

Drawings			
Balance b/d	13,600	Capital a/c	13,600

All other accounts contain only the balances shown in the trial balance.

A. Dillon

Trading and profit and loss account for the year ended 31 March 20X3

	£	£		£
Inventory at 1 Apr 20X2		8,500	Sales revenue	88,400
Purchases	46,300		Less: returns	5,700
Less: Returns	3,100			82,700
	43,200			
Add: Carriage inwards	2,400	45,600		
		54,100		
Less: Inventory at 31 Mar 20X3		9,800		
Cost of sales		44,300		
Gross profit c/d to P/L a/c		38,400		
		82,700		82,700
Carriage outwards		1,600	Gross profit b/d from trading a/c	38,400
Wages and salaries		6,800	Discount received	950
Rent		4,100		
Light and heat		3,200		
Telephone and postage		1,700		
Discount allowed		830		
Profit for the period c/d		21,120		
		39,350		39,350
Capital a/c (Profit transferred)		21,120	Profit for the year b/d	21,120
		Capital		
Drawings		13,600	Balance b/d	42,140
Balance b/d		49,660	Profit and loss a/c	21,120
		63,260		63,260
			Balance b/d	49,660

Notes

1 The trading account is combined with the profit and loss account (top half) in this example. The gross profit is the difference between the two sides of the trading account and must be brought down to the opposite side of the profit and loss account.

2 The profit for the period is the difference between the two sides of the profit and loss account. This is brought down to the credit side of the profit and loss account and then transferred to the capital account by debiting the profit and loss account and crediting the capital account. The reason for this transfer is because the profit belongs to the owner and it increases the amount of capital he or she is entitled to withdraw from the business.

3 If the debit side of the profit and loss account exceeds the credit side, this is shown as a net loss (carried down) on the credit side and debited to the capital account.

4 The balance on the drawings account at the end of the period must be transferred to the capital account.

5 Each of the transfers from the ledger accounts to the trading income and profit and loss ledger account should also be entered in the journal.

A. Dillon					
Statement of financial position as at 31 March 20X3					
Credit	**£**	**Debit**	**£**	**£**	
EQUITY AND LIABILITIES		ASSETS			
Equity capital		**Non-current assets**			
Balance at 1 Apr 20X2	42,140	Motor vehicles		23,100	
Add: *Profit for year*	21,120	Fixtures and fittings		12,400	
	63,260			35,500	
Less: *Drawings*	13,600	**Current assets**			
Balance at 31 Mar 20X3	49,660	Inventories	9,800		
Non-current liabilities		Trade receivables	15,300		
Loan from S. Rodd	10,000	Bank	5,800		
Current liabilities		Cash	460		
Trade payables	7,200			31,360	
	66,860			66,860	

6 Notice that the debit balances remaining in the ledger after the profit and loss account has been prepared are shown on the right-hand side of the statement of financial position and the credit balances on the left-hand side. This may seem inconsistent with the debit and credit sides of the ledger being on the left and right, respectively. However, it is a common form of presentation in accounting.

7 Like the trial balance, the total of each side of the statement of financial position should be the same. That is, the total of the ledger accounts with debit balances should equal the total of the ledger accounts with credit balances. If this is not the case, it indicates that an error has occurred in the preparation of the trading income and profit and loss account (or the statement of financial position).

8 The current assets in the statement of financial position are shown in what is called their 'reverse order of liquidity'. The latter refers to how easily assets can be turned into cash.

9 The entries on the statement of financial position in respect of capital are a summary of the movements in the capital account in the ledger.

10 Carriage inwards is added to the cost of purchases because it relates to the haulage costs of goods purchased. Carriage outwards is shown in the statement of profit and loss account because it relates to the haulage costs of goods sold and is thus a selling and distribution expense.

When the statement of profit and loss and statement of financial position are presented to the owner(s) of a business and HM Revenue and Customs, it is common to use a vertical format. This is illustrated next using the data in Example 15.3. This format is adapted from the suggested formats for statements of profit and loss under IAS 1 – *Presentation of Financial Statements* as it is deemed to provide the most useful information to the users; therefore, is utilized in this book from now on.

A. Dillon
Statement of profit and loss for the year ending 31 March 20X3

	£	£	£
Sales revenue			88,400
Less: Returns			5,700
			82,700
Less: Cost of sales:			
Inventory at 1 Apr 20X2		8,500	
Add: Purchases	46,300		
Less: Returns	3,100		
		43,200	
Add: Carriage inwards		2,400	
		54,100	
Less: Inventory at 31 Mar 20X3		9,800	
			44,300
Gross profit			38,400
Add: Discount received			950
			39,350
Less: Expenditure:			
Carriage outwards		1,600	
Wages and salaries		6,800	
Rent		4,100	
Light and heat		3,200	
Telephone and postage		1,700	
Discount allowed		830	18,230
Profit for the year			21,120

A. Dillon
Statement of financial position as at 31 March 20X3

ASSETS	£
Non-current assets	
Motor vehicles	23,100
Fixtures and fittings	12,400
	35,500
Current assets	
Inventories	9,800
Trade receivables	15,300
Bank	5,800
Cash	460
	31,360
Total assets	66,860

```
OWNER'S EQUITY AND LIABILITIES
Owner's capital
Balance at 1 Apr 20X2                          42,140
Add: Profit for year                           21,120
                                               63,260
Less: Drawings                                 13,600
Balance at 31 Mar 20X3                         49,660
Non-current liabilities
Loan from S. Rodd                              10,000
Current liabilities
Trade payables                                  7,200
Total liabilities                              17,200
Total equity and liabilities                   66,860
```

Summary

Final financial statements comprise a statement of profit and loss and a statement of financial position. These are prepared at the end of the accounting year after the trial balance has been completed. The statement of comprehensive income can be split into three parts: the first focuses on calculating the gross profit for the period and is commonly referred to as the 'trading account'; the next part includes all the other realized income and expenditure for the period and determines the profit/loss for the period; and the final part considers other unrealized gains or losses in the period, such as asset revaluation increases. Sole traders prepare a statement of profit and loss because they rarely disclose unrealized gains or losses. The statement of profit and loss enables users to evaluate the performance of the enterprise. The statement of financial position is a list of the assets and liabilities (and capital) of a business at the end of a given accounting year. It enables users to evaluate the financial position of the enterprise, including whether it is likely to be able to pay its debts. In the statement of financial position, assets are classified as either non-current or current, and liabilities as either current or non-current.

The gross profit is the difference between the sales revenue and the cost of sales. The cost of sales is the amount of purchases as adjusted for the opening and closing inventories. The inventory at the end of an accounting year has to be entered in the general ledger by debiting an inventory account and crediting the trading income account. The trading income and profit and loss accounts are then prepared by transferring the balances on the income and expense accounts in the general ledger to these ledger accounts.

The statement of financial position is a list of the balances remaining in the ledger after the trading income and profit and loss ledger accounts have been prepared. It is extracted in essentially the same way as a trial balance, but presented using a more formal layout to show the two groups of both assets and liabilities, and pertinent subtotals.

> ## Key terms and concepts
>
> | | | | |
> |---|---|---|---|
> | capital | 218 | non-current assets | 222 |
> | cost of sales | 219 | non-current liabilities | 223 |
> | current assets | 222 | profit | 218 |
> | current liabilities | 223 | profit for the period | 221 |
> | equity capital | 222 | statement of comprehensive | |
> | final financial statements | 217 | income | 217 |
> | gross profit | 219 | statement of financial position | 222 |
> | inventory | 219 | statement of profit and loss | 217 |
> | loss for the period | 221 | trading account | 219 |

An asterisk after the question number indicates that there is a suggested answer on the Online Learning Centre (www.mcgraw-hill.co.uk/textbooks/thomas).

connect Review questions

15.1 a Explain the purposes of a statement of profit and loss and a statement of financial position.

   b Describe the structure of each.

15.2 Explain the relevance of inventory in the determination of gross profit.

15.3 Explain each of the entries in the following inventory account:

Inventory			
Trading a/c	4,600	Trading a/c	4,600
Trading a/c	6,300		

connect Exercises

BASIC

15.4

A company has 100 units in inventory at the start of the year valued at £1,000. During the year it purchases a further 500 units for £5,000 and sells 400 units for £8,000.

Required

a What is the quantity and value of the closing inventories?

b What is the gross profit for the year?

c Prepare the trading account for the year.

15.5

Balances on the main inventory accounts are as follows:

– sales revenue	£18,000
– purchases	£12,000
– opening inventory	£1,000
– returns inward	£1,500
– returns outward	£500
– carriage outward	£200
– carriage inward	£900
– discount received	£1,000

The closing inventory count reveals inventory of £1,500.

Required

Determine the gross profit.

15.6

Extract the statement of profit and loss for the year ended 31 December 20X2 for M. McKee and the statement of financial position as at 31 December 20X2 from the following.

M. McKee Trial balance at 31 December 20X2		
	Dr	Cr
	£	£
Capital		66,405
Drawings	5,258	
Cash at bank	4,200	
Buildings	30,000	
Fixtures	18,750	
Trade receivables	15,250	
Trade payables		8,750
Motor vans	2,500	
Purchases	86,452	
Sales revenue		109,250
General expenses	5,250	
Salaries	13,560	
Motor expenses	1,365	
Lighting and heating	890	
Insurance	550	
Rent	380	
	184,405	184,405

Additional information

Inventory at the year end was £11,000.

BASIC

15.7*

The following is the trial balance of R. Woods as at 30 September 20X3:

	Debit	Credit
	£	£
Inventory 1 Oct 20X2	2,368	
Purchases	12,389	
Sales revenue		18,922
Salaries and wages	3,862	
Rent and rates	504	
Insurance	78	
Motor expenses	664	
Printing and stationery	216	
Light and heat	166	
General expenses	314	
Premises	5,000	
Motor vehicles	1,800	
Fixtures and fittings	350	
Trade receivables	3,896	
Trade payables		1,731
Cash at bank	482	
Drawings	1,200	
Capital		12,636
	33,289	33,289

The inventory at 30 September 20X3 is valued at £2,946.

Required

Prepare a statement of profit and loss for the year ended 30 September 20X3 and a statement of financial position at that date (publishable format).

15.8

On 31 December 20X3, the trial balance of Joytoys showed the following chart of accounts and balances:

	Debit	Credit
	£	£
Bank	500	
Capital		75,000
Bank loan		22,000
Inventory	12,000	
Purchases	108,000	
Sales revenue		167,000
Rent, rates and insurance	15,000	
Plant and machinery at cost	70,000	
Office furniture and fittings at cost	24,000	
Discount allowed	1,600	
Bank interest	400	
Discount received		3,000
Wages and salaries	13,000	
Light and heat	9,000	
Drawings	10,000	
Returns outwards		4,000
Returns inwards	1,000	
Trade payables		16,000
Trade receivables	22,500	
	287,000	287,000

Additional information

1 The inventory at 31 December 20X3 was valued at £19,500.

2 The bank loan is repayable in five years' time.

Required

Prepare a statement of profit and loss for the year ended 31 December 20X3 and a statement of financial position at that date (publishable format).

15.9*

The following is the trial balance of A. Evans as at 30 June 20X3:

	Debit	Credit
	£	£
Capital		39,980
Drawings	14,760	
Loan – Solihull Bank		20,000
Leasehold premises	52,500	
Motor vehicles	13,650	
Investments	4,980	
Trade receivables	2,630	
Trade payables		1,910
Cash	460	
Bank overdraft		3,620
Sales revenue		81,640
Purchases	49,870	
Returns outwards		960
Returns inwards	840	
Carriage outwards	390	
Inventory	5,610	
Rent and rates	1,420	
Light and heat	710	
Telephone and postage	540	
Printing and stationery	230	
Bank interest	140	
Interest received		620
	148,730	148,730

Additional information

1 The inventory at 30 June 20X3 has been valued at £4,920.

2 The bank loan is repayable on 1 June 20X6.

Required

Prepare a statement of profit and loss for the year ended 30 June 20X3 and a statement of financial position as at that date (publishable format).

15.10

The following is the trial balance of J. Peters as at 30 September 20X3:

	Debit £	Credit £
Capital		32,890
Drawings	5,200	
Loan from A. Drew		10,000
Cash	510	
Bank overdraft		1,720
Sales revenue		45,600
Purchases	29,300	
Returns inwards	3,800	
Returns outwards		2,700
Carriage inwards	960	
Carriage outwards	820	
Trade receivables	7,390	
Trade payables		4,620
Land and buildings	26,000	
Plant and machinery	13,500	
Listed investments	4,800	
Interest paid	1,200	
Interest received		450
Rent received		630
Inventory	3,720	
Repairs to buildings	810	
Plant hire charges	360	
Bank charges	240	
	98,610	98,610

Additional information

1 The inventory at 30 September 20X3 was valued at £4,580.

2 The loan from A. Drew is repayable on 1 January 20X9.

Required

Prepare a statement of profit and loss for the year ended 30 September 20X3 and a statement of financial position as at that date.

15.11

B. Good drew up the following trial balance as at 31 March 20X3. Extract the statement of profit and loss for the year ended 31 March 20X3 and statement of financial position as at that date.

	Debit	Credit
	£	£
Sundry expenses	1,090	
Rent received		200
Office expenses	560	
Insurance	525	
Wages and expenses	4,580	
Telephone	1,250	
Purchases and sales revenue	125,560	189,560
Motor expenses	569	
Rent	2,500	
Rates	1,250	
Carriage outwards	546	
Carriage inwards	200	
Returns outwards		302
Returns inwards	560	
Building	230,000	
Motor vehicle	12,500	
Fixtures	5,365	
Trade receivables and payables	28,560	48,560
Cash	12	
Bank		32,250
Drawings	5,562	
Capital		178,907
Opening inventory	28,590	
	449,779	449,779

Additional information

Inventory at the year end was £35,650.

15.12

The balances extracted from the books of G. Ryan at 31 December 20X2 are given below:

	£
Drawings	7,180
Heating and lighting	1,234
Stationery and postage	268
Carriage outwards	1,446
Insurance	1,818
Wages and salaries	18,910
Inventory at 1 January 20X2	42,120
Purchases	74,700
Sales revenue	131,040
Rent and rates	2,990
General expenses	1,460
Discount received	426
Plant and machinery	9,060
Cash at bank	3,222
Cash in hand	65
Trade receivables	1,920
Trade payables	630
Sales returns	1,310
Purchases returns	747

Additional information

At 31 December 20X2 inventory was valued at £33,990.

Required

a Prepare the statement of profit and loss for the year ended 31 December 20X2.

b Prepare the statement of financial position as at 31 December 20X2.

When you have read this chapter, log on to the Online Learning Centre for *Introduction to Financial Accounting* at www.mcgraw-hill.co.uk/textbooks/thomas, where you will find multiple choice quizzes, case studies, a glossary and mock exams.

15.12

The balances extracted from the books of L. Byrn at 31 December 20X2 are given below:

	£
Drawings	7,180
Heating and lighting	1,634
Postage and carriage	288
Carriage inwards	1,142
Insurance	1,818
Wages and salaries	18,910
Inventory at 1 January 20X2	42,120
Purchases	74,700
Sales revenue	131,040
Rent and rates	2,090
General expenses	980
Discount received	426
Plant and machinery	9,060
Capital bank	13,275
Cash in hand	41
Trade receivables	14,320
Trade payables	690
Sales return	1,870
Purchases return	741

Additional information

At 31 December 20X2 inventory was valued at £33,900

Required

1 Prepare the statement of profit and loss for the year ended 31 December 20X2.

2 Prepare the statement of financial position as at 31 December 20X2.

Depreciation and non-current assets

Learning Objectives

After reading this chapter you should be able to do the following:

1. Explain the meaning of the key terms and concepts listed at the end of this chapter.

2. Distinguish between capital expenditure and revenue expenditure.

3. Describe the nature, recognition and valuation of non-current assets including intangible non-current assets such as goodwill and development expenditure.

4. Apply the criteria relating to the nature of non-current assets to specific transactions and items to determine the most appropriate accounting treatment.

5. Discuss the nature of depreciation.

6. Describe the straight-line, reducing balance and sum of the years' digits methods of depreciating assets including the resulting pattern of charges to the statement of profit and loss over an asset's useful life, and the circumstances in which each might be the most appropriate.

7. Compute the amount of depreciation using the methods in the point above, and show the relevant entries in the journal, general ledger, statement of profit and loss and statement of financial position.

8. Compute the depreciation on an asset in the years of acquisition and disposal, and the profit or loss on disposal; and show the relevant entries in the journal, general ledger, statement of profit and loss and statement of financial position.

16.1 The nature and types of non-current assets

'An asset is a resource controlled by the enterprise as a result of past events and from which future economic benefits are expected to flow to the enterprise' (the *Framework*) (IASC, 1989). The ability to generate future economic benefits is arguably the most important criterion in determining whether expenditure is to be classified as an asset, or not. Assets are categorized as being either current or non-current in the statement of financial position. **Current assets** include assets that are, or will be, turned into cash or near cash in the near future – usually in a period of less than one year. They usually support the operational activities of the entity. Current assets include inventories, trade receivables, short-term financial assets (investments), bank and cash.

Non-current assets are items not specifically bought for resale but to be used in the production or distribution of those goods normally sold by the business. They are durable goods that usually last for several years, and are normally kept by a business for more than one accounting year. However, expenditure on such items is only regarded as a non-current asset if it is of a material amount.

The Accounting Standards Committee (ASC) defines a **non-current asset** as

> an asset that:
>
> a is held by an enterprise for use in the production or supply of goods and services, for rental to others, or for administrative purposes and may include items held for the maintenance or repair of such assets;
>
> b has been acquired or constructed with the intention of being used on a continuing basis; and
>
> c is not intended for sale in the ordinary course of a business.

Money spent on non-current assets is referred to as **capital expenditure**. All other costs and expenses are referred to as **revenue expenditure**. The latter are entered in the statement of profit and loss for the year in which the costs are incurred.

Non-current assets are classified as either tangible or intangible.

Tangible assets

Tangible assets are assets that have physical substance. The accounting for tangible assets can be found in four standards:

1 *International Accounting Standard (IAS) 16 – Property, Plant and Equipment* (IASB, 2010a) is the most relevant when it comes to accounting for sole traders. It outlines the accounting recommended for tangible assets that are most likely to be held by sole traders, such as property, plant and equipment, fixtures and fittings, motor vehicles, office equipment (such as computers) and loose tools. Tools that are only expected to last for less than one year are referred to as 'consumable tools', and treated as revenue expenditure. **Tangible non-current assets** include assets that are held for use in the production or supply of goods or services, or for administrative purposes and are expected to be used during more than one period. This chapter concentrates predominately on the accounting practices suggested in this standard. The other types of tangible asset are now mentioned in brief.

2 *IAS 40 – Investment Property* (IASB, 2010b) provides guidance on accounting for investment properties.

3 *IAS 17 – Leases* (IASB, 2010d) provides guidance on the accounting for leased assets. In brief, captialized leased assets are depreciated in the same manner as assets that are subject to the recommended practices outlined in IAS 16. Leases and accounting for leases is considered to be beyond the scope of this text.

4 *International Financial Reporting Standard 5 – Non-current Assets Held for Sale and Discontinued Operations* (IASB, 2010e) provides guidance on the accounting treatment for assets that are no longer held with long-term prospects in mind. They no longer form part of the business's operational activities. In brief, the standard recommends that these assets be disclosed separately and labelled as being 'held for sale', or 'discontinued', and should be carried at fair value. **Fair value** is defined in the standard as the amount for which an asset could be exchanged between knowledgeable, willing parties in an arm's length transaction – that is, market value. The accounting for non-current assets held for sale and discontinued activities is considered to be beyond the scope of this book.

Intangible assets

Intangible assets are defined in *IAS 38 – Intangible Assets* (IASB, 2010f) as 'identifiable non-monetary assets without physical substance'. Examples include goodwill, patents, trademarks, copyrights, fishing licences, milk quota, franchises, customer or supplier relationships, mortgage servicing rights, customer loyalty, market share, brand name and development expenditure such as expenditure creating computer software.

Non-financial, also called **non-monetary assets**, are assets other than cash, money in a bank cheque or deposit account, investments, and amounts receivable such as trade receivables.

Goodwill usually arises in the statement of financial position because at some time in the past the business has taken over, or been formed from, another business. Recommended accounting for goodwill is provided in *IFRS 3 – Business Combinations* (IASB, 2010f). The figure shown in the statement of financial position for goodwill is the difference between the amount paid for that business and the value of its net assets. Goodwill is sometimes said to represent the potential future profits or sales arising from a business's reputation and the continuing patronage of existing customers. However, it is much more than this, in that it represents the advantages that are gained from taking over an existing business rather than building up a new business from scratch (e.g. not having to recruit staff, find premises or identify suppliers). Goodwill is discussed in Chapter 28 'Changes in Partnerships'.

Financial assets (investments) are also frequently included under the heading of non-current assets. These may consist of shares and/or debentures that are listed (quoted) on a stock exchange and unlisted securities. Investments should only be classified as a non-current asset where they are held on a long-term basis for the purpose of generating income. If this is not the case, investments should be treated as a current asset (available-for-sale).

16.2 The recognition and valuation of non-current assets

The term 'valuation' refers to the amount at which assets are shown in the statement of financial position. IAS 16 allows non-current tangible assets to be valued using two approaches: historical cost and the alternative treatment, revalued amount.

Historical cost

In historical cost accounting, non-current assets are valued at their historical cost less the **aggregate/accumulated depreciation** from the date of acquisition to the date of the statement of financial position. The resulting figure is known as the **written-down value** (WDV), **net book value** (NBV) or **net carrying amount**. Depreciation is discussed below.

Historical cost refers to the purchase price. Where the business is value added tax (VAT) registered the cost excludes VAT (as the business can claim this back). Where the business is not VAT registered, the cost includes VAT as this is a cost of the asset to the business which cannot be reclaimed. The historical cost of a non-current asset may also include a number of additional costs. The cost of land and buildings, for example, may include legal expenses and stamp duty, and the cost of any subsequent extensions and improvements (but not repairs and renewals). Similarly, the cost of machinery is taken to include delivery charges and installation expenses. However, the costs of any extended warranty, maintenance agreement and replacement/spare parts (for future use) that have been included in the purchase price must be removed from the capital account and treated as revenue expenses. Similarly, the cost of vehicles must exclude the first year's road tax and fuel where these have been included in the purchase price.

Revalued amount

The Companies Act 2006 and IAS 16 allow companies to revalue their tangible non-current assets and show them in the statement of financial position at fair value rather than historical cost. This is known as the alternative treatment.

- The carrying value for an asset accounted for under historical cost is its net book value.

- The **carrying amount** for a revalued asset is its fair value at the date of the revaluation less any subsequent accumulated depreciation and subsequent accumulated impairment losses.

Revaluations are most commonly used in the case of land and buildings that were acquired several years previously, and thus their current market value can exceed the historical cost, unless of course the property was purchased in the period before the financial crises of 2007. If it were purchased in this period then is it likely that the asset's fair value is actually below its book value, in which case, regardless of the valuation method adopted, the asset will have to be written down to its net realizable value. This represents a diminution in value (discussed in the next section). The **current value** of a tangible non-current asset to the business is the lower of replacement cost and recoverable amount. The **recoverable amount** is the higher of fair value and value in use.

Where a tangible non-current asset is revalued, all tangible non-current assets of the same class should be revalued. If a company revalues one or more classes of tangible non-current assets, it should continue to adopt the same policy in future years: that is, IAS 16 does not allow one-off revaluations. There must be regular revaluations. In the case of land and buildings, IAS 16 requires that revaluations be made with sufficient regularity to ensure that 'the carrying amount does not differ materially from that which would be determined using fair value at the statement of financial position date'.

Impairment of assets

Non-current assets should also be reviewed for impairment under *IAS 36 – Impairment of Assets* (IASB, 2010c). As mentioned, the recoverable amount is 'the higher of fair value (less costs to sell) and value in use'. If the carrying amount of the asset exceeds the recoverable amount, the asset is impaired and should be written down to its recoverable amount. The accounting for this adjustment is beyond the scope of this book.

For the sake of simplicity the remainder of this chapter assumes that non-current assets are valued at historical cost. Revaluations are discussed further in Chapter 28, 'Changes in Partnerships' and Chapter 31, 'The Final Financial Statements of Limited Companies'.

 ## 16.3   The nature of depreciation

The purchase of a non-current asset occurs in one year but the revenue generated from its use normally arises over a number of years. This is referred to as its **useful (economic) life**. In IAS 16 the useful life of an asset is defined as 'the period over which an asset is expected to be available for use by an entity; or the number of production or similar units expected to be obtained from the asset by an entity'.

If the cost of non-current assets were treated as an expense in the statement of profit and loss in the year of purchase, this would probably result in an excessive loss in that year, and excessive profits in the years in which the revenue arose. This gives a misleading view of the profits and losses of each year and distorts comparisons over time. Thus, the cost of a non-current asset is not treated as an expense in the year of purchase but rather carried forward and written off to the statement of profit and loss over the useful economic life of the asset in the form of depreciation. The part of the cost of an asset that is 'used up' or 'consumed' in each year of the asset's useful economic life must be set against the revenue that this generates (in conjunction with other factors of production). That part of the cost of a non-current asset, which is 'used up' or 'consumed' during an accounting period, is referred to as 'depreciation'. Thus, **depreciation** may be defined as the allocation of the cost of a non-current asset over the accounting periods that comprise its useful economic life to the business according to some criterion regarding the amount that is 'used up' or 'consumed' in each of these periods. IAS 16 defines depreciation as 'the systematic allocation of the depreciable amount of an asset over its useful life' where the **depreciable amount** is 'the cost of the asset, or other amount attributed to that asset, less its residual value'.

The allocation tries to measure the reduction in the economic benefits available from the tangible non-current asset or to capture the economic benefits that have been consumed during the period. **Consumption** is generally considered to include the wearing-out, using-up or other reduction in the useful economic life of a tangible non-current asset. The reduction can be caused by wear and tear as a result of use, the passing of time or obsolescence through either changes in technology or demand for the goods and services produced by the asset.

Obsolescence through technological change refers to the situation where a new model of the asset, which is significantly more efficient or performs additional functions, comes on to the market. **Obsolescence through demand changes** occurs when there is a substantial reduction in demand for the firm's product because of, for example, technological advances in competitors' products. Both of these causes of obsolescence usually result in a sudden, relatively large decrease in value of the asset, particularly where it cannot be used for any other purpose.

A misconception when defining depreciation is that it represents a loss in an asset's value. This misconception is widespread and is what a typical non-accounting individual would define depreciation as. This misconception is not helped by the use of the term 'depreciation' by some companies to indicate a loss in value as portrayed in real world example 16.1.

REAL WORLD EXAMPLE 16.1

What Car?

'What Car?' have a 'depreciation index' on their website so that users of the site can see in advance the potential loss in value of each model of car. For example, the depreciation index returned the following values for the expected future value of a Renault Scenic Grand MPV 1.5 dCi 110 Expression Auto 5dr:

Yr0	Yr1	Yr2	Yr3	Yr4
£20,625	£11,200	£9,287	£7,583	£5,881

This is the expected future sale price of the vehicle.

Source: http://www.whatcar.com/car-depreciation-calculator, July 2010.

Accountants typically deny that the amount of depreciation shown in final financial statements is a reflection of the loss in value of a non-current asset. They argue that accountants are not valuers, and that depreciation is simply the allocation of the cost of a non-current asset over its useful economic life to the business, and that permanent diminutions in value are a separate issue, and are dealt with by a separate standard. They would consider a loss in value to be a diminution in value. The confusion is compounded by the Companies Act (2006) which states that 'provisions for diminution in value shall be made in respect of any non-current asset which has diminished in value, if the reduction in its value is expected to be permanent'. Under accounting standards where an asset suffers diminution in value, then the asset's value is reduced. A provision is not created. The conceptualization of depreciation as being a reflection of the loss in an asset's value leaves unanswered the question of what is meant by 'value'.

A further misconception about depreciation is that it represents a build-up of funds (through the provision) for the replacement of non-current assets. The annual charge for depreciation in the statement of profit and loss represents a setting-aside of some of the income so that over the useful life of the asset sufficient 'funds' are retained in the business to replace the asset. However, it must be emphasized that no money is usually specifically set aside. Thus, when the time comes to replace the asset, the money needed to do so will not automatically be available. Furthermore, where depreciation is based on the historical cost of the asset, the amount of funds set aside will be insufficient to provide for any increase in the replacement cost of the asset.

Finally, it should be noted that IAS 16 requires all tangible non-current assets except land are depreciated. This includes depreciating buildings. The reason is that although the market value of buildings at any point in time may exceed their historical cost, they nevertheless have a finite life and thus should be depreciated over their useful economic life. However, some businesses do not depreciate their buildings on the grounds that the market value at the end of the year, and/or the estimated residual value at the end of their expected useful life, is not less than the original cost. It is also sometimes argued that since repairs and maintenance costs on buildings are charged to the statement of profit and loss, to also charge depreciation on an asset, the useful life of which is being effectively maintained into perpetuity, would amount to a double expense charge and the creation of secret reserves. However, these arguments ignore that depreciation is not a method of valuation of assets but rather a process of allocation of the cost over the asset's useful life which, however long, must still be finite. Buildings, for example, can be entered in the statement of financial position at a revalued amount in excess of their cost, but this revalued amount should still be depreciated. Revaluations are discussed further in Chapter 28, 'Changes in Partnerships' and Chapter 31, 'The Final Financial Statements of Limited Companies'. The accounting for buildings under IAS 16 is different from the accounting for investment properties under IAS 40. IAS 40 allows investment properties not to be depreciated, but to be revalued yearly to fair value, with the movement in value being charged/credited to the statement of profit and loss. IFRS 5 (IASB, 2010e) also allows assets that are held for sale, or discontinued, not to be depreciated but to be revalued at fair value each year with the change in value being charged/credited to the statement of profit and loss. The reason for the different treatment is that the latter are considered to be investments, not tangible non-current assets that are being consumed by the business.

 ## 16.4 Methods of depreciation

A number of different methods have been developed for measuring depreciation, each of which will give a different annual charge to the statement of profit and loss. There is no one method of depreciation that is superior to all others in all circumstances. The most appropriate method will depend on the type of asset and the extent to which it is used in each period.

Whichever method is used to calculate depreciation, at least three pieces of data relating to the asset in question are needed:

1 the historical cost of the asset;

2 the length of the asset's expected useful economic life to the business;

3 the estimated residual value of the asset at the end of its useful economic life.

The useful life of an asset refers to the period that the business regards as being the most economical length of time to keep the particular asset. This will depend on a number of factors, such as the pattern of repair costs. The useful life of an asset may well be considerably shorter than its total life. **Residual value** refers to the estimated proceeds of sale at the end of the asset's useful life to the business. This is usually considerably more than its scrap value. It should be noted that both the useful life and the residual value have to be estimated when the asset is purchased.

As mentioned earlier, the difference between the historical cost of a tangible non-current asset and its residual value is referred to in IAS 16 as the 'depreciable amount'. According to IAS 16, the depreciable amount of a tangible non-current asset should be allocated to reflect the pattern in which the economic benefits are expected to be consumed by the entity. The two most common methods of depreciation in the UK are the **straight-line/fixed instalment method** and **reducing balance method**. Another method more common in the USA is the **sum of the years' digits method (sum of digits)**. These are described below.

The straight-line/fixed instalment method

Under this method the annual amount of depreciation that will be charged to the statement of profit and loss, referred to as the **depreciation expense**, is computed as follows:

$$\text{Depreciation} = \frac{\text{Cost} - \text{Estimated Residual value}}{\text{Estimated useful life in years}}$$

Alternatively the annual rate of depreciation can be expressed as a percentage. The annual amount of depreciation is then calculated by applying this percentage to the cost of the asset.

$$\text{Depreciation} = \text{Rate of depreciation} \times \text{Cost of asset}$$

This method gives the same charge for depreciation in each year of the asset's useful life. It is therefore most appropriate for assets that are depleted as a result of the passage of time (e.g. buildings, leases, pipelines, storage tanks, patents and trademarks). The method may also be suitable where the utilization of an asset is the same in each year.

The main advantages of the straight-line method are that it is easy to understand and the computations are simple. The main disadvantage is that it may not give an accurate measure of the reduction in the useful life of an asset.

The diminishing/reducing balance method

Under this method it is necessary first to compute the annual rate of depreciation as a percentage, as follows:

$$\text{Rate of depreciation} = 100 - \left(\sqrt[ul]{\frac{\text{Residual value}}{\text{Cost}}} \times 100 \right)$$

where ul refers to the estimated useful life.

The annual amount of depreciation that will be charged to the statement of profit and loss is then computed as:

$$\text{Depreciation} = \text{Rate of depreciation} \times \text{WDV of asset (at start of year)}$$

The WDV of the asset refers to its cost less the aggregate depreciation of the asset since the date of acquisition. This method gives a decreasing annual charge for depreciation over the useful life of the asset. It is therefore most appropriate for non-current assets that deteriorate primarily as a result of usage where this is greater in the earlier years of their life (e.g. plant and machinery, motor vehicles, furniture and fittings, office equipment). However, this method may also be suitable even if the utilization is the same in each year. The logic behind this apparently contradictory assertion involves taking into consideration the pattern of repair costs. These will be low in the earlier years of the asset's life and high in later years. Thus, the decreasing annual amount of depreciation combined with the increasing repair costs will give a relatively constant combined annual charge in each year of the asset's useful life that is said to reflect the constant annual usage.

The main criticisms of this method relate to its complexity, and there is an arbitrary assumption about the rate of decline built into the formula.

The sum of the years' digits method

Under this method the annual amount of depreciation that will be expensed in the statement of profit and loss is computed by multiplying the depreciable amount by a fraction. The denominator in this fraction is the same each year, and is the sum of a decreasing arithmetic progression, the first number of which is the useful life of the asset and the last is one. For example, where an asset has a useful life of three years, the denominator is calculated as follows $(3 + 2 + 1 = 6)$, with the numerator in the fraction being the number of years of the asset's remaining useful life at the start of the accounting year in question (e.g. 3 years, 2 years, 1 year). Therefore, in year one the depreciable amount will be multiplied by $\frac{3}{6}$ in year two the depreciable amount will be multiplied by $\frac{2}{6}$ and so on.

This method gives a decreasing annual charge for depreciation over the useful life of the asset that is similar to, but not the same amount as, the reducing balance method. The arguments for and against the sum of the years' digits method are thus the same as those relating to the reducing balance method except that the former is simpler. Moreover, the difference in the annual depreciation expense highlights the arbitrary nature of the different assumptions about the rates of decline that are built into the two methods.

A numerical example of the above methods of depreciation is given in Example 16.1, which follows after the section on explaining the accounting entries for depreciation.

16.5 Accounting policy for depreciation

Most entities provide details of how they value their assets and how they calculate depreciation in their accounting policies. An example can be found in the financial statements of Viridian Group as follows:

Viridian Group

Property, plant and equipment

Property, plant and equipment are included in the balance sheet (now called the 'statement of financial position') at cost, less accumulated depreciation and any recognised impairment loss. The cost of self-constructed assets includes the cost of materials, direct labour and an appropriate portion of overheads. Interest on funding attributable to significant capital projects is capitalized during the period of construction and written off as part of the total cost of the asset.

Freehold land is not depreciated. Other property, plant and equipment are depreciated on a straight-line basis so as to write off the cost, less estimated residual values, over their estimated useful economic lives as follows:

Infrastructure assets – up to 40 years

Generation assets – up to 30 years

Non-operational buildings – freehold and long leasehold – up to 50 years

Fixtures and equipment – up to 25 years

Vehicles and mobile plant – up to 5 years

The carrying values of property, plant and equipment are reviewed for impairment when events or changes in circumstances indicate that carrying value may not be recoverable. Where the carrying value exceeds the estimated recoverable amount, the asset is written down to its recoverable amount.

Source: Viridian Group Holdings Limited, 2008, Annual Report and Accounts 2007–8, group website, www.viridiangroup.co.uk/Site/10/Documents/200708%20VG%20Holdings%20Ltd%20(consolidated).pdf (accessed May 2010).

As can be seen, this comprehensive accounting policy covers how the company defines cost for purchased assets and internally generated assets, the method of accounting for depreciation, how impairments are determined and when the company no longer recognizes an asset.

> **LEARNING ACTIVITY 16.1**
>
> Using the financial statements of any plc for guidance (use the Web to locate a company with tangible assets), draft a pro forma note on tangible non-current assets. This should show the typical movements in a cost account and in a provision for depreciation account with the resultant opening and closing written-down values being highlighted.
>
> Note how the property, plant and equipment note in the company's financial statements reconciles with the figure that is disclosed on the face of the company's statement of financial position.

16.6 Accounting for depreciation

The accounting entries in respect of the annual charge for depreciation are made after the trial balance has been extracted when the statement of profit and loss is being prepared. These consist of the following:

Debit: Depreciation expense account

Credit: Provision for depreciation account

The depreciation expense account is transferred to the profit and loss account thus:

Debit: Profit and loss account

Credit: Depreciation expense account

The effect is to accumulate the provision while making a charge in the statement of profit and loss each year.

> **EXAMPLE 16.1**
>
> D. McDonald has an accounting year ending on 31 December. On 1 January 20X3 he purchased a machine for £1,000, which has an expected useful life of three years and an estimated residual value of £343.
>
> *Required*
>
> a Calculate the amount of depreciation in each year of the asset's useful life using: (i) the straight-line method; (ii) the reducing balance method; and (iii) the sum of the years' digits method.
>
> b Show the journal and ledger entries relating to the purchase and the provision for depreciation in each year (using the amounts calculated from the straight-line method).
>
> c Show the relevant entries on the statement of financial position for 20X4 (using the amounts calculated from the straight-line method).
>
> *Solution*
>
> a *The calculation of depreciation*
>
>   i The straight-line method:
>
> $$\text{Annual depreciation} = \frac{£1{,}000 - £343}{3} = £219 \text{ per annum}$$

ii The reducing balance method:

$$\text{Depreciation rate} = 100 - \left(\sqrt[3]{\frac{343}{1000}} \times 100 \right) = 100 - (0.7 \times 100) = 30 \text{ per cent}$$

The annual amount of depreciation is calculated by applying this rate to the cost of the asset minus the aggregate depreciation of previous years (i.e. the WDV at the start of each year) as follows:

For 20X3:   30% of £1,000 = £300

For 20X4:   30% of (£1,000 − 300) = £210

For 20X5:   30% of [£1,000 − (£300 + £210)] = £147

iii The sum of the years' digits method:

$$\text{Depreciable amount} = £1,000 - £343 = £657$$

$$\text{Sum of the years' digits} = 3 + 2 + 1 = 6$$

Annual depreciation:

For 20X3: $\frac{3}{6} \times £657 = £329$

For 20X4: $\frac{2}{6} \times £657 = £219$

For 20X5: $\frac{1}{6} \times £657 = £109$

b *The ledger entries (straight line only)*

The journal

20X3				
31 Dec	Depreciation expense		Dr	219
	To provision for depreciation		Cr	219
	Being the charge for depreciation on plant for 20X3			
31 Dec	Statement of profit and loss		Dr	219
	To depreciation expense		Cr	219
	Being the entry to close the depreciation expense account at the year end			

		Plant and machinery		
20X3	**Details**	**£**		
1 Jan	Bank	1,000		

		Depreciation expense account				
20X3	**Details**	**£**	**20X3**	**Details**		**£**
31 Dec	Provision for depreciation A/C	219	31 Dec	P/L A/C (depreciation charge)		219
20X4			**20X4**			
31 Dec	Provision for depreciation A/C	219	31 Dec	P/L A/C (depreciation charge)		219
20X5			**20X5**			
31 Dec	Provision for depreciation A/C	219	31 Dec	P/L A/C (depreciation charge)		219

Provision for depreciation on plant and machinery					
20X3	**Details**	**£**	**20X3**	**Details**	**£**
31 Dec	Balance c/d	219	31 Dec	Depreciation expense a/c	219
20X4			**20X4**		
			1 Jan	Balance b/d	219
31 Dec	Balance c/d	438	31 Dec	Depreciation expense a/c	219
		438			438
20X5			**20X5**		
			1 Jan	Balance b/d	438
31 Dec	Balance c/d	657	31 Dec	Depreciation expense a/c	219
		657			657
			20X6		
			1 Jan	Balance b/d	657

The entries for 20X4 and 20X5 would be exactly the same.

c *The statement of financial position at 31 December 20X4* would appear as follows:

Non-current assets	£
Plant and machinery at cost	1,000
Less: provision for depreciation	438
Written down value (WDV)	562

Alternatively, where there are several types of non-current asset, it is easier to present the non-current assets in columnar form as follows:

Non-current assets			
	Cost	Provision for depreciation	WDV
	£	£	£
Plant and machinery	1,000	438	562

Notes

1 The entries on the statement of financial position comprise the balance on the non-current asset ledger account at the end of the year and the balance on the provision for depreciation ledger account at the end of the year. The latter is referred to as the **provision for, aggregate** or **accumulated depreciation** and is deducted from the historical cost to give the WDV. In sole trade and partnership financial statements both the cost and provision accounts are disclosed on the face of the statement of financial position, with the WDV also being provided. However, in company financial statements, details of these ledger accounts are given in the notes to the financial statements with only the WDV being disclosed in the statement of financial position.

2 Because the entries in the depreciation expense account only ever consist of a single debit and credit of the same amount, most people do not use this ledger account. Instead, the annual charge is credited to the provision for depreciation ledger account and debited directly to the profit and loss ledger account. This practice will be adopted in future examples and answers to exercises.

16.7   Profits and losses on the disposal of non-current assets

Almost without exception, when an asset is sold at the end of (or during) its useful life the proceeds of sale differ from the estimated residual value (or written-down book value (WDV) if sold during its useful life). Where the proceeds are less than the WDV, this is referred to as a **loss on sale**. Where the proceeds are greater than the WDV, this is referred to as a **profit on sale**. This can be illustrated using Example 16.1. Suppose the asset was sold on 31 December 20X5 for £400. The WDV is the difference between the cost of the asset and the aggregate depreciation up to the date of disposal; that is, £1,000 − £657 = £343. The profit (or loss) on sale is the difference between the proceeds of sale and the WDV of the asset. There is thus a profit on sale of £400 − £343 = £57.

When a non-current asset is sold the cost of the asset is transferred from the non-current asset account to an asset disposals account. This is sometimes referred to as an 'asset realization account'. The aggregate depreciation on the asset that has been sold, the proceeds of sale, and the cost of the asset are all entered in the disposals account. The balance on this account is either a profit or a loss on sale. This will be transferred to the profit and loss account.

Profit and losses on the disposal of non-current assets

Specific steps

1 Credit the proceeds of sale to the disposals account.

2 Transfer the aggregate depreciation for the asset sold up to the date of disposal from the provision for depreciation account to the disposals account.

3 Transfer the cost of the asset from the cost account to the disposals account.

4 Calculate the loss or profit on sale. A loss on sale should then be credited to the realization asset account and debited to the profit and loss account. A profit on sale would be debited to the realization asset account and credited to the profit and loss account.

This is illustrated with the continuation of Example 16.1 and the additional data above in Example 16.1.

The journal

20X5				
31 Dec	Provision for depreciation	Dr	657	
	To: asset disposals account	Cr		657
	Being the aggregate depreciation at the date of sale of the asset removed from the ledger account.			
31 Dec	Asset disposals account	Dr	1,000	
	To: Plant and machinery	Cr		1,000
	Being the cost of the asset at the date of sale removed from the ledger account			
31 Dec	Plant and machinery	Dr	57	
	To: profit and loss account	Cr		57
	Being the profit on sale of plant and machinery to P/L A/C			

◀ **The ledger entries**

Plant and machinery						
20X3	**Details**	**£**	**20X5**	**Details**		**£**
	Bank – purchase	1,000	31 Dec	Asset disposals a/c		1,000
		1,000				1,000

Provision for depreciation					
20X5	**Details**	**£**	**20X5**	**Details**	**£**
31 Dec	Asset disposals	657	31 Dec	Balance b/d	657

Asset disposals account (Plant and machinery)					
20X5	**Details**	**£**	**20X5**	**Details**	**£**
31 Dec	Plant and machinery	1,000	31 Dec	Bank – proceeds of scale	400
			31 Dec	Provision for Depreciation	657
31 Dec	Profit and loss a/c (profit on sale)	57	31 Dec	Profit and loss a/c (any loss on sale)	
		1,057			1,057

Profit and loss account			
	£		**£**
Loss on sale of non-current assets	–	Profit on sale of plant and machinery	57

16.8 The depreciation charge on an asset in the years of acquisition and disposal: partial year depreciation

The previous example dealt with the highly unlikely situation of an asset being purchased and sold on the first day and last day of an accounting year, respectively. In practice, these transactions could occur on any day of the year. The way in which depreciation would then be computed depends on the usual practice of the business, or in examinations on what you are explicitly or implicitly instructed to do. Unless the question states otherwise, the depreciation must be calculated on a strict time basis for the period the asset is owned. In examination questions, assets tend to be purchased and sold on the first or last day of a calendar month for simplicity of calculation. It can be argued that in practice one should also calculate depreciation on a strict time basis. The charge for depreciation in the year of purchase would be as follows:

$$\text{Rate of depreciation} \times \text{Cost of asset} \times \frac{\text{Number of months (or days) between the date of purchase and the end of the accounting year in which the asset is purchased}}{12 \text{ (or 365)}}$$

The charge for depreciation in the year of sale would be as follows:

$$\text{Rate of depreciation} \times \text{Cost of asset (or WDV)} \times \frac{\text{Number of months (or days) between the start of the accounting year in which the asset is sold and the date of sale}}{12 \text{ (or 365)}}$$

In practice, to avoid these tedious calculations, some firms have a policy of charging a full year's depreciation in the year of purchase and none in the year of sale. There is little theoretical justification for this. Also, in examination questions, where the date of purchase or sale is not given, this is usually an indication to adopt this policy.

The accounting entries in respect of depreciation on acquisitions and disposals are illustrated in Example 16.2.

EXAMPLE 16.2

P. Smith has an accounting year ending on 31 December. On 31 December 20X2 her ledger contained the following accounts:

	£
Motor vehicles	50,000
Provision for depreciation on vehicles	23,000

Vehicles are depreciated using the straight-line method at a rate of 20 per cent per annum on a strict time basis.

The following transactions occurred during 20X3:

1 Apr   Purchased a van for £5,000.

31 Aug   Sold a vehicle for £4,700. This cost £7,500 when it was bought on 31 July 20X0.

30 Sep   Used one car as part exchange for another. The part exchange allowance on the old car was £4,100 and the balance of £3,900 was paid by cheque. The old car cost £10,000 when it was bought on 1 January 20X1.

You are required to show the entries in the motor vehicles and provision for depreciation accounts in respect of the above for 20X3.

Date of acquisitions and disposals	Details	Total depreciation on disposals	Depreciation charge for year ending 31 Dec 20X3
		£	£
	Depreciation on disposals		
31 July 20X1	For year ending 31/12/X1:		
	$20\% \times £7,500 \times \frac{5}{12}$	625	
	For year ending 31/12/X2:		
	$20\% \times £7,500$	1,500	
31 Aug 20X3	For year ending 31/12/X3:		
	$20\% \times £7,500 \times \frac{8}{12}$	<u>1,000</u>	1,000
		<u>3,125</u>	
	Book value at 31/8/X3:		
	£7,500 – £3,125 = £4,375		
	Profit on sale		
	£4,700 – £4,375 = £325		
1 Jan 20X1	For year ending 31/12/X1:		
	$20\% \times £10,000$	2,000	
	For year ending 31/12/X2:		
	$20\% \times £10,000$	2,000	

30 Sept 20X3	For year ending 31/12/X3:		
	$20\% \times £10,000 \times \frac{9}{12}$	<u>1,500</u>	1,500
		5,500	
	Book value at 30/9/X3:		
	£10,000 − £5,500 = £4,500		
	Loss on sale		
	£4,500 − £4,100 = £400		
	Depreciation on acquisitions		
1 Apr 20X3	$20\% \times £5,000 \times \frac{9}{12}$		750
30 Sept 20X3	$20\% \times (£3,900 + £4,100) \times \frac{3}{12}$		400
	Depreciation on remainder		
	$20\% \times (£50,000 − £7,500 − £10,000)$		<u>6,500</u>
			10,150

Note

1 The 'depreciation on the remainder' of the vehicles is calculated on the vehicles owned at the start of the year that were not disposed off during the current year. Those items that were bought and sold during the year have already been depreciated in the previous calculations.

The ledger

Motor vehicles

20X3	Details	£	20X3	Details	£
1 Jan	Balance b/d	50,000	31 Aug	Disposals account	7,500
1 Apr	Bank	5,000	31 Sep	Disposals account	10,000
30 Sep	Bank	3,900	31 Dec	Balance c/d	45,500
30 Sep	Disposals account – part exchange	4,100			
		63,000			63,000
20X4					
1 Jan	Balance b/d	45,500			

Motor vehicles disposals

20X3	Details	£	20X3	Details	£
31 Aug	Motor vehicles	7,500	31 Aug	Bank	4,700
31 Aug	Profit and loss a/c		31 Aug	Provision for depreciation	3,125
	– profit on sale	325	30 Sep	Motor vehicles	
30 Sep	Motor vehicles	10,000		– part exchange	4,100
			30 Sep	Provision for depreciation	5,500
			30 Sep	Profit and loss a/c	
				– loss on sale	400
		17,825			17,825

Provision for depreciation					
20X3	**Details**	**£**	**20X3**	**Details**	**£**
31 Aug	Vehicles	3,125	1 Jan	Balance b/d	23,000
30 Sep	Vehicles	5,500	31 Dec	Profit and loss a/c	10,150
31 Dec	Balance c/d	24,525			
		33,150			33,150
			20X4		
			1 Jan	Balance b/d	24,525

There should never be a balance on the disposals account at the end of the year after the statement of profit and loss has been prepared.

Notes

1 When one asset is put in part exchange for another, the part exchange allowance is debited to the asset cost account and credited to the asset disposals account and referred to as a 'contra'. The credit entry represents the proceeds of sale of the old asset, and the debit entry represents a part payment for the new asset. The balance that has to be paid for the new asset in cash is debited to the asset account in the normal way. This, together with the debit contra, represents the total cost of the new asset.

2 The transfer from the provision for depreciation account to the non-current asset account relating to the aggregate depreciation on disposals must include the depreciation on disposals in respect of the current year. This therefore cannot be done until the total depreciation for the current year has been ascertained. Thus, all the entries in the provision for depreciation account are usually made at the end of the year after the trial balance has been prepared. It is important to note that this also means that any balance on a provision for depreciation account shown in a trial balance must relate to the balance at the end of the previous year.

16.9 Creative accounting and depreciation

As an accounting adjustment that is subjective, depreciation can be used to manipulate profit. For example, selecting a short useful economic life and a lower expected residual value will result in a larger depreciation charge and lower reported profits. This may be attractive to a business that is doing well now but is uncertain about how its performance will be in the future. Alternatively, selecting a long useful economic life and a high residual value will result in a lower deprecation charge and will be attractive when a business is not performing very well, as recorded profits will be higher. This variation is highlighted in real world example 16.3.

REAL WORLD
EXAMPLE
16.3
Tesco

In 2010 a Citigroup analyst accused Tesco of using aggressive accounting methods for revenue recognition, depreciation, the allocation of profits from property, capitalized interest expense and pension accounting. The methods used are reported to be very different from those used by its competitors. The analyst suggests that the outcome of this is that Tesco's profit cannot be compared with other companies in the industry. Indeed, the analyst reported that Tesco's increase in profit in the year of £3.4 billion would have been £800,000 less had similar methods to those used by its competitors been used. For example, if Tesco had used the same period to depreciation their buildings and fittings, their depreciation charge would have been 15 per cent higher to that reported.

Source: adapted from Finch, 2010, www.guardian.co.uk/business/2010/jun/30/tesco-accounting-comment (accessed May 2011).

Smith (1992) commented that 'one popular choice of creative bookkeeping is altering the calculation of depreciation'. In a research study on creative accounting, Phillips and Drew (1992) reported that depreciation was used by 9 per cent (17 out of the 185 companies investigated) of major UK companies to manipulate profit figures. In the US the depreciation charge is a deductible expense that is recognized by the Revenue and, as such, depreciation has been used for tax evasion purposes. This is evident from real world example 16.4.

REAL WORLD
EXAMPLE
16.4
Depreciation, tax evasion and Beaulieu Group LLC

In 2007 a multinational company based in the US, Beaulieu Group LLC, was found guilty of using creative accounting to evade tax. The worldwide tax investigation centered on several European countries including the UK and Ireland. One of the techniques used to reduce profits and hence reduce the tax bill was to overstate the depreciation charge for assets owned. Over an eight-year period, the company provided excess depreciation of $5,919,093 on four carpet-spinning machines which it purchased in Europe and $1,049,836 in excess depreciation was claimed on 29 Volkman twisters.

The result of the fraud was that Beaulieu had to repay $22 million in unpaid tax and a penalty of $7.7 million to the revenue. In addition, they had to pay a criminal fine of $2.2 million and court costs of $800,000.

Note: depreciation is not a deductable expense in the UK, hence cannot be used to manipulate the tax liability.

Sources: US Immigration and Customs, Enforcement and US Department of Justice, 2007 (see References).

Summary

A non-current asset is an asset that is held by an enterprise for use in the production or supply of goods and services, has been acquired with the intention of being used on a continuing basis, and is not intended for sale in the ordinary course of business. It is also usually expected to generate revenue over more than one accounting year. Non-current assets are classified as either tangible (land and buildings), or intangible (such as goodwill), or financial assets (investments). Money spent on non-current assets is referred to as 'capital expenditure'. All other costs are referred to as 'revenue expenditure'. Non-current assets in sole trader and partnership financial statements are normally valued in the statement of financial position at historical cost, which refers to their purchase price.

All non-current assets except for land and investment properties must be depreciated in the final financial statements. Depreciation is 'the systematic allocation of the depreciable amount of an asset over its useful life' where the depreciable amount is 'the cost of the asset, or other amount attributed to that asset less its residual value'.

There is a range of acceptable depreciation methods. Management should select the method regarded as most appropriate to the type of asset and its use in the business so as to allocate depreciation as fairly as possible to the periods expected to benefit from the asset's use. The depreciation method adopted should reflect the consumption, wearing-out, using-up or other reduction in the useful economic life of a non-current asset whether arising from use, effluxion of time or obsolescence. The two most common methods are the straight-line/fixed instalment method and **diminishing/reducing balance method**. The former gives the same charge for depreciation in each year of the asset's useful life. The latter results in a decreasing annual charge over the useful life of the asset.

Where an asset is acquired or disposed of during the accounting year, it is normal to compute the depreciation for that year according to the period over which the asset was owned. When an asset is disposed of during the accounting year, this usually also gives rise to profit or loss on sale. This is the difference between the proceeds of sale and the written-down or **book value** of the asset. The WDV is the difference between the historical cost and the accumulated/aggregate depreciation from the date of acquisition to the date of disposal.

The ledger entries for depreciation are to credit a provision for depreciation ledger account and debit a depreciation expense ledger account with the annual amount of depreciation. The balance on the depreciation expense ledger account is transferred to the profit and loss ledger account representing the charge for the year. The balance on the provision for depreciation account is shown on the statement of financial position as a deduction from the cost of the non-current asset to give the WDV, which enters into the total of the statement of financial position. When an asset is sold, all the original entries relating to that asset are reversed to an asset disposals account. The cost and any adjustments to cost and the aggregate depreciation on non-current assets disposed of during the year must be transferred from the cost ledger account and from the provision for depreciation ledger account to a disposals account. The receipt (or trade-in value) for the asset is credited to the disposals account also. The balance on this account will represent either a profit or a loss on disposal. This is transferred to the profit and loss ledger account.

Key terms and concepts

An asterisk after the question number indicates that there is a suggested answer on the Online Learning Centre (www.mcgraw-hill.co.uk/textbooks/thomas).

Review questions

connect

16.1 Explain the nature of non-current assets.

16.2 a Explain the difference between capital expenditure and revenue expenditure.

b What criteria would you use to decide whether expenditure should be classified as relating to a non-current asset?

16.3 Briefly explain the circumstances in which each of the following would be regarded as a non-current asset: (a) tools; (b) investments; and (c) advertising expenditure.

16.4 a Explain the difference between tangible and intangible non-current assets.

b What is goodwill and how does it usually arise in a statement of financial position?

16.5 a Describe how non-current assets are valued under historical cost accounting.

b How would you account for expenditure on double-glazing? Explain your reasons.

16.6 Explain fully the nature of depreciation.

16.7 'Depreciation is the loss in value of a non-current asset'. Discuss.

16.8 Describe the data needed in order to compute depreciation.

16.9 Describe two common methods of depreciation including the resulting pattern of charges to the statement of profit and loss for depreciation expense over an asset's useful economic life. In what circumstances might each of these be the most appropriate method and why?

16.10 'Although the straight-line method of depreciation is the simplest to apply, it may not always be the most appropriate'. Explain and discuss.

16.11 In the year to 31 December 20X3, Amy bought a new non-current asset and made the following payments in relation to it:

	£	£
Cost as per supplier's list	12,000	
Less: agreed discount	1,000	11,000
Delivery charge		100
Erection charge		200
Maintenance charge		300
Additional component to increase capacity		400
Replacement parts		250

Required

a State and justify the cost figure that should be used as the basis for depreciation.

b What does depreciation do, and why is it necessary?

c Briefly explain, without numerical illustration, how the straight-line and reducing balance methods of depreciation work. What different assumptions does each method make?

d It is common practice in published financial statements in Germany to use the reducing balance method for a non-current asset in the early years of its life, and then to change to the straight-line method as soon as this would give a higher annual charge. What do you think of this practice? Refer to relevant accounting conventions in your answer.

(ACCA)

connect Exercises

BASIC

16.12

You bought a lorry for £5,000.

Its useful life is estimated at four years.

The residual value is expected to be £1,000 after the four years.

Required

Calculate the depreciation charge for each of the four years using the straight line, reducing balance and the sum of digits methods.

BASIC

16.13

On 31 December 20X2, plant and machinery acquired at a cost of £200,000 in 20W9 was sold for £30,000. The accumulated depreciation to date was £130,000.

Required

Calculate the profit or loss on disposal (show all ledger account entries).

BASIC

16.14

Plant was purchased in the year for £10,000. It has been decided to provide for depreciation on a reducing balance basis (25 per cent). A full year's depreciation is charged in the year of purchase.

Required

a Show the entries in the ledgers for the first two years.

b Provide extracts to show the disclosures in the statement of profit and loss and in the statement of financial position for both years.

16.15

An item of plant and machinery was sold within the year for £5,000.

The asset cost the company £10,000 over two years ago.

The balances on the cost account and accumulated depreciation account were £118,000 and £18,000.

It is company policy to provide for depreciation in the year of purchase but not in the year of sale. (Two years' depreciation charged at 20 per cent straight line per year had been expensed in relation to this asset.)

Required

Calculate the profit or loss on disposal (show all ledger account entries).

16.16

Pusher commenced business on 1 January 20X0 with two lorries – A and B. A cost £1,000 and B cost £1,600. On 3 March 20X1, A was written off in an accident and Pusher received £750 from the insurance company. This vehicle was replaced on 10 March 20X1 by C which cost £2,000.

A full year's depreciation is charged in the year of acquisition and no depreciation is charged in the year of disposal.

a You are required to show the appropriate extracts from Pusher's statement of financial position and statement of profit and loss for the three years to 31/12/X0, 31/12/X1 and 31/12/X2 assuming that:

  i   the vehicles are depreciated at 20 per cent on the straight-line method.

  ii the vehicles are depreciated at 25 per cent on the reducing balance method.

b Comment briefly on the pros and cons of using the straight line and reducing balance methods of depreciation.

(ACCA)

16.17*

A. Black & Co. Ltd owned two machines that had been purchased on 1 October 20X2 at a combined cost of £3,100 ex works. They were identical as regards size and capacity and had been erected and brought into use on 1 April 20X3. The cost of transporting the two machines to the factory of A. Black & Co. Ltd was £130 and further expenditure for the installation of the two machines had been incurred totalling £590 for the foundations, and £180 for erection.

Provision for depreciation using the straight-line method has been calculated from the date on which the machines started work, assuming a life of 10 years for the machines. The first charge against profits was made at the end of the financial year, 30 September 20X3.

One of the machines was sold on 31 March 20Y1 for £800 ex factory to H. Johnson. The work of dismantling the machine was undertaken by the staff of A. Black & Co. Ltd at a labour cost of £100. This machine was replaced on 1 May 20Y1, by one exactly similar in every way, which was purchased from R. Adams at a cost of £2,800, which covered delivery, erection on the site of the old machine, and the provision of adequate foundations. This new machine was brought into general operation on 1 July 20Y1.

Required

a Show the journal entries that should be made on 31 March and 1 May 20Y1.

b Show how you would arrive at the amount of the provision for depreciation as regards the three machines for the year ended 30 September 20Y1.

Note: It is the practice of the company to charge depreciation on a pro rata time basis each year, and to operate a machinery disposal account where necessary.

16.18

Makers and Co. is a partnership with a small factory on the outskirts of London. They decide to erect an extension to their factory.

The following items appear in the trial balance of the firm, as at 31 December 20X2:

	Debit	Credit
	£	£
Purchases	12,800	
Wages	16,400	
Hire of machinery	520	
Plant and machinery at cost to 31 December 20X1	5,900	
Plant and machinery purchased during the year	2,540	
Plant and machinery sold during the year (cost in 20W4 £900; depreciation to 31 December 20X1 £540)		160
Freehold premises at cost to 31 December 20X1 (Land £3,000; Buildings £4,000)	7,000	
Freehold land purchased during the year for a factory extension	2,800	
Provision for depreciation of plant and machinery at 31 December 20X1		2,400
Legal charges	280	

In the course of your examination of the books you ascertain that:

1 building materials used in building the extension and costing £1,800 had been charged to the purchases account;

2 wages paid to men engaged in building the extension amounted to £1,500 and had been charged to the wages account;

3 the hire charge was in respect of machinery used exclusively in the construction of the extension;

4 the legal charges, apart from £50 relating to debt collecting, were incurred in the purchase of the land.

It is decided that depreciation on plant and machinery is to be provided at $12\frac{1}{2}$ per cent on the closing book value.

Required

a Write up the following ledger accounts:

Factory extensions, freehold premises, plant and machinery, and provision for depreciation of plant and machinery.

b Show the particulars that should appear on the firm's statement of financial position at 31 December 20X2.

(ACCA)

16.19*

Wexford Ltd, who prepare their financial statements on 31 December each year, provide for depreciation of their vehicles by a reducing balance method, calculated as 25 per cent on the balance at the end of the year. Depreciation of plant is calculated on a straight line basis at 10 per cent per annum on cost; a full year's depreciation is charged in the year in which plant is acquired and none in the year of sale.

The statement of financial position for 31 December 20X1 showed:

	Vehicles	Plant
	£	£
Original cost	25,060	96,920
Accumulated depreciation	14,560	50,120
Net book value	10,500	46,800

During the year ended 31 December 20X2, the following transactions took place:

Purchase of vehicles	£4,750
Purchases of plant	£33,080

	Year of purchase	Original cost	Proceeds of sale
		£	£
Sale of vehicle 1	20W9	3,200	1,300
Sale of vehicle 2	20X0	4,800	2,960
Sale of plant	20W6	40,000	15,000

Required

a Present the ledger accounts relating to the purchases and sales of vehicles and plant for the year ended 31 December 20X2.

b Show the journal entries for depreciation for the year.

16.20

The statement of financial position of Beta Ltd as at 30 June 20X2 shows motor vehicles as follows:

	£
Motor vehicles at cost	61,850
Less: depreciation	32,426
Net book value	29,424

Vehicles are depreciated on the straight line basis over a five-year life. Depreciation is charged pro rata to time in the year of acquisition but no charge is made in the year of disposal. The disposal account is written up on the last day of each year.

During 20X2–X3 the following vehicle transactions took place:

30 Sep	Purchased delivery van: £8,600
31 Oct	Purchased sales manager's car: £10,700
28 Feb	Purchased lorry: £4,000

The lorry was second-hand and originally cost £9,600.

Sales of vehicles:

31 Oct	Car	£300 originally cost £2,800
31 Dec	Tractor	£540 originally cost £2,400
31 Mar	Van	£420 originally cost £1,900

261

The car was originally purchased on 1 July 20W8, the tractor on 30 November 20W9 and the van on 1 April 20X0.

You are required to write up the accounts for vehicles, vehicle depreciation and vehicle disposals.

(ACCA)

References

Finch, J. (2010) 'Tesco Numbers Game Spooks Investors: Citigroups analysis of Tesco's aggressive' accounting brings down share price', *Guardian*, 30 June 2010, www.guardian.co.uk/business/2010/jun/30/tesco-accounting-comment (accessed May 2011).

International Accounting Standards Board (2010a) *International Accounting Standard 16 – Property, Plant and Equipment* (IASB).

International Accounting Standards Board (2010b) *International Accounting Standard 40 – Investment Property* (IASB).

International Accounting Standards Board (2010c) *International Accounting Standard 36 – Impairment of Assets* (IASB).

International Accounting Standards Board (2010d) *International Accounting Standard 17 – Leases* (IASB).

International Accounting Standards Board (2010e) *International Financial Reporting Standard 5 – Non-current Assets Held for Sale and Discontinued Operations* (IASB).

International Accounting Standards Board (2010f) *International Accounting Standard 38 – Intangible Assets* (IASB).

International Accounting Standards Board (2010g) *International Financial Reporting Standard 3 – Business Combinations* (IASB).

International Accounting Standards Committee (1989) Adopted by the International Accounting Standards Board 2001, *Framework for the Preparation and Presentation of Financial Statements* (IASC).

Phillips and Drew (1992) *Ranking of Creative Accounting Practices used by 185 Major UK Companies*, cited by Mike Jones in his slide show on 'Creative Accounting, Fraud and Accounting Scandals', http://www.docstoc.com/docs/3414029/Creative-Accounting-Fraud-and-Accounting-Scandals

Smith, T. (1992) *Accounting for Growth: Stripping the Camouflage from Company Accounts*, Century Business Publications, London.

US Department of Justice (2007) 'Beaulieu pleads guilty to tax fraud', US Attorney David E. Nahmias, Press Release, US Department of Justice website, www.justice.gov/tax/usaopress/2007/txdv0706-15-07.pdf (accessed May 2011).

US Immigration and Customs Enforcement (2007) 'Beaulieu Pleads Guilty to Tax Fraud', http://www.ice.gov/pi/news/newsreleases/articles/070615rome.htm (last updated 17/11/2008, accessed July 2010).

When you have read this chapter, log on to the Online Learning Centre for *Introduction to Financial Accounting* at www.mcgraw-hill.co.uk/textbooks/thomas, where you will find multiple choice quizzes, case studies, a glossary and mock exams.

Bad debts and provisions for bad debts

Learning Objectives

After reading this chapter you should be able to do the following:

1. Explain the meaning of the key terms and concepts listed at the end of the chapter.

2. Explain the nature of bad debts, provisions and provisions for doubtful debts.

3. Distinguish between specific and general provisions for doubtful debts.

4. Show the entries for bad debts and provisions for doubtful debts in the journal, general ledger, statement of profit and loss and statement of financial position.

17.1 The nature of, and ledger entries for, bad debts

When goods are sold on credit, it sometimes transpires that the customer is unwilling or unable to pay the amount owed. This is referred to as a **bad** or **irrecoverable debt**. The decision to treat a debt as bad is a matter of judgement. A debt may be regarded as irrecoverable for a number of reasons, such as being unable to trace the credit customer, it not being worthwhile financially to take the credit customer to court, or the credit customer being bankrupt. However, if a credit customer is bankrupt, this does not necessarily mean that the whole of the debt is irrecoverable. When a person is bankrupt, his or her possessions are seized and sold in order to pay the creditors. Such payments are often made in instalments known as 'dividends'. Frequently, the dividends do not consist of the repayment of the whole of the debt. Thus, when the 'final dividend' is received, the remainder of the debt is irrecoverable.

This is common in practice as shown in real world example 17.1.

REAL WORLD EXAMPLE 17.1 Distribution on the liquidation of Global Trader Europe Ltd

Global Trader Europe Ltd, a UK broking firm with 200 clients went into administration on 14 February 2008. Its acting insolvency practitioner, Smith and Williamson, announced on 25 March 2009 that Global's 'segregated fund clients would receive up to 95p in the pound and the total financial dividend for unsecured creditors is expected to be in the region of 68p'

Source: Smith and Williamson, 2009, www.smith.williamson.co.uk/news. (see References)

When a debt is regarded as irrecoverable the entries in the ledger are as follows:

Debit: Bad debts ledger account

Credit: Trade receivables ledger account (the individual credit customer's account would also be amended in the sales ledger)

Occasionally, debts previously written off as bad are subsequently paid. When this happens, the ledger entries are the reverse of the above, and the trade receivables ledger account is credited with the money received in the normal way.

Debit: Trade receivables ledger account (the individual credit customer's account would be amended in the sales ledger)

Credit: Bad debts ledger account

At the end of the accounting year the balance on the bad debts account is transferred to the statement of profit and loss.

17.2   The nature of, and ledger entries for, provisions for bad debts

A **provision** is the setting-aside of income to meet a known or highly probable future liability or loss, the amount and/or timing of which cannot be ascertained exactly, and is thus an estimate. An example would be a provision for damages payable resulting from a legal action where the verdict had gone against the business but the amount of the damages had not been fixed by the court at the end of the accounting year. If the damages had been fixed, these would be treated not as a provision but as a liability. Another example of a provision is depreciation.

It should be noted that when accountants talk of setting aside income, what they mean is that 'funds' are being retained in the business but not put into a separate bank account. The funds are automatically retained in the business by designating part of the income as a provision, since this reduces the profit that is available for withdrawal by the owner(s) of the business.

The need for a **provision for bad/doubtful debts** essentially arises because goods sold and recognized as sales revenue in one accounting year may not become known to be a bad debt until the following accounting year. Thus, the profit of the year in which the goods are sold would be overstated by the amount of the bad debt. In order to adjust for this, a provision in respect of probable bad debts is created in the year of sale (matching concept).

A provision for bad debts may consist of either a **specific provision** or a **general provision**, or both. A specific provision involves ascertaining which particular credit customers at the year end are unlikely to pay their debts. A general provision is an estimate of the total amount of bad debts computed using a percentage (based on previous years' figures) of the trade receivables at the end of the current year. Where both specific and general provisions are made, the two amounts are added together and the total is entered in the general ledger.

The accounting entries in respect of a provision for bad debts are made after the trial balance has been extracted when the statement of profit and loss is being prepared. It is important to appreciate that any balance on a provision for bad debts account shown in a trial balance must therefore relate to the balance at the end of the previous year. A charge (or credit) is made to the statement of profit and loss in each year that consists of an amount necessary to increase (or decrease) the provision at the end of the previous year to the amount required at the end of the current year.

An increase in a provision always consists of:

Debit: Profit and loss account (increase in provision for bad debts)

Credit: Provision for bad debts account

A decrease in a provision is entered:

Debit: Provision for bad debts account

Credit: Profit and loss account (decrease in provision for bad debts)

The balance on the provision for bad debts account at the end of the year is deducted from trade receivables in the statement of financial position to give the net amount that is expected to be received from credit customers – that is, their net realizable value. The principle is similar to that applied in the case of a provision for depreciation where the accumulated depreciation at the end of the year, as shown by the balance on the provision for depreciation account, is deducted from the cost of the non-current asset in the statement of financial position. All other provisions such as for legal costs, damages or fines are shown in the statement of financial position as a current liability or non-current liability, depending on whether they are payable within one year or more from the date of the statement of financial position. The treatment of bad debts and provisions for bad debts is illustrated in Examples 17.1 and 17.2.

EXAMPLE 17.1

A. Jones has an accounting year ending on 30 November. At 30 November 20X2 his ledger contained the following accounts:

	£
Trade receivables	20,000
Provision for bad debts	1,000

The trade receivables at 30 November 20X3 were £18,900. This includes an amount of £300 owed by F. Simons that was thought to be irrecoverable. It also includes amounts of £240 owed by C. Steven, £150 owed by M. Evans and £210 owed by A. Mitchell, all of which are regarded as doubtful debts.

You have been instructed to make a provision for bad debts at 30 November 20X3. This should include a specific provision for debts regarded as doubtful and a general provision of 5 per cent of trade receivables.

Show the ledger entries in respect of the above and the relevant statement of financial position extract.

Provision for bad debts at 30 November 20X3	£
Specific provision – C. Steven	240
M. Evans	150
A. Mitchell	210
	600
General provision – 5% × (£18,900 – £300 – £600)	900
	1,500

The ledger

(*Note*: Assume the individual customer accounts are maintained in the general ledger; A. Jones does not keep a sales ledger.)

F. Simons (trade receivable)					
20X3	Details	£	20X3	Details	£
30 Nov	Balance b/d	300	30 Nov	Bad debts	300

Bad debts					
20X3	**Details**	**£**	**20X3**	**Details**	**£**
30 Nov	F. Simons	300	30 Nov	Profit and loss a/c	300

Provision for bad debts					
20X3	**Details**	**£**	**20X2**	**Details**	**£**
30 Nov	Balance c/d	1,500	1 Dec	Balance b/d	1,000
			20X1		
			30 Nov	Profit and loss a/c	500
		1,500			1,500
			20X3		
			1 Dec	Balance b/d	1,500

Profit and loss account				
20X3	**Details**	**£**		
30 Nov	Bad debts	300		
30 Nov	Provision for bad debts	500		

Statement of financial position (extract)	
Current assets	**£**
Trade receivables (£18,900 – £300)	18,600
Less: Provision for bad debts	1,500
	17,100

Notes

1 No entries are made in the accounts of those credit customers that comprise the specific provision, since these are only doubtful debts and thus not yet regarded as irrecoverable.

2 The balance carried down on the provision for bad debts account at the end of the year is always the amount of the new provision. The amount charged to the profit and loss account is the difference between the provision at the end of the current year and that at the end of the previous year. In this example the provision is increased from £1,000 to £1,500 by means of a credit to the provision for bad debts account of £500 and a corresponding debit to the profit and loss account.

3 In computing the amount of the general provision, any bad debts and specific provisions must be deducted from trade receivables. Otherwise, the specific provision would be duplicated and a provision would be made for debts already written off as bad.

4 The bad debts written off must also be removed from trade receivables in preparing the statement of financial position.

5 There is another method of accounting for bad debts and provisions for bad debts that essentially involves combining these two accounts. This is shown below.

(Provision for) bad debts						
20X3	**Details**	**£**	**20X2**	**Details**		**£**
30 Nov	F Simons	300	1 Dec	Balance b/d		1,000
30 Nov	Balance c/d	1,500	**20X3**			
			30 Nov	Profit and loss a/c		800
		1,800				1,800
			20X3	**Details**		
			1 Dec	Balance b/d		1,500

Profit and loss account				
20X3	**Details**	**£**		
30 Nov	Bad debts	800		

The combined charge to the statement of profit and loss for the year in respect of bad debts and the provision for bad debts is the difference between the two sides of the (provision for) bad debts account after inserting the amount of the provision at 30 November 20X3 as a balance carried down. The charge to the statement of profit an loss under both methods is always the same in total.

EXAMPLE 17.2

This is a continuation of Example 17.1.

During the year ended 30 November 20X4 C. Steven was declared bankrupt and a first dividend of £140 was received from the trustee. M. Evans was also declared bankrupt and a first and final dividend of £30 was received from the trustee. A. Mitchell paid his debt in full. A further debt of £350 owed by R. Jackson that is included in trade receivables at 30 November 20X3 proved to be bad.

The trade receivables at 30 November 20X4 were £24,570. This figure is after recording all money received but does not take into account bad debts.

You have been instructed to make a provision for bad debts at 30 November 20X4. This should include a specific provision for doubtful debts and a general provision of 5 per cent of trade receivables.

Show the ledger entries in respect of the above and the relevant statement of financial position extract.

Provision for bad debts at 30 November 20X4	
	£
Specific provision – C. Steven (£240 – £140)	100
General provision – 5% × (£24,570 – £120 – £350 – £100)	1,200
	1,300

The ledger

(*Note*: Assume the individual customer accounts are maintained in the general ledger, i.e., A. Jones does not keep a sales ledger.)

C. Steven (trade receivable)

20X3	Details	£	20X4	Details	£
1 Dec	Balance b/d	240	30 Nov	Bank	140
			30 Nov	Balance c/d	100
		240			240
20X4					
1 Dec	Balance b/d	100			

M. Evans (trade receivable)

20X3	Details	£	20X4	Details	£
1 Dec	Balance b/d	150	30 Nov	Bank	30
			30 Nov	Bad debts	120
		150			150

R. Jackson (trade receivable)

20X3	Details	£	20X4	Details	£
1 Dec	Balance b/d	350	30 Nov	Bad debts	350

Bad debts

20X4	Details	£	20X4	Details	£
30 Nov	M. Evans	120	30 Nov	Profit and loss a/c	470
30 Nov	R. Jackson	350			
		470			470

Provision for bad debts

20X4	Details	£	20X3	Details	£
30 Nov	Profit and loss a/c	200	1 Dec	Balance b/d	1,500
30 Nov	Balance c/d	1,300			
		1,500			1,500
			20X4		
			1 Dec	Balance b/d	1,300

Profit and loss account

		£			£
30 Nov	Bad debts	470	30 Nov	Provision for bad debts	200

Statement of financial position

Current assets	£
Trade receivable (£24,570 − £120 − £350)	24,100
Less: Provision for bad debts	1,300
	22,800

Alternative method					
(Provision for) bad debts					
20X4	Details	£	20X3	Details	£
30 Nov	M. Evans	120	1 Dec	Balance b/d	1,500
30 Nov	R. Jackson	350	20X4		
30 Nov	Balance c/d	1,300	30 Nov	Profit and loss a/c	270
		1,770			1,770
			20X4		
			1 Dec	Balance b/d	1,300

Notes

1 The amount due from M. Evans is written off as a bad debt because the final dividend in bankruptcy was declared, which means that no more money will be received in respect of this debt. However, the amount due from C. Steven is not written off as a bad debt, despite the fact that he was declared bankrupt, because further dividends are expected. Thus, this debt is the subject of a specific provision in respect of the amount still outstanding.

2 No entries are required where a debt that was previously treated as a specific provision is subsequently paid, as in the case of A. Mitchell.

3 The main method shown above (that has separate bad debt and provision for bad debts accounts) is the most common in practice. However, this tends to obscure the logic behind provisions for bad debts, because it accounts for the provision separately from the bad debts. The 'alternative method' shown above allows the logic to be demonstrated as follows. The bad debts for the year (£120 + £350 = £470) are set against the provision at the end of the previous year (£1,500). Any under- or overprovision (£1,500 − £470 = overprovision of £1,030) is written back to the comprehensive income account. The amount of the provision required at the end of the current year (£1,300) is then created in full by debiting the comprehensive income account with this amount. This can be illustrated as follows.

(Provision for) bad debts					
20X4	Details	£	20X3	Details	£
30 Nov	M. Evans	120	1 Dec	Balance b/d	1,500
30 Nov	R. Jackson	350	20X4		
30 Nov	Profit and loss a/c overprovision	1,030	30 Nov	Profit and loss a/c	1,300
30 Nov	Balance c/d	1,300			
		2,800			2,800
			20X4		
			1 Dec	Balance b/d	1,300

The debit entry of £1,030 is the reversal of the overprovision. The credit entry of £1,300 is the creation of the new provision. The net effect is the same as in the previous answer – a debit to the profit and loss account of £270 and a balance on the (provision for) bad debts account of £1,300. However, it should be observed that the overprovision of £1,030 as calculated above is an oversimplification. This is not usually readily identifiable, since the bad debts normally comprise not only those relating to sales in the previous year for which a provision was created, but also bad debts arising from sales in the current year. The charge to the profit and loss account shown in the 'alternative method' therefore usually comprises:

1 a reversal of the under- or overprovision;

2 the bad debts arising from sales in the current year;

3 the amount of the new provision at the end of the current year.

Furthermore, it should be stressed that nobody would prepare a (provision) for bad debts account in the manner shown immediately above since it involves the unnecessary calculation of the under- or overprovision. However, the illustration serves to demonstrate that:

1 the underlying logic behind the provision for bad debts is essentially to shift the bad debts back into the year in which the goods were sold;

2 this requires an estimate of the provision;

3 the estimate usually gives rise to an under- or overprovision that has to be reversed. However, this can be done without identifying the under- or overprovision separately by means of a single charge to the statement of profit and loss when the new provision for bad debts at the end of the current year has been created.

Accounting policy for provision for bad debts

Most entities provide details of how they value their trade receivables and how they calculate the provision for bad debts in their accounting policies. An example can be found in the financial statements of Viridian Group as follows:

Viridian Group

Extract from the accounting policies note

Trade debtors

Trade receivables do not carry any interest and are recognised and carried at the lower of their original invoiced value and recoverable amount. Provision is made when there is objective evidence that the asset is impaired. Balances are written off when the probability of recovery is assessed as being remote.

Source: Viridian (2010), Viridian Group Holdings Limited Annual Report and Accounts 2009–10, http://www.viridiangroup.co.uk/default.aspx?CATID=226 (accessed 11 July 2011).

Using a plc's financial statements (search the Web) for guidance, draft a pro forma note on the provision for bad debts. This should show the typical movements to be expected in a provision and a trade receivables account.

Note how the company you have selected provides details on the age of their outstanding debts. This can be used to determine if the provision is realistic, or not.

Accounting manipulation and provisions for doubtful debts

Like most accounting adjustments there is an element of subjectivity about estimating the extent of general provision that is required. Research has found that movements in the provision for doubtful debts are used to manipulate accounting profits (see Smith, 1992 and Phillips and Drew, 1992). An example is provided in real world example 17.3.

REAL WORLD EXAMPLE 17.3

Accounting irregularities – the provision for bad debts

In 2009 the UK sub-prime lending company 'Cattle' sacked six executives after an under-provision for bad debts was uncovered amounting to £700,000. The outcome of this revelation was that Cattle's future was called into question, trading in the company's shares were suspended by the stock market and the publication of the company's accounts were delayed, pending investigation (Inman, 2009). Hyde's Brewery, a Manchester-based firm, was also found to have accounting irregularities which included under-providing for bad debts. It had to restate its financial statements in 2008 to include an increase in the provision for bad debts of £675,000 and in the year to 2009 a further provision of £369,000 was required.

Source: Gerrard, 2010, www.caterersearch.com/Articles/2010/01/26/331868/Hydes-Brewery-reports-1631.3m-annual-pre-tax-loss.htm (accessed July 2010).

Summary

A debt is treated as irrecoverable if a credit customer is unwilling or unable to pay, and the enterprise decides it is uneconomical to pursue the matter further. The ledger entry for irrecoverable debts is to credit the credit customers' trade receivable personal account and debit a bad debts account. The balance on the bad debts account is transferred to the statement of profit and loss account at the end of the accounting year.

A provision is the setting-aside of income to meet a known or highly probable future liability or loss, the amount and/or timing of which cannot be ascertained exactly, and is thus an estimate. The most common examples are provisions for depreciation and doubtful/bad debts.

A provision for bad debts may consist of a specific provision and/or a general provision. The accounting entries in respect of a provision for bad debts are made after the trial balance has been extracted when the statement of profit and loss and statement of financial position are being prepared. A charge (or credit) is made to the statement of profit and loss that consists of an amount necessary to increase (or decrease) the provision at the end of the previous year to the amount required at the end of the current year. The ledger entries are to debit (or credit) the profit and loss account and credit (or debit) a provision for bad debts account. The latter is shown on the statement of financial position as a deduction from trade receivables to give a net figure representing the amount that the enterprise expects to receive from these credit customers during the forthcoming accounting year.

Key terms and concepts

bad debt	263	provision	264
general provision	264	provision for bad/doubtful debts	264
irrecoverable debt	263	specific provision	264

An asterisk after the question number indicates that there is a suggested answer on the Online Learning Centre (www.mcgraw-hill.co.uk/textbooks/thomas).

connect Review questions

17.1 What do you understand by the term 'bad debts'? In what circumstances might a debt be treated as irrecoverable?

17.2 a Explain the nature of a provision, including how this differs from a liability.

  b Give one example of a provision other than provisions for bad debts and depreciation.

17.3 a Explain the nature of a provision for bad debts.

  b Explain the difference between a specific and general provision for bad debts.

17.4 Examine the purpose and logic behind a provision for bad debts, with particular reference to the timing of profits and losses arising from credit sales.

17.5 a Which accounting concepts directly influence the creation of a provision for doubtful debts?

  b Explain your reasoning.

17.6 a Businesses often create a provision for bad debts

  i Of which concept is this an example? Explain.

  ii What is the purpose for creating a provision for bad debts?

  iii How might the amount of a provision for bad debts be calculated?

  b What is the difference between bad debts and provision for bad debts?

connect Exercises

BASIC

17.7*

A business has an accounting year ending on 31 July. It sells goods on credit and on 31 July 20X3 had trade receivables of £15,680. This includes debts of £410 due from A. Wall and £270 from B. Wood, both of which were regarded as irrecoverable.

The business has decided to create a provision for bad debts at 31 July 20X3 of 4 per cent of trade receivables. Previously there was no provision for bad debts.

You are required to show the ledger entries in respect of the above bad debts and provision for bad debts.

BASIC

17.8*

B. Summers has an accounting year ending on 30 April. At 30 April 20X2 his ledger contained the following accounts:

	£
Trade receivables	25,000
Provision for doubtful debts	750

The trade receivables at 30 April 20X3 were £19,500. This includes £620 due from A. Winters and £880 from D. Spring, both of which are thought to be irrecoverable.

You have been instructed to make a provision for bad debts at 30 April 20X3 of 3 per cent of trade receivables.

Show the ledger entries in respect of the bad debts and provision for bad debts.

17.9

YEAR 1

1 The balance on trade receivables at the year end is £110,000.

2 Two of the balances in the sales ledger have to be written off. One is £4,500 the other is £5,500.

3 The company is to provide 5 per cent for a provision for doubtful debts and 5 per cent for a provision for discounts.

YEAR 2

The sales in the year were £10,000 lower than the cash received in the year (consider the impact of this on the closing balance).

1 One of the debts that had been written off last year (£5,500) is now recoverable.

2 At the end of this year the auditor has identified £500 of the sales ledger balances as bad debts. These should be written off.

3 The provision for discounts should be increased to 10 per cent.

4 The provision for bad debts should be adjusted to 2 per cent.

Required

Show the transactions in the sales ledger and the general ledger accounts and the extract entries from the statement of comprehensive income and statement of financial position for the two years.

17.10

The financial statements for the year ended 30 November 20X3 of Springboard Ltd included a provision for doubtful debts at that date of £900.

During the year ended 30 November 20X4, the company received £500 from Peter Lyon towards the settlement of a debt of £700 that had been written off as irrecoverable by the company in 20X1. There is no evidence that Peter Lyon will be able to make any further payments to the company.

Trade receivables at 30 November 20X4 amounted to £22,000, which includes the following debts:

	£
Mary Leaf	800
Angus Way	300

It has now been decided to write off these debts as bad.

In its financial statements for the year ended 30 November 20X4, the company is to continue its policy of maintaining a provision for doubtful debts of 5 per cent of trade receivables at the year end.

(*Note*: Bad debts written off or recovered are not to be recorded in the provision for doubtful debts account.)

Required

a Prepare the journal entry (or entries) in the books of the company necessitated by the receipt from Peter Lyon.

Notes:

1 Journal entries should include narratives.

2 For the purposes of this question, assume that cash receipts are journalized.

b Prepare the provision for doubtful debts account in the books of the company for the year ended 30 November 20X4.

c Show the entry for trade receivables which will be included in the statement of financial position as at 30 November 20X4 of the company.

(AAT, adapted)

17.11

INTERMEDIATE

The following transactions are to be recorded. At the beginning of year 1 a provision for doubtful debts account is to be opened. It should show a provision of 2 per cent against trade receivables of £50,000. During the year bad debts of £2,345 are to be charged to the provision account. At the end of year 1 the bad debts provision is required to be 2 per cent against trade receivables of £60,000.

In year 2 bad debts of £37 are to be charged against the account. At the end of year 2 a provision of 1 per cent against trade receivables of £70,000 is required.

Required

Prepare provision for doubtful debts account for the two years. Show in the account the double entry for each item, and carry down the balance at the end of each year.

(ACCA, adapted)

17.12

INTERMEDIATE

The statement of financial position as at 31 December 20X2 of Zoom Products Ltd included:

	£
Trade receivables	85,360

The financial statements for the year ended 31 December 20X2 included a provision for doubtful debts at 31 December 20X2 of 3 per cent of the balance outstanding from credit customers. During 20X2, the company's sales totalled £568,000, of which 90 per cent, in value, was on credit and £510,150 was received from credit customers in settlement of debts totalling £515,000. In addition, £3,000 was received from J. Dodds in a settlement of a debt that had been written off as bad in 20X2; this receipt has been credited to J. Dodds's account in the sales' ledger.

On 30 December 20X3, the following outstanding debts were written off as bad:

	£
J . White	£600
K. Black	£2,000

Entries relating to bad debts are passed through the provision for doubtful debts account, whose balance at 31 December 20X3 is to be 3 per cent of the amount due to the company from credit customers at that date.

Required

a Write up the provision for doubtful debts account for the year ended 31 December 20X3, bringing down the balance at 1 January 20X4.

b Prepare a computation of the amount to be shown as trade receivables in the company's statement of financial position at 31 December 20X3.

(AAT, adapted)

17.13

Because of the doubtful nature of some debts, P. Rudent instructed his accountants to make a specific provision in the financial statements for the year ended 30 June 20X3 against the following debts:

	£
J. Black	28
C. Green	6
B. Grey	24
Fawn Ltd	204

He also instructed that a general provision of 5 per cent for doubtful debts should be created on the other trade receivables, which at 30 June 20X3 amounted to £8,000.

No further business transactions were entered into with any of these credit customers during the year ended 30 June 20X4, but an amount of £9 was received from J. Black's trustee in bankruptcy by way of a first dividend; a first and final dividend of £70 was received from the liquidator of Fawn Ltd and B. Grey paid his debt in full. A further debt of £95 due from S. White proved to be bad.

On 30 June 20X4 P. Rudent instructed his accountants to maintain the provision existing against C. Green's debt and to provide for the balance owing by J. Black, and to make further provision for debts owing by J. Blue £19 and R. Brown £15. The other trade receivables amounted to £7,500 and the accountants were instructed to make the provision for doubtful debts equal to 5 per cent of these debts.

Show what entries should be made in P. Rudent's nominal ledger to record these facts.

(ACCA, adapted)

17.14*

M. Shaft has an accounting year ending on 31 December. At 31 December 20X2 the ledger contained the following balances:

	£
Plant and machinery	30,000
Provision for depreciation on plant and machinery	12,500
Trade receivables	10,760
Provision for bad debts	1,260

The provision for bad debts consisted of a general provision of £500 and specific provisions comprising: A. Bee £320; C. Dee £180; and F. Gee £260.

The following transactions occurred during 20X3:

31 Mar   Part exchanged one piece of plant for another. The part exchange allowance on the old plant was £4,000 and the balance of £1,000 was paid by cheque. The old plant cost £8,000 when it was purchased on 1 July 20X1.

30 Apr   A. Bee was declared bankrupt and a first dividend of £70 was received from the trustee.

15 June   A debt of £210 owed by J. Kay that is included in trade receivables at 31 December 20X2 was found to be bad.

3 Aug   C. Dee paid his debt in full.

7 Oct   F. Gee was declared bankrupt and a first and final dividend at £110 was received from the trustee.

Plant and machinery is depreciated using the reducing balance method at a rate of 25 per cent per annum on a strict time basis. The trade receivables at 31 December 20X3 were £12,610. This figure is after recording all money received but does not take into account any of the above bad debts. The relevant specific provisions and a general provision for bad debts of 5 per cent should be maintained at 31 December 20X3.

Required

a Show the ledger entries in respect of the above, including the charges to the statement of profit and loss and the balances at 31 December 20X3. Show your workings clearly and take all calculations to the nearest £.

b Briefly discuss the similarities between provisions for bad debts and depreciation.

References

Gerrard, N. (2010) 'Hyde's Brewery Reports £1.3m annual pre-tax loss', http://www.caterersearch.com/Articles/2010/01/26/331868/Hydes-Brewery-reports-1631.3m-annual-pre-tax-loss.htm (accessed July 2010).

Inman, P. (2009) 'Sub-Prime Lender Sacks executives over £700m accounting hole: Cattle reveals managers jeopardized firm by failing to make proper provision for bad debts', *Guardian*, 1 July 2009, http://www.guardian.co.uk (accessed July 2010).

Phillips and Drew (1992) *Ranking of Creative Accounting Practices used by 185 Major UK Companies*, cited by Mike Jones in his slide show on 'Creative Accounting, Fraud and Accounting Scandals', http://www.docstoc.com/docs/3414029/Creative-Accounting-Fraud-and-Accounting-Scandals

Smith, T. (1992) *Accounting for Growth: Stripping the Camouflage from Company Accounts*, Century Business Publications, London.

Smith and Williamson (2009) 'News Regarding Global Trader Europe Limited (in Liquidation)', http://www.smith.williamson.co.uk/news, (25/03/09) (accessed July 2010).

Viridian (2010) Viridian Group Holdings Limited Annual Report and Accounts 2009–10, http://www.viridiangroup.co.uk/default.aspx?CATID=226 (accessed 11 July 2011).

When you have read this chapter, log on to the Online Learning Centre for *Introduction to Financial Accounting* at www.mcgraw-hill.co.uk/textbooks/thomas, where you will find multiple choice quizzes, case studies, a glossary and mock exams.

Accruals and prepayments

Learning Objectives

After reading this chapter you should be able to do the following:

1 Explain the meaning of the key terms and concepts listed at the end of the chapter.

2 Explain the conceptual foundation of accruals and prepayments, including the nature of the resulting charge to the statement of comprehensive income (statement of profit and loss).

3 Describe the nature of accruals and prepayments and how the amounts can be ascertained in practice.

4 Show the entries for accruals and prepayments in the journal, general ledger, statement of profit and loss and statement of financial position.

5 Prepare simple final financial statements from a trial balance making the required adjustments for accruals and prepayments.

18.1   The nature of, and ledger entries for, accrued expenses

As discussed in Chapter 5, 'Accounting Principles, Concepts and Policies', the accruals concept dictates that costs are recognized as they are incurred, not when money is paid. That is, goods and services are deemed to have been purchased on the date they are received. This gives rise to **accrued expenses/ accruals**. Accruals are 'payables' in respect of services received that have not been paid for at the end of the accounting year. Accrued expenses can obviously only occur where services are paid for in arrears, such as electricity or gas.

An accrual may comprise either or both of the following:

1 Invoices received (for expenses) that have not been paid at the end of the accounting year.

2 The value of services received for which an invoice has not been rendered at the end of the accounting year.

In the case of the latter, this requires an estimate to be made of the amount of the services consumed during the period between the date of the last invoice and the end of the accounting year. This may be based on any one of the following:

1 A meter reading taken at the end of the accounting year.

2 The amount consumed over a corresponding period during the current year.

3 The amount consumed during the same period of the previous year as adjusted for any change in the unit price.

However, in practice, final financial statements are often not prepared until some time after the end of the accounting year. By that time the invoice covering the period in question is likely to have been received and can thus be used to ascertain the value of the services consumed during the relevant period. The accrual convention has been used in the past to manipulate reported earnings (profits) in a fraudulent manner. It is for this reason that auditors afford special attention to the determination of accrual amount and cut-off periods. An example is now provided:

REAL WORLD EXAMPLE 18.1

Sirena Apparel Group Inc.

Serina Apparel Group Inc (Serina) is a women's swimwear manufacturer located in the US. The SEC took action against the company's former chairman and chief financial officer for violation of the accruals and matching concept, wherein they ordered staff to hold open the March 1999 sales ledger until 12 April, when sales targets were met and did not record the related costs which were incurred in making the products available for sale. The overall impact of this action was to overstate the company's revenue by $3.6 million and its earnings by $1.3 million. Serina's staff were also ordered to create false shipping documents for the auditors that were dated March, instead of April.

Source: http://www.sec.gov/news/press/2000-142.txt

Although accrued expenses are essentially payables, rather than have a separate accruals' account it is usual to enter accruals in the relevant expense account. This consists of debiting the amount owing at the end of the year to the expense account as a balance *carried down* and crediting the same account as a balance *brought down* in the next period. Thus, the amount that will be transferred to the income account consists of the amount paid during the year plus the accrual at the end of the year (less the accrual at the start of the year). This will reflect the total value of the services that have been received during the current accounting year. The balance brought down is entered on the statement of financial position as a current liability. A pro forma ledger account showing typical entries is now provided (see Figure 18.1). This can be used to check that entries have been correctly posted.

		Light and heat				
20X2	**Details**		**£**	**20X2**	**Details**	**£**
	Bank		XX	1 Jan	Opening accrual b/d	X
31 Dec	Closing accrual c/d		X	31 Dec	Profit and loss a/c	XX
			XX			XX
				20X3		
				1 Jan	Opening accrual b/d	X

Figure 18.1 A pro forma expense ledger account showing typical entries for expense accruals

The shaded entry is the entry that is derived when the account is closed. This is the charge for the year. The opening accrual on the 1 January 20X3 is the payable that will be disclosed under current liabilities in the statement of financial position. The journal to record (post) the year end accrual shown in Figure 18.1 is as follows:

Debit: Light and heat account current period (this will end up in the current year profit and loss charge)

Credit: Light and heat account new period (opening accrual in the next period – this balance will form part of the profit and loss charge in the next period)

The mechanics of calculating the yearly charge is illustrated in Example 18.1.

EXAMPLE 18.1

D. Spring has an accounting year ending on 31 December. The following amounts have been paid for electricity:

Date paid	Quarter ended	£
29 Mar 20X2	28 Feb 20X2	96
7 July 20X2	31 May 20X2	68
2 Oct 20X2	31 Aug 20X2	73
5 Jan 20X3	30 Nov 20X2	82
3 Apr 20X3	28 Feb 20X3	105

You are required to show the entries in the light and heat account for the year ended 31 December 20X2 and the relevant statement of financial position extract.

Workings

$$\text{Accrual at 1 Jan 20X2} = \tfrac{1}{3} \times £96 = £32$$

$$\text{Accrual at 31 Dec 20X2} = £82 + (\tfrac{1}{3} \times £105) = £117$$

Light and heat					
20X2	**Details**	**£**	**20X2**	**Details**	**£**
29 Mar	Bank	96	1 Jan	Accrual b/d	32
7 July	Bank	68	31 Dec	Profit and loss a/c	322
2 Oct	Bank	73			
31 Dec	Accrual c/d	117			
		354			354
			20X3		
			1 Jan	Accrual b/d	117

Statement of financial position as at 31 December 20X2	(extract)
	£
Current liabilities	
Accrued expenses	117

Note

1 The amount transferred to the statement of profit and loss is the difference between the two sides of the light and heat account after entering the accrual at the end of the year.

18.2 The nature of, and ledger entries for, prepaid expenses

The accruals concept also gives rise to **prepaid expenses/prepayments**. Prepayments are 'receivables' in respect of services that have been paid for but not received at the end of the accounting year. Prepayments can obviously only occur where services are paid for in advance, such as rent, local government taxes, road tax and insurance.

The amount of the prepayment is ascertained by determining on a time basis how much of the last payment made during the accounting year relates to the services that will be received in the following accounting year.

Although prepaid expenses are essentially receivables, rather than have a separate prepayment account, it is usual to enter the prepayment in the relevant expense account. This consists of crediting the amount of the prepayment to the expense account as a balance *carried down* and debiting the same account as a balance *brought down*. Thus, the amount that will be transferred to the profit and loss account consists of the amount paid during the year minus the prepayment at the end of the year (plus the prepayment at the start of the year). This will reflect the total value of the services that have been received during the current accounting year. The balance brought down is entered on the statement of financial position as a current asset. A pro forma ledger account showing the relevant entries is provided in Figure 18.2. This can be used to check entries.

	Rent				
20X2		**£**	**20X31**		**£**
1 July	Opening prepayment b/d	X	30 June	Profit and loss a/c	XX
1 Sep	Bank	XX	30 June	Closing prepayment c/d	X
		XX			XX
20X3					
1 July	Opening prepayment b/d	X			

Figure 18.2 A pro forma expense ledger account showing typical entries for expense prepayments

The shaded entry is the entry that is derived when the account is closed. This is the charge for the year. The opening prepayment on the 1 July 20X3 is the receivable that will be disclosed under current assets in the statement of financial position. The mechanics of calculating the yearly charge is illustrated in Example 18.2.

EXAMPLE 18.2

M. Waters has an accounting year ending on 30 June. The following amounts have been paid as rent:

Date paid	Quarter ended	£
2 Jun 20X2	31 Aug 20X2	600
1 Sep 20X2	30 Nov 20X2	600
3 Dec 20X2	28 Feb 20X3	660
5 Mar 20X3	31 May 20X3	660
4 Jun 20X3	31 Aug 20X3	720

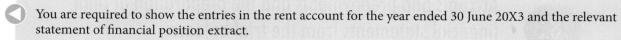

You are required to show the entries in the rent account for the year ended 30 June 20X3 and the relevant statement of financial position extract.

Workings

$$\text{Prepaid at 1 July 20X2} = \tfrac{2}{3} \times £600 = £400$$

$$\text{Prepaid at 30 June 20X31} = \tfrac{2}{3} \times £720 = £480$$

		Rent				
20X2	**Details**	**£**	**20X3**	**Details**	**£**
1 Jul	Prepayment b/d	400	30 Jun	Profit and loss a/c	2,560
1 Sep	Bank	600			
3 Dec	Bank	660			
20X3					
5 Mar	Bank	660			
4 Jun	Bank	720	30 Jun	Prepayment c/d	480
		3,040			3,040
20X3					
1 Jul	Prepayment b/d	480			

Statement of financial position as at 30 June 20X3	(extract)
	£
Current assets	
Prepayments	480

Note

1 The amount transferred to the statement of profit and loss is the difference between the two sides of the rent account after entering the prepayment at the end of the year.

LEARNING ACTIVITY 18.1 Obtain copies of the electricity bills for the house in which you live. From these prepare a light and heat account relating to the last complete calendar year. Repeat this exercise for insurance.

18.3 Accruals and prepayments and the preparation of final financial statements from the trial balance

The statement of profit and loss is usually prepared from the trial balance. This involves adjusting the amounts shown for any accruals and prepayments at the end of the accounting year. It is important to appreciate that, because the trial balance is taken out at the end of the accounting year, the amounts shown in it include any accruals and prepayments at the start of the year. Thus, when preparing an statement of profit and loss from the trial balance, it is only necessary to add to the amount shown in the trial balance any accrual at the end of the accounting year and to subtract any prepayment.

EXAMPLE 18.3

Extract from the trial balance of A. Trader at the year end:

	Debit £	Credit £
Trade receivables	20,000	
Trade payables		6,000
Heat and light	4,000	
Rent	6,000	
	XXXX	XXXX

Additional information

1 There is an accrual at the year end of £200 for heat and light

2 Rent amounting to £1,000 was prepaid at the reporting period end.

Required

a Prepare the ledger accounts showing the year-end adjustments.

b Show the adjusted trial balance.

c Provide extracts from the statement of financial position to show the relevant disclosures for the accrual and the prepayment.

Heat and light	£		£
Balance b/d from TB	4,000		
Closing accrual c/d	200	Profit and loss a/c	4,200
	4,200		4,200
		Opening accrual b/d	200

Rent	£		£
Balance b/d from TB	6,000	Profit and loss a/c	5,000
		Closing prepayment c/d	1,000
	6,000		6,000
Opening prepayment b/d	1,000		

◀ Amended trial balance

	Debit £	Credit £
Trade receivables	20,000	
Trade payables		6,000
Heat and light	4,200	
Rent	5,000	
		200
Accruals		
Prepayments	1,000	
	XXXX	XXXX

The shaded area shows the accounts that have changed.

Extract from the statement of financial position as at XX	
ASSETS	£
Current assets	
Inventories	XX
Trade receivables	20,000
Prepayments	1,000
Bank	XX
Cash	XX
	X
Total assets	XXX
OWNER'S EQUITY AND LIABILITIES	
Owner's capital	XXX
Current liabilities	
Trade payables	6,000
Accruals	200
	6,200
Total equity and liabilities	XXX

18.4 Further year-end adjustment (inventories of tools, stationery and fuels)

As explained in Chapter 16 'Depreciation and Non-current Assets', **loose tools** are regarded as non-current assets, whereas **consumable tools** are designated as revenue expenditure. Thus, any inventories of consumable tools, such as inventories of stationery and fuel, are treated as current assets. However, irrespective of their classification, the accounting adjustments in respect of these items are essentially the same. That is, the value of the items in inventories at the end of the accounting year is entered in the relevant ledger account as a balance *carried down* on the credit side and as a balance *brought down* on the debit side (in exactly the same way as with prepaid expenses). The difference between the two sides of the ledger account is then transferred to the profit and loss account. In the case of loose tools this is described as 'depreciation', which is referred to as having been computed using the revaluation method.

The principle that is applied to each of these items is as follows:

Inventory at end of previous year at valuation

Add: Purchases during the year

Less: Inventory at end of current year at valuation

= Charge to statement of profit and loss

In the ledger this will be presented as follows:

Stationery/oil/tools					
20X2	**Details**	**£**	**20X2**	**Details**	**£**
1 Jan	Opening inventory b/d	XX	30 Nov	Profit and loss a/c	XXX
	Payments mid-year	XXX	31 Dec	Closing inventory c/d	XX
		XXX			XXX
20X3					
1 Jan	Opening inventory b/d	XX			

The charge to the profit and loss account represents the value of stationery, fuel or tools that has been consumed during the year. The same principle is also applied in the financial statements of farming businesses with respect to livestock and growing crops, and in retailing businesses when accounting for containers and packing materials.

Summary

The accruals concept dictates that costs are recognized as they are incurred, not as money is paid. That is, goods and services are deemed to have been purchased on the date they are received. This gives rise to accrued and prepaid expenses. Accrued expenses are payables in respect of services received that have not been paid for at the end of an accounting year. Prepaid expenses are receivables in respect of services that have been paid for, but not received, at the end of an accounting year.

After a trial balance has been extracted, the final financial statements are prepared, which necessitates adjustments relating to accrued and prepaid expenses. These adjustments are made in the relevant expense accounts in the form of a balance at the end of the year. The remaining difference between the two sides of the expense account is transferred to the profit and loss account, and represents the cost of services received during the year. The balance on the expense account is shown on the statement of financial position as a current liability in the case of accruals, or as a current asset in the case of prepayments.

Key terms and concepts

accrued expenses/accruals	277	prepaid expenses	280
consumable tools	283	prepayments	280
loose tools	283		

An asterisk after the question number indicates that there is a suggested answer on the Online Learning Centre (www.mcgraw-hill.co.uk/textbooks/thomas).

Review questions

connect

18.1 **a** Explain the nature of accrued and prepaid expenses.

b Describe how the amount of each may be ascertained.

Exercises

connect

18.2*

BASIC

K. Wills has an accounting year ending on 31 December. The following amounts were paid in respect of rent and gas:

Expense	Date paid	Quarter ended	£
Rent	1 Nov 20X1	31 Jan 20X2	900
Rent	29 Jan 20X2	30 Apr 20X2	930
Gas	6 Mar 20X2	28 Feb 20X2	420
Rent	2 May 20X2	31 July 20X2	930
Gas	4 Jun 20X2	31 May 20X2	360
Rent	30 Jul 20X2	31 Oct 20X2	930
Gas	3 Sep 20X2	31 Aug 20X2	270
Rent	5 Nov 20X2	31 Jan 20X3	960
Gas	7 Dec 20X2	30 Nov 20X2	390
Gas	8 Mar 20X3	28 Feb 20X3	450

You are required to show the ledger entries in the rent and light and heat accounts for the year ended 31 December 20X2.

BASIC

18.3

Oriel Ltd, whose financial year runs from 1 June to the following 31 May, maintains a combined rent and rates account in its ledger.

Rent is fixed on a calendar year basis and is payable quarterly in advance. Rent was £2,400 for the year ended 31 December 20X2 and is £3,000 for the year ending 31 December 20X3.

Oriel Ltd has made the following payments of rent by cheque:

Date	Amount	Details
20X2	£	
3 Jan	600	Quarter to 31 Mar 20X2
1 Apr	600	Quarter to 30 Jun 20X2
1 July	600	Quarter to 30 Sep 20X2
1 Oct	600	Quarter to 31 Dec 20X2
20X3		
3 Jan	750	Quarter to 31 Mar 20X3
1 Apr	750	Quarter to 30 Jun 20X3

Rates are assessed annually for the year from 1 April to the following 31 March and are payable in one lump sum by 30 September. The rates assessment was £2,040 for the year ended 31 March 20X3 and £2,280 for the year ending 31 March 20X4.

Oriel Ltd paid the rates for the year ended 31 March 20X3 by cheque on 30 September 20X2 and intends to pay the rates for the year ended 31 March 20X4 on 30 September 20X3.

Required

a Prepare the rent and rates account for the year ended 31 May 20X3 only as it would appear in the ledger of Oriel Ltd.

b Explain with particular reference to your answer to (a) the meaning of the term 'matching'.

(AAT, adapted)

BASIC

18.4

Munch Catering Ltd, whose financial year runs from 1 December to the following 30 November, maintains a 'Building occupancy costs' account in its general ledger. This account is used to record all payments in respect of rent, insurance and property taxes on the company's business premises.

Rent is fixed on a calendar year basis and is payable quarterly in advance. Rent was £1,800 for the year ended 31 December 20X2 and is £2,100 for the year ended 31 December 20X3.

Munch Catering Ltd has made the following payments of rent by cheque:

Date	Amount	Details
20X2	£	
29 Sep	450	Quarter to 31 Dec 20X2
29 Dec	525	Quarter to 31 Mar 20X3
20X3		
30 Mar	525	Quarter to 30 Jun 20X3
29 Jun	525	Quarter to 30 Sep 20X3
28 Sep	525	Quarter to 31 Dec 20X3

Munch Catering Ltd paid its building contents insurance premium of £547 for the year to 30 November 20X3 on 17 November 20X2. This policy was cancelled as from 31 May 20X3 and Munch Catering Ltd received a cheque for £150 as a rebate of premium on 21 June 20X3. A new buildings contents insurance policy was taken out with a different insurance company with effect from 1 June 20X3. The premium on this policy was £400 and this was paid in full by cheque by Munch Catering Ltd. on 18 May 20X3.

Property taxes are assessed annually for the year from 1 April to the following 31 March and are payable in one lump sum by 30 September. Munch Catering Ltd's assessment was £840 for the year to 31 March 20X3 and £1,680 for the year to 31 March 20X4. Munch Catering Ltd paid the assessment for the year ended 31 March 20X3 by cheque on 2 October 20X2 and the assessment for the year ended 31 March 20X4 by cheque on 26 September 20X3.

Required

Prepare the 'Building occupancy costs' account for the year ended 30 November 20X3 only as it would appear in the general ledger of Munch Catering Ltd.

(AAT)

18.5

BASIC

a Commission: received in advance at the start of the year £50; received in the year £5,600; receivable at the year end £250.

b Rates: paid in the year £950; prepaid at the start of the year £220; prepaid at the year end £290.

c Motor insurance: prepaid at the start of the year £75; paid in the year £744; owing at the year end £100.

d Stationery: paid in the year £1,800; owing at the start of the year £250; owing at the end of the year £490.

e Rent income: receives £550 for rent in the year. Tenant owed £180 at the start of the year and £210 at the end of the year.

f Insurance: paid in the year £420; prepaid at the year end £35.

Required

Prepare the ledger account for the above transactions.

18.6

BASIC

a Stationery: During the year to 31 December 20X2 £1,300 was paid in respect of stationery. The amount owing at 31 December 20X1 was £140 and the amount owing at 31 December 20X2 was £200.

b Rent: Kristal received rent of £3,000 during the year ended 31 December 20X2. The tenant owed Kristal £210 on 31 December 20X1 and owed her £340 on 31 December 20X2.

Required

Draft 'T' accounts for the above transactions including the balances transferred to the statement of profit and loss account for 20X2 and the balances brought down to 20X3.

BASIC

18.7

The company's year end is 31 December 20X3. Prepare ledger accounts for the following accounts showing the adjustments that are necessary for the year-end accruals and prepayments and the balances that would appear in the financial statements.

a The opening accrual for heat and light was £100. The company paid £4,500 in the year. The last payment was in December for the period 1 September to the 30 November. This amounted to £1,500.

b The inventory of toiletries on 1 January 20X3 was £250. An additional £580 was purchased in the year. At the year end there were 10 packets of toilet rolls left costing £20 each.

c The rates bill paid last year was £1,200. It was accounted for correctly using the accruals concept. The rates bill paid this year in April amounted to £1,800 (rates bills cover the period 1 April to 31 March in the next year).

d In December 20X2 our tenant paid us £1,200 for the period 1 December to 28 February. During the year we received another £5,000, including £1,500 in December for the three months to 29 February 20X4.

e At the start of the year an agent for a product owed us £400 commission for sales targets we met last year. This year we made the target sales again. They paid us £6,000 but still owe us £900 at the year end.

BASIC

18.8*

The ledger of RBD & Co. included the following account balances:

	At 1 June 20X2	At 31 May 20X3
	£	£
Rents receivable: prepayments	463	517
Rent and rates payable:		
prepayments	1,246	1,509
accruals	315	382
Trade payables	5,258	4,720

During the year ended 31 May 20X3 the following transactions had arisen:

	£
Rents received by cheque	4,058
Rent paid by cheque	7,491
Rates paid by cheque	2,805
Credit suppliers paid by cheque	75,181
Discounts received from credit creditors	1,043
Purchases on credit	to be derived

Required

Post and balance the appropriate accounts for the year ended 31 May 20X3, deriving the transfer entries to the statement of profit and loss, where applicable.

(ACCA, adapted)

18.9

The balances on certain accounts of Foster Hardware Co. as at 1 April 20X3 were:

	£
Rent and rates payable – accruals	2,200
– prepayments	1,940
Rent receivable – prepayments	625
Vehicles (at cost)	10,540
Provision for depreciation of vehicles	4,720
During the financial year the business	
paid rent by cheque	5,200
paid rates by cheque	3,050
received cheque for rent of sublet premises	960
traded in vehicle – original cost	4,710
– accumulated depreciation	3,080
– part exchange allowance	1,100
paid balance of price of new vehicle by cheque	5,280
Closing balances as at 31 March 20X4 were:	
Rent and rates payable – accruals	2,370
– prepayments	1,880
Rent receivable – prepayments	680
Vehicles (at cost)	to be derived
Provision for depreciation of vehicles	3,890

Required

Post and balance the appropriate accounts for the year ended 31 March 20X4, deriving the transfer entries to the statement of profit and loss where applicable.

(ACCA, adapted)

18.10

The trial balance of Snodgrass, a sole trader, at 1 January 20X3 is as follows:

	Debit £'000	Credit £'000
Capital		600
Non-current assets (net)	350	
Trade receivables	200	
Prepayments – rent	8	
– insurance	12	
Trade payables		180
Accruals – electricity		9
– telephone		1
Inventories	200	
Bank	20	
	790	790

The following information is given for the year:

	£'000
Receipts from credit customers	1,000
Payments to credit suppliers	700
Payments for: rent	30
insurance	20
electricity	25
telephone	10
wages	100
Proprietor's personal expenses	50
Discounts allowed	8
Bad debts written off	3
Depreciation	50

At 31 December 20X3 the following balances are given:

	£'000
Trade receivables	250
Prepayments – rent	10
– telephone	2
Trade payables	160
Accruals – electricity	7
– insurance	6
Inventories	230

Required

Prepare a statement of profit and loss for the year, and a statement of financial position as at 31 December 20X3.

(ACCA, adapted)

18.11

Bush, a sole trader, commenced trading on 1 January 20X2.

a *Telephone expense details*

The quarterly rental payable in advance on 1 January, 1 April, 1 July and 1 October is £30. Telephone calls are payable in arrears: January to March 20X2 paid 1 April 20X2 £318; April to June 20X2 paid 1 July 20X2 £422; and July to September 20X2 paid 1 October 20X2 £172.

He is to prepare his first financial statements to 31 October 20X2 and estimates that the cost of his calls for October 20X2 will be £44.

Rent expense details

Bush also pays rent quarterly in advance for his premises and has made payments as follows:

1 January 20X2	£800
1 April 20X2	£950
1 July 20X2	£950
1 October 20X2	£950

Required

Prepare Bush's ledger accounts for telephone and rent for the period from 1 January 20X2 to 31 October 20X2, showing clearly the amounts to be transferred to his statement of profit and loss for the period together with any balances carried forward on 31 October 20X2.

b At 1 November 20X2, the following balances were brought forward in the ledger accounts of Bush:

Rates payable account	Dr	£1,500
Electricity account	Cr	£800
Interest receivable account	Dr	£300
Provision for doubtful debts account	Cr	£4,800

You are told the following:

Rates are payable quarterly in advance on the last day of December, March, June and September, at the rate of £4,000 per annum.

Interest was received during the year as follows:

2 November 20X2	£250 (for the six months to 30 October 20X2)
3 May 20X3	£600 (for the six months to 30 April 20X3)

You estimate that interest of £300 is accrued at 31 October 20X3.

Electricity is paid as follows:

5 December 20X2	£1,000 (for the period to 30 November 20X2)
10 March 20X2	£1,300 (for the period to 31 December 20X3)
8 June 20X3	£1,500 (for the period to 31 May 20X3)
7 September 20X3	£1,100 (for the period to 31 August 20X3)

At 30 October 20X3, the electricity meter shows that £900 has been consumed since the last bill was received.

At 30 October 20X3, the balance of trade receivables amounts to £250,000. The provision for doubtful debts is to be amended to 10 per cent of trade receivables.

Required

Write up the ledger accounts for:

1 rates payable;

2 electricity;

3 interest receivable;

4 provision for doubtful debts.

and bring down the balances at 31 October 20X3.

c Explain two accounting concepts that govern the treatment of the above items in the financial statements of Bush.

When you have read this chapter, log on to the Online Learning Centre for *Introduction to Financial Accounting* at www.mcgraw-hill.co.uk/textbooks/thomas, where you will find multiple choice quizzes, case studies, a glossary and mock exams.

The final financial statements of sole traders (advanced)

Learning Objectives

After reading this chapter you should be able to do the following:

1 Explain the meaning of the key terms and concepts listed at the end of the chapter.

2 Prepare an extended trial balance taking into account adjustments for inventories, depreciation, provisions for bad debts, accruals, prepayments, and so on.

3 Prepare a statement of profit and loss and a statement of financial position from an extended trial balance.

19.1 Introduction

As explained in Chapter 15, 'The Final Financial Statements of Sole Traders (Introductory)', final financial statements are prepared after the trial balance has been produced and this involves transferring the balances on various income and expense accounts to the statement of profit and loss. In addition, the process of preparing final financial statements involves a number of **adjustments**, some of which have been described in Chapters 16–18.

These may be summarized as follows:

1 accounting for inventories and work-in-progress;

2 provisions for depreciation;

3 provision for bad debts;

4 accruals and prepayments;

5 the correction of omissions and errors such as bad debts not written off during the year.

This chapter brings together all the information/adjustments that typically impact on an entity's financial statements post-trial balance stage.

19.2 The extended trial balance

As explained above, the preparation of final financial statements involves various adjustments. In the preceding three chapters these were described mainly in terms of the necessary ledger entries. However, in practice and in examinations, final financial statements are usually prepared from the trial balance, the ledger entries being done at some later date when the final financial statements are completed.

Because the preparation of final financial statements from the trial balance involves a large number of adjustments, in practice it is usual to make these adjustments using an **extended trial balance**. This may take a number of forms, but a useful approach is to set it up to comprise eight columns made up of four pairs as follows:

1 **The trial balance debit side**

2 **The trial balance credit side**

3 *Adjustments to the debit side*

4 *Adjustments to the credit side*

5 **The profit and loss account debit side**

6 **The profit and loss account credit side**

7 *The statement of financial position debit side*

8 *The statement of financial position credit side*

The first two columns are the normal trial balance. Columns 3 and 4 are used to make adjustments to the figures in the trial balance in respect of provisions for depreciation and bad debts, accruals and prepayments, and so on. Columns 5 and 6 are used to compute the amounts that will be entered in the statement of profit and loss. Columns 7 and 8 are used to ascertain the amounts that will be shown in the statement of financial position.

Columns 3 and 4 relating to the adjustments are used like the journal in that items entered in these columns are intended to represent entries that will be made in the ledger. For example, one simple adjustment is the transfer of drawings to the capital account. This takes the form of an entry in the credit adjustment column on the line containing the balance on the drawings account, with a corresponding entry in the debit adjustment column on the line containing the balance on the capital account, in the trial balance.

Furthermore, adjustments may take the form of an entry in one of the adjustments columns and one of the statement of profit and loss columns. This is because the adjustment columns and the statement of profit and loss columns relate to entries that will be made in the ledger. However, no adjustments must be entered in the statement of financial position columns because the statement of financial position does not involve entries in the ledger.

The most common adjustments found in the extended trial balance are as follows:

1 *Provisions for depreciation*: Debit the statement of profit and loss column and credit the adjustment column on the line containing the balance on the provision for depreciation account in the trial balance with the depreciation charge for the year.

2 *Provision for bad debts*: Debit the statement of profit and loss column and credit the adjustment column on the line containing the balance on the provision for bad debts account with any increase in the provision (opposite for any decrease).

3 *Accruals and prepayments*: Debit and credit the adjustment columns on the line relating to the expense in question.

4 *Inventory at the end of the year*: Debit the adjustment column and credit the statement of profit and loss column. To avoid confusion this may be done on a new line separate from the inventory at the start of the year, as in Example 19.1.

After all the necessary adjustments have been made in the adjustment and profit and loss account columns, the amounts that will be entered in the statement of profit and loss and statement of financial position columns can be ascertained. These are found by cross-casting the amounts relating to each ledger account shown in the original trial balance. For example, if the original trial balance contained a rent account with a debit balance, any prepayment shown in the credit adjustment column would be deducted from this and the difference entered in the statement of profit and loss debit column. The prepayment shown in the debit adjustment column would also be extended across and entered in the statement of financial position debit column. Expenses with accrued charges are treated in a similar way.

When all the amounts have been entered in the statement of profit and loss and statement of financial position columns, the profit (or loss) can be computed in the normal manner as the difference between the two statement of profit and loss columns. The profit is entered in the statement of profit and loss debit column and the credit adjustment column. The latter is then extended into the statement of financial position credit column and eventually added to the capital account balance.

When all the items in the trial balance have been extended across into the statement of profit and loss and statement of financial position columns and the profit has been ascertained, the amounts in these columns are entered in the final version of the statement of profit and loss and statement of financial position. An illustration of the use of the extended trial balance is given in Example 19.1.

EXAMPLE 19.1

T. King has an accounting year ending on 30 April. The following trial balance was prepared for the year ended 30 April 20X3:

	Debit £	Credit £
Capital		59,640
Drawings	7,600	
Bank overdraft		1,540
Cash	1,170	
Plant and machinery	87,000	
Provision for depreciation on plant		27,000
Sales revenue		68,200
Purchases	42,160	
Trade receivables	15,200	
Trade payables		12,700
Provision for bad debts		890
Bad debts	610	
Rent	4,200	
Light and heat	3,700	
Stationery	2,430	
Inventories	5,900	
	169,970	169,970

Additional information

1 Plant and machinery is depreciated using the reducing balance method at a rate of 10 per cent per annum.

2 The provision for bad debts at 30 April 20X3 should be 5 per cent of trade receivables.

3 There is an accrual at 30 April 20X3 in respect of gas amounting to £580, and rent prepaid of £600.

4 Inventory at 30 April 20X3 was £7,220.

You are required to prepare an extended trial balance at 30 April 20X3 and final financial statements in vertical form.

Workings

1 Depreciation = 10% × (£87,000 − £27,000) = £6,000

2 Provision for bad debts = (5% × £15,200) − £890 = £130 decrease

The journal to post these two adjustments is as follows:

Date	Details (account in which the ledger entry is to be made)	Folio	Debit amount	Credit amount
20X3			£	£
30 April	Profit and loss a/c – Depreciation	Dr	6,000	
	Provision for depreciation	Cr		6,000
	Being the depreciation on plant and machinery for the year now posted.			
30 April	Provision for bad debts account	Dr	130	
	Profit and loss a/c – Decrease in provision for bad debts	Cr		130
	Being the decrease in the provision for bad debts at the year end now posted.			

The extended trial balance is shown on the next page.

	Trial balance		Adjustments		Income Statement a/c		Statement of financial position	
	Dr	**Cr**	**Dr**	**Cr**	**Dr**	**Cr**	**Dr**	**Cr**
	£	£	£	£	£	£	£	£
Capital		59,640	7,600					52,040
Drawings	7,600			7,600				
Bank overdraft		1,540						1,540
Cash	1,170						1,170	
Plant and machinery	87,000						87,000	
Provision for depreciation on plant		27,000		6,000	6,000			33,000
Sales revenue		68,200				68,200		
Purchases	42,160				42,160			
Trade receivables	15,200						15,200	
Trade payables		12,700						12,700
Provision for bad debts		890	130			130		760
Bad debts	610				610			
Rent	4,200		600	600	3,600		600	
Light and heat	3,700		580	580	4,280			580
Stationery	2,430				2,430			
Inventories at 1 May 20X2	5,900				5,900			
Inventories at 30 April 20X3			7,220			7,220	7,220	
Profit for the period				10,570	10,570			10,570
	169,970	169,970			75,550	75,550	111,190	111,190

T. King
Extended trial balance as at 30 April 20X3

T. King		
Statement of profit and loss for the year ended 30 April 20X3		
	£	£
Sales revenue		68,200
Less: Cost of sales:		
Inventories at 1 May 20X2	5,900	
Add: Purchases	42,160	
	48,060	
Less: Inventories at 30 April 20X3	7,220	40,840
Gross profit		27,360
Less: Expenditure		
Rent	3,600	
Reduction in the provision for bad debts	(130)	
Light and heat	4,280	
Stationery	2,430	
Bad debts	610	
Depreciation on plant	6,000	16,790
Profit for the period		10,570

T. King: Statement of financial position as at 30 April 20X3			
ASSETS	£	£	£
Non-current assets	Cost	Acc. Depn	WDV
Plant and machinery	87,000	33,000	54,000
Current assets			
Inventories			7,220
Trade receivables		15,200	
Less: Provision for bad debts		760	14,440
Prepayments			600
Cash			1,170
			23,430
Total assets			77,430
OWNER'S CAPITAL AND LIABILITIES			
Owner's capital			
Opening balance			59,640
Add: Net profit			10,570
			70,210
Less: Drawings			7,600
Closing balance			62,610
Current liabilities			
Bank overdraft			1,540
Trade payables			12,700
Accruals			580
Total current liabilities			14,820
Total capital and liabilities			77,430

Finally, it should be observed that although the extended trial balance is common in practice (it is particularly used at the start of a trainee accountants contract to refresh double-entry knowledge), the time allocated to answering examination questions is unlikely to allow for full presentation of the extended trial balance, and this is rarely a requirement. Without the extended trial balance, it becomes difficult to answer final financial statement questions in a logical and accurate manner. Some students therefore find it helpful to make use of the trial balance printed on the question paper. Adjustment columns can be drawn on the right-hand side of the trial balance on the question paper, and the necessary adjustments made in rough form to permit the final financial statements to be prepared in the examination answer book.

LEARNING ACTIVITY 19.1

Write out the journal entries in full for the accrual and inventory adjustment in Example 19.1.

19.3 The ledger accounts

Another approach to adjusting the trial balance is to reopen the ledger accounts and post the omitted transaction/adjustment and then to amend the trial balance, as is shown in Example 18.3 in the previous chapter. The exercises at the end of this chapter use both approaches.

> **LEARNING ACTIVITY 19.2**
>
> To see how an extended trial balance operates in practice, go to the website identified in the following real world example. Go to the worked example link at the bottom of the site – this will give you access to a half-completed extended trial balance that has been created using Microsoft Excel.

> **REAL WORLD EXAMPLE 19.1**
>
> ## VT Final Accounts
>
> VT Final Accounts runs in Microsoft Excel and produces professionally formatted statutory, sole trader and partnership accounts. A trial balance and up to 250 journals can be entered and a nominal report printed. A trial balance can also be imported from VT Transaction+, VT Cash Book and most other accounting packages.
>
> *Source*: http://www.vtsoftware.co.uk/final_accounts/index.htm, March 2010.

Summary

The process of preparing final financial statements from a trial balance involves a number of adjustments relating to accounting for inventories, provisions for depreciation, provisions for bad debts, and accruals and prepayments. In addition, it will be necessary to make further adjustments in respect of any inventories of tools, stationery, fuel, and so on. These are treated as a debit balance on the relevant expense account, and shown on the statement of financial position as a current asset. The remaining difference between the two sides of the expense account is transferred to the statement of profit and loss account, and represents the value of goods consumed during the year.

When trainee accountants start their training contract it is common practice to prepare final financial statements using an extended trial balance. This comprises the usual trial balance money columns but with additional money columns to the right. The first pair of these comprises adjustment columns that are used to make the adjustments referred to above. The second pair represents the entries in the statement of profit and loss; and the third pair represents the amounts shown in the statement of financial position. The amounts that are entered in the statement of profit and loss and statement of financial position columns are ascertained by cross-casting the figures relating to each ledger account shown in the original trial balance and the adjustment columns.

Key terms and concepts

adjustments	293	extended trial balance	294

An asterisk after the question number indicates that there is a suggested answer on the Online Learning Centre (www.mcgraw-hill.co.uk/textbooks/thomas).

Exercises

BASIC

19.1

The trial balance for Jock at 31 December 20X3 is as follows:

	Debit £	Credit £
Sales revenue		10,000
Trade receivables	5,000	
Provision for bad debts		250
Purchases	2,000	
Trade payables		1,000
Provision for discounts allowable		100
Rent	200	
Rates	300	
Inventories	100	
Motor car	10,000	
Provision for depreciation		2,000
Bank	5,000	
Capital account		9,250
	22,600	22,600

Additional information

1 Closing inventory value is £500.

2 The rates in the trial balance cover the 15 months to 31 March 20X4.

3 The motor car is depreciated using 20 per cent straight-line method.

4 A credit customer with a balance on his account of £1,000 is bankrupt.

5 Remove the provision for discounts and provide for a 10 per cent bad debt provision.

Required

a Prepare the statement of profit and loss for Jock for the year ended 31 December 20X3.

b Prepare the statement of financial position at the same date.

(*Note*: An adjusted trial balance is not required. Show all the adjustments to the ledger accounts.)

19.2

B. Good drew up the following trial balance as at 31 March 20X3.

	Debit £	Credit £
Sundry expenses	1,090	
Rent received		200
Office expenses	560	
Insurance	525	
Wages and expenses	4,580	
Telephone	1,250	
Purchases and sales revenue	125,560	189,560
Motor expenses	569	
Rent	2,500	
Rates	1,250	
Carriage outwards	546	
Carriage inwards	200	
Returns outwards		302
Return inwards	560	
Building	230,000	
Motor vehicle	12,500	
Fixtures	5,365	
Trade receivables and payables	28,560	48,560
Cash	12	
Bank		32,250
Drawings	5,562	
Capital		178,907
Opening inventories	28,590	
	449,779	449,779

Closing information included the following:

1 Inventories at the year end were valued at £35,650.

2 An accrual for wages of £400 has still to be posted.

3 The last rent payment (on 15 February) for £1,000 covered the period 1 February to 31 May 20X3.

4 A rates prepayment has been calculated at £250.

5 An accrual for sundry expenses of £110 has still to be posted.

6 Rent income owing at the year end amounted to £100.

Required

Prepare the statement of profit and loss for the year ended 31 March 20X3 and the statement of financial position as at 31 March 20X3.

(*Note*: An adjusted trial balance is not required. Show all the adjustments to the ledger accounts.)

BASIC

19.3

The balances extracted from the books of Cara Van at 31 December 20X2 are given below:

	£
Drawings	7,180
Heating and lighting	1,234
Stationery and postage	268
Carriage outwards	1,446
Insurance	1,818
Wages and salaries	18,910
Inventories at 1 January 20X2	42,120
Purchases	74,700
Sales revenue	131,040
Rent and rates	2,990
General expenses	1,460
Discount received	426
Plant and machinery	9,060
Cash at bank	3,222
Cash in hand	65
Trade receivables	1,920
Trade payables	630
Sales returns	1,310
Purchases returns	747

Required

a Prepare the trial balance.

b What is the missing account?

Additional information

At 31 December 20X2:

1 inventories are valued at £33,990;

2 rent amounting to £310 is still owing;

3 insurance paid in advance is £220.

Required

c Prepare the statement of profit and loss for the year ended 31 December 20X2 and a statement of financial position at that date, after adjusting for the other information that has come to light.

(*Note*: An adjusted trial balance is not required; show the adjustments to the ledger accounts.)

19.4

The following trial balance has been prepared from the books and records of Sulphur Products as at 30 September 20X3. We are also told that the figures have to be amended to take into account further adjustments (see below).

Sulphur Products Trial balance at 30 September 20X3	Debit £	Credit £
Capital		99,000
Drawings	9,000	
Vehicles	60,000	
Trade payables		47,000
Trade receivables	37,000	
Inventories (1 October 20X2)	12,000	
Rent	15,400	
Telephone	1,800	
Postage	300	
Electricity	2,100	
Bank	22,000	
Returns inwards	4,000	
Returns outwards		2,500
Provision for doubtful debts		900
Purchases	213,000	
Sales revenue		370,000
Plant and equipment	147,000	
Discounts received		6,000
Bank charges	1,800	
	525,400	525,400

Additional information

1 A bad debt of £2,000 has yet to be written off.

2 The provision for doubtful debts is to be 3 per cent of trade receivables.

3 There are unpaid bills for electricity £200 and telephone £300.

4 Rent is payable at £3,300 per quarter, and has been paid until the end of November 20X3.

5 The value of inventories at 30 September 20X3 is £16,500.

6 Depreciation is to be provided on Plant and Equipment (25 per cent reducing balance method).

Required

Prepare a statement of profit and loss for Sulphur Products for the period ending 30 September 20X3 and a statement of financial position at that date.

(*Note:* An adjusted trial balance is not required. Show all the adjustments to the ledger accounts).

19.5*

The following is the trial balance of C. Jones as at 31 December 20X3:

	Debit £	Credit £
Owner's capital		45,214
Drawings	9,502	
Purchases	389,072	
Sales revenue		527,350
Wages and salaries	33,440	
Rent and rates	9,860	
Light and heat	4,142	
Bad debts	1,884	
Provision for doubtful debts		3,702
Trade receivables	72,300	
Trade payables		34,308
Cash at bank	2,816	
Cash in hand	334	
Inventories	82,124	
Motor car – cost	7,200	
– depreciation		2,100
	612,674	612,674

Additional information

1 Inventories at 31 December 20X3 are valued at £99,356.

2 The rent of the premises is £6,400 per annum, payable half-yearly in advance on 31 March and 30 September.

3 Rates for the year ending 31 March 20X4 amounting to £1,488 were paid on 10 April 20X3.

4 Wages and salaries to be accrued amount to £3,012.

5 Depreciation on the car is to be provided using the straight-line method at a rate of 20 per cent per annum.

6 It has been agreed that further debts amounting to £1,420 are to be written off against specific customers, and the closing provision is to be adjusted to 5 per cent of the revised trade receivables' figure.

Required

Prepare the statement of profit and loss for the year ended 31 December 20X3, and a statement of financial position at that date. This should be done using an extended trial balance.

19.6*

The following is the trial balance of J. Clark at 31 March 20X3:

	Debit £	Credit £
Capital		60,000
Drawings	5,600	
Purchases/sales revenue	34,260	58,640
Returns inwards/outwards	3,260	2,140
Carriage inwards	730	
Carriage outwards	420	
Discount allowed/received	1,480	1,970
Plant and machinery at cost	11,350	
Provision for depreciation on plant		4,150
Motor vehicles	13,290	
Provision for depreciation on vehicles		2,790
Goodwill	5,000	
Quoted investments	6,470	
Freehold premises at cost	32,000	
Mortgage on premises		10,000
Interest paid/received	1,000	460
Inventories	4,670	
Bank and cash	2,850	
Salaries	7,180	
Rent and rates	4,300	
Provision for bad debts		530
Trade receivables/payables	8,070	4,340
Light and heat	2,640	
Stationery	450	
	145,020	145,020

Additional information

1 Goods on sale or return have been treated as sales. These cost £300 and were invoiced to the customer for £400.

2 The provision for bad debts is to be adjusted to 10 per cent of trade receivables.

3 At 31 March 20X3 there is electricity accrued of £130 and rates prepaid amounting to £210.

4 Inventories at 31 March 20X3 were valued at £3,690.

5 During the year the proprietor has taken goods costing £350 from the business for his own use.

6 Depreciation on plant is 25 per cent on the reducing balance method and on vehicles 20 per cent by the same method.

7 Unrecorded in the ledger is the sale on credit on 1 July 20X2 for £458 of a motor vehicle bought on 1 January 20X1 for £1,000.

8 There are bad debts of £370 that have not been entered in the ledger.

9 There was an inventory of stationery at 31 March 20X3, which cost £230.

Required

Prepare a statement of profit and loss for the year and a statement of financial position at the end of the year.

INTERMEDIATE

19.7

The following trial balance has been extracted from the ledger of Andrea Howell, a sole trader, as at 31 May 20X3, the end of her most recent financial year.

	Debit	Credit
	£	£
Property, at cost	90,000	
Equipment, at cost	57,500	
Provision for depreciation (as at 1 June 20X2)		
– property		12,500
– equipment		32,500
Inventories as at 1 June 20X2	27,400	
Purchases	259,600	
Sales revenue		405,000
Discounts allowed	3,370	
Discounts received		4,420
Wages and salaries	52,360	
Bad debts	1,720	
Loan interest	1,560	
Carriage out	5,310	
Other operating expenses	38,800	
Trade receivables	46,200	
Trade payables		33,600
Provision for bad debts		280
Cash on hand	151	
Bank overdraft		14,500
Drawings	28,930	
13% loan		12,000
Capital, as at 1 June 20X2		98,101
	612,901	612,901

The following additional information as at 31 May 20X3 is available:

1 Inventories as at the close of business were valued at £25,900.

2 Depreciation for the year ended 31 May 20X3 has yet to be provided as follows:

Property: 1 per cent using the straight-line method.

Equipment: 15 per cent using the straight-line method.

3 Wages and salaries are accrued by £140.

4 'Other operating expenses' include certain expenses prepaid by £500. Other expenses included under this heading are accrued by £200.

5 The provision for bad debts is to be adjusted so that it is 0.5 per cent of trade receivables as at 31 May 20X3.

6 'Purchases' include goods valued at £1,040 that were withdrawn by Mrs Howell for her own personal use.

Required

Prepare Mrs Howell's statement of profit and loss for the year ended 31 May 20X3 and her statement of financial position as at 31 May 20X3.

(AAT, adapted)

19.8

INTERMEDIATE

S. Trader carries on a merchandising business. The following balances have been extracted from his books on 30 September 20X3:

	£
Capital – S. Trader, at 1 Oct 20X2	24,239
Office furniture and equipment	1,440
Cash drawings – S. Trader	4,888
Inventories on hand – 1 Oct 20X2	14,972
Purchases	167,760
Sales revenue	203,845
Rent	1,350
Light and heat	475
Insurance	304
Salaries	6,352
Stationery and printing	737
Telephone and postage	517
General expenses	2,044
Travellers' commission and expenses	9,925
Discounts allowed	517
Discounts received	955
Bad debts written off	331
Trade receivables	19,100
Trade payables	8,162
Balance at bank to S. Trader's credit	6,603
Petty cash in hand	29
Provision for doubtful debts	143

The following further information is to be taken into account:

1 Inventories on hand on 30 September 20X3 were valued at £12,972.

2 Provision is to be made for the following liabilities and accrued expenses as at 30 September 20X3: rent £450; lighting and heating £136; travellers' commission and expenses £806; accountancy charges £252.

3 Provision for doubtful debts is to be raised to 3 per cent of the closing trade receivable balance.

4 Office furniture and equipment is to be depreciated by 10 per cent on book value.

5 Mr Trader had removed inventory costing £112 for his own use during the year.

Required

a Prepare a statement of profit and loss for the year ended 30 September 20X3 grouping the various expenses under suitable headings; and

b a statement of financial position as at that date.

(ACCA, adapted)

19.9

F. Harrison is in business as a trader. A trial balance taken out as at 31 January 20X3 was as follows:

	Debit	Credit
	£	£
Purchases	42,400	
Sales revenue		50,240
Returns inwards and outwards	136	348
Salaries and wages	4,100	
Rent, rates and insurance	860	
Sundry expenses	750	
Bad debts	134	
Provision for doubtful debts at 1 February 20X2		280
Inventories on hand at 1 February 20X2	13,630	
Fixtures and fittings:		
At 1 February 20X2	1,400	
Additions on 30 September 20X2	240	
Motor vehicles:		
At 1 February 20X2	920	
Sale of vehicle (book value at		
1 February 20X2 £80)		120
Sundry trade receivables and payables	4,610	3,852
Cash at bank and in hand	3,820	
F Harrison: Capital a/c		20,760
F. Harrison: Drawings a/c	2,600	
	75,600	75,600

The following information is to be taken into account:

1 Included in sales are goods on sale or return that cost £240 and which have been charged out with profit added at 20 per cent of sale price.

2 Outstanding amounts not entered in the books were: rent £36, sundry expenses £90.

3 Prepayments were: rates £60, insurance £10.

4 Inventories on hand on 31 January 20X3 were valued at £15,450.

5 Provision for doubtful debts is to be £340.

6 Depreciation is to be provided for as follows: fixtures and fittings 10 per cent per annum, motor vehicles 25 per cent per annum.

Required

Prepare a statement of profit and loss for the year ended 31 January 20X3, and draw up a statement of financial position as on that date.

(ACCA, adapted)

19.10

INTERMEDIATE

The trial balance extracted from the books of Mary, a sole trader, as at 31 December 20X3 was as follows:

	Debit £	Credit £
Capital		112,190
Furniture and equipment (cost £21,000)	16,400	
Motor vans (cost £17,000)	11,200	
Purchases	362,910	
Sales revenue		456,220
Rent and rates	8,000	
Salaries	39,690	
Bad debts	2,810	
General expenses	10,620	
Bank balance	3,080	
Provision for doubtful debts		2,690
Inventory at 1 January 20X3	87,260	
Trade receivables	42,890	
Trade payables		31,640
Drawings	17,880	
	602,740	602,740

Additional information

1 Inventory on hand on 31 December 20X3 is £94,280.

2 Rates paid in advance at 31 December 20X3 are £600.

3 General expenses unpaid at 31 December 20X3 are £1,660.

4 Provision for doubtful debts is to be adjusted to £2,410.

5 A motor van purchased on 1 January of this year at a cost of £8,000 was traded in for £3,500 on 31 December 20X3 and a new van purchased at a cost of £10,000 on the same day. The amount due on the new van was payable on 1 January 20X4. No entries had been made in the books in respect of this transaction when the trial balance at 31 December 20X3 was extracted.

6 Depreciation is to be charged on furniture and equipment at the rate of 5 per cent per annum on cost and at the rate of 25 per cent per annum (reducing balance method) on motor vehicles.

Required

Prepare Mary's statement of profit and loss for the year ended 31 December 20X3 and statement of financial position as at 31 December 20X3.

After you have read this part, log on to the Online Learning Centre for *Introduction to Financial Accounting* at www.mcgraw-hill.co.uk/textbooks/thomas where you will find Self Test Questions for these chapters, a glossary with definitions of key terms plus extra resources for revision.

Internal control and check

The bank reconciliation statement

Learning Objectives

After reading this chapter you should be able to do the following:

1 Explain the meaning of the key terms and concepts listed at the end of the chapter.

2 Explain the purpose and nature of bank reconciliations.

3 Identify and correct errors and omissions in a cash book.

4 Prepare a bank reconciliation statement.

20.1 The purpose and preparation of bank reconciliations

The purpose of preparing a **bank reconciliation statement** is to ascertain whether or not the balance shown in the cash book at the end of a given accounting period is correct by comparing it with that shown on the bank statement supplied by the bank. In practice, these two figures are rarely the same because of errors, omissions and the timing of bank deposits and cheque payments.

The bank reconciliation is not done in a book of account and thus is not a part of the double-entry system. It must be prepared at least yearly before the final financial statements are compiled. Because most businesses usually have a large number of cheque transactions, they often prepare a bank reconciliation statement either monthly or at least quarterly. The bank reconciliation should always be prepared by someone who is not involved in either writing cheques or dealing with lodgements (not the cashier). There should be segregation of duties. The bank reconciliation is not only the first step to take when preparing an entities financial statements, it also has a very important control function within a company's accounting systems as it helps to verify the validity and accuracy of transactions and serves as an important deterrent to fraud. An example of fraud where this control was not being exercised is given in real world example 20.1.

The first step in the preparation of a bank reconciliation involves identifying payments, and sometimes receipts that are on the bank statement but which have not been entered in the cash book. These are called **unrecorded cheques**. Such payments may include dishonoured cheques, bank charges and interest, standing orders for hire purchase instalments, insurance premiums and loan interest. Occasionally, receipts such as interest and dividends received by credit transfer are also found to be on

REAL WORLD EXAMPLE 20.1

The Sports Institute Northern Ireland

Fraud that could have been avoided had there been segregation of duties in respect of bank transactions

In a report to the Northern Ireland Assembly, the Comptroller and Auditor General (the Government Auditor) explained that action had been taken against a former senior member of staff of the Sports Institute for Northern Ireland. This member of staff had committed fraud by stealing about £70,000 from the Institute's bank account over an 11-month period from October 2005 to August 2006. The fraud involved the fraudster writing and cashing company cheques to his wife and daughter, whom he had included as being staff in the entities payroll system. He also used the company's online banking system to make payments for private use. The Comptroller said the fraud was possible because of a lack of internal controls in the Institute. In particular there was no separation of duties when it came to the finance section, and there was inadequate management supervision of the finance department personnel. The Comptroller was confident that had the appropriate controls been implemented, the fraud would not have taken place, or it would have been uncovered much more quickly than it had been.

Source: NIAO, 2008, http://www.niauditoffice.gov.uk/pubs/onepress.asp?arc=False&id=208&dm=0&dy=0

the bank statement but not in the cash book. These are called **unrecorded lodgements**. When these omissions of receipts and payments occur, the remedy is to enter them in the cash book and compute a new balance. However, in examination questions the student is sometimes required to build them into the bank reconciliation statement instead.

In addition to the above omissions, there are nearly always receipts and payments in the cash book that at the date of the reconciliation have not yet been entered by the bank on the bank statement. These consist of:

1 Cheques and cash received that have been paid into the bank and entered in the cash book but which have not yet been credited on the bank statement at the end of the accounting period when the bank reconciliation statement is being prepared. These are referred to as **amounts not yet credited**, **unpresented lodgements** or **outstanding lodgements**.

2 Cheques drawn that have been sent to the payee and entered in the cash book but which have not yet been presented to the bank for payment or which have not yet passed through the bank clearing system and thus do not appear on the bank statement at the end of the accounting period when the bank reconciliation statement is being prepared. These are referred to as **cheques not yet presented**, **unpresented cheques** or **outstanding cheques**.

The differences are summarized as follows:

1 *Timing differences*:
   - unpresented/outstanding cheques (a cheque that has been entered into the cash book but has not yet been presented to the bank for payment);
   - outstanding lodgements (a receipt entered into the cash book that has not yet been recorded by the bank).

2 *Omitted items*:
   - unrecorded lodgements (standing order/direct debit to the bank account – no record of it in the books);
   - unrecorded cheque (standing order/direct debit from the bank account – no record of it in the books (e.g. bank charges and interest)).

3 *Other/errors*:

- bounced cheques (dishonoured cheques);
- out-of-date cheques;
- a transposition error has occurred (e.g. a cheque for £189 has been entered into the cash book as £198).

The reconciliation procedure

Step 1: Tick off the items that appear in both the cash book and the bank statement.

Step 2: Identify all the items that have not been ticked.

Step 3: Adjust the bank ledger account in our books for items in the bank statement of which we have no record.

Step 4: Reconcile the adjusted balance in the cashbook to the balance on the bank statement in a bank reconciliation statement – differences are those of timing.

Example 20.1 shows the procedure involved in preparing a bank reconciliation statement.

EXAMPLE 20.1

The following is the cash book of J. Alton for the month of June 20X2

Cash book							
20X2	Details	£		20X2	Details	£	
1 June	Balance b/d	1,000		2 June	D. Cat	240	√
11 June	A. Hand	370	√	13 June	E. Dog	490	√
16 June	B. Leg	510	√	22 June	F. Bird	750	
24 June	C. Arm	620		30 June	Balance c/d	1,200	
30 June	Cash	180					
		2,680				2,680	

The following is the statement of J. Alton received from his bank:

Bank statement

Date	Details	Debit £		Credit £		Balance £
20X2						
1 June	Balance					1,000
5 June	D. Cat	240	√			760
15 June	A. Hand			370	√	1,130
18 June	E. Dog	490	√			640
20 June	Dividend received			160		800
21 June	B. Leg			510	√	1,310
30 June	Bank charges	75				1,235

In practice, bank statements do not usually show the names of the people from whom cheques were received and paid. It is therefore necessary to identify the payments by means of the cheque number. However, the use of names simplifies the example for ease of understanding. The procedure is essentially the same.

The first step is to tick all those items which appear in both the cash book and on the bank statement during the month of June. A note is then made of the items which are unticked:

1 *Outstanding lodgements*: Cheques and cash paid into the bank and entered in the cash book but not credited on the bank statement by 30 June 20X2 = C. Arm £620 + Cash £180 = £800.

2 *Outstanding cheques*: Cheques drawn and entered in the cash book not presented for payment by 30 June 20X2 = F. Bird £750.

3 *Unrecorded lodgements*: Amounts received by credit transfer shown on the bank statement not entered in the cash book = Dividends £160.

4 *Unrecorded cheques*: Standing orders and other payments shown on the bank statement not entered in the cash book = Bank charges £75.

Clearly, items 1 and 2 above will eventually appear on the bank statement in a later month. Items 3 and 4 must be entered in the cash book. However, the purpose of the bank reconciliation statement is to ascertain whether the difference between the balance in the cash book at 30 June 20X2 of £1,200 and that shown on the bank statement at the same date of £1,235 is explained by the above list of unticked items. Alternatively, are there other errors or omissions that need to be investigated?

The bank reconciliation statement will appear as follows:

J. Alton: Bank reconciliation statement as at 30 June 20X2		
	£	£
Balance per cash book		1,200
Add: Dividends received not entered in cash book	160	
Cheques not yet presented	750	910
		2,110
Less: Bank charges not entered in cash book	75	
Amounts not yet credited	800	875
Balance per bank statement		1,235

It can thus be seen that since the above statement reconciles the difference between the balances in the cash book and on the bank statement, there are unlikely to be any further errors or omissions.

Notes

1 The dividends received are added to the cash book balance because it is lower than the bank statement balance as a result of this omission. In addition, it will increase by this amount when the dividends are entered in the cash book.

2 The bank charges are deducted from the cash book balance because the bank statement balance has been reduced by this amount but the cash book balance has not. In addition, the cash book balance will decrease by this amount when the bank charges are entered in the cash book.

3 The cheques not yet presented are added to the cash book balance because it has been reduced by this amount whereas the bank statement balance has not.

4 The amounts not yet credited are deducted from the cash book balance because it has been increased by this amount whereas the bank statement balance has not.

Sometimes in examination questions the student is not given the cash book balance. In this case the bank reconciliation statement is prepared in reverse order as follows:

		£	£
Balance per bank statement			1,235
Add:	Amounts not yet credited	800	
	Payments on bank statement not in the cash book	75	875
			2,110
Less:	Cheques not yet presented	750	
	Receipts on bank statement not in the cash book	160	910
= Balance per cash book			1,200

An alternative method of dealing with bank reconciliation is to amend the cash book for any errors and omissions, and only include in the bank reconciliation statement those items that constitute timing differences. Pro forma cash book (ledger account) entries are now prepared for reference when doing questions (see Figures 20.1 and 20.2), as is the bank reconciliation.

Bank 'T'/ledger account adjustments				
Bank account				
Bal b/d	XX	Bounced cheques	XX	
Unrecorded lodgements	XX	Unrecorded cheques	XX	
Errors	X	Errors	X	
		Bal c/d	XX	
	XXX		XXX	
Bal b/d	XX			

Figure 20.1 A pro forma example of the entries required to adjust the cash book (ledger account) when performing a bank reconciliation

Bank statement adjustments	
Balance per statement	XX
Add: outstanding lodgements	XX
	XX
Less: outstanding cheques	XX
Balance per adjusted cashbook	XX

Figure 20.2 A pro forma example of a bank statement reconciliation

This approach is illustrated in Example 20.2, along with some other items frequently found in examination questions.

EXAMPLE 20.2

The following is a summary from the cash book of Home Shopping Ltd for March 20X2:

Cash book			
	£		£
Opening balance b/d	5,610	Payments	41,890
Receipts	37,480	Closing balance c/d	1,200
	43,090		43,090

When checking the cash book against the bank statement the following discrepancies were found:

1 Bank charges of £80 shown in the bank statement have not been entered in the cash book.

2 The bank has debited a cheque for £370 in error to the company's account.

3 Cheques totalling £960 have not yet been presented to the bank for payment.

4 Dividends received of £420 have been credited on the bank statement but not recorded in the cash book.

5 There are cheques received of £4,840 that are entered in the cash book but not yet credited to the company's account by the bank.

6 A cheque for £170 has been returned by the bank marked 'refer to drawer' but no entry relating to this has been made in the books.

7 The opening balance in the cash book should have been £6,510 and not £5,610.

8 The bank statement shows that there is an overdraft at 31 March 20X3 of £1,980.

Required

a Make the entries necessary to correct the cash book.

b Prepare a bank reconciliation statement as at 31 March 20X3.

Cash book			
	£		£
Balance b/d	1,200	Bank charges	80
Dividends	420	Refer to drawer	170
Error in balance	900	Balance c/d	2,270
	2,520		2,520
Balance b/d	2,270		

Home Shopping Ltd		
Bank reconciliation statement as at 31 March 20X3		
	£	£
Balance per cash book		2,270
Add: Cheques not yet presented		960
		3,230
Less: Amounts not yet credited	4,840	
Cheque debited in error	370	5,210
Balance per bank statement (overdrawn)		(1,980)

Notes

1 The cheque debited in error is shown in the bank reconciliation statement rather than the cash book because it will presumably be corrected on the bank statement in due course and thus will not affect the cash book.

Sometimes in examination questions the cash book contains a credit (i.e. overdrawn) balance. In this case, the bank reconciliation statement is prepared by reversing the additions and subtractions that are made when there is a favourable cash book balance. The bank reconciliation statement will thus appear as follows:

Balance per cash book (credit/overdrawn)

Add: **Amounts not yet credited**

Less: **Cheques not yet presented**

= Balance per bank statement

Alternatively, if the cash book balance is not given in the question and the bank statement contains an overdrawn balance, the bank reconciliation statement would be prepared as follows:

Balance per bank statement (debit/overdrawn)

Add: **Cheques not yet presented**

Less: **Amounts not yet credited**

= Balance per cash book

LEARNING ACTIVITY 20.1

Find your most recent bank statement and your cheque book. Prepare a reconciliation of the balance shown on your bank statement with that shown on your record of cheques received and drawn. If you do not keep a continuous record of your cheque receipts and payments, and thus the current balance, do so in future and repeat the exercise when you receive your next bank statement.

Summary

After extracting a trial balance but before preparing final financial statements at the end of each accounting year, the first thing that needs to be done is to check the accuracy of the cash book (or bank account in the ledger). This takes the form of a bank reconciliation, which involves reconciling the balance in the cash book at the end of the year with that shown on the statement received from the bank. These will probably be different for two main reasons. First, there may be errors or omissions where amounts shown on the bank statement have not been entered properly in the cash book. These should be corrected in the cash book. Second, there are likely to be timing differences. These consist of cheques paid into the bank and cheques drawn entered in the cash book, but not shown on the bank statement at the end of the year. These timing differences are entered on the bank reconciliation statement as explanations for the difference between the balance in the cash book and that on the bank statement. If the timing differences provide a reconciliation of the two balances, the cash book balance is deemed to be correct. Otherwise, the reasons for any remaining difference will need to be investigated.

Key terms and concepts

amounts not yet credited	314	unpresented cheques	314
bank reconciliation statement	313	unpresented lodgements	314
cheques not yet presented	314	unrecorded cheques	313
outstanding cheques	314	unrecorded lodgements	314
outstanding lodgements	314		

An asterisk after the question number indicates that there is a suggested answer on the Online Learning Centre (www.mcgraw-hill.co.uk/textbooks/thomas).

 Review questions

20.1 Explain the purpose of a bank reconciliation statement.

20.2 Describe the procedures involved in the collection of the data needed to prepare a bank reconciliation statement.

 Exercises

INTERMEDIATE

20.3

The following is the cash book of T. Trading for the month of September 20X2:

20X2		£	20X2		£
1 Sept	Balance b/d	2,000	2 Sept	Cheque 101	480
11 Sept	Lodgement	740	13 Sept	Cheque 102	980
16 Sept	Lodgement	1,020	22 Sept	Cheque 103	1,500
24 Sept	Lodgement	1,240	30 Sept	Balance c/d	2,400
30 Sept	Lodgement	360			
		5,360			5,360

The following is the bank statement received for T. Trading for the month of September 20X2:

Date	Details	Debit	Credit	Balance
20X2				
1 Sept	Balance			2,000
5 Sept	101	480		1,520
15 Sept	Lodgement		740	2,260
18 Sept	102	980		1,280
20 Sept	Credit transfer		320	1,600
21 Sept	Lodgement		1,020	2,620
30 Sept	Bank charges	150		2,470

Required

Prepare the bank reconciliation as at 30 September 20X2.

20.4

The following is a summary from the cash book of Hozy Co. Ltd for October 20X2:

Cash book				
	£			£
Opening balance b/d	1,407	Payments		15,520
Receipts	15,073	Closing balance c/d		960
	16,480			16,480

On investigation you discover that:

1 Bank charges of £35 shown on the bank statement have not been entered in the cash book.

2 A cheque drawn for £47 has been entered in error as a receipt.

3 A cheque for £18 has been returned by the bank marked 'refer to drawer', but it has not been written back in the cash book.

4 An error of transposition has occurred in that the opening balance in the cash book should have been carried down as £1,470.

5 Three cheques paid to suppliers for £214, £370 and £30 have not yet been presented to the bank.

6 The last page of the paying-in book shows a deposit of £1,542 that has not yet been credited to the account by the bank.

7 The bank has debited a cheque for £72 in error to the company's account.

8 The bank statement shows an overdrawn balance of £124.

Required

a Show what adjustments you would make in the cash book.

b Prepare a bank reconciliation statement as at 31 October 20X2.

(ACCA, adapted)

20.5*

The following is a summary of the cash book of Grow Ltd for March 20X3:

Cash book			
	£		£
Opening balance b/d	4,120	Payments	46,560
Receipts	45,320	Closing balance c/d	2,880
	49,440		49,440

On investigation you discover that at 31 March 20X3:

1 The last page of the paying-in book shows a deposit of £1,904 that has not yet been credited by the bank.

2 Two cheques paid to suppliers for £642 and £1,200 have not yet been presented to the bank.

3 Dividends received of £189 are shown on the bank statement but not entered in the cash book.

4 Bank charges of £105 shown on the bank statement have not been entered in the cash book.

5 A cheque for £54 has been returned by the bank marked 'refer to drawer', but it has not been written back in the cash book.

6 A cheque drawn for £141 has been entered in error as a receipt in the cash book.

7 The bank has debited a cheque for £216 in error to the company's account.

Required

a Show the adjustments that should be made in the cash book.

b Prepare a bank reconciliation statement at 31 March 20X3.

20.6*

On 15 May 20X3 Mrs Lake received her monthly bank statement for the month ended 30 April 20X3. The bank statement contained the following details:

Date	Particulars	Payments	Receipts	Balance
		£	£	£
1 Apr	Balance			1,053.29
2 Apr	236127	210.70		842.59
3 Apr	Bank Giro Credit		192.35	1,034.94
6 Apr	236126	15.21		1,019.73
6 Apr	Charges	12.80		1,006.93
9 Apr	236129	43.82		963.11
10 Apr	427519	19.47		943.64
12 Apr	236128	111.70		831.94
17 Apr	Standing Order	32.52		799.42
20 Apr	Sundry Credit		249.50	1,048.92
23 Apr	236130	77.87		971.05
23 Apr	236132	59.09		911.96
25 Apr	Bank Giro Credit		21.47	933.43
27 Apr	Sundry Credit		304.20	1,237.63
30 Apr	236133	71.18		1,166.45

For the corresponding period, Mrs Lake's own records contained the following bank account:

Date	Details	£	Date	Details	Cheque No	£
1 Apr	Balance	827.38	5 Apr	Purchases	128	111.70
2 Apr	Sales revenue	192.35	10 Apr	Electricity	129	43.82
18 Apr	Sales revenue	249.50	16 Apr	Purchases	130	87.77
24 Apr	Sales revenue	304.20	18 Apr	Rent	131	30.00
30 Apr	Sales revenue	192.80	20 Apr	Purchases	132	59.09
			25 Apr	Purchases	133	71.18
			30 Apr	Wages	134	52.27
			30 Apr	Balance		1,310.40
		1,766.23				1,766.23

Required

a Prepare a statement reconciling the balance at 30 April as given by the bank statement to the balance at 30 April as stated in the bank account.

b Explain briefly which items in your bank reconciliation statement would require further investigation.

(ACCA, adapted)

20.7

INTERMEDIATE

A young and inexperienced bookkeeper is having great difficulty in producing a bank reconciliation statement at 31 December. He gives you his attempt to produce a summarized cash book, and also the bank statement received for the month of December. These are shown below. You may assume that the bank statement is correct. You may also assume that the trial balance at 1 January did indeed show a bank overdraft of £7,000.12.

Cash book summary – draft				
	£	£	£	
1 Jan			35,000.34	Payments Jan–Nov
Opening overdraft		7,000.12		
Jan–Nov receipts	39,500.54			
Add: Discounts	500.02			
		40,000.56	12,000.34	Balance 30 Nov
		47,000.68	47,000.68	
1 Dec		12,000.34		Payments Dec
				Cheque No.
Dec receipts	178.19		37.14	7654
	121.27		192.79	7655
	14.92		5,000.00	7656
	16.88		123.45	7657
		329.26	678.90	7658
			1.47	7659
Dec receipts	3,100.00		19.84	7660
	171.23		10.66	7661
	1,198.17	4,469.40	10,734.75	Balance c/d
		16,799.00	16,799.00	
31 Dec balance		10,734.75		

323

Bank statement – 31 December					
	Withdrawals	Deposits			Balance
	£	£			£
			1 Dec	O/D	800.00
7650	300.00	178.19			
7653	191.91	121.27			
7654	37.14	14.92			
7651	1,111.11	16.88			
7656	5,000.00	3,100.00			
7655	129.79	171.23			
7658	678.90	1,198.17			
Standing order	50.00	117.98			
7659	1.47				
7661	10.66				
Bank charges	80.00		31 Dec	O/D	3,472.34

Required

a A corrected cash book summary and a reconciliation of the balance on this revised summary with the bank statement balance as at 31 December, as far as you are able.

b A brief note as to the likely cause of any remaining difference.

(ACCA)

20.8

The statement of financial position and statement of profit and loss of Faults Ltd show the following two items:

Bank balance – overdrawn	£3,620
Statement of profit and loss – profit for year	£23,175

However, the balance as shown on the bank statement does not agree with the balance as shown in the cash book. Your investigation of this matter reveals the following differences, and additional information:

1 Cheque payments entered in the cash book but not presented to the bank until after the year end – £3,138.

2 Bankings entered in the cash book but not credited by the bank until after the year end – £425.

3 Cheques for £35 and £140 received from customers were returned by the bank as dishonoured, but no entries concerning these events have been made in the cash book.

4 Items shown on bank statements but not entered in the cash book:

- Bank charges, £425.

- Standing order – hire purchase repayments on purchase of motor car, 12 @ £36.

- Standing order – being quarterly rent of warehouse, £125, due on each quarter day.

- Dividend received on investment, £90.

5 The cheques were returned by the bank for the following reasons: the £35 cheque requires an additional signature and should be honoured in due course; the £140 cheque was unpaid due to the bankruptcy of the drawer and should be treated as a bad debt.

6 The hire purchase repayments of £36 represent £30 capital and £6 interest.

7 A cheque for £45 received from a customer in settlement of his account had been entered in the cash book as £450 on the payments side, analysed to the purchases ledger column and later posted.

Required

a Prepare a statement reconciling the cash book balance with the bank statement.

b A statement showing the effect of the alterations on the profit for the period.

(ACCA, adapted)

20.9

The bank statement for G. Graduate for the period ended 30 June 20X3 was received. On investigation it emerged that the balance per the statement was different to the balance per the cash book. The cash book showed a debit balance of £5,944. On examination the following differences were found:

1 Cheques issued amounting to £9,350 were still outstanding and did not go through the bank until July 20X3.

2 A customer, who received a cash discount of 5 per cent on his account of £500, paid the company by cheque on 15 June 20X3. The bookkeeper, in error, entered the gross amount in the cash book.

3 A deposit of £984 paid into the bank on 29 June 20X3 had not yet appeared on the bank statement.

4 Bank charges of £140 were omitted from the cash book.

5 In March the company had entered into an agreement to pay for its electricity bill by direct debit on the 28 of each month. The amount relating to June was £52. No entries appeared for this in the cash book.

6 A cheque for £82 had been lodged on 20 June. On 22 June this appeared on the debit side with the cheque being returned to the company as out of date. A new cheque has been requested from the customer.

7 Two customers paid amounts directly into the bank account by standing order on 28 June. The amounts were £998 and £1,314. No entries had been made in the cash book.

8 £768 paid into the bank had been entered twice in the cash book.

9 A standing order to a charity for £130 had not been entered in the cash book.

10 On 15 June the manager had given the bookkeeper a cheque for £500 to lodge into his personal account. By mistake the bookkeeper lodged it to the business account and recorded it in the cash book.

After correcting the cash book and adjusting the balance on the bank statement, both balances reconciled.

Required

a Show the necessary adjustments in the cash book of G. Graduate, highlighting the corrected balance at 30 June 20X3.

b Prepare a bank reconciliation at that date showing the balance per the bank statement.

20.10

Catherine Big has a cash balance of £52,900 on 1 June 20X3. She opens a current account on that date, with Belfast Bank, depositing £50,000. Her transactions during the next three days included the following:

1 June

- Cash sales £4,500.

- Received a cheque for £25,200 from Sean Dargan, a customer.

- Paid £2,400 as rent by cheque number 0001.

- Paid £48 as wages in cash.

- Paid the petty cashier £168 as the week's imprest. The petty cashier has a cash float of £500 at the beginning of each week and has produced vouchers to the cashier to evidence the payment out of petty cash of £168 in the last week of May.

- Deposited all amounts into bank, leaving a cash float with the cashier of £4,000.

2 June

- Paid £76 for stationery by cheque number 0002.

- Cash sales £3,680.

- £9,600 is paid as business rates by a standing order.

- Paid £290 for electricity by cheque number 0003.

- Paid £72 as wages in cash.

- Received a cheque for £36,800 from Tony Kirk, a customer.

- Deposited all amounts into bank, retaining a float of £4,000.

3 June

- Sean Dargan's cheque for £25,200 is returned to Catherine Big marked 'refer to drawer'. Catherine telephoned Sean, who apologized that he was temporarily short of funds and requested Catherine to re-present the cheque to the bank on 4 June.

- The bank approves a loan to the business of £20,000. Catherine is informed that this is lodged to the current account.

- Paid £56,000 for a car by cheque number 0004.

- Wrote cheque number 0005 to draw £1,200 in cash for office use.

- Catherine drew £2,000 cash for her personal use.

Required

a Write up the cash account and the bank account.

Catherine Big receives the following bank statement on 4 June:

Statement of Catherine Big				
BELFAST BANK plc, 50 Main Street, Belfast, BT1 3HO.				
Date	Details	Debits	Credits	Balance
20X3		£	£	£
2 Jun	Deposit		50,000	50,000
2 Jun	Deposit		28,384	78,384
3 Jun	Standing order	9,600	–	68,784
3 Jun	Cheque 0001	400	–	68,384
3 Jun	Loan		20,000	88,384
3 Jun	Cheque 0003	290	–	88,094
3 Jun	Cheque dishonour	25,200	–	62,894
3 Jun	Cheque 0005	1,200	–	61,694
3 Jun	Bank charges	20	–	61,674

Required

b Prepare the bank reconciliation as at 3 June 20X3.

20.11

The following is an extract of the cashbook for J. Robin:

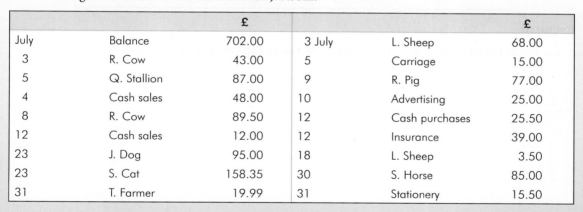

		£			£
July	Balance	702.00	3 July	L. Sheep	68.00
3	R. Cow	43.00	5	Carriage	15.00
5	Q. Stallion	87.00	9	R. Pig	77.00
4	Cash sales	48.00	10	Advertising	25.00
8	R. Cow	89.50	12	Cash purchases	25.50
12	Cash sales	12.00	12	Insurance	39.00
23	J. Dog	95.00	18	L. Sheep	3.50
23	S. Cat	158.35	30	S. Horse	85.00
31	T. Farmer	19.99	31	Stationery	15.50

The bank statement of J. Robin in the account with the Bank of ABC is as follows:

			Dr £	Cr £	Balance £
July	1	Balance c/f			702.00
	3	Interest received		15.00	717.00
	3	Bank charges	5.50		711.50
	4	Cash sales		48.00	759.50
	5	Cheque 100	86.00		673.50
	6	Cheque 101	15.00		658.50
	7	Deposit		43.00	701.50
	8	Deposit		87.00	788.50
	9	Deposit		98.50	887.00
	10	S/O: F. Hen		112.00	999.00
	11	Bounced cheque	87.00		912.00
	12	Deposit		12.00	924.00
	15	S/O: F. Wren		108.00	1032.00
	17	Cheque 104	25.50		1006.50
	18	D/D: Guinness	125.58		880.92
	18	Cheque 105	93.00		787.92
	27	Deposit		253.35	1041.27
	27	D/D: Rent	125.00		916.27
	31	Cheque 103	25.00		891.27

Required

a Complete the cash book and prepare the bank reconciliation as at 31 July 20X2.

20.12

David Greene, the bookkeeper for Botanic, a wholesale distributor of garden equipment, prepares accounts without the aid of a computerized accounting system. He carries out a bank reconciliation on a monthly basis. The details of the cash book for December 20X2 are set out below:

Botanic Cash Book							
Receipts				Payments			
Date	No	Details	£	Date	No	Details	£
20X2				20X2			
1 Dec		Balance b/d	1,501.80	1 Dec	100	P. Potter	55.00
2 Dec	001	Lodgement	1,500.00	1 Dec	101	T. Taylor	222.33
16 Dec	002	Lodgement	1,456.32	6 Dec	102	S. Summer	329.00
21 Dec	003	Lodgement	560.00	6 Dec	103	W. White	1,200.00
30 Dec	004	Lodgement	171.00	8 Dec	104	M. Moore	10.00
				8 Dec	105	R. Rover	52.00
				10 Dec	106	Y. Young	18.50
				10 Dec	107	E. Edwards	32.00
				15 Dec	108	H. Howard	21.50
				15 Dec	109	G. George	180.00
				15 Dec	110	K. Kelly	700.56
				23 Dec	111	F. French	211.00
				23 Dec	112	V. Vance	150.00
				23 Dec	113	D. Downes	89.00
				31 Dec		Balance c/d	1,918.23
			5,189.12				5,189.12

David received Botanic's monthly bank statement for December 20X2 on 6 January 20X3. Details of the bank statement are set out below:

Date	Details	Dr	Cr	Balance
20X2		£	£	£
3 Dec	Balance b/fwd			2,905.11
4 Dec	Cheque no. 101	222.33		2,682.78
5 Dec	Bank Giro Credit (Customer A)		298.34	2,981.12
6 Dec	Lodgement 001		1,500.00	
6 Dec	Cheque no. 099	1,189.19		3,291.93
10 Dec	Cheque no. 100	55.00		3,236.93
11 Dec	N.E. Electricity S.O.	100.00		3,136.93
12 Dec	Transfer to savings a/c	1,500.00		
12 Dec	Cheque no. 097	312.12		1,324.81
13 Dec	Cheque no. 105	25.00		1,299.81
14 Dec	Interest	104.23		1,195.58
17 Dec	Cheque no. 102	329.00		866.58
18 Dec	Lodgement 002		1,456.32	2,322.90
19 Dec	Cheque no. 107	32.00		
19 Dec	D.C. 00300 (Customer B)	109.00		
19 Dec	Fee for dishonoured cheque	5.00		2,176.90
20 Dec	Cheque no. 103	1,200.00		
20 Dec	AB Insurance D.D.	550.00		426.90
21 Dec	Cheque no. 110	700.56		−273.66
24 Dec	T.Y. Ltd.		140.00	−133.66
25 Dec	Lodgement 003		560.00	426.34
26 Dec	G.T. Properties S.O.	300.00		126.34
31 Dec	Cheque no. 098	352.00		−225.66
D.C.: Dishonoured Cheque				
D.D.: Direct Debit				
S.O.: Standing Order				

Additional information

1 All of the cheque payments in December 20X2 were made to suppliers.

2 The cheques paid to suppliers during November 20X2 and not presented to the bank by 30 November 20X2 were:

097	£312.12
098	£352.00
099	£1,189.19

3 David Greene has made a transposition error when entering the opening balance for December 20X2 into the cash book. It should have read £1,051.80 debit instead of £1,501.80 debit.

4 The credit appearing in the bank statement in respect of T.Y. Ltd. is a dividend.

5 The standing order for G.T. Properties has been debited to Botanics bank account in error by the bank. David Greene has written to the bank highlighting the error and has asked for the funds to be credited back to Botanic's account as soon as possible. This was the only error made by the bank in December's bank statement.

6 Customer A and Customer B are both credit customers.

7 N.E. Electricity has an account in the creditors' ledger. However, since payments made to AB Insurance vary on a monthly basis, Botanic has decided not to open an account for them in the creditors' ledger.

Required

a Show the adjustments that should be made to Botanic's cash book for December 20X2.

b Prepare a bank reconciliation statement at 31 December 20X2.

c Identify the entries required in Botanic's ledgers as a result of the adjustments in a above.

Reference

NIAO, 2008 'Internal Fraud in the Sports Institute for Northern Ireland', *Report to the Northern Ireland Assembly by the Comptroller and Auditor General*, 19/11/2008, http://www.niauditoffice.gov.uk/pubs/onepress.asp?arc=False&id=208&dm=0&dy=0 (accessed May 2011).

When you have read this chapter, log on to the Online Learning Centre for *Introduction to Financial Accounting* at www.mcgraw-hill.co.uk/textbooks/thomas, where you will find multiple choice quizzes, case studies, a glossary and mock exams.

Control accounts

Learning Objectives

After reading this chapter you should be able to do the following:

1 Explain the meaning of the key terms and concepts listed at the end of the chapter.

2 Describe the division of the general ledger into several different ledgers.

3 Explain the nature of control accounts, including the sources of the entries.

4 Prepare sales ledger control and purchases ledger control accounts.

5 Explain the purposes of control accounts.

6 Identify and correct errors and omissions relating to the different personal ledgers and control accounts.

21.1 The nature and preparation of control accounts

In practice, it is usual for the general ledger to be split into at least three different ledgers, consisting of the following:

1 A **sales ledger**, which contains all the personal accounts of credit customers. The personal accounts are also referred to as 'debtors' in the UK. The total of the credit customer balances are known as the 'trade receivables' of an entity.

2 A **purchases ledger**, which contains all the personal accounts of credit suppliers. The personal accounts are also referred to as creditors in the UK. The total of the credit suppliers balances are known as the 'trade payables' of an entity.

3 An **impersonal ledger**, which contains all other accounts (also called the **general ledger**). These comprise the nominal (i.e. sales, purchases, wages and expense) accounts, capital, and assets and liabilities other than trade receivables and trade payables.

The main reasons for dividing the general ledger into three ledgers in a manual accounting system are:

1 Where there are a large number of transactions (in a manual bookkeeping system), a single ledger becomes physically too heavy to handle.

2 It allows more than one person to work on the ledgers at the same time.

3 It provides a means of **internal control** for checking the accuracy of the ledgers, facilitates the location of errors, and can deter fraud and the misappropriation of cash. This is achieved through the use of control accounts that are described below.

The above also serves to highlight that the advantages of dividing the general ledger, and having control accounts (where the accounting system is computerized) are largely confined to security matters such as restricting access to minimize the possibility of fraud.

In a manual accounting system with the above three ledgers, it is usual for the impersonal ledger to contain a **control account** for each of the other ledgers. These will comprise a **sales ledger control account** and a **purchases ledger control account** (sometimes also referred to as **total accounts**). These control accounts contain *in total* the entries that are made in the personal ledgers, and are normally written up monthly from the totals of the relevant books of prime entry. For example, in the case of credit sales, the individual invoices shown in the sales day book are entered in each of the credit customer's personal accounts in the sales ledger, and the total sales for the month as per the sales day book is debited to the sales ledger control account in the impersonal ledger and credited to the sales account.

Where an impersonal ledger contains sales ledger and purchase ledger control accounts, these constitute part of the double entry and therefore enter into the trial balance that would be prepared for the impersonal ledger alone. In these circumstances the balances on the sales and purchases ledgers are outside the double-entry system and are thus not entered in the trial balance.

The entries to a typical sales ledger control account are set out in Figure 21.1 (this can be used for reference).

Pro forma sales ledger control account			
	£		£
Balances b/d	XX	Cash/cheques received	XXX
Credit sales	XXX	Cash discount allowed	XX
Returned cheques	XX	Sales returns	XX
Interest charged	XX	Bad debts written off	XX
		Set-off/contra entries	XX
		Balance c/d	XX
	XXX		XXX
Balance b/d	XX		

Figure 21.1 A pro forma of the typical entries required to prepare a sales ledger control account

The entries to a typical purchases ledger control account are set out in Figure 21.2 (this can be used for reference).

Purchases ledger control account			
	£		£
Cash/cheques paid	XXX	Balance b/d	XX
Cash discount received	XX	Credit purchases	XXX
Purchases returns	XX	Interest charged	XX
Set-off/contra entries	XX		
Balance c/d	XX		
	XXX		XXX
		Balance b/d	XX

Figure 21.2 A pro forma of the typical entries required to prepare a purchase ledger control account

A simple illustration of the preparation of control accounts is shown in Example 21.1.

EXAMPLE 21.1

The books of Copper Tree Ltd include three ledgers comprising an impersonal ledger, sales ledger and purchases ledger. The impersonal ledger contains sales ledger and purchases ledger control accounts as part of the double entry.

The following information relates to the accounting year ended 30 June 20X3:

	£
Sales ledger control account balance on 1 July 20X2 (debit)	5,740
Purchases ledger control account balance on 1 July 20X2 (credit)	6,830
Sales revenue	42,910
Purchases	38,620
Cheques received from credit customers	21,760
Cheques paid to credit suppliers	19,340
Returns outwards	8,670
Returns inwards	7,840
Carriage outwards	1,920
Carriage inwards	2,130
Discount received	4,560
Discount allowed	3,980
Bills of exchange payable	5,130
Bills of exchange receivable	9,720
Bad debts	1,640
Provision for bad debts	2,380
Amounts due from customers as shown by the sales ledger, transferred to purchases ledger	950
Cash received in respect of a debit balance on a purchases ledger account	810

Required

Prepare the sales ledger and purchases ledger control accounts.

Sales ledger control				
	£			£
Balances b/d	5,740	Bank		21,760
Sales revenue	42,910	Returns inwards		7,840
		Discount allowed		3,980
		Bills receivable		9,720
		Bad debts		1,640
		Transfer to the purchase ledger (contra entry)		950
		Balance c/d		2,760
	48,650			48,650
Balance b/d	2,760			

Purchase ledger control				
	£			£
Bank	19,340	Balance b/d		6,830
Returns outwards	8,670	Purchases		38,620
Discount received	4,560	Cash		810
Bills payable	5,130			
Transfer from the sales ledger (contra entry)	950			
Balance c/d	7,610			
	46,260			46,260
		Balance b/d		7,610

Notes

1 The carriage inwards, carriage outwards and provision for bad debts are not entered in the control accounts since they do not appear in the individual credit customers' or credit suppliers' accounts in the personal ledgers.

2 The transfer of £950 between the sales ledger and the purchase ledger control accounts (called a **contra entry**) is intended to reflect the total of the transfers between the sales and purchases ledgers during the year. These usually occur where the business buys from and sells goods to the same firm. Thus, instead of exchanging cheques, the amount due as shown in the sales ledger is set against the amount owed as shown in the purchases ledger (or vice versa depending on which is the smaller).

3 The cash received of £810 in respect of a debit balance on a purchase ledger account is credited to the credit supplier's account and the purchases ledger control account. A debit balance in the purchases ledger usually arises because a supplier has been overpaid as a result of either duplicating a payment or paying for goods that are the subject of a credit note. The cash received is a refund to correct the previous overpayment.

4 Bills of exchange were explained briefly at the end of Chapter 9, 'Basic Documentation and Books of Account'. The most relevant characteristics are that bills of exchange are a method of payment where the business, which owes the money, signs a document undertaking to make payment after the expiry of a specified period (usually 30, 60 or 90 days). This document is referred to as a **bill of exchange receivable** in the case of a trade receivable and a **bill of exchange payable** in the case of a trade payable. The essential point is that in the credit customers' and credit suppliers' personal accounts, the debt is treated as paid on the date the bill of exchange is signed (and not when the money is actually received or paid, which is at a later date). The same therefore applies in the control accounts.

5 The balances carried down on the control accounts at the end of the period are the difference between the two sides of the accounts.

6 Some examination questions contain amounts described as a *credit* balance on the sales ledger control account and/or a *debit* balance on the purchases ledger control account (at the beginning and/or end of the period). Although individual credit customers' and credit suppliers' personal accounts can have credit or debit balances, respectively (for the reasons outlined in note 3 above), it is unclear how the control accounts can have such balances. Each control account can only throw up one balance, which is the difference between the two sides of the account. However, if these perverse balances are encountered in an examination question, the following procedure should be adopted: a credit balance on the sales ledger control account should be entered as a credit balance brought down (and debit balance carried down), and the closing debit balance calculated as the difference between the two sides of the control account in the normal way. Similarly, a debit balance on the purchases ledger control account should be entered as a debit balance brought down (and credit balance carried down), and the closing credit balance calculated as the difference between the two sides of the control account in the normal way.

7 The entries for any bad debts recovered are the reverse of those for bad debts. Allowances given and allowances received should be treated in the same way as returns inwards and outwards, respectively. Any interest charged on overdue (credit customers') accounts should be debited to the sales ledger control account and credited to an interest receivable account.

21.2 The purpose of control accounts

The main purpose of a control account is to provide a check on the accuracy of the ledger to which it relates. Since the entries in the control account are the same (in total) as those in the ledger to which it relates, the balance on the control account should equal the total of a list of balances of the individual personal accounts contained in the ledger. If the balance on the control account is the same as the list of balances, this proves that the ledger is arithmetically accurate and that all the items in the books of prime entry have been entered in the ledger on the correct side.

The main function of control accounts is therefore to facilitate the location of errors highlighted in the trial balance by pinpointing the personal ledger in which these errors are likely to be found. Furthermore, the existence of control accounts is likely to deter fraud and the misappropriation of funds since it is usually prepared by the accountant as a check on the clerk who is responsible for the personal ledger.

The importance of having controls over purchasing is highlighted in real world example 21.1.

Fraud at the Office of Fair Trading (OFT) – the importance of having controls over purchasing

The use of proper internal controls including control accounts cannot be emphasized enough. Though the OFT (a government body which has the aim of protecting consumers) provides advice on how to identify and prevent fraud, it was the subject of a £250,000 fraud over a two year period from 2007/08 to 2008/09. The OFT reported in its Annual Report that the losses were due to control weaknesses in the 'accounts payable' procedures.

Source: http://www.jstfinancial.co.uk/articles/homeowner-loans/391/oft-affected-by-%C2%A3250000-fraud.

Finally, control accounts facilitate the preparation of (monthly or quarterly) final financial statements since the total values of trade receivables and trade payables are immediately available. The use of control accounts in the location of errors is illustrated in Example 21.2.

EXAMPLE 21.2

The books of C. Hand Ltd include three ledgers comprising an impersonal ledger, a sales ledger and a purchases ledger. The impersonal ledger contains sales ledger and purchases ledger control accounts as part of the double entry.

The following information relates to the accounting year ended 30 April 20X3:

	£
Sales ledger control account balance on 1 May 20X2 (debit)	8,460
Cheques received from credit customers	27,690
Sales revenue	47,320
Returns outwards	12,860
Returns inwards	7,170
Carriage inwards	3,940
Bills receivable	8,650
Bills payable	4,560
Discount received	5,710
Discount allowed	2,830
Provision for bad debts	1,420
Bad debts	970
Proceeds of bills receivable	6,150
Amounts due from customers as shown by sales ledger transferred to purchases ledger	830
Total of balances in the sales ledger on 30 April 20X3	9,460

a You are required to prepare the sales ledger control account for the year ended 30 April 20X3.

b After the preparation of the control account the following errors were identified:

 i The total of the sales returns day book has been overcast by £360.

 ii A cheque received for £225 has been entered on the wrong side of a credit customer's personal account.

iii The total of the discount allowed column in the cash book is shown as £2,830 when it should be £3,820.

iv A sales invoice for £2,000 has been entered in the sales day book as £200 in error.

Required

Prepare a statement showing the amended balances on the sales ledger and the sales ledger control account. Compute the amount of any remaining undetected error.

a

Sales ledger control account

	£		£
Balances b/d	8,460	Bank	27,690
Sales revenue	47,320	Returns inwards	7,170
		Bills receivable	8,650
		Discount allowed	2,830
		Bad debts	970
		Transfer to the purchase ledger	830
		Balance c/d	7,640
	55,780		55,780
Balance b/d	7,640		

b

Sales ledger

	£
Original balances	9,460
Add: Sales day book error (£2,000 − £200)	1,800
	11,260
Less: Cheque received posted to wrong side of a credit customers' account (£225 × 2)	
	450
Amended balance	10,810

Sales ledger control account

		£
Original balance		7,640
Add: Sales returns day book overcast	360	
Sales day book error (£2,000 − £200)	1,800	2,160
		9,800
Less: Discount allowed undercast		990
Amended balance		8,810
Undetected error = £10,810 − £8,810 = £2,000		

Notes

1 The returns outwards, carriage inwards, bills payable, discount received and provision for bad debts are not entered in the sales ledger control account. The proceeds of bills of exchange receivable should also not be entered in the sales ledger control account. As explained above, the entry in the control account in respect of bills receivable of £8,650 is made when the bills were signed as accepted by the credit customer and not when the proceeds are received. This is dealt with in a separate account, shown below.

Bills receivable			
	£		£
Sales ledger control a/c	8,650	Bank	6,150
		Balance c/d	2,500
	8,650		8,650
Balance b/d	2,500		

2 The difference of £2,000 between the amended balances on the sales ledger and the sales ledger control account indicates that there are still one or more errors in the sales ledger and/or the sales ledger control account.

3 Instead of computing the amended balance on the sales ledger control account in vertical/statement form above, some examination questions require this to be done in the sales ledger control account. This method can take two forms. One way is to prepare a control account containing the correct amounts for all the items. The other method is to prepare a control account with the original (uncorrected) amounts and, after computing the closing balance, show the entries necessary to correct the errors. Notice that this is essentially the same procedure as that shown in Example 20.2 relating to bank reconciliations. The first method is usually expected where an examination question describes the errors before stating the requirement to prepare a control account. The second method is usually expected where an examination question states the requirement to prepare a control account before describing the errors, such as in Example 21.2 above, but unlike the example above, does not explicitly require a statement showing the amended balance on the control account. In this case the items shown in the answer to Example 21.2 that have been added to the 'original' sales ledger control account balance would be simply debited to the control account, and those that have been deducted would be credited to the control account. In practice, errors are not normally identified until after the control accounts have been prepared and thus these would usually be corrected as separate entries in the control accounts.

21.3 Alternative systems

Sometimes, in practice, control accounts are not part of the double entry in the impersonal ledger. Instead, they are prepared on a loose sheet of paper and are thus purely memoranda. The entries still consist of totals from the relevant day books and other books of prime entry. However, in this case the impersonal and personal ledgers must be taken together to produce a trial balance. The values of trade receivables and trade payables in such a trial balance are therefore a list of the balances in the personal ledgers.

Summary

It is common for medium and large enterprises to divide their general ledger into at least three ledgers including: a general ledger (otherwise known as the impersonal ledger as it does not contain any customer/supplier names), a sales ledger and a purchases ledger. The general ledger usually contains a control account for each of the other two personal ledgers. These constitute a part of the double entry and are thus included in the trial balance that would be prepared for the general ledger alone. Thus, sales and purchases ledgers are maintained separately on a single-entry memorandum basis and are not included in the trial balance.

The purchases and sales ledger control accounts are written up from the totals of the relevant books of prime entry. The main purpose of a control account is to provide a check on the accuracy of the ledger to which it relates, and facilitate the location of errors. The balance on a control account should equal the total of a list of balances in the ledger to which it relates. If this is not the case the reasons for the difference will need to be investigated.

Key terms and concepts

bill (of exchange) payable	337	internal control	334
bill (of exchange) receivable	337	purchases ledger	333
contra entry	336	purchases ledger control account	334
control account	334	sales ledger	333
general ledger	333	sales ledger control account	334
impersonal ledger	333	total accounts	334

An asterisk after the question number indicates that there is a suggested answer on the Online Learning Centre (www.mcgraw-hill.co.uk/textbooks/thomas).

Review question

connect

21.1 Explain the main purposes of control accounts.

Exercises

connect

21.2

BASIC

The following information has been extracted from the books of a trader at 1 July 20X2:

	£
Amount owing by credit customers	40,000
Amount owing by credit suppliers	31,200
The transactions during the year ended 30 June 20X3 were as follows:	
Returns inwards	15,750
Returns outwards	8,660
Discount received	3,187
Discount allowed	5,443
Sales revenue	386,829
Purchases	222,954
Bad debts written off	3,400
Cheques received from credit customers	230,040
Cheques paid to credit suppliers	108,999

Required

Write up the sales ledger control account and the purchases ledger control account for the year ended 30 June 20X3.

BASIC

21.3

The books of original entry for James Plc showed the following for the month ended 31 March 20X3:

Cash book:	£
Discounts allowed	7,300
Cash and cheques received from credit customers	294,100
Discounts received	3,150
Cash and cheques paid to credit suppliers	249,200
Journal:	
Bad debts written off	1,500
Purchase day book	253,200
Sales day book	316,250
Returns inward	5,100
Returns outward	4,710
Contra	1,000

Previous trade receivable/trade payable balances were £53,450/£42,150.

Required

Prepare the sales ledger and the purchase ledger control accounts.

INTERMEDIATE

21.4

A list of balances on the individual customer accounts in the sales ledger did not agree with the balance on the sales ledger control account.

Sales ledger	£205,640
Sales ledger control account	£225,000

You are told that:

1 A sales invoice of £12,900 included in the sales day book had not been posted to the personal account in the sales ledger.

2 Discounts allowed to customers of £1,260 had been credited to the individual accounts in the sales ledger but no other entry was made for them in the books.

3 The returns inwards journal was wrongly totalled: it was overcast by £3,000.

4 A sales invoice for £9,400 had been entirely omitted from the books.

5 A debit balance of £7,400 on the personal account of a customer had been included in the list of balances as £4,700.

6 The balance on a customer account in the sales ledger of £5,500 had been omitted from the list of balances.

Required

a Write up the control account to correct it for those errors that affect it.

b Revise the list of customer balances for errors.

21.5

Formica purchases inventory on credit from a large number of suppliers. The company maintains a purchases ledger control account as an integral part of its double-entry system and in addition maintains supplier accounts on a memorandum basis in a purchases ledger. At the end of October 20X2 the balance of £25,450 on the purchases ledger control account failed to agree with the total of the balances from the purchases ledger. The total of the list of credit suppliers' balances is £27,620. The following errors have been subsequently discovered:

1 Goods costing £350 purchased on credit from Yellow had been entered into the purchases day book at £600.

2 An amount of £1,500 paid to Hunt had been correctly entered into the cash book but had been entered into Jack's account at £1,550.

3 The return of goods purchased on credit costing £800 had been completely omitted from the books.

4 The purchase day book has been undercast by £2,220.

Required

a Adjust the purchase ledger control account to show the amendments to the original balance.

b Adjust the list of balances in the purchases ledger to agree with the control account.

21.6

The following particulars relating to the year ended 31 March 20X3 have been extracted from the books of a trader:

	£
Sales ledger control account balance on 1 April 20X2 (debit)	7,182
Sales revenue	69,104
Cash received from credit customers	59,129
Discounts allowed	1,846
Discounts received	1,461
Returns inwards	983
Returns outwards	627
Bills receivable accepted by credit customers	3,243
Bad debts written off	593
Cash paid in respect of a credit balance on a sales ledger account	66
Amounts due from customers as shown by sales ledger transferred to purchases ledger	303
Interest charged on credit customers overdue account	10
Credit balance on sales ledger control account on 31 March 20X3	42

Prepare the sales ledger control account for the year ended 31 March 20X3, using relevant figures selected from the data shown above.

(ACCA)

21.7*

The books of Trader Ltd include three ledgers comprising an impersonal ledger, sales ledger and purchases ledger. The impersonal ledger contains sales ledger and purchases ledger control accounts as part of the double entry.

The following information relates to the month of January 20X3:

	£	
Sales ledger control account balance on 1 January 20X3	4,200	debit
Sales ledger control account balance on 1 January 20X3	300	credit
Purchases ledger control account balance on 1 January 20X3	250	debit
Purchases ledger control account balance on 1 January 20X3	6,150	credit
Credit sales for the month	23,000	
Credit purchases for the month	21,500	
Returns inward	750	
Returns outward	450	
Carriage inwards	25	
Carriage outwards	15	
Cheques received from credit customers	16,250	
Cheques paid to credit suppliers	19,800	
Discount allowed	525	
Discount received	325	
Irrecoverable debts	670	
Provision for bad debts	400	
Cheques received from credit customers, dishonoured	1,850	
Bills of exchange payable, accepted by us	4,500	
Bills of exchange receivable, accepted by credit customers	5,300	
Bad debts recovered	230	
Cash received from bills receivable	4,850	
Credit customers balances set against accounts in the purchases ledger	930	
Cash paid on bills payable	3,700	
Interest charged on credit customers overdue accounts	120	
Allowances received	280	
Allowances given	340	
Sales ledger control account balance on 31 January 20X3	240	credit
Purchases ledger control account balance on 31 January 20X3	420	debit

Required

Prepare the sales ledger and purchases ledger control accounts for January 20X3.

21.8*

INTERMEDIATE

The following particulars relating to the year ended 31 March 20X3 have been extracted from the books of Ball and Chain Ltd. All sales have been recorded in personal accounts in the sales ledger, and the sales ledger control account is part of the double entry in the impersonel ledger.

	£
Sales ledger control account balance on 1 April 20X2 (debit)	14,364
Sales revenue	138,208
Cheques received from credit customers including bad debts recovered of £84	118,258
Discounts allowed	3,692
Discounts received	2,922
Returns inwards	1,966
Returns outwards	1,254
Bills receivable	6,486
Bad debts written off	1,186
Provision for bad debts	1,800
Cash paid in respect of a credit balance on a sales ledger account	132
Amounts due from customers as shown by the sales ledger transferred to the purchases ledger	606
Interest charged on credit customers overdue accounts	20
Total of balances in the sales ledger on 31 March 20X3 (debit)	20,914

Required

a Prepare the sales ledger control account for the year ended 31 March 20X3 using relevant figures selected from the data shown above.

b Subsequently, the following errors have been discovered:

  i   The total of the sales day book has been undercast by £1,000.

  ii An entry of £125 in the returns inward book has been entered on the wrong side of the credit customer's personal account.

  iii Discount allowed of £50 had been entered correctly in a credit customer's personal account but no other entries have been made in the books.

  iv A cheque for £3,400 from a credit customer has been entered correctly in the cash book but has been posted to the credit customer's personal account as £4,300.

Required

Prepare a statement showing the amended balances on the sales ledger and the sales ledger control account.

21.9*

The books of K. Wills include three ledgers comprising the impersonal ledger, sales ledger and purchases ledger. The impersonal ledger contains sales ledger and purchases ledger control accounts as part of the double entry.

The following information relates to the accounting year ended 30 June 20X3:

	£
Sales ledger control account balance on 1 July 20X2 (debit)	17,220
Purchases ledger control account balance on 1 July 20X2 (credit)	20,490
Cheques received from credit customers	45,280
Cheques paid to credit suppliers	38,020
Sales revenue	98,730
Purchases	85,860
Returns outwards	16,010
Returns inwards	18,520
Bills of exchange payable	21,390
Bills of exchange receivable	29,160
Discount received	7,680
Discount allowed	6,940
Bad debts	4,920
Cash received in respect of a debit balance on a credit supplier's ledger account	2,430
Amount due from credit customers as shown by sales ledger, transferred to purchases ledger	2,850
Total balances in purchases ledger on 30 June 20X3 (credit)	20,700

Required

a You are required to prepare the sales ledger and purchases ledger control accounts.

b After the preparation of the above control accounts the following errors were discovered:

   i   The total of the purchases day book has been overcast by £500.

   ii Returns outwards of £180 have been entered on the wrong side of the personal account concerned.

   iii Discount received of £120 has been entered correctly in the appropriate personal account but is shown in the cash book as £210.

   iv A cheque paid for £340 has been entered correctly in the cash book but has been posted to the credit supplier's personal account as £3,400.

Required

Prepare a statement showing the amended balances on the purchases ledger and the purchases ledger control account. Compute the amount of any remaining undetected error.

21.10

The following figures relating to the year ended 31 March 20X3 have been extracted from the books of a manufacturer:

	£
Total of sales ledger balances as per list	8,300
Total of bought ledger balances as per list	1,270
Balance on sales ledger control account	8,160
Balance on bought ledger control account	1,302

The balances on the control accounts, as shown above, have been included in the trial balance and in this trial balance the total of the credit balances exceeded the total of the debit balances by £58.

Subsequently, the following errors have been discovered:

1 Goods returned by a customer to the value of £10 have been entered on the wrong side of his personal account.

2 The total of the sales day book for the month of March has been undercast by £80.

3 The total of the purchases for the month of March had been correctly shown as £653 in the bought day book and control account, but incorrectly posted to the purchases account as £635.

4 An allowance of £10 made by a supplier because of a slight defect in the goods supplied had been correctly entered in the personal account concerned, but no other entries had been made in the books.

5 A credit balance of £22 on a supplier's personal account had been overlooked and therefore did not appear in the list of bought ledger balances.

An undetected error still remained in the books after the discovery of the above-mentioned errors.

Required

a Prepare a statement showing the amended totals of the balances on the sales and bought ledgers and the amended balances on each of the control accounts assuming that the errors discovered have been corrected.

b Calculate the amount of undetected error and state where in the books you consider such an error is to be found.

(ACCA)

21.11

Fox & Co. maintain control accounts, in respect of both the sales ledger and purchases ledger, within their nominal ledger. On 31 December 20X2 the net total of the balances extracted from the sales ledger amounted to £9,870, which did not agree with the balance shown on the sales ledger control account. An examination of the books disclosed the following errors and omissions, which when rectified resulted in the corrected net total of the sales ledger balances agreeing with the amended balance of the control account.

1 £240 standing to the credit of Rice's account in the purchase ledger had been transferred to his account in the sales ledger, but no entries had been made in the control accounts in respect of this transfer.

2 Debit balances of £42 in the sales ledger had been extracted as credit balances when the balances were listed at 31 December 20X2.

3 £8,675, a month's total in the sales day book, had been posted to the control account as £8,765 although posted correctly to the sales account.

4 A balance of £428 owing by Stone had been written off to bad debts as irrecoverable, but no entry had been made in the control account.

5 Entries on the debit side of Hay's account in the sales ledger had been undercast by £100.

6 The following sales ledger balances had been omitted from the list of balances at 31 December 20X2 – debits £536, credits £37.

7 The sale of goods to Croft amounting to £60 had been dealt with correctly and debited to his account. Croft had returned such goods as not being up to standard and the only treatment accorded thereto was the crossing out of the original entry in Croft's account.

8 £22 allowed to Field as discount had been correctly recorded and posted. Subsequently, this discount had been disallowed and a like amount had been entered in the discounts received column in the cash book and posted to Field's account in the purchases ledger and included in the total of discounts received.

Required

a Give the journal entries, where necessary, to rectify these errors and omissions, and, if no journal entry is necessary, state how they should be rectified.

b Prepare the sales ledger control account showing the balance before and after rectification has been made, and reconcile the balance carried forward on this account with the total of balances extracted from the sales ledger.

(ACCA)

INTERMEDIATE 21.12

Prepare the sales ledger control account and the individual credit customer's accounts for the month of November 20X2 from the details provided below.

(*Note*: see questions 12.8 and 13.8 – you should already have prepared many of the ledger account entries.)

Balances in sales ledger		£
1 November 20X2	Boycey	200
	Del Boy	100
	Rachel	100
	Rodney	150
		550

Cash book (receipts side)		Discount allowed £	Amount received from credit customers £
8 Nov	Boycey	20	180
11 Nov	Rodney	15	135
14 Nov	Del Boy	10	90
		45	405

Credit sales		£
8 Nov	Boycey	320
11 Nov	Rodney	250
14 Nov	Del Boy	80
		650

Sales returns		£
16 Nov	Boycey	70

It was decided that Rachel would not pay her debt as she is away in America pursuing her singing career and cannot be contacted.

21.13

The following particulars relating to the year ended 31 March 20X3 have been extracted from the books of Heel and Toe, footwear wholesalers. All sales have been recorded in personal accounts in the sales ledger, and the sales ledger control account is part of the double-entry system in the general ledger.

	£
Sales ledger control account balance at 1 April 20X2 (debit)	28,728
Credit sales	276,416
Cheques received from credit customers including bad debts recovered of £168	249,488
Discounts allowed	7,384
Discounts received	5,844
Returns inwards	3,932
Returns outwards	2,508
Bad debts written off	2,372
Provision for bad debts	3,600
Cash paid in respect of a credit balance on a sales ledger account	264
Amounts due from credit customers as shown by sales ledger transferred to purchases ledger	1,212
Interest charged on credit customer overdue account	40
Total of balances in sales ledger on 31 March 20X3 (debit)	41,828

Required

a Prepare the sales ledger control account for the year ended 31 March 20X3 using relevant figures selected from the data shown above.

b Subsequently, the following errors have been discovered:

- The total of the sales day book has been undercast by £2,000.

- An entry of £250 in the returns inward book has been entered on the wrong side of the credit customer's personal account.

- Discount allowed of £100 had been entered correctly in a credit customer's personal account but no entries have been made in the books.

- A cheque for £6,800 from a credit customer has been entered correctly in the cash book but has been posted to the credit customer's personal account as £8,600.

Prepare a statement showing the amended balances on the sales ledger and the sales ledger control account.

c Discuss the purposes of control accounts.

21.14

INTERMEDIATE

(*Note*: See questions 12.9 and 13.9 – you should already have prepared many of the ledger account entries.)

The balance of the purchases ledger control account in the general ledger of A. Brook and Co. at 1 September is £1,984.50, the details being as follows:

J. Smith & Co	£378.71
A. Brown	£459.33
C. Jones	£235.38
M. Mann	£684.17
Payne & Co	£245.18
	£2,002.77
Less: debit – J. Cann & Co	£18.27
	£1,984.50

The following are the transactions relating to the purchases ledger accounts in September:

		£	£
Sep 4	Paid J. Smith & Co		150.00
	J Cann & Co. – Goods purchased from Brook		48.38
	A. Gray – Goods		30.55
	Paid A. Brown	268.08	
	Discount	8.25	276.33
Sep 11	Paid C. Jones	169.93	
	Discount	5.25	175.18
	C. Jones – Goods		39.33
	A. Brown – Goods		75.48
Sep 18	Goods returned to A. Brown		9.80
	Paid M. Mann		300.00
	M. Mann contra for goods purchased by him		89.80
	Paid Payne & Co	164.14	
	Discount	5.08	169.22
	Payne & Co – Goods		83.33
25 Sep	A. Read – Goods		120.15
30 Sep	Allowance by Gray for soiled goods		3.50
	Trade discount allowed by A. Read		24.03
	(Not previously deducted from the invoice)		

Required

a Open accounts in the purchases ledger with balances at 1 September and post therein the above transactions. Bring down balances, list and total them.

b Open and write up a control account and bring down balance to agree.

Reference

JST Financial Solutions Limited (2009) 'OFT affected by £250,000 Fraud' (Published 13 August 2009 in *Homeowner Loans* and included on JST Financial Solutions Website), http://www.jstfinancial.co.uk/ articles/homeowner-loans/391/oft-affected-by-%C2%A3250000-fraud

When you have read this chapter, log on to the Online Learning Centre for *Introduction to Financial Accounting* at www.mcgraw-hill.co.uk/ textbooks/thomas, where you will find multiple choice quizzes, case studies, a glossary and mock exams.

Errors and suspense accounts

Learning Objectives

After reading this chapter you should be able to do the following:

1. Explain the meaning of the key terms and concepts listed at the end of the chapter.

2. Describe the types of error that do and do not cause a trial balance to disagree.

3. Explain the purposes of a suspense account.

4. Show journal and ledger entries for the correction of both errors that do and do not cause a trial balance to disagree, including those relating to suspense accounts.

5. Prepare a revised income statement and statement of financial position after the correction of errors.

22.1 Introduction

As explained in Chapter 11 'The Balancing of Accounts and the Trial Balance', one of the main purposes of the trial balance is to check the accuracy of the ledger. If a trial balance agrees this indicates the following:

1 There are no arithmetic errors in the ledger accounts.

2 Every transaction recorded in the ledger has been entered once on each side.

However, there can still be errors in the ledger that do not cause a trial balance to disagree. These are explained below.

22.2 Types of error that do not cause a trial balance to disagree

Error of principle

An **error of principle** occurs when a transaction has been entered on both sides of the ledger but one of the entries is in the wrong *class/type* of account. For example, an expense has been debited to an asset account in error (or vice versa), or income credited to a liability account in error (or vice versa). Another common example is where the proceeds of sale of a non-current asset have been credited to the sales account in error.

Error of commission

An **error of commission** occurs when a transaction has been entered on both sides of the ledger correctly and in the correct *class/type* of account, but one of the entries is in the wrong account. For example, stationery has been entered in the purchases account in error, or cheques are posted to the wrong personal account.

Error of omission

An **error of omission** occurs when a transaction has not been recorded anywhere in the books of account. A typical example is bank charges omitted from the cash book.

Error of original/prime entry

An **error of original/prime entry** occurs when an incorrect amount has been entered in a book of prime entry. That is, the amount entered in the book of prime entry is different from that shown on the original document. This will mean that the wrong amount has been entered on both sides of the ledger. For example, a sales invoice for £980 entered in the sales day book as £890 will result in both the sales and sales ledger (control) accounts containing a figure of £890 instead of £980.

Compensating errors

A **compensating error** is two separate errors that are totally unrelated to each other except that they are both of the same amount. Neither of these two errors is of the four types above but rather would individually cause a trial balance to disagree.

Double posting error

This refers to where the correct amount has been entered in a day book (of prime entry) but the wrong amount is shown on both sides of the ledger. Another type of **double posting error** can be said to have occurred when the correct amount of a transaction has been entered on the wrong side of both of the accounts to which it has been posted. A slightly different example is rent received recorded as rent paid.

Illustrations of these errors and their correction are shown in Example 22.1. The errors are presented in the same order as the above list.

EXAMPLE 22.1 State the title of each of the following errors and show the journal entries needed for their correction.

1 Plant that was acquired at a cost of £5,000 has been credited in the cash book but debited to the purchases account in error.

2 The purchase of consumable tools for £80 has been debited to the repairs account in error.

3 Bank charges of £27 shown on the bank statement have not been entered in the cash book.

4 A purchase invoice received from A. Creditor for £1,000 has been entered in the purchases day book as £100.

5 Wages paid of £40 have not been posted to the wages account, and the debit side of the purchases account has been overcast by £40.

6 Rent received of £400 has been entered in both the cash book and the ledger as rent paid.

The journal		Debit £	Credit £
1 Plant and machinery	Dr	5,000	
To purchases account	Cr		5,000
Being correction of error principle			
2 Consumable tools	Dr	80	
To repairs account	Cr		80
Being correction of error of omission			
3 Bank charges	Dr	27	
To cash book	Cr		27
Being correction of error of omission			
4 Purchases account	Dr	900	
To A. Creditor/purchase ledger control account	Cr		900
Being correction of error of prime entry			
(no correction of purchases day book is necessary)			
5 Wages account	Dr	40	
To purchases account	Cr		40
Being correction of compensating error			
– wages not posted and purchases account overcast			
6 Cash book	Dr	800	
To rent payable account	Cr		400
To rent receivable account	Cr		400
Being correction of rent receivable of £400 entered as rent payable			

Inventory error example

Sometimes, in examination questions, goods on sale or return are recorded as sales. This is an error and must be reversed by means of the following entries:

Debit: sales account
Credit: trade receivables
} with the selling price of the goods

Debit: inventories account
Credit: income statement account
} with the cost price of the goods

Note that the entries in the inventory account and the income statement account take the form of increasing the amount of closing inventory.

 ## Types of error that cause a trial balance to disagree

As explained above, one of the purposes of a trial balance is to ascertain whether the total of the debit balances in the ledger is the same as the total of the credit balances. The reason why this may not be the case is because of the existence of one or more of the following errors:

1 Arithmetic errors, such as the incorrect addition of the amounts on one side of an account, and/or in the calculation of a balance. Adding in accounting is sometimes referred to as to **cast (add)** the account. So **overcast** means the balance was over-stated, and **undercast** means the balance was under-stated.

2 Posting errors. These may take three forms:

  a where a transaction has been entered on one side of the ledger but not on the other side;
  b where a transaction has been entered twice on the same side; or
  c where the correct amount of a transaction has been entered on one side of the ledger account but the wrong amount has been entered on the other side. The most common errors of the latter type are of two forms:

    i where a zero is omitted from the end of an amount (for example, a transaction for £33,000 entered on one side of the ledger as £3,300), and
    ii **transposed figures**, where the correct amount of a transaction has been entered on one side of the ledger but two or more of the figures have been reversed when the entry was made on the other side (for example, an amount of £323 entered on one side as £332). A difference of 9, 90, or another number divisible by 9 on the trial balance may indicate that there is a transposition error.

3 Extraction error, where the correct balance is shown in the ledger account but the wrong amount is entered on the trial balance, or the correct amount is put on the wrong side of the trial balance.

The first two types of error have to be corrected by a one-sided ledger entry. The correction may be done by changing the figure to the correct amount. However, it is argued that the correction should take the form of double entry so that some record exists of the correction of the error. Furthermore, in practice it is frequently impractical to correct errors by simply changing a figure to the correct amount, since this usually also necessitates numerous other changes to subsequent totals and balances (e.g. an error in the bank account which occurred several months previously). Where an error is corrected by means of another entry, it is essential that the details of the correction indicate where the original error is located. For these reasons, it is recommended that suspense accounts be created to capture the net error balances and double entry to this account be used to fix the original errors. An illustration of the types of error described above and their correction is given in Example 22.2.

EXAMPLE 22.2 The following examples are shown in the same order as the types of error described above:

Error	Correction
1 The debit side of the cash account has been overcast by £1,000 and this is reflected in the balance brought down	**1** Credit the cash account with £1,000
2a Cash purchases of £200 have been credited in the cash account but not entered in the purchases account	**2a** Debit the purchases account with £200
2b Rent paid of £50 has been credited in the cash account but also credited in error to the rent account	**2b** Debit the rent account with £100 (i.e. £50 × 2)
2c Bank charges of £23 shown in the bank account have been debited to the bank charges account as £32	**2c** Credit the bank charges account with £9
3 The sales revenue account shows a balance of £2,000, which has been entered on the trial balance as £200	**3** Delete the wrong figure on the trial balance and insert the correct amount

These types of error are typically corrected with the use of a suspense account.

22.4 Suspense accounts

Suspense accounts are used for two purposes:

1 *Recording undefined transactions*: That is, where money is received or paid but there is no record of what it relates to, the amount would be entered in the cash book and posted to a suspense account. When the nature of the transaction is known, the amount is transferred from the suspense account to the appropriate account.

2 *To record in the ledger any difference on a trial balance and thus make it agree*: If a trial balance fails to agree by a relatively small amount and the error(s) cannot be found quickly, the difference is inserted in the trial balance (to make it agree) and in a suspense account. The entry in the suspense account must be on the same side of the ledger as the entry in the trial balance. At a later date when the error(s) are located they are corrected by double entry – by means of an entry in the suspense account and the other in the account containing the error. This correction through the suspense account is necessary because the original entry in the suspense account (which made the trial balance agree) in effect corrected all the errors in total. Thus, the correction must effectively be moved from the suspense account to the account that contains the error.

An illustration of the use of suspense accounts is given in Example 22.3.

EXAMPLE
22.3
A trial balance failed to agree because the debit side exceeds the credit side by £2,509. A suspense account has been opened into which the difference is entered. Subsequently, the following errors were identified:

1 The debit side of the cash book has been overcast by £1,000.

2 Goods bought by cheque for £200 have been credited in the cash book but not entered in the purchases account.

3 Rent paid of £50 has been credited in the cash book but also credited in error to the rent account.

4 Car repairs of £23 shown in the cash book have been debited to the motor expenses account as £32 in error.

5 The sales account contains a balance of £2,000 but this has been entered in the trial balance as £200.

You are required to prepare the journal entries needed to correct the above errors and show the entries in the suspense account.

The journal			Debit £	Credit £
1	Suspense account	Dr	1,000	
	Cash book	Cr		1,000
	Being correction of arithmetic error			
2	Purchases account	Dr	200	
	Suspense account	Cr		200
	Being correction of posting error			
3	Rent account	Dr	100	
	Suspense account	Cr		100
	Being correction of posting error (£50 × 2)			
4	Suspense account	Dr	9	
	Motor expenses	Cr		9
	Being correction of transposed figures			
5	Suspense account	Dr	1,800	
	Trial balance (no ledger entry)	Cr		1,800
	Being correction of extraction error			

Suspense account				
Cash book	1,000	Difference on trial balance		2,509
Motor expenses	9	Purchases		200
Extraction error on sales	1,800	Rent		100
	2,809			2,809

Notes

1 It should be noted that only errors of the type that cause a trial balance to disagree are corrected by means of an entry in the suspense account; that is, arithmetic and posting errors described in

Chapter 11, 'The Balancing of Accounts and the Trial Balance'. This is because errors that cause a trial balance to disagree give rise to the original entry in the suspense account.

2 The correction of errors via a suspense account always involves a double entry to the individual ledger account, with one exception. This relates to the correction of extraction errors, such as item 5 above, where the only ledger entry is in the suspense account. A useful way of working out whether the entry in the suspense account is a debit or credit is to imagine what entry is needed to correct the trial balance; the entry in the suspense account will be on the opposite side of the ledger.

3 Sometimes in examination questions, and in practice, the errors that have been identified are not the only errors. In this case there will still be a balance on the suspense account after the known errors have been corrected. This shows the amount of the remaining errors.

4 Occasionally in examination questions and in practice the final financial statements are prepared before the errors in the suspense account have been found and corrected. In this instance the suspense account will be shown on the statement of financial position. In practice, it will disappear when the errors in the suspense account are corrected along with the necessary changes to the items in the final financial statements that are incorrect. However, instead of correcting the final financial statements, some examination questions require students to prepare a statement amending the original/draft (i.e. wrong) figure of profit. In this case it will be necessary also to show the effect of correcting each error on the original profit, as an addition to or subtraction from this figure, thus arriving at a revised amount of profit.

EXAMPLE 22.4

When Jane, a senior accountant from Balance Accountancy Services, extracted the trial balance from the general ledger of Smith Applepie's Limited she noticed that the trial balance did not agree. The debit side was £504 more than the credit balance. Jane is an experienced accountant and she knows from experience that the bookkeeper in Smith Applepie Limited is well trained and normally has everything posted correctly.

What will her first steps be to finding out the source of this error?

As an experienced accountant, Jane's first reaction will be to check her own totals. Then it is likely that she will divide the difference by nine. £504/9 = 56. If the difference is divisible by 9 then it is likely that the error is due to a transposition error. The next step will be to check the trial balance figures to the ledger balances with a focus on ensuring that the balances have been transposed correctly. If this does not uncover the problem, the bank reconciliation, the sales and purchases control accounts and the balances on the corresponding day books will all be checked. If all this is clear then it is likely that the problem lies in the other accounts. This process helps to narrow down the areas that require very labour-intensive review. It is likely that Jane will also get the bookkeeper to help to locate the error.

Errors in bookkeeping are typically corrected internally and, unless material or unethical, are rarely brought to the attention of stakeholders. In some instances, entities make errors that are deemed to be so material that the financial statements require restatement (i.e. to be re-prepared) and reissued to the market. In some instances the regulators will demand restatement in light of their review of the financial statements. The next real world example concerns an error of principle.

WNS (Holdings) Limited

WNS (Holdings) Limited, a leading provider of global business process outsourcing (BPO) services, today provided a business update for the fiscal year ended 31 March 2010.

WNS's financial statements for the year ended 31 March 2010 are subject to finalization and the conclusion of the external audit, and more specifically, adjustments relating to the accounting treatment for referral fees earned from garages, and revenues and costs on completed but unbilled repairs, in its Auto Claims BPO segment (the AutoClaims business).

As background, for automobile accident management services, where WNS arranges for the repairs through a network of repair centres, it invoices the client for the amount of the repair. When it directs a vehicle to a specific repair centre, it receives a referral fee from that repair centre. In the past WNS had recognized the referral fees from garages and the repair payments from clients, net of the amount of referral fees that are passed back to clients, as revenues, and had recognized the payments to the repair centres as cost of revenues. WNS had also not recognized as revenues the amount of completed but unbilled repairs due from clients and similarly had not recognized the corresponding costs of these repairs as cost of revenues.

WNS, in consultation with its Audit Committee, has concluded that it should not include the referral fees from garages within revenues, and should instead subtract them from the costs of revenues for the AutoClaims business. WNS has also concluded that it should recognize the revenues and costs of completed but unbilled repairs as revenues and costs of revenues, respectively. WNS will accordingly restate the 'revenue' and 'cost of revenue' lines of its audited financial statements for the years ended 31 March 2009 and 2008 (as well as selected financial information for the years ended 31 March 2007 and 2006 and the quarterly information for fiscal 2009 and 2010) to reflect these accounting changes.

WNS is currently determining the impact of these accounting changes where the reduction in revenues for the AutoClaims business will be largely matched by the reduction in cost of revenues. WNS currently expects the impact of these changes will be material with respect to revenues of the AutoClaims business. However, the impact of these changes on WNS's net income in its financial statements, as well as adjusted net income is not expected to be material.

Source: http://finance.boston.com/boston/news/read?GUID=12774375.

Summary

If the total of the debit ledger account balances in a trial balance does not equal the total of the credit ledger account balances, this means that certain types of error must have occurred. The types of error that cause a trial balance to disagree comprise arithmetic error, posting error, and extraction error. These need to be corrected by a one-sided entry in the general ledger or trial balance. There are six types of error that do not cause a trial balance to disagree. These consist of errors of principle, errors of commission, errors of omission, errors of original/prime entry, compensating errors and double posting errors. Errors that do not cause a trial balance to disagree are always corrected by means of a two-sided ledger (and journal) entry.

Suspense accounts are used for two purposes. One is to record transactions, the nature of which is unknown. The other is to record in the ledger any difference on a trial balance, and thus make it agree. When the error(s) that gave rise to the difference are located, they are corrected by means of one entry in the suspense account and a corresponding entry in the account containing the error. Only errors that cause a trial balance to disagree are corrected by means of an entry in the suspense account.

Errors giving rise to the creation of a suspense account should be located and corrected before final financial statements are prepared. However, if errors are discovered after the preparation of the final financial statements, the effect of their correction on the income statement and statement of financial position should be taken into consideration. This may involve preparing revised final financial statements.

Key terms and concepts

arithmetic error	356	error of principle	354
cast (add)	356	extraction error	356
compensating errors	354	overcast	356
double posting error	354	posting errors	356
error of commission	354	suspense accounts	357
error of omission	354	transposed figures	356
error of original/prime entry	354	undercast	356

An asterisk after the question number indicates that there is a suggested answer on the Online Learning Centre (www.mcgraw-hill.co.uk/textbooks/thomas).

Review questions

connect

22.1 Describe the types of errors that:

    a cause a trial balance to disagree;

    b do not cause a trial balance to disagree.

22.2 Describe the two main uses of a suspense account.

Exercises

connect

22.3

BASIC

Write journals to correct the following errors. These errors are not suspense account errors.

1 £150 sales invoice posted to the credit customer, D. Brown's account – should have been posted to the credit customer, D. Black's account.

2 £50 stationery paid for in cash was debited to the cash account and credited to the stationery account.

3 £100 paid for equipment by cheque was debited to purchases.

BASIC

22.4

Write journals to correct the following errors. These errors are not suspense account errors.

1 A payment of £4,000 for rent was incorrectly posted to the insurance account.

2 The cost of purchasing a delivery van, £12,400, is incorrectly debited to the motor expenses account.

3 The day's cash sales takings, £13,400, were not paid into the bank or entered into the cash book.

4 A payment of £400 for insurance has been entered in the cash book correctly but posted to the insurance account as £40. This is balanced by a transposition error in posting another payment into the motor expenses account where £480 was posted as £840.

BASIC

22.5

Write journals to correct the following errors (suspense account errors):

1 The debit side of the cash book is undercast by £3,000.

2 A payment of £475 for an electricity bill is correctly entered in the cash book but debited to the telephone account as £457.

3 A payment of £4,750 for an electricity bill is again correctly entered in the cash book but is not debited to the telephone account at all.

4 In preparing the trial balance the debit balance of £1,940 on the electricity bill is omitted.

5 A credit balance of £280 on the heat and light account was not brought forward into the current year.

BASIC

22.6*

A trial balance failed to agree. On investigation the following errors were found:

a Wages of £250 have been credited in the cash account but no other entry has been made.

b The credit side of the sales revenue account has been undercast by £100 and this is reflected in the balance brought down.

c Purchases of £198 shown in the purchases account have been entered in the credit suppliers' account as £189.

d The drawings account contains a balance of £300, but this has been entered on the trial balance as £3,000.

e Bank interest received of £86 has been credited in the bank account and the interest received account.

Required

Describe the entries needed to correct the above errors.

22.7

Arthur started a new business on 1 January 20X3. You are supplied with the following nominal ledger accounts, which have been closed off and a trial balance extracted. These are Arthur's only transactions in this period.

Cash account						Sales revenue account					
Date	**Details**	**£**	**Date**	**Details**	**£**	**Date**	**Details**	**£**	**Date**	**Details**	**£**
6 Jan	Sales	100	9 Jan	H&L	80				6 Jan	Cash	100
8 Jan	Sales	89							8 Jan	Cash	98
									10 Jan	Bank	129
			10 Jan	Bal c/d	119	10 Jan	IS a/c	327			
		189			189			327			327
11 Jan	Bal b/d	119									

Capital introduced account						Bank account					
Date	**Details**	**£**	**Date**	**Details**	**£**	**Date**	**Details**	**£**	**Date**	**Details**	**£**
			1 Jan	Bank	1,000	1 Jan	Cap int.	1,000	2 Jan	H&L	50
						10 Jan	Sales	192	3 Jan	Van	500
10 Jan	Cap a/c	100							10 Jan	Bal c/d	742
		100			100			1,192			1,192
						11 Jan	Bal b/d	742			

Heat and light account (H&L)						Motor vehicle account					
Date	**Details**	**£**	**Date**	**Details**	**£**	**Date**	**Details**	**£**	**Date**	**Details**	**£**
2 Jan	Bank	50				3 Jan	Bank	500			
9 Jan	Cash	80	10 Jan	IS a/c	130				10 Jan	S I a/c	500
		130			130			500			500

Trial balance for Arthur as at 10 January 20X3:

	Debit	Credit
	£	**£**
Cash	119	
Sales		372
Capital introduced		100
Bank account	742	
Heat and light	130	
Motor vehicles	500	
	1,491	572

The trial balance should balance.

There are seven errors (six are double-entry errors, the other is a description error).

Required

a Describe the entries required to correct the errors.

b Redraft the amended ledger accounts and trial balance as on 10 January 20X3.

INTERMEDIATE 22.8

Chocolate is a confectionery shop owned by Thomas McKee. Thomas operates a manual bookkeeping system and employs a cashier and a bookkeeper. When writing up the books of account for the year ended 31 December 20X2, the following errors were discovered:

1 The sale of cakes for £128 was not recorded in the cash book or ledger.

2 Payment of £1,600 as rent was recorded as £16,000 in the cash book and ledger.

3 £500 received from a supplier for returned goods was recorded in the cash book only.

4 A payment of £16,000 for a vehicle was recorded in the cash book as a 'purchase'.

5 A payment (£750) to a supplier 'Stephen McCann' was recorded in his account but not in the cash book.

6 £70 paid for stationery was posted to the telephone account in the ledger.

7 £425 paid for advertising has not been posted in the ledger.

Required

In respect of each of the errors you are to identify:

a which member of the staff is responsible for the error;

b whether the balancing of the trial balance would have been affected;

c the journal required to correct the error (with description).

INTERMEDIATE 22.9

The draft trial balance of Regent Ltd as at 31 May 20X3 agreed. The business proceeded with the preparation of the draft final financial statements and these showed a profit of £305,660.

However, a subsequent audit revealed the following errors:

1 Bank charges of £56 had been omitted from the cash book.

2 The purchases journal had been overcast by £400.

3 The sales journal had been undercast by £100.

4 An invoice for £127 received from Alpha Ltd had been entered into the purchases journal as £217. (This is quite independent of the error made in the purchases journal referred to above.)

5 It is now considered prudent to write off the balance of £88 on P. Shadey's account as bad.

6 An invoice from Caring Garages Ltd for £550 in respect of servicing Regent Ltd's motor vehicles had been posted to the debit of motor vehicles account.

7 Depreciation of 10 per cent per annum has been provided for on motor vehicles inclusive of the £550 invoice referred to in point 6 above.

Regent Ltd maintains control accounts for credit sales and credit purchases in its general ledger. Individual accounts for credit customers and credit suppliers are maintained on a memorandum basis only.

Required

a   Prepare journal entries to show how the above errors would be corrected.
    (*Note*: Dates and narratives not required.)

b   What is the profit for the year after correcting the above errors?

(AAT)

22.10*

INTERMEDIATE

When preparing a trial balance the bookkeeper found it disagreed by £600; the credit side being that much greater than the debit side. The difference was entered in a suspense account. The following errors were subsequently found:

1   A cheque for £32 for electricity was entered in the cash book but not posted to the ledger.

2   The debit side of the wages account is overcast by £28.

3   There is a debit in the rent account of £198 that should be £918.

4   The purchase of a van for £3,000 has been posted to the debit side of the purchases account in error.

5   A cheque received from A. Watt for £80 has been credited to A. Watson's account in error.

6   The sale of some old loose tools for £100 had been credited to sales account in error.

7   An amount of £17 paid for postage stamps has been entered in the carriage outwards account in error.

8   Bank charges of £41 shown on the bank statement have not been entered in the books.

9   An amount of £9 for stationery has been entered in the cash book but not posted to the stationery account. Cash sales of £43 are entered correctly in the cash book but posted to the sales account as £34.

10   A credit sale to J. Bloggs of £120 was entered in the sales day book as £12.

11   A credit balance of £62 shown in the discount received account has been entered on the debit side of the trial balance.

Required

Prepare the journal entries necessary to correct the above errors and show the suspense account.

22.11

INTERMEDIATE

At the end of January 20X3 a trial balance extracted from the ledger of Gerald Ltd did not balance and a suspense account was opened for the amount of the difference. Subsequently, the following matters came to light:

1   £234 had been received during January from a credit customer who owed £240. No entry has been made for the £6 outstanding but it is now decided to treat it as a cash discount.

2   Returns to suppliers during January were correctly posted individually to personal accounts but were incorrectly totalled. The total, overstated by £100, was posted to the returns account.

3   A bank statement drawn up to 31 January 20X3 showed a credit balance of £120 while the balance of the bank account in the trial balance was an overdraft of £87. The difference was found on reconciliation to comprise:

    a   a direct debit for the annual subscription to a trade association of £70, for which no entry had been made in the books of account;

   b an entry in the bank account for payment to a supplier shown as £230 instead of £320;

   c unpresented cheques on 31 January totalled £327;

   d the remainder of the difference was due to an addition error in the bank account.

4 A cheque for £163 was received during January in full settlement of a debt that was written off in the previous financial year. It was correctly entered in the bank account but not posted elsewhere, pending instructions.

5 A credit customer's account with a balance of £180 had been taken out of the looseleaf ledger when a query was investigated and not replaced at the time the trial balance was extracted.

6 A credit note for £5 sent to a customer in respect of an allowance had been posted to the wrong side of the customer's personal account.

Required

Show what correcting entries need to be made in the ledger accounts in respect of these matters. Set out your answer as follows:

Item	Account(s) to be debited £	Account(s) to be credited £

(ACCA, adapted)

INTERMEDIATE

22.12

Chi Knitwear Ltd is an old-fashioned firm with a handwritten set of books. A trial balance is extracted at the end of each month, and an income statement and statement of financial position are computed. This month, however, the trial balance does not balance, the credits exceeding debits by £1,536.

You are asked to help and after inspection of the ledgers, you discover the following errors:

1 A balance of £87 on a credit customer's account has been omitted from the schedule of outstanding balances, the total of which was entered as trade receivables in the trial balance.

2 A small piece of machinery purchased for £1,200 had been written off to repairs.

3 The receipts side of the cash book had been undercast by £720.

4 The total of one page of the sales day book had been carried forward as £8,154, whereas the correct amount was £8,514.

5 A credit note for £179 received from a supplier had been posted to the wrong side of his account.

6 An electricity bill in the sum of £152, not yet accrued for, is discovered in a filing tray.

7 Mr Smith, whose past debts to the company had been the subject of a provision, at last paid £731 to clear his account. His personal account has been credited but the cheque has not yet passed through the cash book.

Required

a Write up the suspense account to clear the difference.

b State the effect on the accounts of correcting each error.

(ACCA)

22.13

The draft final financial statements of RST Ltd for the year ended 30 April 20X3 showed a net profit for the year of £78,263.

During the subsequent audit, the following errors and omissions were discovered. At the draft stage a suspense account had been opened to record the net difference.

1 Trade receivables were shown as £55,210. However:

   a bad debts of £610 had not been written off;

   b the existing provision for doubtful debts, £1,300, should have been adjusted to 2 per cent of trade receivables;

   c a provision of 2 per cent for discounts on trade receivables should have been raised.

2 Rates of £491, which had been prepaid at 30 April 20X2, had not been brought down on the rates account as an opening balance.

3 A vehicle held as a non-current asset, which had originally cost £8,100 and for which £5,280 had been provided as depreciation, had been sold for £1,350. The proceeds had been correctly debited to bank but had been credited to sales. No transfers had been made to a disposals account.

4 Credit purchases of £1,762 had been correctly debited to the purchases account but had been credited to the supplier's account as £1,672.

5 A piece of equipment costing £9,800 and acquired on 1 May 20X2 for use in the business had been debited to the purchases account. (The company depreciates equipment at 20 per cent per annum on cost.)

6 Items valued at £2,171 had been completely omitted from the closing inventory figure.

7 At 30 April 20X3 an accrual of £543 for electricity charges and an insurance prepayment of £162 had been omitted.

8 The credit side of the wages account had been under-added by £100 before the balance on the account had been determined.

Required

Using relevant information from that given above:

a Prepare a statement correcting the draft net profit.

b Post and balance the suspense account. (*Note*: The opening balance of this account has not been given and must be derived.)

(ACCA)

ADVANCED

22.14*

Miscup showed a difference on their trial balance of £14,650. This was posted to a suspense account so that the financial statements for the year ended 31 March 20X3 could be prepared. The following statement of financial position was produced:

Statement of financial position for Miscup as at 31st March 20X3			
ASSETS	£	£	£
Non-current assets	Cost	Deprec	NBV
Tangible assets			
Freehold premises	60,000	–	60,000
Motor vehicles	25,000	11,935	13,065
Fixtures and fittings	1,500	750	750
	86,500	12,685	73,815
Current assets			
Inventories			75,410
Trade and other receivables			37,140
Cash			75
			112,625
Suspense account			14,650
Total assets			201,090
OWNERS' EQUITY AND LIABILITIES			
Equity and reserves			
Equity share capital			125,000
Reserves			33,500
			158,500
Current liabilities			
Trade and other payables			41,360
Bank overdraft			1,230
Total liabilities			42,590
Total equity and liabilities			201,090

On checking the books to eliminate the suspense account you find the following errors:

1 The debit side of the cash book is undercast by £10,000.

2 A credit item of £5,000 in the cash book on account of a new building has not been posted to the nominal ledger.

3 The purchase day book has been summarized for posting to the nominal ledger but an item of purchases of £100 has been entered in the summary as £1,000 and a further transport charge of £450 has been entered as £45.

4 An item of rent received, £45, was posted twice to the nominal ledger from the cash book.

5 The debit side of the sales ledger control account was undercast by £100.

6 On reconciling the bank statement with the cash book, it was discovered that bank charges of £3,250 had not been entered in the cash book.

7 Depreciation of motor vehicles was undercharged by £500.

8 Inventories were undervalued by £1,250.

9 Suppliers' invoices totalling £2,110 for goods included in inventory had been omitted from the books.

Required

a Show the journal entries necessary to eliminate the balance on the suspense account.

b Show the statement of financial position of Miscup as at 31 March 20X3, after correcting all the above errors.

(ACCA)

22.15

Jacobs Ltd has recently completed its draft financial statements for the year ended 30 December 20X2, which showed a draft profit for the year of £300,000. During the audit a number of mistakes and omissions were uncovered. These are listed below.

1 A cheque from a credit customer amounting to £7,100 had been received on 27 December 20X2 but had not been banked or included in the financial statements.

2 Depreciation on a non-current asset had been incorrectly calculated. The assets cost was £125,000, it was being depreciated on a straight-line basis over four years. £16,250 was charged in the financial statements.

3 Although included in inventory an invoice for goods sold by Jacobs amounting to £17,500, dated 26 December 20X2, had not been included in the financial statements.

4 Two items of inventory, currently valued at a total cost of £35,000, are now considered obsolete. The director estimates that they will only realize about £10,000 between them.

5 The company accountant forgot to include a charge for interest on the 10 per cent long-term loan of £240,000 for the final six months of the year.

6 Rates of £1,500 for the year to 1 April 20X2 were paid for in April 20X1. No entries have been made in the financial statements in relation to this item other than correctly recording the original payment.

7 An item of capital worth £3,000 had been incorrectly entered into the prepayments account instead of non-current assets. The asset has a useful life of three years and a residual value of £600. The accounting policy states that the reducing balance method is most appropriate for this type of asset.

8 One of the credit customers contacted Jacobs Ltd to inform them that the cashier had not given him the correct agreed trade discount of 20 per cent. The invoices affected were noted by the accountant as follows:

30 November 20X2	£3,500
2 December 20X2	£1,500
15 December 20X2	£2,000

Required

a For each of the items (1) to (8) above, state and describe the effect on the profit for the year and calculate the total effect on Jacobs' draft profit figure.

b For each of the items (1) to (8) above, describe the changes, if any, which will have to be made on the statement of financial position of Jacobs Ltd.

Reference

WNS Holdings Limited (2010) 'WNS Provides Fiscal 2010 Business Update; Year End Audit in Progress; Announces Restatement of Previously Issued Financial Statements', Thursday, 22 April 2010, Marketwire News Releases, http://finance.boston.com/boston/news/read?GUID=12774375 (accessed March 2011).

When you have read this chapter, log on to the Online Learning Centre for *Introduction to Financial Accounting* at www.mcgraw-hill.co.uk/textbooks/thomas, where you will find multiple choice quizzes, case studies, a glossary and mock exams.

Single entry and incomplete records

Learning Objectives

After reading this chapter you should be able to do the following:

1 Explain the meaning of the key terms and concepts listed at the end of the chapter.

2 Describe the different forms of incomplete records.

3 Prepare final financial statements from incomplete records and single entry.

23.1 Introduction

Incomplete records is a general term given to a situation where the transactions of an organization have not been recorded in double-entry form (or using a computer system), and thus there is not a full set of records of the enterprise's transactions. This is quite common in practice in the case of sole traders. It is often too expensive for small businesses to maintain a complete system of double-entry book-keeping. In addition, many sole traders often claim to have little practical use for any records other than to know how much money they have, and the amounts of trade receivables and trade payables. Many sole traders are usually able to remember, without records, what non-current assets they own, and any non-current liabilities they owe. In the case of small businesses the accountant is therefore usually engaged not to write up the books, but to ascertain the profit of the business for tax purposes. Often, but not always, a statement of financial position is also prepared.

In practice, there are three different forms of incomplete records:

1 *Incomplete records of revenue income and expenditure*: That is, there are no basic documents or records of revenue income and expenditure, or the records are inadequate. This situation usually arises where the books and documents have been accidentally destroyed (e.g. in a fire) or the owner failed to keep proper records. In these circumstances it is not possible to construct a statement of profit and loss. However, it may still be possible to ascertain the profit for the period provided there is information available relating to the assets and liabilities of the business at the start and end of the relevant period.

2 *Single entry*: This term is used to describe a situation where the business transactions have only been entered in a book of prime entry, usually a cash book, and not in the ledger. However, one would also expect to be able to obtain documents or information relating to the value of non-current assets, inventories, trade receivables, trade payables, accruals, prepayments and any non-current liabilities. Given that this is available, it would be possible to prepare a statement of profit and loss and statement of financial position.

3 *Incomplete single entry*: This term may be used to describe a variation on point 2 where there are no books of account (or these are incomplete) but the receipts and payments can be ascertained from the bank statements and/or supporting documents. In this case it would be necessary to produce a cash book summary from the information given on the bank statements, paying-in book and cheque book stubs. The final financial statements will then be prepared from the cash book summary together with the supporting documents and information referred to in point 2.

The procedure for preparing final financial statements from these three different forms of incomplete records is described below.

 ## 23.2 Incomplete records of revenue income and expenditure

As explained in the introduction to this chapter, in these circumstances it is not possible to construct a statement of profit and loss. However, it may still be possible to ascertain the profit for the relevant period provided that the information to prepare a statement of financial position at the start and end of the period is available.

This involves the application of the comparative static approach to profit measurement described in Chapter 8, 'The Accounting Equation and its Components'. The profit (or loss) is found by calculating the difference between the net asset value of the business at the start and end of the period as shown by the two statements of financial position. The logic behind this computation is that an increase in net assets can only come from two sources, either additional capital introduced by the owner or profits generated from the sale of goods and/or other assets. This is illustrated below.

Statement of financial position as at 1 January 20X3	
ASSETS	£
Total assets	25,000
EQUITY AND LIABILITIES	
Capital	20,000
Liabilities	5,000
Total equity and liabilities	25,000

Statement of financial position as at 31 December 20X3	
ASSETS	£
Total assets	38,000
EQUITY AND LIABILITIES	
Capital	30,000
Liabilities	8,000
Total equity and liabilities	38,000

Ignoring the possibility of additional capital introduced during the year, this business has a profit for the year of £30,000 − £20,000 = £10,000. This is computed by ascertaining the increase in either the net assets or the capital. Both must give the same answer. Any decrease in net assets or capital will mean there has been a loss for the year.

However, part of the increase in net assets and capital may be due to additional capital being introduced during the year of, say, £3,000. In this case the profit for the year is that part of the increase in net assets and capital, which is not the result of additional capital introduced during the year, thus:

	£
Net/assets/capital at end of year	30,000
Less: Net assets/capital at start of year	20,000
Increase in capital	10,000
Less: Capital introduced	3,000
Profit for the year	7,000

In addition, the owner of the business may have made drawings during the year of, say, £4,000. These will reduce the capital and net assets at the end of the year. In this case the profit for the year is the increase in net assets/capital less the capital introduced, plus the drawings for the year – that is, £10,000 − £3,000 + £4,000 = £11,000.

In summary, profits (or losses) are reflected in an increase (or decrease) in the net asset value of a business over a given period. The net asset value corresponds to the capital. The profit or loss can thus be ascertained by computing the change in capital over the year and adjusting this for any capital introduced and/or drawings during the year. This is presented in the form of a statement, as shown below. Notice that this statement is simply a reordering of the entries normally shown in the capital account of a sole trader, as presented in the statement of financial position.

Statement of changes in owner equity for the year ended 31 December 20X3	
	£
Capital at end of current year	30,000
Less: Capital at end of previous year	20,000
Increase in capital	10,000
Add: Drawings during the year including any goods taken by the proprietor for his or her own use	4,000
	14,000
Less: Capital introduced during the year either in the form of cash or any other asset	3,000
Profit for the year	11,000

Before this statement can be prepared, it is necessary to calculate the capital at the end of the current year and at the end of the previous year. This is done by preparing a statement of financial position at each of these dates. These are referred to as a **statement of affairs**. This is illustrated in Example 23.1.

EXAMPLE 23.1

A. Ferry has been in business for the last 10 years as an electrical retailer, and has asked you to compute her profit for the year ended 31 December 20X2.

She has no business bank account and kept no records of her income and expenditure apart from the purchase and sale of non-current assets, inventory, trade receivables and trade payables, and a running cash balance. She has been able to give you the following information relating to her affairs:

1 At 31 December 20X2 the business owns freehold land and buildings used as a shop and workshop. This cost £10,000 on 1 July 20W6.

2 During the year ended 31 December 20X2 the business owned the following vehicles:

Date of purchase	Cost	Date of sale	Proceeds
31 Mar 20W9	£1,000	31 Oct 20X2	£625
1 May 20X0	£1,200	unsold at 31 Dec 20X2	
1 July 20X2	£2,000	unsold at 31 Dec 20X2	

You estimate that the above vehicles have a useful working life of five years and no residual value. In previous years these have been depreciated using the straight-line method.

3 During the year ended 31 December 20X2 the owner has put £5,280 in cash into the business and has taken out £15,900 as drawings.

4 Amounts outstanding at:

	31 Dec 20X1	31 Dec 20X2
	£	£
Trade receivables	865	645
Trade payables	390	480
Accruals	35	20
Prepayments	40	25

Included in trade receivables at 31 December 20X2 are doubtful debts of £85.

5 Inventories have been valued at £565 on 31 December 20X1, and £760 on 31 December 20X2. The latter amount includes a television that cost £60 and was worthless at that date due to it having been accidentally damaged beyond repair.

6 The cash balances at 31 December 20X1 and 20X2 were £285 and £165, respectively.

Required

Calculate the profit for the year ended 31 December 20X2, showing clearly your workings.

Workings

20X1	£	£
Motor vehicles owned at 31 December 20X1		
Purchased 31/3/W9	1,000	
Purchased 1/5/X0	1,200	
Total cost	2,200	
Depreciation using the straight-line method		
20% × £1,000 × 2 years 9 months	550	
20% × £1,200 × 1 year 8 months	400	
		950
Written-down value at 31 December 20X1		1,250

20X2	£	£
Motor vehicles owned at 31 December 20X2		
Purchased 1/5/X0	1,200	
Purchased 1/7/X2	2,000	
Total cost	3,200	
Depreciation using the straight-line method		
20% × £1,200 × 2 years 8 months	640	
20% × £2,000 × 6 months	200	
		840
Written down value at 31 December 20X2		2,360

A. Ferry
Statement of financial position as at 1 January 20X2

ASSETS	£
Non-current assets	
Freehold land and buildings	10,000
Motor vehicles	1,250
	11,250
Current assets	
Inventories	565
Trade receivables	865
Prepayments	40
Cash	285
	1,755
Total assets	13,005
EQUITY AND LIABILITIES	
Capital	12,580
Liabilities	
Trade payables	390
Accruals	35
	425
Total equity and liabilities	13,005

Statement of financial position as at 31 December 20X2			
	£ Cost	£ Deprec	£ NBV
ASSETS			
Non-current assets			
Freehold land and buildings	10,000	–	10,000
Motor vehicles	3,200	840	2,360
	13,200	840	12,360
Current assets			
Inventories (£760 – £60)			700
Trade receivables		645	
Provision for doubtful debts		85	560
Prepayments			25
Cash			165
			1,450
Total assets			13,810
EQUITY AND LIABILITIES			
Capital			13,310
Liabilities			
Trade payables			480
Accruals			20
			500
Total equity and liabilities			13,810

Statement of changes in owner equity for the year ended 31 December	
	£
Capital at 31 December 20X2	13,310
Less: Capital at 31 December 20X1	12,580
	730
Add: Drawings	15,900
	16,630
Less: Capital introduced	5,280
Net profit for the year	11,350

Notes

1 There is no need to compute the profit or loss on disposals of non-current assets since this will automatically be reflected in the increase in net assets/capital. However, it is necessary to compute the written-down value (or possibly market value) of non-current assets at the end of each year as shown in the workings in order to prepare the statements of financial position.

2 The inventory at 31 December 20X2 excludes the cost of the television that was damaged beyond repair of £60.

3 Doubtful debts have been provided for by reducing the amount of trade receivables at 31 December 20X2.

4 The amounts for capital in the statement of affairs are the difference between the two sides of these statements of financial position.

5 It is usual to treat the statement of financial position at the end of the previous year as workings not requiring any formal presentation. However, the statement of financial position at the end of the current year should contain the usual headings and subtotals and be in a form presentable to the owner and other interested parties such as HM Revenue and Customs.

23.3 Single entry

As explained in the introduction, **single entry** refers to the situation where a business has some record of its receipts and payments, non-current assets, inventories, trade receivables, trade payables, accruals, prepayments and non-current liabilities. However, these records are not in double-entry form and usually consist of just a cash book.

One possibility is for the accountant to complete the records by posting the receipts and payments to the appropriate accounts in the ledger either in full or summarized form. The final financial statements are then prepared from the trial balance in the normal way. This is common in practice. However, in very small businesses this may be too expensive and/or impractical. In this case the final financial statements are prepared directly from the cash book or a summary thereof, and the appropriate adjustments made for trade receivables, trade payables, provisions, accruals, prepayments, and so on. Examination questions on this topic also usually take the same form. An illustration of this treatment of single-entry records is given in Example 23.2. Because of the importance and length of the workings, the procedure for answering the question is presented as a series of steps. These are well worth memorizing as a model for answering such questions.

EXAMPLE 23.2

The following is the statement of financial position of L. Cook at 31 December 20X1:

Statement of financial position as at 1 January 20X2	
	£
ASSETS	
Non-current assets	
Freehold land and buildings	12,500
Motor vehicles (cost £5,000)	2,900
	15,400
Current assets	
Inventories	1,650
Trade receivables	3,270
Prepayments (rates)	60
Bank	1,500
	6,480
Total assets	21,880
EQUITY AND LIABILITIES	
Capital	19,240
Liabilities	
Trade payables	2,610
Accruals (electricity)	30
	2,640
Total equity and liabilities	21,880

The only book kept by Cook is a cash book, a summary of which for the year ended 31 December 20X2 has been prepared as follows:

Cash book			
	£		£
Balance b/d	1,500	Rates	140
Cash takings banked	4,460	Salaries	2,820
Cheques from credit customers	15,930	Electricity	185
Additional capital	500	Bank charges	10
		Motor expenses	655
		Payments to credit suppliers	16,680
		Stationery	230
		Sundry expenses	40
		Balance c/d	1,630
	22,390		22,390

From the supporting documents it has been ascertained that:

1 The following amounts have been paid from cash takings before they were banked:

Drawings	£22,000
Purchases	£560
Petrol	£85
Repairs to buildings	£490

2 Cook has taken goods out of the business for his own use that cost £265.

3 Motor vehicles have been depreciated in past years at 20 per cent per annum by the reducing balance method.

4 Inventory at 31 December 20X2 was valued at £1,960.

5 The trade receivables and trade payables outstanding at the end of the year are £2,920 and £2,860, respectively.

6 At 31 December 20X2 there are rates prepaid of £70 and electricity accrued of £45.

7 You expect to charge Cook £100 for your services.

Required

Prepare a statement of profit and loss for the year ended 31 December 20X2 and a statement of financial position at that date. Show all your workings clearly.

Workings/procedure

1 If necessary, prepare a statement of financial position as at the end of the previous year to ascertain the capital at that date.

2 If necessary, prepare a summarized cash book from the bank statements, and so on, to ascertain the balance at the end of the year and the total amounts received and spent on each type of income and expenditure, and assets.

3 a Compute the net credit purchases by preparing a purchase ledger control account as follows:

Purchase ledger control account					
20X2	**Details**	**£**	**20X2**	**Details**	**£**
31 Dec	Bank	16,680	1 Jan	Balance b/d	2,610
31 Dec	Balance c/d	2,860	31 Dec	Net purchases	16,930
		19,540			19,540

The net purchases figure is the difference between the two sides.

b Compute the cash and cheque purchases and then the total purchases:

$$\text{Total purchases} = £560 + £16,930 = £17,490$$

4 a Compute the net credit sales by preparing a sales ledger control account as follows:

Sales ledger control account					
20X2	**Details**	**£**	**20X2**	**Details**	**£**
1 Jan	Balance b/d	3,270	31 Dec	Bank	15,930
31 Dec	Net sales	15,580	31 Dec	Balance c/d	2,920
		18,850			18,850

The net sales figure is the difference between the two sides.

b Compute the cash and cheque sales and then the total sales:

$$\text{Cash sales} = £4,460 + £22,000 + £560 + £85 + £490 = £27,595$$

$$\text{Total sales} = £27,595 + £15,580 = £43,175$$

Note that sometimes the computations in (a) and (b) have to be combined. This is necessary when the cash and/or cheque sales are not given separately from the cheques received from credit customers. In this case the total cash and cheques received in respect of sales are credited to the control account. The same principle would also have to be used in the case of purchases when cash and/or cheque purchases are not given separately from cheques paid to credit suppliers.

5 Compute the charges to the statement of profit and loss for those expenses with accruals or prepayments by preparing the relevant ledger accounts. Alternatively, in examinations this may be shown as workings in the statement of profit and loss.

Light and heat					
20X2	**Details**	**£**	**20X2**	**Details**	**£**
31 Dec	Bank	185	1 Jan	Accrual b/d	30
31 Dec	Accrual c/d	45	31 Dec	Profit and loss a/c	200
		230			230

Rates					
20X2	**Details**	**£**	**20X2**	**Details**	**£**
1 Jan	Prepayment b/d	60	31 Dec	Profit and loss a/c	130
31 Dec	Bank	140	31 Dec	Prepayment c/d	70
		200			200

6 Compute the charges and/or credits to the statement of profit and loss in respect of any provision for bad debts, depreciation, sales of non-current assets, and so on. Alternatively, if these are relatively simple, in examinations, they may be shown as workings in the statement of profit and loss.

Motor vehicles

$$\text{Depreciation expense} = 20\% \times £2,900 = £580$$

$$\text{Aggregate depreciation} = (£5,000 - £2,900) + £580 = £2,680$$

7 Prepare the final financial statements, remembering to add together any cheque and cash expenditure of the same type (e.g. motor expenses in this example), and include any non-current assets acquired, drawings (e.g. goods taken by the proprietor), capital introduced, and so on.

L. Cook		
Statement of profit and loss for the year ended 31 December 20X2		
	£	£
Sales revenue		43,175
Less: cost of sales		
Inventories at 1 Jan 20X2	1,650	
Add: Purchases (£17,490 − £265)	17,225	
	18,875	
Less: Inventories at 31 Dec 20X2	1,960	16,915
Gross profit		26,260
Less: expenditure		
Rates (£60 + £140 − £70)	130	
Salaries	2,820	
Light and heat (£185 + £45 − £30)	200	
Bank charges	10	
Motor expenses (£655 + £85)	740	
Stationery	230	
Sundry expenses	40	
Repairs to buildings	490	
Depreciation on vehicles (20% × £2,900)	580	
Accountancy fees	100	5,340
Profit for the year		20,920

L. Cook Statement of financial position as at 31st December 20X2	£ Cost	£ Prov depn	£ WDV
ASSETS			
Non-current assets			
Freehold land and buildings	12,500	–	12,500
Motor vehicles	5,000	2,680	2,320
	17,500	2,680	14,820
Current assets			
Inventories			1,960
Trade receivables			2,920
Prepayments			70
Bank			1,630
			6,580
Total assets			21,400
EQUITY AND LIABILITIES			
Equity capital (owners)			
Balance at 1 Jan 20X2			19,240
Add: Capital introduced			500
Net profit			20,920
			40,660
Less: Drawings (£22,000 + £265)			22,265
Balance at 31 Dec 20X2			18,395
Current liabilities			
Trade payables			2,860
Accruals (£45 + £100)			145
Total liabilities			3,005
Total equity and liabilities			21,400

Notes

1 The goods taken by the proprietor for his own use of £265 have been added to drawings and deducted from purchases (rather than added to sales) because the question gives their cost.

2 In the workings for the sales ledger control account, the term 'net sales' is used to emphasize that this is after deducting returns, the amount of which is unknown and cannot be ascertained. However, if the returns were known, these would be entered in the sales ledger control account and the statement of profit and loss in the normal manner. More importantly, if the value of any bad debts, discount allowed, and so on, were known, these would have to be entered in the sales ledger control account and statement of profit and loss in the normal way. The same principles apply to the purchases ledger control account where there are returns, discount received, and so on.

3 In some single-entry questions there are petty cash balances at the start and end of the accounting year. Where the balance in cash at the end of the year is greater than at the start, the increase must be added to the cash takings that were banked in order to ascertain the cash sales (in Workings 4(b) above). The reason is simply because the increase in the cash float must have come from cash sales. Put another way, the cash takings banked are after deducting/excluding the increase in the cash balance. To ascertain the cash sales therefore necessitates adding back any increase in the cash float, or deducting any decrease from the cash takings that were banked. Where there are cash balances/floats at the start and end of the year, an alternative to the one-line computation of cash sales shown in Workings 4(b) above is to prepare a petty cash account. The cash sales will be the difference between the two sides of the account after entering the opening and closing cash balances, the amounts paid from the cash takings, and the takings that were banked. This may have the added advantage of reminding students to include the various items of petty cash expenditure in the final financial statements.

4 Many businesses accept credit cards such as Visa or MasterCard in payment for goods that they sell to the public. This gives rise to special problems where there are incomplete records in the form of single entry. Most credit card companies charge a commission of up to 5 per cent of the value of goods sold. Thus, if a business sells goods with a selling price of, say, £200 the amount it receives will be £190 (i.e. 95 per cent of £200). The normal ledger entries for this sale will be to credit the sales account with £200 and debit a credit card trade receivable account with the amount it expects to receive of £190. The difference of £10 commission should be debited to a commission account that will be transferred to the statement of profit and loss at the end of the year.

Where there is only single entry, the accounting records in respect of **credit card sales** will consist of a debit in the cash book of the amounts received from the credit card company during the year. It is therefore necessary to compute the value of sales before deducting the commission. This is done in two stages. The first stage is to calculate the total credit card sales for the year after deducting commission by means of a credit card receivables account in which the amount received is adjusted to take into account the opening and closing amounts owing. The second stage is to gross up the total credit card sales after deducting commission to ascertain the total credit card sales before deducting commission. Using the example above, this would be $100/95 \times £190 = £200$. The £200 is then included in sales in the trading account, and the difference of $£200 - £190 = £10$ commission is shown as a separate item of expense in the statement of profit and loss.

> **LEARNING ACTIVITY**
> **23.1**
>
> Construct a list of your personal assets and liabilities from one year ago (for example, car, phone, etc.). Construct a list of your personal assets and liabilities today. How has your, tangible net worth changed?

Summary

There are three different forms of incomplete records. The first is incomplete records of and expenditure. This refers to where there are no documents or records of revenue incor ture. It is therefore not possible to prepare a statement of profit and loss. However, the profit tained by calculating the difference between the capital/net asset value of the business at th of the year by preparing a statement of financial position at each of these dates. The pro adjusting the change in capital over the year for any capital introduced and/or drawings.

The second form of incomplete records is known as 'single entry'. This refers to where the b actions have been entered in a cash book but not posted to a ledger. The third form of incon is incomplete single entry. This refers to where there are no books of account but a cash bo can be prepared from the bank statements and/or supporting documents.

In the case of incomplete single entry and single entry, it is therefore possible to prepare a state profit and loss and statement of financial position. This can be done by posting the amounts shown i summarized cash book to the ledger, extracting a trial balance and preparing final financial statements i the normal way. Alternatively, students are normally required in examinations to prepare final financial statements from the summarized cash book by means of workings. These usually take the form of purchases ledger and sales ledger control accounts, in order to ascertain the purchases and sales, respectively, together with those expense accounts that have accruals and/or prepayments at the start and end of the year.

Key terms and concepts

credit card sales	382	single entry	377
incomplete records	371	statement of affairs	373

An asterisk after the question number indicates that there is a suggested answer on the Online Learning Centre (www.mcgraw-hill.co.uk/textbooks/thomas).

Review question   connect

23.1 Describe the different forms of incomplete records with which you are familiar.

Exercises   connect

23.2

BASIC

Capital at the end of 20X2 is £2,000.

Capital at the end of 20X3 is £3,000.

There were no drawings; and no capital had been introduced.

Required

Calculate the profit for the year ended 20X3 from the above information.

al at the end of 20X2 is £2,000.

...tal at the end of 20X3 is £3,000.

...awings were £700.

Required

Calculate the profit for the year ended 20X3 from the above information.

23.4

Happy did not keep proper books of account. At 31 August 20X1 his balances were:

	£
Lorry (at valuation)	3,000
Tools	4,000
Inventories	16,740
Trade receivables	11,890
Bank	2,209
Cash	115
Trade payables	9,052

Details of transactions in year to 31 August 20X2:

Tools purchased	2,000
Drawings	7,560
Legacy	2,800

At 31 August 20X2 the assets and liabilities were:

Depreciation on tools £600, lorry now valued at £2,500, trade receivables £15,821, prepaid expenses £72, inventories £21,491, trade payables £6,002, payables for expenses £236, cash £84, bank overdraft £165.

Required

Draw up a statement showing the profit or loss made by Happy for the year ended 31 August 20X2.

23.5*

The following is the statement of financial position of Round Music as at 30 June 20X2:

Statement of financial position for Round Music as at 30 June 20X2	
ASSETS	£
Non-current assets	WDV
Plant	31,000
	31,000
Current assets	
Inventories	9,720
Trade receivables	6,810
Prepayments	150
Bank	820
	17,500
Total assets	48,500
EQUITY AND LIABILITIES	
Equity capital (owners)	42,770
Current liabilities	
Trade payables	5,640
Accruals (electricity)	90
Total liabilities	5,730
Total equity and liabilities	48,500

During the year ended 30 June 20X3 there was a fire that destroyed the books of account and supporting documents. However, from questioning the proprietor you have been able to obtain the following information:

1 The plant at 30 June 20X2 cost £50,000 and has been depreciated at 10 per cent per annum by the straight-line method on a strict time basis. Additional plant was purchased on the 1 April 20X3 at a cost of £20,000. Plant costing £10,000 on 1 January 20X0 was sold on 1 October 20X2 for £4,450.

2 Inventories at 30 June 20X3 were valued at £8,630. This includes goods costing £1,120 that are worthless because of fire damage.

3 Trade receivables and trade payables at 30 June 20X3 were £6,120 and £3,480, respectively. Trade receivables include doubtful debts of £310.

4 Accruals and prepayments at 30 June 20X3 were £130 and £80, respectively.

5 There was a bank overdraft at 30 June 20X3 of £1,430.

6 During the year the business had borrowed £7,000 from Lickey Bank, which was repayable on 1 January 20X6.

7 During the year the owner introduced additional capital of £5,000 and made drawings of £18,500 by cheque. The proprietor also took goods costing £750 from the business for his own use.

You are required to compute the profit for the year ended 30 June 20X3 and prepare a statement of financial position at that date. Show separately the cost of non-current assets and the aggregate depreciation in the statement of financial position.

.6

INTERME

Jane Grimes, retail fruit and vegetable merchant, does not keep a full set of accounting records. However, the following information has been produced from the business's records:

1 Summary of the bank account for the year ended 31 August 20X3:

Bank account			
	£		£
1 Sep 20X2 balance brought forward	1,970	Payments to credit suppliers	72,000
Receipts from		Purchase of motor van (E471 KBR)	13,000
credit customers	96,000	Rent and rates	2,600
Sale of private yacht	20,000	Wages	15,100
Sale of motor van (A123 BWA)	2,100	Motor vehicle expenses	3,350
		Postage and stationery	1,360
		Drawings	9,200
		Repairs and renewals	650
		Insurances	800
		31 Aug 20X3 balance carried forward	2,010
	120,070		120,070

2 Assets and liabilities, other than balance at bank:

As at	1 Sept 20X2	31 Aug 20X3
	£	£
Trade payables	4,700	2,590
Trade receivables	7,320	9,500
Rent and rates accruals	200	260
Motor vans:		
A123 BWA – At cost	10,000	–
Provision for depreciation	8,000	–
E471 KBR – At cost	–	13,000
Provision for depreciation	–	To be determined
Inventory in trade	4,900	5,900
Insurances prepaid	160	200

3 All receipts are banked and all payments are made from the business bank account.

4 A trade debt of £300 owing by Peter Blunt and included in the trade receivables at 31 August 20X3 (see point 2 above) is to be written off as a bad debt.

5 It is Jane Grime's policy to provide depreciation at the rate of 20 per cent on the cost of motor vans held at the end of each financial year; no depreciation is provided in the year of sale or disposal of a motor van.

6 Discounts received during the year ended 31 August 20X3 from credit suppliers amounted to £1,000.

Required

a Prepare Jane Grime's statement of profit and loss for the year ended 31 August 20X3.

b Prepare Jane Grime's statement of financial position as at 31 August 20X3.

(AAT)

23.7*

The following is the statement of financial position of A. Fox at 31 July 20X2.

Statement of financial position for A. Fox as at 31 July 20X2			
	£	£	£
	Cost	Prov depn	WDV
ASSETS			
Non-current assets			
Freehold land and buildings	35,000	–	35,000
Fixtures and fittings	10,000	4,200	5,800
	45,000	4,200	40,800
Current assets			
Inventories			3,300
Trade receivables			6,540
Prepayments (telephone)			120
Bank			3,000
			12,960
Total assets			53,760
EQUITY AND LIABILITIES			
Equity capital (owners)			48,480
Current liabilities			
Trade payables			5,220
Accruals (electricity)			60
Total liabilities			5,280
Total equity and liabilities			53,760

The only book kept by A. Fox is a cash book in which all transactions passed through the bank account are recorded. A summary of the cash book for the year ended 31 July 20X3 has been prepared as follows:

Cash book			
	£		£
Balance b/d	3,000	Wages	5,640
Cash takings banked	18,920	Telephone	280
Cheques from credit customers	31,860	Electricity	370
Additional capital	1,000	Motor expenses	1,810
		Payments to credit suppliers	33,360
		Printing	560
		Purchases	4,500
		Balance c/d	8,260
	54,780		54,780

From the supporting documents it has been ascertained that:

1 The following amounts have been paid from the cash takings before they were banked:

	£
Drawings	4,000
Purchases	1,120
Car repairs	980
Window cleaning	170

2 Inventory at 31 July 20X3 was valued at £3,920.

3 At 31 July 20X3 there are telephone charges prepaid of £140 and electricity accrued of £290.

4 The trade receivables and trade payables outstanding at the end of the year are £5,840 and £5,720, respectively.

5 Fox has taken goods out of the business for his own use that cost £530.

6 Fixtures and fittings have been depreciated in past years at 20 per cent per annum by the reducing balance method.

Required

Prepare a statement of profit and loss for the year ended 31 July 20X3 and a statement of financial position at that date.

ADVANCED

23.8

Jock is a clothing retailer. At 31 December 20X2 he asks you to prepare his final financial statements from very incomplete records. You were able to extract the following information from the limited records that were available.

	31/12/X1	31/12/X2
	£	£
Fixtures and fittings (valued)	9,900	19,648
Motor vehicle	1,000	1,500
Building	25,000	24,500
Inventories	39,050	34,255
Trade receivables	2,500	4,500
Trade payables	7,435	9,995
Cash in hand	925	2,350
Cash at bank	9,500	16,850
Rent accrual	500	–
Cash received in settlement of fire claim for goods (cost £1,050) lost by fire	–	1,050

Accruals and prepayments

In addition to the above Jock extracted the following invoices, which need to be adjusted for.

Rates		
Invoice date	Period covering	Amount paid
		£
30/03/X1	01/04/X1–31/03/X2	£800
20/03/X2	01/04/X2–31/03/X3	£880

Electricity

Electricity bills are paid for in arrears. The quarters are end of February, May, August and November. The bill paid on 15 March 20X2 was £315. It is expected that the February 20X3 bill will be 20 per cent higher than last year's bill.

Jock records cash received and paid, except for his own drawings.

Jock's cash transactions for the year are as follows:

Payments by cash	£
Wages	25,560
General expenses	1,350
Goods for resale	10,352
Receipts by cash	**£**
Cash received from credit customers	185,650
Sale of motor car	750
Paid into bank	
Cheques and cash	123,704

Jock always paid credit suppliers in sufficient time to avail of a cash discount of 5 per cent. A summary of the cheque payments are as follows:

Payments by cheque	£
Fixtures and fittings	15,654
Rent and rates	5,625
Trade suppliers (credit)	86,500
Heat and light	3,215
Personal expenditure	3,560
New car	1,800

Jock did not keep record of his own personal cash takings.

Required

a Prepare an opening statement of financial position for Jock as at 1 January 20X2.

b Prepare the sales, purchases, bank, cash, accruals, prepayments (with corresponding expense accounts) and non-current asset adjustment accounts.

c Draft a statement of profit and loss for the year ended 31 December 20X2 and a statement of financial position at that date.

(*Note*: All workings must be provided.)

23.9

ADVANCED

Miss Fitt owns a retail shop. The statement of profit and loss and statement of financial position are prepared annually by you from records consisting of a bank statement and a file of unpaid suppliers and outstanding trade receivables.

The following balances were shown on her statement of financial position at 1 January 20X2:

	£
Shop trade payables	24,500
Shop fittings (cost £25,000) at written-down value	20,000
Inventory in hand	47,500
Trade receivables	5,000
Cash at bank	11,000
Cash float in till	1,000

The following is a summary of her bank statement for the year ended 31 December 20X2:

	£
Takings banked	698,300
Payments to credit suppliers	629,000
Rent of premises to 31 December 20X2	40,000
A. Smith – shop fitters	8,500
Advertising in local newspaper	5,000
Sundry expenses	3,800

You obtain the following additional information:

1 Takings are banked daily and all suppliers are paid by cheque, but Miss Fitt keeps £1,500 per week for herself, and pays her assistant £1,100 per week out of the takings.

2 The work done by A. Smith was for new shelving and repairs to existing fittings. The cost of new shelves was estimated at £5,000.

3 The cash float in the till was considered insufficient and raised to £1,500.

4 Miss Fitt took £7,500 worth of goods for her own use without payment.

5 Your charges will be £2,500 for preparing the financial statements.

6 The outstanding accounts file shows £23,000 due to credit suppliers, £1,000 due in respect of sundry expenses, and £8,500 outstanding trade receivables.

7 Depreciation on shop fittings is provided at 10 per cent on cost, a full year's charge being made in year of purchase.

8 Inventory in hand at 31 December 20X2 was £71,000.

You are required to prepare Miss Fitt's statement of profit and loss for the year ended 31 December 20X2, and her statement of financial position as at that date.

(ACCA, adapted)

ADVANCED

23.10

A year ago, you prepared financial statements for A. Wilson, a retailer. His closing position was then:

Statement of financial position for A. Wilson as at 31 March 20X2			
	£	£	£
	Cost	Prov depn	WDV
ASSETS			
Non-current assets			
Delivery van (cost £4,800 in May 20X0)	4,800	1,920	2,880
Current assets			
Inventories			6,410
Trade receivables		1,196	
Less: provision for doubtful debts		72	1,124
Owing from Askard Ltd			196
			7,730
Total assets			10,610
EQUITY AND LIABILITIES			
Equity capital (owners)			7,726
Current liabilities			
Bank overdraft			70
Trade payables			2,094
Accruals (accountant's fee)			120
Provision for legal claim			600
Total liabilities			2,884
Total equity and liabilities			10,610

Mr Wilson does not keep full records (despite your advice) and once again you have to use what information is available to prepare his financial statements to 31 March 20X3. The most reliable evidence is a summary of the bank statements for the year. It shows:

	£	£
Balance at 1 Apr 20X2 (overdraft)		(70)
Cash and cheques from credit customers		33,100
Cheques from Askard Ltd.		7,840
		40,870
Less: cheques drawn for:		
Wilson's personal expenses	7,400	
Van – tax, insurance, repairs	440	
Rent, rates and general expenses	2,940	
Cash register	400	
Accountant's fee	120	
Trade payables	28,284	
Legal claim settled	460	40,044
Balance at 31 Mar 20X3		826

For some of the sales Askard credit cards are accepted. Askard Ltd charges 2 per cent commission. At the end of the year the amount outstanding from Askard Ltd was £294.

Some other sales are on credit terms. Wilson keeps copies of the sales invoices in a box until they are settled. Those still in the 'unpaid' box at 31 March 20X3 totalled £1,652, which included one for £136 outstanding for four months – otherwise they were all less than two months old. Wilson thinks he allowed cash discounts of about £150 during the year. The debt of £72 outstanding at the beginning of the year for which a provision was made was never paid.

The amount of cash and cheques received from credit customers and from cash sales were all paid into the bank except that some cash payments were made first. These were estimated as:

	£
Part-time assistance	840
Petrol for van	800
Miscellaneous expenses	200
Wilson's drawings	2,000

Invoices from suppliers of goods outstanding at the year end totalled £2,420. Closing inventory was estimated at £7,090 (cost price) and your fee has been agreed at £200. It has been agreed with the Inspector of Taxes that £440 of the van expenses should be treated as Wilson's private expenses.

Required

Prepare the statement of profit and loss for Wilson's business for the year to 31 March 20X3 and a statement of financial position at that date.

(ACCA)

ADVANCED

23.11

David Denton set up in business as a plumber a year ago, and he has asked you to act as his accountant. His instructions to you are in the form of the following letter.

Dear Henry

I was pleased when you agreed to act as my accountant and look forward to your first visit to check my records. The proposed fee of £2,500 p.a. is acceptable. I regret that the paperwork for the work done during the year is incomplete. I started my business on 1 January last, and put £65,000 into a business bank account on that date. I brought my van into the firm at that time, and reckon that it was worth £36,000 then. I think it will last another three years after the end of the first year of my business use.

I have drawn £900 per week from the business bank account during the year. In my trade it is difficult to take a holiday, but my wife managed to get away for a while. The travel agent's bill for £2,800 was paid out of the business account. I bought the lease of the yard and office for £65,000. The lease has 10 years to run, and the rent is only £3,000 a year payable in advance on the anniversary of the date of purchase, which was 1 April. I borrowed £40,000 on that day from Aunt Jane to help pay for the lease. I have agreed to pay her 10 per cent interest per annum, but have been too busy to do anything about this yet.

I was lucky enough to meet Miss Prism shortly before I set up on my own, and she has worked for me as an office organiser right from the start. She is paid a salary of £30,000 per annum. All the bills for the year have been carefully preserved in a tool box, and we analysed them last week. The materials I have bought cost me £96,000, but I reckon there was £5,800's worth left in the yard on 31 December. I have not paid for them all yet; I think we owed £7,140 to the suppliers on 31 December. I was surprised to see that I had spent £48,000 on plumbing equipment, but it should last me five years or so. Electricity bills received up to 30 September came to £11,220; motor expenses were £9,120, and general expenses £13,490 for the year. The insurance premium for the year to 31 March next was £8,000. All these have been paid by cheque but Miss Prism has lost the rate demand. I expect the Local Authority will send a reminder soon since I have not yet paid. I seem to remember that the rates came to £1,800 for the year to 31 March next.

Miss Prism sent out bills to my customers for work done, but some of them are very slow to pay. Altogether the charges made were £298,630, but only £256,130 had been received by 31 December.

Miss Prism thinks that 10 per cent of the remaining bills are not likely to be paid. Other c̶ ̶ ̶ ̶ ̶ ̶s ̶for
jobs too small to bill have paid £34,180 in cash for work done, but I only managed to ban̶ for
this money. I used £4,000 of the difference to pay the family's grocery bills, and Miss Prism ̶0 ̶of
for general expenses, except for £1,230 which was left over in a drawer in the office on 31 De̶st

Kind regards,

Yours sincerely,

David.

Required

Draw up a statement of profit and loss for the year ended 31 December, and a statement of fi
position as at that date.

(ACCA, ad̶

23.12

Bugs Bunny, a wholesale dealer in ready-made menswear, achieves a gross profit ratio of 50 per ̶
The statement of financial position of the business as at 30 June 20X2 was as follows:

Bugs Bunny Statement of financial position as at 30 June 20X2			
	£ Cost	£ Prov depn	£ WDV
ASSETS			
Non-current assets			
Motor vehicles	60,000	24,000	36,000
Fixtures and fittings	43,000	12,900	30,100
	103,000	36,900	66,100
Current assets			
Inventories			79,300
Trade receivables less provision			76,475
Cash and bank			17,125
			172,900
Total assets			239,000
EQUITY AND LIABILITIES			
Equity capital			
Opening balance			114,750
Profit for the year			38,900
			153,650
Drawings			29,150
Closing balance			124,500
Current liabilities			
Trade payables			94,472
Accruals – (salary)			9,200
Accruals – (other expenses)			10,828
Total current liabilities			114,500
Total equity and liabilities			239,000

date the accounting function has been neglected. However, on the basis of records in his
diary, Bugs Bunny confirms the following:

At 30 June 20X3, £138,000 is due from credit customers and £108,000 is owed to credit suppliers.

During the year ended 30 June 20X3, the payments set out below have been made:

	£
Paid for purchases	252,000
Staff salaries	80,130
Rent for shop premises	10,000
Entertainment	2,250
Office equipment	15,200
Motor vehicles	17,500
Other expenses	33,020
Personal expenses	13,250

3 A vehicle acquired for £15,000 on 1 April 20W9 was sold for £3,830 in the year to 30 June 20X2. Motor vehicles and equipment are depreciated at 20 per cent and 10 per cent per annum on cost, respectively. The depreciation policy is to charge a full year's depreciation in the year of acquisition and none in the year of disposal.

4 A provision for doubtful debts is maintained at 5 per cent of trade receivables outstanding at the year end. Debts amounting to £22,000 were written off in the year.

5 Accruals as at 30 June 20X3 consisted of salaries £10,200, rent £3,000 and other expenses amounting to £13,000.

6 Cash in hand and at bank on 30 June 20X3 is £400.

7 Inventories in trade on 30 June 20X3 (valued at cost) is £99,405.

8 With Bugs Bunny's permission, his teenage sons have been regularly helping themselves to ready-made garments from the shop.

9 All sales and purchases are on credit.

Required

Prepare the statement of profit and loss for Bugs Bunny for the year ended 30 June 20X3 and the statement of financial position as at that date.

(*Note*: All workings must be shown.)

23.13

T. Murray has prepared the following bank ledger account for the year ended 31 March 20X3:

Bank account				
	£			**£**
Balance at 1 April 20X2	782	Repairs		256
Commission	4,930	Renewals		507
Rent income	567	Heat and light		350
Sundry income	58	Telephone		125
Capital introduced	652	Salary and wages		3,328
Bank interest	120	Extension to premises		800
Sale of land	3,600	General expenses		89
Sales	3,250	Stationery		25
		Rent		3,300
		Purchases		2,800
		Rates		200
		Furniture		250
		Motor vehicle		1,250
		Motor expenses		354
		Balance c/d – Cash	100	
		– Bank	225	325
	13,959			13,959

T. Murray has also supplied you with the following information.

a Commissions received included £85, which had been in arrears at 31 March 20X2, and £55, which had been paid for the year commencing 1 April 20X3. In addition, three customers still owed commission for the year to 31 March 20X3. One was commission for a type A product (£15) the other two were commission for the sale of type B products (£45).

b The land that was sold was valued in the company's books at £1,500.

c Depreciation is to be charged as follows.

Buildings	5 per cent per annum straight line basis
Motor vehicle	Sum of digits method over five years
Fixtures and fittings	25 per cent reducing balance method
Furniture	20 per cent reducing balance method

A full year's depreciation is charged in the year of purchase but none is charged in the year of sale.

d Accrued expenses:

	31/03/X2	31/03/X3
	£	**£**
Stationery	15	656
Wages	560	545

The electricity bill for the period to 30 April 20X3 (£450) was paid for on 23 May 20X3.

The rent paid in advance was to cover three full financial years including 20X2.

The interest received in the year is for the period from 1 April 20X2 to 31 December 20X2.

e General expenses includes an amount of £35 for a telephone bill that was posted here in error.

f The closing inventory has been valued at £990.

g Repairs include £200, which was paid for a brand new pool table.

h The following balances are from T. Murray's books at 31 March 20X2:

	£
Land at cost	8,000
Buildings at cost	6,400
Buildings provision for depreciation	800
Fixtures and fittings at cost	1,250
Fixtures provision for depreciation	250
Furniture at cost	580
Furniture provision for depreciation	180
Commission in arrears (including £15 from a bankrupt client)	100
Commission in advance	30
Inventories	250

Required

a Prepare the opening statement of financial position for T. Murray as at 31 March 20X2.

b Prepare the statement of profit and loss for T. Murray for the year ended 31 March 20X3.

c Prepare the statement of financial position for T. Murray as at 31 March 20X3.

Further questions on incomplete records arise in Chapter 26, 'The Final Financial Statements of Clubs' and Chapter 27, 'The Final Financial Statements of Partnerships'.

When you have read this chapter, log on to the Online Learning Centre for *Introduction to Financial Accounting* at www.mcgraw-hill.co.uk/ textbooks/thomas, where you will find multiple choice quizzes, case studies, a glossary and mock exams.

Preparing final financial statements for manufacturing entities

Part contents

Inventory valuation

Learning Objectives

After reading this chapter you should be able to do the following:

1 Explain the meaning of the key terms and concepts listed at the end of the chapter.

2 Describe the methods for valuing work-in-progress (WIP) and explain the relationship between these methods and the treatment of WIP in manufacturing accounts.

3 Discuss the method of valuation of finished goods inventory including its impact on gross profit.

4 Describe the perpetual inventory system.

5 Describe the main methods of identifying the cost of fungible inventories and demonstrate their application in the valuation of inventories and the cost of sales.

6 Discuss the circumstances in which each of the main methods of identifying the cost of fungible inventories may be justifiable, and describe their impact on gross profit.

24.1 Introduction

Accounting for inventories is a perfect example of the matching concept. Goods purchased, or manufactured, in one period that are not sold, are carried into the next period to be matched against the sales revenue when it occurs. The accounting for inventory is examined in Chapter 15, though this chapter only considers inventory that has been purchased for resale. In practice different entities have different types of inventory. For example, the inventory in service-type organizations (such as accountancy firms or law firms) is typically partly completed service roles, such as half an audit. This type of inventory is called **work-in-progress**. Chapter 25 examines accounting within manufacturing entities, which have four different types of inventory as identified in Figure 24.1.

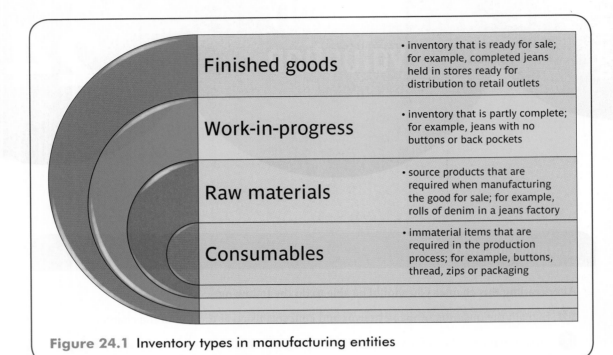

Figure 24.1 Inventory types in manufacturing entities

A retail entity is likely to have only two types of inventory:

1 *Goods for sale* – clothes, shoes, and so on.

2 *Consumables* – immaterial items such as coat hangers, price stickers, plastic bags, and so on.

 Monitoring inventory

There are several different methods used to monitor inventory within an entity, and two are considered briefly in this chapter – the perpetual and periodic inventory control systems. These are explained briefly in Figure 24.2.

Periodic inventory control system	• The number of items in inventory are physically checked periodically (monthly, quarterly, yearly) and orders for more items are made in light of expected demand relative to the number of items in stores • The review period is usually fixed and hence high levels of inventory are typically held • In many instances the business closes for the counts, or it is performed overnight
Perpetual inventory control systems	• Constant monitoring of inventory levels and frequent reorders • Computerized control system usually with point of sale technology which records inventory receipts and issues from stores • Physical counts take place continuously, are organized and focus on rotated areas (for example, in a large supermarket, baby products may be covered in one day, vegetables the next, cereals the next, etc.)

Figure 24.2 Inventory control systems

24.3 The valuation of goods for sale and raw materials

Though the accounting for inventories is relatively straightforward, the valuation of inventory has been manipulated in the past to window-dress financial statements. **Window-dressing** is a term used to describe the selection of valuation techniques and presentation ploys to portray the performance and financial position of an entity in a more favourable light than perhaps it should be. Inventories are material in many entities, and changes in valuation directly impacts on profitability; therefore, the accounting and valuation of inventories is afforded its own standard, *International Accounting Standard 2 – Inventories* (IASB, 2010). The remainder of this chapter focuses on the valuation of inventories.

IAS 2 recommends that inventories be valued at the lower of purchase cost and **net realizable value** (NRV). Where purchase cost includes:

1 invoice price, net of trade discount and value added tax (VAT is recoverable);

2 import duties (if sourced in a foreign country) and other taxes that are not recoverable;

3 transport costs (delivery costs);

4 handling costs;

5 other costs that are directly attributable to obtaining the inventory.

Raw materials should be valued in the same manner.

Sometimes goods in inventory may have to be sold at a price that is below their cost. If there are goods in inventory at the end of a given accounting year that are expected to result in a loss, those goods should be valued and entered in the financial statements at their expected NRV and not their cost. NRV is the estimated proceeds from the sale of items of inventory less all costs to be incurred in marketing, selling and distributing that are directly related to the items in question. The comparison of cost and NRV needs to be made in respect of each item of inventory separately (see Example 24.1).

EXAMPLE 24.1

Martin is a clothes retailer. At the year-end his inventory was valued at its cost price of £21,560. Included in this inventory is a line of clothing that is no longer in fashion. The inventory cost £5,600. Martin is sure that this inventory can be sold at 80 per cent of its cost price. It will cost £200 to market the line.

Required

Calculate the value of inventory that should appear in the financial statements of Martin.

Workings

The £5,600 needs to be written down to its NRV, which is its sale value less any costs of sale.

$$£5,600 \times 80\% = £4,480 \text{ less } £200 = £4,280.$$

This amounts to a total reduction of £1,320 (£5,600 − £4,280).

Therefore, the inventory will appear in the financial statements of Martin valued at £20,240 (£21,560 − £1,320).

Accounting policy for valuing inventory

Most entities provide details of how they value their inventories. An example can be found in the financial statements of Wm Morrison Supermarkets PLC as follows:

Wm Morrison Supermarkets PLC

REAL WORLD EXAMPLE 24.1

Stocks are measured at the lower of cost and net realisable value. Cost is calculated on a weighted average basis and comprises purchase price, import duties and other non-recoverable taxes less rebates. Stocks represent goods for resale. Net realizable value is the estimated selling price in the ordinary course of business, less the estimated costs necessary to make the sale.

Source: Extract from the accounting policies note Annual Report and Financial Statements 2010.

LEARNING ACTIVITY 24.1

Using Wm Morrison Supermarket plc's financial statements (to be found on their website) for guidance, draft a pro forma note showing a breakdown of an inventory note for a company that manufactures furniture.

24.4 The valuation of **finished goods** and work-in-progress

IAS 2 provides guidance on how to value inventories – 'the cost of inventories shall comprise all costs of purchase, costs of conversion and other costs incurred in bringing inventories to their present location and condition'. The costs of purchase are covered in the previous section. The **costs of conversion** comprise:

1 costs directly attributable to the units of production; for example, direct labour, direct materials and subcontract work;

2 allocated production overheads (fixed and variable):

  a *Fixed production overheads* – indirect costs of production that remain relatively constant regardless of the production quantity. Examples include depreciation of the factory building, maintenance of the factory building, factory rent and rates, factory management costs and factory administration costs.

  b *Variable production overheads* – indirect costs of production that vary with production volume. Examples include indirect labour and indirect materials.

The specific costs that impact on the valuation of internally produced inventory are discussed in more detail in the next chapter that focuses on manufacturing entities.

Fungible inventory: cost flow assumptions

In the case of both manufacturing and non-manufacturing businesses, the determination of the cost/purchase price of goods in inventory often presents a major problem. It is frequently not possible to identify the particular batch(es) of goods that were purchased, which are in inventory at the end of the year. These are referred to as **fungible inventories**, which means substantially indistinguishable goods. In these circumstances it is necessary to make an *assumption* about the cost of goods in inventory. There are a number of possible assumptions, but the most reasonable assumption will depend on the type of good involved, the procedure for handling the receipt and sale of inventories, prices, and so on. The most appropriate assumption is one that provides a fair approximation to the expenditure actually incurred.

To provide a systematic method of valuing this type of inventory, most large businesses operate what is called a **perpetual inventory system**, which is a continuous record of the quantity and value of inventory. It includes a stores ledger containing an account for each type of good that is purchased. The **stores ledger** accounts are used to record the quantities and prices of goods purchased, the quantities and cost of goods sold (or issued to production in the case of direct materials in manufacturing entities), and the balance and cost of goods in inventories after each receipt and sale. This system requires an assumption or decision on how to attribute value to the goods that leave the stores (cost of goods sold/produced) and the inventory that remains. This is required as all the inventory in stores may have been purchased at different times and at different costs.

There are a number of possible assumptions, or what are referred to as bases/methods of identifying/pricing the cost of inventories. The bases make assumptions about the flow of items in inventory. These flow assumptions are not selected as a result of the actual way in which inventory is used but to reflect a particular view of the economic effects of inventory usage in financial statements; hence, they are called the **cost flow assumptions**. Three common approaches are:

1 first in, first out (FIFO);

2 last in, first out (LIFO);

3 average cost (AVCO), sometimes referred to as the **weighted average method**.

These assume, respectively, that:

1 the oldest inventory is sold first (FIFO);

2 the most recently purchased inventory is sold first (LIFO);

3 the cost of sales comprises the average cost of all the purchases in inventory (AVCO).

Each of these methods is described using Example 24.2.

 EXAMPLE 24.2 P. Easton commenced business on 1 January 20X3 as a dealer in scrap iron. The following purchases and sales were made during the first six months of 20X3:

Jan Purchased 40 tonnes at £5 per tonne

Feb Purchased 50 tonnes at £6 per tonne

Mar Sold 30 tonnes at £10 per tonne

Apr Purchased 70 tonnes at £7 per tonne

May Sold 80 tonnes at £15 per tonne

Required

a Prepare a perpetual inventory record of the quantities and values of goods purchased, sold and inventory.

b Prepare a statement of profit and losses showing the gross profit for the six months to 30 June 20X3 given that the above are the only purchases and sales.

State any assumptions that you make.

LEARNING ACTIVITY 24.2

Attempt part (b) of Example 24.2 before proceeding further.

EXAMPLE 24.2 CONTINUED

1 First in, first out (FIFO)

The FIFO assumption is that the goods sold are those that have been in inventories for the longest time. The inventory is therefore composed of the most recent purchases and the cost of inventories is the price paid for these. Given the FIFO assumption, the answer to Example 24.2 will be as follows.

Stores ledger account

Date	Purchases			Cost of sales			Balance in inventory		
	Units	Price	Value	Units	Price	Value	Units	Price	Value
Jan	40	5	200				40	5	200
Feb	50	6	300				40	5	200
							50	6	300
							90		500
Mar				30	5	150	10	5	50
							50	6	300
							60		350
Apr	70	7	490				10	5	50
							50	6	300
							70	7	490
							130		840
May				10	5	50			
				50	6	300			
				20	7	140	50	7	350
				80		490			
Totals	160		990	110		640	50		350

The FIFO method is based on the premise that the physical movement of goods over time will have this sequence of events, particularly where the goods are perishable. The use of the FIFO method is favoured by IAS 2 and by HM Revenue and Customs.

P. Easton		
Statement of profits and losses for the six months ended 30 June 20X3		
	£	£
Sales revenue: 30 tonnes @ £10	300	
80 tonnes @ £15	1,200	1,500
Less: Cost of sales –		
Purchases	990	
Less: Inventories at 30 June 20X3	350	640
Gross profit		860

2 Last in, first out (LIFO)

The LIFO assumption is that the goods sold are those that have been in inventory for the shortest time. The inventory is therefore composed of those goods that have been held for the longest time, and the cost of inventory is the price paid for these. Given the LIFO assumption, the answer to Example 24.2 will be as follows:

Stores ledger account

Date	Purchases			Cost of sales			Balance in inventory		
	Units	Price	Value	Units	Price	Value	Units	Price	Value
Jan	40	5	200				40	5	200
Feb	50	6	300				50	6	300
							40	5	200
							90		500
Mar				30	6	180	20	6	120
							40	5	200
							60		320
Apr	70	7	490				70	7	490
							20	6	120
							40	5	200
							130		810
May				70	7	490			
				10	6	60	10	6	60
				80		550	40	5	200
							50		260
Totals	160		990	110		730	50		260

P. Easton		
Statement of profits and losses for the six months ended 30 June 20X3		
	£	£
Sales revenue		1,500
Less: Cost of sales –		
Purchases	990	
Less: Inventories at 30 June 20X3	260	730
Gross profit		770

The LIFO method may be in accordance with the physical movement of goods in some circumstances. For example, purchases of coal, iron ore, sand and gravel are likely to be piled one on top of the other, and thus goods taken from the top of the heap will probably consist of the most recent purchases. In most other instances it is an unrealistic assumption. However, even where this is the case, the LIFO method may be justified in times of rising prices on the grounds that the cost of sales will reflect the most recent prices. This is said to give a more realistic figure of profit since the most recent price is an approximation of the current cost of the goods sold (i.e. their replacement cost). Thus, one argument for the LIFO method is that where historical cost accounting is used it gives a 'true and fair view' of the profit in times of changing prices.

The LIFO method is not allowed under IAS 2 or by HM Revenue and Customs. The arguments put forward against its use are that LIFO 'results in inventories being stated in the statement of financial position at amounts that bear little relationship to recent cost levels, and it is a poor substitute for a proper system of accounting for changing prices'.

3 Weighted average method (AVCO)

The weighted average method is based on the assumption that the goods sold and the inventory comprise a mixture of each batch of purchases. The cost of sales and inventory is therefore taken to be a weighted average of the cost of purchases. Given the weighted average assumption, the answer to Example 24.2 will be as follows (notice that a new weighted average is computed after each purchase):

Stores ledger account

Date	Purchases			Cost of sales			Balance in inventory		
	Units	Price	Value	Units	Price	Value	Units	Price	Value
Jan	40	5	200				40	5.000	200
Feb	50	6	300				90	5.556[1]	500
Mar				30	5.556	167	60	5.556	333
Apr	70	7	490				130	6.331[2]	823
May				80	6.331	506	50	6.331	317
Totals	160		990	110		673	50		317

Workings for weighted average cost:

1 February = £500 ÷ 90 units = £5.556

2 April = £823 ÷ 130 units = £6.331

All calculations to three decimal places.

P. Easton		
Statement of profits and losses for the six months ended 30 June 20X3		
	£	£
Sales revenue		1,500
Less: Cost of sales –		
Purchases	990	
Less: Inventories at 30 June 20X3	317	673
Gross profit		827

Where purchases are mixed together, the weighted average method can be justified on the grounds that it is in accordance with the physical events. This often occurs when goods are stored in a single container that is rarely completely emptied, such as in the case of nuts and bolts, liquids and granular substances, and so on. Another justification is that when prices are fluctuating it gives a more representative normal price and thus more comparable cost of sales figures.

The weighted average method is approved by IAS 2 and is acceptable to HM Revenue and Customs.

24.5 FIFO and LIFO compared

Clearly, each of the methods of calculating the cost of inventory results in different values for inventory and profit. In times of constantly rising prices, FIFO will give a higher figure of profits and value of inventory than LIFO because it matches older, lower costs against revenues. A business should choose whichever method is appropriate to its particular circumstances and apply this consistently in order that meaningful comparisons can be made. FIFO is by far the most common method used in practice in the UK because it is favoured by the UK accounting standard *SSAP 9 – Stocks and Long Term Contracts* (ASC, 1988), by IAS 2 and by HM Revenue and Customs. The valuation of inventories is a controversial issue in accounting, and is one of the areas most open to deliberate manipulation as can be seen in the following real world example.

REAL WORLD EXAMPLE 24.2

Inventory manipulation in General Tire and Rubber

Laux (2007) discusses some of the practical ways that financial statements have been manipulated using inventory. She notes that it is often the inventory choice itself (LIFO, for example) that results in income manipulation. She cites General Tire and Rubber as an example. This company, she claimed, accelerated raw material purchases at the end of the year to minimize profits and taxes. This meant that the year-end inventory value was manipulated (by accelerating low-cost purchases near year-end) to cause higher cost of goods sold and hence lower taxable income. A further example is the drugstore chain, Phar-Mor. They used phoney inventory figures. The resulting cost was a financial fraud resulting in at least half a billion dollars of losses.

Source: Laux, 2007, www.cluteinstitute-onlinejournals.com/PDFs/105.pdf.

Summary

Work-in-progress and finished goods inventories are usually valued at their factory cost. Direct materials inventories and goods purchased for resale are normally valued at cost. However, IAS 2 dictates that if the NRV of any of these inventories is lower than their cost, they must be included in the final financial statements at their NRV. Furthermore, it is frequently not possible to identify the cost of goods in inventories. This is referred to as 'fungible inventories', which means that the goods are substantially indistinguishable from each other. In these circumstances it is necessary to make an assumption about the cost of goods in inventory and thus the cost of goods sold (or issued to production in the case of direct materials in manufacturing entities). The most common assumptions are first in, first out (FIFO), last in, first out (LIFO), and a weighted average cost (AVCO). In times of changing prices, each will give a different value of inventories, cost of sales and thus profit.

Key terms and concepts

An asterisk after the question number indicates that there is a suggested answer on the Online Learning Centre (www.mcgraw-hill.co.uk/textbooks/thomas).

connect Review questions

24.1 Work-in-progress and finished goods inventories should be valued at the cost of purchase and conversion. Explain.

24.2 Explain how the matching principle is applied to the valuation of inventories.

24.3 Explain the circumstances in which inventories might be shown in the financial statements at a value different from their historical cost.

24.4 Explain fully the basis on which finished goods and work-in-progress inventories should be valued in final financial statements.

24.5 a What is a perpetual inventory system?

    b Describe three methods of calculating the cost of fungible inventories.

    c Explain the circumstances in which each of these methods may be justifiable.

24.6* 'In selecting a method of calculating the cost of inventory, management should ensure that the method chosen bears a reasonable relationship to actual costs. Methods such as . . . LIFO do not usually bear such a relationship' (ASC, 1988). Discuss.

connect Exercises

INTERMEDIATE 24.7

On 1 April 20X2 Modern Dwellings Ltd commenced business as builders and contractors. It spent £14,000 on the purchase of six acres of land with the intention of dividing the land into plots and building 72 houses thereon.

During the year ended 31 March 20X3 roads and drains were constructed for the project at a total cost of £8,320. Building was commenced, and on 31 March 20X3 30 houses had been completed and eight were in the course of construction.

During the year the outlay on houses was as follows:

	£
Materials, etc.	36,000
Labour and subcontracting	45,000

The value of the work-in-progress on the uncompleted houses at 31 March 20X3 amounted to £8,500, being calculated on the actual cost of materials, labour and subcontracting to date.

During the year, 24 houses had been sold, realizing £80,000.

Required

Prepare a statement of profit and loss for the year ended 31 March 20X3. It can be assumed that the plots on which the 72 houses are to be built are all of equal size and value.

(ACCA, adapted)

24.8

After stocktaking for the year ended 31 May 20X2 had taken place, the closing inventory of Cobden Ltd was aggregated to a figure of £87,612.

During the course of the audit that followed, the undernoted facts were discovered:

1 Some goods stored outside had been included at their normal cost price of £570. They had, however, deteriorated and would require an estimated £120 to be spent to restore them to their original condition, after which they could be sold for £800.

2 Some goods had been damaged and were now unsaleable. They could, however, be sold for £110 as spares after repairs estimated at £40 had been carried out. They had originally cost £200.

3 One inventory sheet had been overadded by £126 and another under-added by £72.

4 Cobden Ltd had received goods costing £2,010 during the last week of May 20X2 but because the invoices did not arrive until June 20X2, they have not been included in inventories.

5 An inventory sheet total of £1,234 had been transferred to the summary sheet as £1,243.

6 Invoices totalling £638 arrived during the last week of May 20X2 (and were included in purchases and in trade payables) but, because of transport delays, the goods did not arrive until late June 20X2 and were not included in closing inventory.

7 Portable generators on hire from another company at a charge of £347 were included, at this figure, in inventories.

8 Free samples sent to Cobden Ltd by various suppliers had been included in inventories at the catalogue price of £63.

9 Goods costing £418 sent to customers on a sale or return basis had been included in inventories by Cobden Ltd at their selling price, £602.

10 Goods sent on a sale or return basis to Cobden Ltd had been included in inventories at the amount payable (£267) if retained. No decision to retain had been made.

Required

Using such of the above information as is relevant, prepare a schedule amending the inventory figure as at 31 May 20X2. State your reason for each amendment or for not making an amendment.

(ACCA, adapted)

24.9*

Universal Shoes Ltd is a Northern Ireland company that sells a range of casual, dress and work footwear through the internet. The accountant has asked you to calculate the value of the company's closing inventory at 31 December 20X2 for inclusion in the financial statements. The following additional information is available:

a Pairs of shoes counted in the warehouse at the year-end stock take were as follows:

Casual	10,000 pairs
Work	5,000 pairs
Dress	2,000 pairs

b 2,000 pairs of casual footwear were received into stores on 3 January 20X3. The goods were ordered on 23 December 20X2 and invoiced on 24 December, but were still in transit from the US supplier when the stock take was being performed. The invoice for these goods is included in the purchase ledger and the trade payable has been recognized at 31 December 20X2.

c Due to an increase in the price of toughened leather, the supplier of work shoes had to increase the cost of each pair from 1 November 20X2. Since this date, Universal Shoes has received 3,000 pairs into its stores.

d Due to sharp change in fashion over the months of November and December 20X2, dress shoes in inventory have become worthless. They cannot be sold in Northern Ireland. However, the sales manager has secured a contract with a shoe retailer in Sweden. This retailer has agreed to purchase all of the dress shoes at a reduced price.

e Selling price and cost per pair of shoes in 20X2.

	Casual shoes	Work shoes	Dress shoes
	£	£	£
Selling prices in 20X2	30	55	75
Selling prices in 20X3	30	55	40
Purchase cost:			
01/01/X2–01/11/X2	5	10	45
01/11/X2–Present	5	15	45
Carriage inwards per pair	1	2	2
Marketing costs per pair:			
In 20X2	3	5	10
Expected in 20X3	3	5	10

f It is company policy to use the FIFO method of recording the flow of inventory cost.

Required

a Prepare a schedule showing the calculation of the value of inventories to be included in the year end (31 December 20X2) financial statements, in accordance with IAS 2 – *Inventories*.

b Write a brief memorandum to the chief accountant explaining the reasons (under IAS 2) for valuing the inventories on the bases you applied in (a).

24.10

Anna started a picture framing business on 1 July 20X3. The following transactions occurred in the six months ended 31 December 20X3:

Purchases		Sales	
20/07/X3	150 units at £20 each	18/09/X3	305 units at £45 each
25/08/X3	225 units at £30 each	02/10/X3	50 units at £45 each
15/11/X3	410 units at £40 each	20/12/X3	100 units at £75 each

Additional information

1 On 1 July 20X3 Anna started the business by putting £10,000 into the bank account.

2 Two months' credit is taken from suppliers.

3 One month's credit is given to customers.

4 Expenses of £1,400 are paid each month as incurred.

Required

a Calculate the value of closing inventory using the first in, first out (FIFO) method and the average cost (AVCO) method.

b Prepare extracts from the statement of profit and loss for the six months to 31 December 20X3 and the statement of financial position at that date, to show the presentation of the above information, for each cost flow assumption used to value inventories.

24.11

John Ltd starts selling mobile phones in 20X2. Details of purchases in the year are as follows:

Date completed	Number purchased	Unit cost of mobile phone
		£
01/06/X2	100	150
05/08/X2	150	160
21/10/X2	75	176
25/12/X2	100	180
	425	

Details of sales in the year are as follows:

Date of sale	Number sold	Unit sale price
		£
05/06/X2	50	200
10/08/X2	115	220
23/12/X2	50	210
30/12/X2	150	240
	365	

Required

a Calculate the cost of sales for the year ended 31 December 20X2 and detail the value of the closing inventory using the FIFO and weighted average inventory valuation cost flow methods (inventory movement sheets are required).

b Prepare the statement of profit and loss for the year ended 31 December 20X2 based on both valuation methods.

24.12

Brian Ltd starts selling footballs in 20X2. Although each ball looks the same, the unit cost of manufacture (which is done in batches) has fluctuated during the period. Details of the costs are as follows:

Date completed	Number completed	Unit costs
		£
02/07/X2	200	75
01/08/X2	300	80
24/12/X2	150	88
15/03/X3	200	90
	850	

Details of sales are as follows:

Date of sale	Number sold	Unit sale price
		£
05/07/X2	100	100
10/08/X2	230	110
30/12/X2	100	105
16/03/X3	300	120
	730	

The closing inventory was counted on 30 June and found to be 70 units.

Required

a Calculate the cost of sales for the year ended 30 June 20X3 and detail the value of the closing inventory using the FIFO, LIFO and weighted average inventory valuation cost flow methods (inventory movement sheets are required).

b Prepare extracts fom the statement of profit and loss for the year ended 30 June 20X3 based on the three valuation methods – explain why a different profit is reported under each method.

c What inventory valuation method is not permitted under IAS 2?

d Explain in which circumstances (if any) it would be appropriate to use the following cost flow assumptions:

   i   first in first out (LIFO) assumption;

   ii last in, first out (LIFO) assumption;

   iii specific identification assumption;

   iv weighted average cost assumption.

24.13

Your company sells, for £275 each unit, a product that it purchases from several different manufacturers, all charging different prices. The manufacturers deliver at the beginning of each week throughout each month. The following details relate to the month of February.

		Quantity	Cost each	Sales (units)
Opening inventories		10	£145	
Deliveries:	Week 1	20	£150	15
	Week 2	34	£165	33
	Week 3	50	£145	35
	Week 4	30	£175	39

From the above data you are required to:

a Prepare inventory records detailing quantities and values using the following pricing techniques:

  i   last in, first out (LIFO);

  ii first in, first out (FIFO);

  iii weighted average cost (calculated monthly to the nearest £).

b Prepare statements of profit and loss using each of the inventory cost flow pricing methods in (a) above and show the gross profit for each method.

c Compare the results of your calculations and state the advantages and disadvantages of FIFO and LIFO pricing methods in times of inflation.

(JMB, adapted)

24.14*

A businessman started trading with a capital in cash of £6,000, which he placed in the business bank account at the outset.

His transactions, none of which were on credit, were as follows (in date sequence) for the first accounting period. All takings were banked immediately and all suppliers were paid by cheque. He traded in only one line of merchandise.

Purchases		Sales	
Quantity	Price per unit	Quantity	Price per unit
No.	£	No.	£
1,200	1.00		
1,000	1.05	800	1.70
600	1.10	600	1.90
900	1.20	1,100	2.00
800	1.25	1,300	2.00
700	1.30	400	2.05

In addition, he incurred expenses amounting to £1,740, of which he still owed £570 at the end of the period.

Required

Prepare separately using the FIFO (first in, first out), the LIFO (last in, first out) and (AVCO) weighted average cost (calculated for the period to the nearest penny) methods of inventory valuation:

a a statement of cost of sales for the period;

b a statement of financial position at the end of the period.

Note: Workings are an integral part of the answer and must be shown (ACCA, adapted).

ADVANCED

24.15

S. Bullock, a farmer, makes up his financial statements to 31 March each year. The trial balance extracted from his books as at 31 March 20X3 was as follows:

	Debit	Credit
	£	£
Purchases – livestock, seeds, fertilizers, fodder, etc.	19,016	
Wages and National Insurance	2,883	
Rent, rates, telephone and insurance	1,018	
Farrier and veterinary charges	34	
Carriage	1,011	
Motor and tractor running expenses	490	
Repairs – Farm buildings	673	
– Implements	427	
Contracting for ploughing, spraying and combine work	308	
General expenses	527	
Bank charges	191	
Professional charges	44	
Sales revenue		29,162
Motor vehicles and tractors – as at 1 April 20X2	1,383	
– Additions	605	
Implements – as at 1 April 20X2	2,518	
– Additions	514	
Valuation as at 1 April 20X2:		
Livestock, seeds, fertilizers, fodder, etc.	14,232	
Tillages and growing crops	952	
Loan from wife		1,922
Minister Bank		4,072
S. Bullock – capital at 1 April 20X2		6,440
Current account at 1 April 20X2		6,510
Drawings during the year	1,280	
	48,106	48,106

On 31 March 20X3:	£	£
Trade receivables and prepayments were:		
Livestock sales	1,365	
Motor licence	68	
Liabilities were: seeds and fertilizers		180
Rent, rates and telephone		50
Motor and tractor running expenses		40
Professional charges		127
Contracting		179
General expenses		54

Included in the above-mentioned figure of £50 is £15 for rent and this is payable for the March 20X3 quarter. In arriving at this figure the landlord has allowed a deduction of £235 for materials purchased for repairs to the farm buildings, which were carried out by S. Bullock, and is included in the 'Repairs to farm buildings' shown in the trial balance. In executing these repairs it was estimated that £125 labour costs were incurred and these were included in 'Wages and National Insurance'. This cost was to be borne by S. Bullock.

The valuation as at 31March 20X3 was:

	£
Livestock, seeds, fertilizers, fodder, etc.	12,336
Tillages and growing crops	898

Depreciation, calculated on the book value as at 31 March 20X3, is to be written off as follows:

– Motor vehicles and tractors 25 per cent per annum

– Implements 12 per cent annum

Required

a Prepare the statement of profit and loss for the year ended 31 March 20X3.

b Prepare the statement of financial position as at that date.

(ACCA, adapted)

References

Accounting Standards Committee (1988) *Statement of Standard Accounting Practice 9 – Stocks and Long-term Contracts* (ICAEW).

International Accounting Standards Board (2010) *International Accounting Standard 2 – Inventories* (IASB).

Laux, J. (2007) 'Accounting Issues: An Essay Series (Part III – Inventory)', *Journal of College Teaching & Learning*, 4, 8, 1–5, http://www.cluteinstitute-onlinejournals.com/PDFs/105.pdf.

When you have read this chapter, log on to the Online Learning Centre for *Introduction to Financial Accounting* at www.mcgraw-hill.co.uk/textbooks/thomas, where you will find multiple choice quizzes, case studies, a glossary and mock exams.

Financial statements for manufacturing entities

Learning Objectives

After reading this chapter you should be able to do the following:

1 Explain the meaning of the key terms and concepts listed at the end of the chapter.

2 Describe the main differences between the final financial statements of a commercial enterprise and those of a manufacturing business.

3 Explain the classification of costs into direct and indirect costs.

4 Describe the different categories of inventories found in a manufacturing business and show how these are treated in the ledger and final financial statements.

5 Explain the purpose of a manufacturing account and the various subtotals normally found in this account.

6 Prepare a manufacturing account, a statement of profit and loss and a statement of financial position for a manufacturing business.

7 Explain the nature of manufacturing profits and show the entries in final financial statements.

25.1 Introduction

The main differences between the financial statements of commercial and manufacturing businesses stem from the former buying goods for resale without further processing, whereas the latter buy raw materials and components that are processed into **finished goods** to be sold. This makes it necessary for a manufacturing business to calculate the total factory cost of goods produced. The amount is computed in what is termed 'a manufacturing account' and the result shown in place of 'purchases' in the statement of profit and loss of a non-manufacturing business. Furthermore, the inventories in the statement of profit and loss are the inventories of finished goods unsold at the start and end of the accounting year. Apart from these differences the statement of profit and loss of a manufacturing business is the same as that of a commercial business, in that they both contain selling and distribution costs/overheads, administrative expenses/overheads and financial charges (such as interest). However, unlike a sole trader, the costs are analysed into these categories and subtotals for each are determined. The statement of financial position is also the same, except a manufacturing business will also include a number of different categories of inventory, which will be described later. The manufacturing account does not form part of the published financial statements. It is for internal management use, therefore does not fall within the presentation requirements of *International Accounting Standard (IAS) 1 – Presentation of Financial Statements* (IASB, 2010b).

Bespoke accounting packages for manufacturing accounts

REAL WORLD EXAMPLE 25.1

Manufacturing accounts provide vital information for manufacturing entities and bespoke accounting packages are widely available with relevant charts of accounts (a tailored journal) and the ability to deal with the allocation of direct costs and factory overhead costs to work-in-progress and finished goods. Examples include DBA manufacturing software and JD Edwards EnterpriseOne Manufacturing.

Source: Author.

25.2   The classification of costs

One of the major differences between the financial statements of a commercial and manufacturing business concerns the classification of costs. In a manufacturing business, costs are usually classified as either direct costs or indirect costs/overheads. **Direct costs** are those that can be traced, attributed to or identified with a particular product.

Examples of direct costs are:

1 direct material – raw materials;

2 direct labour – machine operators' wages;

3 other direct expenses – royalties, consumables.

Direct materials consist of any goods that form a part of the final product. These are composed of the raw materials and components that a manufacturing business turns into its finished product. For example, iron ore is a raw material in the manufacture of engines for motor vehicles. Material inputs do not just consist of raw materials – for example, a car manufacturer may purchase steel, which is the finished product of another industry. Similarly, many companies find it cheaper to buy rather than manufacture parts of their finished product. For example, car manufacturers buy components such as tyres and lighting equipment from outside suppliers. Thus, direct materials consist of raw materials and various types of components that make up the final product.

Direct labour typically comprises the wages of those employees who physically work on the products or operate the machines that are used to produce the finished products. Wages paid to foremen, supervisors, cleaners, maintenance staff, and so on, are not direct wages.

Direct expenses are any expenses that are directly attributable to a specific product. The most common direct expenses are royalties paid for the right to produce the finished product, the cost of any special drawings and subcontracted work. **Indirect costs/overheads** are those costs that cannot be traced, attributed to or identified with a particular product, and comprise **factory/production/manufacturing overheads**, **selling and distribution overheads**, and **administrative overheads**.

Examples of factory overheads are:

1 indirect wages – supervisors' wages, cleaners' wages, foremen's wages, maintenance staff wages;

2 power, factory heat and light;

3 depreciation of plant and machinery;

4 depreciation of the factory building;

5 repairs to plant and machinery;

6 factory running costs such as factory rent (if rented), factory rates, factory insurance, factory stationery, and so on;

7 consumable tools;

8 other.

25.3 Categories of inventory

A manufacturing business also differs from a commercial business in that it has a number of different categories of inventories. These were mentioned in the previous chapter and are now revisited in the context of manufacturing entities.

Inventory types

Direct materials

This category is composed of raw materials and components that have been purchased but not put into production at the end of the accounting year.

Work-in-progress (WIP)

This refers to goods that are partially complete (part way through the production process) at the end of the accounting period.

Finished goods

This category consists of goods that are fully complete and are available for sale but which are unsold at the end of the accounting year. These goods have exited the production process.

25.4 Purposes and preparation of a manufacturing account

As has already been mentioned, the main purpose of a **manufacturing account** is to calculate the **factory cost of completed production**. This replaces purchases in the statement of profit and loss. Therefore, it is prepared after the trial balance has been extracted but before the statement of profit and loss is completed. In calculating the cost of the products that have been completed during the accounting year, it is usual to show the following in the manufacturing account (in the order shown below):

1 *The direct material cost* of goods that have been put into production during the year. To calculate this, it will be necessary to adjust the cost of purchases of direct materials for the opening and closing inventories thus:

> Direct materials in inventories at start of year
>
> *add*: Purchases of direct materials during year
>
> *less*: Direct materials in inventories at end of year
>
> = Cost of direct materials put into production during year

It is also common to add any carriage inwards to the cost of purchases.

2 *The direct labour costs*

3 *The direct expenses*

4 *The **prime cost** of production*

This is the sum of the direct materials, direct labour and direct expenses.

5 *The factory overheads*

6 *The **total factory costs***

This is the sum of the prime costs and the factory overheads.

7 *The factory cost of completed production.*

The total factory costs relate to both those products that have been completed during the year and those which are only partially completed at the end of the year. To arrive at the factory cost of completed production, it is therefore necessary to make an adjustment for the opening and closing WIP thus:

> **WIP at start of year**
>
> *add*: **Total factory costs**
>
> *less*: **WIP at end of year**
>
> = **Factory cost of completed production**

The pro forma shown in Figure 25.1 should serve as a useful guide for the preparation of the manufacturing account.

The factory cost of completed production is transferred to the statement of profit and loss in place of 'purchases' in a non-manufacturing business. The cost of sales is computed by adjusting the factory cost of completed production for the opening and closing inventories of finished goods:

> **Inventories of finished goods at start of year**
>
> *add*: **Factory costs of completed production**
>
> *less*: **Inventories of finished goods at end of year**
>
> = **Cost of goods sold**

Pro forma manufacturing account for 'X' for the year ended 31/12/X2	£	£
Production cost for the period		
Opening inventory of raw materials	XX	
Direct materials	XX	
Raw material returns	(XX)	
Carriage inwards	X	
	XX	
Closing inventory of raw materials	(XX)	
Cost of raw materials consumed		XX
Direct labour		XX
Direct expenses		XX
Prime cost		XX
Factory overhead expenses		
Indirect wages	XX	
Factory rent	XX	
Factory rates	XX	
Factory cleaners wages	XX	
Total factory overheads		XXX
Total factory costs		XXX
Opening work-in-progress		XX
		XXX
Closing work-in-progress		(XX)
Factory cost of completed production c/d *(to statement of P&L)*		XXX

Figure 25.1 A pro forma of the layout of a manufacturing account

The expenses in the statement of profit and loss in a manufacturing entity are normally categorized into distribution expenses, administration expense and finance costs.

Examples of distribution expenses are:

1 salesmen salaries;
2 credit control staff salaries;
3 commission;
4 advertising;
5 marketing;
6 depreciation on salesmen's motor vehicles;
7 depreciation on delivery trucks;
8 carriage outwards;
9 bad debts;
10 increases/(decreases) in the provision for bad debts.

Sometimes bad debts and the movement in the provision for bad debts are regarded as being administrative expenses. It depends whether the credit control department is regarded as being either selling or administration. In this book we are treating the credit control department as a selling department.

Therefore, this should be assumed unless a question states that the administration department has control over the granting of credit and the collection of debts.

Examples of administrative costs are:

1 salaries of accounting staff;

2 office overheads, heat and light, insurance, rent, rates, and so on;

3 cleaners' wages;

4 depreciation on office fixtures and fitting;

5 depreciation of the office manager's motor vehicle;

6 depreciation of the general manager's motor vehicle;

7 stationery.

The last category is finance costs.

Examples of finance costs are:

1 loan interest;

2 bank charges;

3 discounts allowed.

The pro forma shown in Figure 25.2 should serve as a useful guide for the preparation of the statement of comprehensive income (statement of profit and loss) for a manufacturing entity.

Pro forma statement of profit and loss for 'X' for the year ended 31/12/X2	£	£
Revenue		XXX
Cost of sales		(XX)
Gross profit		XX
Other income		X
Distribution expenses		(X)
Administrative expenses		(X)
Other expenses		(X)
Finance costs		(X)
Profit before income tax		X
Income tax expense		(X)
Profit for the period		X

Figure 25.2 A pro forma of the layout of a statement of a statement of profit and loss for a manufacturing entity

Note that all the adjustments in respect of direct materials inventories, WIP and finished goods are applications of the matching principle. An illustration of the preparation of a manufacturing account is shown in Example 25.1.

EXAMPLE 25.1

The following information relating to the year ended 30 April 20X3 has been extracted from the books of A. Bush, a motor vehicle component manufacturer:

	£		£
Sales revenue	298,000	Sales staff salaries	41,700
Inventories of direct materials at 1 May 20X2	7,900	Accounting staff salaries	38,200
Inventories of direct materials at 30 Apr 20X3	6,200	Royalties paid for products produced under licence	17,500
Work in progress at 1 May 20X2	8,400		
Work in progress at 30 Apr 20X3	9,600	Cost of power for machinery	9,200
Inventories of finished goods at 1 May 20X2	5,400	Repairs to plant	6,700
Inventories of finished goods at 30 Apr 20X3	6,800	Bad debts	5,100
Purchase of direct materials	68,400	Interest on bank loan	7,400
Direct wages	52,600	Depreciation on plant	18,600
Production supervisors' salaries	34,800	Depreciation on delivery vehicles	13,200
		Depreciation on accounting office equipment	11,500

Required

Prepare a manufacturing account and a statement of profit and loss for the year ended 30 April 20X3, showing clearly the total direct/prime costs, manufacturing/factory costs, cost of completed production and cost of sales.

Manufacturing account for A. Bush for the year ended 30/4/X3		
	£	£
Production cost for the period		
Opening inventory of raw materials	7,900	
Direct materials	68,400	
	76,300	
Closing inventory of raw materials	(6,200)	
Cost of raw materials consumed		70,100
Direct labour		52,600
Direct expenses		17,500
Prime cost		140,200
Factory overhead expenses		
Supervisors' salaries	34,800	
Power	9,200	
Repairs to plant	6,700	
Depreciation on plant	18,600	
Total factory overheads		69,300
Total factory costs		209,500
Opening work-in-progress		8,400
		217,900
Closing work-in-progress		(9,600)
Factory cost of completed production c/d *(to statement of P&L)*		208,300

Notes

1 Any proceeds from the sale of scrap direct materials are normally credited to the manufacturing account, thus reducing the cost of completed production.

Statement of profit and loss for A. Bush for the year ended 30/4/X3		
	Note	£
Sales revenue		298,000
Cost of goods produced	1	206,900
Gross profit		91,100
Distribution expenses	2	60,000
Administrative expenses	3	49,700
Finance costs	4	7,400
(Loss) for the period		(26,000)

Notes

1 Cost of sales

Opening inventory of finished goods	5,400
Factory cost of completed production (b/d from manufacturing account)	208,300
	213,700
Closing inventory of finished goods	(6,800)
	206,900

2 Distribution expenses

Sales staff salaries	41,700
Depreciation on delivery vehicles	13,200
Bad debts	5,100
	60,000

3 Administration expenses

Accounting staff salaries	38,200
Depreciation on office equipment	11,500
	49,700

4 Finance costs

Interest on loan	7,400
	7,400

25.5 Manufacturing profits

In some businesses, manufactured goods are transferred from the factory to the warehouse at market prices, or an approximation thereof in the form of cost plus a given percentage for profit. This is intended to represent the price that the warehouse would have to pay if it bought the goods from an external supplier, or the price that the factory would receive if it sold the goods to an external customer. This is commonly referred to as the **transfer price**. The purpose of having internal transfer prices is to make the managers in the factory and warehouse more aware of the impact of market forces, to increase motivation and to facilitate the evaluation of their performance.

The accounting entries are relatively straightforward. The figure for completed production carried down from the manufacturing account to the statement of profit and loss will simply be at some transfer price or valuation other than cost. This gives rise to a **manufacturing profit** (or loss), which will be the difference between the two sides of the manufacturing account. The double entry for this profit (or loss) is to credit (or debit) the profit and loss account. While this accounting treatment of the manufacturing profit (or loss) may be adopted in the final financial statements prepared for internal management purposes, it would not be acceptable for external reporting because it contravenes IAS 2, which requires that finished goods inventories are valued at the lower of factory cost (discussed later) and net realizable value (NRV) (discussed in the previous chapter). The finished goods inventories will have been valued at the transfer price, which means that the manufacturing profit includes unrealized profit contained in any increase in finished goods inventories over the year. Any such unrealized profit should be transferred to a provision for unrealized (manufacturing) profit account by crediting this account and debiting the profit and loss account. Where there is a decrease in finished goods inventories over the year, the entries are the opposite. After these entries have been made, there should be a balance on the provision for unrealized profit account equal to the manufacturing profit contained in the finished goods inventory at the end of the year. This is deducted from the value of finished goods inventories (at transfer price) in the statement of financial position, thus reducing it to factory cost.

EXAMPLE 25.2

Using the information from Example 25.1, assume that the manufacturing division of A. Bush has a transfer price, for the goods that have left the production process, of £220,000.

Required

Prepare a summarized manufacturing account and a summarized statement of profit and loss for the year ended 30 April 20X3 showing the split in profits between the manufacturing division and the trading division.

Manufacturing account for A. Bush for the year ended 30/4/X3	
	£
Transfer price	220,000
Factory cost of completed production	208,300
Gross profit on manufacturing	11,700

Statement of profit and loss for A. Bush for the year ended 30/4/X3		
		£
Sales revenue		298,000
Cost of goods produced		206,900
Gross profit	1	91,100
Distribution expenses	2	60,000
Administrative expenses	3	49,700
Finance costs	4	7,400
(Loss) for the period		(26,000)

Notes

1 Cost of sales (internal use)

Opening inventory of finished goods	5,400
Factory cost of completed production (b/d from manufacturing account)	220,000
	225,400
Closing inventory of finished goods	(6,800)
	218,600

2 Gross profit (internal use)

Manufacturing	11,700
Trading	79,400
Total gross profit (manufacturing and trading)	91,100

25.6 The valuation of finished goods and work-in-progress

The work-in-progress (WIP) shown in the manufacturing account is usually valued at production/factory cost; that is, prime costs plus factory overheads. This is why the adjustment for the opening and closing WIP is made after the total factory costs have been computed. Similarly, the finished goods inventory shown in the statement of profit and loss is normally valued at factory cost. This is consistent with the valuation of the completed production, which is also included in the statement of profit and loss at factory cost. Thus, neither the WIP nor finished goods inventory includes other overheads such as selling and distribution costs, administrative expenses and interest. Sometimes WIP is valued at prime cost: that is, excluding factory overheads. In this case the adjustment for WIP must be made before the factory overheads in the manufacturing account.

The above assertions relating to the valuation of WIP and finished goods inventories can be explained further by reference to *IAS 2 – Inventories* (IASB, 2010a). This states that 'the cost of inventories shall comprise all costs of purchase, costs of conversion and other costs incurred in bringing the inventories to their present location and condition'. This expenditure should include, in addition to cost of purchase (of direct materials), such costs of conversion as are appropriate to the location and condition. Both purchase price and the costs of conversion are outlined in the previous chapter. In brief, purchase price includes all costs that are incurred in obtaining inventory (invoice price, delivery, handling, etc.). The **costs of conversion** comprise costs that are specifically attributable to units of production, that is, direct labour, direct expenses and subcontracted work and production overheads. This does not include selling and distribution overheads, administrative overheads or finance costs.

LEARNING ACTIVITY 25.1

Visit the website of a known manufacturing company and review their financial statements. For example, Bombardier – a Canadian-based company which manufactures aeroplanes, trains, etc. This Canadian company has a subsidiary in Belfast (called Shorts) (http://www.bombardier.com/en/corporate/investor-relations/financial-results).

Examine the format of their published financial statements. These will typically follow the format for company financial statements (see Chapters 1 or 31 for a proforma) as the details provided in manufacturing accounts would be deemed to be too sensitive to be made available for competitors to see! However, you will see non-standard items separately identified, such as research and development.

Summary

Manufacturing businesses usually classify all their costs as either direct or indirect/overheads. Direct costs comprise direct materials, direct labour and direct expenses. Overheads are classified as either factory overheads, selling and distribution costs, or administrative expenses. Manufacturing businesses also normally have a number of different types of inventory that comprise inventories of direct materials, WIP and finished goods.

The main difference between preparing the financial statements of manufacturing businesses and preparing the financial statements of commercial undertakings is that the former includes preparing a manufacturing account. This is used to ascertain the cost of completed production that is entered in the statement of profit and loss in place of the purchases of a non-manufacturing business. The computation of the cost of completed production necessitates certain adjustments in respect of inventories of direct materials and WIP that are similar to those relating to the calculation of the cost of sales.

Key terms and concepts

administrative overheads	418	finished goods	417
costs of conversion	427	indirect costs/overheads	418
direct costs	418	manufacturing account	419
direct expenses	418	manufacturing profit	425
direct labour	418	prime cost	420
direct materials	418	selling and distribution overheads	418
factory cost of completed production	419	total factory costs	420
factory/production/manufacturing overheads	418	transfer price	425

An asterisk after the question number indicates that there is a suggested answer on the Online Learning Centre (www.mcgraw-hill.co.uk/textbooks/thomas).

connect Review questions

25.1 a Explain the difference between direct costs and overheads.

   b Describe the different types of direct cost and overhead found in a manufacturing business.

25.2 Describe the different categories of inventory normally held by a manufacturing business.

25.3 a Explain the main purpose of a manufacturing account.

   b Describe the structure and main groups of costs found in a manufacturing account.

25.4 a Explain the difference between the total factory cost of production and the factory cost of completed production.

   b What is the justification for adjusting the total factory cost for work-in-progress rather than, say, the total prime/direct cost?

connect Exercises

BASIC

25.5

	£
Inventories, 1 January 20X3	
Raw materials	7,500
Finished goods	14,300
Work-in-progress	10,070
Wages and salaries	
Factory direct	98,500
Factory indirect	17,500
Purchases – raw materials	90,600
Power and fuel	28,260
Sales revenue	385,400
Insurance	6,640
Returns inwards (finished goods)	6,000
Inventories, 31 December 20X3	
Raw materials	9,200
Finished goods	8,600
Work-in-progress	8,700

Additional information

1 The manufacturing entity's machinery cost £102,000.

2 Provision for depreciation at the start of the period is £47,000. The company has a policy of providing deprecation at the rate of 20 per cent per year calculated using the reducing balance method.

3 At the year end £740 is outstanding for fuel and power.

4 In addition, the manager informs you that insurance of £240 is prepaid at the year end. The factory proportion of this is 75 per cent, whereas the administration is to be allocated 25 per cent of the expense.

Required

Prepare the manufacturing account and the statement of profit and loss for the year ended 31 December 20X3.

25.6*

The trial balance extracted at 30 April 20X3 from the books of Upton Upholstery, a furniture manufacturer, is given below.

	Debit	Credit
	£	£
Factory machinery at cost	28,000	
Factory machinery depreciation 1/5/X2		5,000
Office equipment	2,000	
Office equipment depreciation 1/5/X2		800
Trade receivables and payables	15,000	16,000
Cash and bank	2,300	
Bank loan		11,000
Inventories 1/5/X2 – Raw materials	4,000	
– Incomplete production	16,400	
– Finished goods	9,000	
Carriage inwards	1,200	
Carriage outwards	700	
Purchases – raw materials	84,000	
Light and heat	3,000	
Rent and rates	6,600	
Direct factory wages	19,900	
Office wages	5,200	
Sales commission to selling agents	1,400	
Sales of finished goods		140,000
Capital account		35,000
Drawings	9,100	
	207,800	207,800

Notes

1 At 30 April 20X3 accrued direct factory wages amounted to £600 and office wages £100; rent paid included £600 paid on 20 January 20X3 for the period 1 January to 30 June 20X3.

2 Records showed that, at the year end, inventory values were as follows; raw materials £5,400; incomplete production £17,000; finished goods £8,000.

3 Depreciation should be allowed for factory machinery on the straight line method over seven years, and office equipment on the reducing balance method at 25 per cent per annum.

4 A provision of £1,000 should be made for doubtful debts.

5 Light and heat should be apportioned between the factory and office in the ratio 4 : 1, respectively; rent and rates in the ratio 3 : 1, respectively.

Required

Prepare a manufacturing account and a statement of profit and loss for the year ended 30 April 20X3 and a statement of financial position at that date.

INTERMEDIATE

25.7*

From the following information prepare a manufacturing account and a statement of profit and loss for the year ended 31 December 20X2. Show clearly the prime cost, factory cost of completed production, cost of sales, gross profit, selling and distribution overheads, administrative overhead, and net profit.

	£
Inventory of raw materials at 1 January 20X2	2,453
Work-in-progress valued at factory cost at 1 January 20X2	1,617
Inventory of finished goods at 1 January 20X2	3,968
Purchases of raw materials	47,693
Purchases of finished goods	367
Raw materials returned to suppliers	4,921
Carriage outwards	487
Carriage inwards	683
Direct wages	23,649
Administrative salaries	10,889
Supervisors' wages	5,617
Royalties payable	7,500
Electricity used in factory	2,334
Light and heat for administrative offices	998
Sales staff salaries and commission	8,600
Bad debts	726
Discount received	2,310
Discount allowed	1,515
Depreciation – plant	13,400
– delivery vehicles	3,700
– office fixtures and furniture	1,900
Rent and rates (factory $\frac{3}{4}$ office $\frac{1}{4}$)	4,800
Delivery expenses	593
Postage and telephone	714
Printing and stationery	363
Proceeds from the sale of scrap metal	199
Interest payable on loan	3,000
Bank charges	100
Insurance on plant	1,750
Advertising	625
Repairs to plant	917
Sales revenue	145,433
Purchases of raw materials includes £2,093, and direct wages £549, for materials and work done in constructing an extension to the factory.	
Inventory of raw materials at 31 December 20X2	3,987
Work-in-progress valued at factory cost at 31 December 20X2	2,700
Inventory of finished goods at 31 December 20X2	5,666

25.8

INTERMEDIATE

W. Wagner, a manufacturer, provided the following information for the year ended 31 August 20X3:

	£
Inventories at 1 September 20X2	
– Raw materials	25,000
– Work-in-progress	15,900
– Finished goods	26,600
Raw materials purchased	176,600
Factory general expenses	14,800
Direct wages	86,900
Repairs to plant and machinery	9,900
Factory lighting and heating	20,010
Carriage inwards	1,910
Carriage outwards	2,500
Sales revenue	320,000
Raw materials returned	7,800
Factory maintenance wages	19,000
Administrative expenses	30,000
Selling and distribution expenses	15,100
Plant and machinery at cost	178,000
Freehold land and buildings at cost	160,000
Provision for depreciation on plant and machinery (1/9/X2)	80,000

Additional information

1 Amounts owing at 31 August 20X3:

	£
Direct wages	4,800
Factory heating and lighting	1,500

2 Depreciation on plant and machinery is to be provided at 10 per cent per annum on cost. There were no sales or purchases of plant and machinery during the year.

3 All manufactured goods are transferred to the warehouse at factory cost plus 10 per cent.

4 Inventories at 31 August 20X3:

	£
Raw materials	30,000
Work-in-progress	17,800
Finished goods	35,090

The raw materials are valued at cost, the work-in-progress at factory cost, while the inventory of finished goods is valued at the factory transfer price.

Required

a A manufacturing account for the year ended 31 August 20X3.

b A statement of profit and loss for the year ended 31 August 20X3.

(AEB, adapted)

ADVANCED

25.9

Veronica is the owner of a manufacturing business. The following trial balance was extracted from her books as at 31 December 20X2:

	Dr	Cr
	£	£
Cash in hand	200	
Bank		7,220
Purchase ledger balances		7,160
Sales ledger balances	12,200	
Provision for doubtful debts		2,000
Administration expenses	5,620	
Electricity and power	12,000	
Sales expenses	2,880	
Repairs to building	2,000	
Rates and insurance	3,200	
Factory wages	27,280	
Administration wages	10,800	
Sales department wages	6,000	
Sales revenue		132,000
Raw material purchases	37,000	
Purchases of tools and utensils	1,600	
Opening inventories		
– Raw materials	6,600	
– Work-in-progress	5,000	
– Finished goods	12,000	
– Loose tools and utensils	2,400	
Motor vehicles (selling and distribution)	8,000	
Provision for depreciation on motor vehicles		5,600
Plant and machinery	29,000	
Provision for depreciation on plant and machinery		14,000
Land	30,000	
Capital account		45,800
	213,780	213,780

The following information was also made available:

1 Expenses are to be allocated as follows:

	Factory	Administration
Electricity and power	90%	10%
Repairs	80%	20%
Rates and insurance	70%	30%

2 Closing inventories included: raw materials £5,600; loose tools and utensils £3,200; finished goods £7,800; and work-in-progress £5,000.

3 Bad debts amounting to £1,000 are to be written off and the provision for doubtful debts reduced to £1,200.

4 The following amounts have yet to be provided for in the trial balance: electricity and power £1,600 and new machinery £1,000.

5 The following amounts have been prepaid as at the year end: rates £600 and vehicle licences on sales representatives' cars £80.

6 A vehicle costing £3,000 and written down to £1,000 was sold for £1,200. None of these entries have been recorded in the trial balance as the bookkeeper did not know how to adjust for the sale.

7 Annual depreciation on plant and machinery and on motor vehicles is to be provided using the reducing balance method. The rates used for each class of asset are 15 per cent (plant and machinery) and 20 per cent (motor vehicles).

8 An invoice for £200 for repairs to the building had been incorrectly posted to the administration expenses account.

9 A building costing £100,000 was purchased using a long-term loan on 1 January 20X2. Interest payable on the loan is 10 per cent per year. No entries for this transaction have been included in the trial balance. It has been decided to depreciate buildings at 5 per cent on cost.

Required

Prepare the following:

a The manufacturing account and the statement of profit and loss for the year ended 31 December 20X2.

b The statement of financial position as at 31 December 20X2.

(*Note*: All workings must be shown including adjustments to ledger accounts.)

25.10

ADVANCED

Zacotex Ltd, a manufacturer, produced the following financial information for the year ended 31 March 20X3.

	£
Raw material purchases	250,000
Direct labour	100,000
Direct expenses	80,900
Indirect factory labour	16,000
Factory maintenance costs	9,700
Machine repairs	11,500
Sales of finished goods during the year	788,100
Inventories at 1 April 20X2	
– Raw materials	65,000
– Finished goods	48,000
– Work-in-progress	52,500
Other factory overhead	14,500
Factory heating and lighting	19,000
Factory rates	11,500
Administration expenses	22,000
Selling and distribution expenses	36,800

Additional information

1 The inventories held at 31 March 20X3 were:

Raw materials	£51,400
Finished goods	£53,800
Work-in-progress	£41,000

Note: Raw materials are valued at cost; finished goods at factory cost; work-in-progress at factory cost. Of the raw materials held in inventories at 31 March 20X3, £15,000 had suffered flood damage and it was estimated that they could only be sold for £2,500. The remaining raw material inventory could only be sold on the open market at cost less 10 per cent.

2 One-quarter of the administration expenses are to be allocated to the factory.

3 The raw materials purchases figure for the year includes a charge for carriage inwards. On 31 March 20X3 a credit note for £1,550 was received in respect of a carriage inwards overcharge. No adjustment had been made for this amount.

4 Expenses in arrears at 31 March 20X3 were:

	£
Direct labour	6,600
Machine repairs	1,700
Selling and distribution expenses	4,900

5 Plant and machinery at 1 April 20X2

	£
At cost	250,000
Aggregate depreciation	75,000

During the year an obsolete machine (cost £30,000, depreciation to date £8,000) was sold as scrap for £5,000. On 1 October 20X2 new machinery was purchased for £70,000 with an installation charge of £8,000.

The company depreciates its plant and machinery at 10 per cent per annum on cost on all items in company ownership at the end of the accounting year.

6 An analysis of the sales of finished goods revealed the following:

	£
Goods sold for cash	105,000
Goods sold on credit	623,100
Goods sold on sale or return: returned	25,000
Goods sold on sale or return: retained and invoice confirmed	35,000
	788,100

7 On 1 April 20X2 the company arranged a long-term loan of £250,000 at a fixed rate of interest of 11 per cent per annum. No provision had been made for the payment of the interest.

Required

Prepare for the year ended 31 March 20X3

a A manufacturing account showing prime cost and factory cost of goods produced.

b A statement of profit and loss.

(AEB, adapted)

25.11

ADVANCED

Ashley Ltd is a manufacturing firm. The bookkeeper supplies you with the following financial information for the year ended 31 March 20X3.

	£
Factory buildings	100,000
Provision for depreciation on buildings	15,000
Plant and equipment	500,000
Provision for depreciation on plant	150,000
Motor vehicles (administration)	25,000
Provision for depreciation on motor vehicles	9,000
Trade receivables	156,000
Bank	8,000
Cash	700
Trade payables	56,000
Other selling and distribution expenses	33,600
Other administration expenses	24,000
Raw material purchases	500,000
Factory rates	23,000
Direct labour	200,000
Factory heat and light	38,000
Direct expenses	161,800
Other factory overheads	29,000
Indirect factory labour	32,000
Inventories at 1 April 20X2	
– Raw materials	130,000
– Finished goods	96,000
– Work-in-progress	105,000
Factory maintenance costs	176,000
Machine repairs	23,000
Sales of finished goods in the year	1,903,400
Sales representatives' salaries	30,000
Commission to sales representatives	10,000
Bad debts	4,000
Bookkeeper's salary	15,000
Postage	1,000

Other information

1 On 1 April 20X2 the company arranged a long-term loan of £500,000 at a fixed rate of interest of 10 per cent per annum. The loan was used to buy a building worth £300,000, plant worth £150,000 (including an installation charge of £16,000) and three sales representatives' vehicles for £50,000. No provision had been made for the payment of the interest.

2 During the year an obsolete machine costing £60,000, but written down to £44,000, was sold as scrap for £10,000.

3 The company depreciates its assets as follows:

Buildings	5 per cent per annum
Plant and equipment	20 per cent reducing balance
Motor vehicles (administration)	25 per cent reducing balance
Motor vehicles (sales representatives) over four years using the sum of digits method. A full year's depreciation is provided for all assets in ownership at the end of the year.	

4 The inventories held at the end of the year were:

	£
Raw materials per inventory sheet	102,800
Finished goods	107,600
Work in progress	82,000

Of the raw materials held in inventories at the year end, £30,000 had suffered fire damage. It was estimated that they could be sold for £5,000.

5 The raw material purchases figure included in the list above includes £100,000 for carriage inwards. A credit note for £3,000, correcting an overcharge on an original invoice for carriage, was received on 31 March 20X3. The figures had not been adjusted for this.

6 Accruals and prepayments at the year end were:

	£
Direct labour accrued	13,200
Machine repairs accrued	3,400
Factory maintenance prepaid	2,000

Required

Prepare the following:

a The manufacturing account and the statement of profit and loss for the year ended 31 March 20X3.

b The statement of financial position as at 31 March 20X3.

(*Note*: All workings must be shown including the adjustments to ledger accounts.)

25.12

ADVANCED

(*Note*: This question should be attempted after the chapter on incomplete records has been studied.)

ABC manufacturing entity (sole trader) has provided you with the following information at the year ended 31 July 20X2:

	£
Inventories:	
– Raw materials	25,000
– Work-in-progress	6,700
– Finished goods	100,000
Trade payables	47,500
Trade receivables	68,000
Bank	3,500
Administration expenses prepaid	300
Non-current assets (cost £60,000)	59,400

During the year ended 31 July 20X3 the following transactions took place:

	£
Sales invoiced	254,000
Cash received from customers	245,700
Discounts allowed	5,900
Bad debts written off	900
Purchases invoiced	92,000
Purchase returns	1,500
Payments to suppliers	93,500
Discounts received	1,800
Factory wages paid	42,600
Manufacturing expenses paid	51,500
Administration expenses paid	15,800
Selling and distribution expenses paid	18,100
Payments to purchase plant and machinery	28,000

ABC informed you that the balances at 31 July 20X3 were as follows:

	£
Inventories:	
— Raw materials	24,000
— Work-in-progress	5,900
— Finished goods	102,000
Trade payables	?
Trade receivables	?
Bank	?
Administration expenses accrued	1,000
Non-current assets (cost £88,000)	59,000

Additional information

1 Depreciation on non-current assets should be apportioned between manufacturing (60 per cent), administration (25 per cent) and selling and distribution (15 per cent).

2 Discounts allowed and bad debts are regarded as selling expenses.

3 Discounts received should be regarded as administration expenses.

Required

a Compute the balances on the trade receivables account, the trade payables account and the bank account at 31 July 20X3 *(the ledger accounts should be provided)*.

b Prepare the manufacturing account and the statement of profit and loss for the company for the year ended 31 July 20X3.

References

International Accounting Standards Board (2010a) *International Accounting Standard 2 – Inventories* (IASB).

International Accounting Standards Board (2010b) *International Accounting Standard 1 – Presentation of Financial Statements* (IASB).

After you have read this part, log on to the Online Learning Centre for *Introduction to Financial Accounting* at www.mcgraw-hill.co.uk/ textbooks/thomas where you will find Self Test Questions for these chapters, a glossary with definitions of key terms plus extra resources for revision.

Clubs

PART SIX

The final financial statements of clubs

26

Learning Objectives

After reading this chapter you should be able to do the following:

1. Explain the meaning of the key terms and concepts listed at the end of the chapter.

2. Describe the main differences between the final financial statements of a business enterprise and those of a club, with particular reference to its capital.

3. Show the accounting entries in respect of annual subscriptions and explain their conceptual foundation.

4. Prepare the final financial statements of clubs, including from incomplete records, comprising a receipts and payments account, a bar trading account, an income and expenditure account and a statement of financial position.

5. Show the accounting entries in respect of various items usually only arising in the financial statements of clubs and explain their conceptual foundation.

26.1 Introduction

Most accounting students gain their first experience of 'practical' accounting by becoming treasurers of a club of which they are a member. A **club** is an organization whose primary aim is to provide a service to its members (e.g. sports and social clubs) and/or some section of the community (e.g. senior citizens). One of its main financial objectives is therefore not to earn a profit but often simply to break even. Thus, in the final financial statements of clubs, the statement of profit and loss is replaced with an **income and expenditure account**. Any difference between the income and expenditure for the year is referred to as an **excess of income over expenditure**, or vice versa (i.e. not a profit or loss). The income and expenditure account is prepared using the same principles as the statement of profit and loss: namely, the matching and accrual of revenue income and expenditure. However, the contents differ in that income will take the form of subscriptions, **entrance fees** from sports activities, surpluses on a bar, dances, raffles, gaming machines, annual dinners, and so on.

Another major difference between clubs and business enterprises is that clubs are usually managed by voluntary officers. Members of the club therefore frequently expect them to provide an account of the money that has been received and the way in which it has been spent. Thus, final financial statements of clubs often include a **receipts and payments account**. This is simply a summary of the cash book showing the opening and closing cash and bank balances and the total amounts received and spent on each type of income and expenditure, assets, and so on.

Many clubs are quite small and may have few, if any, assets and liabilities other than cash. It therefore serves little purpose to prepare a statement of financial position, particularly if a receipts and payments account has been produced. However, some clubs are relatively large. In this case the final financial statements should include a statement of financial position which is also sometimes called a **statement of affairs**. It will take the same form as for business enterprises with one major difference, which is that the capital account is replaced by an **accumulated/general fund**. This is an accumulation of previous years' surpluses (less deficits) of income over expenditure, and represents the net worth of the club. Unlike the capital account of business enterprises, there cannot be capital introduced or drawings against the accumulated fund. The only other significant difference between the statement of financial position of a business enterprise and that of a club is that the latter usually has subscriptions in arrears and subscriptions in advance.

Although clubs are not primarily trading organizations, they frequently engage in certain activities that are intended to make a profit/surplus as a way of raising additional funds or subsidizing other functions – for example, the sale of drinks and snacks, gaming machines, raffles and dances. Where these involve material amounts of money, it is usual to compute the profit or loss on the activity in a separate account such as a **bar trading account**. Where the amounts are less significant, the income, expenditure and resulting surplus (or deficit) should be shown in the income and expenditure account: for example, annual dinner or dance.

 ## 26.2 Annual subscriptions

Many clubs require their members to pay an annual subscription. These are usually accounted for on an accruals basis – that is, applying the accruals concept. This means that the amount credited to the income and expenditure account in respect of subscriptions is the amount due for the year, irrespective of whether this has all been received.

The application of the accruals concept gives rise to subscriptions in arrear and subscriptions in advance in the final financial statements. Where some members have not paid their subscriptions at the end of a given accounting year, these are referred to as **subscriptions in arrears**, and treated as receivables. Where some members have paid their subscriptions for the following accounting year, these are referred to as **subscriptions in advance**, and treated as payables. However, as in the case of accrued and prepaid expenses, receivables and payables in respect of subscriptions are not entered in separate personal accounts. Instead, these are recorded in a subscriptions account. Subscriptions in arrears are entered in the subscriptions account as a balance carried down on the credit side and a balance brought down on the debit side. Subscriptions in advance are entered in the subscriptions account as a balance carried down on the debit side and a balance brought down on the credit side. A pro forma subscriptions account would have the following entries (see Figure 26.1):

Subscriptions account			
	£		£
Opening subscriptions in arrears (receivable) b/d	XX	Opening subscriptions received in advance b/d	XX
Bad debts	X	Received in year (bank/cash)	XX
Income and expenditure account	XXX		
Closing subscriptions received in advance c/d	XX	Closing subscriptions in arrears (receivable) c/d	XX
	XXX		XX
Next year		*Next year*	
Subscriptions in arrears (receivable) b/d	XX	Subscriptions received in advance b/d	XX

Figure 26.1 A pro forma showing the typical entries required in a subscriptions ledger account

The shaded area usually represents the missing figure – that is, the correct accruals adjusted subscriptions for the period being considered. This will be credited to the club's income and expenditure account.

Subscriptions in arrears are shown in the statement of financial position as a current asset and subscriptions in advance are shown as a current liability.

Sometimes subscriptions are recorded in the income and expenditure account on a strict cash-received basis and not an accruals basis. In this case there will not be any subscriptions in arrear or in advance in the final financial statements. It is sometimes justified on the grounds that members, unlike other receivables, are more likely to fail to pay subscriptions in arrear, and clubs are unlikely to take legal or other action to force payment. However, the use of the cash received basis is not common in examination questions and should only be applied where specifically required.

LEARNING ACTIVITY **26.1**

If you are a member of a club, you are entitled to obtain a copy of their financial statements. If you have not already received these, request them and observe the differences between the income and expenditure account format and the IFRS-adopted formats for reporting income and expenditure that has been adopted in the rest of this textbook. Look for any unusual items and list these. Try to categorize them according to the main elements in a set of financial statements (asset, liability, income expenditure).

26.3 The preparation of final financial statements of clubs

It is common to find that the books of accounts of a club have been kept on a **single-entry** basis. This means that the procedure to be followed in the preparation of the final financial statements will be as described in Chapter 23, 'Single Entry and Incomplete Records'. This is illustrated in Example 26.1.

EXAMPLE
26.1

City Football Club has the following assets and liabilities at 1 July 20X2: freehold land and buildings at cost £50,000; equipment at written down value (WDV) £12,200; grass mower at cost £135; bar trade payables £1,380; subscriptions in advance £190; subscriptions in arrear £105; bar inventories £2,340; rates in advance £240; electricity accrued £85.

A summary of the receipts and payments during the year ended 30 June 20X3 is as follows:

Bank account			
	£		£
Bank balance at 1 July 20X2	695	Rates	490
Bar takings banked	5,430	Electricity	255
Subscriptions received	3,610	Purchase of new grass mower	520
Sale of dance tickets	685	Bar steward's wages	2,200
Gate money received	8,490	Bar credit suppliers	4,980
		Band for dance	490
		Postage and telephone	310
		Printing and stationery	175
		Bank balance at 30 June 20X3	9,490
	18,910		18,910

Additional information

1 Bar inventories at 30 June 20X3, £2,560.

2 Bar trade payables at 30 June 20X3, £980.

3 Rates paid include £400 for the six months to 30 September 20X3.

4 Electricity in arrear at 30 June 20X3, £70.

5 Subscriptions in arrear at 30 June 20X3, £95.

6 Subscriptions in advance at 30 June 20X3, £115.

7 The following amounts have been paid from bar takings before they were banked: sundry expenses £25, bar purchases £235, office salaries £1,200, stationery £45, and travelling expenses £140.

8 The new grass mower was purchased by putting in part exchange the old one, for which the trade-in value was £180.

9 Depreciation on the equipment is 20 per cent per annum using the reducing balance method. No depreciation is charged on the grass mower.

Required

a A bar trading account for the year ended 30 June 20X3.

b An income and expenditure account for the year ended 30 June 20X3.

c A statement of financial position as at 30 June 20X3.

Show clearly all your workings.

Workings/procedure

1 If necessary, prepare a statement of financial position as at the end of the previous year in order to ascertain the accumulated/general fund.

City Football Club	
Statement of financial position as at 30 June 20X2	
ASSETS	
Non-current assets	£
Freehold land and buildings at cost	50,000
Equipment at NBV	12,200
Grass mower at cost	135
	62,335
Current assets	
Inventories	2,340
Prepaid expenses	240
Subscriptions in arrears	105
Bank	695
	3,380
Total assets	65,715
CAPITAL AND LIABILITIES	
Members' capital	
Accumulated fund at 30 June 20X2	64,060
Current liabilities	
Trade payables	1,380
Accrued expenses	85
Subscriptions in advance	190
Total liabilities	1,655
Total members' capital and liabilities	65,715

The shaded number is not provided in the question. It is missing and is found by woking back using total assets less total current liabilities.

2 If necessary, prepare a receipts and payments account for the year in order to ascertain the bank and cash balance at the end of the year and the total amounts received and spent on each type of income and expenditure, and on assets.

3 **a** Compute the net credit bar purchases by preparing a purchase ledger control account:

Purchase ledger control				
20X3		£	**20X2**	£
30 June	Bank	4,980	1 July Balance b/d	1,380
30 June	Balance c/d	980	**20X3**	
			30 June Net purchases	4,580
		5,960		5,960

The figure for net credit purchases is the difference between the two sides.

b Compute the cash and cheque bar purchases and then the total bar purchases:

Total purchases = £235 + £4,580 = £4,815

4 **a** Compute the net credit bar sales, if any, by preparing a sales ledger control account.

b Compute the cash and cheque bar sales and then the total bar sales:

Cash and total sales = £5,430 + £25 + £235 + £1,200 + £45 + £140 = £7,075

5 Ascertain the income for the year in respect of subscriptions by preparing the ledger account. Alternatively, in examinations this may be shown as workings in the income and expenditure account.

	Subscriptions				
20X2		£	**20X2**		£
1 July	Subs in arrears b/d	105	1 July	Subs in advance b/d	190
20X3			**20X3**		
30 June	Subs for year	3,675	30 June	Bank	3,610
30 June	Subs in advance c/d	115	30 June	Subs in arrears c/d	95
		3,895			3,895

The figure for subscriptions for the year of £3,675 is the difference between the two sides. It is credited to the income and expenditure account.

6 Compute the expenditure for the year in respect of those expenses with accruals and prepayments by preparing the relevant ledger accounts.

	Rates				
20X2		£	**20X3**		£
1 July	Prepayment b/d	240	30 June	Income and expenditure a/c	530
20X3			30 June	Prepayment c/d ($\frac{3}{6} \times 400$)	200
30 June	Bank	490			
		730			730

	Light and heat				
20X3		£	**20X2**		£
30 June	Bank	255	1 July	Accrual b/d	85
30 June	Accrual c/d	70	**20X3**		
			30 June	Income and expenditure a/c	240
		325			325

7 Ascertain the depreciation charges for the year and any profit or loss on the sale of non-current assets:

Depreciation on equipment = 20 per cent × £12,200 = £2,440

Profit on sale of grass mower = £180 − £135 = £45

8 Prepare the bar trading account, income and expenditure account, and statement of financial position, remembering to add together any cheque and cash expenditure of the same type (e.g. stationery) and make any other necessary adjustments, such as the purchase of non-current assets.

City Football Club		
Bar trading account for the year ended 30 June 20X3		
	£	£
Sales revenue		7,075
Less: Cost of sales –		
Inventory at 1 July 20X2	2,340	
Add: Purchases	4,815	
	7,155	
Less: Inventory at 30 June 20X3	2,560	4,595
Gross Profit		2,480
Other bar costs–		
Steward's wages	2,200	2,200
Profit on bar		280

City Football Club		
Income and expenditure account for the year ended 30 June 20X3		
	£	£
Income		
Gate receipts		8,490
Subscriptions		3,675
Profit on bar		280
Income from dance	685	
Cost of dance	(490)	
Surplus on dance		195
Profit on sale of non-current asset		45
Total income		12,685
Less: Expenditure		
Rates (£490 + £240 − £200)	530	
Light and heat (£255 + £70 − £85)	240	
Postage and telephone	310	
Printing and stationery (£175 + £45)	220	
Sundry expenses	25	
Office salaries	1,200	
Travelling expenses	140	
Depreciation on equipment	2,440	5,105
Excess of income over expenditure		7,580

City Football Club			
Statement of financial position as at 30 June 20X3			
ASSETS	£	£	£
Non-current assets	*Cost*	*Prov. for depn*	*NBV*
Freehold land and buildings at cost	50,000	–	50,000
Equipment at NBV	12,200	2,440	9,760
Grass mower (£520 + £180)	700	–	700
	62,900	2,440	60,460
Current assets			
Inventories			2,560
Subscriptions in arrears			95
Prepayments			200
Bank			9,490
			12,345
Total assets			72,805
MEMBERS' CAPITAL AND LIABILITIES			
Members' capital			
Accumulated fund			
Balance at 30 June 20X2			64,060
Add: Excess of income over expenditure for the year			7,580
Balance at 30 June 20X3			71,640
Current liabilities			
Trade payables			980
Subscriptions in advance			115
Accruals			70
Total current liabilities			1,165
Total members' capital and liabilities			72,805

26.4 Special items

As seen above, clubs have a variety of different forms of income, many of which are not found in business enterprises. Some of these are not common in practice but provide examples that examiners can use to test important principles. Those most frequently encountered in examinations are now discussed.

Donations, bequests and gifts

Small **donations**, **bequests** and **gifts** in the form of money are credited to the income and expenditure account on receipt. Donations and gifts in the form of domestic goods (such as furniture for the club-house or old clothes for resale) with a relatively small value are not usually recorded in the income and expenditure account (until they are sold, when just the sale proceeds are recorded).

Where donations of money or other assets are of a material amount (i.e. large in relation to the size of the club's normal income), the generally accepted practice is to credit such items direct to the accumulated fund instead of the income and expenditure account. This is because it would probably be misleading to credit the income and expenditure account with large amounts of income that is of a non-recurring nature. Members might be misled into thinking that the resulting surplus for the year was likely to be repeated in future years and thus could be used to cover additional recurring expenditure or reduced bar prices! The corresponding debit entry would be in the receipts and payments account in the case of money, or to the relevant asset account where the donation or bequest takes some other form, such as land, buildings or paintings. In the latter case the amount entered in the financial statements would be market value at the date of the donation.

Membership/entrance fees

Clubs that have valuable assets that are in great demand, such as golf and other sports facilities, often require new members to pay an entry or joining fee (in addition to the annual subscription). To treat these **membership/entrance fees** as income for the year in which it was received by crediting the income and expenditure account would be a breach of the matching principle, the reason being that this fee is a prepayment by the member for services which the club is obliged to provide over his or her period of membership, which is usually several years.

Such fees are referred to as **deferred income**, and the matching principle dictates that these should be credited to the income and expenditure account over the number of years that the club expects to have to provide the member with its services. Clearly, the decision relating to the length of this period is highly subjective. One possibility is the average number of years that people remain members of the club. However, in practice, a more arbitrary period may be selected depending on the nature of the club's services and the size of the membership fee.

The accounting entries in respect of joining fees are thus to credit these to a deferred income account, and each year to transfer a given proportion (e.g. 10 per cent, if it is to be spread over 10 years) to the income and expenditure account. The balance on the deferred income account is shown on the statement of financial position after (and separate from) the accumulated fund.

Life membership subscriptions

Instead of paying an annual subscription, some clubs permit their members to make a once-only payment that entitles them to membership for life. These are referred to as **life membership subscriptions** and, like entrance fees above, are in the nature of a prepayment by the member for services that the club is obliged to provide over the remainder of his or her life. They must therefore not be credited to the income and expenditure account as income of the year they are received.

Life membership subscriptions are a form of deferred income, and the matching principle dictates that they be spread over the number of years that the club expects to have to provide the life member with its services. Clearly, the decision relating to the length of this period is highly subjective. One possibility is the average number of years between people becoming life members and their death. However, in practice, a more arbitrary period may be selected depending on the nature of the club's services. For example, the period may be considerably longer for a golf club or social club than an athletics club or senior citizens club, since the period of life membership of the latter is restricted by physical and age constraints.

The accounting entries in respect of life membership subscriptions are thus to credit these to a deferred income account, and each year to transfer a given proportion (e.g. 5 per cent if it is to be spread over 20 years) to the income and expenditure account. The balance on the deferred income account is shown on the statement of financial position after (and separate from) the accumulated fund.

There is an alternative treatment of life membership subscriptions, however, it could be argued that this treatment is not in the spirit of the accounting principles as it is overly prudent, ignores the accruals and matching concept and the economic substance of the transaction. Clubs that use the alternative treatment argue that because the period of membership cannot be predicted with reasonable certainty, the income should not be recognized until the member dies. Thus, all the life membership subscriptions are credited to a fund account, and when a member dies his or her subscription is transferred to the accumulated fund (or possibly the income and expenditure account). The life membership subscription fund account is shown in the statement of financial position just below the accumulated fund and separate from any items that have been treated as deferred income, such as membership/entrance fees. This method of treating life membership subscriptions would be adopted in examination questions that do not give any indication of the length of time over which these should be credited to income, and which give details of how many life members died during the accounting year.

> **LEARNING ACTIVITY 26.2**
>
> Visit the website of a large charity and find a copy of their latest annual report and financial statements. Prepare a list of the main differences between this document and the annual report of any plc (that is not a club). Alternatively, perform the same task using the annual report of a football club. However, this is likely to be less relevant since professional football clubs are not clubs as such, but rather, like some charities are limited companies, a few of them, such as Tottenham Hotspur and Millwall FC, have their shares listed/quoted on the Alternative Investment Market of the London Stock Exchange.

Prize funds

Some clubs give prizes or other monetary awards to their members and/or other people that they wish to honour or assist for educational reasons. These are frequently financed from a separate fund, which may have been created by the club or from money that was donated for the express purpose of making the award. When the fund is set up the money donated for this purpose is invested in securities that provide some sort of income. This often takes the form of government bonds carrying a fixed rate of interest. The prizes or awards are usually paid out of the interest received and not the original donation, which remains invested.

The accounting entries for **prize funds** can be confusing, partly because they involve two related accounts. The first is a prize fund account that appears on the statement of financial position along with other funds, such as the accumulated fund and any life membership subscription fund. The other is a prize fund investment account which is usually treated as a non-current asset. When the fund is set up, the money set aside or donated for this purpose is debited to the prize fund investment account and credited to the prize fund account.

When income is received from the prize fund investments, this is debited in the receipts and payments account and credited to the prize fund account. When the prizes are awarded, the amounts are credited in the receipts and payments account and debited to the prize fund account. This is illustrated in Example 26.2.

> **EXAMPLE 26.2**
>
> Parkview plc donated £10,000 to the City Club on 31 December 20X1. It was agreed that the annual income from this is to be used to make a grant to members' children for educational purposes. The donation was invested in 10 per cent Government bonds on 1 January 20X2. The annual income of £1,000 was received on 31 December 20X2 and this was given to J. Smith as a grant on 1 January 20X3.

Show how this would be recorded in the ledger of City Club.

Receipts and payments (R & P)					
20X1		£	**20X2**		£
31 Dec	Grant fund – Parkview donation	10,000	1 Jan	Grant fund investments	10,000
20X2			**20X3**		
31 Dec	Grant fund – interest	1,000	1 Jan	Grant fund – J. Smith	1,000

Grant fund investments			
20X2	£		£
1 Jan R & P	10,000		

Parkview grant fund			
20X3	£	**20X1**	£
1 Jan R & P – J. Smith	1,000	31 Dec R & P	10,000
		20X2	
		31 Dec R & P – interest	1,000

Note

1 The balance on the grant fund at the end of each accounting year is normally the same as that on the grant fund investment account. However, as in the above example, these may differ because of time lags between the receipt of investment income and the payment of the grant.

Club bespoke expenditure

Every club will have their own unique types of income and expenditure. When a club has a form of expenditure that club members are particularly interested in, they typically disclose all income, expenditure, assets and liabilities in relation to the respective items separately. For example, in football clubs stakeholders are particularly interested in player transfer transactions, and most football clubs disclose information on this activity separately from their other trading activities (see, for example, Arsenal Holdings plc http://www.arsenal.com). Information disclosed in the annual return of the club for the period ended 31 May 2009 on player transfers is reproduced as follows:

REAL WORLD EXAMPLE 26.1

Arsenal Holdings plc (year ended 31 May 2009)

Player Trading

'The sale of player registrations generated a profit of £23.2 million (2008 – £26.5 million) which, together with fees of £3.6 million from the loan of players, meant that the overall result from player trading was a surplus of £2.9 million (2008 – £5.2 million).

The main contributions to the disposal profit came from the sales of Alexander Hleb and Justin Hoyte and the sell-on shares receivable in connection with moves by former players David Bentley and Lassana Diarra. The Board's policy continues to be that all proceeds from player sale transactions are made available to Arsène Wenger for re-investment back into the development of the team.'

Source: www.arsenal.com (see Reference).

LEARNING ACTIVITY 26.3

Revisit the financial statements of the club obtained for Learning Activity 26.1. Look for any unusual items and list these. In two lines explain what each item is and categorize them according to the main elements in a set of financial statements (asset, liability, income expenditure).

Summary

The final financial statements of clubs differ from those of business enterprises in a number of ways. Because clubs are non-profit-seeking organizations, the statement of profit and loss is replaced by an income and expenditure account. However, this is prepared using the same principles, such as the accruals concept. Clubs are also usually managed by voluntary officers whom the members expect to provide a summarized cash book known as a 'receipts and payments account'. The statement of financial position of clubs is much the same as that of a business except that the capital is replaced by a general/accumulated fund, which is an accumulation of previous years' excesses of income over expenditure. Some clubs engage in trading activities such as a bar, in which case it is necessary to include in the final financial statements a bar trading account.

Another major difference between clubs and businesses is that the former often have a variety of different forms of income not normally associated with the latter – in particular annual subscriptions. These are usually accounted for in the income and expenditure account on an accrual basis. This gives rise to subscriptions in advance and in arrears which are shown on the statement of financial position as a current liability or current asset, respectively. However, sometimes subscriptions are accounted for on a strict cash received basis.

The books of account of clubs are often kept on a single-entry basis. In this case the final financial statements will be prepared using the same procedure as described in Chapter 23 'Single Entry and Incomplete Records', with the addition of workings relating to the subscriptions account.

The final financial statements of clubs also sometimes contain a number of special items not normally found in the financial statements of businesses, but which involve the application of certain common principles. Two of these are entrance/joining fees and life membership subscriptions. The matching principle dictates that these be treated as deferred income. Furthermore, donations, bequests and gifts of a material amount should be credited direct to the club's accumulated fund rather than the income and expenditure account where it is of a non-recurring nature. Finally, a club may operate a prize or grant fund. This must be accounted for by means of a fund separate from the general/accumulated fund, and a separate prize fund investment account.

Key terms and concepts

accumulated/general fund	442	income and expenditure account	441
bar trading account	442	life membership subscriptions	449
bequests	448	membership/entrance fees	449
club	441	prize funds	450
deferred income	449	receipts and payments account	442
donations	448	single-entry	443
entrance fees	441	statement of affairs	442
excess of income over expenditure	441	subscriptions in advance	442
gifts	448	subscriptions in arrears	442

An asterisk after the question number indicates that there is a suggested answer on the Online Learning Centre (www.mcgraw-hill.co.uk/textbooks/thomas).

Review questions

26.1* Explain the difference between a receipts and payments account and an income and expenditure account.

26.2 Explain the nature of an accumulated fund in the statement of financial position of a club.

26.3 Describe the entries in the financial statements of a club for each of the following and explain the justification for each treatment:

a Donation of second-hand clothing for resale.

b A gift of a large amount of cash.

c A bequest of premises to be used as a clubhouse.

26.4 Describe two possible methods of accounting for each of the following in the financial statements of clubs and explain the theoretical/conceptual justification for each method:

a Membership/entrance fees.

b Life membership subscriptions.

26.5 Explain the nature and accounting entries in respect of prize funds in the accounts of clubs.

Exercises

26.6

INTERMEDIATE

The secretary of the Woodland Hockey Club gives you the following summary of his cash book for the year ended 31 May 20X2:

Cash book			
	£		£
Balances at commencement of year:		Rent	234
– At bank	63	Printing and stationery	18
– In hand	10	Affiliation fees	12
Subscriptions:		Captain's and secretary's expenses	37
– Supporters	150	Refreshments for visiting teams	61
– Supporters 20X2–20X3 season	20	Annual social	102
Fees per game	170	Equipment purchased	26
Annual social	134	Balance at close of year:	
		– At bank	49
		– In hand	8
	547		547

The secretary also gives you the following information:

	31 May 20X1	31 May 20X2
	£	£
Amounts due to the club:		
Supporters' subscriptions	14	12
Fees per game	78	53
Re annual social	6	–
Amounts owing by the club:		
Rent	72	54
Printing	–	3
Secretary's expenses	4	8
Refreshments	13	12

On 31 May 20X1 the club's equipment appeared in the books at £150. It is desired that 12 per cent be written off the book value of the equipment as it appears on 31 May 20X1.

Required

a Show your computation of the club's accumulated fund as on 31 May 20X1.

b Prepare the income and expenditure account showing the result for the year ended 31 May 20X2, and the statement of financial position as on that date.

(ACCA)

INTERMEDIATE

26.7

The treasurer of the Senior Social Club has prepared the following summary of the club's receipts and payments for the year ended 30 November 20X2.

Senior Social Club			
Receipts and payments account for the year ended 30 November 20X2			
	£		£
Cash and bank balances b/f	810	Secretarial expenses	685
Members' subscriptions	4,250	Rent	2,500
Donations	1,480	Visiting speakers' expenses	1,466
Sales of competition tickets	1,126	Donations to charities	380
		Prizes for competitions	550
		Purchase of equipment	1,220
		Stationery and printing	469
		Balance c/f	396
	7,666		7,666

On 1 December 20X1 the club owned equipment that had cost £3,650 and which was valued at £2,190. The club's equipment as at 30 November 20X2 (inclusive of any purchases during the year) was valued at £1,947.

The following information is available:

As at	1 Dec 20X1	30 Nov 20X2
	£	£
Inventory of prizes	86	108
Owing to suppliers of prizes	314	507
Subscriptions in arrears	240	580
Subscriptions in advance	65	105

Required

a Calculate the value of the accumulated fund of the club as at 1 December 20X1.

b Prepare a subscriptions account for the year ended 30 November 20X2 showing clearly the amount to be transferred to the club's income and expenditure account for the year.

c Prepare a statement showing the surplus or deficit made by the club on competitions for the year ended 30 November 20X2.

d Prepare an income and expenditure account for the year ended 30 November 20X2.

e Prepare the club's statement of financial position as at 30 November 20X2.

(AAT)

26.8*

The Elite Bowling and Social Club prepares its annual financial statements to 31 October. The following receipts and payments account has been prepared by the treasurer:

Receipts and payments account			
	£		£
Cash in hand, 31/10/20X1	10	Bar purchases	1,885
Balances at bank, 31/10/20X1:		Wages	306
– Current account	263	Rent and rates	184
– Deposit account	585	Lighting and heating	143
Spectators' entrance fees	54	New mower (less allowance for old one £40)	120
Subscriptions: – To 31/10/X1	30	General expenses	132
– To 31/10/X2	574	Catering purchases	80
– To 31/10/X3	44	Additional furniture	460
Bar takings	2,285	Cash in hand at 31/10/X2	8
Deposit account interest	26	Balances at bank 31/10/X2:	
Catering receipts	120	– Current account	176
		– Deposit account	497
	3,991		3,991

Additional information

1 The book values of the non-current assets on 31 October 20X1 were: furniture, fixtures and fittings £396 (cost £440), and mower £20 (cost £120).

2 The current assets and liabilities were as follows:

	31 Oct 20X1	31 Oct 20X2
	£	£
Bar inventory at cost	209	178
Amount owed to the brewery for bar purchases	186	248
Due for rent and rates	12	26
Due for lighting and heating	9	11
Subscriptions in arrears	30	50

3 During the year the steward commenced to provide light refreshments at the bar and it has been agreed that in the annual financial statements provision should be made for the payment to him of a bonus of 40 per cent of the gross profit arising from this catering venture.

4 Depreciation to furniture, fixtures and fittings is to be provided at a rate of 10 per cent on cost. No depreciation is to be provided on the new mower, but a full year on the new furniture.

Required

a Prepare a statement showing the accumulated fund of the club as on 31 October 20X1.

b Prepare an income and expenditure account for the year ended 31 October 20X2 (showing separately gross profit on bar sales and catering).

c Prepare statement of financial position as at 31 October 20X2.

(ACCA)

ADVANCED

26.9*

The treasurer of a club has given you the following account of its activities during the year ended 30 June 20X3.

Receipts	£	Payments	£
Bank balance at 1/7/X2 (including £75 received during the year ended 30/6/X2 on the prize fund investments)	390	Additional billiard table with accessories bought 1/7/X2	300
		Repairs to billiard tables	50
Annual subscriptions (including £20 relating to previous year)	340	Purchases for bar	3,680
		Steward's wages and expenses	400
Life membership subscriptions (5 × £16)	80	Rates	140
Sundry lettings	180	Lighting and heating	72
Bar receipts	4,590	Cleaning and laundry	138
Receipts for billiards	275	Sundry expenses	80
Gifts from members	3,500	Prizes awarded for previous year from income available at 1/7/X2	75
Income from £1,500 5 per cent defence bonds allocated specifically for a prize fund	75	Repayment of 5 per cent mortgage on 30/6/X3 with interest for two years	4,400
		Bank balance at 30/6/X3	95
	9,430		9,430

Additional information

1 The freehold building, owned and occupied by the club, was purchased for £6,000 many years ago.

2 On 1 July 20W7 the club acquired six billiard tables for which they paid £1,200, and it is considered that the tables have a life of 12 years.

3 The bar inventory at 1 July 20X2 was £150 and at 30 June 20X3 is £180.

4 Annual subscriptions outstanding from members at 30 June 20X3 amounted to £10.

5 On 1 July 20X2 there were 25 life members who had paid subscriptions of £16 each. During the year ended 30 June 20X3 three of these members had died.

Required

Prepare an income and expenditure account and statement of financial position showing clearly how you have treated the subscriptions of life members and the prize fund.

(ACCA)

26.10

ADVANCED

You have agreed to take over the role of bookkeeper for the AB sports and social club. The summarized statement of financial position on 31.12.X1 as prepared by the previous bookkeeper contained the following items. All figures are in £s.

Assets	£	£
Heating oil for clubhouse		1,000
Bar and café inventories		7,000
New sportswear, for sale, at cost		3,000
Used sportswear, for hire, at valuation		750
Equipment for grounds person – cost	5,000	
– depreciation	(3,500)	1,500
Subscriptions due		200
Bank – current account		1,000
– deposit account		10,000
Claims		
Accumulated fund		23,150
Payables – bar and café goods		1,000
– sportswear		300

The bank account summary for the year to 31.12.X2 contained the following items.

	£
Receipts	
Subscriptions	11,000
Bankings – bar and café	20,000
– sale of sportswear	5,000
– hire of sportswear	3,000
Interest on deposit account	800
Payments	
Rent and repairs of clubhouse	6,000
Heating oil	4,000
Sportswear	4,500
Grounds person	10,000
Bar and café purchases	9,000
Transfer to deposit account	6,000

You discover that the subscriptions due figure as at 31.12.X1 was arrived at as follows.

	£
Subscriptions unpaid for 20X0	10
Subscriptions unpaid for 20X1	230
Subscriptions paid for 20X2	40

Corresponding figures at 31.12.X2 are:

	£
Subscriptions unpaid for 20X0	10
Subscriptions unpaid for 20X1	20
Subscriptions unpaid for 20X2	90
Subscriptions paid for 20X3	200

Subscriptions due for more than 12 months should be written off with effect from 1.1.X2.

	£
Asset balances at 31.12.X2 include:	
Heating oil for clubhouse	700
Bar and café inventories	5,000
New sportswear, for sale, at cost	4,000
Used sportswear, for hire, at valuation	1,000

	£
Closing payables at 31.12.X2 are:	
For bar and café inventories	800
For sportswear	450
For heating oil for clubhouse	200

Two-thirds of the sportswear purchases made in 20X2 had been added to inventories of new sportswear in the figures given in the list of assets above, and one-third had been added directly to the inventory of used sportswear for hire.

Half of the resulting 'new sportswear for sale at cost' at 31.12.X2 is actually over two years old. You decide, with effect from 31.12.X2, to transfer these older items into the inventory of used sportswear at a valuation of 25 per cent of their original cost.

No cash balances are held at 31.12.X1 or 31.12.X2. The equipment for the grounds person is to be depreciated at 10 per cent per annum, on cost.

Required

Prepare the income and expenditure account and statement of financial position for the AB sports club for 20X2, in a form suitable for circulation to members. The information given should be as complete and informative as possible within the limits of the information given to you. All workings must be submitted.

(ACCA)

26.11

ADVANCED

The N. I. Jock United Social Club was started in 20W0 to provide facilities for Jock United Football Supporters in Northern Ireland. At 1 January 20X2 there were 400 paid-up members for 20X1 (£20 per annum) and 20 members who still owed their dues for 20X1. Ten members had already paid their subscriptions for 20X2 before the current year (in advance). Refreshments were served at each match and a group of members provided the meals at cost plus 20 per cent. Travel to matches was arranged and any surplus was put into club funds. Functions during the winter were varied and many were open to the public. The Club rented premises, which they furnished at a cost (in 20W8) of £3,000, and had hired gaming machines on which they paid 30 per cent of the takings.

On 1 January 20X2 the Club owed money to three companies for merchandise. The amounts owed are as follows:

Sam Ltd	£100
Jockie Ltd	£200
Bisto Ltd	£150

During the year the Club received goods from these companies worth the following:

3 February 20X2	Sam Ltd	£1,500
5 August 20X2	Jockie Ltd	£1,200
6 September 20X2	Bisto Ltd	£500

They returned goods to Bisto Ltd worth £500 as they were unhappy with the quality of the products. Sam Ltd gave 10 per cent discount as the Club paid that account within one month.

On the 31 December 20X2 there were unpaid accounts for secretarial expenses of £450 and printing brochures for trips/outings to matches in England of £200. Rates of £600 had been paid to 31 March 20X3. The rates paid last year amounted to £500. The last electricity bill amounting to £600 was paid for on 15 December 20X2 for the period to 31 October 20X2. The bill for the period to 31 January 20X3 has not yet been received.

The following is the cash record for the year to 31 December 20X2:

Cash account			
	£		£
Balance 1 January 20X2	2,500	Merchandise – Sam Ltd	1,350
Subscriptions	8,300	– Jockie Ltd	1,300
Ticket receipts for matches	660	– Bisto Ltd	150
Sale of refreshments	1,100	Refreshments and food	800
Gaming machine receipts	1,600	Printing and stationery:	
Travel to matches	600	– Dances	100
Competition entry fees	200	– Matches	200
Dance receipts	500	Rent	2,000
		Rates	600
		Light and heat	2,000
		General expenses	790
		Dance expenses	400
		Matches – Coach	150
		– Meals	120
		Competition expenses	500
		Secretary's expenses	560
		Filing cabinet	1,000
		Freezer	150
		Balance 31 December 20X2	3,290
	15,460		15,460

Required

a Open personal accounts in the purchases ledger and post the transactions. Write up the purchase ledger control account and reconcile the balance on the control account with the balances on the personal accounts.

b Prepare an income and expenditure account for the year ended 31 December 20X2, taking into consideration that the furnishings have been depreciated at the rate of 10 per cent per annum (reducing balance method) since purchase; that at 1 January 20X2 there was an inventory of refreshments of £300 and that at 31 December 20X2 the inventory had been reduced to £100.

c Prepare a statement of financial position for the club as at 31 December 20X2.

26.12

The treasurer of Murray Golf Club has prepared the following receipts and payments account for the year ended 31 March 20X3:

Receipts and payments accounts				
	£			£
Balance at 1 April 20X2	782	Repairs		256
Subscriptions	4,930	Functions		507
Functions	567	Heat and light		350
Sundry income	58	Telephone		125
Bequest	652	Salary and wages		3,328
Bank interest	120	Extension to clubhouse		800
Sale of land	3,600	General expenses		89
Donations	50	Stationery		25
Bar takings	3,200	Rent		3,300
		Bar purchases		2,800
		Bar rates		200
		Furniture		250
		Motor vehicle		1,250
		Motor expenses		354
		Balance c/d – Cash	100	
		– Bank	225	325
	13,959			13,959

The treasurer has also supplied you with the following information:

1 Subscriptions received included £85, which had been in arrear at 31 March 20X2, and £55, which had been paid for the year commencing 1 April 20X3. In addition three members still owed their fees for the year to 31 March 20X3. One was a junior (membership £15) the other two were senior members (£45 per membership).

2 The land that was sold was valued in the Club's books at £1,500.

3 Depreciation is to be charged as follows.

Buildings	5 per cent per annum straight-line basis.
Motor vehicle	Sum of digits method over 5 years.
Fixtures and fittings	25 per cent reducing balance method.
Furniture	20 per cent reducing balance method

A full year's depreciation is charged in the year of purchase but none is charged in the year of sale.

461

4 Accrued expenses:

	31 March 20X2	31 March 20X3
	£	£
Stationery	15	656
Wages	560	545

The electricity bill for the period to 30 April 20X3 (£450) was paid for on 23 May 20X3.

The rent paid in advance was to cover three full financial years including 20X3.

The interest received in the year is for the period from 1 April 20X2 to 31 December 20X2.

5 It is estimated that 60 per cent of staff wages related to bar work. General expenses includes an amount of £35 for cleaning the windows in the bar for the year.

6 The closing bar inventories have been valued at £990.

7 Repairs include £200, which was paid for a brand new pool table.

8 The following balances are from the Club's books at 31 March 20X2:

	£
Land at cost	8,000
Buildings at cost	6,400
Buildings provision for depreciation	800
Fixtures and fittings at cost	1,250
Fixtures provision for depreciation	250
Furniture at cost	580
Furniture provision for depreciation	180
Subscriptions in arrears (including £15 from a lapsed member)	100
Subscriptions in advance	30
Bar inventories	250

9 At a board meeting it was agreed that the bequest should be capitalized.

Required

a Prepare the opening statement of financial position for Murray Golf Club as at 31 March 20X2.

b Prepare the bar trading income account for Murray Golf Club for the year ended 31 March 20X3.

c Prepare the income and expenditure account for Murray Golf Club for the year ended 31 March 20X3.

d Prepare the statement of financial position for Murray Golf Club as at 31 March 20X3.

26.13

When a Welfare Association was formed on 1.1.20X2, the tenants of all 820 flats on University Street joined as members. The membership fee was agreed at £20 per month. Five hundred and sixty of these tenants agreed also to pay an additional fee of £50 per month for crèche facilities. The council promoted the Association by donating a three-roomed flat, rent-free, for use as offices and approving an annual grant of £50,000. At the end of the first year the Association prepared its Receipts and Payments account as follows.

University Street Flat Tenants' Welfare Association Receipts and payments account for the year to 31.12.20X2			
Receipts	**£**	**Payments**	**£**
Membership fees for year 20X2	133,600	Security Guard's salary	39,200
Membership fees for year 20X3	12,800	Crèche wages	77,600
Crèche fees for year 20X2	251,000	Furniture	32,800
Crèche fees for year 20X3	2,500	Grounds maintenance	25,600
Grant from borough council	50,000	Snooker tables	32,000
Sale: Xmas raffle tickets	14,900	Crèche consumables	42,900
		Xmas party raffle	9,000
		Xmas party expenses	10,300
		Sports consumables	22,400
		Admin. expenses	27,300

Other information

1 Expenditure unpaid at the end of the year is as follows:

Note

Crèche employee's salary	£25,600
Security guard's salary	£2,700
Supplier of crèche consumables	£13,500

2 Sports consumables costing £3,000 remain unused as at 31.12.20X2.

3 Membership fees and crèche fees due for a seven-month period were written off because a tenant had left the country.

4 One-tenth of the cost of furniture should be written off as depreciation.

5 The snooker tables should be depreciated over four years using the sum of digits method.

6 £300 of administration expenses paid relate to next year.

7 £1,000 was posted to crèche wages instead of to the wages of the security guards.

Required

Prepare the income and expenditure account for the year ended 31 December 20X2 and a statement of financial position as at that date.

(*Note*: All workings must be shown.)

ADVANCED

26.14

Belfast Darts Club, though formed in 20W8, never maintained proper books of account. Their transactions, however, were always recorded through the bank account. They have two types of membership: player members pay £40 per month and social members pay £30 per month. A non-refundable fee of £500, charged on joining, is regarded as part of the income for the year. The bank statements for the year ended 31.12.20X2 have been summarized as stated below.

		In respect of the years			
Balance at bank on 1 Jan 20X2					8,500
	20W8–20X0	*20X2*	*20X3*		
Player membership fees	22,400	237,600	3,840		263,840
Social membership fees	26,880	116,100	7,920		150,900
Joining fees					43,000
Collections for charity					15,300
Bar takings					130,960
Sale of refreshments					42,690
Staff salary (20 per cent bar, 10 per cent refreshments, rest general)					(140,960)
Bar rates					(8,000)
Purchase of refreshments					(33,700)
Furniture and fittings					(60,000)
Donations to the charity					(12,400)
Repayment of mortgage loan					(50,000)
Interest on the mortgage loan					(13,750)
Purchase of player consumables					(45,200)
Bar purchases					(133,200)
Membership welfare					(28,520)
Administrative expenses					(53,360)
Clubhouse maintenance					(44,900)
Travel expenses on away matches reimbursed					(28,520)
Balance at bank on 31 December 20X2					2,680

You have gathered the following additional information:

1   £24,880 of player membership subscriptions and £9,500 of social membership subscriptions are to be written off in the year.

2   Regular till collections are made on match days for the benefit of those mentally handicapped.

3 The assets and liabilities of the club include the following:

	31.12.20X1	31.12.20X2
	£	£
Clubhouse at cost	480,000	480,000
Furniture at book value	145,000	?
Trade receivables for player membership fees	56,800	81,020
Trade receivables for social membership fees	38,900	56,920
Inventories of player consumables	22,500	29,100
Inventories of bar supplies	49,300	43,000
Trade receivables for bar sales	12,900	33,100
Subscription in advance – players' membership	2,900	?
Subscription in advance – social membership	5,100	?
Trade payables for bar supplies	11,300	8,800
Trade payables for refreshment supplies	3,120	9,900
Bar rates owing	5,000	6,000
Owed to charity	8,500	?
Loan on mortgage of club house premises	250,000	?

4 The clubhouse is not *depreciated*; one-fifth of the year-end book value of furniture is written off as depreciation.

Required

Prepare the following for Belfast Darts Club, for the year ended 31 December 20X2:

a the opening statement of financial position;

b the bar income account;

c the refreshments income account;

d the income and expenditure account; and

e the closing statement of financial position.

(*Note*: All workings must be shown.)

Reference

Arsenal Holdings PLC (2009) Financial Report for the year ended 31 May 2009, Arsenal Holdings PLC website www.arsenal.com/assets/_files/documents/sep_09/gun_1254124328_PLUS_ANNOUNCEMENT_29-9-09.pdf (accessed May 2011).

When you have read this chapter, log on to the Online Learning Centre for *Introduction to Financial Accounting* at www.mcgraw-hill.co.uk/textbooks/thomas, where you will find multiple choice quizzes, case studies, a glossary and mock exams.

Partnerships

Partnerships

The final financial statements of partnerships

Learning Objectives

After reading this chapter you should be able to do the following:

1 Explain the meaning of the key terms and concepts listed at the end of the chapter.

2 Describe the main characteristics of partnerships.

3 Explain how profits may be shared between partners, including the nature and purpose of partners' salaries, interest on capital and interest on drawings.

4 Explain the difference between partners' capital, current and drawings accounts.

5 Show the journal and ledger entries relating to those items normally found in partners' capital, current and drawings accounts.

6 Prepare partnership final financial statements, including an appropriation account.

7 Show the entries in the ledger and final financial statements relating to partners' commission and a guaranteed share of profit.

8 Explain the difference between a partnership and a limited liability partnership.

27.1 The law and characteristics of partnerships

For a number of commercial reasons, it may be mutually advantageous for two or more people to form a partnership. The Partnership Act 1890 defines a **partnership** as 'the relation which subsists between persons carrying on business in common with a view of profit'. It cannot have fewer than two partners and, at one time, the Act set a limit of 20 partners. However, with the introduction of the Companies Act 1967, this maximum has been relaxed in the case of a number of professional firms, such as accountants and solicitors.

Since partnerships are not able to limit their liability to creditors and other members of the public, there is no need for any special legislation to protect these groups. Thus, partners are largely free to make whatever agreements between themselves that they wish to cover their mutual relationships. The powers and rights of the partners between themselves are governed by any written agreement they may make. This is referred to as the **articles** or **deed of partnership**. It is important for partners to reach an agreement on matters such as detailed in Figure 27.1:

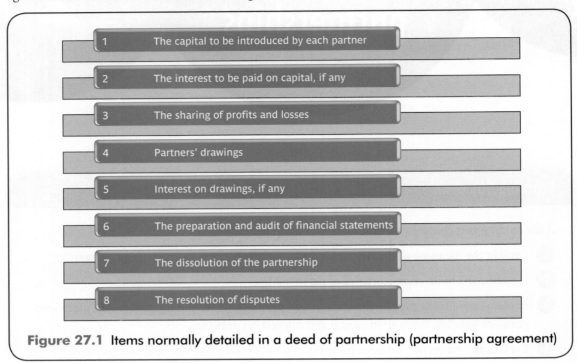

1	The capital to be introduced by each partner
2	The interest to be paid on capital, if any
3	The sharing of profits and losses
4	Partners' drawings
5	Interest on drawings, if any
6	The preparation and audit of financial statements
7	The dissolution of the partnership
8	The resolution of disputes

Figure 27.1 **Items normally detailed in a deed of partnership (partnership agreement)**

In the absence of any partnership agreement, or if the agreement is silent on any of the items 1–8 above then the partnership is subject to the provisions of the Partnership Act 1890, which includes the following:

1 Each partner has **unlimited liability**. That is, if the debts of the partnership cannot be paid because the business has insufficient assets to do so, the creditors have recourse to the private property of the individual partners. The partners are said to be jointly and severally liable for the debts of the firm and therefore a creditor may sue the partnership or any individual partner.

2 Voting powers: in the ordinary day-to-day running of a partnership, individual partners often make routine business decisions without consulting the other partners. At the other extreme, certain fundamental decisions, such as to change the type of business in which the partnership is engaged, or the admission of a new partner, require the consent of all the partners. Other major decisions are supposed to be determined by a majority vote. Each partner has one vote. However, a partnership deed may specify some other distribution of voting power.

3 Every partner is entitled to take part in the management of the business. However, some partnership agreements provide for certain partners to be sleeping or limited partners. Neither of these normally takes part in the management of the business.

4 Every partner is entitled to have access to the books and papers of the partnership. This includes sleeping and limited partners.

5 Each partner is an agent of the partnership and can thus sign contracts on behalf of the partnership, which will then be legally bound to honour them.

6 A new partner can only be admitted to the partnership if all the existing partners give their consent. However, a partnership deed may specify otherwise.

7 A partnership will be dissolved by:

  a any partner giving notice to the other partner(s) of his or her intention to leave the partnership;

  b the death, insanity or bankruptcy of a partner.

27.2 The sharing of profits between the partners

> **LEARNING ACTIVITY 27.1**
>
> Consider the following situation. A and B enter into partnership; A is to work full time in the business while B will only spend a few hours each week on partnership business; B is to put into the business £100,000 as capital whereas A is to contribute capital of only £10,000. You are asked by A and B to suggest how the profits might be shared so as to recompense A for working more hours than B in the business, and to compensate B for having put into the business (and therefore put at risk) substantially more capital than A.

The way this is normally achieved is to give each partner a prior share of the profits as: (1) a **partnership salary** related to the amount of time each devotes to the business; and (2) **interest on the capital** each invests. The remaining profit, which is often referred to as the **residual profit/loss**, can then be divided between the partners according to whatever they agree is fair. This might be equal, since both have already been compensated for the unequal time and capital they contribute.

Another aspect of sharing partnership profits concerns **interest on drawings**. This is intended to compensate the partner who has annual drawings that are less than those of the other partner. Each partner is charged interest on drawings for the period from the date of the drawings to the end of the accounting year in which the drawings took place.

It is important to appreciate that partners' 'salaries', 'interest on capital' and 'interest on drawings' are not actual payments of money; they are only part of a profit-sharing formula. If any such payments are made to a partner, these should be treated as drawings. Indeed, as a general rule *all* payments to partners must be treated as drawings. It should also be observed that salaries, interest on capital and interest on drawings will still arise even if the business makes a loss. In these circumstances they effectively become part of a loss-sharing formula.

If there is no agreement between the partners concerning how profits and losses should be shared, section 24 of the Partnership Act 1890 would be applied as follows:

1 Profits and losses are to be shared equally between the partners.

2 No partner will receive a salary or interest on capital, or be charged interest on drawings.

3 Any loans made by a partner to the business (as distinct from capital introduced) will be entitled to interest at the rate of 5 per cent per annum.

27.3 Capital and current accounts

In the financial statements of sole traders, there is a capital account and usually a drawings account. In the books of a partnership there will be:

1 a **capital account** for each partner. Unlike the capital account of a sole trader, this will only contain the original capital put into the business plus any further capital introduced at a later date. It is regarded as a long-term investment by the partners in the partnership.

2 a **current account** for each partner, in which is entered:

    a drawings of money or goods taken by the partner for his or her own use (debit);

    b interest charged on drawings (debit);

    c interest on loans to the partnership (credit);

    d salary (credit);

    e interest on capital (credit);

    f the partner's share of the residual profit or loss.

There may also be a separate **drawings account** for each partner in which all goods or money taken by the partners during the year are entered instead of putting them in the partners' current accounts. However, at the end of the year these are transferred to the partners' current accounts. Note also that current accounts are sometimes labelled 'drawings accounts'.

The partners' capital accounts are shown on the statement of financial position in the same place as the capital account of a sole trader. Underneath these are entered the balances on the partners' current accounts at the end of the year. If a current account has a debit balance, it may be entered after the net current assets but it is more common to deduct (in parentheses) this from the other partners' current accounts.

 27.4 ## The appropriation account

In partnership final financial statements the statement of profit and loss contains exactly the same entries as that of a sole trader.

After the statement of profit and loss has been prepared, the profit (or loss) for the year is carried down to an **appropriation account** in which is shown the sharing of the profit (or loss) between the partners. The basis for sharing may include partners' salaries, interest on capital and interest on drawings. It will also always contain the division of the remaining amount (the residual profit or loss) in some agreed proportion. The appropriation account is part of the double entry in the ledger and as a general rule it is worth remembering that the double entry for each item in the appropriation account is on the opposite side of the relevant partner's current account. The typical contents of an appropriation account (ledger style) are shown in Figure 27.2. This can be used as a reference to check your double entry.

Appropriation account			
Salaries		*Profit*	*XXX*
– Salary A (to current account)	XX		
– Salary B (to current account)	XXX	*Interest on drawings*	
Interest on capital X%		– A (to current account)	X
– A (to current account)	X	– B (to current account)	X
– B (to current account)	X	– C (to current account)	X
– C (to current account)	X		
Balance (to current account)			
– A 40%	XXX		
– B 40%	XXX		
– C 20%	XX		
	XXX		XXX

Figure 27.2 A pro forma layout of a typical partnership appropriation account (ledger style)

The corresponding pro forma entries to the current account are shown in Figure 27.3.

Current account							
	A	B	C		A	B	C
Drawings	XX	XX	XX	Balance b/d	XX	XX	XX
Interest on drawings	X	X	X	Salary	XX	XXX	–
				Interest on capital	X	X	X
Balance c/d	XX	XX	XX	Profit	XXX	XXX	XX
	XXX	XXX	XXX		XXX	XXX	XXX
				Balance b/d	XX	XX	XX

Figure 27.3 A pro forma example of the layout of a typical partnership current account

The contents of the appropriation account are illustrated in Example 27.1.

EXAMPLE 27.1

Bonnie and Clyde are in partnership sharing profits in the ratio 2 : 1. From the following, you are required to prepare the appropriation account for the year ended 31 December 20X2 and show the relevant items in the statement of financial position at that date.

	Bonnie	Clyde
	£	£
Capital at 31 Dec 20X1	100,000	80,000
Current account balances at 31 Dec 20X1	16,340	28,290
Drawings – 1 Apr 20X2	4,000	8,000
31 Aug 20X2	6,000	9,000
30 Sep 20X2	8,000	–
Salaries	20,000 p.a.	25,000 p.a.
Interest on capital	10% p.a.	10% p.a.
Interest on drawings	5% p.a.	5% p.a.

Clyde introduced additional capital of £10,000 on 1 January 20X2 and Bonnie lent the business £20,000 on 30 June 20X2. The profit for the year ended 31 December 20X2 was £78,700.

Before dividing the profit between the partners, the partners' capital accounts need to be adjusted. These ledger accounts are often prepared in columnar form as follows:

Capital account							
		Bonnie	Clyde			Bonnie	Clyde
		£	£			£	£
20X2				20X2			
				1 Jan	Balance b/d	100,000	80,000
31 Dec	Balance c/d	100,000	90,000	1 Jan	Bank		10,000
		100,000	90,000			100,000	90,000
				20X3			
				1 Jan	Balance b/d	100,000	90,000

The loan from Bonnie is not entered in his capital account but rather in a separate loan account, which constitutes a non-current liability.

Next, it may be useful to prepare a schedule which shows the division of the profits as follows:

	Bonnie	Clyde	Total
	£	£	£
Profit for 20X2			78,700
Loan interest ($\frac{6}{12} \times 5\% \times £20,000$)	500	–	(500)
Partners' salaries	20,000	25,000	(45,000)
Interest on capital:			
10% × £100,000	10,000	–	(10,000)
10% × £90,000	–	9,000	(9,000)
	30,500	34,000	14,200
Interest on drawings (see note 3)	(350)	(450)	800
	30,150	33,550	15,000
Share of residual profit (2 : 1)	10,000	5,000	(15,000)
Totals	40,150	38,550	–

Notes

1 The interest on partners' loans is computed using the rate of 5 per cent per annum specified in the Partnership Act 1890, unless you are told that some other rate has been agreed by the partners.

2 The interest on capital is computed using the balances on the partners' capital accounts and not the current accounts, unless you are told the contrary. Note also that in this example the balance on the capital account at the end of the year can be used because the additional capital was introduced at the start of the year. Where additional capital is introduced at some other date, it will be necessary to compute the interest on a strict time basis.

3 The interest on drawings is calculated on a monthly basis as follows:

Bonnie	$\frac{9}{12} \times 5\% \times £4,000 = 150$
	$\frac{4}{12} \times 5\% \times £6,000 = 100$
	$\frac{3}{12} \times 5\% \times £8,000 = \underline{100}$
	$\underline{350}$
Clyde	$\frac{9}{12} \times 5\% \times £8,000 = 300$
	$\frac{4}{12} \times 5\% \times £9,000 = \underline{150}$
	$\underline{450}$

4 The sum of the total of each column in the profit appropriation schedule should always equal the profit for the year (i.e. £40,150 + £38,550 = £78,700; £30,150 + £33,550 + £15,000 = £78,700, etc.)

The above appropriation schedule can be used to make the necessary entries in the appropriation account and the partners' current accounts in the ledger. The preparation of a schedule is very efficient because the total of each of the columns, showing each partner's total share of the annual net profit, can be entered in the appropriation account and partners' current accounts as single amounts thus:

		Debit	Credit
Debit:	Appropriation account	£78,700	
Credit:	Current accounts: – Bonnie		£40,150
	– Clyde		£38,550

However, for a fuller presentation and to emphasize the double entry, the separate elements are all shown below:

Bonnie and Clyde appropriation account for the year ended 31 December 20X2					
	£	£		£	£
Loan interest – Bonnie			Net profit for year b/d		78,700
$(\frac{6}{12} \times 5\% \times £20,000)$		500	Interest on drawings:		
Salaries – Bonnie	20,000		– Bonnie	350	
– Clyde	25,000	45,000	– Clyde	450	800
Interest on capital :					
– Bonnie (10% × £100,000)	10,000				
– Clyde (10% × £90,000)	9,000	19,000			
Shares of residual profit:					
– Bonnie (2/3)	10,000				
– Clyde (1/3)	5,000	15,000			
		79,500			79,500

The double entry for the items in the appropriation account is in the partners' current accounts, which are usually prepared in columnar form as follows:

Current accounts					
	Bonnie	Clyde		Bonnie	Clyde
	£	£		£	£
Drawings	18,000	17,000	Balance b/d	16,340	28,290
Interest on drawings	350	450	Loan interest	500	–
Balance c/d	38,490	49,840	Salaries	20,000	25,000
			Interest on capital	10,000	9,000
			Shares of profit	10,000	5,000
	56,840	67,290		56,840	67,290
			Balance b/d	38,490	49,840

The relevant balances will then be included in the statement of financial position as follows:

Bonnie and Clyde statement of financial position as at 31 December 20X2		
	£	£
EQUITY AND LIABILITIES		
Owners' equity		
Capital		
– Bonnie		100,000
– Clyde		90,000
		190,000
Current accounts		
– Bonnie	38,490	
– Clyde	49,840	88,330
		278,330
Non-current liabilities		
Loan – Bonnie		20,000
Total non-current liabilities		20,000
Total equity and liabilities		298,330

Alternatively, these can be shown on the statement of financial position in columnar form, as follows:

	Bonnie	Clyde	Total
EQUITY AND LIABILITIES			
Owners' equity			
	£	£	£
Capital	100,000	90,000	190,000
Current accounts	38,490	49,840	88,330
Total owners' equity	138,490	139,840	278,330
Non-current liabilities			
Loan – Bonnie			20,000
Total non-current liabilities			20,000
Total equity and liabilities			298,330

In practice and when answering examination questions it is not usual to show final financial statements in account form. Thus, the appropriation account is not normally prepared in account form. Instead this can either be presented as a schedule, as shown above, or in a vertical format as illustrated below. Whichever presentation is adopted, it is advisable to show each of the entries in the partners' current accounts relating to salaries, interest on capital, and so on as above, rather than the totals of each of the partner's columns in the schedule. Moreover, the vertical format shown below is generally preferable to a schedule because the use of an analysis column for each partner serves little purpose when the entries in the partners' current accounts are done individually. This format has thus been used in the solutions to the exercises in the student OLC.

Bonnie and Clyde appropriation account for the year ended 31 December 20X2			
	£	£	£
Profit for the year			78,700
Add : Interest on drawings:			
– Bonnie		350	
– Clyde		450	800
			79,500
Less : Loan interest – Bonnie		500	
Salaries:			
– Bonnie	20,000		
– Clyde	25,000	45,000	
Interest on capital:			
– Bonnie	10,000		
– Clyde	9,000	19,000	64,500
Residual profit			15,000
Shares of residual profit:			
– Bonnie			10,000
– Clyde			5,000
			15,000

Notes

1 Interest on partners' loans is commonly entered in the appropriation account, particularly in examination questions that do not require the preparation of a statement of profit and loss. However, this is not strictly an appropriation of profit but rather an expense that should be entered in the statement of profit and loss as a charge/deduction in arriving at the profit (or loss) for the year.

2 Where money which is described as 'salaries' has actually been paid to the partners this must be treated as drawings and not included in the statement of profit and loss as wages and salaries. However, this may be interpreted as indicating that the partners wish to give themselves a prior share of profits in the form of a salary. In this case the amounts paid must still be treated as drawings but an equivalent amount is also entered in the appropriation account as salaries, as described above.

3 Additional capital introduced during the year may include assets other than cash. This would usually be entitled to interest on capital from the date the assets were introduced until the end of the year in question (and subsequent years).

4 Interest is usually only charged on cash and cheque drawings and not on goods taken by the partners for their own use.

5 Losses would be shared in the same ratio as profit. If, in the case of Example 27.1, the profit for the year had been only £55,000, the schedule of division of profits would be as follows:

	Bonnie	Clyde	Total
	£	£	£
Profit for year			55,000
Loan interest	500	–	(500)
Salaries	20,000	25,000	(45,000)
Interest on capital	10,000	9,000	(19,000)
	30,500	34,000	(9,500)
Interest on drawings	(350)	(450)	800
	30,150	33,550	(8,700)
Shares of residual loss (2 : 1)	(5,800)	(2,900)	8,700
	24,350	30,650	–

Note that loan interest, salaries, interest on capital and interest on drawings are included even if there is a net loss for the year (i.e. before the appropriation). Salaries, and so on, simply increase the amount of the residual loss.

27.5 Partners' commission

Some partnership businesses are departmentalized, with each of the selling departments being managed by a different partner. In such circumstances it is common for partners' salaries to take the form of an agreed **partners' commission** expressed as a percentage of the profit of their department. This necessitates the preparation of a trading account for each department, which normally takes the form of a columnar trading account, containing columns on both the debit and credit sides for each department. Computing the profits of each partner's department is done in the same way as departmental accounts, a short description of which is given in Appendix A (p.481) to this chapter. Having ascertained the profit of each department, the partner's commission can be calculated and then accounted for in exactly the same way as partners' salaries.

27.6 A guaranteed share of profit

Some partnership agreements include a clause which states that if a particular partner's share of profit in any year is below some agreed figure, then all or certain other partners will make it up to the agreed amount from their shares of profit. The agreed amount is referred to as a **guaranteed share of profit**; the amount by which the actual share of profit falls short of the guaranteed amount is usually shared (i.e. made up) by the other partners in their profit-sharing ratio. Such a guarantee is fairly common in professional firms as an enticement to an employee to become a partner while at the same time being guaranteed an amount equal to the employee's existing remuneration. The guaranteed amount may include or exclude the partner's interest on capital and/or salary, but in the absence of information to the contrary it is usually taken to be the residual profit share that is guaranteed. Example 27.2 shows how to account for a guaranteed share of profit.

If, in the amended Example 27.1, when profits are only £55,000, Bonnie was guaranteed a share of residual profit of at least £2,000, the profit-sharing schedule would appear as follows:

	Bonnie	Clyde	Total
	£	£	£
Profit for year	–	–	55,000
Salaries, interest on loan, capital, and drawings	30,150	33,550	(63,700)
Share of residual loss	2,000	(10,700)	8,700
	32,150	22,850	–

Limited liability partnerships

Limited liability partnerships (LLP) were introduced in the UK under the Limited Liability Partnership Act 2000 and the Limited Liability Partnerships Act (Northern Ireland) 2002. They have some characteristics that are similar to companies – the partners are seen as being legally independent from the partnership, which has its own legal identity. Just like a company, the responsibility of the partners for the debts of the LLP is limited to the amounts invested by the partners – hence their liability is limited. However, the partners are taxed in a similar manner to partners in a normal partnership. Many accountancy and law partnerships have became LLPs in response to negligence claims being made against partnerships (see real world example 27.1).

REAL WORLD EXAMPLE 27.1

Deloitte opts for limited liability

'Deloitte & Touche yesterday became the last of the Big Four accounting firms to say it would adopt limited liability status in an attempt to protect partners from Enron-style negligence claims.

The UK arm, which absorbed Andersen's former partners and much of its business after the firm's collapse last year, announced its intention to convert in early summer. PricewaterhouseCoopers, Ernst & Young and KPMG have switched already.

Sources said the firm had little choice because recruitment has become increasingly difficult following Andersen's demise. Partners, who share the firm's liabilities as well as its profits, are concerned that a successful negligence claim could leave them destitute.

Limited liability ringfences the liability only around those partners involved in a failed audit, leaving others in the partnership unaffected. As a condition, however, the firm must open up its books like a public company.'

Source: Daily Telegraph 26/03/03; http://www.accountancy.com.pk/newsprac.asp?newsid=237

**LEARNING
ACTIVITY
27.2**

Visit the Deloitte LLP website and view their financial statements for the most recent year (http://www.deloitte.com). Note how the format of LLP financial statements is consistent with that of a company, not a partnership. *Also, in the UK the heading Balance Sheet is still used by many companies instead of Statement of Financial Position.*

Summary

A partnership exists when between 2 and 20 persons (or more in the case of professional firms) carry on business with a view of profit. One of the main characteristics of partnerships is that the partners have unlimited liability. They are thus jointly and severally liable for the partnership debts. Each partner is also an agent of the partnership, entitled to take part in the management, and has equal voting rights.

However, the articles or deed of partnership may contain any form of agreement relating to the rights of partners between themselves. This is particularly important with regard to the sharing of profits and losses. Where partners contribute unequal amounts of capital and/or time, it is common to find a profit-sharing formula that includes giving each partner a prior share of profits as interest on capital and/or a salary. Similarly, where partners have unequal amounts of drawings, they may decide to charge each other interest on drawings as a part of the profit-sharing formula.

The statements of profit and loss of partnerships are the same as those of sole traders. However, the net profit (or loss) is carried down into an appropriation account in which is shown the shares of profit appropriated to each partner. The statement of financial position of partnerships is the same as that of a sole trader, except that instead of having a single capital account there is a capital and current account for each partner.

Sometimes partners' salaries take the form of a commission that is expressed as a percentage of the gross (or net) profit of a department or branch that is managed by each partner. Some partnership agreements also contain a clause guaranteeing a particular partner a minimum amount as his or her share of the annual profit. In this case, the amount by which the actual share of the annual profit falls short of the minimum is made up from the other partners' share(s) of profit (in their profit-sharing ratio).

Key terms and concepts

appropriation account	472	interest on drawings	471
articles/deed of partnership	470	limited liability partnerships (LLP)	479
capital account	471	partners' commission	478
current account	472	partnership	469
drawings account	472	partnership salary	471
guaranteed share of profit	478	residual profit/loss	471
interest on the capital	471	unlimited liability	470

Appendix A: Departmental accounts

Where it is decided to produce separate profit or loss results for each trading department within a business, in addition to identifying the sales for each unit and tracking costs that are specifically identifiable to the departments, it is necessary to apportion (i.e. divide up on the basis of ratios) the untraceable overhead costs. No matter how carefully the apportionment ratios are selected, they will depend on the exercise of judgement, and to that extent are arbitrary. The basis should be chosen to attempt to reflect the extra cost likely to be caused by the particular department or, failing that, the benefits the department receives. An illustration of the preparation of departmental financial statements is given in Example 27.3.

EXAMPLE 27.3

Status Stores run three sales departments; clothing, footwear and stationery. For accounting purposes departmental financial statements are to be prepared, apportioning building costs (rent, etc.) on the basis of floor space occupied and office administration in proportion to gross profit. The following information has been extracted from the store's accounting records for the year ended 31 December 20X3:

	Clothing	Footwear	Stationery
	£	£	£
Sales revenue	47,000	27,000	26,000
Purchases	23,000	16,000	10,500
Wages	2,500	2,100	1,800
Inventories at 1 Jan 20X3	6,000	1,000	500
Inventories at 31 Dec 20X3	4,000	2,000	1,000
Floor space (in sq. m)	3,000	2,000	1,000
Rent, rates, lighting, heating and building maintenance (all departments)		£13,800	
Administration and office salaries, etc.		£20,000	

Status Stores

Departmental statement of profit and loss for the year ended 31 December 20X3

	Clothing		Footwear		Stationery	
	£	£	£	£	£	£
Sales revenue		47,000		27,000		26,000
Less: Cost of sales:						
Opening inventory	6,000		1,000		500	
Add: Purchases	23,000		16,000		10,500	
	29,000		17,000		11,000	
Less: Closing inventory	4,000	25,000	2,000	15,000	1,000	10,000
Gross profit		22,000		12,000		16,000
Less: Wages	2,500		2,100		1,800	
Building costs (3 : 2 : 1)	6,900		4,600		2,300	
Administration (22 : 12 : 16)	8,800	18,200	4,800	11,500	6,400	10,500
Profit for the year		3,800		500		5,500

It is not usual to have separate statements of financial position for each department.

An asterisk after the question number indicates that there is a suggested answer on the Online Learning Centre (www.mcgraw-hill.co.uk/textbooks/thomas).

connect Review questions

27.1 a Define a partnership.

b What are the legal limits on the number of partners?

c Outline the principal matters normally found in the articles or deed of partnership.

27.2* Describe the main characteristics of a partnership.

27.3 If there is no partnership agreement the provisions of the Partnership Act 1890 apply. List the main provisions of this Act with regard to the rights of partners between themselves, including the sharing of profits or losses.

27.4 Explain each of the following in the context of partnership profit sharing:

a partners' salaries;

b interest on capital;

c interest on drawings;

d residual profit.

27.5 Lane and Hill have decided to form a partnership. Lane is to contribute £150,000 as capital and Hill £20,000. Hill is to work full time in the business and Lane one day a week. Because Hill has no other income, she anticipates making drawings of £1,000 per month from the partnership. Lane expects to make drawings of about £1,000 per quarter.

You have been asked to advise the partners on how to share profits in such a way as to compensate each of them for their unequal contributions of capital and labour and withdrawals.

27.6 Explain the difference between each of the following ledger accounts in the books of a partnership:

a capital account;

b current account;

c drawings account.

connect Exercises

BASIC

27.7*

Clayton and Hammond are in partnership sharing profits and losses equally. The partnership agreement provides for annual salaries of Clayton: £17,000 and Hammond: £13,000. It also provides for interest on capital of 8 per cent per annum and interest on drawings of 4 per cent per annum.

The following additional information relates to the accounting year ending 30 June 20X3:

	Clayton	Hammond
	£	£
Capital at 1 July 20X2	90,000	60,000
Current account at 1 July 20X2	16,850	9,470
Drawings – 1 October 20X2	3,000	2,000
– 1 March 20X3	5,000	1,000
Capital introduced – 1 November 20X2	10,000	–
Loan by Hammond – 1 April 20X3	–	20,000

The profit for the year shown in the statement of profit and loss for the year ended 30 June 20X3 was £67,500.

Required

Prepare the appropriation account, capital account and current account. Show all the accounts in account format.

27.8

BASIC

Mary and Seamus are in partnership sharing profits and losses equally. The partnership agreement provides for annual salaries of £34,000 for Mary and £22,000 for Seamus. It also provides for interest on capital of 8 per cent per annum and interest on drawings of 5 per cent per annum.

You are given the following additional information relating to the accounting year ending 30 June 20X3.

	Mary	Seamus
	£	£
Capital at 1 July 20X2	180,000	60,000
Current account at 1 July 20X2	33,850	20,470
Drawings – 1 October 20X2	6,000	5,000
– 1 March 20X3	12,000	4,000
Capital introduced – 1 November 20X2	30,000	–
Loan by Seamus (5%) – 1 April 20X3	–	50,000

The profit for the year shown in the statement of profit and loss for the year ended 30 June 20X3 was £150,000.

Required

a Prepare the following accounts:

  i Appropriation account

  ii Capital accounts

  iii Current accounts

b Describe the main characteristics of a partnership.

BASIC

27.9

Anna and Thomas are in partnership sharing profits and losses equally. The partnership agreement provides for an annual salary to Anna of £57,000. It also provides for interest on capital of 10 per cent per annum and interest on drawings of 12 per cent per annum.

The following additional information relates to the accounting year ending 30 June 20X3:

	Anna	Thomas
	£	£
Opening capital balance	150,000	50,000
Opening current account balance	5,000	12,000
Drawings – 1 July 20X2	10,000	10,000
Drawings – 1 October 20X2	10,000	15,000
Drawings – 1 December 20X2	12,000	10,000
Drawings – 1 March 20X3	5,000	8,000
Capital introduced – 1 December 20X2	50,000	
Loan by Anna – 1 December 20X2 (15%)	100,000	

The profit for the year shown in the statement of profit and loss for the year ended 30 June 20X3 was £180,000.

Required

a Prepare the following accounts:

  i   Appropriation account

  ii Capital accounts

  iii Current accounts

BASIC

27.10

Light and Dark are in partnership sharing profits and losses in the ratio 7 : 3, respectively. The following information has been taken from the partnership records for the financial year ended 31 May 20X3:

Partners' capital accounts, balances as at 1 June 20X2:

Light	£200,000
Dark	£140,000

Partners' current accounts, balances as at 1 June 20X2:

Light	£15,000 Credit
Dark	£13,000 Credit

During the year ended 31 May 20X3 the partners made the following drawings from the partnership bank account:

Light	£10,000 on 31 August 20X2
	£10,000 on 30 November 20X2
	£10,000 on 28 February 20X3
	£10,000 on 31 May 20X3
Dark	£7,000 on 31 August 20X2
	£7,000 on 30 November 20X2
	£7,000 on 28 February 20X3
	£7,000 on 31 May 20X3

Interest is to be charged on drawings at the rate of 12 per cent per annum. Interest is allowed on capital accounts and credit balances on current accounts at the rate of 12 per cent per annum. Dark is to be allowed a salary of £15,000 per annum.

The net profit of the partnership for the year ended 31 May 20X3 is £102,940.

Required

a A computation of the amount of interest chargeable on each partner's drawings for the year ended 31 May 20X3.

b The partnership appropriation account for the year ended 31 May 20X3.

c A computation of the balance on each partner's current account as at 31 May 20X3.

(AAT)

27.11

INTERMEDIATE

The partnership of Sewell, Grange and Jones has just completed its first year in business. The partnership agreement stipulates that profits should be apportioned in the ratio of Sewell 3, Grange 2 and Jones 1 after allowing interest on capital at 12 per cent per annum and crediting Sewell with a salary of £15,000.

The following information relates to their first financial year that ended on 31 October 20X3:

1 The partners introduced the following amounts as capital on 1 November 20X2:

	£
Sewell	50,000
Grange	40,000
Jones	20,000

2 Cash drawings during the year were:

	£
Sewell	3,900
Grange	4,500
Jones	2,400

3 The draft statement of profit and loss for the year showed a profit for the year of £61,720.

4 Included in the motor expenses account for the year was a bill for £300 that related to Grange's private motoring expenses.

5 No entries had been made in the financial statements to record the following:

a As a result of a cash flow problem during April, Grange invested a further £10,000 as capital with effect from 1 May 20X3, and on the same date Jones brought into the business additional items of equipment at an agreed valuation of £6,000. In addition, in order to settle a debt, Jones had privately undertaken some work for Foster, a creditor of the partnership. Foster accepted the work as full settlement of the £12,000 the partnership owed her for materials.

b Sewell had accepted a holiday provided by Miller, a credit customer of the partnership. The holiday, which was valued at £1,000, was accepted in full settlement of a debt of £2,500 that Miller owed to the partnership and that he was unable to pay.

c Each partner had taken goods for his own use during the year at cost as follows:

	£
Sewell	1,400
Grange	2,100
Jones	2,100

Note: It is the policy of the firm to depreciate equipment at the rate of 10 per cent per annum based on the cost of equipment held at the end of each financial year.

Required

a The appropriation account for the year ended 31 October 20X3 showing clearly the corrected profit from the first year's trading.

b The capital and current accounts of Sewell, Grange and Jones for the year ended 31 October 20X3.

(AEB)

27.12*

The following is the trial balance of Peace and Quiet, grocers, as at 31 December 20X2.

	Debit	Credit
	£	£
Capital: Peace		10,000
Capital: Quiet		5,000
Current account: Peace		1,280
Current account: Quiet		3,640
Purchases/sales revenue	45,620	69,830
Trade receivables/trade payables	1,210	4,360
Leasehold shop at cost	18,000	
Equipment at cost	8,500	
Depreciation on equipment		1,200
Shop assistants' salaries	5,320	
Light and heat	1,850	
Stationery	320	
Bank interest and charges	45	
Inventory	6,630	
Bank	3,815	
Drawings – Peace 1 May 20X2	2,200	
– Quiet 1 September 20X2	1,800	
	95,310	95,310

Additional information

1 The inventory at 31 December 20X2 was valued at £5,970.

2 There is electricity accrued at the end of the year of £60.

3 Stationery unused at 31 December 20X2 was valued at £50.

4 The equipment is depreciated at 10 per cent per annum on the reducing balance method.

5 There is a partnership deed that says that each partner is to be credited with interest on capital at 10 per cent per annum; salaries of £6,200 per annum for Peace and £4,800 per annum for Quiet; and charged interest on drawings of 8 per cent per annum The remainder of the profit is to be divided equally between the partners.

6 Included in the capital of Peace is capital introduced of £1,000 on 1 April 20X2 and a loan to the partnership of £2,000 on 1 October 20X2.

You are required to prepare the statement of profit and loss and appropriation account for the year and a statement of financial position at 31 December 20X2.

27.13

Peter and Paul, whose year end is 30 June, are in business as food wholesalers. Their partnership deed states that:

a profits and losses are to be shared equally;

b salaries are: Peter £20,000 per annum; Paul £18,000 per annum;

c interest on capital of 10 per cent is allowed;

d interest on drawings of 5 per cent is charged;

e interest on loans from partners is given at the rate shown in the Partnership Act 1890.

The trial balance as at 30 June 20X3 is as follows:

	Debit	Credit
	£	£
Capital – Peter		100,000
– Paul		80,000
Current accounts – Peter	804	
– Paul		21,080
Loan at 1 July 20X2 – Peter		12,000
Freehold premises at cost	115,000	
Plant and machinery at cost	77,000	
Provision for depreciation on plant		22,800
Motor vehicles at cost	36,500	
Provision for depreciation on vehicles		12,480
Loose tools at 1 July 20X2	1,253	
Inventories	6,734	
Trade receivables	4,478	
Trade payables		3,954
Bank	7,697	
Electricity accrued at 1 July 20X2		58
Paid for electricity	3,428	
Purchases	19,868	
Sales revenue		56,332
Warehouse wages	23,500	
Rates	5,169	
Postage and telephone	4,257	
Printing and stationery	2,134	
Provision for bad debts		216
Selling expenses	1,098	
	308,920	308,920

You also ascertain the following:

1 Inventory at 30 June 20X3 is £8,264.

2 Depreciation by the straight line method is 10 per cent per annum on plant and machinery and 20 per cent per annum on motor vehicles. The latter are used by the administrative staff. The revaluation method of depreciation is used for loose tools. These have a value at 30 June 20X3 of £927.

3 Included in wages are drawings of £6,000 by Peter on 1 March 20X3 and £8,000 by Paul on 1 October 20X2.

4 The provision for bad debts at 30 June 20X3 is to be £180.

5 Trade receivables include bad debts of £240.

6 Sales revenue includes goods that are on sale or return at a price of £200. The cost price of these is £160.

7 Electricity accrued at 30 June 20X3 amounts to £82.

8 Rates prepaid at 30 June 20X3 are £34.

Required

Prepare a statement of profit and loss and appropriation account for the year ended 30 June 20X3 and a statement of financial position at that date. Present your answer in vertical form.

27.14*

ADVANCED

Simon, Wilson and Dillon are in partnership. The following trial balance has been prepared on 31 December 20X2:

	Debit £	Credit £
Capital accounts – Simon		35,000
– Wilson		25,000
– Dillon		10,000
Current accounts – Simon		5,600
– Wilson		4,800
– Dillon	1,800	
Freehold land and buildings	65,000	
Inventories	34,900	
Bank	10,100	
Delivery vehicles at cost	30,000	
Provision for depreciation on vehicles		18,000
Goodwill at cost	11,000	
8% mortgage on premises		40,000
Salesmen's salaries	19,480	
Sales ledger control account	28,000	
Purchases ledger control account		25,000
Unquoted investments	6,720	
Loose tools at valuation	1,200	
Sales revenue		130,000
Investment income		800
Returns	400	600
Purchases	64,000	
Rates	12,100	
Motor expenses	2,800	
Provision for bad debts		400
Mortgage interest paid	1,600	
Printing and stationery	1,100	
Extension to premises	5,000	
	295,200	295,200

Additional information

1 The inventory at 31 December 20X2 was valued at £31,000.

2 There is investment income accrued at 31 December 20X2 of £320.

3 The inventory of stationery at 31 December 20X2 was £170.

4 At the same date there were motor expenses accrued of £240 and rates paid in advance of £160.

5 The provision for bad debts at 31 December 20X2 is to be adjusted to 2 per cent of trade receivables.

6 Mortgage interest accrued should be provided for at the end of the year.

7 Depreciation on vehicles, on a strict time basis, is 10 per cent per annum using the straight-line method.

8 The loose tools in inventory at 31 December 20X2 were valued at £960.

9 The following errors have been found:

   a unrecorded in the ledger is the sale of a delivery vehicle on credit on 1 November 20X2 for £1,900 – this vehicle cost £2,400 when it was purchased on 1 April 20X0;

   b bad debts for this year of £2,000 have not been written off;

   c bank charges of £130 have been omitted from the books.

Simon and Dillon are to be allocated salaries of £15,000 and £10,000 per annum, respectively. All partners will be entitled to interest on capital of 10 per cent per annum. The remaining profit or loss is shared between Simon, Wilson and Dillon in the ratio of 2 : 2 : 1, respectively.

You are required to prepare in vertical form a statement of profit and loss and appropriation account for the year ended 31 December 20X2 and a statement of financial position at that date.

ADVANCED

27.15

A, B, C and D were partners in a garage business comprising (1) petrol sales, (2) repairs and servicing and (3) second-hand car dealing. A was responsible for petrol sales, B for repairs and servicing and C for second-hand car deals, while D acted purely in an advisory capacity.

The partnership agreement provided the following:

1 Interest on fixed capital is to be provided at a rate of 10 per cent per annum.

   a Each working partner is to receive commission of 10 per cent of the gross profit of that partner's own department.

   b Profits are shared as follows: A: $\frac{2}{10}$, B: $\frac{3}{10}$, C: $\frac{3}{10}$, D: $\frac{2}{10}$

   c Financial statements are to be made up annually to 30 September.

A trial balance extracted from the books at 30 September 20X3 showed the following balances:

	Debit	Credit
	£	£
A Capital account		3,500
Current account		1,350
Drawings account	6,000	
B Capital account		7,500
Current account		7,500
Drawings account	13,250	
C Capital account		6,500
Current account		5,500
Drawings account	10,500	
D Capital account		12,500
Current account		2,150
Drawings account	3,500	
Freehold premises at cost	25,000	
Goodwill at cost	10,000	
Servicing tools and equipment at cost	9,000	
Servicing tools and equipment – accumulated depreciation to 1 October 20X2		1,350
Bank balance		10,105
Inventories at 1 October 20X2 – petrol	950	
– spares	525	
– second-hand cars	6,350	
Trade receivables	4,350	
Cash in hand	125	
Trade payables		2,350
Sales – petrol		68,650
– servicing and repairs		86,750
– cars		156,000
Purchases – petrol	58,500	
– spares	51,650	
– second-hand cars	118,530	
Wages – forecourt attendants	5,750	
– mechanics	31,350	
– car sales staff	8,550	
– office personnel	1,850	
Rates	2,500	
Office expenses	1,800	
Heating and lighting	550	
Advertising	775	
Bank interest	350	
	371,705	371,705

Additional information

1 Inventories at 30 September 20X3:

	£
Petrol	1,050
Spares	475
Second-hand cars	9,680

2 Depreciation on tools and equipment is to be provided at 5 per cent per annum by the straight-line method.

3 Your fees for preparation of the financial statements will be £175.

4 The service department did work valued at £11,300 on the second-hand cars.

5 The service department used old cars valued at £550 for spare parts in services and repairs.

Required

a Prepare a statement of profit and loss for the year ended 30 September 20X3.

b Prepare a statement of financial position at 30 September 20X3.

c The partners' current accounts in columnar form for the year.

(ACCA)

27.16

INTERMEDIATE

a When accounting for the relationship of partners *inter se*, the partnership agreement provides the rules which, in the first instance, are to be applied.

What information would you expect to find in a partnership agreement to provide such rules, and what should you do if the agreement fails to deal with any aspect of the partnership relationship that affects the financial statements?

b A, B and C are in partnership, agreeing to share profits in the ratio 4 : 2 : 1. They have also agreed to allow interest on capital at 8 per cent per annum; a salary to C of £5,000 per annum; and to charge interest on drawings made in advance of the year end at a rate of 10 per cent per annum.

A has guaranteed B a minimum annual income of £6,500, gross of interest on drawings. The statement of financial position as at 30 June 20X2 disclosed the following:

EQUITY AND LIABILITIES		£	£
Owners' equity			
Capital	A	50,000	
	B	30,000	
	C	10,000	90,000
Current accounts	A	2,630	
	B	521	
	C	(418)	2,733
			92,733
Non-current liabilities			
Loan account	A		15,000
Total equity and liabilities			107,733
Drawings during the year were: A £6,400; B £3,100; C £2,000.			
Profit for the year to 30 June 20X3 was £24,750.			

You are required to prepare the current accounts for the partners as at 30 June 20X3.

(ACCA, adapted)

27.17

Brick, Stone and Breeze carry on a manufacturing business in partnership, sharing profits and losses: Brick one-half, Stone one-third and Breeze one-sixth. It is agreed that the minimum annual share of profit to be credited to Breeze is to be £2,200, and any deficiency between this figure and her true share of the profits is to be borne by the other two partners in the ratio that they share profits. No interest is to be allowed or charged on partners' capital or current accounts.

The trial balance of the firm as on 30 June 20X3 was as follows:

	Debit	Credit
	£	£
Inventory on 1 July 20X2	7,400	
Purchases	39,100	
Manufacturing wages	8,600	
Salaries	5,670	
Rates, telephone and insurance	1,744	
Incidental trade expenses	710	
Repairs and renewals	1,250	
Cash discounts allowed	280	
Cash discounts received		500
Office expenses	3,586	
Carriage inwards	660	
Carriage outwards	850	
Professional charges	500	
Sales revenue		69,770
Provision for doubtful debts as at 1 July 20X2		400
Provision for depreciation as at 1 July 20X2:		
Machinery and plant		2,500
Motor vehicles		1,300
Capital accounts:		
Brick		9,000
Stone		5,000
Breeze		4,000
Current accounts as at 1 July 20X2:		
Brick		1,900
Stone	500	
Breeze		400
Freehold buildings, at cost	9,800	
Machinery and plant, at cost	8,200	
Motor vehicles, at cost	2,500	
Bank balance	750	
Sales ledger balances	7,000	
Bought ledger balances		4,330
	99,100	99,100

Additional information

1 An amount of £3,000, for goods sent out on sale or return, has been included in sales. These goods were charged out to customers at cost plus 25 per cent and they were still in the customers' hands on 30 June 20X3, unsold.

2 Included in the item, repairs and renewals is an amount of £820 for an extension to the factory.

3 Telephone and insurance paid in advance amounted to £424 and £42 was owing in respect of a trade expense.

4 A debt of £80 has turned out to be bad and is to be written off.

5 The provision for doubtful debts is to be increased to £520.

6 Provision for depreciation on machinery and plant and on motor vehicles is to be made at the rate of 10 per cent and 20 per cent per annum, respectively, on the cost.

7 The value of the inventory on hand on 30 June 20X3 was £7,238.

8 Each month Brick has drawn £55, Stone £45 and Breeze £20, and the amounts have been included in salaries.

Required

a Prepare the statement of profit and loss for the year ended 30 June 20X3.

b Write up the partners' current accounts, in columnar form, for the year.

c Draw up the statement of financial position as on 30 June 20X3.

(ACCA)

ADVANCED

27.18

A. Cherry owned a farmhouse and land, the latter being used by him and his sons, Tom and Leo, in carrying on a fruit and poultry business in partnership. The partnership agreement stipulated that the father should take one-sixth of the profits, such to be not less than £1,200 per annum, the sons sharing the remainder equally.

The following are extracts from the trial balance of the business as on 31 December 20X3:

	Debit	Credit
	£	£
Purchases – poultry	2,160	
– feeding stuffs	30,720	
– sprays and fertilizers	14,510	
– spraying machine	4,600	
Wages	29,080	
General expenses (not apportionable)	8,420	
Sales – fruit		60,220
– poultry		5,580
– eggs		58,430
– motor mower (cost £900 written down to £500)		460
Capital accounts – A. Cherry		64,500
– Tom		33,400
– Leo	8,400	
Drawings – A. Cherry	9,300	
Equipment at 1 January 20X3 at cost	34,200	
Equipment at 1 January provision for depreciation		15,100

Inventories on hand were as follows:

	31 Dec 20X2	31 Dec 20X3
	£	£
Sprays and fertilizers	3,100	2,890
Poultry	3,200	1,540
Feeding stuffs	3,630	4,120

Additional information

1 Drawings by Tom and Leo have been £150 and £140 per week, respectively. The amounts have been included in the wages account. Of the wages, one-quarter is to be charged to the fruit department and three-quarters to the poultry department.

2 The father and son Tom live in the farmhouse and are to be charged jointly per annum £300 for fruit, and £680 for eggs and poultry, such charges being shared equally. Leo is to be charged £380 for fruit and £620 for eggs and poultry.

3 Independent of the partnership, Leo kept some pigs on the farm and in respect of this private venture he is to be charged £1,400 for feeding stuffs and £400 for wages.

4 A. Cherry is to be credited with £3,600 for rent of the land (to be charged as to two-thirds to the fruit and one-third to the poultry departments), and Tom is to be credited with £840 by way of salary for packing eggs and dressing poultry.

5 Eggs sold in December 20X3 and paid for in January 20X4 amounted to £2,430 and this sum was not included in the trial balance.

6 An account to 31 December 20X3 for £240 was received from a veterinary surgeon after the trial balance had been prepared. This account included a sum of £140 in respect of professional work as regards Leo's pigs, which he himself paid.

7 Annual provision was to be made for depreciation on equipment at 10 per cent on cost at the end of the year.

Required

a A trading account (showing separately the trading profit on the fruit and poultry departments) and appropriation accounts for the year ended 31 December 20X3.

b The partners' capital accounts in columnar form showing the balances as on 31 December 20X3.

(ACCA)

27.19

Field, Green and Lane are in partnership making up financial statements annually to 31 March. Owing to staff difficulties proper records were not maintained for the year ended 31 March 20X3, and the partners request your assistance in preparing the financial statements for that year.

The statement of financial position on 1 April 20X2 was as follows:

ASSETS	£	£	£
Non-current assets	Cost	Acc depn	WDV
Fixed plant	15,000	6,000	9,000
Motor vehicles	4,000	1,000	3,000
Fixtures and fittings	500	250	250
	19,500	7,250	12,250
Current assets			
Inventories			19,450
Trade receivables			10,820
Prepayments			250
Cash			75
			30,595
Total assets			42,845
OWNERS' EQUITY AND LIABILITIES			
Owners' equity			
Capital accounts			
– Field		10,000	
– Green		10,000	
– Lane		2,500	22,500
Current accounts			
– Field		5,000	
– Green		2,000	
– Lane		500	7,500
			30,000
Current liabilities			
Bank overdraft			6,370
Trade payables			1,125
Accruals			5,350
Total current liabilities			12,845
Total capital and liabilities			42,845

The accruals in the statement of financial position comprised: audit fee £600, heat and light £400 and advertising £125. The prepayment of £250 was in respect of rates.

A summary of the bank statement provides the following information for the year to 31 March 20X3.

	£
Takings banked	141,105
Purchases	111,805
Wages	6,875
Rates and water	6,850
Heat and light	1,720
Delivery and travelling	3,380
Repairs and renewals	1,475
Advertising	375
Printing and stationery	915
Sundry office expenses	215
Bank charges	1,100
Audit fee	600

The following items were paid from the takings before they were banked:

- Wages: cleaner £5 per week; van driver's mate £10 per week
- Casual labour for the year: £555
- Paraffin for shop heating: £445
- Advertising: £75
- Sundry office expenses: £515
- Purchases for resale: £12,635
- Hire of delivery vehicle: £20 per week
- Partners' drawings per week: Field £40, Green £30, Lane £30.

Additional information

1 The partners are allowed interest of 5 per cent per annum on their capital accounts.

2 Profits or losses are shared in the ratio Field 5, Green 3, Lane 2, with the proviso that Lane is guaranteed by Field an income of £3,000 per annum, excluding his interest on capital.

3 Certain goods had been appropriated by the partners during the year. The selling price of these goods was £460, allocated as follows: Field £235; Green £110; Lane £115.

4 Depreciation on non-current assets is to be provided at the following rates: fixed plant 5 per cent; motor vehicles 25 per cent; and fixtures and fittings 10 per cent; using the straight-line method.

5 Accrued charges for heat and light at 31 March 20X3 were £450.

6 Rates of £750 were prepaid at 31 March 20X3.

7 Your charges for the 20X2/X3 audit were estimated at £650.

8   At 31 March 20X3, inventories were £22,345, trade receivables £11,415, trade payables £5,920 and cash in till £100.

Required

a   Prepare the partnership's statement of profit and loss, and appropriation account for the year ended 31 March 20X3.

b   Prepare the statement of financial position as at 31 March 20X3. (Movements in the partners' current accounts should be shown on the face of the statement of financial position.)

(ACCA)

When you have read this chapter, log on to the Online Learning Centre for *Introduction to Financial Accounting* at www.mcgraw-hill.co.uk/textbooks/thomas, where you will find multiple choice quizzes, case studies, a glossary and mock exams.

Changes in partnerships

Learning Objectives

After reading this chapter you should be able to do the following:

1. Explain the meaning of the key terms and concepts listed at the end of the chapter.

2. Discuss the nature, valuation and accounting treatment of goodwill. Compute the value of goodwill.

3. Show the journal and ledger entries for the admission of a new partner and/or an outgoing partner, including those relating to goodwill and the effects of revaluing assets.

4. Show the journal and ledger entries relating to a change in partners' profit-sharing ratio, including the appropriation of profits in the year of the change.

5. Prepare the appropriation account and statement of financial position of a partnership where there is a change in partners or there is a change in their profit-sharing ratio.

28.1 Introduction

When a partner leaves a partnership owing to, for example, retirement or death or whenever a new partner is admitted, it has the effect of bringing the old partnership to an end and transferring the business to a new partnership. The retiring partner(s) will want to take out their share of the business assets and any new partner(s) may be expected to introduce capital. Furthermore, a new profit-sharing agreement must be reached. The situation would be relatively simple, in accounting terms, if three conditions could be met:

1. The change occurs at the start or end of an accounting year.

2. The separate assets and liabilities of the business are all included in the financial statements at values that the partners agree to be current.

3. No account is taken of 'goodwill'.

The difficulties that arise when these conditions do not apply (which is nearly always) is discussed later in this chapter. The term 'goodwill' has special significance in accounting and explanation of this is also introduced.

As explained, when a partner leaves and/or a new partner is admitted, the law states that the old partnership is dissolved and a new partnership is created. The new partnership frequently takes over the assets and liabilities of the old partnership, normally retains the name of the old partnership (with perhaps a minor amendment to reflect the change of partners) and thus from the perspective of third parties often has the appearance of being a continuing business. For these reasons the partnership usually continues to use the same set of books of account with various adjustments to the capital and current accounts to reflect the change of partners. These are described below.

28.2 Retirement of a partner

This can be considered initially using the simplifying assumptions 1, 2 and 3 set out earlier. The first step in dealing with the retirement of a partner is to ensure that the financial statements are complete at the date of retirement, including crediting the partner's current account with the partner's share of profit and debiting the current account with the partner's drawings to this date. The retiring partner's share of the partnership assets is then represented by the sum of the balances on his or her current and capital accounts. As soon as the individual ceases to be a partner, that person no longer has capital invested in the partnership and must thus be treated as a loan creditor. The balances on the former partner's current and capital accounts are, therefore, transferred to a loan account in the individual's name. This loan is eliminated either by one payment, or alternatively there may be a clause in the partnership agreement to make repayment by instalments over time. Since the person is no longer a partner, any interest payable on this loan is an expense of the partnership to be charged in the statement of profit and loss and not an appropriation of profits as in the case of interest on loans made by partners.

The accounting entries relating to the retirement of a partner are illustrated in Example 28.1.

EXAMPLE 28.1

Britten, Edwards and Howe are partners sharing profits equally after interest on partners' loans of 5 per cent per annum. Edwards retires on 1 January 20X4 and is to be repaid one year later. Interest on money due to her is to be at 8 per cent per annum.

The statement of financial position at 31 December 20X3 is summarized as below, before the appropriation of profit:

EQUITY AND LIABILITIES		
Owners' equity	£	£
Capital accounts		
– Britten	10,000	
– Edwards	6,000	
– Howe	5,000	21,000
Current accounts		
– Britten	1,000	
– Edwards	1,500	
– Howe	1,100	3,600
Income statement – profit for year		1,000
		25,600
Non-current liabilities		
Partners' loan from Edwards		2,000
Total equity and liabilities		27,600

First, the appropriation of profits should be carried out as follows:

	B £	E £	H £	Total £
Profit for year				1,000
Interest on loan (5% × £2,000)		100		(100)
				900
Shares of residual profit	300	300	300	(900)
	300	400	300	–

The journal and ledger entries in respect of Edwards' interest on loan and share of profit will be as follows:

			£	£
Debit:	Appropriation account	Dr	400	
Credit:	Current account – Edwards	Cr		400

This produces a balance on Edwards' current account of £1,500 + £400 = £1,900. The balances on the retiring partner's capital, current and loan accounts are then transferred to a new loan account as shown by the following journal entries:

			£	£
Debit:	Capital account – Edwards	Dr	6,000	
Debit:	Current account – Edwards	Dr	1,900	
Debit:	Partners' loan account – Edwards	Dr	2,000	
Credit:	Loan account – Edwards	Cr		9,900
			9,900	9,900

After crediting the other partners' current accounts with their shares of profit the statement of financial position on 1 January 20X4 after Edwards' retirement will be as follows:

EQUITY AND LIABILITIES		
Owners' equity	£	£
Capital accounts		
– Britten	10,000	
– Howe	5,000	15,000
Current accounts		
– Britten	1,300	
– Howe	1,400	2,700
		17,700
Non-current liabilities		
Loan – Edwards		9,900
Total equity and liabilities		27,600

28.3   Admission of a new partner

When a new partner is admitted to a partnership, the value of the assets he or she introduces into the business will be debited to the appropriate asset accounts (e.g. bank) and credited to the new partner's capital account. If the new partner is admitted in the circumstances set out in the introduction to this chapter as three conditions or simplifying assumptions, then these are the only entries that are necessary to account for the admission of a new partner.

However, such circumstances are rarely the case. In particular, the change of partners may not occur at the start or end of an accounting year, but more likely at some time during the accounting year. We will thus now examine the accounting requirements when this condition does not apply, but the other two are still met.

When a new partner is admitted (or an existing partner leaves) part way through an accounting year it is usual, at least in examination questions, to retain the same accounting year. This means that it will be necessary to ascertain the partners' shares of profit for the period from the start of the accounting year to the date of the change, separately from that for the period from the date of the change until the end of the accounting year.

One possibility is to start by preparing two statements of profit and loss, one for each of these two periods. However, it is more common, at least in examination questions, to assume that the profit has arisen evenly over the accounting year, and thus simply prepare a statement for profit and loss for the year and divide the profit (or loss) between the two periods on a time basis. Two appropriation accounts are then prepared: one for the period from the start of the accounting year to the date of the change; and the other from the date of the change until the end of the accounting year. The reason for this is that the partners' shares of profit will be different for each period, as may be their salaries, rates of interest on capital and interest on drawings. Note that the salaries, interest on capital and interest on drawings for each of the two periods will have to be computed separately, and on a strict time basis.

The two appropriation accounts are usually prepared in columnar form since this is quicker and easier. Moreover, it means that each partner's salary, interest on capital, interest on drawings and share of residual profit for each of the two periods can be added together to give the total of each for the year. Obviously, this only applies to those partners who were partners before and after the change.

An illustration of the preparation of an appropriation account where a new partner is admitted part way through an accounting year is given in Example 28.2. Notice that there is no impact on the statement of profit and loss, and the only effects on the statement of financial position relate to the capital introduced by the new partner and the appropriation of profit to the partners' current accounts.

EXAMPLE
28.2

Brick and Stone are in partnership sharing profits and losses Brick $\frac{3}{5}$ and Stone $\frac{2}{5}$ after giving each partner 6 per cent per annum interest on capital and annual salaries of £28,000 to Brick and £22,000 to Stone.

On 1 July 20X2 Wall was admitted as a partner. From this date profits or losses will be shared equally after giving each partner 10 per cent per annum interest on capital and annual salaries of £34,000 to Brick, £26,000 to Stone and £24,000 to Wall.

The financial statements are made up to 31 December of each year. The profit for the year ended 31 December 20X2 was £150,000 and this is believed to have arisen evenly over the year. The following is the statement of financial position at 31 December 20X2 before the appropriation of the profit between the partners:

ASSETS	£'000	£'000
Non-current assets		675
Current assets		180
Total assets		855
EQUITY AND LIABILITIES		
Owners' equity		
Capital accounts:		
– Brick	300	
– Stone	200	
– Wall	100	600
Current accounts:		
– Brick	27	
– Stone	23	50
Profit for the year		150
Total owners' equity		800
Current liabilities		55
Total equity and liabilities		855

The above balances on the capital accounts of Brick and Stone have not changed since 31 December 20X1. The balance on Wall's capital account is the capital she introduced on 1 July 20X2.

You are required to prepare:

a An appropriation account for the year ended 31 December 20X2;

b A statement of financial position as at 31 December 20X2 showing all the entries in the partners' current accounts after giving effect to the change in partners.

a

Workings	Brick £'000	Stone £'000	Wall £'000
From 1 Jan to 30 June 20X2:			
Salaries			
$\frac{6}{12} \times £28,000$	14		
$\frac{6}{12} \times £22,000$		11	
Interest on capital			
$\frac{6}{12} \times 6\% \times £300,000$	9		
$\frac{6}{12} \times 6\% \times £200,000$		6	
From 1 July to 31 Dec 20X2:			
Salaries			
$\frac{6}{12} \times £34,000$	17		
$\frac{6}{12} \times £26,000$		13	
$\frac{6}{12} \times £24,000$			12
Interest on capital			
$\frac{6}{12} \times 10\% \times £300,000$	15		
$\frac{6}{12} \times 10\% \times £200,000$		10	
$\frac{6}{12} \times 10\% \times £100,000$			5

Brick, Stone and Wall
Appropriation account for the year ended 31 December 20X2

	Total £'000	£'000	1 Jan to 30 June £'000	£'000	1 July to 31 Dec £'000	£'000
Profit for the year		150		75		75
Less: salaries						
– Brick	31		14		17	
– Stone	24		11		13	
– Wall	12		–		12	
	67		25		42	
Less: interest on capital						
– Brick	24		9		15	
– Stone	16		6		10	
– Wall	5		–		5	
	45		15		30	
		112		40		72
Residual profit		38		35		3
Shares of residual profit:						
– Brick		22		21		1
– Stone		15		14		1
– Wall		1		–		1
		38		35		3

504

b

Brick, Stone and Wall Statement of financial position as at 31 December 20X2				
ASSETS	£'000	£'000	£'000	£'000
Non-current assets				675
Current assets				180
Total assets				855
EQUITY AND LIABILITIES				
Owners equity	*Brick*	*Stone*	*Wall*	*Total*
Capital accounts	300	200	100	600
Current accounts:				
Balance at 1 Jan 20X2	27	23	–	
Add: – salaries	31	24	12	
– interest on capital	24	16	5	
– shares of residual profit	22	15	1	
Balance at 31 Dec 20X2	104	78	18	200
Total equity	404	278	118	800
Current liabilities				55
Total equity and liabilities				855

Notes

1 In some examination questions the profit does not accrue evenly over the accounting year. These questions usually specify the amounts of profit before and after the change in partners. With this exception the same principles as above would be applied to the preparation of the appropriation account. It is unlikely, but students may be required to compute the amounts of profit before and after the change, in which case the necessary information would have to be supplied in the question. This will probably involve apportioning some expenses between the two periods on a time basis.

2 When a partner leaves part-way through an accounting year, the above principles and procedure would also have to be applied to the appropriation of profits. However, where the outgoing partner leaves the amount due to him or her in the partnership as an interest-bearing loan, it will be necessary to prepare the appropriation account for the period up to the change in partners before that for the period after the change. This is because the outgoing partner's share of profit, salary, and so on, will need to be credited to his or her current account and then transferred to a loan account at the date of the change in partners. The balance on this account will then be used to ascertain the interest on the loan that needs to be deducted in arriving at the net profit of the period after the change in partners.

LEARNING ACTIVITY 28.1

Imagine you are in business with assets and capital of £100,000. You decide to admit me to your business as a partner. I will bring in capital of £100,000 in cash, and we will share profits and losses equally. The assets of your old business have a market value of £150,000, but we have agreed that they will remain in the books at their historical cost of £100,000 on the grounds of prudence. The day after my admission I give you notice to dissolve our partnership, and the assets of your old business are sold for £150,000. The profit of £150,000 – £100,000 = £50,000 must be shared equally, and thus our capital is now £100,000 + £25,000 = £125,000 each. This is repaid in cash and I therefore walk away with a gain of £25,000 after only having been a partner for two days.

Describe your feelings about the way in which the profit on realization of the assets has been shared, and whether in retrospect you would have done anything differently. The answer is given on p.506.

28.4 The revaluation of assets on changes in partners

The values of assets and liabilities shown in the ledger and the statement of financial position (i.e. the book values) are not normally the current market values. Therefore, when a new partner is admitted to a business or an existing partner dies or retires, it is usually necessary to revalue all the assets and liabilities. The reason for this revaluation is that since assets are normally shown in the financial statements at their historical cost, there will be **unrealized holding gains and losses** that have not been recorded in the books (e.g. arising from an increase in the market value of property since the date of purchase). These must be taken into account by means of a **revaluation**, and each old partner's capital account credited with their share of the unrealized gains (or debited with their share of any unrealized losses).

Thus, when an existing partner dies or retires, the revaluation ensures that the former partner receives his or her share of any unrealized holding gains. Similarly, when a new partner is admitted, the revaluation is necessary to ensure that the old partners receive recognition of their shares of the unrealized holding gains. If this was not done the new partner would be entitled to a share of these gains when they were eventually realized, despite the fact that they arose prior to the partner's admission to the partnership.

LEARNING ACTIVITY 28.2

Answer

You should not have agreed to the assets remaining in the books at their historical cost. The whole of the difference between their market value and historical cost belongs to you. The principle of prudence does not apply because the assets of your old business were sold to the new partnership, and thus the gain was realised. You should have brought the revaluation of the assets into the books before admitting me as a partner. That way, the whole of the gain would have been credited to your capital account.

An illustration of the ledger entries relating to the revaluation of assets on changes in partners is given in Example 28.3.

So far, consideration has only been given to situations where any deceased or retiring partners' capital accounts have credit balances and the remaining partners are required to make payments to them. If there is a debit balance on a capital account, a retiring partner will be due to pay this to the partnership. However, if the retiring partner is unable to make this payment, there will be a deficiency to be shared among the remaining partners. The partnership agreement may specify how this sharing is to take place. In the absence of such an agreement, then the precedence of a court ruling in the case of **Garner v. Murray** will apply under English law. Under this rule, the deficiency is shared in proportion to the partners' credit balances on their capital accounts at the last statement of financial position date before the retirement. Subsequent revaluations are not taken into account in calculating these proportions, nor are profit-sharing ratios.

EXAMPLE 28.3

Bill and Harry are in partnership sharing profits equally. On 1 July 20X3 Harry retired and Jane was admitted as a partner. She is to contribute cash of £9,000 as capital. Future profits are to be shared, Bill three-fifths and Jane two-fifths.

The statement of financial position at 30 June 20X3 was as follows:

ASSETS	£	£	£
Non-current assets	Cost	Acc Depn	WDV
Plant	13,500	3,300	10,200
Fixtures and fittings	10,500	2,700	7,800
	24,000	6,000	18,000
Current assets			
Inventories			13,800
Trade receivables			9,450
Cash			3,900
			27,150
Total assets			45,150
OWNERS' EQUITY AND LIABILITIES			
Owners' equity			
Capital accounts			
– Bill		17,000	
– Harry		17,500	34,500
Current accounts			
– Bill		4,800	
– Harry		2,100	6,900
Total owners' equity			41,400
Current liabilities			
Trade payables			3,750
Total current liabilities			3,750
Total capital and liabilities			45,150

It was decided that inventory is to be valued at £12,000 and fixtures are to be valued at £10,350. Of the trade receivables, £1,350 are considered to be doubtful debts.

The ledger entries relating to the above revaluation and change of partners are required.

It is necessary first to set up a revaluation account in the ledger and enter the increases and decreases in value of all the assets. The resulting profit or loss on revaluation must then be shared between the old partners in their old profit-sharing ratio and entered in their capital accounts. The cash introduced by the new partner is simply credited to her capital account. This is shown below.

Fixtures

Balance b/d	10,500	Provision for depreciation	2,700
Revaluation a/c	2,550	Balance c/d	10,350
	13,050		13,050
Balance b/d	10,350		

Inventory

Balance b/d	13,800	Revaluation a/c	1,800
		Balance c/d	12,000
	13,800		13,800
Balance b/d	12,000		

Provision for bad debts

		Revaluation a/c	1,350

Revaluation a/c

Write down of inventory	1,800	Write up of fixtures		2,550
Provision for bad debts	1,350	Loss on revaluation –		
		Capital Bill	300	
		Capital Harry	300	600
	3,150			3,150

Capital

	Bill	Harry	Jane		Bill	Harry	Jane
Revaluation a/c	300	300	–	Balance b/d	17,000	17,500	–
Balance c/d	16,700	17,200	9,000	Bank	–	–	9,000
	17,000	17,500	9,000		17,000	17,500	9,000
				Balance b/d	16,700	17,200	9,000

Finally, the transfers in respect of Harry's capital and current accounts must be made, which would involve the following journal entry:

		Debit	Credit
Debit:	Capital account – Harry	17,200	
Debit:	Current account – Harry	2,100	
Credit:	Loan account – Harry		19,300
		19,300	19,300

28.5 The nature of goodwill

The precise nature of goodwill is difficult to define in a theoretically sound manner. However, it is generally recognized that goodwill exists, since a value is normally attached to it when a business is purchased. Goodwill usually arises in the financial statements where another business has been purchased at some time in the past. Its value frequently takes the form of the excess of the purchase price of the other business over the market value of its net assets. The existence of this excess shows that the purchaser of a business is prepared to pay for something in addition to the net assets. Goodwill is the label given to that something. *IFRS 3 – Business Combinations* (IASB, 2010b), states that (in a business combination) **goodwill** represents a 'payment made by the acquirer in anticipation of future economic benefits from assets that are not capable of being individually identified and separately recognised'. Goodwill is therefore by definition incapable of realization separately from the business as a whole. **Separable/identifiable net assets** are the assets and liabilities of an entity that are capable of being disposed of or settled separately, without necessarily disposing of the business as a whole. **Fair value** is the amount at which an asset or liability could be exchanged in an arm's length transaction.

Where the value of a business as a whole exceeds the total value of its separable net assets this is described as **positive goodwill**. Where the value of a business as a whole is less than the total value of its separable net assets, this is referred to as **negative goodwill**. This usually arises where a business is expected to make future losses because of a poor reputation, and so on.

Most ongoing businesses are normally worth more as a going concern than is shown by the value of their net tangible assets; otherwise, it would probably be better to shut the business down and sell the separate assets. From this standpoint, goodwill may be said to represent the present value of the future profits accruing from an existing business. Thus, goodwill arises from a number of attributes that an ongoing business possesses, such as the following:

1 The prestige and reputation attaching to the name of a business or its products and thus the likelihood that present customers will continue to buy from the business in future (e.g. Rolls-Royce, Microsoft).

2 Existing contracts for the supply of goods in the future (e.g. construction, aerospace, defence equipment).

3 The location of the business premises (e.g. a newsagent next to a railway station) and other forms of captive customers (e.g. a milk distributor's clientele).

4 The possession of patents, trademarks, brand names and special technical knowledge arising from previous expenditure on advertising and research and development. However, some of these may be accounted for as separate assets.

5 The existence of known sources of supply of goods and services, including the availability of trade credit.

6 The existing staff, including particular management skills. The costs of recruiting and training present employees give rise to an asset that is not recorded in the statement of financial position but nevertheless represents a valuable resource to the business. Furthermore, these costs would have to be incurred if a business were started from scratch.

7 Other set-up factors. An existing business has the advantage of having collected together the various items of equipment and other assets necessary for its operations. Obtaining and bringing together these assets usually involves delay and expense, and avoiding this is an advantage of an ongoing business.

Goodwill is classified as either acquired or non-acquired. **Acquired goodwill** is measured in *IFRS 3* as 'the residual cost of the business combination after recognising the acquiree's identifiable assets, liabilities and contingent liabilities'. It thus essentially refers to the amount paid for goodwill when one business takes over another business. **Non-acquired goodwill** is the **internally generated goodwill** of a business. *IAS 38 – Intangible Assets* (IASB, 2010a) does not allow the capitalization of any internally generated intangible asset that cannot be separately identified and reliably measured. Therefore, goodwill is not recognized in financial statements.

28.6 The recognition of goodwill in partnership financial statements

As explained above, all businesses possess either positive or negative goodwill. However, this may or may not be recorded in the books and thus appear on the statement of financial position as an intangible non-current asset. IFRS 3 recommends that positive purchased goodwill should be capitalized as an intangible asset on the statement of financial position at cost. Then goodwill should be reviewed for impairment on a regular basis. When it is clear that there is impairment, the capitalized value should be written down to its current fair value. Internally generated, that is non-purchased goodwill, is not allowed to be recognized as an asset. The main reason for this is that the valuation of non-acquired goodwill is regarded as highly subjective and thus contravenes the principle of reliability.

> **REAL WORLD EXAMPLE 28.1**
>
> ## Impairment of goodwill
>
> 'The most highly publicized write-downs of goodwill have been in the banking sector. Wachovia (a US bank) alone reported a goodwill impairment charge of nearly $19 billion in the third quarter of 2008. The phenomenon was not limited to U.S. banks. The Royal Bank of Scotland Group wrote off £15.5 billion of goodwill in 2008 related to series of mergers, including £7.7 billion for ABN AMRO, £4.4 billion for Citizens and Charter One, and £2.7 billion for NatWest.'
>
> *Source*: Gore and Zimmerman (2010), www.cpajournal.com/acc.htm (pp. 46–48).

Although the financial statements of sole traders and partnerships do not have to be prepared in accordance with accounting standards, it is nevertheless highly unlikely that these will include goodwill except possibly when another business has been purchased. In the case of a partnership, this includes where a new partner is admitted or an existing partner retires or dies. The law states that in each instance the old partnership is dissolved, and thus effectively taken over by the new partnership. The financial statements of the new partnership may therefore include goodwill acquired from the purchase of the old partnership. This is examined in detail later in the chapter.

The accounting for goodwill has changed dramatically over the past three decades; at one time goodwill was written off directly to reserves. However, this was argued not to reflect economic reality: that is, an asset has been purchased. Another view was that the value of goodwill declined with the passage of time; hence, it had a finite life. To account for this, the acquired goodwill was recorded in the financial statements and amortized (i.e. depreciated) over its useful economic life. There was another school of thought that argued that the value of goodwill could be perpetuated by, for example, expenditure on advertising and training, and thus has an infinite life. The supporters of the latter view argued that it was not necessary to amortize goodwill. At one time there was even a choice of how to treat goodwill (amortize or write off). Having a choice was deemed to reduce the quality of information being prepared by entities, as it hindered comparability.

The current established thinking is that acquired goodwill is an asset that has a cost. Its value is impacted on by changes in the economic climate, changes in business trends, changes in human capital (personnel), changes in intellectual capital, and so on. The value may increase, or decrease. Therefore, the best way to determine whether there has been a change in the economic value (its ability to generate future income) of goodwill is to review it periodically for impairment (goodwill is never revalued upwards). In simple terms, an **impairment review** is essentially a revaluation to ensure that the value of goodwill has not fallen below its book/carrying value. Some indicators that might spark a full impairment review include a decline in sales, or the introduction into the market of a new competitor. These events may be taken as indicators that the future earnings to be expected from goodwill have declined and its value is not as it once was. Determining the new value is subjective and is beyond the scope of this text. Any exercises in this text that deal with capitalized goodwill will provide the impairment amount. At this level, an awareness of how to account for the impairment is sufficient.

28.7 The valuation of goodwill

As explained previously, the cost of acquired goodwill is deemed to be the excess of the purchase price of a business over the market/fair value of its net assets. In the case of company financial statements, the value of goodwill is usually computed in precisely this manner. However, in the case of sole traders and partnerships, the purchase price of a business is frequently arrived at by valuing the net tangible assets (often at market prices) and, as a separate item, goodwill. This is particularly common where a new partner is admitted or an existing partner leaves.

There are several methods of valuing goodwill. These reflect the customs/conventions of businesses generally and certain trades and professions in particular. It should be emphasized that in practice the amount arrived at using one of these methods is frequently regarded as a starting point in negotiating a final value for goodwill. The most common methods are as follows:

1 A given multiple of annual turnover. The multiple is intended to represent the number of years' future sales that are likely to result from the goodwill presently attaching to the business. The turnover may be an estimate of future sales, or more likely an average of a given number of past periods. This method is common in the case of retail businesses and professional firms such as accountants and solicitors.

2 A given multiple of annual profit. Again, the multiple is intended to represent the number of years' future profits that are likely to be generated from the existing goodwill. The annual profit may be either an estimate of the future profit or more likely an average of a given number of past years. The profits used in the computation may be those shown in the audited financial statements or alternatively what is termed the **abnormal** or **super profit**. This refers to the profit shown in the financial statements minus a notional charge for interest on capital and proprietors' salaries. It is essentially a hypothetical form of residual profit. The super profit is intended to represent the return from risking money in a business over and above what could be earned by depositing that money elsewhere at a fixed rate of interest and taking employment with a guaranteed salary. This method of valuing goodwill may be particularly appropriate in riskier industries with fluctuating profits, such as engineering and building construction.

3 The excess of the capitalized value of (past or forecasted) annual (average) profit (or super profit) over the current (market) value of the net tangible assets of the business. The capitalized value is normally computed by multiplying the annual profit by the average price–earnings (P/E) ratio of similar size companies in the same industry whose shares are listed on a stock exchange. The capitalized value is intended to reflect the total value of the business as a going concern. This method may be most appropriate in the case of a large business that is not a company or whose shares are not quoted on a stock exchange.

28.8 The admission of a new partner and the treatment of goodwill

When a new partner is admitted to a partnership, an adjustment to the old partners' capital accounts is necessary to recognize the value of goodwill that they have created and therefore belongs to them. The principle is exactly the same as with the revaluation of assets except that the goodwill has not previously been recorded in the books. There are three main ways of dealing with this, each of which is described below and illustrated using Example 28.4.

EXAMPLE 28.4

A and B are in partnership sharing profits in the ratio 3 : 2. The balances on their capital accounts are: A £15,000 and B £20,000.

On 31 December 20X2 they decide to admit C as a partner who is to bring in £42,000 as her capital and will receive half of all future profits. The old partners' profit-sharing ratio will continue to be 3 : 2.

Goodwill is to be calculated at twice the average super profits of the last three years. The super profits are after charging interest on capital of 5 per cent per annum and partners' salaries of £12,500 per annum each.

The profits transferred to the appropriation account are as follows:

	£
Year ended 31/12/X0	28,560
Year ended 31/12/X1	29,980
Year ended 31/12/X2	32,210

The value to be ascribed to goodwill would first be calculated as follows:

Year ended	Net profits	Salaries	Interest on capital	Super profits
	£	£	£	£
31/12/X0	28,560	25,000	1,750	1,810
31/12/X1	29,980	25,000	1,750	3,230
31/12/X2	32,210	25,000	1,750	5,460
				10,500

$$\text{Goodwill} = 2 \times \frac{£10,500}{3} = £7,000$$

Note that the new profit-sharing ratio will be A3 : B2 : C5. This can be explained thus: since C is to receive one-half of all future profits, A's share will be 3 divided by 3 + 2 multiplied by the remaining one-half, i.e. $\frac{3}{5} \times \frac{1}{2} = \frac{3}{10}$. Similarly, B's share will be $\frac{2}{5} \times \frac{1}{2} = \frac{2}{10}$. Thus, the new profit-sharing ratio is A $\frac{3}{10}$, B $\frac{2}{10}$ and C $\frac{5}{10}$, or A3 : B2 : C5.

The different methods of treating goodwill on the admission of a new partner can now be shown as follows.

Method 1

The value of goodwill is debited to a goodwill account and credited to the old partners' capital accounts in their old profit-sharing ratio. This method recognizes the existence of the previously unrecorded asset of goodwill by bringing it into the books. The goodwill is shared between the old partners in their old profit-sharing ratio because it is an asset created by the old partnership which thus belongs to the old partners.

Goodwill						
20X2		£	**20X2**			£
31 Dec	Capital A	4,200				
31 Dec	Capital B	2,800	31 Dec	Balance c/d		7,000
		7,000				7,000
20X3						
1 Jan	Balance b/d	7,000				

Capital									
		A	B	C			A	B	C
20X2		£	£	£	**20X2**		£	£	£
					31 Dec	Balance b/d	15,000	20,000	—
					31 Dec	Bank	—	—	42,000
31 Dec	Balance c/d	19,200	22,800	42,000	31 Dec	Goodwill	4,200	2,800	—
		19,200	22,800	42,000			19,200	22,800	42,000
					20X3				
					1 Jan	Balance b/d	19,200	22,800	42,000

Method 2

Earlier in this chapter it was pointed out that goodwill should be impaired. In partnerships it is common practice to write the goodwill off against the partners' capital accounts. In Method 1 above, the goodwill would be impaired. Method 2 is the alternative treatment. The value of goodwill is first debited to a goodwill account and credited to the old partners' capital accounts in their old profit-sharing ratio (as in Method 1). Then the goodwill is written off by crediting the goodwill account and debiting all the partners in the new partnership in their new profit-sharing ratio. The debit to the partners' capital accounts is in their new profit-sharing ratio because the writing off of goodwill effectively amounts to recognizing a (paper) loss that would otherwise have been charged to future years' statements of profit and loss (as the impairment of goodwill) and thus shared between the new partners in their new profit-sharing ratio.

Goodwill					
20X2		£	**20X2**		£
31 Dec	Capital A	4,200	31 Dec	Capital A	2,100
31 Dec	Capital B	2,800	31 Dec	Capital B	1,400
			31 Dec	Capital C	3,500
		7,000			7,000

Capital								
	A	B	C			A	B	C
20X2	£	£	£	20X2		£	£	£
31 Dec Goodwill	2,100	1,400	3,500	31 Dec	Balance b/d	15,000	20,000	—
				31 Dec	Bank	—	—	42,000
31 Dec Balance c/d	17,100	21,400	38,500	31 Dec	Goodwill	4,200	2,800	—
	19,200	22,800	42,000			19,200	22,800	42,000
				20X3				
				1 Jan	Balance b/d	17,100	21,400	38,500

The entries in the goodwill account are a waste of time and paper, and thus Method 2 normally involves only the two sets of entries for goodwill on each side of the partners' capital accounts. Note that this method should be used when you are told that no account for goodwill is to be kept/maintained in the books or that goodwill is not to be recorded in the books.

It should also be observed that this method has the effect of charging the new partner with what is referred to as a premium of £3,500, in that her capital introduced has been reduced by £3,500. This premium represents the purchase by the new partner of her share of goodwill, that is $\frac{1}{2}$ of £7,000 = £3,500. She will get this back when the goodwill is eventually realized (if the business is sold) or she leaves.

Method 3

This method is essentially a further shortcutting of Method 2. The net effects of the entries for goodwill in the partners' capital accounts in Method 2 are: C is debited with £3,500; A is credited with £4,200 − £2,100 = £2,100; and B is credited with £2,800 − £1,400 = £1,400. Method 3 consists of simply entering in the partners' capital accounts these net effects, which are referred to as a **premium contra**. The amount of the premium is debited to the new partners' capital account and credited to the old partners' capital accounts in their old profit-sharing ratio A $\frac{3}{5} \times$ £3,500 = £2,100 and B $\frac{2}{5} \times$ £3,500 = £1,400.

Capital								
	A	B	C			A	B	C
20X2	£	£	£	20X2		£	£	£
31 Dec Premium	—	—	3,500	31 Dec	Balance b/d	15,000	20,000	—
				31 Dec	Bank	—	—	42,000
31 Dec Balance c/d	17,100	21,400	38,500	31 Dec	Premium	2,100	1,400	—
	17,200	21,400	42,000			17,100	21,400	42,000
				20X3				
				1 Jan	Balance b/d	17,100	21,400	38,500

This method should normally only be used where you are told that the new partner is to pay a premium representing the purchase of his or her share of goodwill. The premium is usually given but can be calculated from the goodwill. In this example the premium can be calculated as $\frac{1}{2}$ of £7,000 = £3,500. The ledger entries would be as shown immediately above. It must be emphasized that this method only gives a correct answer where the old partners share profits (and losses) in the new partnership in the same ratio as the old partnership. If this is not the case, Method 2 must be used instead.

Sometimes it is not possible to compute the premium from the figure of goodwill because the partners have not agreed a method of valuation for goodwill. Instead, you may be told something along the lines that the new partner receives an interest in the new partnership equity/assets, which is less than the amount he or she is to invest/pay into the firm.

EXAMPLE
28.5

Using the data in Example 28.4 this can be illustrated as follows. C is to be admitted as a partner with a one-half interest in both capital and profits in exchange for £42,000. C's interest in the capital/assets is computed as follows:

	£
Capital/assets/equity of old partnership (£15,000 + £20,000)	35,000
Investment by C	42,000
Capital/assets/equity of new partnership	77,000
C's share of equity of new partnership	
($\frac{1}{2} \times$ £77,000)	38,500

The premium which C is being charged is therefore £42,000 – £38,500 = £3,500. The ledger entries will be similar to those in Method 3. However, these can be shortened to the following:

Journal			Debit	Credit
			£	£
Debit:	Bank		42,000	
Credit:	Capital – C			38,500
Credit:	Capital – A			2,100
Credit:	Capital – B			1,400
			42,000	42,000

Remember that this method only gives the correct answer where the old partners continue to share profits in the same ratio. If this is not the case Method 2 must be used, which will require a notional figure for goodwill to be computed by multiplying the premium by the inverse of the new partner profit-sharing ratio (i.e. £3,500 $\times \frac{2}{1}$ = £7,000).

Finally, it should be mentioned that it is possible for the new partner to receive an interest greater than the amount he or she is to invest. This results in a **negative premium**, sometimes referred to as a 'bonus', and negative goodwill.

28.9 An outgoing partner and the treatment of goodwill

When a partner leaves, the balances on his or her capital and current accounts are repaid. However, it is necessary first to make an adjustment to the partners' capital accounts in recognition of the value of goodwill that has been created, some of which belongs to the outgoing partner. There are three main ways of dealing with this, which correspond to Methods 1 to 3 (Example 28.4), respectively, of treating goodwill on the admission of a new partner.

1 The value of goodwill is debited to a goodwill account and credited to the old partners' capital accounts in their old profit-sharing ratio.

2 The value of goodwill is credited to the old partners' capital accounts in their old profit-sharing ratio and debited to the remaining partners' capital accounts in their new profit-sharing ratio. This effectively results in the remaining partners purchasing the outgoing partners' share of goodwill. No goodwill account is maintained in the books.

3 The outgoing partner's share of goodwill is credited to his or her capital account and debited to the remaining partners' capital accounts in their new profit-sharing ratio. Again, no goodwill account is maintained in the books. This method only gives a correct answer where the remaining partners share profits in the new partnership in the same ratio as the old partnership. If this is not the case, Method 2 must be used instead.

Sometimes it is not possible to compute the outgoing partner's share of goodwill from the figure of goodwill, because the partners have not agreed a method of valuation for goodwill. Instead, you may be told something along the lines that the outgoing partner is to receive more than the balance of his or her capital account. This excess is the outgoing partner's share of goodwill. If necessary, a notional figure for goodwill can be computed by multiplying this excess by the inverse of the outgoing partner's profit-sharing ratio.

28.10 Incoming and outgoing partners and goodwill

We have thus far dealt with the revaluation of assets on changes in partners and the treatment of goodwill where there is either an incoming or outgoing partner. The final step is to combine all of these and examine the situation where there is both an incoming and outgoing partner. This is a fairly simple step since the treatment of goodwill involves exactly the same principles whether there is an incoming or outgoing partner. An illustration is given in Example 28.6.

EXAMPLE 28.6

Beech and Oak are in partnership, sharing profits and losses in the ratio 3 : 5, respectively. The statement of financial position drawn up on 31 December 20X2 showed the following position:

ASSETS	£	£
Non-current assets		NBV
Premises		16,000
Fixtures		6,000
		22,000
Current assets		
Inventories		4,000
Trade receivables		3,000
Cash		5,000
		12,000
Total assets		34,000
OWNERS' EQUITY AND LIABILITIES		
Owners' equity		
Capital accounts		
– Beech	11,000	
– Oak	14,000	25,000
Current liabilities		
Trade payables		9,000
Total current liabilities		9,000
Total capital and liabilities		34,000

Beech retired as from 1 January 20X3 and at the same date Maple was admitted to the partnership. For the purpose of these changes, the premises were revalued at £19,500, fixtures at £4,500, inventories at £5,800 and goodwill was agreed at £10,000. A provision for bad debts of £200 is also to be created. The new valuations are to be included in the business books but no account for goodwill is to be maintained. In the new partnership, profits or losses will be divided in the proportions 3 : 2 between Oak and Maple, respectively. Maple will introduce cash of £15,000 and Beech is to receive payment for his capital in cash, but no other cash is to change hands between partners in implementing the change.

Required

Show the above changes in the revaluation account and the partners' capital accounts.

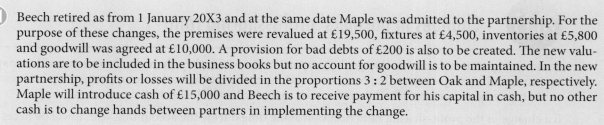

Revaluation account				
	£			£
Fixtures	1,500	Premises		3,500
Provision for bad debts	200	Inventory		1,800
Profit on revaluation				
— Beech ($£3,600 \times \frac{3}{8}$)	1,350			
— Oak ($£3,600 \times \frac{5}{8}$)	2,250	3,600		
		5,300		5,300

Capital accounts							
	Beech	Oak	Maple		Beech	Oak	Maple
Goodwill contra	—	6,000	4,000	Balance b/d	11,000	14,000	—
Cash	16,100	—	—	Profit on			
Balance c/d	—	16,500	11,000	revaluation	1,350	2,250	—
				Goodwill contra	3,750	6,250	—
				Cash	—	—	15,000
	16,100	22,500	15,000		16,100	22,500	15,000
				Balance c/d	—	16,500	11,000

Notes

1 The double entry for the items in the revaluation account will be in the respective asset accounts and the provision for bad debts account.

2 The goodwill is credited to the old partners' capital accounts in their old profit-sharing ratio (Beech $\frac{3}{8} \times £10,000 = £3,750$; Oak $\frac{5}{8} \times £10,000 = £6,250$) and debited to the new partners' capital accounts in their new profit-sharing ratio (Oak $\frac{3}{5} \times £10,000 = £6,000$; Maple $\frac{2}{5} \times £10,000 = £4,000$).

3 The cash paid to Beech of £16,100 is the balance on his capital account after the revaluation of assets and adjustments for goodwill.

28.11 Changes in partners' profit-sharing ratio

Sometimes partners decide to change the proportions in which they share profits or losses. This may occur when the partners agree that one partner is to spend more (or less) time on partnership business, or alternatively one partner's skills have become more (or less) valuable to the partnership.

If a change in the profit-sharing ratio occurs at some time during the accounting year, it will be necessary to divide the profit before appropriations into the periods before and after the change. This is usually done on a time basis. The interest on capital and on drawings, salaries and shares of residual profit are then computed for each period separately. It should be noted that this procedure is the same as when a new partner is admitted and/or a partner leaves during the accounting year.

When there is a change in the profit-sharing ratio, it is also necessary to revalue the assets, including goodwill. As in the case of changes in partners, the profit or loss on revaluation is computed in a revaluation account and transferred to the partners' capital accounts. An adjustment must also be made in respect of goodwill, using the principles already described. A simple illustration is given in Example 28.7 and a more complicated version is shown in Example 28.8.

EXAMPLE 28.7

X and Y are in partnership sharing profits and losses equally. They have decided that as from 1 October 20X2 the profit-sharing ratio is to become X three-fifths and Y two-fifths.

The financial statements are made up to 31 December each year. The profit for the year ended 31 December 20X2 was £60,000. The statement of financial position at 31 December 20X2 prior to sharing profits is as follows:

	£
Net assets	210,000
Capital X	80,000
Capital Y	70,000
Profit for the year	60,000
	210,000

It was decided that the impact of the change in profit-sharing ratio on each partner's share of the assets would be effected at 31 December 20X2 when the net assets were valued at £250,000. The goodwill was valued at £25,000. No goodwill account is to be maintained in the books.

You are required to show the entries in the partners' capital accounts and a statement of financial position at 31 December 20X2.

Distribution of profit 20X2			
	£	£	£
	Total	1 Jan–30 Sep	1 Oct–31 Dec
Profit for the year apportioned on a time basis	60,000	45,000	15,000
Share of profit – X	31,500	22,500	9,000
– Y	28,500	22,500	6,000
	60,000	45,000	15,000

Revaluation account				
Profit on revaluation:			Net assets	40,000
– Capital X	20,000		(£250,000 – £210,000)	
– Capital Y	20,000	40,000		
		40,000		40,000

Capital accounts						
	X	Y			X	Y
Goodwill contra	15,000	10,000	Balance b/d		80,000	70,000
			Share of profit		31,500	28,500
			Profit on revaluation		20,000	20,000
Balance c/d	129,000	121,000	Goodwill contra		12,500	12,500
	144,000	131,000			144,000	131,000
			Balance b/d		129,000	121,000

X and Y statement of financial position as at 31 December 20X2	
	£
TOTAL ASSETS	250,000
EQUITY AND LIABILITIES	
Owners' equity	
– Capital X	129,000
– Capital Y	121,000
Total equity and liabilities	250,000

EXAMPLE 28.8

Hill and Dale are in partnership sharing profits and losses Hill three-fifths and Dale two-fifths after giving each partner 8 per cent per annum interest on capital and annual salaries of £28,000 to Hill and £18,000 to Dale.

They have decided that as from 1 July 20X2 the profits or losses will be shared equally after giving each partner 10 per cent per annum interest on capital and annual salaries of £32,000 to Hill and £30,000 to Dale.

The financial statements are made up to the 31 December of each year. The profit for the year ended 31 December 20X2 was £150,000 and this is believed to have accrued evenly over the year. The following is the statement of financial position at 31 December 20X2 before the appropriation of the profit between the partners and any other entries relating to the change in the partners' profit-sharing ratio:

ASSETS		
Non-current assets	£'000	£'000
Freehold land and buildings at cost		600
Current assets		
Inventories		105
Trade receivables		45
Bank		25
		175
Total assets		775
EQUITY AND LIABILITIES		
Owners' equity		
Capital accounts:		
– Hill	300	
– Dale	250	550
Current accounts:		
– Hill	26	
– Dale	14	40
Profit for the year		150
Total owners' equity		740
Current liabilities		
Trade payables		35
Total current liabilities		35
Total equity and liabilities		775

The forementioned balances on the partners' capital accounts and the land and buildings account are as at 31 December 20X1.

On 1 July 20X2 the freehold land and buildings were revalued at £650,000. The partners have also agreed that the book values of the other assets and liabilities at 1 July 20X2 were their current net realizable values. The goodwill at 1 July 20X2 was valued at £100,000 but no goodwill account is to be maintained in the books.

Required

Prepare:

a the partners' capital accounts as at 1 July 20X2 showing the effects of the change in the partners' profit-sharing ratio on their claims on the partnership assets;

b an appropriation account for the year ended 31 December 20X2;

c a statement of financial position as at 31 December 20X2 showing all the entries in the partners' current accounts after giving effect to the change in the partners' profit-sharing ratio.

a

				Capital accounts		
	Hill	**Dale**			**Hill**	**Dale**
	£'000	**£'000**			**£'000**	**£'000**
Goodwill	50	50		Balance b/d	300	250
Balance c/d	340	260		Profit on revaluation		
				(£650k – £600k)	30	20
				Goodwill	60	40
	390	310			390	310
				Balance b/d	340	260

b

Workings	Hill £'000	Dale £'000
From 1 Jan to 30 June 20X2:		
Salaries		
$\frac{6}{12} \times £28,000$	14	
$\frac{6}{12} \times £18,000$		9
Interest on capital		
$\frac{6}{12} \times 8\% \times £300,000$	12	
$\frac{6}{12} \times 8\% \times £250,000$		10
From 1 July to 31 Dec 20X2:		
Salaries		
$\frac{6}{12} \times £32,000$	16	
$\frac{6}{12} \times £30,000$		15
Interest on capital		
$\frac{6}{12} \times 10\% \times £340,000$	17	
$\frac{6}{12} \times 10\% \times £260,000$		13

Hill and Dale

Appropriation account for the year ended 31 December 20X2

	Total £'000	Total £'000	1 Jan to 30 June £'000	1 Jan to 30 June £'000	1 July to 31 Dec £'000	1 July to 31 Dec £'000
Profit for the year		150		75		75
Less: salaries						
– Hill	30		14		16	
– Dale	24		9		15	
	54		23		31	
Less: interest on capital						
– Hill	29		12		17	
– Dale	23		10		13	
	52		22		30	
		106		45		61
Residual profit		44		30		14
Shares of residual profit:						
– Hill		25	$\frac{3}{5}$	18	$\frac{1}{2}$	7
– Dale		19	$\frac{2}{5}$	12	$\frac{1}{2}$	7
		44		30		14

c

Current accounts						
	Hill £'000	Dale £'000			Hill £'000	Dale £'000
			Balance b/d		26	14
			Salaries		30	24
			Interest on capital		29	23
			Share of residual profit		25	19
Balance c/d	110	80			110	80
	110	80				
			Balance b/d		110	80

Hill and Dale			
Statement of financial position as at 31 December 20X2			
ASSETS	£'000	£'000	£'000
Non-current assets			
Freehold land and buildings			650
Current assets			
Inventories			105
Trade receivables			45
Bank			25
			175
Total assets			825
EQUITY AND LIABILITIES			
Owners' equity	Hill	Dale	Total
Capital accounts	340	260	600
Current accounts:	110	80	190
Total owners' equity	450	340	790
Current liabilities			
Trade payables			35
Total current liabilities			35
Total equity and liabilities			825

Notes

1 The requirement in part 'a' of the example, to prepare the partners' capital accounts, is not always explicitly required by examination questions. However, it is always necessary in these circumstances and, where there is interest on capital, will need to be done first.

2 Then the appropriation account, for the periods prior to and after the change in the partners' profit-sharing ratio are prepared. These could be done as two separate accounts but it is quicker and easier to show them in columnar form, as in the above answer. Each partner's salary, interest on capital and share of residual profit for the year shown in the total column of the appropriation account is found by simply adding together the respective amounts for each of the periods prior to and after the change in the profit-sharing ratio.

Summary

When a new partner is admitted to a partnership, an existing partner leaves or there is a change in the profit-sharing ratio, it is usually necessary to revalue all the assets and liabilities. This ensures that the existing/old partners receive their share of the unrealized holding gains (and losses) that arose prior to the change.

When assets are revalued, it is also usually necessary to make certain adjustments to the partners' capital accounts in respect of goodwill. According to IFRS 3 goodwill is a 'payment made by the acquirer in anticipation of future economic benefits from assets that are not capable of being individually identified and separately recognised'. It is valued as 'the residual cost of the business combination after recognising the acquiree's identifiable assets, liabilities and contingent liabilities'. In the case of partnerships, goodwill is normally valued as a given multiple of the annual sales or profits. When there is a change of partners, goodwill is brought into the books by debiting a goodwill account and crediting the capital accounts of the existing/old partners in their old profit-sharing ratio. The goodwill must either be capitalized at cost and impaired, or alternatively, written off against the new partners' capital accounts in their profit-sharing ratio (assuming it is just an accounting adjustment). This latter treatment can be short-cut by means of adjusting entries on both sides of the partners' capital accounts.

Subsequent to the revaluation of assets and goodwill adjustments, when a new partner is admitted, the capital introduced is credited to his or her capital account. When a partner leaves, the balance on this partner's capital, current and any loan account is transferred to a new loan account, which is repaid in due course.

Key terms and concepts

abnormal profit	511	negative premium	515
acquired goodwill	509	non-acquired goodwill	510
fair value	509	positive goodwill	509
Garner v. *Murray*	506	premium contra	514
goodwill	509	revaluation	506
impairment review	511	separable/identifiable net assets	509
internally generated goodwill	510	super profit	511
negative goodwill	509	unrealized holding gains and losses	506

An asterisk after the question number indicates that there is a suggested answer on the Online Learning Centre (www.mcgraw-hill.co.uk/textbooks/thomas).

Review questions

connect

28.1* a Explain the nature of goodwill.

b Describe the business attributes that are thought to give rise to goodwill.

28.2 a What is the difference between positive and negative goodwill?

b What **is** the difference between purchased goodwill and non-purchased goodwill?

28.3 a Explain the circumstances in which goodwill might appear in the books of a partnership.

b Describe how it would be treated in the statement of financial position.

28.4 A member of the board of Shoprite Enterprises plc has suggested two accounting policies for consideration by the financial director in preparing the latest set of financial statements. These have been summarized as follows:

1 The incorporation of goodwill in the financial statements as a permanent non-current asset in recognition of the favourable trading situations of several of the business's outlets and also to reflect the quality of management experience in the business.

2 No depreciation to be provided in future on the buildings owned by the company, because their market value is constantly appreciating and, in addition, this will result in an increase in the profit of the company.

Required

a Briefly explain your understanding of each of the following:

i goodwill;

ii depreciation.

b Discuss the acceptability of each of the above suggested accounting policies, highlighting any conflict with accounting concepts and standards.

(AEB)

28.5 Describe three different methods of valuing goodwill where the purchase price is unknown.

connect Exercises

BASIC

28.6

Al and Bert are in partnership sharing profits equally. At 30 June they have balances on their capital accounts of £12,000 (Al) and £15,000 (Bert). On that day they agree to bring in their friend Hall as a third partner. All three partners are to share profits equally from now on. Hall is to introduce £20,000 as capital into the business. Goodwill on 30 June is agreed at £18,000.

Required

a Show the partners' capital accounts for 30 June and 1 July on the assumption that the goodwill, previously unrecorded, is to be included in the financial statements.

b Show the additional entries necessary to eliminate goodwill again from the financial statements.

c Explain briefly what goodwill is. Why are adjustments necessary when a new partner joins a partnership?

(ACCA)

28.7*

Brown and Jones are in partnership sharing profits and losses equally. The statement of financial position drawn up on 31 March 20X2 showed the following position:

ASSETS	
Non-current assets	£
Premises	80,000
Fixtures	60,000
	140,000
Current assets	
Inventories	40,000
Trade receivables	30,000
Cash	85,000
	155,000
Total assets	295,000
EQUITY AND LIABILITIES	
Equity capital	
— Brown	110,000
— Jones	87,000
Total equity	197,000
Current liabilities	
Sundry payables	98,000
Total current liabilities	98,000
Total equity and liabilities	295,000

Brown retired as from 1 April 20X2 and at the same date Smith was admitted to the partnership. For the purpose of these changes, the premises were revalued at £115,000, fixtures at £68,000, inventory at £36,000 and goodwill was agreed at £90,000. A provision for bad debts of £3,000 is also to be created. The new valuations are to be included in the business accounts, but no account for goodwill is to be maintained. In the new partnership, profits and losses will be divided in the proportion 3 : 2 between Jones and Smith, respectively. Smith will introduce cash of £100,000 and Brown is to receive payment for his capital in cash but no other cash is to change hands between partners in implementing the change.

Required

Show the above changes in the revaluation account and partners' capital accounts.

28.8*

Blackburn, Percy and Nelson are in partnership, sharing profits equally. On 1 January 20X2 Nelson retired and Logan was admitted as a partner. Nelson has agreed to leave the amounts owing to her in the business as a loan until 31 December 20X2. Logan is to contribute £6,000 as capital. Future profits are to be shared; Blackburn one-half and Percy and Logan one-quarter each.

A goodwill account is to be opened and kept in the books. The goodwill should be valued at the difference between the capitalized value of the estimated super profits for the forthcoming year and the net asset value of the partnership at 31 December 20X1 after revaluing the assets. The capitalized value of the expected super profits is to be computed using the price–earnings ratio, which for this type of business is estimated as 8. The super profits are after deducting notional partners' salaries but not interest on capital. The profit for 20X2 is estimated as £48,750 and it is thought that the partners could each earn £15,000 a year if they were employed elsewhere.

The statement of financial position at 31 December 20X1 was as follows:

ASSETS	Cost	Prov for depn	WDV
Non-current assets	£	£	£
Plant	9,000	2,200	6,800
Vehicles	7,000	1,800	5,200
	16,000	4,000	12,000
Current assets			
Inventories			9,200
Trade receivables			6,300
Prepaid expenses			2,600
			18,100
Total assets			30,100
EQUITY AND LIABILITIES			
Equity capital			
Capital			
– Blackburn		10,000	
– Percy		8,000	
– Nelson		5,000	23,000
Current accounts			
– Blackburn		1,300	
– Percy		1,900	
– Nelson		1,400	4,600
Total equity capital			27,600
Current liabilities			
Trade payables			2,500
Total current liabilities			2,500
Total equity and liabilities			30,100

It was decided that inventory is to be valued at £8,000 and vehicles at £6,700. Of the trade receivables £900 are considered doubtful debts.

Required

Show the ledger entries relating to the above revaluation and change of partners.

28.9

Gupta, Richards and Jones are in partnership sharing profits and losses in the ratio 5 : 4 : 3. On 1 January 20X3 Richards retired from the partnership and it was agreed that Singh should join the partnership, paying a sum of £30,000. From this date, profits are to be shared equally between the three partners and, in view of this, Jones agrees to pay a further £10,000 into the partnership as capital.

The statement of financial position at 31 December 20X2 showed:

ASSETS	£	£
Non-current assets		
Property		60,000
Fixtures		30,000
		90,000
Current assets		
Inventories		30,000
Trade receivables		15,000
Bank		5,000
		50,000
Total assets		140,000
EQUITY AND LIABILITIES		
Owners' equity		
Capital accounts		
– Gupta	60,000	
– Richards	40,000	
– Jones	25,000	125,000
Current accounts		
– Gupta	1,000	
– Richards	2,500	
– Jones	1,500	5,000
Total equity		130,000
Current liabilities		
Trade payables		10,000
Total current liabilities		10,000
Total equity and liabilities		140,000

It was agreed that in preparing a revised opening statement of financial position of the partnership on 1 January 20X3, the following adjustments should be made:

1 Property is to be revalued at £70,000 and fixtures are to be revalued at £32,000.

2 Inventory is considered to be shown at a fair value in the financial statements. A provision for doubtful debts of £1,200 is required.

3 Professional fees of £600 relating to the change in partnership structure are to be regarded as an expense of the year to 31 December 20X2, but were not included in the statement of profit and loss of that year. They are expected to be paid in March 20X3.

4 Goodwill of the partnership as at 31 December 20X2 is estimated at £30,000. No account for goodwill is to be entered in the books, but appropriate adjustments are to be made in the partners' capital accounts.

5 On retirement, Richards is to be paid a sum of £40,000. The balance owing to her will be recorded in a loan account carrying interest of 12 per cent, to be repaid in full after two years.

6 All balances on current accounts are to be transferred to capital accounts. All balances on capital accounts in excess of £20,000 after this transfer are to be transferred to loan accounts carrying interest at 12 per cent.

Required

a Compute the balances on the loan accounts of Richards and the new partners on 1 January 20X3, following completion of these arrangements.

b Prepare an opening statement of financial position for the partnership on 1 January 20X3, following completion of these arrangements.

c Explain briefly *three* factors to be taken into account when establishing profit-sharing arrangements between partners.

(JMB, adapted)

ADVANCED

28.10

Street, Rhode and Close carried on business in partnership sharing profits and losses, in the ratio 5 : 4 : 3. Their draft statement of financial position as on 31 March 20X2 was as follows:

ASSETS	Cost	Prov for depn	WDV
Non-current assets	£	£	£
Leasehold premises	8,000	800	7,200
Plant and machinery	9,200	2,700	6,500
	17,200	3,500	13,700
Current assets			
Inventories			5,400
Trade receivables		4,200	
Provision for doubtful debts		(750)	3,450
Bank			8,000
			16,850
Total assets			30,550
EQUITY AND LIABILITIES			
Equity capital			
Capital			
— Street		8,500	
— Rhode		6,000	
— Close		4,500	19,000
Current accounts			
— Street		850	
— Rhode		1,300	
— Close		1,150	3,300
Total equity			22,300
Non-current liabilities			
Loan: Street			4,000
Total non-current liabilities			4,000
Current liabilities			
Trade payables			4,250
Total current liabilities			4,250
Total equity and liabilities			30,550

Street retired from the partnership on 31 March 20X2 and Rhode and Close decided to carry on the business and to admit Lane as a partner who is to bring in capital of £10,000. Future profits are to be shared equally among Rhode, Close and Lane.

By agreement, the following adjustments were to be incorporated in the books of account as at 31 March 20X2:

1 Plant and machinery to be increased to £6,900 in accordance with a valuer's certificate.

2 Inventory to be reduced to £4,860, since some items included therein were regarded as unsaleable.

3 The provision for doubtful debts to be increased to £830.

4 Provision to be made for the valuer's charges, £140.

The partnership deed provided that on the retirement of a partner, the value of goodwill was to be taken to be an amount equal to the average annual profit of the three years ending on the date of retirement. The profits of such three years were:

Year ended 31 Mar 20X0	£7,800
Year ended 31 Mar 20X1	£9,400
Year ended 31 Mar 20X2	£11,600

The partners agreed that, in respect of the valuing of goodwill, the profits should be regarded as not being affected by the revaluation. It was decided that an account for goodwill should not be opened in the books, but that the transactions between the partners should be made through their capital accounts.

£3,000 was repaid to Street on 1 April 20X2 and she agreed to leave £12,000 as a loan to the new partnership. Rhode, Close and Lane promised to repay the balance remaining due to Street within six months.

Required

You are required to prepare:

a the revaluation account.

b the partners' capital accounts (in columnar form).

c Street's account showing the balance due to her.

d the statement of financial position of Rhode, Close and Lane as on 1 April 20X2.

(ACCA, adapted)

INTERMEDIATE

28.11

Matthew, Mark and Luke were in partnership sharing profits and losses in the ratio 5 : 3 : 2, financial statements being made up annually to 30 June. Fixed capitals were to bear interest at the rate of 5 per cent per annum, but no interest was to be allowed or received on current accounts or drawings. Any balance on current accounts was to be paid at each year end.

Luke left the partnership on 30 September 20X2, but agreed to leave his money in the business until a new partner was admitted, provided interest at 5 per cent was paid on all amounts due to him.

John was admitted to the partnership on 1 January 20X3, providing capital of £2,000. It was agreed that the new profit-sharing ratio be Matthew 5, Mark 4, John 1, but Mark was to guarantee John an income of £3,000 per annum in addition to his interest on capital.

At 1 July 20X2 each partner had a fixed capital of £4,000.

Drawings during the year 20X2/20X3 were as follows:

Matthew	£750
Mark	£600
Luke	£220 (to 30 September 20X2)
John	£80

The profit for the year to 30 June 20X3 was £20,000, which may be assumed to have accrued evenly over that period.

You are required to show:

a the appropriation account;

b the partners' current accounts for the year ended 30 June 20X3.

(ACCA)

INTERMEDIATE

28.12

Hawthorn and Privet have carried on business in partnership for a number of years, sharing profits in the ratio of 4 : 3 after charging interest on capital at 4 per cent per annum. Holly was admitted into the partnership on 1 October 20X2, and the terms of the partnership from then were agreed as follows:

1 Partners' annual salaries to be: Hawthorn £1,800, Privet £1,200, Holly £1,100.

2 Interest on capital to be charged at 4 per cent per annum.

3 Profits to be shared: Hawthorn four-ninths, Privet three-ninths, Holly two-ninths.

On 1 October 20X2 Holly paid £7,000 into the partnership bank and of this amount £2,100 was in respect of the share of goodwill acquired by her. Since the partnership has never created, and does not intend to create, a goodwill account, the full amount of £7,000 was credited for the time being to Holly's capital account at 1 October 20X2.

The trial balance of the partnership at 30 June 20X3 was as follows:

	Debit	Credit
	£	£
Cash at bank	3,500	
Inventories at 1 July 20X2	11,320	
Purchases	102,630	
Sales revenue		123,300
Wages and salaries	6,200	
Rates, telephone, lighting and heating	2,100	
Printing, stationery and postage	530	
General expenses	1,600	
Bad debts written off	294	
Capital accounts: – Hawthorn		22,000
– Privet		11,000
– Holly		7,000
Current accounts: – Hawthorn	2,200	
– Privet	1,100	
– Holly	740	
Trade receivables and trade payables	27,480	13,744
Freehold premises	12,000	
Furniture, fixtures and fittings at 1 July 20X2	5,800	
Bad debts reserve		450
	177,494	177,494

After taking into account the following information and the adjustment required for goodwill, prepare a statement of profit and loss for the year ended 30 June 20X3 and a statement of financial position as on that date. On 30 June 20X3:

1 Inventory was £15,000.

2 Rates (£110) and wages and salaries (£300) were outstanding.

3 Telephone rental paid in advance was £9.

4 Provision for bad debts is to be adjusted to 2.5 per cent of trade receivables.

5 Depreciation is to be provided on furniture, fixtures and fittings at 10 per cent.

Apportionments required are to be made on a time basis.

(ACCA)

28.13

A, B and C are in partnership sharing profits and losses in the ratio of 50 : 25 : 25 per cent. Each partner receives a salary of £40,000 and interest on opening capital balance of 15 per cent per year. The draft statement of financial position at the year end 31 March 20X2 is as follows:

Draft statement of financial position for ABC as at 31 March 20X2			
ASSETS	Cost	Prov for depn	WDV
Non-current assets	£'000	£'000	£'000
Fixtures	500	300	200
Motor vehicles	240	120	120
	740	420	320
Current assets			
Inventories			280
Trade receivables		200	
Provision for doubtful debts		(40)	160
Bank			240
			680
Total assets			1,000
EQUITY AND CAPITAL			
Equity capital			
Capital accounts:			
– A		80	
– B		160	
– C		80	320
Current accounts:			
– A		40	
– B		(20)	
– C		60	80
			400
Profit for the year (not yet apportioned)			320
Total equity			720
Non-current liabilities			
Long-term loan			80
Total non-current liabilities			80
Current liabilities			
Trade payables			200
Total current liabilities			200
Total equity and liabilities			1,000

The partners agreed to admit D on 31 March 20X2. D agreed to introduce £200,000 of capital. The partners have agreed to share the profits as follows A (40 per cent), B (30 per cent), C (20 per cent) and D (10 per cent). Goodwill on that date is valued at £600,000 and is not to be brought into the books. It is agreed that inventories are worth £360,000 and trade receivables £140,000. All other entries are of similar value to the book value amounts shown in the above statement of financial position.

You are required to prepare the:

a appropriation account for the year ended 31 March 20X2;

b revaluation account;

c partners' capital and current accounts;

d revised final statement of financial position at 31 March 20X2, after the introduction of D as partner.

28.14

X, Y and Z are in partnership sharing profits and losses in the ratio 4 : 2 : 2. Z died on 30 June 20X2. The partnership statement of financial position as at that date was:

Statement of financial position for X, Y and X partners on 30 June 20X2		
ASSETS	£'000	£'000
Non-current assets		280
Current assets		800
Total assets		1,080
EQUITY AND LIABILITIES		
Owners' equity		
Partner capital accounts		
– X	200	
– Y	240	
– Z	160	600
Partner current accounts		
– X	60	
– Y	100	
– Z	40	200
Total owners' equity		800
Current liabilities		280
Total equity and liabilities		1,080

Additional information

It was agreed between X, Y and Z's representatives that on 30 June 20X2 (for the purposes of settling the affairs of Z) that goodwill be valued at £120,000 and the freehold land (the only non-current asset) at £360,000. The balance owing to Z will remain on loan to the partnership for five years at a rate of 10 per cent interest per annum. X and Y agree that goodwill should not be reflected as an asset in the financial statements; however, the new value of freehold land should. They also agree that in the future they will share profits and losses equally.

Required

a Prepare the capital and current accounts for the three partners, the revaluation account and the opening statement of financial position for the new X and Y partnership.

b Explain goodwill and outline why it is important to be able to value it in the context of partnership financial statements.

References

Gore, R., Zimmerman, D. (2010) 'Is Goodwill an Asset?', *The CPA Journal*, June 2010, www.cpajournal.com/acc.htm (pp. 46–48).

International Accounting Standards Board (2010a) *International Accounting Standard 38 – Intangible Assets* (IASB)

International Accounting Standards Board (2010b) *International Financial Reporting Standard 3 – Business Combinations* (IASB).

When you have read this chapter, log on to the Online Learning Centre for *Introduction to Financial Accounting* at www.mcgraw-hill.co.uk/textbooks/thomas, where you will find multiple choice quizzes, case studies, a glossary and mock exams.

Partnership dissolution and conversion to a limited company

Learning Objectives

After reading this chapter you should be able to do the following:

1. Explain the meaning of the key terms and concepts listed at the end of the chapter.

2. Show the journal and ledger entries for the dissolution of a partnership.

3. Show the journal and ledger entries relating to the conversion of a partnership to a limited company.

29.1 Introduction

The previous chapter dealt with changes to a partnership that continued in operation into the future. This chapter focuses on the accounting for a complete cessation of the partnership. This usually happens in two circumstances: when the partnership is dissolved; and when the partnership converts to a limited company. Accounting for limited companies is covered in detail in Part 8 of this book. This chapter will only deal with the basic format of company financial statements. The two types of permanent cessation are now considered.

29.2 Dissolution of partnerships

As explained in the previous chapter, when a partner leaves and/or a new partner is admitted, the law states that the old partnership is dissolved and a new partnership is created. However, the phrase 'dissolution of partnerships' refers to the circumstances where all the partners wish to leave, and thus the activities of the partnership are wound up without a new partnership being created. Partnerships are usually dissolved because either it is unprofitable to carry on trading or the partners no longer wish to be associated with each other for personal reasons.

Accounting for the dissolution of partnerships can be quite complicated when the assets are disposed of over a prolonged period; known as the piecemeal realization of assets, and/or one or more of the partners is insolvent, which may involve the application of the *Garner* v. *Murray* rule described in Chapter 28 in the section on the 'Revaluation of assets on changes in partners'. However, these circumstances are not covered in this book. The basic model of accounting for the dissolution of partnerships is relatively simple, at least after having grasped the contents of Chapter 28.

The chronological sequence of events on the dissolution of partnerships is as follows:

1 Prepare a set of final financial statements from the end of the previous accounting year to the date of dissolution, including the usual entries in the partners' current accounts. These will be no different from the usual final financial statements apart from relating to a period of less than one year.

2 The assets will be disposed of usually by sale (although some may be taken over by the partners) and the money collected from trade receivables.

3 The liabilities are repaid in the order – trade payables, loans and then any partners' loans.

4 The balances on the partners' capital (and current) accounts are paid to them.

A simplifying assumption is usually made that all the above events occur on the date of dissolution or within a short period thereafter.

The simplest and also a perfectly acceptable way of accounting for a dissolution is to transfer *all* the balances on the asset (except for bank/cash), liability and provision accounts to a realization account. Then, all the money received from the sale of assets (including that collected from trade receivables) and paid to trade payables and loan creditors is entered in this account. If any assets (or liabilities) are taken over by the partners, the value placed on these will be entered in the realization account with a double entry to the relevant partners' capital accounts.

However, since liabilities such as trade payables and loans are technically not realized, some accountants do not enter these in the realization account. Instead, the amounts paid are entered in the relevant liability accounts, and any difference between the book values and amounts paid, such as discount received, are transferred to the realization account.

This highlights an important feature of the realization account concerning its purpose, and brings us to the next stage in the accounting procedure. The realization account performs a similar function to the revaluation account except that instead of being used to determine the profit or loss on revaluation, it is used to ascertain the profit or loss on dissolution. This is then transferred to the partners' capital accounts in their profit-sharing ratio.

Finally, the balances on the partners' current accounts are transferred to their capital accounts, and the resulting balances on the capital accounts are paid to the partners. This will eliminate the balance on the bank and cash accounts, leaving all the ledger accounts now closed. One last complication arises if the resulting balance on any of the partners' capital accounts, before repaying the partners, is a debit balance. At foundation level students are usually expected to assume that the partner is solvent and thus will pay to the partnership any debit balance on his or her capital account. This should then provide enough money with which to repay the other partners the credit balances on their capital accounts.

An illustration of accounting for the dissolution of partnerships is given in Example 29.1.

EXAMPLE 29.1

Tom and Jerry, whose accounting year end is 31 December, have been in partnership for several years sharing profits equally. They have decided to dissolve the partnership as on 14 February 20X2. You have already prepared a statement of profit and loss for the period 1 January 20X2 to 14 February 20X2 and a statement of financial position as at the latter date as follows:

	Cost	Depn	NBV
ASSETS	£	£	£
Non-current assets			
Motor vehicles	20,000	6,600	13,400
Current assets			
Inventories			6,700
Trade receivables		5,900	
Provision for bad debts		(600)	5,300
Prepaid expenses			500
			12,500
Total assets			25,900
EQUITY AND LIABILITIES			
Equity capital			
Capital – Tom		8,000	
– Jerry		4,200	12,200
Current accounts – Tom		4,800	
– Jerry		(1,900)	2,900
Total equity capital			15,100
Current liabilities			
Bank overdraft			1,600
Trade payables			3,200
Bank loan			2,000
Loan – Tom			4,000
Total current liabilities			10,800
Total equity and liabilities			25,900

One of the motor vehicles was taken over by Jerry at an agreed valuation of £5,700. The remainder were sold for £6,200. The inventory realized £7,100 and £4,900 was received from trade receivables. A refund of the full amount of prepaid expenses was also received.

There were selling expenses in respect of advertising the vehicles and inventory for sale of £800. Trade payables were paid £2,900 in full settlement. The bank loan was repaid, including an interest penalty for early settlement of £400.

The partnership also sold its business name and a list of its customers to a competitor for £1,000.

You are required to show all the ledger entries necessary to close the partnership books.

Motor vehicles			
Balance b/d	20,000	Realization	20,000

Provision for depreciation			
Realization	6,600	Balance b/d	6,600

Inventory			
Balance b/d	6,700	Realization	6,700

Trade receivables			
Balance b/d	5,900	Realization	5,900

Provision for bad debts			
Realization	600	Balance b/d	600

Prepaid expenses			
Balance b/d	500	Realization	500

Trade payables			
Bank	2,900	Balance b/d	3,200
Realization	300		
	3,200		3,200

Bank loan			
Bank	2,400	Balance b/d	2,000
		Realization (Interest penalty)	400
	2,400		2,400

Loan – Tom			
Bank	4,000	Balance b/d	4,000

Realization account

Vehicles	20,000	Provision for depreciation		6,600
Inventories	6,700	Provision for bad debts		600
Trade receivables	5,900	Bank – vehicles		6,200
Prepaid expenses	500	Bank – inventories		7,100
Loan interest	400	Bank – trade receivables		4,900
Bank–expenses	800	Bank – prepayments		500
		Bank – goodwill		1,000
		Trade payables		300
		Capital – Jerry		5,700
		Loss on realization:		
		– Capital Tom	700	
		– Capital Jerry	700	1,400
	34,300			34,300

Current accounts

	Tom	Jerry		Tom	Jerry
Balance b/d	–	1,900	Balance b/d	4,800	–
Capital	4,800	–	Capital	–	1,900
	4,800	1,900		4,800	1,900

Capital accounts

	Tom	Jerry		Tom	Jerry
Current account	–	1,900	Balance b/d	8,000	4,200
Realization – vehicle	–	5,700	Current a/c	4,800	–
Loss on realization	700	700	Bank	–	4,100
Bank	12,100	–			
	12,800	8,300		12,800	8,300

Bank

Realization – vehicles	6,200	Balance b/d		1,600
Inventories	7,100	Trade payables		2,900
Trade receivables	4,900	Bank loan		2,400
Prepayments	500	Realization – expenses		800
Goodwill	1,000	Loan – Tom		4,000
Capital – Jerry	4,100	Capital – Tom		12,100
	23,800			23,800

Conversion to a limited company

Sometimes the partners in a partnership decide to convert their partnership into a limited company. This may be to limit their personal liability to the creditors of the partnership, or it may be for tax reasons.

'Why would a partnership wish to convert to a limited liability company?'

The main reason for a partnership firm becoming incorporated is to enable the partners not to be personally liable for the debts of the business. A partnership has no separate legal identity and each partner has joint and several liability for the debts of the firm. However, a shareholder in a limited company is not responsible for the debts of the company in the event of its insolvency. A shareholder's liability is limited to any amount still unpaid on the issue of the shares. If the shares were issued fully paid (as they normally are), then the shareholder has no liability.

Further, as a company the business should find it easier to attract new capital, as investors become shareholders and not partners. In the long run, companies can be floated on a stock exchange. However, before incorporating the business as a company, the partners will have to carefully consider the tax implications'.

Source: extract from an article by Tom Clendon 1999, www.accaglobal.com/archive/sa_oldarticles/30891#top (accessed May 2011).

A practical example of the benefits to of limited liability are provided in the next real world example:

The BDO Binder Hamlyn Case

The High Court in this case ordered the partners of BDO Binder Hamlyn (BDO) to pay £65 million to ADT (an electronic security group) in damages and £105 million in court costs. This was a famous case as it was highest-ever award against a firm of auditors. At this time (1996) BDO was not an LLP, and the insurance company did not cover the full claim, meaning that the partners had to make good on the outstanding debt from their personal assets.

The history of the case is as follows: BDO audited the financial statements of Britannia Security Systems (Britannia). When ADT were undertaking their due diligence audit before acquiring Britannia, they reviewed ADT's financial statements and a representative of ADT met the BDO audit partner who had signed the audit report 11 weeks earlier. The audit partner provided assurances to the ADT representative over the truth and fairness of the audited financial statements. The court concluded that these assurances meant that the BDO partner had accepted responsibility for the audited financial statements and had known about the influence the financial statements had on the decision by ADT to acquire Britannia. After acquisition, ADT discovered that Britannia was worth about £65 million less than the £105 million paid for the company and that the financial statements had contributed to the overvaluation.

Had BDO been an LLP, ADT would not have had recourse for the balance due to them from the partners' (shareholders') personal assets.

Source: http://www.thelawyer.com/reasons-to-be-careful/92609.article

LEARNING ACTIVITY 29.1

Download the Winter 2007 publication by *CPA Protect (Kennedy's – legal advice in black and white)*. Read the article that discusses the BDO case in the previous real life example and in addition familiarize yourself with the 'Bannerman case'. This famous case influenced the wording of audit reports, as auditors took steps to limit their liability from claims made by parties who had used audited financial statements for economic decision making (such as lending funds to the entity, or acquiring the entity) but found out subsequently that the financial statements did not faithfully represent the true performance and financial position of the entity.

Source: Sharrock (2007), the website address is in the References section.

The result of a conversion to a limited company is that the partnership ceases to exist and all the partnership accounts have to be closed and a new company is established with new ledger accounts. The steps to take to convert a partnership to a company are as follows:

1 Open a realization account and transfer all assets and liabilities to this (the exception is cash/bank). In addition, some questions may state that items have to be paid, or credit accounts settled before the **conversion** takes place.

2 Transfer the partners' current accounts to the capital accounts.

3 Open a 'company personal account' and debit the consideration being given for the partnership to this account. Credit the realization account with the other side of this entry.

4 Close off the realization account, transferring the profit, or loss, on realization to the partners in their profit-sharing ratio.

5 Credit the 'company personal account' with the share capital, debentures and cash (this account will now also balance and can be closed) and debit the partnership accounts with the shares, cash or debentures in the portions stipulated in the question.

6 The balance on the partners' capital accounts will be the amount owing to them from the partnership, or the amount they owe to the partnership.

7 Finally, write cheques to settle any balances remaining as owing to the partners (credit bank, debit partners' capital accounts), or get the partners to introduce cash when they owe the partnership funds (debit bank, credit partners' capital accounts). At this point the cash account should be closed with no balance and the capital accounts will be closed with no balances. Indeed, all accounts will now be closed.

The transactions also have to be recorded in the books of the new company. This is normally done through a **purchase of consideration account**. The assets are usually taken over at fair value and these values are the ones that should be used as the opening balances in the new company. The steps to take when setting up the accounts in the new company are as follows:

1 Determine the value of goodwill (excess of the purchase consideration over the fair value of the assets and liabilities). This is commonly taken to be the balance on the purchase consideration account.

2 Open a purchase of consideration account. Debit it with the purchase consideration and credit the source of the purchase consideration; for example, share capital, bank, loan or debentures.

3 Credit the purchase consideration account with the asset values and debit the new asset accounts.

4 Debit the purchase consideration account with the liabilities value and credit the new liabilities accounts.

5 Post the balance (goodwill) to a goodwill account.

When the goodwill is negative, then it is important to review the fair values of the assets being recorded; it is likely that they are overstated.

<table>
<tr><td rowspan="2">EXAMPLE
29.2</td><td colspan="4">Anna and Mary, who share profits 3 : 2, decide to become a limited company on 31/03/X3. The statement of financial position at this date is as follows:</td></tr>
</table>

Statement of financial position for Anna and Mary as at 31 March 20X3			
	Cost	Prov for depn	WDV
ASSETS	£	£	£
Non-current assets			
Motor vehicles	10,000	8,000	2,000
Equipment	6,000	2,000	4,000
	16,000	10,000	6,000
Current assets			
Inventories			3,200
Trade receivables			4,400
Cash			800
			8,400
Total assets			14,400
EQUITY AND LIABILITIES			
Owners' equity	Anna	Mary	
Capital account	6,000	3,000	9,000
Current account	960	(160)	800
	6,960	2,840	9,800
Current liabilities			
Trade payables			4,600
Total equity and liabilities			14,400

The company is to be called McKees Ltd.

The purchase consideration is £12,500 to be settled by issuing 10,000 equity shares of £1 each, allotted at £1.20 per share, and £500 cash.

Assume the transfer is at book values.

Required

a Close the accounts of the partnership.

b Prepare the opening statement of financial position of the new company.

Motor vehicles			
Balance b/d	10,000	Realization account	10,000

Provision for depreciation–motor vehicles			
Realization a/c	8,000	Balance b/d	8,000

Equipment			
Balance b/d	6,000	Realization account	6,000

Provision for depreciation—equipment

Realization a/c	2,000	Balance b/d	2,000

Inventories

Balance b/d	3,200	Realization account	3,200

Trade receivables

Balance b/d	4,400	Realization account	4,400

Trade payables

Realization a/c	4,600	Balance b/d	4,600

Personal account

Realization account (Purchase consideration)	12,500	Cash		500
		Shares allocated:		
		– Anna ($\frac{3}{5}$)	7,200	
		– Mary ($\frac{2}{5}$)	4,800	12,000
	12,500			12,500

Realization account

Motor vehicles	10,000	Provision for depreciation:	
Equipment	6,000	– Motor vehicles	8,000
Inventories	3,200	– Equipment	2,000
Trade receivables	4,400	Trade payables	4,600
		Personal account–purchase consideration	12,500
Profit on realization:			
– Anna ($\frac{3}{5}$)	2,100		
– Mary ($\frac{2}{5}$)	1,400	3,500	
		27,100	27,100

Current accounts

	Anna	Mary		Anna	Mary
Balance b/d	–	160	Balance b/d	960	–
Capital account	960	–	Capital account	–	160
	960	160		960	160

Capital accounts					Anna	Mary
	Anna	**Mary**			**Anna**	**Mary**
Current account	–	160	Balance b/d		6,000	3,000
Equity shares	7,200	4,800	Current account		960	–
			Profit on realisation		2,100	1,400
Bank	1,860	–	Bank		–	560
	9,060	4,960			9,060	4,960

Bank account			
Balance b/d	800	Anna	1,860
Personal account	500		
Mary	560		
	1,860		1,860

Note

1 Mary has to introduce £560 to the partnership, whereas Anna will receive a cheque from the partnership for £1,860.

EXAMPLE 29.3

Required

Using the information from Example 29.2 prepare the opening statement of financial position of the new company.

Note: the purchase of business account should be completed, but it is unnecessary to open all the ledger accounts.

Purchase of business account			
Trade payables account	4,600	Motor vehicles account	2,000
Purchase consideration:		Equipment account	4,000
– Bank overdraft account	500	Inventories account	3,200
– Equity share capital account	12,000	Trade receivables account	4,400
		Goodwill account	3,500
	17,100		17,100

Statement of financial position for McKees Ltd as at 31/03/X3		
ASSETS		
Non-current assets	£	£
Tangible assets		
Motor vehicles		2,000
Equipment		4,000
		6,000
Intangible assets		
Goodwill		3,500
Total non-current assets		9,500
Current assets		
Inventories		3,200
Trade receivables		4,400
		7,600
Total assets		17,100
EQUITY AND LIABILITIES		
Equity and reserves		
Share capital		12,000
Current liabilities		
Bank overdraft		500
Trade payables		4,600
Total current liabilities		5,100
Total equity and liabilities		17,100

The next real world example is taken from the Companies House website and deals with the creation of an LLP from a limited company.

Can I convert from being a limited company to an LLP?

REAL WORLD EXAMPLE 29.3

'The LLP legislation does not allow for a 'conversion process' – in the way that a limited company can convert to PLC status under the Companies Act, for example. Anyone with a current limited company wishing to transfer their existing company name to a new LLP should contact the LLP Team Leader. The process will involve a closely controlled company change of name and an LLP incorporation. Establishing contact prior to submitting the necessary forms will help ensure that this process is completed as smoothly as possible.

What are the LLP disclosure requirements?

They are similar to those of a company. LLPs are required to provide financial information equivalent to that of companies, including the filing of annual accounts. Among other things, they are also required to:

- File an annual return;
- Notify any changes to the LLP's membership;
- Notify any changes to their members names and residential addresses;
- Notify any change to their Registered Office Address.

What are the duties of a designated member?

Designated members are responsible for carrying out certain duties including some of those that would normally be carried out by a company director or secretary. They include such things as:

- Signing the annual accounts;
- Filing the annual accounts and annual returns with Companies House;
- In the event of insolvency proceedings, providing any statement setting out the affairs of the business i.e. assets, debts and liabilities.'

Source: www.companieshouse.gov.uk (see References).

REAL WORLD EXAMPLE 29.4

Limited liability agreements

The UK Companies Act 2006 allows auditors to conclude liability limitation agreements with their clients. Chapter 7 contains important provisions about auditors' liability that enable auditors to enter into liability limitation agreements (LLAs) with their clients. An LLA is an agreement that purports to limit an auditor's liability to a company in respect of any negligence, default, breach of duty or breach of trust by the auditor vis-à-vis the company, and which occurs during the audit of the accounts. For more detailed information on this, read the article by Sharrock (2007).

Source: Author. (Sharrock, 2007)

Summary

When a partnership's activities cease there is a dissolution of the partnership. All the assets are realized and the liabilities paid. Any profit or loss on realization is ascertained via a realization account and transferred to the partners' capital accounts. The balances on the partners' capital and current accounts are then repaid.

Key terms and concepts

conversion	541	purchase of consideration	
dissolution	535	account	541

An asterisk after the question number indicates that there is a suggested answer on the Online Learning Centre (www.mcgraw-hill.co.uk/textbooks/thomas).

Review questions

connect

29.1* What are the main reasons for dissolving a partnership?

29.2 What happens to the assets and liabilities of a partnership on dissolution?

Exercises

connect

29.3*

INTERMEDIATE

Martin and Stephen share profits in the ratio 2 : 1. They decide to terminate their partnership on 31 December 20X2. Their statement of financial position being as follows:

Statement of financial position for Martin and Stephen as at 31 December 20X2			
	Cost	Depn	NBV
ASSETS	£	£	£
Non-current assets	6,000	2,400	3,600
Current assets			
Inventory			4,150
Trade receivables			3,850
Cash			250
			8,250
Total assets			11,850
EQUITY AND LIABILITIES			
Equity capital	*Martin*	*Stephen*	
Capital	5,000	3,000	8,000
Current	150	(100)	50
Total equity	5,150	2,900	8,050
Non-current liabilities			
Loan account: Martin			1,000
Total non-current liabilities			1,000
Current liabilities			
Trade payables			2,800
Total current liabilities			2,800
Total equity and liabilities			11,850

The dissolution progressed as follows:

1 £350 of trade receivables could not be recovered.
2 Trade payables gave 10 per cent discount when settled.
3 Non-current assets realized £2,950.
4 Realization costs of £50 were paid.
5 Inventory realized 20 per cent more than anticipated.
6 Partners' claims were met and the books closed.

Required

Prepare the ledger accounts showing the final distributions to be paid to each partner.

ADVANCED

29.4

Alpha, Beta and Gamma were in partnership for many years sharing profits and losses in the ratio 5 : 3 : 2 and making up their financial statements to 31 December each year. Alpha died on 31 December 20X1, and the partnership was dissolved as from that date.

The partnership statement of financial position at 31 December 20X1 was as follows:

Alpha, Beta and Gamma			
Statement of financial position as at 31 December 20X1			
	Cost	Aggregate depreciation	Net book value
ASSETS			
Non-current assets	£	£	£
Freehold land and buildings	350,000	50,000	300,000
Plant and machinery	220,000	104,100	115,900
Motor vehicles	98,500	39,900	58,600
	668,500	194,000	474,500
Current assets			
Inventories			110,600
Trade and sundry receivables			89,400
Cash at bank			12,600
			212,600
Total assets			687,100
EQUITY AND LIABILITIES			
Owners' equity			
Capital accounts:			
– Alpha			233,600
– Beta			188,900
– Gamma			106,200
			528,700
Non-current assets			
Loan – Delta (carrying interest at 10 per cent)			40,000
Current liabilities			
Trade and sundry payables			118,400
Total equity and liabilities			687,100

In the period January to March 20X2 the following transactions took place and were dealt with in the partnership records:

1	Non-current assets	
		£
	Freehold land and buildings – sold for:	380,000
	Plant and machinery – sold for:	88,000
	Motor vehicles: Beta and Gamma took over the cars they had been using at the following agreed values:	
	– Beta	9,000
	– Gamma	14,000
	The remaining vehicles were sold for:	38,000
2	Current assets	
	Inventory – taken over by Gamma at agreed value:	120,000
	Trade and sundry receivables:	
	Cash received	68,400
	Remainder taken over by Gamma at agreed value	20,000
3	Current liabilities	
	The trade and sundry payables were all settled for a total of:	115,000
4	Non-current liabilities	
	Delta's loan was re paid on 31 March 20X2 with interest accrued since 31 December 20X1	
5	Expenses of dissolution £2,400 were paid	
6	Capital accounts	
	The final amounts due to or from the estate of Alpha, Beta and Gamma were paid/received on 31 March 20X2	

Required

Prepare the following accounts as at 31 March 20X2 showing the dissolution of the partnership:

a realization account;

b partners' capital accounts;

c cash book (cash account).

Ignore taxation and assume that all partners have substantial resources outside the partnership.

(ACCA)

ADVANCED

29.5

Peter, Paul and Mary have been in partnership for several years sharing profits and losses in the ratio 1 : 2 : 3. Their last statement of financial position is as follows:

| Peter, Paul and Mary | | | |
| Statement of financial position as at 30 June 20X2 | | | |
ASSETS	£	£	£
Non-current assets	40,000	12,000	28,000
Current assets			
Inventories			10,000
Trade receivables			42,000
			52,000
Total assets			80,000
EQUITY AND LIABILITIES			
Owners' equity			
Capital accounts			
– Peter			4,000
– Paul			8,000
– Mary			8,000
Total equity			20,000
Current liabilities			
Bank			26,000
Trade payables			34,000
Total current liabilities			60,000
Total equity and liabilities			80,000

The partnership had become very dependent on one customer, Jefferson, and in order to keep his custom the partners had recently increased his credit limit until he owed them £36,000. Jefferson has just been declared bankrupt and the partnership is unlikely to get any money from him. Reluctantly, the partners have agreed to dissolve the partnership on the following terms:

1 The inventory is to be sold for £8,000.

2 The non-current assets will be sold for £16,000 except for certain items with a book value of £10,000, which will be taken over by Mary at an agreed valuation of £14,000.

3 The trade receivables, except for Jefferson, are expected to pay their accounts in full.

4 The costs of dissolution will be £1,600 and discounts received from trade credit suppliers are expected to be £1,000.

5 Peter is unable to meet his liability to the partnership out of his personal funds.

Required

Prepare the:

a realization account

b partners' capital accounts recording the dissolution of the partnership.

29.6

ADVANCED

Maraid, Wendy and Diane have been in partnership for a number of years sharing profits $\frac{2}{5}$, $\frac{2}{5}$ and $\frac{1}{5}$, respectively. They decide to form a limited company on 1 January 20X2, called McKee Ltd, to carry on the business. The statement of financial position of the partnership on 31 December 20X1 is as follows:

Statement of financial position for Maraid, Wendy and Diane as at 31 December 20X1			
	Cost	Dep'n	NBV
ASSETS	£	£	£
Non-current assets			
Land	190,000	–	190,000
Plant and equipment	40,000	23,650	16,350
Fixtures and fittings	18,000	8,000	10,000
	248,000	31,650	216,350
Current assets			
Inventories			38,000
Trade receivables		186,490	
Provision for doubtful debts		(12,000)	174,490
Bank			20,500
Cash			510
			233,500
Total assets			449,850
EQUITY AND LIABILITIES			
Owners' equity			
Capital accounts:			
– Maraid			84,950
– Wendy			45,000
– Diane			30,000
Total equity			159,950
Non-current liabilities			
10% Loan			120,000
Current liabilities			
Trade payables			169,900
Total equity and liabilities			449,850

Additional information

The updated statement of financial position information at 31 December 20X1 is as follows:

1 The land is valued at £210,000 on the 31 December 20X1.

2 A machine that was purchased for £10,000 on 1 January 20W9 is now considered to be worthless. Machines are depreciated using the sum of digits method over a period of four years. On 1 January 20X2 the partners considered that this machine would have a residual value of £2,000. (The figures in the statement of financial position above have been adjusted for 20X1's depreciation charge.)

3 The financial statements for the period ended 31 December had omitted the accountancy fee for that period of £3,000.

4 During a review of the inventory on 31 December 20X1, items valued in the books at £9,000 were considered to be worth £1,000.

5 The partners received information that one of their customers, 'Seamus', is declared bankrupt. On investigation, it is estimated that Seamus will only be able to pay 20p for each £1 he owes. Seamus owes the partnership £50,000.

6 A full year's interest is still outstanding and has not yet been accrued in the above draft figures.

Required

Provide the relevant entries required for amending the statement of financial position to take account of the new up-to-date information and prepare the new updated statement of financial position.

(*Note*: All workings must be shown.)

ADVANCED

29.7

Use the amended information from Exercise 29.6 as a starting point.

Dissolution information

1 On 1 January 20X2 the partners decide to form a company and issue £140,000 worth of shares in the company to the partners. They raise an additional loan (£60,000) and raise £70,000 in cash from the bank by way of an overdraft to enable the newly created company to purchase the partnership. The full £270,000 is to be used to purchase the assets and liabilities of the partnership, with the exception of the loan and the interest owing on the loan.

2 The shares and loan are to be divided between the partners as follows: Maraid (50 per cent), Wendy (25 per cent) and Diane (25 per cent).

3 The expenses associated with the conversion to a limited company are £3,500. These are payable by the partnership.

4 The partnership loan and interest owing must be repaid in full before the conversion takes place.

Required

a Provide the relevant entries required for dissolution of the partnership (each partner will withdraw, or introduce cash to close their capital account). Prepare all the necessary ledger accounts, showing all workings.

b Prepare purchase of business account and the statement of financial position of McKee Ltd as on 1 January 20X2 (the opening accounts in the new business are not required).

References

Clendon, T. (1999) 'Conversion of a Partnership to a Limited Company', 1 October 1999, ACCA website, http://www.accaglobal.com/archive/sa_oldarticles/30891#top (accessed May 2011).

Companies House UK (2011) 'Limited Liability Partnerships (FAQs), Companies House website www.companieshouse.gov.uk/infoAndGuide/faq/11pFAQ.shtml (accessed May 2011).

The Lawyer (1996) 'Reasons to be careful', http://www.thelawyer.com/reasons-to-be-careful/92609.article (accessed March 2011).

Sharrock, C. (2007) 'Limiting the Risk', *CPA Protect: Kennedy's legal advice in black and white*, Winter 2007, http://www.kennedys-law.com/media/docs/CPAProtectWinter2007_2312008.pdf (accessed March 2010).

Skrine, R. (2007) 'Limiting and disclaiming liability: one clause can make all the difference', *CPA Protect: Kennedy's legal advice in black and white*, Winter 2007, http://www.kennedys-law.com/media/docs/CPAProtectWinter2007_2312008.pdf (accessed March 2010).

Spicer, P. and Fahy, A. (2011) 'The Benefits of Incorporating your Audit Practice', *Accountancy Ireland*, Vol. 43, No. 1, pp. 34–36.

When you have read this chapter, log on to the Online Learning Centre for *Introduction to Financial Accounting* at www.mcgraw-hill.co.uk/textbooks/thomas, where you will find multiple choice quizzes, case studies, a glossary and mock exams.

Companies

The nature of limited companies and their capital

Learning Objectives

After reading this chapter you should be able to do the following:

1. Explain the meaning of the key terms and concepts listed at the end of the chapter.

2. Describe the main characteristics of limited companies with particular reference to how these differ from partnerships.

3. Describe the different classes of companies limited by shares.

4. Outline the legal powers and duties of limited companies with reference to their Memorandum and Articles of Association.

5. Explain the nature and types of shares and loan capital issued by limited companies.

6. Outline the procedure relating to the issue of shares and debentures.

7. Explain the nature of a share premium, debenture discount, preliminary expenses, interim and final dividends.

8. Discuss the contents and purpose of the auditors' report.

9. Describe the contents of a company's statutory books.

10. Describe the purpose and proceedings of a company's annual general meeting.

30.1   Introduction

As discussed in Chapter 1, there are several different legal forms of organization. These can be grouped into two categories, known as **bodies sole** and **bodies corporate**. Bodies sole, or **unincorporated bodies**, consist of sole traders and partnerships. All other forms of organization are bodies corporate. A key feature of bodies corporate, or **incorporated bodies**, is that they are recognized by law as being a legal entity separate from their members.

A body corporate is one that is created either by Royal Charter, such as the Institute of Chartered Accountants in England and Wales, or by Act of Parliament. The Act of Parliament may either relate to the creation of a specific organization, such as the British Broadcasting Corporation, or alternatively permit the creation of a particular form of legal entity by any group of individuals. The most common forms of legal entity that can be created under such Acts of Parliament include building societies, life assurance and friendly societies, and companies.

A **company** can thus be defined as a legal entity that is formed by registration under the Companies Act 2006 (this supersedes all prior Companies Act legislation). There are four types of company: companies whose liability is limited by shares, companies with unlimited liability, companies whose liability is limited by guarantee and companies limited by shares and guarantee. Companies limited by guarantee include organizations such as some professional bodies where the liability of its members is limited to the amount of their annual subscription. The remainder of this chapter deals with companies whose liability is limited by shares. These are commonly known as 'limited companies'.

The characteristics of companies limited by shares

1 A company is a legal entity that is separate from its shareholders (owners). This means that companies enter into contracts as legal entities in their own right. Thus, creditors and others cannot sue the shareholders of the company but must take legal proceedings against the company. This is referred to as not being able to lift the **veil of incorporation**.

2 A company has perpetual existence in that the death of one of its shareholders does not result in its dissolution. This may be contrasted with a partnership, where the death of a partner constitutes a dissolution.

3 The liability of a company's shareholders is limited to the nominal value of their shares. **Limited liability** means that if a company's assets are insufficient to pay its debts, the shareholders cannot be called upon to contribute more than the nominal value of their shares towards paying those debts.

4 The shareholders of a company do not have the right to take part in its management as such. They appoint directors to manage the company. However, a shareholder may also be a director (or other employee).

5 Each voting share carries one vote at general meetings of the company's shareholders (e.g. in the appointment of directors). There may be different classes of shares, each class having different rights and, possibly, some being non-voting.

6 A limited company must have at least two shareholders but there is no maximum number.

30.3 The classes of companies limited by shares

There are two classes of companies limited by shares, namely public and private. Under the Companies Act a **public limited company** must be registered as such and is required to have a minimum authorized and allotted/issued share capital of £50,000. The principal reason for forming a public limited company is to gain access to greater amounts of capital from investment institutions and members of the public. The shares of many, but not all, public companies in the UK are quoted on the London Stock Exchange.

All other limited companies are **private companies**. These are not allowed to offer their shares for sale to the general public and thus do not have a stock exchange quotation. One of the main reasons for forming a private rather than a public company is that it enables its owners to keep control of the business, for example, within a family.

The name of a public company must end with the words 'public limited company' or the abbreviation 'plc'. The name of a private company must end with the word 'limited' or the abbreviation 'Ltd'. A business that does not have either of these descriptions after its name is not a limited company even if its name contains the word 'company' (the only exception being certain companies that have private company status, such as charities, who are permitted under licence to omit the word limited from their name).

30.4 The legal powers and duties of limited companies

A company is formed by sending certain documents and the appropriate fee to the Registrar of Companies. The most relevant of these documents are the Memorandum and Articles of Association. These define a company's powers and duties. The key contents of the **Memorandum of Association** are contained in Figure 30.1.

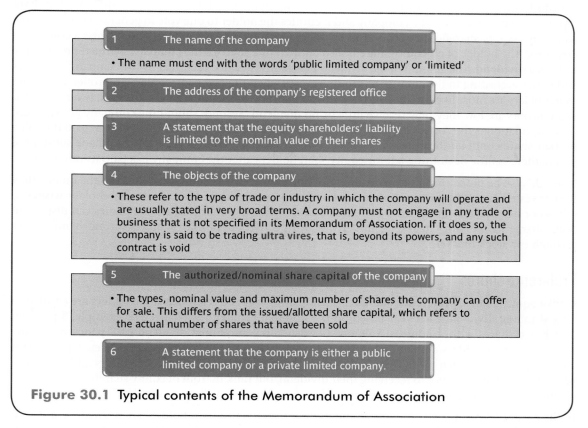

1 The name of the company
- The name must end with the words 'public limited company' or 'limited'

2 The address of the company's registered office

3 A statement that the equity shareholders' liability is limited to the nominal value of their shares

4 The objects of the company
- These refer to the type of trade or industry in which the company will operate and are usually stated in very broad terms. A company must not engage in any trade or business that is not specified in its Memorandum of Association. If it does so, the company is said to be trading **ultra vires**, that is, beyond its powers, and any such contract is void

5 The authorized/nominal share capital of the company
- The types, nominal value and maximum number of shares the company can offer for sale. This differs from the issued/allotted share capital, which refers to the actual number of shares that have been sold

6 A statement that the company is either a public limited company or a private limited company.

Figure 30.1 Typical contents of the Memorandum of Association

Any of the above can be subsequently changed by a **special resolution** passed at a general meeting of the company's shareholders. Such a resolution requires at least 75 per cent of the votes cast.

The **Articles of Association** can best be described as a rule book that sets out the rights of a company's shareholders between themselves. It contains regulations relating to the issue of shares, conduct of meetings, borrowing powers, the appointment of directors, and so on. When a company is registered, it is issued with what might be described as a birth certificate by the Register of Companies. This is called a **Certificate of Incorporation**. However, before a public limited company can commence trading, it must satisfy the Registrar that certain regulations relating to its capital structure have been complied with. When this is done the Registrar issues a **Trading Certificate**, on receipt of which the company can commence trading.

The costs of forming a company, including the above documents, are referred to as **preliminary, promotion or formation expenses**.

30.5 The nature and types of share and loan capital

Companies are financed predominantly by the issue (sale) of shares, loan stock and **debentures**, and by retaining part of each year's profit. In the UK all shares, loan stock and debentures have a fixed **nominal, par or face value**. This is often £1 or 25 pence in the case of shares and £100 for debentures and loan stock. There are several different types of share and loan capital, each of which is described below.

Equity shares

An **equity share** is also referred to as an **ordinary share** in the UK. Possession of an **equity voting share** represents part ownership of a company and it entitles the holder to one vote in general meetings of the company's equity shareholders. This gives shareholders the power to appoint and dismiss a company's directors. The holder of an equity share is also entitled to a share of the company's annual profit in the form of a **dividend**. The amount of the dividend per share is decided each year by the company's directors and varies according to the amount of profit. In years when the company earns high profits, the equity shareholders are more likely to receive a large dividend. However, equity shareholders run two risks. First, when profits are low they may receive little or no dividend. Second, should the company go bankrupt (into liquidation is the correct legal term) the equity shareholders are not entitled to be repaid the value of their shares until *all* the other debts have been paid. Often, where a company has made substantial losses, there is little or nothing left for equity shareholders after the company has paid its other debts.

It should also be noted that a company does not normally repay its equity shareholders the money they have invested except in the event of liquidation (or by court order). If an equity shareholder wishes to sell his or her shares, a buyer must be found. Shareholders in public limited companies can dispose of their shares in the stock market. Similarly, a prospective buyer may acquire 'second-hand' shares through the stock market.

Preference shares

Unlike equity shares, **preference shares** carry no voting rights. Preference shareholders are entitled to a fixed rate of dividend each year based on the nominal value of the shares. For example, 8 per cent preference shares with a nominal value of £1 each carry an annual dividend of 8 pence per share. Preference shareholders are entitled to their dividend after all the company's expenses, tax and debt commitments have been paid. Therefore, they rank behind normal company creditors and lenders in yearly terms when it comes to receiving their dividend, but rank in front of equity shareholders and will receive their dividend before equity shareholders can get any distribution (dividend).

In the event of a company going into liquidation, the preference shareholders are normally entitled to be repaid the nominal value of their shares before the equity shareholders. However, if no money is left after paying the other debts they would receive nothing.

As in the case of equity shares, companies do not normally repay preference shareholders the money they have invested except in the event of liquidation. Should a preference shareholder wish to dispose of shares, he or she must find a buyer or sell them in the stock market, if the company has a quotation for the preference shares.

There are two advantages of preference shares from the point of view of a company. One is that, since the rate of dividend is fixed, the company knows in advance what its future annual commitment is in respect of preference dividends. The second advantage is that preference shares are a permanent source of long-term capital, which does not have to be repaid. However, since the introduction of the corporation tax system in 1965, it has become unpopular to issue preference shares, because the dividend is not an allowable charge against income for tax purposes, while interest on debt is allowable. This makes debt a relatively more attractive source of fixed return finance for most companies. Small companies may be able to take advantage of the tax rules applicable to them to offset this difference.

There are a number of different types of preference share with rights that vary from those described above as detailed in Figure 30.2.

Cumulative preference shares
- The holders of **cumulative perference shares** will receive any arrears of dividends owing to them (before any equity shareholder receives a dividend) in the first subsequent year that there is sufficient profit to cover the dividend. Most of the preference shares quoted on the London Stock Exchange are cumulative

Redeemable preference shares
- **Redeemable preference shares** repayable by the company on a date fixed when the shares are issued. Because such a reduction in capital may endanger the creditor's interests, the Companies Act states that when a redemption takes place, the company must either make a new issue of shares with the same total nominal value, or capitalize an equivalent amount of profits. Capitalization refers to a transfer of retained profits to a capital reserve (usually called a **capital redemption reserve**). This means that the amount transferred cannot be distributed as dividends

Participatimg preference shares
- In addition to receiving a fixed rate of dividend, holders of **participating preference shares** are entitled, along with the equity shareholders, to a share of the profit remaining after deducting preference dividends

Figure 30.2 Types of preference share

Accounting for and disclosing preference shares and preference share dividends in the financial statements

Classifying preference shares is quite difficult under international accounting standards. They can be considered to be debt or equity. The terms of each preference share issue needs to be considered to determine the economic substance of the issue, with a view to classifying the shares as either a form of finance (debt), or new owners (equity). Preference shares are not strictly equity as they do not represent a share in the ownership of a company. Yet, in some instances, they have the same rights as owners. For example, they might be classed as equity: when they have voting rights attached that are the same as the voting rights of equity shareholders; when they are non-cumulative and directors can waive the yearly dividend; when they are non-redeemable; and when they are participating. In these circumstances preference shares are more like equity shares than debt.

In the UK most preference shares are cumulative and are non-participating. Some are redeemable. In these instances, though preference shares are called share capital, it is argued that their economic substance is closer to debt. Like debt, they have no voting rights and the company has to pay a finance charge yearly (the dividend). Therefore, unless otherwise stated, it is assumed, in this book, that preference shares are a form of non-current liability and their dividend is a finance charge, albeit a non-taxable deduction.

Debentures/loan stock

These are often referred to in the press as **corporate bonds**. Debentures and loan stock are not shares and have no voting rights. They represent a loan to the company and carry a fixed rate of interest per annum based on the nominal value. For example, 10 per cent debentures with a nominal value of £100 each carry an annual interest of £10 per debenture. A company may make several issues of debentures or loan stock at different times, each of which can have a different rate of interest. Debenture holders are entitled to their interest before the preference and equity shareholders receive their dividends, and the interest must be paid even if there is a loss. The interest on debentures is thus referred to as a charge against profit, whereas dividends constitute an **appropriation of profit**.

In the event of a company going into liquidation, debenture holders are entitled to be repaid the nominal value of their debentures before the preference and equity shareholders. Such debentures are usually referred to as **unsecured** – although they rank before shareholders, they are not entitled to be repaid until after all other creditors. However, some issues of debentures are **secured** on certain of the company's assets by either a **fixed charge** or a **floating charge**. A fixed charge is usually on specified assets such as property, plant or vehicles, and means that the company cannot dispose of those assets. A floating charge is usually on assets such as inventory. In this case the company can sell the assets but must replace them with similar assets of an equivalent value.

When debentures are secured, an accountant or solicitor may be appointed by the company to act as a trustee for the debenture holders. It is the trustee's responsibility to ensure that the value of the assets is always sufficient to repay the debenture holders. If this is not the case, or if the company may not be able to pay the annual interest on the debentures, the trustee may take legal possession of the assets, sell them and repay the debenture holders. Such drastic action usually results in the company going into liquidation.

Debentures and loan stock are usually repayable at some future date, which is specified when they are issued. This date is often several decades after they are issued. Should debenture holders wish to dispose of their debentures, they must find a buyer or sell them through a stock exchange such as the London Stock Exchange, or the Irish Stock Exchange, if the company has a quotation for the debentures.

The main advantage of debentures to a company is that the annual interest on debentures is an allowable charge against income for tax purposes.

A variation on debentures that has proved popular is **convertible loan stock/debentures**. These are debentures with a fixed annual rate of interest that also carry the right, at the holder's option, to convert them into a specified number of equity shares within a given time period, which is fixed when they are issued. The attraction of convertible loan stock is that the holder hopes to make a capital gain on conversion at some time in the future by virtue of the conversion rate being such that the equity shares can be acquired at an effective cost, which is lower than the market price at the date of conversion. Suppose, for example, a company issues £100 convertible loan stock at a price of £108, the rate of conversion being 90 equity shares for every £100 loan stock. At the date of the issue, the equity shares are quoted on the stock exchange at a price of £1 each. If at some future date the market price of the shares rises to, say, £1.50, it is beneficial to convert, since the shares would effectively cost £1.20 each (i.e. £108 ÷ 90 shares) compared with a market price of £1.50. These could then be sold for 90 @ £1.50 = £135 to give a capital gain of £135 − £108 = £27. Where the effective cost is more than the current market price, it would not be beneficial to convert and so the debentures should be retained.

A summary of the characteristics of shares and loan stock is given in Figure 30.3. A more detailed summary of the different types of preference shares and loan stock is shown in Figure 30.4.

Equity shares	Preference shares	Loan stock/debentures
1 Owners of the company who are normally entitled to vote at general meeting of the company's shareholders (e.g. to elect directors)	**1** No voting rights	**1** No voting rights
2 Receive a dividend the rate of which is decided annually by the company's directors. It varies each year depending on the profit and is an appropriation of profit	**2** Receive a fixed rate of dividend each year which constitutes an appropriation of profit. Have priority over equity dividends	**2** Receive a fixed rate of interest that constitutes a charge against income in computing the profit. Have priority over preference dividends
3 Last to be repaid the value of their shares in the event of the company going into liquidation. Also entitled to any surpluses/profits on liquidation	**3** Repaid before the equity shareholders in the event of liquidation	**3** Repaid before the equity and preference shareholders in the event of liquidation
4 Non-repayable except on the liquidation of the company	**4** All but one particular type are non-repayable except on liquidation	**4** Normally repayable after a fixed period of time
5 Rights specified in Articles of Association	**5** Rights specified in Articles of Association	**5** Rights specified in the terms of issue
6 Dividends non-deductible for tax purposes	**6** Dividends non-deductible for tax purposes	**6** Interest deductible for tax purposes

Figure 30.3 Summary of the characteristics of shares and loan stock

---

Types of preference shares

1 Non-cumulative – do not receive arrears of dividends.
2 Cumulative – if the dividend on these shares is not paid in any year, the holders are entitled to it in the next year that there are sufficient profits – before any other shareholder receives a dividend. The dividend becomes a liability of the company.
3 Redeemable – the only type of preference share that is repaid by the company after the expiration of a period specified when they were issued.
4 Participating – in addition to receiving a fixed annual rate of dividend, the holders are also entitled to a further dividend, which is related to profit levels and is similar in nature to a dividend on equity shares.

Issuing preference shares

Advantages: (a) non-repayable (except point 3 above); (b) the annual cost/dividend is known, thus facilitating planning; (c) in extreme circumstances the annual dividend can be waived.

Disadvantages: the dividends are not deductible for tax purposes.

Types of loan stock/debentures

1 Unsecured/naked – in the event of the company going into liquidation these are repaid before the equity and preference shareholders, but after other creditors.
2 With a fixed charge – secured on assets that the company cannot dispose of without the trustee for the debenture holders' permission. In the event of the security being in jeopardy, or the company not paying the annual interest, the trustee can take legal possession of the asset(s), sell them and repay the debenture holders.
3 With a floating charge – the same as debentures with a fixed charge, except that the asset(s) on which the debentures are secured can be sold by the company, but must be replaced with asset(s) of an equivalent value.
4 Convertible loan stock – carry the right, at the holder's option, to convert them into equity shares within a given time period fixed when they are issued. The rate of conversion is usually such that the holder obtains equity shares at a price that is lower than the market price of the shares at the date of conversion.

Issuing loan stock/debentures

Advantages: (a) the annual cost/interest is known; (b) the interest is deductible for tax purposes.

Disadvantages: (a) they have to be repaid after the expiration of the period specified when they were issued; (b) the interest must be paid before the equity and preference shareholders receive any dividend. This can be a burden when the proceeds of the issue have been used to finance expansion that may not result in revenue during the early years or where there is a reduction in the annual profit or high interest rates.

Figure 30.4 Summary of the types of preference shares and loan stock

30.6   The issue of shares and debentures

Shares can be, and usually are, issued (sold) by the company at a price in excess of their nominal value. The amount by which the issue price exceeds the nominal value is referred to as a **share premium**. In the case of a public limited company whose shares are listed on a stock exchange, the price at which the shares are quoted is usually different from both the nominal value and the issue price. The market price may be either above or below the issue price and the nominal value.

Debentures can be issued by the company at a price that is either greater or less than their nominal value. The latter is referred to as a **debenture discount**.

When shares and debentures are issued, the price may be payable by instalments. These consist of amounts payable: (a) on application; (b) on allotment/allocation of the shares by the company; and (c) any number of further instalments, referred to as **calls**.

Public limited companies offer shares, loan stock and debentures for sale to members of the public by means of a document known as a **prospectus**. This usually takes the form of a booklet sent by the company to anyone who expresses an interest in the issue. It may also consist of a full-page advertisement in a national newspaper, such as the *Financial Times*. The contents of a prospectus include as a minimum: (a) the total number of shares the company wishes to issue and the minimum subscription (i.e. the smallest number for which the applicant can apply); (b) the price of each share, stating the amounts payable on application, allotment and any calls; (c) details of the rights attaching to all classes of shares; and (d) a report by the company's auditors on the profits and dividends of the last five years, and the assets and liabilities at the end of the previous accounting year.

30.7   Interim and final dividends

Most large companies pay both interim and final dividends on their equity and preference shares. An **interim dividend** is paid halfway through the accounting year, when the profit for the first six months is known. The amount is decided by the directors. The **final dividend** is additional to the interim dividend and, although it relates to the same accounting year, is paid just after the end of the year. This is because the final dividend has to be approved by the equity shareholders at the annual general meeting (AGM), and this is always held after the end of the accounting year when the profit for the year is known.

Interest on loan stock and debentures is also often paid in two instalments, one halfway through the accounting year and the other at the end of the year. However, the amount relating to the latter half of the year may be outstanding at the end of the accounting year.

30.8   The books of account and published financial statements

Companies are required by law to keep proper books of account, and to prepare a set of published financial statements each year (i.e. a statement of comprehensive income, a statement of financial position, a statement of cash flows and the related notes), which conform with the books of account. The 'books of account' need not necessarily actually be in the form of books, but there must be some set of records of the business transactions (e.g. a computerized system). A copy of the published financial statements must be sent to each equity shareholder and the Registrar of Companies. The latter are available for inspection by the general public at Companies House. Most public limited companies also publish a copy of their full final financial statements on their website.

LEARNING ACTIVITY

30.1

You have already been able to view the final financial statements of a large public limited company, Ryanair plc or Diageo plc.

Using search engines, locate and view the full financial statements of five other large UK companies.

To fully appreciate the extent of standardization in company annual reports, prepare a table of the main contents as is found at the start of the Ryanair plc's annual report (e.g. it includes directors' report, remuneration report, etc.). Put the contents in rows in the table. Turn to the contents of each of the other companies' annual reports and match them to the table you created from Ryanair plc's annual reports (you could create columns for each company and tick if the same report is included).

Then view the statement of comprehensive income and statement of financial position; note the similarity in presentation.

Compare the presentation of accounting information in the financial statements of these companies to that recommended by IAS 1. This is given as a pro forma presentation for companies in Chapter 1 (simple version) and again in more detail in Chapter 31.

30.9 The auditors' report

Most limited companies are required by law to have their books and annual final financial statements audited by an independent qualified accountant. The financial statements covered by the audit consist of the statement of comprehensive income, the statement of financial position, the statement of cash flows (covered in Chapter 32) and the notes to the financial statements.

Although paid by the company, the auditors act on behalf of the equity shareholders and are appointed by them at the AGM. The auditors' function is to ascertain, or rather form an opinion of, whether or not *the financial statements give a true and fair view of the state of affairs and the profit of the company and have been properly prepared in accordance with the Companies Act 2006*. Their opinion is given in the **auditors' report**, which is attached to the final financial statements, and uses wording similar to that in italics in the previous sentence. If the financial statements are considered not to give a true and fair view or do not comply with the Companies Acts in some other way, the nature of the departure is usually stated in the auditors' report. This is referred to as a **'qualified' audit report**.

It is important to appreciate that the auditor does not guarantee that fraud or errors have not taken place. In the UK shareholders and loan creditors would be unlikely to receive damages from the auditors if a company subsequently went into liquidation or discrepancies were discovered, unless the auditors are shown to have been negligent. Furthermore, the auditors' report is not intended to be interpreted as passing an opinion on how efficiently and effectively the directors have used the company's assets.

LEARNING ACTIVITY

30.2

Revisit the audit report to the members of Wm Morrison Supermarkets plc (this is reproduced in Chapter 7). Read the audit report again, highlighting the wording of the opinion, and the scope limitation, which specifically details the fact that an audit is not a guarantee that fraud and errors have not taken place.

Statutory books

Companies are obliged by law to maintain certain records relating to their capital and directors. These are known as **statutory books** and consist of the following:

1 Register of Members, containing the name, address and number of shares held by each shareholder.

2 Register of Debenture Holders, containing the name, address and number of debentures/loan stock held by each debenture holder.

3 Register of Directors and Company Secretary, stating the name, address and occupation of each.

4 Register of Directors' Shareholdings, showing the number of shares held by each director.

5 Register of Mortgages and Other Charges secured on the company's assets, showing the name and address of the lender and the amount of each loan.

6 Minute Book of General Meetings of the company's equity shareholders, containing details of the proceedings and resolutions.

7 Minute Book of Directors' Meetings, containing details of the resolutions.

Companies are also required by law to submit an annual return to the Registrar of Companies each year, showing changes in the entries in the statutory books during that year. This information is available for inspection by the general public at Companies House. The statutory books (except the Minutes of Directors' Meetings) are also required by law to be available for inspection by members of the public at the company's registered office.

 ## The annual general meeting

The law demands that companies hold an **annual general meeting** (AGM). This is a meeting of the equity shareholders at which they are entitled to vote on a number of matters. These include the following:

1 To receive and adopt the report of the directors and the published financial statements for the year. This provides shareholders with an opportunity to question the directors on the contents of the financial statements. The financial statements are usually adopted, but if shareholders think that the financial statements are inaccurate or misleading, they may vote not to accept the financial statements. If the shareholders vote not to adopt the financial statements, this does not mean that another set has to be prepared.

2 To declare and adopt a proposed final dividend for the year on the equity shares. The amount of the final dividend is proposed by the directors. The shareholders cannot propose some other figure. Thus, if the shareholders vote not to adopt the proposed dividend, they will receive no final dividend for that year.

3 To elect directors. This is a source of the shareholders' power, in that if they are dissatisfied with the financial statements, the dividend or the company's performance, they may vote not to re-elect the existing directors. Shareholders also have the right to nominate other people as directors.

4 To appoint auditors and fix their remuneration. The directors normally suggest a specific firm of auditors, and the power to fix their remuneration is often delegated to the directors by the shareholders at the AGM. Large companies usually appoint a reputable national or international firm of accountants to act as auditors.

| REAL WORLD EXAMPLE 30.1 | **Shareholders becoming more active?** |

The Walker Report (2009) suggests that owners (shareholders) should protect their own interests by taking a more active role in ensuring that the company is governed appropriately. Shareholders *have* become more active and have used their power to exercise control over director decision-making. For example, in June 2010 at Tesco's Annual General Meeting 47 per cent of shareholders failed to back the remuneration report (Bowers and Finch, 2010). Figures from Pirc, the UK governance advisory group, show that the number of companies with 10 per cent or more opposition to their remuneration reports jumped from zero in 2000 to 65 in 2009 (Pirc website, 2010). At a British Airways Annual General Meeting (in 2010) one disgruntled shareholder got a round of applause when he reportedly told the board *'you do seem to be feathering your own nests at the expense of the shareholders you are supposed to serve'*.

Source: Author. (Walker Report, 2009; Bowers and Finch, 2010; Pirc website, 2010)

Summary

A limited company is a separate legal entity that has perpetual existence, and is managed by directors appointed by the members. The liability of its shareholders is limited to the nominal value of their shares. There are two classes of companies limited by shares, known as private limited companies (Ltd) and public limited companies (plc). A company's powers and the rights of the shareholders are contained in its Memorandum and Articles of Association.

Limited companies are financed predominantly by the issue of equity and preference shares, debentures and loan stock. These have a fixed face or nominal value but may be issued at a premium. Equity shares usually carry voting rights that give their holders the power to elect directors. They are also entitled to a share of the annual profits as a dividend that can vary each year. Equity shares are the last to be repaid in the event of the company going into liquidation. Preference shares are also entitled to an annual dividend but this is at a rate fixed at the time of issue. They may be cumulative, redeemable or participating. Preference shares are repaid before the equity shares in the event of liquidation. Most shares are non-repayable except on liquidation. All dividends are an appropriation of profits, and may include both an interim and final dividend. Debentures and loan stock represent a loan to the company. These carry a fixed rate of interest that is a charge against income. Debentures and loan stock are repaid before the shares in the event of liquidation, and may be secured by either a fixed or floating charge on company assets.

Companies are required by law to keep proper records of their transactions and prepare annual financial statements. In most cases these must be audited by independent qualified accountants who prepare a report expressing an opinion on whether the financial statements give a true and fair view of the profit and financial state of affairs. A copy of the published financial statements and auditors' report must be sent to all the equity shareholders. Companies are also required by law to maintain statutory books, and hold an AGM. At the AGM the equity shareholders vote on whether to adopt: the published financial statements; the dividend proposed by the directors; and the election of directors and auditors.

Key terms and concepts

An asterisk after the question number indicates that there is a suggested answer on the Online Learning Centre (www.mcgraw-hill.co.uk/textbooks/thomas).

connect Review questions

30.1* Describe the characteristics of companies limited by shares.

30.2 How does a public limited company differ from a private limited company?

30.3 Describe the contents of the Memorandum and Articles of Association. What are the purposes of these documents?

30.4 What are preliminary expenses?

30.5 Explain how each of the following arises:

a a share premium;

b a debenture discount.

30.6 Outline the main contents of a prospectus.

30.7 What is the difference between an interim dividend and a final dividend?

30.8 What is the auditors' report? How useful do you think this is in its present form and with its current legal standing in the UK?

30.9 Describe the contents of the statutory books of companies. What is the purpose of each of these books?

30.10 What is the annual general meeting of a company? Describe the proceedings at such a meeting.

30.11 Explain the main difference between a limited company and a sole trader.

30.12* Explain the main similarities and differences between equity shares, preference shares and debentures/loan stock.

30.13 Describe the different kinds of preference share.

Exercises

connect

30.14*

INTERMEDIATE

Design a table highlighting the attributes of a preference share that might cause it to be regarded as being equity, and the attributes that are more likely to cause it to be regarded as debt.

30.15

INTERMEDIATE

Rank the following stakeholders in terms of who would have priority when a company is settling claims of the stakeholders against it. Note, a rank of 1 means this stakeholder should be paid first.

- debenture holders;
- loan stock holders;
- preference shareholders;
- trade supplier;
- equity shareholder;
- bank.

30.16

INTERMEDIATE

What is the difference between a fixed charge and a floating charge?

30.17

INTERMEDIATE

Describe the main kinds of debenture loan stock.

References

Bowers, S. and Finch, J. (2010) 'Shareholders fight back over executive pay and bonuses', *Guardian*, Sunday, 11 July 2010, http://www.guardian.co.uk/business/ (accessed January 2011).

Milmo, D. and agencies (2010) 'BA boss Willie Walsh heckled at AGM over strike claims', *Guardian*, Tuesday, 13 July 2010, http://www.guardian.co.uk/business/ (accessed January 2011).

Pensions, Investments, Research Consultants Limited (PIRC) (2010) *PIRC Shareholder Voting Guidelines 2010*, www.pirc.co.uk (accessed December 2010).

Walker Report (2009) *A Review of Corporate Governance in UK Banks and other Financial Industry Entities*, The Walker Review Secretariat, London, 16 July.

When you have read this chapter, log on to the Online Learning Centre for *Introduction to Financial Accounting* at www.mcgraw-hill.co.uk/textbooks/thomas, where you will find multiple choice quizzes, case studies, a glossary and mock exams.

The final financial statements of limited companies

Learning Objectives

After reading this chapter you should be able to do the following:

1 Explain the meaning of the key terms and concepts listed at the end of the chapter.

2 Describe the main differences between the final financial statements of sole traders and companies, with particular reference to those arising from the latter being a separate legal entity.

3 Explain the nature and types of reserves.

4 Show the journal and ledger entries relating to the treatment of preliminary expenses. debenture interest, company income tax, dividends and transfers to reserves.

5 Demonstrate a basic understanding of the legal format of published company final financial statements and the main provisions of International Accounting Standard (IAS) 1 and International Financial Reporting Standards (IFRS) 5.

6 Prepare a simple set of final financial statements in a form suitable for publication and which complies with IAS (and with the Companies Act 2006).

7 Explain the nature and accounting treatment of discontinued operations, material items, prior period adjustments, events after the reporting period and contingencies.

31.1 Introduction

The Companies Act 2006 requires companies to send their equity shareholders a copy of the annual final financial statements. These are contained in the annual report and referred to as **published accounts**. They include a statement of comprehensive income, a statement of financial position and related notes. Larger entities also have to provide a statement of cash flows. There are detailed legal requirements relating to the content and format of company final financial statements. The first two sections of this chapter deal with the preparation of company final financial statements prior to putting them in a form suitable for publication. The remaining sections describe some of the legal requirements relating to their presentation in published form.

 ## Published financial statements

The final financial statements of companies that are published and sent to equity shareholders in the annual report must be presented in a form that complies with the Companies Act 2006. The Companies Acts laid down specific guidance on formats: financial statements must comprise a profit and loss account (statement of comprehensive income) and a balance sheet (statement of financial position). The statement of financial position must portray a true and fair view of the state of the affairs of the entity at the end of the year and the statement of comprehensive income must portray a true and fair view of the profit or loss of the entity for the year.

In terms of format, financial statements now have to be prepared either in accordance with IASs, or in accordance with any guidance/provision laid down by the Secretary of State (s396 of the 2006 Companies Act). The latter currently allows presentation under two statutory instruments: the Small Companies and Groups (Accounts and Directors Report) Regulations 2008; and the Large and Medium Sized Companies and Group (Accounts and Report) Regulations 2008. This book is focusing on IFRS; therefore, the formats presented in *IAS 1 – Presentation of Financial Statements* are utilized. The pro forma formats provided in IAS 1 include certain items with which the student will be unfamiliar and go beyond what is required at introductory level. The formats do not include disclosures for group entities as this is considered in 'An Introduction to Consolidated Financial Statements', available online at www.mcgrawhill/textbooks/thomas. With the exception of deferred tax, the remainder should be understandable at this level. Deferred tax is not usually examined at this level. The formats are reproduced in full for reference purposes in Figures 31.1, 31.2, 31.3 and 31.4.

 ## Determining the profit or loss for the period

IAS 1 allows two options for presenting the profit or loss for an entity for a period of time (usually one year). The first option is to combine all income, whether recognized or not, into a statement called the 'statement of comprehensive income'. This has two parts: the first part deals with realised profits or losses and is called the statement of profit and loss for the period. This ranges from 'revenue' to 'profit for the year'. The second part of this statement is called 'statement of other comprehensive income'. The statement of comprehensive income is as shown in Figure 31.1.

The second option is to present this information in two statements, the 'statement of profit and loss' and the 'statement of other comprehensive income net of tax'. In this instance the above format is split into the two statements as shown in Figure 31.2 and 31.3.

The statement of other comprehensive income is relatively simple, at least at introductory level. It will contain any unrealized surplus on the revaluation of non-current assets. The purpose of this statement is to show the gains (and losses) accruing to the company's shareholders, be they either realized, such as the profit for the year, or unrealized, as in the case of revaluation surpluses.

The IASB have stated a preference for a single statement approach and it is likely that published financial statements will use this format. However, it is more likely than not that private companies who comply with IAS will use the two statement approach as this is similar to the current approach being utilized in the UK, wherein companies who prepare their financial statements using UK standards, prepare a statement of total recognised gains and losses (the UK standards equivalent of the statement

Company name	
Statement of comprehensive income for the year ended 31 March 20X2	
	£
Revenue	XXX
Cost of sales	(XXX)
Gross profit	XXX
Other income	XX
Distribution costs	(XXX)
Administration expenses	(XXX)
Other expenses	(XXX)
Finance costs	(XXX)
Profit before tax	XX
Income tax expense	(XX)
Profit for the year	XX
Other comprehensive income	
Gains on property revaluation	XX
Exchange differences on translating foreign operations	XX
Income tax on other comprehensive income	(X)
Other comprehensive income net of tax	XX
Total comprehensive income for the year	XXX

Figure 31.1 A pro forma of the layout of a statement of comprehensive income for a company

Company name	
Statement of comprehensive income for the year ended 31 March 20X2	
	£
Revenue	XXX
Cost of sales	(XXX)
Gross profit	XXX
Other income	XX
Distribution costs	(XXX)
Administration expenses	(XXX)
Other expenses	(XXX)
Finance costs	(XXX)
Profit before tax	XX
Income tax expense	(XX)
Profit for the year	XX

Figure 31.2 A pro forma of the layout of a statement of profit and loss for a company

Company name	
Statement of other comprehensive income for the year ended 31 March 20X2, after tax	
Other comprehensive income for the year, after tax:	£
Gains on property revaluation	XX
Exchange differences on translating foreign operations	XX
Income tax on other comprehensive income	(X)
Other comprehensive income net of tax	XX
Total comprehensive income for the year	XXX

Figure 31.3 A pro forma of the layout of an 'other comprehensive income' statement for a company

of other comprehensive income, after tax) and a profit and loss account (the UK equivalent of the statement of profit and loss).

The contents of the statement of profit and loss for companies are the same as for sole traders and partnerships, with the following exceptions.

In arriving at the profit for the year, certain items not found in the financial statements of sole traders and partnerships are deducted.

- *Expenses*: these consist of directors' emoluments/remuneration (e.g. fees, salaries, pensions, compensation for loss of office), auditors' fees and expenses, interest on debentures, preliminary/ formation/promotion expenses and taxation. Preliminary/formation/promotion expenses refers to the costs incurred in forming a company, such as registration fees, and preparation of the Memorandum and Articles of Association. Preliminary expenses must not be retained in the financial statements as an asset.

- *Income tax expense (tax on income)*: Since a company is a separate legal entity, it is liable for taxation on its annual profit, which takes the form of income tax. This is called **corporation tax** in the UK, but is disclosed as income tax (an international label for the taxation of companies). The income tax is deducted from the profit before tax to give profit for the year. The double entry for the income tax *charge* on the annual profit is to debit the statement of profit and loss (or a separate income tax expense account, which is then transferred to the statement of profit and loss at the year end) and credit a current liability account in the name of 'HM Revenue and taxation', or more likely, 'income tax'.

- *Preference share dividends*: As mentioned previously, the economic substance of preference share capital is usually regarded as being a form of debt. Therefore, the dividends payable on preference share capital are included as a finance cost and treated as an expense of the company for accounting purposes. However, it is noted that dividends on preference shares are not an allowable expense for taxation purposes, therefore have to be added back in a tax computation to determine the taxable profit. Preference dividends comprise any interim dividend paid plus the final dividend proposed. The interim dividend paid will have been debited to the preference share dividends account in the ledger and thus shown in the trial balance. The final dividend may be outstanding at the end of the accounting year, in which case it is necessary to create an accrual in the preference dividends account and to show the amount owing on the statement of financial position as a current liability. The total of the interim and final dividends is then transferred from the preference share dividend account to the profit and loss account by debiting the profit and loss account with the yearly charge, with a corresponding credit in the preference share dividends account.

Where an examination question contains no income tax expense, the profit before tax is referred to as **profit for the year**. The key point at this stage is that the separate items that make up the cost of sales, distribution costs, administrative expenses, finance costs and other income should not be shown on the face of the statement of profit and loss. It is therefore necessary to first ascertain the total of each of these as workings. Note that distribution costs include selling expenses. Guidance on this was provided in Chapter 25, 'Financial Statements for Manufacturing Entities'.

Some of the items that are to be classified as either distribution costs or administrative expenses may be obvious from their descriptions (e.g. salespersons' commission, administrative salaries). Others are either less obvious or based on generally accepted conventions. In particular, distribution costs are usually taken to include advertising, carriage outwards, bad debts, changes in the provision for bad debts, discount allowed, motor expenses of delivery vehicles (including depreciation, profit/losses on disposal), and any costs associated with a warehouse such as wages, repairs to and depreciation of fork-lift trucks and similar 'plant and machinery'. There are few generally accepted conventions regarding the composition of administrative expenses. Examination questions normally need to specify which costs are regarded as administrative expenses, failing which, as a last resort, these may be taken to include auditors' fees and expenses, discount received, directors' remuneration, office salaries, rent and rates, light and heat, telephone and postage, and so on. Frequently, examination questions also require some items (such as those in the previous sentence) to be apportioned between distribution costs and administrative expenses. This is a relatively simple arithmetic exercise in which the amounts are divided between distribution costs and administrative expenses using the basis of apportionment (i.e. percentages for each) given in the question.

31.4 The statement of financial position

IAS 1 – Presentation of Financial Statements (IASB, 2010a) presents the financial position of the entity in the form of the accounting equation: assets = capital + liabilities. Assets and liabilities are analysed into current and non-current (see Figure 31.4).

The content of the statement of financial position of companies is the same as that of sole traders and partnerships, with the following exceptions:

1 The 'trade receivables' includes prepayments, and the 'trade and other payables' includes trade payables and accruals.

2 Property, plant and equipment includes the cost accounts for all tangible non-current assets and their provisions for depreciation.

3 The current liabilities of companies also usually include current tax payable (which is the income tax due on the annual profit), current portions of long-term borrowing (debt capital that is repayable within one year), short-term provisions, accrued debenture interest and the outstanding final dividends on preference shares (the latter two will be included with the other finance charges outstanding at the year end – in *trade and other payables*).

4 The non-current liabilities of companies also often include the nominal value of loan stock, debentures and long-term provisions.

5 The financing of a company is categorized as being either equity capital or liabilities. Under the heading 'equity attributable to the owners of the parent', the equity share capital (not preference share capital), retained earnings and other components of equity are disclosed.

Where this format is followed exactly in answering examination questions, it will be necessary to prepare workings that clearly show how the amounts of, in particular, property, plant and equipment and trade and other payables (both current and long term) have been computed. This is discussed later in this chapter.

Company name	
Statement of financial position as at 31 March 20X2	
ASSETS	£'000
Non-current assets	
Property, plant and equipment	XXX
Goodwill	XX
Other intangible assets	XX
Available-for-sale investments	XX
	XXX
Current assets	
Inventories	XX
Trade receivables	XX
Other current assets	XX
Cash and cash equivalents	XX
	XXX
Total assets	XXX
EQUITY AND LIABILITIES	
Equity attributable to owners	
Share capital	XXX
Retained earnings	XX
Other components of equity	XX
Total equity	XXX
Non-current liabilities	
Long-term borrowing	XX
Deferred tax	X
Long-term provisions	XX
Total non-current liabilities	XX
Current liabilities	
Trade and other payables	XX
Short-term borrowing	XX
Current portion of long-term borrowing	XX
Current tax payable	XX
Short-term provision	XX
Total current liabilities	XXX
Total liabilities	XXX
Total equity and liabilities	XXX

Figure 31.4 A pro forma of the layout of financial statement for a company

Equity attributable to the owners of the parent

Details about equity share capital should be provided, either on the face of the statement of financial position, the statement of changes in equity or in a note to the financial statements (IAS 1). Three items are usually disclosed.

1 **Authorized/nominal share capital:** This refers to the types, nominal value and maximum number of shares that the company is permitted by its Memorandum of Association to issue.

2 **Allotted share capital:** This refers to the total nominal value of the number of shares that have actually been issued at the date of the statement of financial position. It is sometimes referred to as the issued share capital.

3 **Called-up share capital:** This refers to that part of the allotted share capital that the company has required the equity shareholders to pay. It will consist of the amounts payable on application and allotment plus any calls that have been made by the company up to the date of the statement of financial position.

In addition, a reconciliation of the number of shares outstanding at the start of the year and at the end of the year is required, along with details of the rights, preferences and restrictions attaching to each class of share including restrictions on the distribution of dividends and the repayment of capital (restrictive covenants). IAS 1 also requires disclosure of the details of any shares held in the entity by the entity itself, or any of its subsidiaries or associates, and details of shares reserved for issue under options and contracts for the sale of shares, including terms and amounts.

The figure for share capital that enters into the total of the statement of financial position under 'equity attributable to the owners of the parent' is the called-up equity share capital. This is frequently the same as the allotted share capital. However, if these are different, the allotted capital must be shown as a memorandum figure (i.e. not entering into the total of the statement of financial position). The authorized capital must always be disclosed as a memorandum amount. The memorandum authorized and allotted share capital is disclosed in a note to the financial statements. An example of the typical disclosures are as follows.

REAL WORLD EXAMPLE 31.1

Tesco Plc

Note 13 Called up share capital

	2010 Ordinary shares of 5p each		2009 Ordinary shares of 5p each	
	Number	£m	Number	£m
Authorised:				
At beginning of year	10,858,000,000	543	10,858,000,000	543
Authorised during the year	2,500,000,000	125	–	–
At end of year	13,358,000,000	668	10,858,000,000	543
Allotted, called up and fully paid:				
At beginning of year	7,895,344,018	395	7,863,498,783	393
Share options	62,329,535	3	57,060,046	3
Share awards	27,370,504	1	–	–
Share buy-back	–	–	(25,214,811)	(1)
At end of year	7,985,044,057	399	7,895,344,018	395

During the financial year, 62 million (2009 – 57 million) shares of 5p each were issued in relation to share options for aggregate consideration of £166m (2009 – £130m).

During the financial year, 27 million (2009 – nil) shares of 5p each were issued in relation to share bonus awards for consideration of £1m (2009 – £nil).

During the year, the Company purchased and subsequently cancelled no shares of 5p each (2009 – 25,214,811), representing 0% (2009 – 0%) of the called up share capital, at an average price of £nil (2009 – £3.98) per share. The total consideration, including expenses, was £nil (2009 – £100m). The excess of the consideration over the nominal value has been charged to retained earnings.

Source: Tesco PLC Annual Report and Financial Statements 2010, p. 129, www.tescoplc.com.

Reserves are difficult to define because they take a variety of forms. However, they usually represent some sort of gain or profit, and constitute part of a company's capital. Reserves may be of two types, either distributable or non-distributable. These are also frequently referred to as revenue and capital reserves, respectively. **Revenue/distributable reserves** are those that can be distributed to equity shareholders as dividends. These include any **retained earnings** and other revenue reserves/general reserves that are made up from transfers from retained earnings. These reserves consist of retained profits of the current and previous accounting years.

Capital/non-distributable reserves cannot be distributed as dividends. These may take a number of forms. The most common is the balance on a **share premium** account. This arises from shares having been issued at a price in excess of their nominal value. The excess is credited to a share premium account. Another non-distributable reserve is a **revaluation reserve**. This arises if a non-current asset (usually land and buildings) is revalued and shown in the statement of financial position at an amount that exceeds its historical cost. The excess is credited to a revaluation reserve account. A third form of non-distributable reserve is a **capital redemption reserve (CRR)**. This is formed by transfers from retained earnings. This is a statutory reserve, being identified in the Companies Act. It arises when shares are redeemed or purchased back from shareholders. Attention is given to the CRR and share repurchase in 'Changes in Share Capital', available online at www.mcgraw-hill.uk/textbooks/thomas.

The total amount of reserves is added to the called-up share capital and shown on the statement of financial position as the '**Total equity attributable to owners**'. IAS 1 requires that the company discloses a description of the nature and purpose of each reserve within equity. This information is commonly provided for in a note.

 ## 31.5 Statement of changes in equity

Changes in equity reserves and gains and losses in equity that do not form part of the statement of profit and loss (but form part of the other statement of comprehensive income) impact on an additional statement, the **statement of changes in equity**. This statement focuses on reconciling the opening and closing equity position. It provides details on the movements in share capital, reserves, including the share premium account, any revaluation reserve, and the statement of profit and loss (i.e. retained earnings). Movements on these reserves will arise from the issue of shares at a premium, a surplus on the revaluation of non-current assets and the retained earnings for the year, respectively. A pro forma is provided in IAS 1, as shown in Figure 31.5.

Statement of changes in equity for the year ended 31 March 20X2					
	Share capital	Other components of equity	Revaluation reserve	Retained earnings	Total
	£'000	£'000	£'000	£'000	£'000
Balance at 1 April 20X1	XXX	XX	XX	XXX	XXX
Changes in accounting policy	–	–	–	(X)	(X)
Restated balance	XXX	XX	XX	XXX	XX
Changes in equity for 20X2					
Issue of share capital	XXX	–	–	–	XXX
Dividends	–	–		(XX)	(XX)
Total comprehensive income for the period	–	–	XX	XXX	XXX
Balance at 31 March 20X2	XXX	XX	XX	XXX	XXX

Figure 31.5 A pro forma of the layout of a statement of changes in equity for a company

Items that do not form part of comprehensive income, but are changes in equity

Equity share dividends

These are *not* entered in the statement of comprehensive income. They are not an expense. They should be deducted from retained earnings in the statement of changes, and/or disclosed in a note to the financial statements. Equity dividends comprise an interim dividend paid plus a proposed final dividend. The interim dividend paid will have been debited to the equity share dividends account and thus shown in the trial balance. The proposed final dividend will always be outstanding at the end of the accounting year. However, it is *not* a liability at the statement of financial position date. It does not become a liability until it is agreed by the equity shareholders at the Annual General Meeting (AGM), at which point the financial statements are approved by the equity holders. Therefore, it is *not* an accrual. The amount proposed is however disclosed in a note to the financial statements. What is debited to **general reserves** will be the total amount of equity dividend paid in the year, which usually comprises *last year's proposed dividend and the interim dividend paid for this year.*

Transfers to other distributable reserves

The profit for the year is added to the 'retained earnings reserve account'. Note that it is not transferred to the capital account, as in the case of sole traders. However, sometimes companies transfer a part of their retained earnings to a reserve account (though this is not as common now). The reason for this is to indicate to equity shareholders that the directors do not intend to distribute it as dividends but rather have earmarked it for some other use, such as expansion of the business by purchasing additional non-current assets. The entry for a transfer to a reserve is to debit the retained earnings account and credit the reserve account.

An illustration of the preparation of the final financial statements of limited companies is given in Example 31.1.

EXAMPLE
31.1

The following is the trial balance of XYZ Ltd at 31 March 20X2:		
	£	£
Equity shares of £1 each, fully paid		100,000
5% preference shares of £1 each, fully paid		20,000
8% debentures		30,000
Share premium		9,500
Revaluation reserve		10,000
General reserve		2,000
Retained profit from previous years		976
Motor vehicles at revaluation	210,000	
Depreciation on vehicles		19,000
Inventories	14,167	
Trade receivables/trade payables	11,000	8,012
Provision for doubtful debts		324
Bank balance	9,731	
Purchases/sales revenue	186,000	271,700
Wages and salaries	16,362	
General expenses	3,912	
Directors' remuneration	15,500	
Preliminary expenses	1,640	
Debenture interest	1,200	
Equity dividend paid (interim)	2,000	
	471,512	471,512

Additional information:

1 Inventory at 31 March 20X2 is valued at £23,487.

2 Depreciation of motor vehicles is to be provided at the rate of 10 per cent per annum on the fixed instalment method (straight-line method).

3 The provision for doubtful debts is to be made equal to 5 per cent of the trade receivables at 31 March 20X2.

4 Debenture interest of £1,200 and preference share dividends of £1,000 are outstanding at 31 March 20X2.

5 Provision is to be made for taxation on the year's profit amounting to £9,700.

6 There is a proposed final equity dividend of 5p per share.

7 The directors have decided to increase the general reserve by a further £3,000.

8 The authorized share capital consists of: (a) 200,000 equity shares of £1 each; and (b) 50,000 5 per cent preference shares of £1 each. The value of the shares shown in the trial balance is the allotted and called-up capital.

You are required to prepare in publishable form the statement of comprehensive income for the year ended 31 March 20X2, the statement of financial position at that date and the statement of changes in equity.

Workings

These could be done arithmetically but are shown below in the form of ledger accounts to help students understand the double entry.

Provision for doubtful debts			
Balance c/d	550	Balance b/d	324
(5% x £11,000)		Profit and loss a/c	226
	550		550
		Balance b/d	550

Provision for depreciation			
Balance c/d	40,000	Balance b/d	19,000
		Profit and loss a/c	21,000
	40,000		40,000
		Balance b/d	40,000

Debenture interest			
Bank	1,200	Profit and loss a/c	2,400
Accrual c/d	1,200		
	2,400		2,400
		Accrual b/d	1,200

Preference dividend			
Balance c/d	1,000	Profit and loss a/c	1,000
	1,000		1,000
		Balance b/d	1,000

Equity dividends			
Bank	2,000	Retained earnings	2,000
		(statement of changes in equity)	
	2,000		2,000

In a note to the financial statements the amount of final dividend proposed (100,000 × 5p = £5,000) would be disclosed.

Income tax			
Closing payable c/d	9,700	Profit and loss a/c	9,700
		Opening payable c/d	9,700

General reserve			
Balance c/d	5,000	Balance b/d	2,000
		Retained earnings account	3,000
	5,000		5,000
		Balance b/d	5,000

XYZ Ltd	
Statement of profit and loss for the year ended 31 March 20X2	
	£
Revenue	271,700
Cost of sales	(176,680)
Gross profit	95,020
Distribution costs	(21,226)
Administration expenses	(35,774)
Other expenses	(1,640)
Finance costs	(3,400)
Profit before tax	32,980
Income tax expense	(9,700)
Profit for the year	23,280

XYZ Ltd	
Statement of financial position as at 31 March 20X2	
ASSETS	£
Non-current assets	
Property, plant and equipment	170,000
	170,000
Current assets	
Inventories	23,487
Trade receivables	10,450
Bank	9,731
	43,668
Total assets	213,668
EQUITY AND LIABILITIES	
Equity	
Share capital	100,000
Share premium	9,500
Retained earnings	19,256
General reserve	5,000
Revaluation reserve	10,000
Total equity	143,756
Non-current liabilities	
Preference shares	20,000
Debentures	30,000
Total non-current liabilities	50,000
Current liabilities	
Trade and other payables	10,212
Current tax payable	9,700
Total current liabilities	19,912
Total liabilities	69,912
Total equity and liabilities	213,668

Statement of changes in equity for the year ended 31 March 20X2						
	Share capital	Share premium	Revaluation reserve	General reserve	General earnings	Total
	£	£	£	£	£	£
Balance at 1 April 20X1	100,000	9,500	10,000	2,000	976	122,476
Changes in equity for 20X2						
Equity dividends paid	–	–	–	–	(2,000)	(2,000)
Total comprehensive income for the period	–	–	–	–	23,280	23,280
Transfer to general reserve	–	–	–	3,000	(3,000)	–
Balance at 31 March 20X2	100,000	9,500	10,000	5,000	19,256	143,756

Notes

1 The cost of sales is calculated as follows:

Inventories at 1 Apr 20X1	14,167
Add: Purchases	186,000
	200,167
Less: Inventories at 31 Mar 20X2	23,487
Cost of sales	176,680

2 Expenditure is allocated as follows:

	Distribution costs	Administration expenses	Other expenses	Finance costs
	£	£	£	£
Wages and salaries		16,362		
General expenses		3,912		
Provision for depreciation	21,000			
Provision for doubtful debts	226			
Directors' remuneration		15,500		
Preliminary expenses			1,640	
Debenture interest				2,400
Preference dividend				1,000
Total	21,226	35,774	1,640	3,400

3 Property, plant and equipment (£170,000) comprises motor vehicles at valuation £210,000 less the amended provision for depreciation £40,000.

4 Trade receivables £10,450 is net of the amended year end provision for doubtful debts (£11,000 − £550).

5 The amount of the proposed final dividend on equity shares is computed by multiplying the dividend per share by the number of shares that have been issued/allotted as shown in the trial balance; that is, 5p × (£100,000 ÷ £1) = £5,000. Sometimes the dividend per share is expressed as a percentage. In this case the percentage is applied to the nominal value of the issued/allotted equity share capital (e.g. 5% × £100,000 = £5,000). Where additional equity shares have been issued during the year, these are usually entitled to the full amount of any dividends that are declared after they have been allotted, such as the proposed final dividend for the year. In answering examination questions students should make this assumption unless told otherwise.

Note: The dividend on the new shares is *not* computed on a time basis because it is not a fixed annual rate.

6 It is important to ensure that the amounts entered in the statement of profit and loss in respect of debenture interest and preference share dividends are the amounts paid plus any that are outstanding at the end of the year. Sometimes in examination questions students are not told how much is outstanding or even that anything is outstanding. In these circumstances the total amount to be entered in the statement of profit and loss is ascertained using the information given in the question relating to the rates of debenture interest and preference dividends as follows:

$$8 \text{ per cent debentures £30,000}$$

$$\therefore \text{Annual interest} = 8\% \times £30,000 = £2,400.$$

$$5\% \text{ preference shares £20,000}$$

$$\therefore \text{Annual dividend} = 5\% \times £20,000 = £1,000.$$

The amounts to be entered as current liabilities in the statement of financial position can then be found by subtracting the amounts paid as shown in the trial balance as follows:

$$\text{Debenture interest outstanding} = £2,400 - £1,200 = £1,200$$

$$\text{Preference dividends outstanding} = £1,000 - £0 = £1,000$$

The reason for adopting this procedure in the case of debenture interest is that the debentures could have been issued at any time during a previous accounting year and thus the interest may be payable on dates other than the end of the accounting year and halfway through the year. This means that the amount of interest outstanding at the end of the accounting year will not necessarily be the total for the year or the last six months. Thus, one cannot assume that the accrual should be 6/12 of the total interest for the year, even though it often is in examination questions. Where debentures or preference shares have been issued during the year, the amount of interest/dividends that is entered in the statement of profit and loss needs to be calculated on a strict time basis.

7 It is generally accepted practice to prepare the final financial statements of companies in vertical form. However, the statement of profit and loss must also be prepared in the ledger by transferring all the balances on the income and expense accounts to this account in the normal manner. The retained earnings of the current year (after deducting any transfers to reserves) is added to the retained earnings reserve and the resulting figure is carried forward to the next year in the statement of financial position. This movement is shown in the statement of changes in equity. It should also be remembered that journal entries are supposed to be made for all the above entries in the ledger.

8 As explained earlier in this chapter, the law allows revenue reserves such as the general reserve and the balance in retained earnings at the end of the previous year to be distributed to shareholders as dividends. This can clearly be seen from the statement of changes in equity, wherein dividends are paid out of the available reserves, which is the current year addition and the balance brought forward.

9 As explained earlier in this chapter, preliminary expenses must not be retained in the financial statements as an asset. There are two possible ways of dealing with these. One is to charge them to the statement of profit and loss, as in the above example. However, this reduces the profit, which many companies wish to avoid if possible. The alternative, and preferred treatment, is to charge preliminary

expenses against the balance on the share premium account, the double entry being to credit the preliminary expenses account and debit the share premium account. The amount entered on the statement of financial position in respect of the share premium account will then be the difference between the balance shown in the trial balance and the preliminary expenses; that is, the balance on the share premium account after entering the preliminary expenses.

10 Details on share capital will be presented in a note to the financial statements (this information can be provided on the face of the statement of financial position and in the statement of changes in equity).

Share capital	20X2
Authorized	**£'000**
200,000 equity shares of £1 each	200
50,000 5% preference shares of £1 each	50
	250
Allotted and fully paid	
100,000 equity shares of £1 each	100
20,000 5% preference shares of £1 each	20
	120

31.6 Notes to the financial statements

The Companies Act 2006 and IASs also require several 'notes' to be attached to the published statement of comprehensive income and statement of financial position. Those most commonly examined at the introductory level comprise the following:

1 Changes in property, plant and equipment (and accumulated depreciation).

2 A note on allotted, authorized and fully paid share capital.

A note on the composition of property, plant and equipment and the related accumulated depreciation is necessary to provide detail on the single figure that is reported in the statement of financial position. In addition, this note must include the cost of acquisitions and disposals, any revaluation, diminution in value, the depreciation charges for the year and the accumulated depreciation on disposals. An illustration is given later in the book.

An illustration of the preparation of published financial statements including the above notes is given in Example 31.2.

EXAMPLE 31.2

The following is the trial balance of Oasis Ltd as at 30 September 20X2:

	£'000	£'000
Called-up share capital		1,000
Share premium		500
Retained earnings 1 October 20X1		700
10% debentures (repayable 20X6)		600
Land and buildings at cost	2,500	
Buildings – accumulated depreciation		90
Motor vehicles – at cost	1,400	
– accumulated depreciation		470
Inventories	880	
Trade receivables/payables	420	360
Purchases/sales revenue	3,650	6,540
Warehouse wages	310	
Administrative salaries	190	
Sales staff salaries	70	
Bad debts	20	
Directors' remuneration	280	
Advertising expenditure	60	
Motor expenses	230	
Light and heat	180	
Telephone and postage	80	
Bank overdraft		19
Discount allowed	9	
	10,279	10,279

Additional information:

1 The called-up share capital consists of 1 million equity shares of £1 each, fully paid.

2 Inventory at 30 September 20X2 was £740,000.

3 The auditors' fees and expenses for the year are expected to be £71,000.

4 The estimated tax charge on the company's profits for the year is £250,000.

5 The directors have proposed a final dividend on the equity shares in issue at 30 September 20X2 of 10p per share.

6 Depreciation is provided on a straight-line basis at 2 per cent per annum for buildings and 20 per cent per annum on vehicles. A full year's charge is made in the year of acquisition and none in the year of disposal.

7 The following items are to be apportioned between distribution costs and administrative expenses as below:

	Distribution	Administrative
Directors' remuneration	25%	75%
Light and heat, telephone and postage, buildings depreciation	40%	60%
Motor expenses, vehicle depreciation	50%	50%

8 The following items were unrecorded in the ledger on 30 September 20X2:

  a The issue of 500,000 equity shares at £1.50 each fully paid on 31 August 20X2.

  b The acquisition on credit of a motor vehicle costing £100,000 on 31 August 20X2.

  c The sale on credit of a motor vehicle for £40,000 on 31 August 20X2. This cost £50,000 when purchased on 1 February 20X0.

9 The land included in the above trial balance cost £1m. The directors have decided to revalue this on 30 September 20X2 at £1.3m.

Required

Prepare the company's statement of comprehensive income for the year and a statement of financial position as at 30 September 20X2. This should be in a form suitable for publication and should include a statement of other comprehensive income for the period (net of tax), a statement of changes in equity and notes relating to changes in non-current assets and details of equity share capital.

Workings

1 Cost of sales

	£'000
Inventories at 1 Oct 20X1	880
Add: Purchases	3,650
	4,530
Less: Inventories at 30 Sep 20X2	740
Cost of sales	3,790

2 Depreciation

		£'000
a	Buildings at cost (£2,500 − £1,000)	1,500
	Depreciation expense (2% × £1,500)	30
	Accumulated depreciation at 30 Sep 20X1 (£90 + £30)	120
b	Motor vehicles at 1 Oct 20X1 at cost	1,400
	Acquisition	100
		1,500
	Disposal	(50)
	Motor vehicles at 30 Sep 20X2 at cost	1,450
	Disposal –	
	Accumulated depreciation (2 × 20% × £50)	20
	Book value (£50 − £20)	30
	Profit on sale (£40 − £30)	10
	Depreciation expense (20% × £1,450)	290
	Accumulated depreciation at 30 Sep 20X2 (£470 − £20 + £290)	740

3 Distribution costs and administrative expenses

	Distribution	Administrative
	£'000	£'000
Warehouse wages	310	–
Administrative salaries	–	190
Sales staff salaries	70	–
Bad debts	20	–
Directors' remuneration	70	210
Advertising	60	–
Motor expenses	115	115
Vehicle depreciation	145	145
Profit on sale vehicle	(5)	(5)
Light and heat	72	108
Telephone and postage	32	48
Buildings depreciation	12	18
Discount allowed	9	–
Auditors' fees and expenses	–	71
	910	900

4 Trade and other payables

	£'000
Trade payables	360
Auditor's fees and other expenses	71
Car dealer	100
Debenture interest (600 × 10%)	60
	591

Oasis Ltd	
Statement of profit and loss for the year ended 30 September 20X2	
	£'000
Sales revenue	6,540
Cost of sales	(3,790)
Gross profit	2,750
Distribution costs	(910)
Administrative expenses	(900)
Finance costs (10% × £600)	(60)
Profit before taxation	880
Income tax expense	(250)
Profit for the year	630

Oasis Ltd

**Statement of other comprehensive income
for the year ended 30 September 20X2**

	£'000
Other comprehensive income for the year, after tax:	
Gain on property revaluation	300
Other comprehensive income for the year, net of tax	300

Oasis Ltd

Statement of financial position as at 30 September 20X2

ASSETS	£'000
Non-current assets	
Property, plant and equipment (Note 1)	3,390
Current assets	
Inventory	740
Trade receivables	420
Other current assets	40
Cash and cash equivalents (£750 − £19)	731
	1,931
Total assets	5,321
EQUITY AND LIABILITIES	
Equity	
Share capital	1,500
Share premium account	750
Revaluation reserve	300
Retained earnings	1,330
Total equity	3,880
Non-current liabilities	
Debenture loans	600
Total non-current liabilities	600
Current liabilities	
Trade and other payables	591
Current tax payable	250
Total current liabilities	841
Total assets less current liabilities	1,441
Total equity and reserves	5,321

Statement of changes in equity for Oasis Ltd for the year ended 30 September 20X2

	Share capital	Share premium	Revaluation reserve	Retained earnings	Total
	£'000	£'000	£'000	£'000	£'000
Balance at 1 October 20X1	1,000	500	–	700	2,200
Changes in equity for 20X2					
Total comprehensive income for the period	–	–	300	630	930
Issue of share capital	500	250	–	–	750
Balance at 30 September 20X2	1,500	750	300	1,330	3,880

Notes to the financial statements

1 Property, plant and equipment

	Land £'000	Buildings £'000	Vehicles £'000	Total £'000
Cost or valuation				
At 1 Oct 20X1	1,000	1,500	1,400	3,900
Additions	–	–	100	100
Disposals	–	–	(50)	(50)
Revaluation	300	–	–	300
At 30 Sep 20X2	1,300	1,500	1,450	4,250
Accumulated depreciation				
At 1 Oct 20X1	–	90	470	560
Charge for year	–	30	290	320
Disposals	–	–	(20)	(20)
At 30 Sep 20X2	–	120	740	860
Net book value				
At 30 Sep 20X2	1,300	1,380	710	3,390
At 1 Oct 20X1	1,000	1,410	930	3,340

2 Dividends

The company proposed a final dividend of 10p per share (£100,000).

3 Share capital

	20X1
Authorized	£'000
1,000,000 equity shares of £1 each	1,000
Allotted and fully paid	
1,000,000 equity shares of £1 each	1,000

Note

The alternative disclosure for total comprehensive income is to show one statement as follows:

Oasis Ltd	
Statement of comprehensive income for the year ended 30 September 20X2	
	£'000
Sales revenue	6,540
Cost of sales	(3,790)
Gross profit	2,750
Distribution costs	(910)
Administrative expenses	(900)
Finance costs (10% × £600)	(60)
Profit before taxation	880
Income tax expense	(250)
Profit for the year	630
Other comprehensive income	
Gains on property revaluation	300
Total comprehensive income for the year	960

31.7 Reporting financial performance

The Companies Act and various IASs require that certain items be shown separately in published financial statements or as notes to the financial statements. The most significant of these, which have not been discussed thus far, are explained below in brief. However, it is first necessary to appreciate why these items are required to be shown separately.

As explained in Chapter 3, one of the main objectives of published financial statements is to provide information that is useful in the evaluation of the performance of the reporting entity. One of the principal means of evaluating performance involves making comparisons over time, with other companies and/or forecasts. It may also involve making predictions of future profits, cash flows, and so on. Comparisons and predictions of profits are likely to be misleading where the profit includes gains and losses of a non-recurring nature such as relating to operations that have been discontinued. In order to facilitate comparisons and predictions, it is therefore desirable that the following items be disclosed separately in published company financial statements.

31.8 Non-current assets held for sale and discontinued operations

IFRS 5 – Non-current Assets Held for Sale and Discontinued Operations (IASB, 2010d) provides guidance on how to define and account for items, operations, and so on that are no longer being utilized for operational activities and are either being sold or abandoned. IFRS 5 defines a **discontinued operation** as 'a component of an entity that either has been disposed of, or is classified as held for sale, and a represents a separate major line of business or geographical area of operations;

b is part of a single coordinated plan to dispose of a separate major line of business or geographical area of operations; or

c is a subsidiary acquired exclusively with a view to resale.'

A non-current asset (or disposal group) should be classed as **held for sale** if 'its carrying amount will be recovered principally through a sale transaction rather than through continuing use' (IFRS 5). The following conditions have to be met before an asset/disposal group can be classed as held for sale.

a The asset, or disposal group must be available for immediate sale in its present condition and its sale must be highly probable.

b Management should be actively trying to sell the asset, or disposal group.

c The sale should be expected to be completed within one year, though may extend beyond this if events occur that are beyond the company's control.

d It is unlikely that there will be any significant changes to the plan to sell the asset, or disposal group.

Operations not satisfying all these conditions are classified as continuing.

When a non-current asset/disposal group is classed as discontinued or held for sale, then all the assets and liabilities are measured at the lower of carrying amount and fair value less costs to sell. These assets are not depreciated and are disclosed separately on the face of the statement of financial position. In addition, the results (income and expenditure) of the discontinued operation are shown separately from the results from continuing operations on the face of the statement of comprehensive income (net of tax). Though detail on the results of the discontinued activity can be provided on the face of the statement of comprehensive income, they are normally shown in one line, with detail being provided in a note to the financial statements. This note should include an analysis of revenue, expenses, pre-tax profit/loss, the related income tax expense and the gain/loss on the measurement of the discontinued/ held for sale asset to fair value less costs to sell (and the related tax expense). The disclosure on the face of the statement of comprehensive income might be as shown in Figure 31.6.

 ## 31.9 Material/exceptional items

IAS 1 recommends that an entity should 'present additional line items, headings and subtotals in the statement of comprehensive income, when such presentation is relevant to an understanding of the entity's financial performance'. Therefore material items and items, which are not material in size but are material in nature, should be disclosed separately (with the related tax impact) if non-disclosure would mislead the users of the financial statements. Examples of items that might be considered to impact on the users' ability to see trends in the performance of the company can include: profits or losses on the sale or termination of an operation; costs of a fundamental reorganization or restructuring having a material effect on the nature and focus of the reporting entity's operations; profits or losses on the disposal of non-current assets (all types); discontinued activities; one-off redundancy costs; abnormal losses caused by a natural disaster such as a fire, flood, earthquake – where not insured, bad debts, inventory, property, plant or equipment write-downs and subsequent reversal of such write-downs, a legal claim against the company and any other provisions. These items are usually material and if included within, say, administration expenses, would lead users to misinterpret the performance of the company and its management team in the year.

Company name	
Statement of comprehensive income for the year ended 31 March 20X2	
	£
Revenue	XXX
Cost of sales	(XXX)
Gross profit	XXX
Other income	XX
Distribution costs	(XXX)
Administration expenses	(XXX)
Other expenses	(XXX)
Finance costs	(XXX)
Profit before tax	XX
Income tax expense	(XX)
Profit for the year from continuing activities	XX
Loss for the year from discontinuing activities	(X)
Profit for the year	XX
Other comprehensive income	
Gains on property revaluation	XX
Exchange differences on translating foreign operations	XX
Income tax on other comprehensive income	(X)
Other comprehensive income net of tax	XX
Total comprehensive income for the year	XXX

Figure 31.6 A pro forma of the layout of a statement of comprehensive income for a company that has both continuing and discontinuing activities in the reporting period

LEARNING ACTIVITY 31.1

You should find it useful at this point to combine the three numerical examples given above in respect of acquisitions, discontinued operations, **exceptional items** and extraordinary items since these provide a fairly comprehensive model of a published statement of comprehensive income. In addition, students may wish to attempt Exercise 31.24 or use the solution as an example of how to answer examination questions on this topic.

31.10 Prior period adjustments

IAS 8 – Accounting Policies, Changes in Accounting Estimate and Errors (IASB, 2010b) provides guidance on the most common events to cause a **prior period adjustment** – namely, the correction of prior period errors and changes to accounting policies caused by the introduction of a new standard, or the revision of a standard that does not contain specific transitional arrangements (these are normally arrangements that allow the change in accounting policy to be made prospectively). Changes in accounting estimates, such as the useful economic life of a non-current asset, do not require a prior period adjustment. The change is applied prospectively.

According to IAS 8, the relevant errors that require a prior period adjustment are 'material omissions from, or misstatements, in financial statements'. Errors found in current period financial statements should be corrected before the statements are signed off (finalized). Errors in respect of prior years should be corrected by restating the opening balances to what they really should be and by amending the comparatives. Indeed, since January 2009, the revised IAS 1 has required that two years of adjusted comparatives for the statement of financial position only should be provided. When a prior period adjustment has taken place, a note to the financial statements should disclose the nature of the prior period error, the impact that the correction had to each line of the financial statements that it affected (including the tax implications) and the impact of the correction at the beginning of the earliest period presented – the opening retained earnings of the earliest statement of financial position disclosed.

Examples of prior period adjustments are rare but include a change in the method of inventory valuation, and an item previously recorded as a non-current asset that should have been treated as an expense (or vice versa). The most common prior period adjustment arises from the issue of an IFRS that would necessitate a company to change one of its accounting policies.

 ## 31.11   Events after the reporting period

These are defined in *IAS 10 – Events After the Reporting Period* (IASB, 2010c) as 'those events, both favourable and unfavourable, which occur between the statement of financial position date and the date on which the financial statements are authorised for issue'. The statement of financial position date is of course the end of an accounting year. The date on which the financial statements are authorized for issue is the date that they are approved by the board of directors, which is usually before they are approved by the equity shareholders. They are usually authorized for issue a month or two after the end of the accounting year, since it takes this amount of time to prepare the financial statements.

Events after the reporting period are classified as falling into one of two categories as follows:

1 **Adjusting events after the reporting period** are defined as events 'that provide additional evidence of conditions that existed at the end of the reporting period'.

Examples of adjusting events include any evidence of a permanent diminution in value of non-current assets, investments, inventories and work-in-progress, the insolvency of a credit customer, changes in the rates of taxation, amounts received or receivable in respect of an insurance claim outstanding at the reporting date, and errors or frauds which show that the financial statements were incorrect.

IAS 10 requires that a material adjusting event should be included in the financial statements. For example, inventories would be reduced to their net realizable value, a provision created for an insolvent credit customer, errors corrected, and so on.

2 **Non-adjusting events after the reporting period** are defined as 'events that are indicative of conditions that arose after the reporting period'. In other words, the conditions did not exist during the reporting period. Examples include mergers and acquisitions, reconstructions, issues of shares and debentures, purchases and sales of non-current assets and investments, losses on non-current assets and inventories resulting from a fire or flood, government action (e.g. nationalization), strikes and other labour disputes.

IAS 10 requires that details of material non-adjusting events be disclosed as a note to the financial statements. It is not appropriate to include non-adjusting events in the financial statements since they do not relate to conditions that existed during the reporting period. However, it is appropriate to disclose non-adjusting events as a note to ensure that financial statements are not misleading where there is some subsequent material event that affects a company's financial position. These details should refer to the nature of the event and provide an estimate of the financial effect, or a statement that such an estimate cannot be made.

31.12 Provisions and contingencies

These are the subject of *IAS 37 – Provisions, Contingent Liabilities and Contingent Assets* (IASB, 2010e). This defines a **provision** as 'a liability of uncertain timing or amount'. A **liability** is 'a present obligation of a reporting entity arising from past events the settlement of which is expected to result in an outflow from the entity of economic benefits'. A provision should be recognized in the financial statements when it meets the definition of a liability and a reliable estimate can be made of the amount of the obligation. The relevant double entry would be as follows:

Debit: The statement of comprehensive income with the increase in the provision
(the relevant expense)   XXX

Credit: The provision account (a liability in the statement of financial position)   XXX

The notes to the financial statements should disclose for each class of provision: (1) the carrying amount at the start and end of the period; (2) increases and decreases in the provision; (3) amounts charged against the provision; (4) a brief description of the nature of the obligation, and the expected timing of any resulting transfers of economic benefits; and (5) an indication of the uncertainties about the amount or timing of those transfers of economic benefits.

A **contingency** is a condition that exists at the end of the reporting period, where the outcome will be confirmed only on the occurrence, or non-occurrence, of one or more uncertain future events. A **contingent liability** can be possible or probable.

It can be

> a *possible* obligation that arises from past events and whose existence will be confirmed only by the occurrence or non-occurrence of one of more uncertain future events not wholly within the control of the entity
>
> [or]
>
> a *probable* obligation that arises from past events but is not recognised because: (i) it is not probable that an outflow of resources embodying economic benefits will be required to settle the obligation; or (ii) the amount of the obligation cannot be measured with sufficient reliability.

Contingent liabilities should not be recognized in the financial statements. They should be disclosed in a note to the financial statements, except when remote, wherein they should not form part of the financial statements.

A **contingent asset** is 'a possible asset that arises from past events and whose existence will be confirmed only by the occurrence or non-occurrence of one or more uncertain future events not wholly within the control of the entity'. Contingent assets should not be recognized in the financial statements. They should be disclosed in a note to the financial statements, except when remote, wherein they should not form part of the financial statements. The note should disclose a brief description of the nature of the contingent asset at the reporting date and, where practicable, an estimate of their financial effect. If the asset becomes certain, then it is not contingent, it is an asset, which should be recognized.

Contingent liabilities and contingent assets should be reviewed regularly to determine if they are certain liabilities and assets, whereupon they are recognized.

Examples of contingent losses include possible liabilities arising from bills of exchange received that have been discounted, corporation tax disputes, failure by another party to pay a debt that the reporting entity has guaranteed, and a substantial legal claim against the company. The latter is the most common example and refers to where a legal action has been brought against the company but the court has not yet pronounced judgement regarding the company's innocence or guilt. This is often simply referred to as a pending legal action. It is regarded as a contingency because, whether or not a loss or liability will arise, depends on the 'outcome' of the court case (i.e. an 'uncertain future event').

It should also be noted that although contingencies are conditions that exist at the end of the reporting period, their accounting treatment depends on information available up to the date on which the financial statements are approved by the board of directors.

A useful exercise at this point is to consider the similarities and differences between liabilities, provisions and contingent liabilities. A liability is a debt owed to a known party of a known certain amount. A provision is a known or highly probable future liability or loss, the amount and/or timing of which is uncertain (and thus has to be estimated). A contingent liability is uncertain with regard to its existence, timing and amount, and is thus only a possible liability.

> **LEARNING ACTIVITY 31.2**
>
> Examine Wm Morrison Supermarket plc's financial statements for items discussed in this chapter. List the purpose of any provisions made by them. Note any contingencies and related disclosures.

31.13 Accounting for debt

Accounting for debt can be quite complicated depending on the nature of the debt. At introductory level, it is assumed that debt is a liability which is known with certainty. As such the amortized cost of the debt, for example a bank loan, should be capitalized at the outset and the relevant interest and charges should be released using the effective annual interest rate (which may differ to the actual interest payments that have been contracted to be paid) over the period of the loan agreement. The accounting for debt is best explained using an example (Example 31.3).

> **EXAMPLE 31.3**
>
> Magnetic Ltd requires £500,000 to finance a new investment and enters into a loan agreement with their bank, All First Bank. Magnetic Ltd has been a long-standing customer of the bank, and they inform the bank that they need the repayments to be over a five-year period and to be higher in the later stages of the loan agreement due to current liquidity issues. The bank agrees to provide the £500,000 on the following terms. An arrangement fee of £25,000 is payable, though this can be added to the capital portion of the loan; hence does not have to be paid for up-front. The bank requires Magnetic Ltd to pay interest on the capital portion of the loan (the £500,000) of 1% at the end of year 1 and 2, 7 per cent at the end of year 3, 14 per cent at the end of year 4 and 20 per cent at the end of year 5, with all of the capital (£500,000) being repaid on the first day of year 6. The effective annual interest rate is 6.731 per cent.
>
> **Required**
>
> **a** Determine the interest charge for each of the five years.
>
> **b** Show the accounting entries (in journal form) for each of the five years.
>
> **c** Prepare the ledger account for the financial liability (the loan) showing the movement and balance at the end of each period.

a Calculation of the interest charge in each of the five years.

Year	Opening Balance	Interest charge (6.731%)	Repayment	Closing Balance
1	£525,000	£35,340	(£5,000)	£555,340
2	£555,340	£37,380	(£5,000)	£587,720
3	£587,720	£39,560	(£35,000)	£592,280
4	£592,280	£39,870	(£70,000)	£562,150
5	£562,150	£37,850	(£100,000)	£500,000
6	£500,000	–	(£500,000)	–

There is rounding (to the nearest £10) in this table in the interest calculation.

b Initial recognition in year 1

Bank	Dr	£525,000	
Loan account	Cr		£525,000

Journal to post the entries for the financial liability in year 1

Interest expense (statement of P&L)	Dr	£35,340	
Loan account	Cr		£30,340
Bank	Cr		£5,000

Journal to post the entries for the financial liability in year 2

Interest expense (statement of P&L)	Dr	£37,380	
Loan account	Cr		£32,380
Bank	Cr		£5,000

Journal to post the entries for the financial liability in year 3

Interest expense (statement of P&L)	Dr	£39,560	
Loan account	Cr		£4,560
Bank	Cr		£35,000

Journal to post the entries for the financial liability in year 4

Interest expense (statement of P&L)	Dr	£39,870	
Loan account	Dr	£30,130	
Bank	Cr		£70,000

Journal to post the entries for the financial liability in year 5

Interest expense (statement of P&L)	Dr	£37,850	
Loan account	Dr	£62,150	
Bank	Cr		£100,000

Journal to post the entries for the financial liability in year 6

Loan account	Dr	£500,000	
Bank	Cr		£500,000

c

		Loan account			
Year 1	**Details**	**£**	**Year 1**	**Details**	**£**
31 Dec	Bank account	5,000	1 Jan	Bank account	525,000
			31 Dec	P&L Interest	35,340
31 Dec	Balance c/d	555,340			
		560,340			560,340
			Year 2		
			1 Jan	Balance b/d	555,340
31 Dec	Bank account	5,000	31 Dec	P&L Interest	37,380
31 Dec	Balance c/d	587,720			
		592,720			592,720
			Year 3		
			1 Jan	Balance b/d	587,720
31 Dec	Bank account	35,000	31 Dec	P&L Interest	39,560
31 Dec	Balance c/d	592,280			
		627,280			627,280
			Year 4		
			1 Jan	Balance b/d	592,280
31 Dec	Bank account	70,000	31 Dec	P&L Interest	39,870
31 Dec	Balance c/d	562,150			
		632,150			632,150
			Year 5		
			1 Jan	Balance b/d	562,150
31 Dec	Bank account	100,000	31 Dec	P&L Interest	37,850
31 Dec	Balance c/d	500,000			
		600,000			600,000
			Year 6		
1 Jan	Bank account	500,000	1 Jan	Balance b/d	500,000
31 Dec	Balance c/d	–			
		500,000			500,000

Note

1 The effective annual interest rate was calculated by the author using the internal rate of return, though can also be determined using a financial calculator. You will be given the effective annual interest rate in questions at Introductory level.

2 The difference between the effective yearly interest charge and the amount that Magnetic Ltd pays to the bank either increases the financial liability owing, or reduces it, depending on whether the payment is less than or more than the interest charge.

LEARNING ACTIVITY 31.3

Visit the website of a large listed/quoted public limited company and find their latest annual report and financial statements. Examine the contents of the statement of comprehensive income (or equivalent named), statement of financial position and notes to the financial statements, paying particular attention to the items discussed in this chapter.

Summary

The statements of profit and loss of companies contain the same items as those of sole traders but in addition include others such as directors' remuneration, auditors' fees, interest on debentures/loan stock and income tax. Many large companies will also have to provide a statement showing other comprehensive income in the period. Other comprehensive income includes unrealized gains on, for example, the revaluation of property, actuarial gains on pension funds and foreign exchange translation differences. At this level only revaluations are examined. The other comprehensive income can be disclosed as a stand-alone statement, or it can form part of the main statement (called the 'statement of comprehensive income'). When the latter approach is adopted (i.e. a single statement), the whole statement is called the statement of comprehensive income for the period.

The statements of financial position of companies are similar to those of sole traders, except that the capital account is replaced by the called-up share capital and various reserves. These may be of two sorts, either revenue or capital reserves. Revenue reserves such as the retained earnings and general reserves can be distributed as dividends. Capital reserves such as the share premium, revaluation reserve and capital redemption reserve cannot be distributed as dividends. Loan stock and debentures are normally shown on the statement of financial position as non-current liabilities at their nominal value.

The final financial statements that are published and sent to equity shareholders must be presented in a form that complies with the Companies Act 2006 (i.e. contain a statement of profit and loss and a statement of financial position that show a true and fair view of the company's performance for the reporting period and its financial position at the reporting date), IAS 1 and other IASs. One of the main purposes of many accounting standards, particularly IAS 1, IAS 8, IAS 10 and IFRS 5, is to facilitate comparisons and predictions of performance by showing separately in the statement of comprehensive income any items of a non-recurring nature, showing items that belong to the period and adjusting comparatives when non-adjustment would diminish comparability. IFRS 5 requires an analysis of turnover, expenses, profit and tax on discontinued operations to be separately identifiable. In addition, all assets and liabilities of the asset/disposal group that are not classed as disposed, or as being held for sale, are separately disclosed and measured at the lower of realizable value and fair value less the costs of sale. Similarly, IAS 1 also states that some material items should be shown separately in published statements of comprehensive income. Comparisons and predictions may also be distorted where there are material adjustments applicable to prior periods arising from changes in accounting policies or the correction of fundamental errors. These are referred to as 'prior period adjustments'; and IAS 8 requires that the comparative figures for the preceding year be restated. Indeed, two years' adjusted comparatives of the statement of financial position should be disclosed.

In addition to showing certain items separately in final financial statements, the Companies Act 2006 and various accounting standards require notes to form part of the financial statements. These provide a more detailed breakdown, and in some cases, additional information about conditions prevailing at the reporting date, or events that have occurred since. Two examples are contingencies and events after the reporting date, respectively. IAS 10 states that material adjusting events after the reporting period should be provided for in financial statements, and material non-adjusting events after the reporting date be disclosed as a note. Similarly, IAS 37 requires that probable material contingent liabilities be recognized in financial statements as provisions and probable material contingent gains be recognized as assets. Possible but not probable material contingent assets and liabilities should be disclosed in a note to the financial statements.

Key terms and concepts

An asterisk after the question number indicates that there is a suggested answer on the Online Learning Centre (www.mcgraw-hill.co.uk/textbooks/thomas).

connect Review questions

31.1 Explain the difference between the authorized share capital, allotted share capital and called-up share capital of companies.

31.2 Explain the difference between revenue/distributable reserves and capital/non-distributable reserves, giving three examples of the latter.

31.3 Explain the difference between a reserve and a provision.

31.4 Briefly explain the reason(s) for the separate disclosure of components of financial performance such as discontinued operations, exceptional and extraordinary items in published company financial statements.

31.5 a Explain the nature of acquisitions and discontinued operations.

 b Briefly describe the treatment of each of these items in published company financial statements.

31.6 a Explain with examples the nature of exceptional items and extraordinary items.

 b Briefly describe the treatment of each of these items in published company financial statements.

31.7 a Explain with examples the nature of prior period adjustments.

 b Briefly describe the treatment of prior period adjustments in published company financial statements.

31.8 a Explain with examples the nature of events after the reporting period.

 b Describe the treatment of events after the reporting period in published company financial statements.

31.9   **a** Explain with examples the nature of contingent assets and contingent liabilities.

       b Describe the treatment of contingent assets and liabilities in published company financial statements.

31.10 Explain with an example the difference between current liabilities, provisions and contingent liabilities.

Exercises

31.11

Set out below is the capital section of a company's statement of financial position.

	31 Mar 20X2	31 Mar 20X1
	£'000	£'000
Equity share capital	140,000	140,000
Preference share capital	–	30,000
Share premium	20,000	20,000
Capital redemption reserve	30,000	–
Revaluation reserve	9,700	7,200
General reserve	27,000	20,000
Retained earnings	84,900	70,300
	311,600	287,500

You are required to explain the five different reserves that are shown on this company's statement of financial position, including in your answer the possible reasons for their existence.

(JMB)

31.12

a The following items usually appear in the final financial statements of a limited company:

   i   interim dividend;

   ii authorized capital;

   iii general reserve;

   iv share premium account.

Required:

An explanation of the meaning of each of the above terms.

b The following information has been obtained from the books of Drayfuss Ltd:

Authorized capital	100,000 8% £1 preference shares
	400,000 50p equity shares
Retained earnings – 1 Apr 20X0	£355,000
General reserve	£105,000
Issued capital	80,000 8% £1 preference shares (fully paid)
	250,000 50p equity shares (fully paid)
Profit for the year to 31 Mar 20X1	£95,000

The preference share interim dividend of 4 per cent had been paid and the final dividend of 4 per cent had been proposed by the directors. No equity share interim dividend had been declared, but the directors proposed a final dividend of 15p per share. The directors agreed to transfer £150,000 to general reserve.

Required

Prepare the statement of changes in equity for the year ended 31 March 20X1. Ignore taxation.

(AEB, adapted)

31.13

INTERMEDIATE

The following information has been extracted from the statement of financial position of Aston Products Ltd as at 30 April 20X1.

	£'000
Authorized share capital	
Equity shares of 50p each	4,000
6% preference share of £1 each	1,500
	5,500
Allotted and called-up share capital	
Equity shares of 50p each	2,000
6% preference shares of £1 each	1,000
	3,000
Retained profits	950

There were no other reserves in the statement of financial position at 30 April 20X1.

You are given the following additional information relating to the year ended 30 April 20X2.

1 The company issued one million equity shares at a price of 75 pence each on 1 January 20X2.

2 The management have decided to revalue the land and buildings that cost £400,000 at a value of £600,000.

3 The profit before tax for the year ended 30 April 20X2 was £475,000.

4 The income tax charge on the profit for the year ended 30 April 20X2 was estimated to be £325,000.

5 There are no interim dividends during the year ended 30 April 20X2 but the directors have proposed a final dividend on the preference shares, and a dividend of 10 pence each on the equity shares.

6 The directors have agreed to transfer £350,000 to a general reserve at 30 April 20X2.

You are required to prepare in vertical form the statement of comprehensive income for the year ended 30 April 20X2, a statement of financial position extract at that date showing the composition of the equity and a statement of changes in equity.

31.14

INTERMEDIATE

Cold Heart plc, which has a turnover of £100 million and pre-tax profit of £10 million, has its financial statements drawn up on 30 June each year and at 30 June 20X2 the company's accountant is considering the items specified below.

1 The directors have decided that the change in trading prospects evident during the year means that the goodwill shown at 30 June 20X1 at £200,000 has no value at 30 June 20X2.

2 Research and development expenditure of £7 million has been incurred in the year, and has been written off due to the project being abandoned.

3 Unrealized revaluation surplus of £10 million that arose on the revaluation of the company's buildings during the year.

4 A provision for bad debts of £15 million on the collapse of the company's main customer during the year.

5 A loss of £1 million arising from the closure of the company's retailing activities.

You are required to classify each of the above items into one of the following categories, explaining the reasons for the classification:

a material item that requires separate disclosure on the face of the financial statements;

b transfer direct to reserves;

c discontinued operations.

(JMB, adapted)

31.15

INTERMEDIATE

IAS 10 – Events After the Reporting Period defines the treatment to be given to events arising after the statement of financial position date but before the financial statements are approved by the Board of Directors.

Required

a Define the terms 'adjusting events after the reporting period' and 'non-adjustment events after the reporting' as they are used in IAS 10.

b Consider each of the following four events after the reporting period. If you think the event is an adjusting one, show exactly how items in the financial statements should be changed to allow for the event. If you think the event is non-adjusting, write a suitable disclosure note, including such details as you think fit. You may assume that all the amounts are material but that none is large enough to jeopardize the going concern status of the company.

  i The company makes an issue of 100,000 shares that raises £180,000 shortly after the statement of financial position date.

  ii A legal action brought against the company for breach of contract is decided, shortly after the reporting period, and as a result the company will have to pay costs and damages totalling £50,000. No provision has currently been made for this event. The breach of contract concerned occurred within the reporting period.

  iii Inventory included in the financial statements at cost £28,000 was subsequently sold for £18,000.

  iv A factory in use during the reporting period and valued at £250,000 was completely destroyed by fire. Only half of the value was covered by insurance. The insurance company has agreed to pay £125,000 under the company's policy.

(ACCA, adapted)

31.16

INTERMEDIATE

Your managing director is having a polite disagreement with the auditors on the subject of accounting for contingencies. Since the finance director is absent on sick leave, he has come to you for advice.

It appears that your firm is involved in four unrelated legal cases: P, Q, R and S. In case P the firm is suing for £10,000, in case Q the firm is suing for £20,000, in case R the firm is being sued for £30,000 and in case S the firm is being sued for £40,000. The firm has been advised by its expert and expensive lawyers that the chances of the firm winning each case are as follows:

Case	Percentage likelihood of winning
P	8
Q	92
R	8
S	92

Required

Write a memorandum to the managing director that:

1 explains why IAS 37 is relevant to these situations;

2 states the required accounting treatment for each of the four cases in the published financial statements;

3 gives journal entries for any necessary adjustments in the double-entry records;

4 suggests the contents of any Notes to the Financial Statements that are required by the IAS;

5 briefly discusses whether IAS 37 leads to a satisfactory representation of the position.

(ACCA, adapted)

31.17

The trial balance of Norr Ltd at 31 December 20X2 appeared as follows:

	Debit	Credit
	£	£
Equity shares of £1 – fully paid		50,000
Purchases	220,000	
Retained profit		30,000
Freehold property – cost	80,000	
Fixtures – cost	15,000	
Fixtures – accumulated depreciation		9,000
Rates	3,000	
Motor vehicles – cost	28,000	
Motor vehicles – accumulated depreciation		14,000
Insurance	2,000	
Inventories	40,000	
Trade receivables	30,000	
Trade payables		24,000
Sales revenue		310,000
Bank	12,100	
12% debentures		40,000
Debenture interest	2,400	
Wages and salaries	34,000	
Heat and light	4,100	
Professional fees	3,900	
General expenses	1,200	
Motor expenses	2,000	
Provision for bad debts		1,000
Bad debts	300	
	478,000	478,000

Additional information

1 During the year a motor vehicle purchased on 31 March 20W9 for £8,000 was sold for £3,000. The sale proceeds were debited to the bank account and credited to the sales account, and no other entries have been made in the financial statements relating to this transaction.

2 Depreciation has not yet been provided for the year. The following rates are applied on the straight-line basis, with the assumption of no residual value:

Fixtures and fittings   10 per cent

Motor vehicles   20 per cent

The company's policy is to provide a full year's depreciation in the year of acquisition and no depreciation in the year of disposal.

3 Inventory at 31 December 20X2 amounted to £45,000.

4 Rates paid in advance amount to £400. Insurance includes £200 paid in advance. An electricity bill covering the quarter to 31 December 20X2 and amounting to £320 was not received until February 20X3. It is estimated that the audit fee for 20X2 will be £1,500. An accrual also needs to be made in relation to debenture interest.

5 A general provision for bad debts of 4 per cent of trade receivables is to be carried forward.

6 The directors propose a dividend of £10,000.

Required

a Prepare a statement of comprehensive income and statement of financial position on the basis of the above information.

b Explain the meaning of the terms 'provision' and 'reserve', giving one example of each from the statement of financial position you have prepared.

(JMB, adapted)

ADVANCED

31.18

The Cirrus Co. Ltd has the following balances on its books at 31 December 20X2.

	Debit	Credit
	£	£
50p equity shares		20,000
£1 (6%) preference shares		14,000
Purchases	240,000	
Sales revenue		310,000
Inventories at 1 January 20X2	20,000	
Directors' fees	6,000	
Retained earnings at 1 January 20X2		35,700
10% debentures		20,000
Debenture interest paid	1,000	
Discounts allowed	500	
Administrative expenses	18,400	
Sales staff salaries	18,500	
Selling and distribution expenses	4,000	
Heating and lighting	2,500	
Rent and rates	1,700	
Trade receivables	14,000	
Provision for doubtful debts at 1 January 20X2		300
Trade payables		9,700
Land and buildings at cost	65,000	
Vans at cost less depreciation	19,800	
Cash in hand	400	
Bank balance		2,100
	411,800	411,800

The following information is also given:

1 The inventory at 31 December 20X2 has been valued at £32,000. Further investigation reveals that this includes some items originally purchased for £3,000, which have been in inventory for a long time. They need modification, probably costing about £600, after which it is hoped they will be saleable for between £3,200 and £3,500. Other items, included in the total at their cost price of £5,000, have been sent to an agent and are still at his premises awaiting sale. It cost £200 for transport and insurance to get them to the agent's premises and this amount is included in the selling and distribution expenses.

2 The balance on the vans account (£19,800) is made up as follows:

	£
Vans at cost (as at 1 Jan 20X2)	30,000
Less: Provision for depreciation to 1 Jan 20X2	13,800
	16,200
Additions during 20X2 at cost	3,600
	19,800

Depreciation is provided at 25 per cent per annum on the diminishing balance method. The addition during the year was invoiced as follows:

	£
Recommended retail price	3,000
Signwriting on van	450
Undersealing	62
Petrol	16
Number plates	12
Licence (to 31 Dec 20X2)	60
	3,600

3 The directors, having sought the advice of an independent valuer, wish to revalue the land and buildings at £80,000.

4 The directors wish to make a provision for doubtful debts of 2.5 per cent of the balance of trade receivables at 31 December 20X2.

5 Rates prepaid at 31 December 20X2 amount to £400, and sales staff's salaries owing at that date were £443.

6 The directors have proposed an equity dividend of 5p per share and the 6 per cent preference dividend.

7 Ignore value added tax (VAT).

Required

a Explain carefully the reason for the adjustments you have made in respect of points 1, 2 and 3 above.

b Prepare a statement of comprehensive income for the year ended 31 December 20X2, a statement of financial position as at that date and the statement of changes in equity for the year.

c Briefly distinguish between your treatment of debenture interest and proposed dividends.

(ACCA, adapted)

INTERMEDIATE

31.19*

The following is the trial balance of D. Cooper Ltd as at 30 September 20X2:

	Debit	Credit
	£	£
Authorized, allotted and called-up share capital:		
100,000 equity shares of £1 each		100,000
50,000 7% preference shares of 50p each		25,000
Leasehold premises at valuation	140,000	
Goodwill	20,000	
Plant and machinery (cost £80,000)	66,900	
Loose tools (cost £13,000)	9,100	
Inventory	9,400	
Trade receivables/trade payables	11,200	8,300
Bank overdraft		7,800
Purchases/sales revenue	49,700	135,250
Directors' salaries	22,000	
Rates	4,650	
Light and heat	3,830	
Plant hire	6,600	
Interest on debentures	1,200	
Preliminary expenses	1,270	
10% debentures		24,000
Provision for bad debts		910
Share premium		35,000
Retained earnings		2,580
Revenue reserve		10,200
Interim dividend on equity shares paid	3,250	
Audit fees	1,750	
Revaluation reserve		9,860
Bad debts	700	
Listed investments	8,000	
Investment income		650
	359,550	359,550

Additional information

1 Inventory at 30 September 20X2 is valued at £13,480.

2 Rates include a payment of £2,300 for the six months from 1 July 20X2.

3 Depreciation on plant is 15 per cent per annum of cost and the loose tools were valued at £7,800 on 30 September 20X2. Goodwill did not suffer any diminution in value. The company does not depreciate its premises.

4 The provision for bad debts is to be adjusted to 10 per cent of the trade receivables at the end of the year.

5 The preference share dividends are outstanding at the end of the year and the last half year's interest on the debentures has not been paid.

6 The corporation tax on this year's profit is £6,370.

7 The directors propose to declare a final dividend on the equity shares of 13 pence per share and transfer £2,500 to revenue reserves.

You are required to prepare in publishable form a statement of comprehensive income and a statement of changes in equity for the year ended 30 September 20X2, and a statement of financial position at that date.

31.20*

ADVANCED

The following is the trial balance of L. Johnson Ltd as at 31 December 20X1:

	Debit	Credit
	£	£
Authorized capital:		
200,000 equity shares of £1 each		200,000
90,000 5% preference shares of £1 each		90,000
Issued and called-up capital:		
80,000 equity shares		80,000
50,000 5% preference shares		50,000
Freehold buildings (at valuation)	137,000	
Motor vehicle (cost £35,000)	29,400	
Plant and machinery (cost £40,000)	32,950	
Development costs (cost £10,000)	6,600	
Interim dividend on preference shares	1,250	
Provision for bad debts		860
Wages and salaries	5,948	
Bad debts	656	
Discount allowed/received	492	396
Goodwill	10,000	
Listed investments	4,873	
Purchases/sales revenue	78,493	130,846
Capital redemption reserve		9,000
Revaluation reserve		13,500
Formation expenses	250	
Directors' emoluments	13,000	
Returns inwards/outwards	1,629	1,834
Rates	596	
Dividends received		310
Retained earnings		3,126
Light and heat	1,028	
Audit fee	764	
Revenue reserve		8,400
Share premium		5,600
10% debentures		30,000
Inventories	9,436	
Trade receivables/trade payables	11,600	8,450
Bank overdraft		3,643
	345,965	345,965

Additional information

1 Corporation tax of £2,544 will be payable on the profit of 20X1.

2 Rates include £200 for the half year ended on 31 March 20X2.

3 Electricity for the quarter to 31 January 20X2 of £330 is not included in the trial balance.

4 The provision for bad debts is to be adjusted to 5 per cent of the trade receivables at the end of the year.

5 Annual depreciation on the reducing balance method is 25 per cent of vehicles, 20 per cent of plant and 10 per cent of development costs. The value of goodwill did not fall below the value recorded in the trial balance. The company does not depreciate buildings.

6 Formation expenses are to be written off against the share premium account.

7 Inventory at 31 December 20X1 was £12,456.

8 It is proposed to pay a final dividend on the equity shares of 6.25 pence per share.

9 The directors have decided to transfer £4,000 to the revenue reserve this year.

10 The debenture interest for the year and the final dividend on the preference shares are outstanding at the end of the year.

Required

Prepare in publishable form a statement of comprehensive income and a statement of changes in equity for the year ended 31 December 20X1, and a statement of financial position at that date.

31.21*

The following is the trial balance of Oakwood Ltd as at 30 June 20X2:

	Debit	Credit
	£	£
Authorized capital:		
150,000 equity shares of £1 each		150,000
70,000 5% preference shares of £1 each		70,000
Allotted and called-up capital:		
125,000 equity shares		125,000
60,000 5% preference shares		60,000
Freehold buildings at cost	165,000	
Development costs (cost £12,000)	5,400	
Goodwill	8,000	
Delivery vehicles (cost £28,000)	18,700	
Plant and machinery (cost £34,000)	31,900	
Listed investments	3,250	
10% debentures		20,000
Share premium		9,000
Revenue reserve		6,100
Interim dividend on equity shares	2,000	
Interim dividend on preference shares	1,500	
Provision for bad debts		730
Administrative salaries	6,370	
Bad debts	740	
Discount allowed/received	290	440
Purchases/sales revenue	81,230	120,640
Audit fee	390	
Preliminary expenses	200	
Directors' remuneration	14,100	
Returns inwards/outwards	230	640
Carriage inwards	310	
Rates	600	
Interest received		410
Retained earnings		7,700
Light and heat	940	
Postage and telephone	870	
Inventories	8,760	
Trade receivables/trade payables	10,400	7,890
Bank overdraft		2,630
	361,180	361,180

Additional information

1 Corporation tax of £1,080 will be payable on the profit of this year.

2 Rates include a prepayment of £150.

3 Gas used in May and June 20X2 of £270 is not included in the trial balance.

4 Inventory at 30 June 20X2 was £11,680.

5 The provision for bad debts is to be adjusted to 5 per cent of trade receivables at 30 June 20X2.

6 Annual depreciation on the reducing balance method is 20 per cent of plant, 10 per cent of vehicles and 25 per cent of development costs. The value of goodwill did not fall below the value recorded in the trial balance. The company does not depreciate buildings.

7 Sales revenue includes goods on sale or return at 30 June 20X2 that cost £500 and were invoiced to credit customers at a price of £1,000.

8 Included in plant and machinery are consumable tools purchased during the year at a cost of £300.

9 The preliminary expenses are to be written off against the share premium account balance.

10 It is proposed to pay a final dividend on the equity shares of 3.2 pence per share.

11 The directors have decided to transfer £3,000 to the revenue reserve.

Required

Prepare in publishable form a statement of comprehensive income and a statement of changes in equity for the year ended 30 June 20X2, and a statement of financial position at that date.

31.22

The trial balance of Harmonica Ltd at 31 December 20X1 is given below.

	Debit	Credit
	£'000	£'000
Purchases and sales revenue	18,000	28,600
Inventory at 1 January 20X1	4,500	
Warehouse wages	850	
Salespersons' salaries and commission	1,850	
Administrative salaries	3,070	
General administrative expenses	580	
General distribution expenses	490	
Directors' remuneration	870	
Debenture interest paid	100	
Dividends – interim dividend paid	40	
Non-current assets		
– cost	18,000	
– aggregate depreciation, 1 January 20X1		3,900
Trade receivables and payables	6,900	3,800
Provision for doubtful debts at 1 January 20X1		200
Balance at bank		2,080
10% debentures (repayable 20X5)		1,000
Called-up share capital (£1 equity shares)		4,000
Share premium account		1,300
Retained earnings, 1 January 20X1		8,720
Suspense account (see note 3 below)		1,650
	55,250	55,250

Additional information

1 Closing inventory amounted to £5m.

2 A review of the trade receivables total of £6.9m showed that it was necessary to write off debts totalling £0.4m, and that the provision for doubtful debts should be adjusted to 2 per cent of the remaining trade receivables.

3 Two transactions have been entered in the company's cash record and transferred to the suspense account shown in the trial balance. They are:

    a   The receipt of £1.5m from the issue of 500,000 £1 equity shares at a premium of £2 per share.

    b   The sale of some surplus plant. The plant had cost £1m and had a written-down value of £100,000. The sale proceeds of £150,000 have been credited to the suspense account but no other entries have been made.

4 Depreciation should be charged at 10 per cent per annum on cost at the end of the year and allocated 70 per cent to distribution costs and 30 per cent to administration.

5 The directors propose a final dividend of 4 pence per share on the shares in issue at the end of the year.

6 Accruals and prepayments still to be accounted for are:

	Prepayments	Accruals
	£'000	£'000
General administrative expenses	70	140
General distribution expenses	40	90
	110	230

7 Directors' remuneration is to be analysed between distribution costs and administrative expenses as follows:

	£'000
– distribution	300
– administration	570
	870

8 Ignore taxation.

Required

Prepare the company's statement of comprehensive income and statement of changes in equity for the year ended 31 December 20X1, and statement of financial position as at 31 December 20X1 in a form suitable for publication. Notes to the financial statements are not required.

(ACCA adapted)

ADVANCED 31.23

The following balances existed in the accounting records of Koppa Ltd. at 31 December 20X2:

	£'000
Development costs capitalized, 1 January 20X2	180
Freehold land as revalued 31 December 20X2	2,200
Buildings – cost	900
– aggregate depreciation at 1 January 20X2	100
Office equipment – cost	260
– aggregate depreciation at 1 January 20X2	60
Motor vehicles – cost	200
– aggregate depreciation at 1 January 20X2	90
Trade receivables	1,360
Cash at bank	90
Trade payables	820
12% debentures (issued 20W5 and redeemable 20X2)	1,000
Called up share capital – equity shares of 50p each	1,000
Share premium account	500
Revaluation reserve	200
Retained earnings 1 January 20X2	1,272
Sales revenue	8,650
Purchases	5,010
Research and development expenditure for the year	162
Inventories 1 January 20X2	990
Distribution costs	460
Administrative expenses	1,560
Debenture interest	120
Interim dividend paid	200

In preparing the company's statement of comprehensive income and statement of financial position at 31 December 20X2 the following further information is relevant:

1 Inventory at 31 December 20X2 was £880,000.

2 Depreciation is to be provided for as follows:

Land	Nil
Buildings	2 per cent per annum on cost
Office equipment	20 per cent per annum, reducing balance basis
Motor vehicles	25 per cent per annum on cost

Depreciation on buildings and office equipment is all charged to administrative expenses. Depreciation on motor vehicles is to be split equally between distribution costs and administrative expenses.

3 The £180,000 total for development costs as at 1 January 20X2 relates to two projects:

	£'000
Project 836: completed project (balance being amortized over the period expected to benefit from it. Amount to be amortized in 20X2: £20,000)	82
Project 910: in progress	98
	180

4 The research and development expenditure for the year is made up of:

	£'000
Research expenditure	103
Development costs on Project 910 that continues to satisfy the requirements in IAS 38 for capitalization	59
	162

5 The freehold land had originally cost £2,000,000 and was revalued on 31 December 20X2.

6 Prepayments and accruals at 31 December 20X2 were:

	Prepayments	Accruals
	£'000	£'000
Administrative expenses	40	11
Sundry distribution costs	–	4

7 The share premium account balance arose as a result of the issue during 20X2 of 1,000,000 50p equity shares at £1 each. All shares qualify for the proposed final dividend to be provided for (see note below).

8 A final dividend of 20p per share is proposed.

Required

Prepare the company's statement of comprehensive income, a statement of changes in equity for the year ended 31 December 20X2, and statement of financial position as at that date, in a form suitable for publication as far as the information provided permits. No notes are required. Ignore taxation.

(ACCA, adapted)

31.24

ADVANCED

Topaz Ltd makes up its financial statements regularly to 31 December each year. The company has operated for some years with four divisions; A, B, C and D, but on 30 June 20X1 Division B was sold for £8m, realizing a profit of £2.5m. During 20X1 there was a fundamental reorganization of Division C, the costs of which were £1.8m.

The trial balance of the company at 31 December 20X1 included the following balances:

	Division B		Divisions A, C and D combined	
	Debit	Credit	Debit	Credit
	£m	£m	£m	£m
Sales revenue		13		68
Costs of sales	8		41	
Distribution costs (including a bad debt of £1.9m – Division D)	1		6	
Administrative expenses	2		4	
Profit on sale of Division B		2.5		
Reorganization costs, Division C			1.8	
Interest on £10m (10% debenture stock) issued in 20W5			1	
Taxation			4.8	
Interim dividend paid			2	
Revaluation reserve				10

A final dividend of £4m is proposed.

The balance on the revaluation reserve relates to the company's freehold property and arose as follows:

	£'m
Balance at 1 January 20X1	6
Revaluation during 20X1	4
Balance at 31 December X1 per trial balance	10

Required

a Prepare the statement of comprehensive income of Topaz Ltd for the year ended 31 December 20X1, complying as far as possible with the provisions of the Companies Act 2006 and *IAS 1 – Presentation of Financial Statements*.

b Explain why the disclosures in the statement of comprehensive income required by IFRS 5 and IAS 1 improve the quality of information available to users of the financial statements.

(ACCA, adapted)

31.25

INTERMEDIATE

Marmite Ltd obtains a £750,000 loan which is repayable over the next five years. The bank has agreed to accept the following repayments. The repayments are varied to match to periods when Marmite Ltd expect to have surplus future cash flows which can be used to reduce their debt. The repayment schedule is as follows. Marmite Ltd is aware that interest is usually paid up front and has proposed the following split in the agreed repayments for the preparation of the financial statements.

	Interest	Capital	Total repayment
End of Year 1	£20,000	£10,000	£30,000
End of Year 2	£60,000	£40,000	£100,000
End of Year 3	£60,000	£90,000	£150,000
End of Year 4	£50,000	£250,000	£300,000
End of Year 5	£40,000	£360,000	£400,000

You are informed that the effective interest rate is 7.05%.

Required

a Advise Marmite Ltd as to whether the above suggested charge for interest and capital is appropriate under International Financial Reporting Standards.

b Calculate the interest charge that is applicable in each of the five years (under IFRS).

c Prepare journals to post the transactions to the financial liability account (the loan account) for the five-year period.

d Prepare the ledger account for the loan for the five-year period.

References

International Accounting Standards Board (2010a) *International Accounting Standard 1 – Presentation of Financial Statements* (IASB).

International Accounting Standards Board (2010b) *International Accounting Standard 8 – Accounting Policies, Changes in Accounting Estimates and Errors* (IASB).

International Accounting Standards Board (2010c) *International Accounting Standard 10 – Events After the Reporting Period* (IASB).

International Accounting Standards Board (2010d) *International Financial Reporting Standard 5 – Non-current Assets Held for Sale and Discontinued Operations* (IASB).

International Accounting Standards Board (2010e) *International Accounting Standard 37 – Provisions, Contingent Liabilities and Contingent Assets* (IASB).

Tesco plc (2010) Annual Report, www.tescoplc.com.

When you have read this chapter, log on to the Online Learning Centre for *Introduction to Financial Accounting* at www.mcgraw-hill.co.uk/textbooks/thomas, where you will find multiple choice quizzes, case studies, a glossary and mock exams.

International Accounting Standards Board (2010a) *International Accounting Standard 1 – Presentation of Financial Statements* (IASB).

International Accounting Standards Board (2010b) *International Accounting Standard 8 – Accounting Policies, Changes in Accounting Estimates and Errors* (IASB).

International Accounting Standards Board (2010c) *International Accounting Standard 10 – Events After the Reporting Period* (IASB).

International Accounting Standards Board (2010d) *International Financial Reporting Standard 5 – Non-current Assets Held for Sale and Discontinued Operations* (IASB).

International Accounting Standards Board (2010e) *International Accounting Standard 37 – Provisions, Contingent Liabilities and Contingent Assets* (IASB).

Tesco plc (2010) Annual Report, www.tescoplc.com

Statement of cash flows

Learning Objectives

After reading this chapter you should be able to do the following:

1. Explain the meaning of the key terms and concepts listed at the end of the chapter.

2. Explain the nature and purpose of a statement of cash flows.

3. Explain the advantages and limitations of a statement of cash flows.

4. Explain the relationship between a statement of cash flows and the statement of comprehensive income (statement of profit and loss) and the statement of financial position.

5. Prepare a simple statement of cash flows for sole traders and limited companies.

6. Prepare a classified statement of cash flows using the indirect method for sole traders and limited companies in accordance with International Accounting Standard (IAS) 7 (including notes).

7. Explain the nature of the groups of items and subtotals found in a typical classified statement of cash flows conforming to IAS 7.

8. Outline the main differences between the direct and indirect methods of preparing a statement of cash flows.

32.1 The nature and purpose of statements that analyse the cash flows of a business

In simple terms, the purpose of a **statement of cash flows** is to show the reasons for the change in the cash and bank balance over an accounting period. Another common way of expressing this is to show the manner in which cash has been generated and used (or where it has gone). It might be thought that this is relatively straightforward since it could be done in the form of a summarized cash book or receipts and payments account. Unfortunately, however, it is usually not done in this way but rather in the form of changes in the value of the items in the statement of financial position between the end of the previous year and the end of the current year.

32.2 Relationship between statement of cash flows, statement of profit and loss and statement of financial position

Statements of cash flows are intended to complement the statement of profit and loss (statement of comprehensive income) and statement of financial position. The main difference between a statement of cash flows and a statement of profit and loss lies in the observation that profit is not the same as the increase in cash over a given accounting period, but rather is one source of funds. The cash flow statement provides information on the cash that is obtained from operating activities, which are the core objects of an entity and which typically make up most of the entity's ongoing profits/returns. The statement of cash flows also shows the impact on cash of movements in assets, liabilities and capital over the accounting period. Therefore, it provides a link between the statement of financial position at the beginning of the period, the statement of profit and loss for the period, and the statement of financial position at the end of the period.

 32.3 Sources and application of cash: sole traders and partnerships

The first types of statement to analyse the changes in the statement of financial position of an entity, in terms of the impact on cash, classified the changes as either sources or applications of cash funds – the resultant statement being called 'the sources and application of funds statement'. Sources essentially relate to receipts (cash inflows) and applications to payments (cash outflows). In terms of changes in the items in the statement of financial position, sources of cash funds can comprise the following:

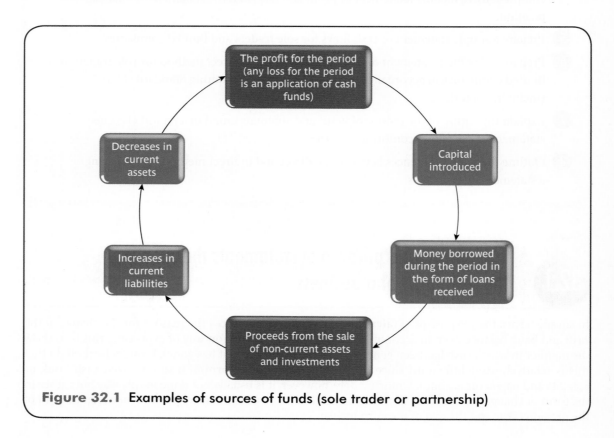

Figure 32.1 Examples of sources of funds (sole trader or partnership)

Profit is a source of cash funds as it represents the excess of income over expenditure. The timing of the source may not equate exactly to cash inflows as some of the sales and purchases/**capital expenditures** may have been on credit; however, they will eventually result in a net cash inflow.

Applications of cash funds are highlighted in Figure 32.2.

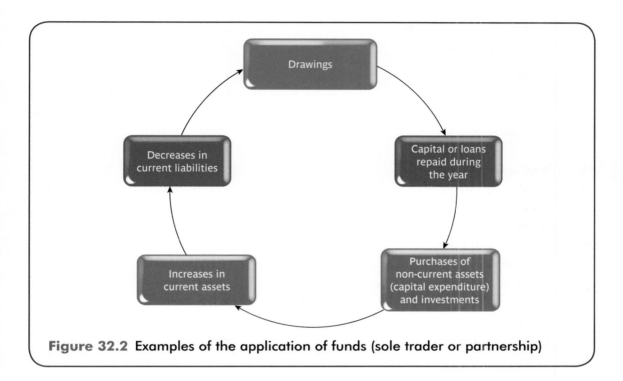

Figure 32.2 Examples of the application of funds (sole trader or partnership)

Probably the most confusing aspect of the source and application of cash flows is the changes in current assets and liabilities. Some simplified examples may thus be helpful. An increase in trade payables is a source of funds because the money that would otherwise have been used to pay these credit suppliers is available for other purposes (less has been paid out – therefore there is more in the bank). A decrease in trade receivables is also a source of funds as the credit customers have paid their accounts earlier, hence there will be more in the bank (assuming sales have remained constant or grown). Similarly, a decrease in inventory is a source of funds because the proceeds of the sale of inventory will mean that there is more money in the bank. Conversely, an increase in inventory is an application of funds since money will have been used to pay for it. Similarly, an increase in trade receivables is an application of funds, because allowing customers additional credit is like giving them a loan. A decrease in trade payables is also an application of funds, since money will have been paid out to them. Frequently, certain sources of funds have corresponding applications. For example, an increase in inventory may be 'financed' by an increase in trade payables.

A simple statement showing the sources and application of cash funds for a sole trader, or a partnership, might consist of the above list of sources and applications of cash funds, including a breakdown of the changes in current assets and current liabilities between trade payables, trade receivables and inventory. This is illustrated in Example 32.1.

EXAMPLE
32.1

The following are the statements of financial position of A. Cashwood as at 30 September 20X2 and 30 September 20X3:

	30 Sep 20X2	30 Sep 20X3
	£	£
ASSETS		
Non-current assets (at cost)	85,000	97,000
Current assets		
Inventory	13,600	10,800
Trade receivables	8,400	9,700
Cash and bank	2,500	3,600
	24,500	24,100
Total assets	109,500	121,100
EQUITY AND LIABILITIES		
Equity		
Capital at start of year	77,700	82,200
Add: Capital introduced	2,800	4,300
Profit for the year	21,600	34,200
	102,100	120,700
Less: Drawings	19,900	20,700
Capital at end of year	82,200	100,000
Non-current liabilities		
Bank loan	20,000	15,000
Total non-current liabilities	20,000	15,000
Current liabilities		
Trade payables	7,300	6,100
Total current liabilities	7,300	6,100
Total liabilities	27,300	21,100
Total equity and liabilities	109,500	121,100

Required

Prepare a statement showing the sources and application of cash for the year ended 30 September 20X3.

A. Cashwood		
Statement of sources and application of cash for the year ended 30 September 20X3		
	£	£
Sources of cash		
Profit for the year		34,200
Capital introduced		4,300
Decrease in inventory (£13,600 – £10,800)		2,800
		41,300
Applications of cash		
Drawings	(20,700)	
Repayment of bank loan (£20,000 – £15,000)	(5,000)	
Purchase of non-current assets (£97,000 – £85,000)	(12,000)	
Increase in trade receivables (£9,700 – £8,400)	(1,300)	
Decrease in trade payables (£7,300 – £6,100)	(1,200)	
		(40,200)
Increase in cash in the year		1,100
Cash and bank balance at 1 Oct 20X2		2,500
Cash and bank balance at 30 Sep 20X3		3,600

This reconciles to the cash and bank balance as disclosed in the statement of financial position.

32.4 Sources and application of cash: companies

The preparation of a statement of cash flows for companies involves some additional considerations as follows.

Sources of cash funds include:

1 the profit for the year before interest, taxation and income from investing activities, for example dividends received (this is because these items are shown separately as sources or applications of funds);

2 investment income: for example, dividends received;

3 capital introduced. This will comprise the amount received from any issues of shares and debentures during the year;

4 proceeds from the sale of non-current assets and investments;

5 increases in current liabilities;

6 decreases in current assets.

Applications of cash funds include:

1 income tax paid during the period;

2 servicing of finance: for example, interest paid;

3 instead of drawings, the amounts paid during the year in respect of equity share dividends. This will normally comprise the interim dividend plus the final dividend of the previous accounting year;

4 capital repaid will consist of any loans repaid during the year and any shares and debentures redeemed during the year;

5 purchases of non-current assets and investments;

6 increases in current assets;

7 decreases in current liabilities.

The preparation of cash flows from operating activities for both sole traders and companies involves some further complications with regard to the figure for profit or loss that is included in the statement. This should reflect the funds generated from a business's operating activities. However, the amount of profit shown in the statement of profit and loss is after deducting (and adding) certain items that do not involve the movement of cash funds. These consist of:

1 provisions for depreciation on non-current assets;

2 profits and losses on the sale of non-current assets;

3 increases and decreases in provisions for bad debts.

All these items are purely accounting adjustments that arise from the preparation of the statement of profit and loss using an accruals/matching basis. They do not represent movements of cash funds. It is therefore necessary to adjust the figure of profit shown in the statement of profit and loss in respect of these items to arrive at the cash funds generated from operations that are entered in the statement of cash flows as follows (see Figure 32.3):

Profit per statement of profit and loss	
Add:	Provisions for depreciation
	Losses on sale of non-current assets
	Increase in provision for bad debts
Less:	Profits on sale of non-current assets
	Decrease in provisions for bad debts
=	*Cash funds generated from operations*

Figure 32.3 An example of the adjustments required to determine cash funds generated from operating activities

In addition, items included in the statement of profit and loss that are regarded as being income from investing activities (dividends received), or payments to service finance (interest paid) are typically removed from the profit and disclosed separately as sources and applications of funds. Taxation is also removed for the same reason. Therefore, investment income is taken off the profit figure, and the interest and taxation expense are added back.

This is illustrated in Example 32.2.

This example, like most examination questions, does not contain a statement of profit and loss. In order to ascertain the profit before tax, it is therefore necessary to reconstruct the lower half of the statement of profit and loss. The income tax must either be given as a note in the question or included under current liabilities on the statement of financial position at the end of the current year. Details on both interim dividends paid and proposed dividend and their respective payment dates must be given as further information in the question. Transfers to reserves and the retained profit of the current year are found by calculating the difference between the amounts shown on the statement of financial position at the end of the current year and the end of the previous year for these items (see Example 32.2.)

EXAMPLE 32.2

The following are the statements of financial position of C. Flowers Ltd as at 31 March 20X2 and 31 March 20X3:

	31 Mar 20X2	31 Mar 20X3
	£	£
ASSETS		
Non-current assets		
Property, plant and equipment	127,000	113,000
Current assets		
Inventory	48,400	56,700
Trade receivables	37,400	34,800
Cash and bank	8,600	17,300
	94,400	108,800
Total assets	221,400	221,800
EQUITY AND LIABILITIES		
Equity		
Equity shares of £1 each	50,000	60,000
Share premium account	18,000	26,000
General reserve	6,400	9,600
Retained earnings	47,900	54,900
Total equity	122,300	150,500
Non-current liabilities		
10% debentures	52,000	20,000
Total non-current liabilities	52,000	20,000
Current liabilities		
Trade payables	31,400	32,800
Current tax payable	15,700	18,500
Total current liabilities	47,100	51,300
Total liabilities	99,100	71,300
Total equity and liabilities	221,400	221,800

Additional information

1

Non-Current Assets	31 Mar 20X2	31 Mar 20X3
	£	£
Property, Plant and Equipment (at cost)	173,000	165,000
Aggregate depreciation	(46,000)	(52,000)
	127,000	113,000

2 Non-current assets that cost £8,000 and had a written-down value of £4,200 were disposed of during the year ended 31 March 20X3 at a price of £3,500. There were no other acquisitions or disposals of non-current assets during the year.

3 The total depreciation on non-current assets for the year was £9,800.

4 Trade receivables are made up of the following:

	31 Mar 20X2	31 Mar 20X3
	£	£
Trade receivables	39,100	36,200
Less: Provision for bad debts	(1,700)	(1,400)
	37,400	34,800

5 The current tax payable at 31 March 20X2 of £15,700 was paid in September 20X2.

6 The proposed final equity dividend for the year 31 March 20X3 is £29,600 (31 March 20X2 – £26,200). If approved at the AGM, the proposed final equity dividend is paid for immediately. The AGM is usually three months after the reporting period end date. In addition, an interim equity dividend is paid each year in October. The interim dividend for 20X3 was £8,600 (20X2 – £5,500).

7 During the year 10,000 equity shares were issued at a price of £1.80 each.

You are required to prepare a statement showing the sources and application of cash for the year ended 31 March 20X3.

Solution		
Computation of profit before interest and taxation	£	£
Increase in balance in retained earnings –		
(£54,900 – £47,900)		7,000
Transfer to general reserve (£9,600 – £6,400)		3,200
Equity dividends paid –		
Proposed final (20X2)	26,200	
Interim (20X3)	8,600	34,800
Interest paid on debentures (£20,000 × 10%)		2,000
Income tax expense		18,500
Profit before taxation		65,500

C. Flowers Ltd		
Statement of sources and application of cash for the year ended 31 March 20X3		
	£	£
Sources of cash funds		
Profit for the year before interest and tax	65,500	
Add (Less): Adjustments for items not involving the movement of funds –		
Provision for depreciation	9,800	
Loss on sale of non-current assets (£4,200 – £3,500)	700	
Decrease in provision for bad debts (£1,700 – £1,400)	(300)	
Cash funds generated from operations		75,700
Issue of shares (10,000 × £1.80)		18,000
Proceeds of sale of non-current assets		3,500
Increase in trade payables (£32,800 – £31,400)		1,400
Decrease in trade receivables (£39,100 – £36,200)		2,900
		101,500
Applications of cash funds		
Income tax paid	(15,700)	
Dividends paid (£26,200 + £8,600)	(34,800)	
Interest on debentures (£20,000 × 10%)	(2,000)	
Repayment of debentures (£52,000 – £20,000)	(32,000)	
Increase in inventory (£56,700 – £48,400)	(8,300)	
		(92,800)
Increase (decrease) in cash and bank balance		8,700
Cash and bank balance at 1 Apr 20X2		8,600
Cash and bank balance at 31 Mar 20X3		17,300

Notes

1 The proceeds from the issue of shares of £18,000 (given in Additional information above) should correspond with the increase in equity share capital (£60,000 – £50,000) and share premium account (£26,000 – £18,000) shown in the statement of financial position (i.e. £10,000 + £8,000). The proceeds from an issue of shares are often not given in the Additional information, and thus have to be calculated in terms of the increase in share capital and share premium accounts.

2 The details relating to the acquisition and disposal of non-current assets, and depreciation (given in additional information) should also correspond with the changes in non-current assets and aggregate depreciation shown in the statement of financial position as follows:

Non-current assets			
20X2	**£**	**20X3**	**£**
1 Apr Balance b/d	173,000	31 Mar Bank	3,500
		31 Mar Provision for depreciation	
		(£8,000 – £4,200)	3,800
		31 Mar Loss on sale	700
		31 Mar Balance c/d	165,000
	173,000		173,000

Provision for depreciation			
20X3	**£**	**20X2**	**£**
31 Mar Non-current assets	3,800	1 Apr Balance b/d	46,000
(£8,000 – £4,200)		**20X3**	
31 Mar Balance c/d	52,000	31 Mar Depreciation expense	9,800
	55,800		55,800

The reason for understanding how the additional information in respect of issues of shares, non-current assets and depreciation corresponds with changes in the statement of financial position is that sometimes not all the information required is given as additional information (e.g. acquisitions of non-current assets, revaluations of assets). The student will then have to ascertain the missing information by examining the changes in the statement of financial positions. A useful way of doing this is in terms of the ledger accounts.

3 In the preparation of a statement of cash flows, investments held as a non-current asset are treated in the same way as other non-current assets. However, investments held as a current asset that are repayable on demand are treated in the same way as cash and bank as per IAS 7 (discussed later). The amount of current asset investments is added to the cash and bank balance and shown on statements of cash flows as 'cash and cash equivalents'.

4 As covered in Chapter 31, dividends do not form part of the statement of profit and loss. They are distributions out of distributable profits (usually retained earnings). They are only taken out of distributable profits when paid, not when proposed. Proposed dividends are just disclosed in the financial statements (not accrued). They are typically paid a couple of months after the reporting period end date – when they have been approved by shareholders at the company's AGM. Therefore, the movement in retained earnings between two reporting dates will have been affected by the dividends paid in the year. Dividends paid in the year will comprise the proposed dividend from the previous period (in this instance £26,200) and any interim dividends paid in the year (in this instance £8,600).

5 The income tax expense used to compute the profit before tax is the amount outstanding at the end of the current accounting year (£15,700) because this will have been deducted in arriving at the retained earnings for the year of £3,600. It is often given as a note in examination questions, failing which the amount can be found as a current liability on the statement of financial position at the end of the current year. In contrast, the income tax shown as an application of funds (£18,500) is that outstanding at the end of the previous year since this will have been paid during the current year. It is often given as Additional information in examination questions, failing which, the amount can be found as a current liability on the statement of financial position at the end of the previous year.

6 The movement in the retained earnings reserves will also include (in addition to the profit for the year after tax) transfers made to other reserves. Therefore, when working back to find the profit before tax, it is necessary to add any transfer to reserves to the movement in the retained earnings balances as shown in the opening and closing statements of financial position. Details of transfers to other reserves may be found in additional information, however, they can also be identified from increases in the reserve balances recorded in the opening and closing statements of financial position.

7 Dividends paid in the period might also be determined from the statement of changes in equity if provided in the examination question.

8 The current assets might include prepaid expenses and the current liabilities may include accrued expenses. These could be dealt with separately in the statement of sources and application of cash as sources or applications of cash. However, another acceptable and more expedient treatment is simply to aggregate prepayments with trade receivables, and accruals with trade payables.

9 It is assumed that the interest on the debentures is paid within the year, therefore there is no opening or closing accruals and the statement of profit and loss charge is equal to the cash flow.

32.5 Statements of cash flows – IAS 7

IAS 7 – Statement of Cash Flows (IASB, 2010) defines **cash flows** as 'inflows and outflows of cash and cash equivalents'. **Cash** is defined as 'cash on hand and demand deposits'. **Demand deposits** are repayable on demand if they can be withdrawn at any time without notice and without penalty, or if they are at maturity, or have a period of notice of not more than 24 hours or one working day has been agreed. **Cash equivalents** are 'short-term, highly liquid investments that are readily convertible to known amounts of cash and which are subject to an insignificant risk of changes in value'.

> **LEARNING ACTIVITY 32.1**
>
> There are two basic concepts of funds: cash funds and working capital funds. Cash funds form the basis of statements of cash flows, and working capital funds form the basis of funds flow statements or statements of source and application of funds. The purpose of a statement of cash flows is to show the reasons for the change in the cash and bank balance over an accounting period.

IAS 7 requires the items that are normally contained in a statement of cash flows to be classified, grouped under three headings, the total of which are reconciled to the opening and closing cash position. A simple summarized format portraying the key cash flow information requirements is shown in Figure 32.4.

The detail making up each of the key classifications of cash (operating, investing and financing) are provided on the face of the statement of cash flows. These are now discussed in turn.

1 Cash flows from operating activities

Operating activities are the principal revenue-producing activities of the entity and other activities that are not investing or financial activities. **Cash flows from operating activities** are primarily made up of the net increase (or decrease) in cash that results from a company's normal trading activities.

B. Good	
Statement of cash flows for the year ended 31 March 20X2	
	£
Net cash from operating activities	XXX
Net cash from investing activities	XX
Net cash from financing activities	XX
Net cash increase in cash and cash equivalents	XXX
Cash and cash equivalents at 1/4/X1	X
Cash and cash equivalents at 31/03/X2	XXX

Figure 32.4 A summary of the key headings included in a statement of cash flows under IAS 7

Therefore, they generally result from the transactions and other events that enter into the determination of profit or loss.

'Cash flow from operating activities' is sometimes crudely referred to as 'cash profit', or more accurately 'operating profit computed on a cash basis'. Under IAS 7 the derivation of the 'cash flow from operating activities' is shown first in the statement of cash flows. It can be derived using two methods: the direct method or the indirect method. Both methods give the same figure for cash flows from operating activities.

The direct method

The **direct method** involves converting all the individual items in the statement of profit and loss from an accruals basis to a cash basis. It therefore shows the cash received from customers, cash paid to suppliers, and cash paid in wages and for operating expenses. This is all new information not shown elsewhere in the published financial statements. A pro forma (adapted from an example provided in the appendix to IAS 7) for calculating cash flows from operating activities using the direct method might look like the one shown in Figure 32.5.

Cash flows from operating activities	£	£
Cash received from customers	XXX	
Cash paid to suppliers	(XXX)	
Cash paid to employees	(XX)	
Cash paid for other operating activities	(XX)	
Cash generated from operations	XXX	
Taxation paid	(XX)	
Net cash from operating activities		XXX

Figure 32.5 A pro forma for calculating cash flows from operating activities using the direct method

The cash generated from operations is before payments to service finance (interest), tax and income from investments.

- *Taxation cash flows.* Tax on operating activities is included in this part of the statement of cash flows and is taken away from 'cash generated from operations' to give 'net cash from operating activities'. The tax cash flows refer to cash received and paid to taxation authorities in respect of a reporting entity's operating activities. If any portion of the tax expense were attributable to, for example, investing activities, then that tax cash flow would be included under that classification. It usually only relates to the income tax (corporation tax) paid on a company's annual profit. It does not include value added tax (VAT) or property taxes. In this introductory textbook, all taxation entries are assumed to arise from operating activities only, so will always be disclosed under the 'cash flows from operating activities' classification.

● *Interest and dividend cash flows.* There is some flexibility within IAS 7 in respect of interest paid, interest received, dividends paid and dividends received. The standard either allows these to be disclosed within 'net cash flows from operating activities' wherein they would be separately disclosed after the 'cash generated from operations' in the same manner as taxation in Figure 32.5. The argument for this treatment stems from the fact that interest and investment income forms part of the determination of profit or loss and, therefore, should be disclosed here. Alternatively, interest and dividends paid in the period can be classified as a financing cash flow as these represent the cost of obtaining and retaining finance such as loans and equity, while interest and dividends received in the period can be classified as cash inflows from investing activities as they are the returns from investment activities, not operating activities. In this textbook, for consistency purposes, the latter approach is adopted and all proformas are portrayed in this manner.

The indirect method

The **indirect method** involves adjusting the profit or loss before tax for:

1 the effects of transactions of a non-cash nature, such as profits and losses on the disposal of non-current assets and movements in provisions (bad debts);

2 deferrals or accruals of past or future operating cash receipts or payments (changes in working capital);

3 items of income or expense associated with investing or financing cash flows (dividends and interest payable and receivable).

Therefore the indirect method calculates the cash flows from operating activities by reconciling the reported profit before taxation in the statement of profit and loss with the cash movements in the assets and liabilities in the statement of financial position that are held for the purposes of generating profits through normal operating activities. A pro forma (adapted from an example provided in the appendix to IAS 7) is provided in Figure 32.6.

Cash flows from operating activities	£	£
Profit before taxation	XXX	
Adjustments for:		
Depreciation	XX	
Investment income	(XX)	
Interest expense	XX	
Loss on sale of non-current asset	XX	
Operating profit before working capital changes	XXX	
Increase in trade and other receivables	(XX)	
Decrease in inventories	XX	
Increase in trade and other payables	(XX)	
Cash generated from operations	XXX	
Income taxes paid	(XX)	
Net cash from operating activities		XXX

Figure 32.6 A pro forma for calculating cash flows from operating activities using the indirect method

Most companies use the indirect method. The reasons are probably because it does not require the disclosure of any new information and if they were to use the direct method this would have to be additional to the indirect method. All the examples and exercises in this book are based on the indirect method.

The amount of cash flows arising from operating activities is a key indicator of the extent to which the operations of an entity have generated sufficient cash flows to repay loans, maintain the operating capability of the entity, pay dividends and make new investments without recourse to external sources of finance.

The requirements of IAS 7 with regard to the application of the indirect method of deriving the net cash inflow from operating activities are illustrated in Example 32.3. This question follows on from Example 32.2. However, in this instance the statement of profit and loss is provided and you do not need to reconstruct it, and investment income is introduced. The statements of financial position and notes 1 to 7 from Example 32.2 are relevant in this example also, though the workings are not revisited.

EXAMPLE 32.3

You are provided with the following statement of profit and loss for C. Flowers Ltd.

C. Flowers Ltd	
Statement of profit and loss for the year ended 31/03/X3	
	£
Revenue	1,429,000
Cost of sales	(1,143,200)
Gross profit	285,800
Other income	5,400
Distribution costs	(136,000)
Administration expenses	(89,700)
Finance costs	(2,000)
Profit before tax	63,500
Income tax expense	(18,500)
Profit for the year	45,000

Additional information

Other income represents interest received on investments made (this was not in Example 32.2).

Required

Prepare the 'cash flows from operating activities' for inclusion in the statement of cash flows for C. Flowers for the year ended 31/03/X3 using the information provided in this question and the information in example 32.2.

 **Solution**

C. Flowers Ltd	
Statement of cash flows for the year ended 31/03/X3	
Cash flows from operating activities	**£**
Profit before taxation	63,500
Adjustments for:	
Depreciation charges	9,800
Interest received	(5,400)
Debenture interest paid	2,000
Loss on sale of tangible non-current assets	700
Provision for bad debts (decrease)	(300)
Operating profit before working capital changes	70,300
Increase in trade payables	1,400
Decrease in trade receivables	2,900
Increase in inventory	(8,300)
Cash generated from operations	66,300
Income taxes paid	(15,700)
Net cash inflow from operating activities	50,600

2 Cash flows from investing activities

According to IAS 7 (IASB, 2010) **investing activities** are 'the acquisition and disposal of non-current assets and other investments not included in cash equivalents'. This refers to cash flows arising from the acquisition and disposal of non-current assets and the ownership of investments and payments to the providers of non-current finance and non-equity shareholders. In respect of investment in capital items, the entries in the statement of cash flows should distinguish between tangible non-current assets and intangible non-current assets. In each case the receipts from disposals must be shown separately from payments in respect of acquisitions.

In terms of investments in financial assets, cash flows comprise the purchase and sale of financial assets (which are not classed as cash equivalents) and interest and dividends received on these assets.

Examples of cash flows from investing activities that are included in IAS 7 are as follows:

- cash payments to acquire property, plant and equipment;
- cash payments to acquire intangible assets;
- cash payments to acquire other non-current assets;
- cash receipts from the sale of property, plant and equipment;
- cash receipts from the sale of intangible assets;
- cash receipts from the sale of other non-current assets;
- cash payments to acquire the equity or debt instruments of other entities (including joint ventures);

- cash receipts from the sale of equity or debt instruments in other entities (including joint ventures);

- cash advances or loans made to other parties (not banks);

- cash receipts from the repayment of advances and loans from other parties (not banks);

- interest received on investments;

- dividends received from investments.

The latter two examples are not included in the pro forma presented in the appendix of IAS 7 since two disclosure options are permissible, as previously discussed. The separate disclosure of cash flows arising from investing activities is important, because the cash flows represent the extent to which expenditures have been made for resources intended to generate future income and cash flows.

3 Cash flows from financing activities

According to IAS 7, **financing activities** are 'activities that result in changes in the size and composition of the contributed equity and borrowings of the entity'. This encapsulates cash received and paid to external providers of finance in respect of the principal amounts of finance and the payments required to service these principal amounts (interest and dividends). The most common external providers of finance are equity shareholders, preference shareholders, loan stock holders and debenture holders.

Examples of **cash flows from financing activities** that are included in IAS 7 are as follows (IASB, 2010):

- cash proceeds from issuing shares;

- cash payments to owners to acquire, or redeem shares;

- cash proceeds from issuing debentures, loans, notes, bonds, mortgages and other short or long-term borrowing;

- cash repayments of amounts borrowed;

- cash payments by a lessee for the reduction of the outstanding liability relating to a finance lease;

- dividends paid on 'financing equity';

- interest paid on 'financing debt'.

The latter two examples are not included in the pro forma presented in IAS 7 since two disclosure options are permissible, as previously discussed.

The separate disclosure of cash flows from financial activities is important because it is useful in predicting claims on future cash flows by providers of capital to the entity.

32.6 Presentation: statement of cash flows

Now that each main part of the statement has been discussed, a complete pro forma is provided in Figure 32.7 for reference. This pro forma is adapted from an example provided in the appendix to IAS 7 (IASB, 2010).

Statement of cash flows (indirect method)		
Cash flows from operating activities	£	£
Profit before taxation	XXX	
Adjustments for:		
Depreciation	XX	
Loss on sale of non-current assets	XX	
Profit on sale of non-current assets	(X)	
Investment income	(XX)	
Finance charges	XX	
Operating profit before working capital changes	XXX	
Decrease in trade and other receivables	XX	
Increase in inventories	(XX)	
Decrease in trade and other payables	XX	
Cash generated from operations	XXX	
Income tax paid	(XX)	
Net cash from operating activities		XXX
Cash flows from investing activities		
Purchase of property, plant and equipment (note 1)	(XXX)	
Proceeds from sale of equipment	XX	
Interest received	XX	
Dividends received	XX	
Net cash used in investing activities		(XX)
Cash flows from financing activities		
Proceeds from the issue of share capital	XXX	
Proceeds from long-term borrowings	XX	
Payment of finance lease liabilities	(XX)	
Interest paid	(XX)	
Dividends paid	(XX)	
Net cash from financial activities		XX
Net increase in cash and cash equivalents		XXX
Cash and cash equivalents at beginning of period (note 2)		XX
Cash and cash equivalents at end of period (note 2)		XXX

Figure 32.7 A pro forma of the layout of a statement of cash flows (indirect method) under IAS 7 (IASB, 2010)

Copyright © 2011 IFRS Foundation
All rights reserved. No permission granted to reproduce or distribute.
Reproduced by McGraw-Hill Education with the permission of the IFRS Foundation.

32.7 IAS 7 — statement of cash flows: companies

The application of IAS 7 (IASB, 2010) recommended formats is shown in Example 32.4. This example uses the information from Example 32.2 and 32.3 to prepare the whole statement.

<table>
<tr><td rowspan="2">EXAMPLE
32.4</td><td colspan="3">C. Flowers Ltd</td></tr>
</table>

	£	£
C. Flowers Ltd		
Statement of cash flows for the year ended 31 March 20X3		
Cash flows from operating activities		
Profit before taxation	63,500	
Adjustments for:		
Depreciation charges	9,800	
Interest received	(5,400)	
Debenture interest paid	2,000	
Loss on sale of tangible non-current assets	700	
Provision for bad debts (decrease)	(300)	
Operating profit before working capital changes	70,300	
Increase in trade payables	1,400	
Decrease in trade receivables	2,900	
In crease in inventory	(8,300)	
Cash generated from operations	66,300	
Income taxes paid	(15,700)	
Net cash flow from operating activities		50,600
Cash flows from investing activities		
Interest received	5,400	
Receipts from sale of tangible non-current assets	3,500	
Net cash from investing activities		8,900
Cash flows from financing activities		
Issue of equity share capital	18,000	
Repayment of debenture loan	(32,000)	
Debenture interest paid	(2,000)	
Equity dividends paid	(34,800)	
Net cash used in financing activities		(50,800)
Net increase in cash and cash equivalents		8,700
Cash and cash equivalents at beginning of period		8,600
Cash and cash equivalents at end of period		17,300

Though the statement of cash flows for C. Flowers Ltd (Example 32.4) shows the cash flows for the current year and uses two columns to display subtotals and totals for each main heading, in practice many companies just show the figures in one column, but also show the comparatives (prior year figures). An example of the latter format can be seen in the financial statements of Tesco plc (2010) as shown in the following real world example.

REAL WORLD EXAMPLE

32.1

Tesco plc
Group cash flow statement

Year ended 27 February 2010	notes	52 weeks 2010 £m	53 weeks 2009 £m
Cash flows from operating activities			
Cash generated from operations	31	**5,947**	4,978
Interest paid		**(690)**	(562)
Corporation tax paid		(512)	(456)
Net cash from operating activities		4,745	3,960
Cash flows from investing activities			
Acquisition of subsidiaries, net of cash acquired		**(65)**	(1,275)
Proceeds from sale of property, plant and equipment		**1,820**	994
Purchase of property, plant and equipment and investment property		**(2,855)**	(4,487)
Proceeds from sale of intangible assets		**4**	–
Purchase of intangible assets		**(163)**	(220)
Increase in loans to joint ventures		**(45)**	(242)
Investments in joint ventures and associates		**(4)**	(30)
Investments in short-term and other investments		**(1,918)**	(1,233)
Proceeds from sale of short-term investments		**1,233**	360
Dividends received		**35**	69
Interest received		81	90
Net cash used in investing activities		(1,877)	(5,974)
Cash flows from financing activities			
Proceeds from issue of ordinary share capital		**167**	130
Increase in borrowings		**862**	7,387
Repayment of borrowings		**(3,601)**	(2,733)
Repayment of obligations under finance leases		**(41)**	(18)
Dividends paid		**(968)**	(883)
Dividends paid to minority interests		**(2)**	(3)
Own shares purchased		(24)	(265)
Net cash from financing activities		(3,607)	3,615
Net (decrease)/increase in cash and cash equivalents		**(739)**	1,601
Cash and cash equivalents at beginning of year		**3,509**	1,788
Effect of foreign exchange rate changes		49	120
Cash and cash equivalents at end of year	19	2,819	3,509

Reconciliation of net cash flow to movement in net debt note

Year ended 27 February 2010	note	52 weeks 2010 £m	53 weeks 2009 £m
Net (decrease)/increase in cash and cash equivalents		(739)	1,601
Investment in Tesco Bank		(230)	–
Elimination of net increase in Tesco bank cash and cash equivalents		(167)	(37)
Debt acquired on acquisition of Homever		–	(611)
Transfer of joint venture loan receivable on acquisition of Tesco Bank		–	(91)
Net cash inflow/(outflow) from debt and lease financing		2,780	(4,636)
Dividend received from Tesco Bank		150	–
Increase in short-term investments		81	873
Increase in joint venture loan receivables		45	242
Other non-cash movements		(249)	(759)
Decrease/(increase) in net debt in the year		1,671	(3,418)
Opening net debt	32	(9,600)	(6,182)
Closing net debet	32	(7,929)	(9,600)

NB. The reconciliation of net cash flow to movement in net debt note is not a primary statement and does not form part of the cash flow statement and forms part of the notes to the financial statements

Source: Tesco PLC Annual Report and Financial Statements 2010, p. 74, http://ar2010.tescoplc.com (accessed May 2011).

32.8 IAS 7 – statement of cash flows: notes

IAS 7 also requires some notes to the statement of cash flows. Normally, a note provides more information on investing activities, highlighting what was invested and how it was financed. IAS 7 requires that an analysis of the opening and closing balance of cash and cash equivalents, as disclosed in the last two lines of the statement of cash flows, is provided in a note.

An illustration of this latter note is shown in a continuation of Example 32.4 using the information in Example 32.2.

EXAMPLE 32.4 CONTINUED

Notes to the statement of cash flows (continued)

1 Cash and cash equivalents

	At 1 April 20X2 £	At 31 Mar 20X3 £
Cash in hand, at bank	8,600	17,300
Total cash and cash equivalents	8,600	17,300

32.9 Purposes and uses of statements of cash flows revisited

The statement of cash flows for C. Flowers Ltd in Example 32.4 can be interpreted as showing the following. The company generated £50,600 from operating activities. There has been no expansion in the company's business activities; indeed, there has been a slight contraction as shown by the net positive **cash flow from investing activities** of which £3,500 comes from the sale of non-current tangible assets. The cash generated from operating activities together with the proceeds from the sale of investments and the proceeds from the issue of additional equity shares have been used to repay part of the debenture loan, the interest on the debenture loan and a dividend of £34,800 to the equity shareholders. In short, this statement of cash flows paints a picture of a company well able to cover its financing charges by cash inflows from operating activities, and which is seeking to reduce its dependence on debt capital by partly replacing it with more permanent equity shares. This scenario is often associated with a process of consolidation likely to result in greater financial stability in times of falling profits that frequently occur during an economic recession.

32.10 IAS 7 — statement of cash flows: sole traders and partnerships

The same principles apply; the cash flows that are particular to sole traders will have to be analysed into cash flows from operating activities, cash flows from investing activities and cash flows from financing activities. Example 32.1 (see Example 32.5) is now revisited and the resultant analysis of cash flows for the year are presented in a format that is consistent with that recommended in IAS 7.

EXAMPLE 32.5

This is a very simple example (using the information from Example 32.1). It is assumed that there is no tax, interest or non-cash items in the statement of profit and loss.

A. Cashwood Statement of cash flows for the year ended 30 September 20X3	£	£
Cash flows from operating activities		
Profit before taxation	34,200	
Adjustments for:		
Decrease in trade payables	(1,200)	
Increase in trade receivables	(1,300)	
Decrease in inventory	2,800	
Net cash flow from operating activities		34,500
Cash flows from investing activities		
Purchase of property, plant and equipment	(12,000)	
Net cash used in investing activities		(12,000)
Cash flows from financing activities		
Repayment of bank loan	(5,000)	
Capital introduced	4,300	
Drawings	(20,700)	
Net cash used in financing activities		(21,400)
Net increase in cash and cash equivalents		1,100
Cash and cash equivalents at beginning of period (note 1)		2,500
Cash and cash equivalents at end of period (note 1)		3,600

1 Cash and cash equivalents

	At 1 Oct 20X2	At 30 Sept 20X3
	£	£
Cash at bank	2,500	3,600
Total cash and cash equivalents	2,500	3,600

32.11 Advantages and limitations of statements of cash flows

The advantages of statements of cash flows are often explained in terms of the deficiencies of statements of profit and loss and statements of financial position. This should not be interpreted to mean that statements of cash flows are an alternative to statements of profit and loss. The statement of profit and loss and statement of financial position have a number of limitations; however, they provide different types of information for users. Statements of cash flows provide useful additional information for the following reasons:

1 Most readers and potential readers (e.g. private shareholders) appreciate the meaning and importance of cash and will therefore find statements of cash flows easier to understand and more relevant. In contrast, the nature of profit and capital and the contents of the statement of profit and loss and statement of financial position are more difficult to understand.

2 Statements of cash flows are more objective in that cash received and paid are observable events. In contrast, the statement of profit and loss and statement of financial position are based on the accruals concept and matching principle, which involve subjective allocations, valuations, and so on.

3 Statements of cash flows therefore permit more meaningful comparisons of performance over time, and between actual performance and forecasts.

4 Profit is only a symbol or measure of performance. The ultimate success and survival of an enterprise depends on its ability to generate and use cash in the most efficient manner. The statement of cash flows provides information that facilitates an evaluation of the efficiency with which cash has been generated and used.

5 Future dividends, the repayment of loans and payments to trade payables depend primarily on the availability of cash and not profits. Statements of cash flows provide information that allows users of company published financial statements to make more accurate predictions of future dividends, insolvency, and so on.

Few accountants would quarrel with the assertion that statements of cash flows provide useful additional information. However, most would be opposed to the idea that they should replace the statement of profit and loss for the following reasons:

1 A statement that is easier to understand is not necessarily more relevant or useful.

2 The preparation of statements of cash flows also involves subjective judgements.

3 The use of statements of cash flows in making comparisons and the evaluation of performance can be misleading. The pattern of cash flows over time is often erratic and therefore not indicative of an enterprise's long-term performance.

4 Statements of cash flows focus on the **financing activities** of an enterprise rather than the economic or trading activities. They therefore do not provide meaningful information on either past or future economic performance.

32.12 The purpose, uses and advantages of classified statements of cash flows

The purpose of a statement of cash flows is often expressed in a number of different ways. At the start of this chapter, it was given in simple terms as being to show the reasons for the change in the cash and bank balance over the accounting year. However, the grouping of items in the classified statement of cash flows permits a more precise definition. According to IAS 7, the purpose of statements of cash flows is to provide information about the historical changes in cash and cash equivalents of an entity by classifying cash flows during the period from operating, investing and financing activities. This enables the users of financial statements to have a basis to assess the ability of the entity to generate cash and cash equivalents and the needs of the entity to utilize those cash flows. The economic decisions that are taken by users require an evaluation of the ability of an entity to generate cash and cash equivalents and to assess the timing and certainty of their generation. In particular, users will wish to assess the liquidity, solvency, investment potential and financial adaptability of the entity. The following objectives may be expanded and expressed in slightly different terms to emphasize the potential uses of statements of cash flows:

1 To enable management, investors, trade payables and others to see how the various activities of the company have been financed (e.g. which activities have net cash outflows and which have net cash inflows).

2 A statement of cash flows, in conjunction with a statement of comprehensive income and statement of financial position, provides information on the financial position and performance as well as liquidity, solvency and financial adaptability of an entity. It also gives an indication of the relationship between profitability and cash-generating ability, and thus of the *quality* of the profit earned. Historical cash flow information could be useful to check the accuracy of past assessments and indicate the relationship between the entity's activities, and its receipts and payments.

3 Historical cash flow information may assist users of financial statements in making judgements on the amount, timing and degree of certainty of future cash flows. The statement of cash flows may therefore be useful to management, investors, trade payables and others in assessing the enterprise's ability to:

a pay its debts (i.e. loan repayment, trade payables, etc.) as and when they become due;

b pay loan interest, dividends, and so on.

c decide whether it will need to raise additional external finance (e.g. issue shares or debentures) in the near future.

4 To explain why an enterprise may have a profit for the year but nevertheless has less cash at the end of that year (or vice versa), and thus, for example, is only able to pay a small dividend.

5 To allow users to see directly the reasons for the difference between the net profit and its associated cash receipts and payments (i.e. the net cash inflow from operating activities).

When answering examination questions, it is often advisable to assume that the function/objective/purpose(s), uses and advantages of statements of cash flows all require similar answers but the amount of detail increases with each, respectively.

LEARNING ACTIVITY 32.2

Examine the most recent financial statements of British Airways plc. Try to construct the statement of cash flows from the information provided in the statement of comprehensive income, the statement of financial position and the related notes where relevant. Some of the entries are beyond the scope of this text; however, you should be able to determine about 80 per cent of the final statement of cash-flow entries. Compare your effort with their published version.

Summary

The purpose of a statement of cash flows is to show the reasons for the change in the cash and bank balance over an accounting year. Another common way of expressing this is that a statement of cash flows shows the manner in which cash has been generated and used. The reasons for the change in cash are shown in this statement as either sources or applications of cash funds. The statement of cash flows is intended to complement the statement of profit and loss and statement of financial position by providing additional information. It is often regarded as an alternative with its own advantages and limitations. However, the statement of cash flows is intended to serve different purposes.

IAS 7 requires that most companies include a classified statement of cash flows in their annual financial statements. The purpose of a classified statement of cash flows is to show the effects on cash flows of an entity's operating, investing and financing activities for a given period. The items normally shown in a statement of cash flows are classified into the three groups: net cash from operating activities, net cash from investing activities and net cash from financing activities. The net cash from operating activities is usually compiled using the indirect method. However, there is another method, referred to as the direct method, which is also permissible but is more difficult to prepare as the information is not readily available. IAS 7 also requires an analysis of the opening and closing cash and cash equivalent balance as disclosed in the statement of cash flows.

Key terms and concepts

An asterisk after the question number indicates that there is a suggested answer on the Online Learning Centre (www.mcgraw-hill.co.uk/textbooks/thomas).

Review questions

32.1 a Explain the purpose(s) of a statement of cash flows.

    b Describe the typical sources and applications of cash funds in an entity.

32.2 Describe the advantages and limitations of statements of cash flows.

32.3 Explain how statements of cash flows differ from: (a) statements of profit and loss; and (b) statements of financial position.

32.4 Explain the meaning of each of the following in the context of statements of cash flows:

    a cash;

    b cash equivalents.

32.5 List and describe the contents of the three headings/groups of items found in a statement of cash flows prepared in accordance with IAS 7.

32.6 Explain the purpose, uses and advantages of classified statements of cash flows prepared in accordance with IAS 7.

32.7 Explain the difference between the direct and indirect methods of ascertaining the 'net cash inflow from operating activities' shown in a statement of cash flows.

32.8 For many years, company financial statements consisted of a statement of financial position and a statement of profit and loss prepared using the accruals basis. Many also have to include a statement of cash flows.

Required

a Explain why a statement of cash flows is considered to add value to the information already available in the statement of financial position and the statement of profit and loss.

b Itemize the different sections that IAS 7 requires to be included in the statement of cash flows and explain the information each one can provide to users.

Exercises

32.9

BASIC

J. White, a sole trader, has produced the following statements of financial position for the years ended 31 March 20X2 and 31 March 20X3.

		J. White		
		Statements of financial position as at 31 March		
ASSETS		20X3		20X2
Non-current assets	£	£	£	£
Freehold premises		10,000		10,000
Shop fittings	1,200		1,000	
Depreciation to date	(870)	330	(750)	250
Motor vehicle	800		800	
Depreciation to date	(600)	200	(400)	400
		10,530		10,650
Current assets				
Inventories		15,400		11,000
Trade receivables		540		1,000
Bank		3,000		9,500
Cash in till		30		50
		18,970		21,550
Total assets		29,500		32,200
EQUITY AND LIABILITIES				
Equity				
Capital		15,000		15,000
Current account	5,200		3,000	
Profits	5,800		5,400	
	11,000		8,400	
Drawings	(4,500)	6,500	(3,200)	5,200
Total equity		21,500		20,200
Current liabilities				
Trade payables		8,000		12,000
Total liabilities		8,000		12,000
Total equity and liabilities		29,500		32,200

J. White is unable to understand why, after he has made a profit for the year ended 31 March 20X3 of £5,800, his bank balance has fallen by £6,500.

Required

Prepare a report explaining how this has occurred.

(Adapted from ACCA)

32.10

Prepare a statement of cash flows in accordance with IAS 7 using the information in Question 32.9. There was no investment income or interest paid during the year ended 31 March 20X3.

32.11

T. Bone is a sole trader and reports the following for the year ended 30 June 20X2:

T. Bone Statements of financial position as at 30 June		
ASSETS	20X2	20X1
Non-current assets	£	£
Motor vans	10,500	14,500
Depreciation to date	(4,448)	(5,628)
	6,052	8,872
Current assets		
Inventories	16,352	12,558
Trade receivables less bad debt provision	5,250	6,580
Bank	4,093	2,358
	25,695	21,496
Total assets	31,747	30,368
EQUITY AND LIABILITIES		
Equity		
Capital	10,808	8,799
Profits	28,689	24,009
	39,497	32,808
Drawings	(24,000)	(22,000)
Total equity	15,497	10,808
Non-current liabilities		
10% loan	6,000	7,000
Total non-current liabilities	6,000	7,000
Current liabilities		
Trade payables	10,250	12,560
Total current liabilities	10,250	12,560
Total liabilities	16,250	19,560
Total equity and liabilities	31,747	30,368

T. Bone		
Statement of profit and loss for the year ended 30 June 20X2 (extract)		
	£	£
Gross profit		56,325
Add: discounts received:		1,026
Less expenses:		57,351
Wages	18,930	
Motor expenses	6,582	
Loan Interest	600	
Bad debts	650	
Increase in bad debts provision	240	
Loss on sale of motor van	570	
Depreciation	1,090	28,662
Profit for the year		28,689

Notes

1 The 20X1 provision for bad debts was £600.

2 The 20X2 provision for bad debts is £840.

3 The motor van was sold for £2,300.

Required

Prepare the statement of cash flows in accordance with IAS 7 for T. Bone for the year ended 30 June 20X2.

32.12

A. Net is a sole trader and reports the following for the year ended 31 December 20X2:

Statement of profit and loss for the year ended 31 December 20X2 (extract)		
	£	£
Gross profit		2,500
Less expenses:		
Wages	300	
Motor expenses	110	
Loss on sale of car	20	
Depreciation	60	490
Profit for the year		2,010

A. Net		
Statements of financial position as at 31 December		
ASSETS	20X2	20X1
Non-current assets	£	£
Motor vehicles	1,500	1,750
Depreciation to date	(150)	(270)
	1,350	1,480
Current assets		
Inventories	1,600	1,200
Trade receivables less bad debt provision	1,200	980
Bank	1,220	500
	4,020	2,680
Total assets	5,370	4,160
EQUITY AND LIABILITIES		
Equity		
Capital	2,060	1,000
Profits	2,010	1,650
	4,070	2,650
Drawings	(950)	(590)
Total equity	3,120	2,060
Non-current liabilities		
Loan	1,800	1,700
Total non-current liabilities	1,800	1,700
Current liabilities		
Trade payables	450	400
Total current liabilities	450	400
Total liabilities	2,250	2,100
Total equity and liabilities	5,370	4,160

Note: The car that was disposed of during the year was sold for £400, which was lodged in A. Net's bank account.

Required

Prepare the statement of cash flows in accordance with IAS 7 for A. Net for the year ended 31 December 20X2.

32.13

The following are the financial statements for A. Tack for the years ended 30 June 20X3 and 20X2:

Statement of profit and loss for the year ended 30 June		
	20X3	20X2
	£'000	£'000
Sales revenue	2,280	1,230
Less: Cost of goods sold	1,318	422
Gross profit	962	808
Less expenses		
Depreciation	320	310
Office expenses	100	110
Interest paid	27	–
Rent	173	150
Profit for the year	342	238

Statements of financial position as at 30 June		
	20X3	20X2
ASSETS	£'000	£'000
Non-current assets (see note)	2,640	2,310
Current assets		
Inventory	450	275
Trade receivables	250	100
Bank	153	23
	853	398
Total assets	3,493	2,708
EQUITY AND LIABILITIES		
Equity		
Capital	2,388	2,050
Capital introduced	300	200
Profits for year	342	238
	3030	2488
Drawings	(252)	(100)
Total equity	2,778	2,388
Non-current liabilities		
9% loan (20X9)	300	–
Total non-current liabilities	300	–
Current liabilities		
Trade payables	415	320
Total current liabilities	415	320
Total liabilities	715	320
Total equity and liabilities	3,493	2,708

Note: Schedule of non-current assets			
	Land & buildings	Plant and machinery	Total
	£'000	£'000	£'000
Cost			
At 1 July 20X2	1,500	1,350	2,850
Additions	400	250	650
At 30 June 20X3	1,900	1,600	3,500
Depreciation			
At 1 July 20X2	–	540	540
Charge for year at 20%	–	320	320
At 30 June 20X3	–	860	860
Net book value at 30 June 20X3	1,900	740	2,640

Required

Prepare a statement of cash flows in accordance with IAS 7 for A. Tack for the year ended 30 June 20X3.

32.14

INTERMEDIATE

The following are the financial statements for S. Low for the years ended 30 April 20X2 and 30 April 20X3:

S. Low Income statements for year ended 30 April				
	20X3		20X2	
	£'000	£'000	£'000	£'000
Sales revenue		4,850		4,400
Less: cost of sales		2,400		2,310
Gross profit		2,450		2,090
Less: expenses				
Depreciation	162		142	
Interest payable	22		18	
Wages	750		670	
Electricity	520		450	
Rent	286	1,740	286	1,566
Profit for the period		710		524

S. Low		
Statements of financial position as at 30 April		
ASSETS	20X3	20X2
Non-current assets	£	£
Property, plant and equipment	1,250	630
Depreciation to date	(432)	(270)
	818	360
Current assets		
Inventories	405	384
Trade receivables less bad debt provision	698	729
Bank	–	47
	1,103	1,160
Total assets	1,921	1,520
EQUITY AND LIABILITIES		
Equity		
Capital	429	220
Profits	710	524
	1,139	744
Drawings	(391)	(315)
Total equity	748	429
Non-current liabilities		
12% loan	180	150
Total non-current liabilities	180	150
Current liabilities		
Bank overdraft	28	–
Trade payables	965	941
Total current liabilities	993	941
Total liabilities	1,173	1,091
Total equity and liabilities	1,921	1,520

Required

Prepare a statement of cash flows in accordance with IAS 7 for S. Low for the year ended 30 April 20X3.

INTERMEDIATE 32.15*

The following are the statements of financial positions of A. Brooks as at 30 June 20X2 and 30 June 20X3:

	30 June 20X2	30 June 20X3
ASSETS	£	£
Non-current assets		
Property, plant and equipment (cost)	65,000	72,000
Aggregate depreciation	(13,000)	(14,500)
	52,000	57,500
Current assets		
Inventory	6,700	7,300
Trade receivables	5,400	4,100
Cash and bank	–	900
	12,100	12,300
Total assets	64,100	69,800
EQUITY AND LIABILITIES		
Equity		
Capital at start of year	38,500	43,000
Capital introduced	2,700	20,000
Profit for the year	14,100	–
	55,300	63,000
Loss for the year	–	(1,800)
Drawings	(12,300)	(7,600)
Total equity capital	43,000	53,600
Non-current liabilities		
Bank loan (5 years)	15,000	10,000
Total non-current liabilities	15,000	10,000
Current liabilities		
Trade payables	4,800	6,200
Bank overdraft	1,300	–
Total current liabilities	6,100	6,200
Total liabilities	21,100	16,200
Total equity and liabilities	64,100	69,800

Additional information

1 There were no disposals of non-current assets during the year.

2 During the year ended 30 June 20X3 there was interest received of £900 and bank interest paid of £1,250.

Required

Brooks cannot understand how there can be a loss for the year 20X2/X3 when there has been an increase in the cash and bank balance. You are required to explain this by preparing a statement of cash flows for the year ended 30 June 20X3.

ADVANCED

32.16

The statement of financial position of C.F. Ltd for the year ended 31 December 20X2, together with comparative figures for the previous year, is shown below.

	20X2	20X1
ASSETS	£'000	£'000
Non-current assets		
Property, plant and equipment (note 4)	180	124
Current assets		
Inventory	50	42
Trade receivables	40	33
Cash	–	11
	90	86
Total assets	270	210
EQUITY AND LIABILITIES		
Equity		
Equity share capital £1 shares	25	20
Share premium	10	8
Retained earnings	93	81
Total equity	128	109
Non-current liabilities		
15% debentures, repayable 20X6	80	60
Total non-current liabilities	80	60
Current liabilities		
Trade and operating payables	33	24
Current tax payable	19	17
Bank overdraft	10	–
Total current liabilities	62	41
Total liabilities	142	101
Total equity and liabilities	270	210

Additional information

1 There were no sales of non-current assets during 20X2.

2 The company declared a final dividend of £26,000 for 20X2 (20X1 – £28,000). This is paid immediately after the AGM that takes place two months after the year end. The company does not pay any interim dividends.

3 New debentures and shares issued in 20X2 were issued on 1 January.

4 Property, plant and equipment is made up of the following:

	20X2	20X1
	£'000	£'000
Equipment	270	180
Provision for depreciation	(90)	(56)
	180	124

Required

a Show your calculation of the operating profit of C.F. plc for the year ended 31 December 20X2.

b Prepare a statement of cash flows for the year, in accordance with *IAS 7 Statement of Cash Flows*.

c State the headings of any other notes that you would be required to include in practice under IAS 7.

d Comment on the implications of the information given in the question, plus the statements you have prepared, regarding the financial position of the company.

e IAS 7 supports the use of the indirect method of arriving at the net cash inflow from operating activities, which is the method you have used to answer part (b) of this question. What is the direct method of arriving at the net cash inflow from operations? State, with reasons, whether you agree with the IAS 7 acceptance of the indirect method.

(ACCA, adapted)

32.17*

ADVANCED

The directors of J. Kitchens Ltd were pleased when their accountants informed them that the company had made a profit of £24,000 during the year ended 31 December 20X2.

However, their pleasure was turned into confusion when the cashier showed them a letter he had received from their banker. This indicated that he had reviewed Kitchens' account and was concerned to note the deterioration in their bank position. During 20X2 a small overdraft of £500 had reached £9,800 and was nearing the limit of their security. The directors would like to see an explanation of this increased overdraft, particularly as they had declared lower dividends than for the previous year. You are given the statements of financial position at 31 December 20X1 and 31 December 20X2:

	20X1	20X2
ASSETS	£	£
Non-current assets		
Property, plant and equipment (note 5)	58,000	59,500
Current assets		
Inventory	14,900	22,500
Trade receivables	11,300	16,400
	26,200	38,900
Total assets	84,200	98,400
EQUITY AND LIABILITIES		
Equity		
Share capital	20,000	20,000
Reserves	44,000	51,000
Total equity	64,000	71,000
Current liabilities		
Trade payables	19,700	17,600
Overdraft	500	9,800
Total current liabilities	20,200	27,400
Total equity and liabilities	84,200	98,400

Notes

1 Dividends

	20X1	20X2
	£	£
Interim paid	3,000	8,000
Final proposed	9,000	—

2 During the year, plant costing £10,000 with a net book value of £6,000 was sold for £6,400.

3 The amount included for trade receivables at 31 December 20X2 is after making a provision for bad debts of £600 (20X1: £400).

4 During the year ended 31 December 20X2 £750 was paid in bank interest.

5 Property, plant and equipment is made up of the following:

	20X1		20X2	
	£	£	£	£
Property, plant and equipment				
Leasehold premises – cost	30,000		30,000	
Provision for depreciation	(6,000)	24,000	(9,000)	21,000
Plant – cost	41,000		48,000	
Provision for depreciation	(7,000)	34,000	(9,500)	38,500
		58,000		59,500

Required

You are required to prepare a statement of cash flows in accordance with IAS 7 for the year 20X2 showing why the overdraft has increased.

ADVANCED

32.18*

The following are the statement of financial positions of L. Tyler Ltd as at 31 May 20X2 and 31 May 20X3:

	20X2	20X3
ASSETS		
Non-current assets	£	£
Property, plant and equipment (note 5)	115,000	94,000
Current assets		
Inventory	21,600	19,400
Trade receivables (note 6)	11,300	13,500
Investments	3,900	17,100
Cash and bank	4,600	12,800
	41,400	62,800
Total assets	156,400	156,800

EQUITY AND LIABILITIES		
Equity		
Equity shares of 50p each	60,000	70,000
Share premium account	25,000	34,000
Revenue reserve	4,200	6,900
Retained earnings	23,000	27,000
Total equity	112,200	137,900
Non-current liabilities		
8% loan stock	30,000	5,000
Total non-current liabilities	30,000	5,000
Current liabilities		
Trade payables	8,400	6,700
Current tax payable	5,800	7,200
Total current liabilities	14,200	13,900
Total liabilities	44,200	18,900
Total equity and liabilities	156,400	156,800

Notes

1 Non-current assets that cost £12,000 and had a book value of £7,500 were sold during the year ended 31 May 20X3 for £8,100. There were no other purchases or sales of non-current assets during that year.

2 The amounts of current tax shown in the statement of financial position as outstanding at 31 May 20X2 were paid during the year ended 31 May 20X3.

3 A dividend of £19,600 was proposed by the directors and later approved by the shareholders for the year ended 20X2 (20X3 − £21,800). In addition, an interim dividend of £6,400 was paid on 1 January 20X3.

4 The company received interest of £1,800 and paid loan stock interest of £1,600 in the year to 31 May 20X3.

5 Property, plant and equipment is made up of the following:

	20X2	20X3
	£	£
Equipment and fixtures at cost	143,000	131,000
Aggregate depreciation	(28,000)	(37,000)
	115,000	94,000

6 Trade receivables is made up of the following:

	20X2	20X3
	£	£
Trade receivables	11,800	14,200
Provision for bad debts	(500)	(700)
	11,300	13,500

Required

Prepare a statement of cash flows in accordance with IAS 7 for the year ended 31 May 20X3.

32.19

The statement of financial position of Euston Ltd as at 31 December 20X2, with corresponding amounts, showed the following:

ASSETS	20X2	20X1
Non-current assets	£'000	£'000
Property, plant and equipment	4,200	4,000
Current assets		
Inventory	470	400
Trade receivables	800	600
Prepayments	60	50
Bank	20	150
	1,350	1,200
Total assets	5,550	5,200
EQUITY AND LIABILITIES		
Equity		
Share capital	2,500	2,500
Retained earnings	1,650	1,530
Total equity	4,150	4,030
Non-current liabilities		
12% debentures	1,000	800
Total non-current liabilities	1,000	800
Current liabilities		
Trade payables	230	200
Current tax payable	100	80
Accruals	70	90
Total current liabilities	400	370
Total liabilities	1,400	1,170
Total equity and reserves	5,550	5,200

Notes relevant to 20X2

1 Property, plant and equipment includes the following:

Property, plant and equipment	20X2		20X1	
	£'000	£'000	£'000	£'000
Freehold property at cost		2,000		2,000
Plant and machinery:				
– Cost	3,500		3,000	
– Provision for depreciation	(1,300)	2,200	(1,000)	2,000
Total		4,200		4,000

2 An item of plant costing £100,000 with a written-down value of £60,000 was sold at a profit of £15,000 during the year. This profit has been included in the statement of profit and loss for the year.

3 The company declared a final dividend at the end of 20X2 of £50,000 (20X1 – £30,000). This was approved by the shareholders one month after the reporting period end and paid two weeks after that. No interim dividend was paid during the year.

4 Tax on company profits is paid nine months after the end of the reporting period.

5 During the year ended 31 December 20X2 there was no interest received but there was debenture interest paid of £108,000. None of the debenture interest was accrued at the end of either 20X1 or 20X2.

Required

Prepare a statement of cash flows in accordance with IAS 7 for the year 31 December 20X2.

(JMB, adapted)

32.20

ADVANCED

The following are the statements of financial positions of Waterloo plc for the last two financial years ended on 30 September.

	20X2	20X1	Notes
	£'000	£'000	
ASSETS			
Non-current assets			
Property, plant and equipment	1,320	1,090	1
Goodwill	200	200	2
	1,520	1,290	
Current assests			
Inventories	420	300	
Trade receivables	220	120	
Balance at bank	–	20	
	640	440	
Total assets	2,160	1,730	
EQUITY AND LIABILITIES			
Equity			
Equity shares, of 50p each, fully paid	750	500	4
Share premium account	100	350	4
Revaluation reserve	300	–	
Retained earnings	340	280	
Total equity	1,490	1,130	
Non-current liabilities			
9% debentures	360	400	
Total non-current liabilities	360	400	
Current liabilities			
Bank overdraft	120	–	
Trade payables	190	200	
Total current liabilities	310	200	
Total liabilities	670	600	
Total equity and liabilities	2,160	1,730	

Explanatory notes to the statement of financial positions are as follows:

1 The movement during the year to 30 September 20X2 in property, plant and equipment was as follows:

	Buildings	Plant and machinery	Total
Cost	£'000	£'000	£'000
At 1 October 20X1	820	600	1,420
Surplus on revaluation	300	–	300
Additions	–	100	100
Disposals	–	(50)*	(50)
	1,120	650	1,770
Provision for depreciation			
At 1 October 20X1	100	230	330
Depreciation on disposal	–	(40)*	(40)
Depreciation for year	50	110	160
At 30 September 20X2	150	300	450
Closing net book value	970	350	1,320
Opening net book value	720	370	1,090

Note:

* The plant and machinery disposed of during the year was sold for £5,000.

2 Goodwill arising from the purchase of a business on 1 November 20X0 was valued at £200,000. Goodwill has not diminished in value over the year.

3 Dividend details for the company are as follows:

	20X2	20X1
Interim paid in year	£25,000	£15,000
Final proposed at year end	£60,000	£45,000

4 There was a bonus issue during the year to 30 September 20X2 of one new equity share for every two held.

Required

Prepare a statement of cash flows for the year ended 30 September 20X2, in accordance with IAS 7. There was no investment income for the year ended 30 September 20X2 but there was debenture interest paid of £35,000 during the year.

(AEB, adapted)

32.21

The summarized statements of financial position as at 31 March 20X1 and 31 March 20X2 of Higher Ltd are as follows:

	20X2	20X1	Additional information
ASSETS	£'000	£'000	
Non-current assets	175	150	1
Current assets	90	80	2
Total assets	265	230	
EQUITY AND LIABILITIES			
Equity			
Equity shares of £1 each	90	80	3
Share premium account	25	20	3
Capital redemption reserve	15	–	
Retained earnings	35	20	
Total equity	165	120	
Non-current liabilities			
Debentures	30	30	
8% redeemable preference shares of 50p each	–	30	3
Total non-current liabilities	30	60	
Current liabilities	70	50	
Total liabilities	100	110	
Total equity and liabilities	265	230	

Additional information

1 Non-current assets

	Cost	Depn	Net book value
	£'000	£'000	£'000
Balance at 31 March 20X1	200	50	150
Additions	60	–	60
Disposals	(40)	(25)	(15)
Depreciation for the year to 31 March 20X2	–	20	(20)
	220	45	175

Non-current assets disposed of during the year were sold for £22,000.

2 Current assets at 31 March for each of the two years comprise the following:

	20X2	20X1
	£'000	£'000
Inventories	35	27
Trade receivables	22	28
Bank	24	22
Cash	9	3
	90	80

3 The preference shares were redeemed during the year ended 31 March 20X2. This redemption was funded by a new issue of equity shares at a premium.

4 During the year the company made a transfer of £15,000 from retained earnings to the capital redemption reserve.

Required

Prepare a statement of cash flows for Higher Ltd for the year ended 31 March 20X2, in accordance with IAS 7. Assume that there was no investment income, interest paid or dividends paid during the year ended 31 March 20X2.

(AEB, adapted)

References

International Accounting Standards Board (2010) *International Accounting Standard 7 – Statement of Cash Flows* (IASB).

Tesco PLC (2010) Annual Report, http://www.tescoplc.com/.

When you have read this chapter, log on to the Online Learning Centre for *Introduction to Financial Accounting* at www.mcgraw-hill.co.uk/textbooks/thomas, where you will find multiple choice quizzes, case studies, a glossary and mock exams.

The appraisal of company financial statements using ratio analysis

Learning Objectives

After reading this chapter you should be able to do the following:

1. Explain the meaning of the key terms and concepts listed at the end of the chapter.

2. Explain the purposes of ratio analysis.

3. Compute various measures of a company's performance, explain what each is intended to measure and evaluate the results.

4. Compute various measures of liquidity and solvency, explain what each is intended to measure, and evaluate the results.

5. Compute various ratios used in the appraisal of working capital, explain what each is intended to measure and evaluate the results.

6. Compute various measures of return on investment and risk, explain what each is intended to measure and evaluate the results.

7. Explain the nature of capital gearing, compute the gearing ratio and describe the effect of gearing on the profit available for distribution as dividends and the earnings per share.

8. Discuss the limitations of ratio analysis.

33.1 Introduction

Ratio analysis involves relating two numbers from an entity's financial statements to each other to form an easily understood number (typically a percentage) which will facilitate comparison to ratios from previous years and across entities of different sizes. Most stakeholders with business knowledge will use ratio analysis to evaluate the performance of an entity, both in terms of their previous performance and relative to competitors in the market. Information is typically extracted from an entity's financial statements. These can be obtained online for most plcs and at Companies House for most limited companies. Alternatively most university libraries have access to database of financial statements (for example, Financial Analysis Made Easy (FAME) contains information on UK and Irish companies; OSIRIS provides information on about 53,000 listed and unlisted companies worldwide; or Thomson One Banker Analytics provides company information worldwide). Copies of sole trader and partnership financial statements are not publicly available and can only be obtained from the sole trader or partners.

The purpose of ratio analysis

The main function of published company final financial statements is to provide information that will enable users of financial statements to evaluate the financial performance and financial position of a company. However, the absolute amount of profit, or assets and liabilities, shown in the financial statements is not usually a particularly meaningful criterion for evaluating the performance or financial position of a business. For example, if Company A has a profit of £200,000 and Company B has a profit of £1 million, one cannot conclude that B has better performance than A. Company B may have used net assets of £10 million to generate this profit whereas Company A may have only used net assets of £0.5 million.

Net assets = Total assets less Total liabilities

Therefore, 'net assets' is the same as equity invested in the company (Assets = Liabilities plus Equity). 'Net assets' is also known as **capital employed**.

Thus, A is said to be more profitable than B because the profit is 40 per cent of the value of its net assets (£200,000/£500,000) compared with only 10 per cent in the case of B (£1,000,000/£10,000,000). Similarly, if Company B had a profit of £900,000 last year, one cannot conclude that it is more profitable this year. The value of the net assets last year may only have been £8 million, which gives a return of 11.25 per cent (£900,000/£8,000,000) compared with 10 per cent this year.

Indeed, the terms '**profitability**' and '**return**' are taken as referring to the relationship between the profit and the value of the net assets/equity capital used to generate that profit. Thus, in order to evaluate a company's performance and financial position over time, or in relation to other companies, it is necessary to compute various accounting ratios and percentages. These are primarily intended for the use of external groups of users such as shareholders, loan creditors and credit suppliers, whose only source of accounting information is that contained in published financial statements.

It is important to appreciate at the outset that accounting ratios and percentages have a number of limitations. One of these stems from the aggregate nature of information in published financial statements. Companies are not required to disclose all the items that enter into the computation of profit or values of assets and liabilities in the statement of financial position. As a result, the information needed to compute some ratios may not be available. This necessitates the use of surrogate data in the calculation of some ratios. Furthermore, comparisons of ratios over time and between companies can be misleading when economic conditions change and/or where the companies concerned are operating in substantially different industries. Ratios must therefore always be interpreted in the light of the prevailing economic climate and the particular circumstances of the company or companies concerned. The limitations of ratio analysis are discussed in the context of each ratio and are summarized at the end of the chapter.

A large number of ratios can be calculated from the information contained in published financial statements. These ratios may be grouped under four main headings, each heading reflecting what the ratios are intended to measure: (1) measures of company performance; (2) measures of solvency and **liquidity**; (3) measures of the control of **working capital** (management efficiency); and (4) measures of return on investment and risk. The most common ratios in each of these four classes are described on the following pages and illustrated using the information in Example 33.1.

EXAMPLE 33.1	The following is an extract from the published financial statements of A. Harry plc, for the year ending 31 January 20X2:

Statement of profit and loss

	£'000
Revenue	5,280
Cost of sales	(3,090)
Gross profit	2,190
Distribution costs	(560)
Administrative expenses	(230)
Finance costs	(400)
Profit before taxation	1,000
Income tax expense	(250)
Profit after taxation	750

Statement of financial position

	£'000
ASSETS	
Non-current assets at cost	9,470
Aggregate depreciation	(2,860)
	6,610
Current assets	
Inventories	550
Trade receivables	1,070
Bank and cash	1,130
	2,750
Total assets	9,360
EQUITY AND LIABILITIES	
Equity	
Called-up share capital: 2,000,000 equity shares of £1 each	2,000
Retained earnings	2,380
Total equity	4,380
Non-current liabilities	
10% loan stock of £100 each	4,000
Total non-current liabilities	4,000
Current liabilities	
Trade payables	730
Current tax payable	250
Total current liabilities	980
Total liabilities	4,980
Total equity and liabilities	9,360

Additional information

1 The equity shares and loan stock are currently quoted on the London Stock Exchange at £4 and £90, respectively.

2 A final dividend for the year of £400,000 is proposed (no interim dividend was paid in the year).

33.2 Measures of a company's performance

The main function of financial statements is to provide information that will enable users to evaluate the financial performance and financial position of a company. Performance may relate to a number of things, such as productivity, energy conservation and pollution control. From the equity shareholders' point of view, financial performance is usually equated with the profit available for distribution as dividends or the **earnings per share** (discussed later). However, the term 'financial performance' is normally associated with an entity view of business enterprises. This section therefore examines various measures of a company's performance from the point of view of its being an economic entity separate from the shareholders, and irrespective of the way in which its assets are financed (i.e. the proportion of debt to equity capital).

Return on capital employed (ROCE)

Various accounting ratios are used to measure different aspects of financial performance. Many of these are derived from a single ratio known as the 'return on capital employed'. The **return on capital employed** is a measure of profitability that is used to indicate how efficiently and effectively a company has utilized its assets during a given accounting period. It is a common means of evaluating a company's profitability over time, and comparing the profitability of different companies. As a rough guide, the typical target ROCE of many large companies is about 15 per cent. This is ascertained as follows:

$$\frac{\text{Profit before tax, interest on non-current loans and preference dividends}}{\text{Net capital employed}} \times 100$$

Net capital employed refers to the shareholders' interests + non-current liabilities. Using the data in Example 33.1 this is calculated thus:

$$\frac{£1,000,000 + £400,000}{£4,380,000 + £4,000,000} \times 100 = 16.7 \text{ per cent}$$

The logic behind this ratio is perhaps more obvious when it is calculated as the **return on assets** as follows:

$$\frac{\text{Profit before tax, interest on non-current loans and preference dividends}}{\text{Total assets less current liabilities}} \times 100$$

$$\frac{£1,000,000 + £400,000}{£9,360,000 - £980,000} \times 100 = 16.7 \text{ per cent}$$

Some authors advocate expressing the return on capital employed in terms of the **gross capital employed**. This refers to the shareholders' interests + non-current liabilities + current liabilities. A somewhat easier way of calculating this is non-current assets + current assets. Clearly, the return on gross capital employed/total assets will be different from the return on net capital employed/total assets less current liabilities. The latter is more common in practice.

Whatever method is used, there is a problem concerning the point at which the capital employed should be measured. In the above computation this was taken as being the end of the accounting year, for simplicity. However, this is not really justifiable because the capital employed includes the retained profit for the year and any additional capital raised during the year. The retained profit for the year was not available to generate the profit throughout this year, and it is unlikely that any capital raised during the year provided a significant contribution to the profit for the year. Given the time lags between capital expenditure and assets becoming productive, it may be more appropriate to use the capital employed at the start of the accounting year. Alternatively, if the additional capital is known to have generated profit during the year, the average capital employed for the year would be used. The same consider-ations apply to the **return on equity** discussed later.

The use of historical cost data in the calculation of this ratio can give a distorted view of the profitability for two reasons. First, during times of rising prices the denominator in the formula comprises a mix-ture of assets acquired at various times when the prevailing levels of prices were different. In times of rising prices, the denominator is also understated because assets are not shown in the statement of financial position at their current value. Second, the numerator tends to be overstated, since the histor-ical cost profit is calculated by matching current selling prices with historical costs. Thus, the effect of historical cost accounting in both the denominator and the numerator is to inflate the return on capital and encourage the retention of old assets.

The profit margin and asset-turnover ratios

The ROCE can be broken down into two further ratios, as follows:

$$ROCE = Profit\ margin \times Asset\text{-}turnover\ ratio$$

The **profit margin** is computed thus:

$$\frac{\text{Profit before tax, interest on non-current loans and preference dividends}}{\text{Revenue}} \times 100$$

Using the data in Example 33.1 this will give:

$$\frac{£1,000,000 + £400,000}{£5,280,000} \times 100 = 26.5\ \text{per cent}$$

The profit margin is often described as a measure of profitability that shows what percentage of sales revenue is profit. Different products have different profit margins. Jewellery and greengrocery, for example, usually have a higher profit margin than electrical goods and clothing. In addition, different sized businesses have different profit margins. Small shops, for example, usually have a higher profit margin than supermarkets. Inter-firm comparisons of profit margins should therefore only be made between companies in the same industry and of a comparable size.

The Companies Act requires the disclosure of an analysis of profit and revenue for each class of busi-ness. It is therefore possible to calculate the profit margin for each class of business. These could be used in inter-firm comparisons of performance. However, this can be misleading because the profit margin constitutes an average for all the products comprising one particular class of business, and few firms sell exactly the same combination of products (i.e. product mix). Time-series analysis of profit margins is likely to be more meaningful. Variations in the profit margin over time can be due to a number of factors relating to changes in the product mix, selling prices, unit costs and overhead costs.

The second of the ratios making up the ROCE is referred to as the **asset-turnover ratio**. It is calculated as follows:

$$\frac{\text{Revenue}}{\text{Total assets less Current liabilities}}$$

Using the data in Example 33.1 this will give:

$$\frac{£5,280,000}{£9,360,000 - £980,000} = 0.63\ \text{times}$$

This shows the amount of sales revenue that has been generated per £ of capital employed. In this instance, £0.63 of revenue has been generated in this year from every £1 invested in the company by equity shareholders and other providers of long-term financing (long-term liabilities). It is a meas-ure of the level of activity and productivity. Different industries have different asset turnover ratios, primarily because of differences in technology. Labour-intensive industries usually have a high asset-turnover ratio, whereas capital-intensive industries tend to have a lower asset-turnover ratio. Inter-firm comparisons of asset-turnover ratios should therefore only be made between companies in the same industry. Time-series analysis of asset-turnover ratios is likely to be more meaningful. Changes in the asset-turnover ratio over time can be due to a number of factors, such as producing at under capacity, labour inefficiency or overstocking.

There is an important relationship between the asset-turnover ratio and the profit margin. In order to achieve a satisfactory return on capital employed, a company with a low asset-turnover ratio (e.g. capital-intensive) will need a high profit margin on its products. Conversely, a company with a high asset-turnover ratio (e.g. labour-intensive) will only require a low profit margin on its products in order to achieve a satisfactory return on capital employed. The former case of a capital-intensive company can be illustrated arithmetically using the asset-turnover ratio, profit margin and ROCE for Example 33.1, as follows:

$$0.63 \times 26.5 \text{ per cent} = 16.7 \text{ per cent}$$

The profit margin ratio may be broken down into a number of other ratios in order to pinpoint more precisely the reasons for changes in performance over time. These are as follows:

Profit margin:

$$\frac{\text{Cost of sales}}{\text{Revenue}} \times 100$$

$$\frac{\text{Gross profit}}{\text{Revenue}} \times 100$$

$$\frac{\text{Distribution costs}}{\text{Revenue}} \times 100$$

$$\frac{\text{Administration expenses}}{\text{Revenue}} \times 100$$

The most important of these is probably the **gross profit ratio**. Using data from Example 33.1, a gross profit percentage of 41.5 per cent results.

$$\frac{£2,190,000}{£5,280,000} \times 100 = 41.5$$

This provides information on the percentage of each pound of revenue that contributes towards covering the entity's fixed overhead costs and to profit. It includes the variable costs associated with each sale, such as the purchase cost of the products in non-manufacturing entities, or the manufacturing cost of the products that are for sale in manufacturing entities. It is affected by the selling price of the products, the purchase price of the products and inventory management (inventory losses).

The asset-turnover ratio can also be analysed further into a number of other ratios to pinpoint more precisely reasons for changes in performance over time. These are as follows:

Asset-turnover ratio:

$$\frac{\text{Revenue}}{\text{Non-current assets}}$$

$$\frac{\text{Revenue}}{\text{Net current assets}}$$

The last ratio can be further subdivided into a number of other ratios relating to each constituent of net current assets. These are discussed in a later section on the appraisal of working capital.

33.3 Measures of solvency and liquidity

The main function of published financial statements is to provide information that will enable users to evaluate the performance and financial position of a company. The phrase 'financial position' is normally taken as including whether or not a company will be able to pay its debts as and when they become due. A business that is unable to do so is said to be **insolvent**, and will usually be forced into compulsory liquidation by its creditors. Sometimes profitable businesses face financial crisis, frequently because of overtrading. This broadly means that a company has invested too much in non-current assets and inventory but too little in liquid assets and is thus short of cash.

Solvency does not mean that at any time a business must have enough money to pay its liabilities. These will fall due at various dates in the future. **Solvency** therefore refers to whether or not liabilities are covered by assets that will be realized as the liabilities fall due. Thus, if the value of current assets is less than the amount of current liabilities, a business may be insolvent.

However, even if current assets are equal to or greater than current liabilities, this is no guarantee of solvency, since some current assets are less liquid than others. Liquidity refers to the ease with which an asset can be turned into cash without loss. Cash in hand and money in a bank current account are the most liquid types of asset, followed by listed investments, trade receivables and inventory. Current assets are usually presented in published financial statements in what is referred to as a reverse order of liquidity.

Two fairly crude but common ratios used to measure liquidity are explained below.

The working capital/current ratio

The **working capital/current ratio** is calculated thus:

$$\frac{\text{Current assets}}{\text{Current liabilities}}$$

Using the data in Example 33.1 this gives:

$$\frac{£2,750,000}{£980,000} = 2.8$$

This is a measure of the extent to which current liabilities are covered by current assets. As a generalization, the current ratio should be between 1.5 and 2, although this depends on the type of industry and the prevailing economic climate. A ratio of lower than 1.5 may indicate a poor liquidity position and thus future insolvency. At the other extreme a business can have too much working capital, which normally means that its assets are not being used as profitably as they otherwise might.

The working capital ratio has a serious limitation as a measure of liquidity, which is that some current assets are less liquid than others. In particular, inventories and work-in-progress are not easily realized without loss in the short term. A better criterion for measuring a company's ability to pay its debts as and when they become due is the **liquidity ratio**. In this ratio, inventories and work-in-progress are excluded from current assets.

The liquidity/quick ratio or acid test

This is calculated thus:

$$\frac{\text{Current assets} - \text{Inventories}}{\text{Current liabilities}}$$

Using the data in Example 33.1 this gives:

$$\frac{£2,750,000 - £550,000}{£980,000} = 2.24$$

Bank overdrafts are frequently excluded from the current liabilities in the calculation of this ratio because, although an overdraft is usually legally repayable at short notice, in practice it is often effectively a non-current liability.

The liquidity ratio indicates whether a company is likely to be able to pay its credit suppliers, current taxation, other current liabilities and dividends proposed (but not accrued) from its cash at bank, the proceeds of sale of listed investments and the amounts collected from trade receivables, that is, without having to raise additional capital or sell non-current assets. As a generalization, the liquidity ratio should therefore be at least 1 (expressed as 1:1). However, this criterion cannot be applied to all types of business. Large retailing companies, for example, often have a liquidity ratio of less than 1. They buy goods on credit, sell them for cash and turn over their inventory rapidly. Thus, inventory is a relatively liquid asset. It is therefore only necessary for the working capital ratio to be at least 1.

A poor liquidity position usually arises from continual losses, though it can also be the result of overtrading. At the other extreme a business can have too much liquidity. Where this is not temporary, the excess should be invested in non-current assets (assuming that there are profitable investment opportunities).

The prediction of insolvency

The working capital and liquidity ratios are, at best, crude conventional measures of liquidity. Most users of published financial statements are interested in liquidity as an indicator of whether a company will be able to pay its debts, or alternatively whether it is likely to go into liquidation in the near future. There is empirical research that demonstrates that the working capital and liquidity ratios are not particularly good predictors of insolvency. However, certain other ratios have been found to be useful in predicting corporate failure. The two most often cited studies of bankruptcy are by Altman (1968) in the USA and Taffler (1982) in the UK. They each identify a set of five accounting ratios that provide successful predictions of company failure. These are as follows:

Altman	*Taffler*
$\dfrac{\text{Profit before interest and tax}}{\text{Total assets}}$	$\dfrac{\text{Profit before interest and tax}}{\text{Opening total assets}}$
$\dfrac{\text{Working capital}}{\text{Total assets}}$	$\dfrac{\text{Working capital}}{\text{Net worth}}$
$\dfrac{\text{Revenue}}{\text{Total assets}}$	$\dfrac{\text{Revenue}}{\text{Average inventory}}$
$\dfrac{\text{Revenue earnings}}{\text{Total assets}}$	$\dfrac{\text{Quick assets}}{\text{Total assets}}$
$\dfrac{\text{Market value of equity}}{\text{Book value of total debt}}$	$\dfrac{\text{Total liabilities}}{\text{Net capital employed}}$

Both of these studies make use of a statistical technique known as 'multiple discriminant analysis'. This involves taking several ratios together in a multiple regression model. The set of five ratios in Altman's model enabled him correctly to classify as bankrupt or non-bankrupt 95 per cent of the cases in a sample of failed and non-failed US companies. He further claims that these ratios can be used to predict bankruptcy up to two years prior to actual failure. Similarly, Taffler correctly classified all but one company in a sample of UK companies, and asserts that his model exhibits predictive ability for about three years prior to bankruptcy. Several other studies have revisited this area (Ohlson, 1980; Dambolena and Khoury, 1980; Ding, 2007) making revisions to the methodology used and the ratios being focused on.

However, there are doubts about the validity of the results of studies such as these for a number of reasons. First, the research is not based on a theory that explains why particular ratios should provide successful predictions of insolvency. Second, these studies make use of historical cost data, the deficiencies of which have already been explained. Finally, there are several problems involved in the use of statistical techniques, such as discriminant analysis, which make the results questionable.

 ## 33.4 The appraisal of working capital

The phrase 'working capital' has two slightly different meanings. In computational terms it relates to the amount of the **net current assets**.

$$\text{Net current assets} = \text{Current assets} - \text{Current liabilities}$$

However, it is also used in a general sense to refer to the current assets and current liabilities. In this section the phrase 'working capital' is intended to be interpreted in the latter sense.

One way of looking at the appraisal of working capital is in terms of the interrelationship between a company's performance and liquidity position. As regards performance, the analysis of working capital is an extension of the asset turnover ratio (or more precisely the ratio of revenue to net current assets), which shows how effective a company's management has been in utilizing the various constituents of working capital. This in turn affects a company's liquidity position.

If there has been a significant change in the working capital and/or liquidity ratios, one would want to try to pinpoint the cause(s). In crude terms, the appraisal of working capital reveals whether too much or too little is invested in, for example, trade receivables and inventory relative to a company's level of activity (i.e. revenue). In theory, there is an optimal level of working capital. However, in practice all that users of published financial statements can do is to identify changes in the relative level of current assets such as trade receivables and inventory. These are taken as prima facie indicators of the effectiveness of credit control and inventory control, respectively.

A number of ratios can be calculated relating to those items that make up the working capital. Each of these must be considered in the light of the particular circumstances of the company, the type of industry and the prevailing economic climate. The most common ratios used in the appraisal of working capital are given below.

The trade receivables' ratio — average period of credit taken by credit customers

This is calculated thus:

$$\frac{\text{Trade receivables}}{\text{Revenue}} \times \text{Number of days in a year}$$

Using the data in Example 33.1 this gives:

$$\frac{£1,070,000}{£5,280,000} \times 365 = 74 \text{ days}$$

Instead of using the trade receivables at the end of the accounting year in the numerator some authors compute the average trade receivables as follows:

Trade receivables at the end of the previous year + Trade receivables at the end of the current year

2

The argument for using this method of computation is that it gives a more representative figure for the 'normal' level of trade receivables. However, the important point is that the ratio should be computed on a consistent basis, otherwise comparisons will be misleading.

As the title suggests, this ratio shows the average number of days' credit taken by trade receivables. The most common terms of credit in the UK are that an invoice is due for payment by the end of the calendar month following the calendar month in which the goods are delivered/invoiced. The minimum average period of credit is thus approximately 45 days (i.e. one and a half months). However, many credit customers take a longer period than this if they can, since it is obviously beneficial for them to do so. An average period of credit of around 75 days (i.e. two and a half months) is therefore not uncommon. Another method of expressing this ratio is referred to as the trade receivables' turnover ratio. It is calculated by inverting the fraction (and excluding the number of days in a year).

$$\frac{\text{Revenue}}{\text{Trade receivables}}$$

Using the data in Example 33.1 this gives:

$$\frac{£5,280,000}{£1,070,000} = 4.9 \text{ times}$$

This means that trade receivables turn over 4.9 times each year.

When the **trade receivables' ratio** is calculated from the information in published financial statements, it may be nothing like any of these figures. This occurs if a company has both cash and credit sales. Since trade receivables arise because of credit sales, the denominator in the ratio should obviously comprise only the credit sales. However, these are not disclosed separately in published financial statements. Consequently, the aggregate of cash and credit sales has to be used in the computation, which results in a lower trade receivables' collection period than if the denominator comprises only the credit sales. This is therefore clearly not the 'real' average period of credit, and a change in the proportion of cash to credit sales can distort the ratio over time.

The trade receivables' collection period can also be abnormally high or low because a business's sales are seasonal, such as where these are heavily concentrated either in the summer (e.g. ice cream, soft drinks) or winter, or at Easter or Christmas. This can result in an exceptionally high or low trade receivables' figure depending on when the accounting year ends, and thus a correspondingly high or low trade receivables' ratio.

The average period of credit taken by credit customers varies between industries and according to the economic situation. Retailers, for example, usually grant little or no credit, whereas wholesalers and manufacturers often allow a considerable period of credit. Comparisons should therefore really only be made between businesses in the same industry and for a particular company over time. Where the period of credit is high compared with other firms (or with the average for the industry), and/or increasing over time, this is normally taken as indicating inadequate credit control procedures.

The trade payables' ratio – average period of credit received from credit suppliers

The basic principle used in the calculation of the ratio for trade receivables can also be applied to trade payables in order to ascertain the average period of credit taken by the reporting entity. This is calculated as follows:

$$\frac{\text{Trade payables}}{\text{Purchases}} \times \text{Number of days in a year}$$

As in the case of trade receivables, the figure of trade payables used in the computation of this ratio may be an average of those at the end of the previous year and the end of the current year. Another method of expressing this ratio is referred to as the 'trade payables' turnover ratio'. It is calculated by inverting the fraction (and excluding the number of days in a year).

$$\frac{\text{Purchases}}{\text{Trade payables}}$$

The amount of purchases is not normally disclosed in published financial statements. However, if the company is a non-manufacturing business, these can be calculated by adjusting the cost of sales figure (given in the statement of profit and loss) by the change in inventory (given in the statement of financial position) over the year as follows:

Cost of sales

Add: inventory at end of current year

Less: inventory at end of previous year

= Purchases

Where the company is a manufacturing business, or the inventory at the end of the previous year is not given as a comparative figure instead of purchases, a surrogate has to be used, such as the cost of sales.

Using the data in Example 33.1 this will give:

$$\frac{£730,000}{£3,090,000} \times 365 = 86 \text{ days}$$

It is beneficial to delay paying credit suppliers for as long as possible. However, this may adversely affect the company's credit rating, and credit suppliers may refuse to supply further goods on credit. In addition, where the period of credit is high compared with other firms (or with the average for the industry) and/or increasing over time, this may be an indication of financial weakness.

The inventory turnover ratio

This is calculated thus:

$$\frac{\text{Cost of sales}}{\text{Inventory (finished goods)}}$$

Using the data in Example 33.1 this will give:

$$\frac{£3,090,000}{£550,000} = 5.6$$

As in the calculation of the average period of credit for trade receivables and trade payables, there is an argument for using an average of the inventory at the end of the previous year and the current year as the denominator in this ratio. Once again, the important point is that a consistent basis of computation should be used to ensure meaningful comparisons. Another method of expressing this ratio is referred to as the 'number of days' sales from inventory'. It is calculated by inverting the fraction and multiplying the answer by 365.

The **inventory turnover ratio** shows the number of times that a business 'turns over'/sells its average/normal level of inventory during the accounting year. In very simple terms, a greengrocer who goes to market once a week and sells all these goods during that week would have an inventory turnover ratio of 52 (because there are 52 weeks in a year). Inventory turnover ratios vary between industries. Food retailers, for example, have a relatively high inventory turnover ratio, whereas jewellery retailers normally have a much lower ratio. Comparisons should therefore really only be made between firms in the same industry and for a particular company over time. Where the inventory turnover ratio is low compared with other firms (or with the average for the industry), and/or decreasing over time, this is normally taken as indicating a lack of adequate inventory control.

33.5   Measures of return on investment and risk

This group of ratios is primarily intended for the use of equity shareholders, although a company's management will probably monitor these ratios as a guide to how investors view the company. There are several investment ratios, some of which are published in the *Financial Times*. These include the following.

The dividend yield

This is calculated as:

$$\frac{\text{Annual equity dividend}}{\text{Current market value of equity shares}}$$

For Example 33.1 this will give:

$$\frac{£400,000 \div 2,000,000}{£4} \quad \text{or} \quad \frac{£400,000}{2,000,000 \times £4} \times 100 = 5 \text{ per cent}$$

The same principle can be used to calculate the **dividend yield** on preference shares and the interest yield on debentures and loan stock.

The dividend yield is said to measure the equity shareholder's annual cash return on investment, and may be compared with what could be obtained by investing in some other company. However, such comparisons can be misleading, for two main reasons. First, companies have different risk characteristics. A comparison of the dividend yields of, for example, a steel company and a large retailer such as Tesco plc would be misleading because the former is a riskier investment than the latter. Second, companies have different dividend policies, in that some distribute a greater proportion of their annual profit than others. Put slightly differently, the annual dividend is only part of an investor's total return, in that the investor will also expect to make a capital gain in the form of an increase in the market price of shares. This partly results from companies retaining a proportion of their annual profits.

The dividend yield is often between 2 and 5 per cent, but varies between companies for the reasons outlined above. Some investors regard the dividend yield as important because they are primarily interested in maximizing their annual cash income (e.g. retired people). However, for other investors the dividend yield may only be of limited importance because they are more interested in capital gains (for tax reasons) resulting from an increase in the share price. They are therefore often attracted to companies with a low dividend yield but high retained profits.

Dividend cover

This is calculated as:

$$\frac{\text{Profit for the year}}{\text{Annual equity dividend}}$$

For Example 33.1 this will give:

$$\frac{£750,000}{£400,000} = 1.875$$

The profit for the year is used in the calculation of this ratio because it represents the profit available for distribution as dividends to equity shareholders.

The **dividend cover** indicates how likely it is that the company will be able to maintain future dividends on equity shares at their current level if profits were to fall in future years. It is thus a measure of risk.

The amount by which the dividend cover exceeds unity represents what might be called 'the margin of safety'. Thus, a company with a high dividend cover would be more likely to be able to maintain the current level of equity dividends than a company with a low dividend cover. The average dividend cover for companies whose shares are listed on the London Stock Exchange is about 2, but clearly this depends on a company's dividend policy.

Earnings per share (EPS)

This is calculated as:

$$\frac{\text{Profit for the year}}{\text{Number of equity shares in issue}}$$

For Example 33.1 this will give:

$$\frac{£750,000}{2,000,000} = £0.375$$

The profit for the year is used in the calculation of this ratio because it represents the profit available for distribution as dividends to equity shareholders. This is referred to as the 'earnings'. There are complex rules for ascertaining the number of equity shares but these are beyond the scope of this book. The rules are applied where the allotted share capital has changed during the year because, for example, there has been an issue of shares during the year. The calculation involves determining an average number of shares for the year (IASB, 2010).

EPS is not strictly a measure of return on investment. However, as will be discussed below, it is included in the calculation of another widely used accounting ratio, the price–earnings ratio (discussed next). Furthermore, EPS is generally regarded as an important consideration in investment decisions, as such, and because of the significance investors place on this ratio, it has been given special attention by the IASB and has its own standard, *IAS 33 – Earnings Per Share* (IASB, 2010). This standard requires that the EPS be disclosed in the published financial statements of all listed companies.

As explained earlier, the absolute amount of profit (in this context, available for distribution as dividends) is not usually a satisfactory measure of performance because it ignores the amount of net assets/capital that has been used to generate that profit. However, EPS takes this into consideration in the form of the number of equity shares and thus provides a useful means of evaluating performance (where performance is defined from the shareholders' point of view as relating to the profit available for distribution as dividends). The trend in EPS over time indicates growth or otherwise in the profit attributable to each equity share. Inter-firm comparisons of EPS are not advisable.

The price–earnings (P/E) ratio

The **price–earnings (P/E) ratio** is calculated as:

$$\frac{\text{Current market price of each equity share}}{\text{EPS}}$$

For Example 33.1 this will give:

$$\frac{£4}{£0.375} = 10.67$$

The P/E ratio is often between 10 and 25 but varies considerably between different industries and companies in the same industry. Many authors shy away from explaining the P/E ratio because its meaning is somewhat ambiguous, despite the fact that this is probably the most widely cited accounting ratio. The P/E ratio is a reflection of risk in that it represents the number of years' earnings that investors are prepared to buy at their current level. This is probably better explained in terms of what is essentially a payback period. The P/E ratio shows the number of years it will take to recoup the current price of the shares at the present level of EPS (the share price being recouped in the form of dividends and retained profits). In the context of A. Harry plc, the P/E ratio can be explained as follows. Share price covers earnings 10.67 times. Therefore, it will take 10.67 years to recoup the share price investment in earnings.

Where an investment is risky, investors will want to get their money back relatively quickly, whereas if an investment is comparatively safe, a longer payback period will be acceptable. Thus, companies in risky industries such as mining and construction tend to have a low P/E ratio, whereas companies in relatively safe industries such as food manufacturers, and those which are diversified, tend to have a high P/E ratio.

The P/E ratio also varies between companies in the same industry. If investors think that a company's earnings are going to decline, the P/E ratio will tend to be lower than the average for the industry. Conversely, if profits are expected to rise, the P/E ratio will tend to be higher, both of which occur because of decreases and increases in the share price, respectively. The P/E ratio is therefore also a reflection of the expected earnings growth potential of a company. This also means that sometimes industries which one would expect to have a high P/E ratio, since they are relatively safe, in fact have a low P/E ratio because the earnings are expected to decline (and vice versa).

It appears that the P/E ratio is sometimes also used in practice to identify shares that are over or underpriced. A share is said to be overpriced if its P/E ratio is higher than the norm for the industry or other similar companies, and underpriced if the P/E ratio is lower than the norm for the industry or other similar companies. However, as explained above, this is probably an oversimplification, because the intrinsic/real value of a share will depend on the expected future earnings of the particular company.

Another way of looking at the P/E ratio is to invert the formula and express the result as a percentage. This is referred to as the **earnings yield**. For Example 33.1 this will give:

$$\frac{£0.375}{£4} = \text{or } \frac{£750,000}{2 \text{ million @ } £4} \times 100 = 9.375 \text{ per cent}$$

The earnings yield is not really a yield in the same sense as the dividend yield, since not all the earnings are distributed as dividends. However, it is often referred to as a measure of return on investment. As in the case of EPS, the earnings yield is a useful means of evaluating performance (where performance is defined from the shareholders' point of view as relating to the profit available for distribution as dividends). The trend in the earnings yield over time indicates how efficiently and effectively a company has utilized the amount of money the shareholders have invested in the company in terms of the current share price. It can also be used to compare the performance of different companies.

> **LEARNING ACTIVITY 33.1**
>
> Obtain two copies of the *Financial Times*, one for a Monday and one for any other day of the week. Turn to the last two pages but one of the section called 'Companies and Markets' headed 'London Share Service'. Look at the last two columns in the Tuesday to Saturday editions headed 'Yield' and 'P/E', which refer to the dividend yield and price–earnings ratio, respectively. Similarly, look at the column in the Monday edition headed 'Div.cov.', which refers to the dividend cover. Examine the values of these three ratios for some large public limited companies in different industries. What do these ratios tell you about those companies?

The return on equity (ROE)

This is calculated as:

$$\frac{\text{Profit for the year}}{\text{Equity}} \times 100$$

For Example 33.1 this will give:

$$\frac{£750,000}{£4,380,000} \times 100 = 17.1 \text{ per cent}$$

Sometimes this ratio is calculated using the profit before tax (but after preference dividends) to avoid the distortions that can arise when comparing companies with different tax positions. As in the ROCE ratio, it is more appropriate to use the equity shareholders' interests at the start of the accounting year, or an average, rather than at the end of the year. The latter is unjustifiable and has only been used in this example because it is the only figure available for simplicity.

The ROE is essentially the same as the earnings yield. The difference is that, instead of expressing the earnings as a percentage of the market price/value of the equity shares, this is expressed as a percentage of the book value of the equity shares in the form of the equity shareholders' interests. Since the latter is not the 'real' (i.e. market) value of the equity shareholders' investment, this ratio can be said to be inferior to the earnings yield.

However, the ROE, like the earnings yield, is a common measure of return on investment which is used to evaluate profitability (where profitability is defined from the equity shareholders' point of view as relating to the profit available for distribution as dividends). It is said to indicate how efficiently and effectively a company's management has utilized the equity shareholders' interests. The ratio may be used to compare the profitability of different companies and/or to examine trends over time.

The gearing ratio

Gearing, or **leverage** as it is called in the USA, refers to the relationship between the amount of fixed interest capital (i.e. loan stock, debentures, preference shares, etc.) and the amount of equity capital (i.e. equity shares). In discussions of gearing, the fixed interest capital is frequently referred to as the **debt capital**, which is taken to include preference shares. As a broad generalization, where the value of fixed interest capital is less than the value of equity, a company is said to have low gearing. Where the value of debt capital is more than the value of equity, a company is said to have high gearing.

There are two main ways of expressing the **gearing ratio**. The basis most commonly used in the financial press is to express the debt capital as a fraction (or percentage) of the equity capital thus:

$$\text{Debt/equity ratio} = \frac{\text{Debt capital}}{\text{Equity capital}} \ (\times 100)$$

However, in accounting it is more common to compute the gearing ratio by expressing the debt capital as a fraction (or percentage) of the total capital thus:

$$\text{Gearing ratio} = \frac{\text{Debt capital}}{\text{Debt capital} + \text{Equity capital}} \ (\times 100)$$

Using the latter basis, the next issue concerns how the debt and equity capital are to be measured/valued. There are three main methods as follows:

1 *Using the nominal values* of fixed interest capital and equity share capital thus:

$$\frac{\text{Nominal value of debt capital}}{\text{Nominal value of debt capital} + \text{Nominal value of equity shares}} \times 100$$

The debt capital refers to the preference shares, loan stock, debentures, bank loans, mortgages and any other non-current borrowing, such as an overdraft for more than one year. An illustration of the calculation of the gearing ratio using this formula is given in Example 33.2. This also highlights the difference between low gearing and high gearing.

	Company with low gearing	Company with high gearing
	£	£
Equity shares of £1 each	400,000	100,000
10% preference shares of £1 each	30,000	150,000
10% debentures of £100 each	70,000	250,000
	500,000	500,000
Gearing ratio	20% or 1:4	80% or 4:1

EXAMPLE 33.2

2 Including the reserves and retained profits as part of the equity capital thus:

$$\frac{\text{Nominal value of debt capital}}{\text{Nominal value of debt capital} + \text{Nominal value of equity}} \times 100$$

Returning to the data in Example 33.1, this would be calculated as follows:

$$\frac{£4,000,000}{£4,000,000 + £4,380,000} \times 100 = 47.7 \text{ per cent}$$

This method of expressing the gearing ratio is considered to be superior to the first because reserves and retained earnings constitute part of the equity shareholders' interests and thus the capital that they provide. The logic behind this is perhaps more obvious when the gearing ratio is calculated in terms of the book value of the assets, thus:

$$\frac{\text{Nominal value of debt capital}}{\text{Total assets} - \text{Current liabilities}} \times 100$$

Using the data in Example 33.1 this would be calculated as follows:

$$\frac{£4,000,000}{£9,360,000 - £980,000} \times 100 = 47.7 \text{ per cent}$$

This formula highlights that the gearing ratio shows the proportion of the assets, which are financed by fixed interest capital.

3 *Using the current market prices* of a company's equity shares and debt capital, thus:

$$\frac{\text{Market value of debt capital}}{\text{Market value of debt capital} + \text{Market value of equity shares}} \times 100$$

Using the data in Example 32.1 this would be calculated as follows:

$$\frac{40,000 @ £90(\text{or } £4,000,000 \times £90/£100)}{(40,000 @ £90) + (2,000,000 @ £4)} \times 100 = 31 \text{ per cent}$$

This is generally regarded as being a more theoretically sound method of expressing the gearing ratio, because market prices are said to represent the 'real' value of the debt capital and shareholders' interests as distinct from the nominal or book values.

There are several other ways of expressing gearing, which show the relationship between the annual amount of interest on debt capital and the profit for the year. However, these are not used very often.

The gearing ratio is a measure of the '**financial risk**' attaching to a company's equity shares that arises because of the prior claim that fixed interest capital has on the annual income and assets (in the event of liquidation). This financial risk is additional to the '**operating risk**' that is associated with the particular industry or industries in which a company is trading.

Companies are said to engage in gearing because it usually produces substantial benefits for the equity shareholders. In crude terms, the money provided by loan creditors is used to generate income in excess of the loan interest. The tax deductibility of interest contributes to this benefit. In technical terms, gearing usually increases the profit available for distribution as dividends to equity shareholders and thus the EPS, although it does have an impact on the riskiness of the earnings. These effects are illustrated numerically in Example 33.3. The data are taken from Example 33.2. These two companies are assumed to be identical in all respects except their gearing. Both have a profit after tax (but before interest) of £50,000 and an EPS of 10 pence in year 1. Although this example is clearly unrealistic, it illustrates vividly the impact of gearing.

EXAMPLE 33.3		Company with low gearing		Company with high gearing	
Year 1	£	£	£	£	
Profit before interest		50,000		50,000	
Preference dividends	3,000		15,000		
Interest	7,000	10,000	25,000	40,000	
Distributable profit		40,000		10,000	
Earnings per share		10p		10p	
Year 2					
Profit before interest		100,000		100,000	
Preference dividends	3,000		15,000		
Interest	7,000	10,000	25,000	40,000	
Distributable profit		90,000		60,000	
Earnings per share		22.5p		60p	

Now suppose the profit of both companies doubles in year 2, as shown in Example 33.3. In the case of the company with low gearing, a 100 per cent increase in the profit after tax (but before interest) in year 2 results in a 125 per cent increase (from £40,000 to £90,000) in the profit available for distribution as dividends to equity shareholders. By contrast, in the case of the highly geared company, a 100 per cent increase in the profit after tax in year 2 results in a 500 per cent increase (from £10,000 to £60,000) in the distributable profit. Similarly, a 100 per cent increase in the profit after tax results in a 125 per cent increase in the EPS of the low-geared company, compared with a 500 per cent increase for the company with high gearing. This can be summarized in the form of a general rule as follows: any increase in profit (before charging interest) will result in a *proportionately greater* increase in the profit available for distribution (and the EPS) of a high-geared company, compared with an equivalent increase for a company with low gearing.

However, gearing is a double-edged sword, in that the same occurs in reverse when there is a decrease in profit, as often happens when there is an economic recession. Imagine that the chronological sequence in Example 33.3 is reversed, giving profit before interest of £100,000 in year 1 and £50,000 in year 2 representing a 50 per cent decrease in the profit after tax (but before interest). This results in a reduction in the distributable profit and EPS of 56 per cent in the case of the low-geared company, compared with 83 per cent for the company with high gearing. This can also be summarized in the form of a general rule as follows: any decrease in the profit (before charging interest) will result in a proportionately greater reduction in the profit available for distribution (and the EPS) of a high-geared company compared with an equivalent decrease for a company with low gearing.

Furthermore, the level of gearing affects a company's break-even point. A company with high gearing will have a larger break-even point than an equivalent company with low gearing. This is because the interest charges of a high-geared company are greater than for an equivalent company with low gearing. In Example 33.3 the break-even point of the high-geared company is £30,000 (i.e. £40,000 − £10,000) higher than that of the low-geared company. This means that a company with high gearing has to earn a greater profit (before interest) before it can declare a dividend compared with an equivalent company that has low gearing. Thus, if the profit after tax of these companies fell to, say, £20,000, the company with low gearing would still be able to declare an equity dividend from the current year's trading profit whereas the high-geared company could not.

To sum up, the equity shareholders in a high-geared company benefit from gearing when profits are relatively large. However, they run two risks. First, when profits are small the dividends will be less than would be the case with low gearing. Second, if the company goes into liquidation, they will not be repaid the value of their shares until after all the fixed interest capital has been repaid. Usually very little or nothing is left for the equity shareholders. Thus, the tendency to assume that gearing is advantageous may be a misconception because, while it frequently results in a proportionately greater increase in the distributable profit, it also makes the equity shares riskier. To use an analogy, one should not bet on an outsider in a horse race merely because the winnings would be greater than betting on the favourite. One must weigh up the possible return in relation to the perceived risk.

> **LEARNING ACTIVITY 33.2**
>
> Assess the liquidity, solvency, profitability, efficiency and investment potential of Ryanair plc. Find the disclosures in respect of their EPS ratio. Try to calculate it using the information provided.

> **LEARNING ACTIVITY 33.3**
>
> Search the Web for a copy of the financial statements of a large public limited. Try to obtain the financial statements of a company that is known to have had recent financial problems. Using the information contained in this document, compute all the ratios discussed in this chapter for the current and previous year. List any apparent material changes in the value of these ratios, and outline their possible causes.

33.6 The limitations of ratio analysis

Example 33.1 was deliberately kept simple for the purpose of illustration. In particular, it contains no comparative figures for the previous year. Thus, no time-series analysis was possible. In addition, in the calculation of some ratios (e.g. EPS, ROE, ROCE) the amount at the end of the accounting year was used when it would have been more appropriate to take the figure at the beginning of the year or an average for the year. Companies are required by law to include comparative figures for the previous year in their published financial statements. These would therefore usually be available and should be used where appropriate.

Ratio analysis has a number of limitations. Most of these have already been explained in the context of particular ratios but can be summarized as follows:

1 Comparisons between companies and for a particular company over time may be misleading if different accounting policies are used to calculate profits and value assets.

2 Ratios usually have to be calculated using historical cost data since few companies publish a current cost statement of comprehensive income and statement of financial position. These ratios will therefore be distorted because of the effects of inflation and thus comparisons may be misleading.

3 The data needed to compute some ratios are not disclosed in published financial statements and thus surrogates have to be used (e.g. the aggregate cash and credit sales in the calculation of the average period of credit taken by trade receivables). This may also mean that comparisons are misleading.

4 The general yardsticks or performance criteria that may be applied to particular ratios (e.g. a liquidity ratio of at least 1) are not appropriate for all types of industry.

5 Changes in a given ratio over time and differences between companies must be considered in the light of the particular circumstances of the reporting entity, the type of industry and the general economic situation. They may also be due to deliberate policy decisions by management such as a build-up of inventories prior to a sales promotion campaign, to rent or own non-current assets, and so on.

6 A single ratio may not be very informative by itself, but a number of related ratios taken together should give a general picture of the company's performance or financial position (e.g. in the prediction of insolvency).

In practice

To aid the interpretation of performance, most plcs include important ratios in a statement at the front of their annual report called the 'Operating and Financial Review', or the 'Operating and Financial Statistics'. This can either be a narrative overview of the performance of the entity or a table highlighting trends in certain ratios. An example is now provided.

REAL WORLD EXAMPLE **33.1**

British Airways plc

Below are the operational and financial statistics for British Airways Plc for the five years ended 31 March 2010:

Total Group operations (note 1)

Financial		**2010**	2009	2008	2007	2006
Passenger revenue per revenue passenger km	p	**6.30**	6.85	6.42	6.44	6.31
Passenger revenue per available seat km	p	**4.94**	5.28	5.08	4.90	4.80
Cargo revenue per cargo tonne km	p	**12.12**	14.51	12.57	12.74	12.94
Average fuel price (US cents/US gallon)		**189.2**	284.1	245.3	209.6	188.2
Interest cover	times	**(2.9)**	(3.6)	15.4	16.7	6.0
Dividend cover	times	**n/a**	(5.2)	n/a	n/a	n/a
Operating margin	%	**(2.9)**	(2.4)	10.0	7.1	8.5
Earnings before interest, tax, depreciation, amortization and rentals (EBITDAR)	m	**642**	645	1,780	1,549	1,666
Net debt/total capital ratio	%	**52.0**	56.3	28.7	29.1	44.2
Net debt/total capital ratio including operating leases	%	**63.1**	62.8	38.2	39.6	53.0
Total traffic revenue per total revenue tonne km	p	**48.31**	53.00	48.91	48.79	47.53
Total traffic revenue per total available tonne km	p	**35.39**	38.17	35.92	34.35	33.28
Total operating expenditure per total revenue tonne km	p	**52.76**	57.38	46.91	49.26	47.26
Total operating expenditure per total available tonne km	p	**38.65**	41.32	34.45	34.68	33.10

Source: extract from the British Airways Annual Report 2010, amended slightly to simplify disclosure: http://www.britishairways.com.

Summary

The main purpose of ratio analysis is to enable users of financial statements to evaluate a company's financial performance and financial position over time, and/or in relation to other companies. Ratios may be grouped under four main headings, each reflecting what the ratios are intended to measure, as follows:

1 *Measures of a company's performance*: These include the return on capital employed, profit margin and asset-turnover ratio.

2 *Measure of solvency and liquidity*: Solvency refers to whether a company is able to pay its debts as they become due. Liquidity refers to the ease with which an asset can be turned into cash without loss. Measures include the current and liquidity ratios.

3 *The appraisal of working capital (management efficiency)*: Measures include the trade receivables' ratio, trade payables' ratio and inventory-turnover ratio.

4 *Measures of return on investment and risk*: These include the dividend yield, dividend cover, earnings per share, price–earnings ratio, earnings yield, return on equity and capital-gearing ratio.

A single ratio may not be very informative, but a number of related ratios taken together can provide strong indications of a company's performance or financial position, such as in the prediction of insolvency. However, these must be interpreted in the light of the particular circumstances of the company, the type of industry and the current economic climate. General yardsticks are not always appropriate. Furthermore, ratios must be interpreted with caution. The use of historical cost and surrogate data, as well as different accounting policies, can distort comparisons.

Key terms and concepts

asset-turnover ratio	665	liquidity ratio	667
capital employed	662	net current assets	669
debt capital	675	operating risk	676
dividend cover	672	price–earnings (P/E) ratio	673
dividend yield	672	profitability	662
earnings per share	664	profit margin	665
earnings yield	674	return	662
financial risk	676	return on assets	664
gearing	675	return on capital employed	664
gearing ratio	675	return on equity	665
gross capital employed	664	solvency	667
gross profit ratio	666	trade payables' ratio	670
insolvent	667	trade receivables' ratio	670
inventory turnover ratio	671	working capital	662
leverage	675	working capital/current ratio	667
liquidity	662		

An asterisk after the question number indicates that there is a suggested answer on the Online Learning Centre (www.mcgraw-hill.co.uk/textbooks/thomas).

Review questions

connect

33.1 Explain what each of the following is intended to measure:

   a return on capital employed;

   b profit margin;

   c asset-turnover ratio;

   d working capital and liquidity ratios;

   e average period of credit taken by trade receivables;

   f inventory turnover ratio.

33.2 Examine the empirical evidence relating to the predictive ability of accounting ratios with regard to insolvency.

33.3 Explain what each of the following is intended to measure: (a) dividend yield; (b) dividend cover; (c) earnings per share; (d) price–earnings ratio; and (e) return on equity.

33.4 a Explain what is meant by capital gearing/leverage.

   b Why might this influence a prospective investor's decision concerning whether or not to buy equity shares in a company?

33.5 Explain the limitations of using accounting ratios in time-series analysis and inter-firm comparisons, giving examples where appropriate.

33.6 How does inflation affect ratio analysis?

33.7 What is the difference between solvency and liquidity?

Exercises

connect

33.8

Dale is in business as a sole trader. You are presented with the following summarized information relating to his business for the year to 31 October 20X2:

Statement of profit and loss for the year to 31 October 20X2		
	£'000	£'000
Sales revenue: cash	200	
credit	600	800
Less: Cost of goods sold –		
opening inventory	80	
purchases	530	
	610	
Less: closing inventory	70	540
Gross profit		260
Expenses		(205)
Profit for the year		55

Statement of financial position at 31 October 20X2	
ASSETS	£'000
Non-current assets	550
Current assets	
Inventories	70
Trade receivables	120
Cash	5
	195
Total assets	745
EQUITY AND LIABILITIES	
Equity	
Capital at 1 November 20X1	410
Net profit for the year	55
	465
Drawings	(50)
Total equity	415
Non-current liabilities	
Loan	200
Total non-current liabilities	200
Current liabilities	
Trade payables	130
Total current liabilities	130
Total liabilities	330
Total equity and liabilities	745

Required

a Based on the above information, calculate eight recognized accounting ratios.

b List what additional information you would need in order to undertake a detailed ratio analysis of Dale's business for the year to 31 October 20X2.

Note: In answering part (a) of the question, each ratio must be distinct and separate. Marks will *not* be awarded for alternative forms of the same ratio.

(AAT)

33.9*

White and Black are sole traders. Both are wholesalers dealing in a similar range of goods. Summaries of the profit calculations and statements of financial position for the same year have been made available to you, as follows:

Statements of profit and loss for the year				
	White		Black	
	£'000	£'000	£'000	£'000
Sales revenue		600		800
Cost of goods sold		(450)		(624)
Gross profit		150		176
Administrative expenses	(64)		(63)	
Selling and distribution expenses	(28)		(40)	
Depreciation – equipment and vehicles	(10)		(20)	
Depreciation – buildings	–	(102)	(5)	(128)
Profit for the year		48		48

Statements of financial position as at end of year		
ASSETS	White	Black
Non-current assets	£'000	£'000
Buildings	29	47
Equipment and vehicles	62	76
	91	123
Current assets		
Inventory	56	52
Trade receivables	75	67
Bank balance	8	–
	139	119
Total assets	230	242
EQUITY AND LIABILITIES		
Equity		
Capital	192	160
Total equity	192	160
Current liabilities		
Trade payables	38	78
Bank balance	–	4
Total current liabilities	38	82
Total equity and liabilities	230	242

Required

Compare the performance and financial position of the two businesses on the basis of the above figures, supporting your comments where appropriate with ratios and noting what further information you would need before reaching firmer conclusions.

(ACCA)

BASIC

33.10

Bastante plc has 40,000 equity shares in issue. They are currently trading at £3.00 each. Bastante plc also has 400 debentures, trading at par.

Required

a Calculate the gearing ratio for Bastante plc using market values.

b Explain the outcome.

INTERMEDIATE

33.11

The following are the summarized financial statements of Alpha and Omega, two companies that operate in the same industry:

Summarized statement of financial position		
	Alpha	Omega
	£'m	£'m
ASSETS		
Non-current assets	790	1,000
Current assets		
Inventories	1,200	1,800
Trade receivables	720	1,200
Bank	190	–
	2,110	3,000
Total assets	2,900	4,000
EQUITY AND LIABILITIES		
Equity		
Capital	1,160	1,756
Retained earnings	340	404
Total equity	1,500	2,160
Non-current liabilities		
Loan	500	–
Current liabilities		
Trade payables	900	1,040
Bank overdraft	–	800
Total current liabilities	900	1,840
Total liabilities	1,400	1,840
Total equity and liabilities	2,900	4,000

Summarized statements of profit and loss					
		Alpha		Omega	
	£m	£m		£m	£m
Revenue		6,000			7,200
Less: Cost of goods sold					
Opening inventory	1,000			1,500	
Add: purchases	4,760			5,916	
	5,760			7,416	
Less: closing inventory	1,200	4,560		1,800	5,616
Gross profit		1,440			1,584
Expenses					
Overhead expenditure		(1,100)			(1,180)
Profit for the year		340			404

Required

a Using ratio analysis, comment on the profitability, efficiency, liquidity and gearing of *both* companies.

b List three limitations of ratio analysis for the purposes of interpreting financial statements.

33.12*

Statement of profit and loss	
	£'000
Revenue	4,230
Cost of sales	(2,560)
Gross profit	1,670
Distribution costs	(470)
Administrative expenses	(380)
Finance costs	(240)
Profit before taxation	580
Income tax	(270)
Profit for the year	310

Blue Light Plc: Statement of financial position	
	£'000
ASSETS	
Non-current assets	4,870
Current assets	
Inventories	480
Trade receivables	270
Bank and cash	320
	1,070
Total assets	5,940
EQUITY AND LIABILITIES	
Equity	
500,000 equity shares of £1 each	500
Retained earnings	1,910
Total equity	2,410
Non-current liabilities	
8% debentures of £100 each	3,000
Total non-current liabilities	3,000
Current liabilities	
Trade payables	260
Current tax payable	270
Total current liabilities	530
Total liabilities	3,530
Total equity and liabilities	5,940

The following is an extract from the published financial statements of Blue Light plc for the year ended 31 March 20X2.

Additional information:

1 The equity shares and debentures are currently quoted on the London Stock Exchange at £5 and £110, respectively.

2 You are required to calculate the ratios that you would include in a report to a prospective investor relating to measures of performance, liquidity, the appraisal of working capital, and return on investment and risk. Comment briefly on the results and the limitations of your analysis.

33.13*

The following is a summary of some of the accounting ratios of two companies in the same industry and of a comparable size for the year ended 30 June 20X2.

	Fish plc	Chips plc
Dividend yield	4%	7%
Dividend cover	3.6	2.1
Earnings per share	17p	23p
P/E ratio	14	8
Return on equity	22%	27%
Return on capital employed	18%	15%
Profit margin	20%	25%
Asset turnover ratio	0.9	0.6
Gearing ratio	28%	76%

Required

Write a report to a prospective investor on the comparative return on investment, risk and performance of these two companies.

33.14*

	20X1	20X2
Working capital ratio	1.5	1.7
Liquidity ratio	1.1	0.8
Inventory turnover	6.3	5.9
Trade receivables' ratio	52 days	63 days
Trade payables' ratio	71 days	78 days

Required

Write a report to one of the company's major shareholders on the change in its liquidity and working capital position over the year ended 30 April 20X2.

33.15

Two retailers show the following financial statements for the year to 31 December 20X2.

Statements of financial position as at 31 December 20X2		
	A. Ltd	B. Ltd
ASSETS	£'000	£'000
Non-current assets		
Premises	5,000	8,000
Fixtures	500	1,000
	5,500	9,000
Current assets		
Inventory	800	900
Trade receivables	50	60
Bank	330	720
	1,180	1,680
Total assets	6,680	10,680
EQUITY AND LIABILITIES		
Equity		
Equity shares of £1	3,000	2,000
Retained earnings	2,030	2,700
Total equity	5,030	4,700
Non-current liabilities		
Long-term loans	800	5,000
Total non-current liabilities	800	5,000
Current liabilities	850	980
Total liabilities	1,650	5,980
Total equity and liabilities	6,680	10,680

Statements of profit and loss for the year ended 31 December 20X2		
	£'000	£'000
Revenue	13,360	16,020
Cost of sales	(8,685)	(10,090)
Gross profit	4,675	5,930
Distribution	(2,300)	(2,870)
Administration	(1,375)	(1,670)
Finance costs	(65)	(400)
Profit for the year	935	990

Additional information

1 A. Ltd paid a dividend of £300,000 during the year.

2 B. Ltd paid a dividend of £400,000 during the year.

Required

a Compute for each of the two companies:

  i one ratio relevant to an assessment of liquidity;

  ii one ratio relevant to an assessment of gearing;

  iii three ratios relevant to an assessment of profitability and performance.

b Summarize briefly the overall strengths and weaknesses of Company A, using each of the ratios you have computed.

(JMB)

33.16

The outline statements of financial position of the Nantred Trading Co. Ltd were as shown below:

Statements of financial position as at 30 September		
ASSETS	20X1	20X2
Non-current assets	£	£
Premises	40,000	98,000
Plant and equipment	65,000	162,000
	105,000	260,000
Current assets		
Inventory	31,200	95,300
Trade receivables	19,700	30,700
Bank and cash	15,600	26,500
	66,500	152,500
Total assets	171,500	412,500
EQUITY AND LIABILITIES		
Equity		
Equity share capital	100,000	200,000
Retained earnings	36,200	43,600
Total equity	136,200	243,600
Non-current liabilities		
7% debentures	–	100,000
Total non-current liabilities	–	100,000
Current liabilities		
Trade payables	23,900	55,800
Current tax payable	11,400	13,100
Total current liabilities	35,300	68,900
Total liabilities	35,300	168,900
Total equity and liabilities	171,500	412,500

Additional information

The only other information available is that the revenue for the years ended 30 September 20X1 and 20X2 was £202,900 and £490,700, respectively, and that on 30 September 20X0 reserves were £26,100.

Required

a Calculate, for each of the two years, six suitable ratios to highlight the financial stability, liquidity and profitability of the company.

b Comment on the situation revealed by the figures you have calculated in your answer to (a) above.

(ACCA)

33.17

You are given below, in draft form, the financial statements of Algernon Ltd for 20X2 and 20X3. They are not in publishable format.

Statements of financial position						
			20X2			20X3
ASSETS	Cost	Depn	Net	Cost	Depn	Net
	£	£	£	£	£	£
Plant	10,000	4,000	6,000	11,000	5,000	6,000
Building	50,000	10,000	40,000	90,000	11,000	79,000
	60,000	14,000	46,000	101,000	16,000	85,000
Financial assets			50,000			80,000
Land			43,000			63,000
Inventory			55,000			65,000
Trade receivables			40,000			50,000
Bank			3,000			–
Total assets			237,000			343,000
EQUITY AND LIABILITIES						
Equity shares £1 each			40,000			50,000
Share premium			12,000			14,000
Revaluation reserve			–			20,000
Retained earnings			45,000			45,000
10% debentures			100,000			150,000
Trade payables			40,000			60,000
Bank			–			4,000
			237,000			343,000

Statements of profit and loss		
	20X2	20X3
	£	£
Sales revenue	200,000	200,000
Cost of sales	(100,000)	(120,000)
Gross profit	100,000	80,000
Expenses	(60,000)	(60,000)
Profit for the year	40,000	20,000

Required

a Calculate for Algernon Ltd, for 20X2 and 20X3, the following ratios:

i   return on capital employed;

ii   return on owners' equity (return on shareholders' funds);

iii trade receivables' turnover;

iv   trade payables' turnover;

v   current ratio;

vi   quick assets (acid test) ratio;

vii gross profit percentage;

viii net profit percentage;

ix   dividend cover;

x   gearing ratio.

b Using the summarized financial statements given, and the ratios you have just prepared, comment on the position, progress and direction of Algernon Ltd.

(ACCA adapted)

33.18

Delta Ltd is an old-established light engineering company. The key performance data for the company between 20W9 and 20X3 are given below.

	20W9	20X0	20X1	20X2	20X3
Profit before interest/revenue (%)	3.6	0.5	0.6	8.1	9.8
Revenue/non-current assets (times)	4.6	3.4	3.3	3.5	3.7
Revenue/net current assets (times)	2.2	2.5	2.9	3.7	5.1
Cost of sales/inventory (times)	1.9	2.0	2.4	2.7	2.9
Trade receivables/ave. days sales (days)	80.0	77.0	75.0	67.0	64.0
Trade payables/ave. days sales (days)	58.0	57.0	61.0	64.0	71.0
Cost of sales/revenue (%)	71.0	73.7	75.0	71.0	69.5
Selling and distribution/revenue (%)	19.0	18.7	18.5	16.0	15.6
Administrative/revenue (%)	6.4	7.1	5.9	4.9	5.1
Current ratio	4.9	2.8	3.3	2.1	1.8

Required

Examine the above data and write a report to the directors of Delta Ltd analysing the performance of the company between 20W9 and 20X3.

(JMB)

ADVANCED

33.19

Aragon (a bank) has recently received a request for a term loan from one of its customers, Valencia plc, a company listed on the Alternative Investment Market of the London Stock Exchange. Valencia plc's directors have requested a further £6 million (five-year floating rate) term loan at an initial interest rate of 12 per cent per annum, in order to purchase new equipment. The equipment will not materially change the company's current average percentage return on investment. Valencia plc's turnover increased by 9 per cent during the last financial year. Prior to receiving the request, the regional commercial manager of Aragon had conducted a review of Valencia plc's financial position, and had decided to ask Valencia plc's management to reduce the company overdraft by 25 per cent within the next six months.

Summarized financial statements for Valencia plc are as follows:

Statements of financial position		
	20X2	**20X1**
ASSETS	**£'000**	**£'000**
Non-current assets		
Property, plant and equipment	16,060	14,380
Current assets		
Inventories	31,640	21,860
Trade receivables	24,220	17,340
Investment	8,760	10,060
Cash and cash equivalents	1,700	960
	66,320	50,220
Total assets	82,380	64,600
EQUITY AND LIABILITIES		
Equity		
Share capital	3,800	3,800
Retained earnings	16,900	13,500
Total equity	20,700	17,300
Non-current liabilities		
Long-term borrowings	6,000	—
Debentures	16,000	16,000
Total non-current liabilities	22,000	16,000
Current liabilities		
Overdraft	16,340	13,220
Trade and other payables	20,920	15,280
Current taxation	2,420	2,800
Total current liabilities	39,680	31,300
Total liabilities	61,680	47,300
Total equity and liabilities	82,380	64,600

Extract information from the statement of profit and loss of Valencia plc

	20X2
	£'000
Revenue	99,360
Profit before interest and taxation	10,760
Finance costs	(3,840)
Profit before tax	6,920
Income tax expense	(2,420)
Profit for the period	4,500
Dividend paid in the year	1,100

The company's debentures are currently trading at £96.50 and equity 10p shares at £1.50.

Comparative ratio information for Valencia plc's industry (averages)

	20X2
Share price	£51.20
Dividend yield	2.5%
Dividend payout ratio	50%
Gross asset turnover	1.4 times
Earnings per share	17.8 pence
Gearing	52.4%
Acid test	1 : 1
Interest cover	4 times
Return on revenue (PBIT)	9%
Return on investment	16.5%

Required

a You are a consultant for Aragon. You are required to produce a reasoned case explaining why the bank should request a 25 per cent reduction in the company's overdraft.

b You are a consultant for Valencia plc:

i Prepare a reasoned case to present to Aragon in support of the new term loan.

ii Make recommendations to the board of Valencia plc in respect of how you think the company's financial position might be improved.

Note: (Clearly state any assumptions made. All assumptions must relate to all parts of the question).

33.20

The directors of Atono plc were informed at a golf outing by fellow directors that it is more valuable to have debt in a company's capital structure than equity, as debt is cheaper than equity. Atono plc currently has no debt in its capital structure, though is considering borrowing funds, which it will use to buy back the more expensive equity capital. The capital structure of Atono plc is as follows:

	Current £'000	Suggested £'000
Assets	10,000	10,000
Equity and reserves	10,000	5,000
Long-term debt	–	5,000
Total equity and liabilities	10,000	10,000
Shares outstanding	500,000	250,000

Additional information:

1 The company's equity shares are currently trading at £20 each, and it is assumed that this value does not change when the suggested capital structure change takes place.

2 The long-term debt attracts an interest rate of 8 per cent.

3 Taxation is 30 per cent.

Required

Calculate the gearing ratio for Atono plc under both scenarios.

33.21

Using the information provided in 33.20, assume the company faces three differing external environment scenarios: boom; steady state; and recession. Each scenario has different income potentials: if there is a boom economy, then earnings before interest and taxation (EBIT) of £1 million are expected; if the economy stays steady, EBIT are expected to remain at £660,000; whereas if the economy goes into recession, EBIT are expected to fall to £450,000.

Required

Calculate the impact of the change in gearing on the *return on equity* and the *earnings per share* for each scenario.

33.22

The following are the summarized financial statements of Ingrid Ltd and Epona Ltd, two firms that operate in identical industries.

Summarized statements of profit and loss		
	Ingrid Ltd	Epona Ltd
	£'000	£'000
Sales revenue	6,000	7,200
Cost of goods sold	(4,560)	(5,616)
Gross profit	1,440	1,584
Overhead expenditure (including interest)	(1,140)	(1,260)
Profit for the year	300	324

Summarized statements of financial position		
ASSETS		
Non-current assets	790	1,000
Current assets		
Inventories	1,200	1,800
Trade receivables	720	1,200
Bank	190	–
	2,110	3,000
Total assets	2,900	4,000
EQUITY AND LIABILITIES		
Equity		
Share capital and retained earnings	1,500	2,160
Non-current liabilities		
8% long-term loan	500	–
Current liabilities		
Trade payables	900	1,040
Bank overdraft	–	800
Total current liabilities	900	1,840
Total liabilities	1,400	1,840
Total equity and liabilities	2,900	4,000

Note: The rate of interest on Epona's overdraft is 10 per cent per annum.

Required

a Calculate three ratios for each company showing profitability and three showing liquidity.

b Discuss three reasons why a potential investor would choose Ingrid Ltd.

c Identify three further pieces of information necessary before making the recommendation in (b) above.

References

Altman, E.A. (1968) Financial ratios, discriminant analysis and the prediction of corporate bankruptcy, *Journal of Finance* (September), 589–609.

International Accounting Standards Board (2010) *IAS 33 – Earnings Per Share* (IASB).

Dambolena, I.G. and Khoury, S.J. (1980) 'Ratio Stability and Corporate Failure', *Journal of Finance*, 35(4), 1017–1026.

Ding, A. (2007, July) 'Early discovery of individual firm insolvency', *IMA Journal of Management Mathematics*, 18(3), 269–295.

Ohlson, J.A. (1980) 'Financial Ratios and the Probabilistic Prediction of Bankruptcy', *Journal of Accounting Research*, 18(1), 109–131.

Taffler, R.J. (1982) 'Forecasting company failure in the UK using discriminant analysis and financial ratio data', *Journal of the Royal Statistical Society*, 145, Part 3.

When you have read this chapter, log on to the Online Learning Centre for *Introduction to Financial Accounting* at www.mcgraw-hill.co.uk/textbooks/thomas, where you will find multiple choice quizzes, case studies, a glossary and mock exams.

Case studies

Case study 1

The following case study shows how to track entries from the book of original entries right through to the preparation of final financial statements for a sole trader. Details and instructions are given on how to complete the relevant sections for Part 2, 'Double-entry Bookkeeping' and for Part 3 'Preparing Final Financial Statements for Sole Traders'.

Trading details and supporting documentation

Mr O'Donnell, a sole trader, has owned and operated an antique furniture store for a number of years. He specializes in the purchase and sale of antique furniture from different countries and deals with a small number of reputable suppliers and reliable customers.

You have been employed by Mr O'Donnell as a qualified accountant to maintain his accounts and prepare his financial statements. Following discussions with Mr O'Donnell, from which he believes he has supplied you with all the necessary details, and after obtaining a copy of all relevant documentation, you have established an opening trial balance at the start of the financial year 1 October 20X1. Furthermore, you identify all his business transactions for the year ended 30 September 20X2. You also ascertain that VAT of 25 per cent applies to the sale, purchase and return of goods. In all other respects VAT can be ignored. VAT and PAYE returns are submitted on an annual basis and are paid by direct debit every December.

O'Donnell's Opening Trial Balance as at 1 October 20X1	Debit	Credit
	£	£
Non-current assets		
Delivery vans (2)	26,000	
Accumulated depreciation on delivery vans		11,500
Fittings	12,000	
Accumulated depreciation on fittings		2,000
Current assets		
Inventories	44,000	
Trade receivables (Murphy £7,000; Foley £7,000)	14,000	
Cash at bank		1,750
Petty cash	130	
Current liabilities		
Trade payables (Cronin £11,000; Broderick £4,000)		15,000
VAT		1,000
PAYE		100
Equity		
Capital		67,150
Drawings		
Selling and distribution expenses		
Motor delivery expenses	600	
Administration expenses		
Postage, stationery and telephone		130
Light and heat		100
Rent	2,000	
	98,730	98,730

The transactions that occurred during the year to 30 September 20X2 are listed below:

October:

2 Sold goods on credit to Murphy for £5,000, invoice no. 580.

6 Purchases goods on credit from Cronin for £3,750.

11 Paid £7 for stationery from petty cash.

23 Received and lodged to bank all money outstanding from Foley (no discount allowed).

November:

4 Returned £1,250 worth of goods purchased from Cronin.

11 Sold goods on credit to Foley for £5,000, invoice no. 581.

19 Paid cheques no. 23985, £45, for electricity and no. 23986, £175, for petty cash.

24 Purchased goods on credit from Broderick for £1,250.

December:

1 Murphy returned goods worth £1,000 and credit note 14 was issued to him.

12 Received and lodged cheque for £3,000 from Murphy and allowed him discount of £100.

19 Paid cheque no. 23987 in the amount of £2,000 to Cronin and received £200 discount.

24 Withdrew £2,500 for personal use.

27 Paid VAT and PAYE outstanding from previous year by direct debit.

30 Paid motor insurance, £1,200 by cheque no. 23988 to cover the following six months.

31 Paid from petty cash: £7 postage; £11 motor repairs; £50 advertising.

January:

7 Sold goods on credit to Foley for £400, invoice no. 582, and to Doolan for £4,000, invoice no. 583.

8 Lodged cash sales of £1,250.

9 Purchased goods on credit for £1,500 from Broderick.

22 Foley returned goods worth £1,000 so credit note 15 was issued to him.

23 Sent cheque no. 23989 for £100 to Foley to cover the cost of returning goods.

30 Paid £6,000 by cheque no. 23990, being rent due for 12 months from 1 February 20X2.

February:

1 Received and lodged all money due from Foley after allowing him discount of £400.

7 Sold goods to Doolan for £3,000, invoice no. 584; paid cheque no. 23991 worth £73 for motor expenses.

17 Purchased goods from Cronin on credit, £7,200.

22 Returned goods to Cronin to the value of £3,000.

30 Paid from petty cash: £12 postage; £20 stationery; £20 petrol.

March:

3 Sold goods on credit to Doyle to the value of £5,000, invoice no. 585.

7 Sold goods on credit to O'Haire, £11,000, invoice no. 586.

11 Paid cheque no. 23992 worth £2,700 to Getaway Travel for a family holiday.

12 Withdrew £3,000 from bank for use on holiday.

April:

7 Returned to find that Doyle was in financial difficulties and his accountant has temporarily suspended all payment. However, you decided to take no action yet.

8 Paid cheque no. 23993 to Cronin to the amount of £3,200 and received a discount of £200.

9 Paid motor tax, £133 by cheque no. 23994.

10 Paid cheque no. 23995 to the value of £400 to cover repairs to delivery van.

17 Sold goods on credit to Brennan for £7,000, invoice no. 587.

19 Purchased goods on credit from Cronin, £3,000.

25 Paid Cronin £5,000 (cheque no. 23996) and received a discount of £200.

31 Paid from petty cash: advertising £22; postage £12; petrol £44.

May:

 7 Sold goods to Kelly on credit for £4,000, invoice no. 588.

10 Received £400 unexpectedly from Doyle's accountants, lodged money immediately.

17 Kelly returned damaged goods worth £2,000. Credit note 16 was issued to him.

22 Purchased goods from Sabura on credit worth £2,000.

23 Received and lodged cheques from Brennan in full settlement after allowing for a discount of £100.

31 Paid from petty cash: stationery £5; motor expenses £81; postage £12.

June:

 2 Sold goods on credit to O'Haire worth £5,000, invoice no. 589.

 3 Purchased goods on credit from Broderick to the value of £3,000.

 9 Purchased goods from Cronin on credit worth £1,750.

17 Lodged cash sales worth £400.

22 Paid Broderick the full amount due less discount £350 (cheque no. 23997).

29 Withdrew £2,000 for personal use. O'Donnell also received letter from bank dated 28 June stating that his bank account was seriously overdrawn and that if money was not lodged soon to reduce it, serious action would have to be taken.

July:

 2 Sold goods on credit to O'Haire for £7,000, invoice no. 590.

 3 Paid cheque no. 23998 to the amount of £300 to petty cash.

11 O'Haire returned goods of £1,000. Credit note 17 was issued.

14 O'Haire settled account in full, less agreed discount of £450. Proceeds lodged.

19 Sold goods on credit to Doolan for £11,000, invoice no. 591.

25 Withdrew £3,000 for personal use.

30 Paid motor insurance of £1,200 by cheque no. 23999 to cover following three months.

August:

 3 Purchased goods on credit from Cronin for £9,000.

 7 Returned goods worth £2,000 to Cronin. Credit note N274 received.

11 Cash sales of £500 lodged.

20 Paid telephone bill of £432 by cheque no. 24000.

20 Sold goods to O'Haire on credit for £500, invoice no. 592.

21 Sold goods on credit to Doolan worth £4,000, invoice no. 593.

26 Paid Cronin £10,000 on account, cheque no. 24001. Discount received £100.

29 Received and lodged £12,000 from Doolan. Discount allowed £500.

30 Doolan returned goods in the amount of £100. Credit note 18 issued.

September:

1 Purchased goods on credit from Slatery worth £5,000.

3 Sold goods on credit to O'Haire for £3,000, invoice no. 594.

6 Received and lodged balance due from O'Haire, less an agreed discount of £100.

7 Paid electricity bill of £298 by cheque no. 24002.

9 Sold goods to Murphy on credit worth £2,000, invoice no. 595 and to Doolan for £3,000, invoice no. 596.

13 Lodged cash sales worth £490.

16 Sold goods to O'Sullivan on credit for £3,000, invoice no. 597.

19 Received and lodged £2,500 from O'Sullivan. Discount allowed £200.

20 Received and lodged £1,000 from Murphy. Discount allowed £50.

21 Paid Cronin by cheque no. 24003 to the amount of £4,000. Discount received £200.

22 Paid Slatery £2,500 by cheque no. 24004. Discount received £100. Cash sales £2,450 lodged by Credit Transfer.

23 Paid Sergi, a temporary employee, to the amount of £1,300 by cheque no. 24005.

24 Withdrew £7,000 for personal use.

30 Paid from petty cash: stationery £42; postage £35; petrol £88; delivery expenses £94.

31 Received and lodged £3,500 from J. Cunningham to whom you sold a delivery van.

Mr O'Donnell's bank, First Time Bank, have supplied you with the following bank statement:

Account Number: 809234

Customer: O'Donnell's Furniture, New Street, Ballydune, Cork

Statement No 9

Date	Details	Debit	Credit	Balance
20X1/20X2		£	£	dr = overdrawn
1 Oct	Balance			1,750 dr
23 Oct	Lodgement		7,000	5,250 cr
22 Nov	Cheque no 23985	45		5,205 cr
25 Nov	Cheque no 23986	175		5,030 cr
12 Dec	Lodgement		3,000	8,030 cr
23 Dec	Cheque no 23987	2,000		6,030 cr
24 Dec	Withdrawal	2,500		3,530 cr
27 Dec	Direct debit 7422986	1,000		2,530 cr
27 Dec	Direct debit 7422987	100		2,430 cr
31 Dec	Cheque no 23988	1,200		1,230 cr
31 Dec	Interest and charges	90		1,140 cr
8 Jan	Lodgement		1,250	2,390 cr
26 Jan	Cheque no 23989	100		2,290 cr
1 Feb	Lodgement		4,000	6,290 cr
6 Feb	Cheque no 23990	6,000		290 cr
12 Mar	Withdrawal	3,000		2,710 dr
20 Mar	Cheque no 23992	2,700		5,410 dr
21 Mar	Cheque no 23991	73		5,483 dr
12 Apr	Cheque no 23994	133		5,616 dr
15 Apr	Cheque no 23995	400		6,016 dr
28 Apr	Cheque no 23996	5,000		11,016 dr
10 May	Lodgement		400	10,616 dr
23 May	Lodgement		6,900	3,716 dr
17 June	Lodgement		400	3,316 dr
17 June	Cheque no 23993	3,200		6,516 dr
28 June	Cheque no 23997	9,400		15,916 dr
29 June	Withdrawal	2,000		17,916 dr
30 June	Interest and charges	1,185		19,101 dr
3 July	Cheque no 23998	300		19,401 dr
14 July	Lodgement		21,550	2,149 cr
25 July	Withdrawal	3,000		851 dr
11 Aug	Lodgement		500	351 dr
25 Aug	Cheque no 24000	432		783 dr
26 Aug	Lodgement		12,000	11,217 cr
30 Aug	Cheque no 24001	10,000		1,217 cr
6 Sep	Lodgement		3,400	4,617 cr
13 Sep	Lodgement		490	5,107 cr
19 Sep	Lodgement		2,500	7,607 cr
20 Sep	Lodgement		1,000	8,607 cr
23 Sep	Cheque no 24004	2,500		6,107 cr
24 Sep	Cheque no 24005	1,300		4,807 cr
24 Sep	Withdrawal	7,000		2,193 dr
30 Sep	Lodgement		3,500	1,307 cr

Required

First, prepare the books of original entry; that is, journals (sales, sales returns, purchases and purchases returns), cheque payments book, cash receipts book and petty cash book. This requires that you make one entry in these books for each transaction listed above.

Next, you must complete the sales and purchases ledgers. To do this you extract the relevant information from the books of original entry, which you have just completed. Include the opening balances for individual credit customers and credit suppliers as shown in the trial balance at 1 October 20X1. You should also extract trade receivables and trade payables schedules. These will be used later to check control account balances.

The next stage is writing up the nominal ledger. Remember to enter the opening balances for the individual relevant ledger accounts shown in the trial balance at 1 October 20X1. You complete this stage by preparing a bank reconciliation statement at 30 September 20X2.

At this point you may extract a preliminary trial balance by extracting balances from the nominal ledger accounts you have just completed. Remember to enter the individual opening balances for the relevant accounts shown in the trial balance at 1 October 20X1.

Note: Case study 2: Preparing final financial statements is a continuation from this point.

(Sandra Brosnan, adapted)

Case study 2

Using the preliminary trial balance you extracted in Case study 1, and taking account of the following post trial balance adjustments, you are required to prepare the statement of profit and loss and statement of financial position for Mr O'Donnell for the year ended 30 September 20X2.

Post-trial balance adjustments:

1 Closing inventory is valued at £35,000.

2 On 30 September 20X2 Mr O'Donnell decided to dispose of one of his vans. This had been acquired in 20W9 at a cost of £10,000 and had been depreciated at a rate of 25 per cent per annum on cost. Sale proceeds amounted to £3,500 and this was lodged by Mr O'Donnell into his account in First Time Bank on 30 September. No other entry relating to this transaction has been made in the books.

3 Mr O'Donnell's depreciation policy is as follows: Depreciation is to be charged on delivery vans at 25 per cent on cost and on fittings at 10 per cent using the reducing balance method. Depreciation is not to be charged in the year of disposal.

4 Light and heat worth £120 and telephone worth £215 are outstanding at the year end.

5 You have decided to charge Mr O'Donnell £2,000 for your accounting services.

6 There is PAYE of £256 outstanding in respect of Sergi that must be forwarded to the tax authorities.

7 The rent payment made on 30 January was in respect of the subsequent 12 months. The motor insurance payment made on 30 July related to the subsequent three months.

8 After discussing matters with Mr O'Donnell, you decide that there is little likelihood of any further payments from Doyle and that the remaining balance should be written off as a bad debt.

9 In the light of the experience with Doyle, you have advised Mr O'Donnell that it would be prudent to create a provision for doubtful debts. He has agreed that a provision equal to 6 per cent of closing trade receivables should be established.

Note: A statement of cash flows may also be requested here.

(Sandra Brosnan, adapted)

Case study 3

This case study tests your understanding of the incomplete records topic. In order to fully answer the questions in the case study, it is necessary to draw upon earlier topics including accruals and prepayments, depreciation, doubtful debts and the purpose of financial statements.

Wendy set up the printing shop business on 2 January 20X2. She is new to running a business, and so has only been able to maintain some basic records, including those of her cash transactions. Wendy has hired you for an agreed fee of £1,000 to prepare her end of year financial statements and to explain some accounting principles that are puzzling her. The agreed fee will be paid after you have completed the accountancy work. She has provided you with the following letter that contains information about her business activities during the year.

Dear Accounting Expert,   31 January 20X3

Thank you very much for agreeing to act as my accountant and also for agreeing to deal with some rather puzzling points which, I have to confess, have been making my brain hurt! I started the printing shop business with just £2,000 in cash, which I deposited in the business bank account on 2 January of this year. All cash transactions have gone through the business bank account. I was fortunate in obtaining a loan of £28,000, from the Sunnydale Bank, on 2 January. I immediately used the loan to purchase some essential desktop printing equipment for £20,000 in cash. I used the remainder of the loan to purchase a van, to be used for delivering printing orders to clients, for £8,000 in cash. I also purchased on 2 January a stock of paper on good credit terms for £30,000. An experienced businesswoman friend of mine has explained that I need to depreciate both my printing equipment and the van. I do not understand this point at all, as I paid for both of the items in cash – surely that is the only cost that matters, as I have paid for both the assets in full? Anyway, my friend tells me that it is standard practice in my line of business to depreciate the printing equipment evenly over its six-year life, and to depreciate the van at 25 per cent on the reducing balance basis. I am told that the printing equipment has a scrap value of £2,000. I am not clear as to what all of this advice on depreciation means, but I am sure that you will be able to explain it and work it all out for me.

During the year, I paid an assistant a salary of £10,000, but I still owe her £1,000 for the overtime which she kindly agreed to work for me in December 20X2. I have also drawn £25,000 in cash for myself out of the business bank account over the year. I obtained premises to rent at the start of the year, and paid rent of £12,000 in advance in cash on 2 January to cover me up to the end of June 20X3. There have been several van expenses which have arisen during the year and have been paid in cash. Petrol expenses amounted to £1,500. Also, there were van repairs which totalled £500 and additional payments for tax and insurance which came to £1,000. Electricity expenses paid in cash during the year amounted to £1,000. This figure for electricity included the last bill for £300 for three months: it covered the months of November and December 20X2 as well as the month of January 20X3. Business rates of £9,600 were paid in cash in advance on 1 April 20X2, and covered the 12 months up to 31 March 20X3. The council kindly agreed not to charge me rates for the first three months of 20X2.

At the end of the year, I was advised by friends to carry out a comprehensive stock-take for the business. This revealed that I had an inventory of paper worth £40,000. I also found that I had spent £60,000 in cash on purchases of paper during the year, and also owed credit suppliers £50,000 for purchases of paper during the year. I have received cash from sales of printing work of £120,000 during 20X2. I also discovered that I had credit customers who owed me £40,000 for printing work, which I had carried out for them during the year. I also appear to have a problem credit customer. The bank has informed me that a cheque from one credit customer, Shark Enterprises, which owes me £4,000, has 'bounced' many times and so unfortunately I am not likely to obtain any money from that firm now or in the future. The bank manager has also suggested that I should make a provision of 10 per cent of the remaining trade receivables in order to allow for possible problems with people who do not settle their debts in future. I am not clear as to how this might be done, but hope that this suggestion makes sense to you when you put all this business information together.

During the year, as you may want to know, I took a modest amount of paper for my own use out of the business. This paper was worth £1,000. Also, I was able to pay the total interest of £3,000 which was due on the loan in cash, and was able to repay £2,000 of the loan to the Sunnydale Bank.

I hope that you can make sense of all the information that I have provided for you above.

I understand that you can prepare some financial statements for me, although I am not really sure if it is necessary to do this. If I can aim just to end up with a cash surplus at the end of the year, then is that not sufficient to show everyone that the business is doing well?

Best wishes

Yours sincerely

Wendy

Required

1 Draw up a statement of profit and loss for Wendy's Printing Shop for the year ended 31 December 20X2 and a statement of financial position as at that date. Include in your workings both the depreciation policies suggested by Wendy's friend and the treatment of bad and doubtful debts suggested by her bank manager.

2 Explain to Wendy the purpose and importance of depreciating non-current assets.

3 Explain to Wendy the purpose and importance of making a provision for doubtful debts.

4 Compare the cash position of Wendy's business at the end of the year with the performance shown by the statement of profit and loss. Explain the difference between the two, and how a statement of profit and loss and a statement of financial position can be useful to Wendy.

(Robert Jupe, adapted)

Case study 4

Mr O'Donnell, originally a sole trader, had owned and operated an antique furniture store in Cork for a number of years. He specialized in the purchase and sale of antique furniture from different countries and dealt with a small number of reputable suppliers and reliable customers. However, due to growing demand and growing opportunities Mr O'Donnell decided two years ago to register as a private limited company named Antique Furniture Supplies Ltd to facilitate expansion into a growing international market and secured a number of interested investors to provide the necessary capital. Antique Furniture Supplies Ltd filed all the necessary documentation (Memorandum of Association and Articles of Association) with the Registrar of Companies in accordance with the Companies Act 2006. Antique Furniture Supplies Ltd maintained all its existing customer base and suppliers but has also attracted a number of large customers that have enabled the company to be quite successful.

You have been employed by Antique Furniture Supplies Ltd, as a qualified accountant, to maintain its company financial statements and prepare the necessary financial statements. Following discussions with Antique Furniture Supplies Ltd, and after obtaining a copy of all relevant documentation, you have established an opening trial balance at the start of the financial year, 1 October 20X1. Furthermore, you identify all his business transactions for the year ended 30 September 20X2. You also ascertain that VAT of 25 per cent applies to the sale, purchase and return of goods. In all other respects VAT can be ignored. VAT returns are submitted on an annual basis and are paid by direct debit every December.

Antique Furniture Supplies Ltd		
Opening trial balance as at 1 October 20X1		
	Debit £	Credit £
Non-current assets		
Delivery vans	42,000	
Accumulated depreciation on delivery vans		11,500
Fittings	16,000	
Accumulated depreciation on fittings		2,000
Premises	200,000	
Accumulated depreciation		40,000
Current assets		
Inventories	54,000	
Trade receivables (Murphy £12,000; Foley £12,000)	24,000	
Cash at bank	35,550	
Petty cash	130	
Current liabilities		
Trade payables (Cronin £11,000; Broderick £4,000)		15,000
VAT		2,400
Income tax		10,000
Equity		
Share capital (200,000 £1 shares)		200,000
Share premium	20,000	
Retained earnings 1 October 20X0		53,150
10 per cent long-term loan		60,000
Selling and distribution expenses		
Motor delivery expenses	600	
Administration expenses		
Postage, stationery and telephone		130
Light and heat		100
Rent	2,000	
	394,280	394,280

The transactions that occurred during the year to 30 September 20X2 are listed below:

October:

2 Sold goods on credit to Murphy for £5,000.

5 Sold goods on credit to Hulgerstein for £20,000.

6 Purchased goods on credit from Cronin for £53,750.

11 Paid £70 for stationery from petty cash.

23 Received and lodged to bank all money outstanding from Foley (no discount allowed).

30 Paid employee wages of £8,000 by direct debit.

November:

4 Returned £10,250 worth of goods purchased from Cronin.

11 Sold goods on credit to Foley for £5,000.

12 Sold goods on credit to Williams for £15,000.

19 Paid cheques no. 23985 for light and heat (£1,450) and no 23986 for petty cash £600.

24 Purchased goods on credit from Broderick for £21,250.

30 Paid employee wages of £8,000 by direct debit.

December:

1 Murphy returned goods in the amount of £1,000 and credit note 14 was issued to him.

2 Received and lodged £19,000 from Hulgerstein after allowing him a 5 per cent discount.

12 Received and lodged cheque in amount of £13,000 from Murphy and allowed him a discount of £650.

19 Paid cheque no. 23987 in amount of £42,000 to Cronin and received £1,500 discount.

24 Received £13,000 from Williams and allowed him a discount of £750.

27 Paid VAT outstanding from previous year by direct debit.

30 Paid motor insurance, £2,400 by cheque no 23988 to cover the following six months.

30 Paid employee wages of £8,000 by direct debit.

31 Paid from petty cash: £27 postage; £350 stationery.

January:

7 Sold goods on credit to Foley for £4,000 and to Doolan for £4,000.

8 Lodged cash sales of £24,500.

9 Purchased goods on credit for £31,500 from Broderick.

22 Foley returned goods worth £1,000 so credit note 15 was issued to him.

26 Murphy lodged the amount outstanding on his account.

30 Paid £8,000 by cheque no. 23989, being rent due for 12 months from 1 February 20X0.

30 Paid employee wages of £8,000 by direct debit.

February:

1　Received and lodged all money due from Foley after allowing him discount of £400.

7　Sold goods to Doolan for £3,000; paid cheque no. 23990 worth £5,300 for motor expenses.

10　Sold goods on credit for £20,000 to Williams.

17　Purchased goods from Cronin on credit, £37,500.

22　Returned goods to Cronin to the value of £3,000.

28　Paid from petty cash: £80 postage; £200 stationery.

28　Paid employee wages of £8,000 by direct debit.

March:

3　Sold goods on credit to Doyle to the value of £8,000.

7　Sold goods on credit to O'Haire, £11,000.

8　Paid £36,750 to Broderick for goods previously purchased (cheque no. 23991).

10　Purchased goods on credit for £21,000 from Broderick.

11　Paid cheque no. 23992 to Cronin to the amount of £33,200 and received a discount of £2,000.

16　Paid for light and heat to the amount of £4,350 with cheque no. 23993.

25　Williams lodged £18,000 into bank account.

26　Paid £3,500 for advertising with cheque no. 23994.

30　Paid employee wages of £8,000 by direct debit.

30　Received a letter from Doyle's accountant to state that Doyle is in financial difficulty and probably will not be able to settle his debt.

April:

7　Paid motor tax, £1,000 by cheque no. 23995.

8　Paid cheque no. 23996 to the value of £900 to cover repairs to delivery van.

17　Sold goods on credit to Brennan for £17,000.

19　Purchased goods on credit from Cronin, £13,000.

20　Sold goods worth £25,000 to Hulgerstein on credit.

25　Paid Cronin £15,000 (cheque no. 23997) and received a discount of £800.

28　Sold a further £50,000 worth of goods on credit to Williams.

30　Received a letter from your bank stating that the company has overdrawn beyond its agreed credit limits and that if the overdraft was not reduced serious action will have to be taken.

30　Paid employee wages of £8,000 by direct debit.

30　Paid £12 from petty cash for postage.

May:

7　Sold goods to Kelly on credit for £4,000.

12　Received £1,000 unexpectedly from Doyle's accountants, lodged money immediately.

17 Kelly returned damaged goods in the amount of £2,000.

19 Hulgerstein paid £20,000 on his account and was allowed a discount of £500.

22 Purchased goods from Sabura on credit worth £2,000.

23 Received and lodged cheques from Brennan in full settlement after allowing for a discount of £100.

30 Paid employee wages of £8,000 by direct debit.

31 Paid from petty cash: stationery £50; postage £12.

June:

2 Sold goods on credit to O'Haire worth £25,000.

3 Purchased goods on credit from Broderick to the value of £13,000.

9 Purchased goods from Cronin on credit worth £15,750.

17 Lodged cash sales worth £14,000.

20 Credit sale of £10,000 to Hulgerstein.

22 Paid Broderick £53,650 due, less discount £350 (cheque no. 23998).

29 Paid motor and delivery expenses of £3,500 (cheque no. 23999)

30 Williams settled his account (no discount allowed).

30 Paid employee wages of £8,000 by direct debit.

July:

2 Sold goods on credit to O'Haire for £17,000.

3 Paid cheque no. 24000 to the amount of £300 to petty cash.

13 O'Haire returned goods of £1,000.

14 O'Haire settled account in full, less agreed discount of £450. Proceeds lodged.

19 Sold goods on credit to Doolan for £11,000.

24 Hulgerstein settled his account (discount allowed of £450).

30 Paid employee wages of £8,000 by direct debit.

31 Paid motor insurance of £2,400 by cheque no. 24001 to cover following three months.

August:

3 Purchased goods on credit from Cronin for £19,000.

7 Returned goods worth £6,000 to Cronin.

10 Sold goods on credit to Baralux Ltd to the amount of £50,000.

11 Cash sales of £6,000 lodged.

20 Paid telephone bill of £4,500 by cheque no. 24002.

20 Sold goods to O'Haire on credit for £5,000.

21 Sold goods on credit to Doolan worth £4,000.

26 Paid Cronin £26,000 on account, cheque no. 24003. Discount received £250.

29 Received and lodged £12,000 from Doolan. Discount allowed £500.

30 Doolan returned goods in the amount of £100.

30 Paid employee wages of £8,000 by direct debit.

September:

1 Purchased goods on credit from Slatery worth £20,000.

3 Sold goods on credit to O'Haire for £6,000.

6 Received and lodged balance due from O'Haire, less an agreed discount of £100.

7 Paid light and heat worth £2,528 by cheque no. 24004.

9 Sold goods to Murphy on credit worth £6,000, and to Doolan for £3,000.

13 Lodged cash sales worth £4,900.

14 Baralux Ltd paid £35,000 on its account. Discount allowed £1,000.

16 Sold goods to O'Sullivan on credit for £3,000.

19 Received and lodged £2,500 from O'Sullivan. Discount allowed £200.

20 Received and lodged £4,000 from Murphy. Discount allowed £100.

21 Paid Cronin by cheque no. 24005 to the amount of £9,000.

22 Paid Slatery £2,500 by cheque no. 24006. Discount received £100. Cash sales £2,450 lodged by credit transfer.

23 Purchased goods on credit from Slatery for £26,000.

30 Paid from petty cash: stationery £42; Postage £35.

30 Received and lodged £5,500 from J. Cunningham to whom you sold a delivery van.

30 Paid employee wages of £8,000 by direct debit.

Antique Furniture Supplies Ltd's bank, First Time Bank, have supplied you with the following bank statement:

Account Number: 659289

Customer: Antique Furniture Supplies Ltd, Link Road, Ballydune, Cork.

Statement No 11

Date	Details	Debit	Credit	Balance
20X1/20X2		£	£	dr = overdrawn
1 Oct	Balance			35,550 cr
23 Oct	Lodgement		12,000	47,550 cr
30 Oct	Direct debit 7422984	8,000		39,550 cr
19 Nov	Cheque no 23985	1,450		38,100 cr
19 Nov	Cheque no 23986	600		37,500 cr
30 Nov	Direct debit 7422985	8,000		29,500 cr
2 Dec	Lodgement		19,000	48,500 cr
12 Dec	Lodgement		13,000	61,500 cr
19 Dec	Cheque no 23987	42,000		19,500 cr
24 Dec	Lodgement		13,000	32,500 cr
27 Dec	Direct debit 7422986	2,400		30,100 cr
30 Dec	Cheque no 23988	2,400		27,700 cr
30 Dec	Direct debit 7422987	8,000		19,700 cr
31 Dec	Interest and charges	1,900		17,800 cr
8 Jan	Lodgement		24,500	42,300 cr
27 Jan	Lodgement		2,350	44,650 cr
30 Jan	Cheque no 23989	8,000		36,650 cr
30 Jan	Direct debit 7422988	8,000		28,650 cr
1 Feb	Lodgement		7,600	36,250 cr
8 Feb	Cheque no 23990	5,300		30,950 cr
28 Feb	Direct debit 7422989	8,000		22,950 cr
15 Mar	Cheque no 23992	33,200		10,250 dr
21 Mar	Cheque no 23991	36,750		47,000 dr
25 Mar	Lodgement		18,000	29,000 dr
28 Mar	Cheque no 23994	3,500		32,500 dr
30 Mar	Direct debit 7422990	8,000		40,500 dr
15 Apr	Cheque no 23995	1,000		41,500 dr
16 Apr	Cheque no 23996	900		42,400 dr
28 Apr	Cheque no 23997	15,000		57,400 dr
30 Apr	Direct debit 7422991	8,000		65,400 dr
12 May	Lodgement		1,000	64,400 dr
20 May	Lodgement		20,000	44,400 dr
23 May	Lodgement		16,900	27,500 dr
30 May	Direct debit 7422992	8,000		35,500 dr
17 June	Lodgement		14,000	21,500 dr
17 June	Cheque no 23993	4,530		26,030 dr

Date	Details	Debit	Credit	Balance
28 June	Cheque no 23998	53,650		79,680 dr
29 June	Cheque no 23999	3,500		83,180 dr
30 June	Lodgement		53,250	29,930 dr
30 June	Interest and charges	1,185		31,115 dr
30 June	Direct debit 7422993	8,000		39,115 dr
3 July	Cheque no 24000	300		39,415 dr
14 July	Lodgement		51,550	12,135 cr
25 July	Lodgement		9,550	21,685 cr
30 July	Direct debit 7422994	8,000		13,685 cr
3 Aug	Cheque no 24001	2,400		11,285 cr
11 Aug	Lodgement		6,000	17,285 cr
25 Aug	Cheque no 24002	4,500		12,785 cr
29 Aug	Lodgement		12,000	24,785 cr
30 Aug	Cheque no 24003	26,000		1,215 dr
30 Aug	Direct debit 7422995	8,000		9,215 dr
6 Sep	Lodgement		10,900	1,685 cr
13 Sep	Lodgement		4,900	6,585 cr
15 Sep	Lodgement		35,000	41,585 cr
20 Sep	Lodgement		2,500	44,085 cr
21 Sep	Lodgement		4,000	48,085 cr
23 Sep	Cheque no 24004	2,528		45,557 cr
24 Sep	Cheque no 24005	9,000		36,557 cr
24 Sep	Lodgement		2,450	39,007 cr
24 Sep	Cheque no 24006	2,500		36,507 cr
30 Sep	Lodgement		5,500	42,007 cr
30 Sep	Direct debit	8,000		34,007 cr

Required

First, prepare the books of original entry, that is, journals (sales, sales returns, purchases and purchases returns), cheque payments book, cash receipts book and petty cash book. This requires that you make one entry in these books for each transaction listed above.

Next, you must complete the sales and purchases ledgers. To do this you extract the relevant information from the books of original entry, which you have just completed.

Include the opening balances for individual credit customers and credit suppliers as shown in the trial balance at 1 October 20X1. You should also extract trade receivables and trade payables schedules. These will be used later to check control account balances.

The next stage is writing up the nominal ledger. Remember to enter the opening balances for the individual relevant accounts shown in the trial balance at 1 October 20X1. You complete this stage by preparing a bank reconciliation statement at 30 September 20X2.

At this point you may extract a preliminary trial balance by extracting balances from the nominal ledger accounts you have just completed. Remember to enter the individual opening balances for the relevant accounts shown in the trial balance at 1 October 20X1.

Using the preliminary trial balance you extracted above, and taking account of the following post-trial balance adjustments, you are required to prepare the statement of profit and loss for Antique Furniture Supplies Ltd for the year ended 30 September 20X2 and a statement of financial position at that date. Also, comment on Antique Furniture Supplies Ltd's cash flow position throughout the year and suggest ways to improve its working capital cycle.

Post trial balance adjustments

1 Closing inventory is valued at £35,000.

2 On the 30 September 20X2 Antique Furniture Supplies Ltd decided to dispose of one of its vans. This had been acquired in 20W9 at a cost of £12,000 and had been depreciated at a rate of 20 per cent per annum on cost. Sale proceeds amounted to £5,500 and this was lodged by Mr O'Donnell into his account in First Time Bank on 30 September. No other entry relating to this transaction has been made in the books.

3 Antique Furniture Supplies Ltd's depreciation policy is as follows. Depreciation is to be charged on both delivery vans and premises at 20 per cent on cost and on fittings at 10 per cent using the reducing balance method. Depreciation is not to be charged in the year of disposal.

4 Light and heat worth £175 and telephone worth £265 are outstanding at the year end along with wages of £2,000.

5 You have decided to charge Antique Furniture Supplies Ltd £12,000 for your accounting services.

6 The rent payment made on 30 January was in respect of the subsequent 12 months. The motor insurance payment made on 30 July related to the subsequent three months.

7 After discussing matters with Antique Furniture Supplies Ltd, you decide that there is little likelihood of any further payments from Doyle and that the remaining balance should be written off as a bad debt.

8 In the light of the experience with Doyle, you have advised Antique Furniture Supplies Ltd that it would be prudent to create a provision for doubtful debts. It is agreed that a provision equal to 5 per cent of closing trade receivables should be established.

9 Income tax for this accounting period is £10,000 and has not been paid.

10 Interest on the long-term loan is outstanding at the year end.

11 It is proposed that a final dividend of 5 per cent equity share capital should be paid.

Note: A statement of cash flows may also be requested here.

(Sandra Brosnan, adapted)

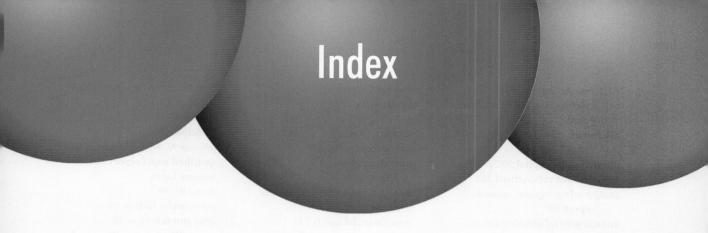

Index

Note: Key terms and concepts are in **bold**.
Page numbers in *italic (715–832)* refer to online chapters.